FOURTH EDITION

D0746993

SOCIAL WELFARE

in Canadian Society

Rosalie Chappell, B.S.W., M.S.W.

NELSON / EDUCATION

NELSON / EDUCATION

**Social Welfare in Canadian Society,
Fourth Edition**

by Rosalie Chappell

Vice-President, Editorial Director:
Evelyn Veitch

Editor-in-Chief, Higher Education:
Anne Williams

Acquisitions Editor:
Anne-Marie Taylor

Marketing Manager:
Ann Byford

Developmental Editor:
Liisa Kelly

Photo Researcher:
Kristiina Paul

Permissions Coordinator:
Kristiina Paul

Production Service:
MPS Limited

Copy Editor:
Rodney Rawlings

Proofreader:
Susan Fitzgerald

Indexer:
Elliot Linzer

Senior Production Coordinator:
Ferial Suleman

Design Director:
Ken Phipps

Managing Designer:
Franca Amore

Interior Design:
Joanne Slouenwhite
with modifications by
Olena Sullivan

Cover Design:
Tammy Gay

Cover Image:
Paul Taylor/Getty Images

Compositor:
MPS Limited

Printer:
Webcom

**Library and Archives Canada
Cataloguing in Publication**

Chappell, Rosalie, 1955–

Social welfare in Canadian society/
Rosalie Chappell. – 4th ed.

Includes bibliographical references
and index.
ISBN 978-0-17-650064-1

1. Social service–Canada.
2. Public welfare–Canada.
I. Title.

HV105.C48 2009   361.971
C2009-902541-8

ISBN-13: 978-0-17-650064-1
ISBN-10: 0-17-650064-2

This one's for Paul, the love of my life.
"Just another 10 clicks."

BRIEF TABLE OF CONTENTS

TABLE OF CONTENTS

PREFACE

The foundations of Canada's social welfare system continue to shift. When the first edition of *Social Welfare in Canadian Society* was released in 1997, Canadian governments had one goal in mind: to eliminate the deficit. During those deficit-fighting years, social welfare programs endured considerable damage and fragmentation. By 2003, the federal and several provincial governments had balanced their budgets, were even showing budget surpluses, and indicated an interest in "social reinvestment." For a variety of reasons, social reinvestment at the federal level never took place to any real extent. Some provinces have nevertheless forged ahead with their own economic and social development plans.

Now, as this fourth edition goes to press, Canada is in a deep economic recession. The federal government is enriching certain social welfare programs—such as Employment Insurance—to help working Canadians weather the worst of the economic storm. However, the future of social welfare as a "system" is uncertain, as is the support that will be available for this country's most disadvantaged citizens.

My research over the past year reconfirms for me that Canadian politicians have no interest in resurrecting the "old" social welfare system (in fact, some politicians shy away from even using the term *social welfare*.) There is no question that a new social welfare system is needed, but what will that new system look like? This fourth edition of *Social Welfare in Canadian Society* explores Canada's traditional approach to social welfare, and glimpses into what the future of social welfare might hold.

TEXT OBJECTIVES

Remaining true to its original objectives, this fourth edition aims to

- strike a balance between historical and current content;
- explore a wide range of social welfare policies and programs in both the public and private sectors;
- provide real-life examples of social welfare programs from across the country;
- discuss practice issues related to various social welfare fields;
- consider the impact of social welfare programs and policies on social groups;

- deliver Canadian content, and draw from the wisdom of Canadian scholars and researchers; and

- provide a critical analysis of issues, approaches, and initiatives.

It is hoped that this fourth edition not only meets these objectives, but also gives students a good sense of Canada's unique approach to social welfare, and an appreciation of the strengths and shortcomings of social welfare programs and services.

As with previous editions, this revised text introduces the basic concepts and processes related to social welfare, current issues in the field, and Canadian programs and services. The book is designed to stimulate further interest in Canada's approach to social welfare. Various resources are available to support readers in this task:

- Appendix A provides a chronology of key events in social welfare and related systems over a hundred-year period. This appendix is an excellent resource for readers wishing to learn about a specific period in the development of Canada's social welfare system, or to track important dates in the evolution of particular programs.

- The glossary can be used to learn a wide range of words and phrases specific to the social welfare field. It is also an excellent resource to students when preparing for examinations.

- The *Social Welfare in Canadian Society* website can be accessed at www.socialwelfare4e.nelson.com for links to the most current information on issues related to social welfare.

ORGANIZATION

This edition retains the basic three-part structure of previous editions. Part I introduces readers to some of the fundamental aspects of Canada's social welfare system, including the nature of its programs and services, its ideological base, approaches to helping, and historical foundations.

Part II is devoted to social welfare's service delivery system. Here readers learn about the various service sectors and the principal activities of social agencies. This section also looks at the range of service providers found in social welfare settings and the approaches they use when helping people.

Part III examines the social issues and concerns of selected populations: low-income groups, families with children, seniors, Aboriginal peoples, recent immigrants, and people with a disability. This section also explores the various social welfare approaches, programs, and services available for each population.

New to this Edition

Readers will be interested in the various themes that are woven throughout this new edition, which reflect some of the more significant trends in Canada's social welfare system. For example, this edition

- gives more attention to **women's issues** in relation to social welfare;
- explores the **business approach** to social welfare, which is rapidly gaining political support in Canada;
- emphasizes the **evidence-base** underlying all new social welfare initiatives;
- provides a more **critical analysis** of social welfare approaches, programs, and services;
- highlights the many types of **partnerships** and collaborations that characterize the Canadian approach to social welfare; and
- examines the **politics** behind initiatives, and why politicians approach social welfare the way that they do.

This edition features a new **Chapter 2** on social policy and the policy-making process. A highlight of this chapter is the section on policy analysis, and the various "lenses" that can be used to critically examine social welfare policy.

Chapter 5 has undergone significant revisions in order to emphasize government's new business approach and the impact of that approach on the voluntary sector.

Chapter 7 expands the focus on service providers, taking into account the increasing reliance not only on professional helpers, but also on volunteers, self-help groups, and unpaid caregivers in the provision of social welfare.

Major revisions to **Chapter 9** emphasize the growing problem of poverty in Canada and its many interrelated consequences. This chapter also considers some of the innovative strategies governments are using to address poverty, including asset-based accounts, and poverty reduction schemes.

Appendix B provides a primer on globalization and its impact on Canada's social welfare system. This appendix is a simple must-read for anyone interested in the economic influences on social welfare over the past few decades.

In addition to new and revised **exhibits** throughout the book, **photographs** have been added to enhance visual appeal and to bring the content alive.

Discussion questions appear throughout each chapter section to draw readers' attention to specific content and issues, and to provoke lively in-class discussions.

Engaging chapter-opening **quotes** set the tone for the content, and hopefully inspire and provoke thought.

Finally, this edition brings students **up to date** on social statistics, policies, initiatives, and issues.

PEDAGOGICAL FEATURES

Reviews of *Social Welfare in Canadian Society* suggest that certain features of previous editions enhance the reader's comprehension and enjoyment of the book. These features include

- a list of learning objectives at the beginning of each chapter to set the direction of the content;
- a variety of exhibits to give a visual reference to points made in the text;
- definitions of terms in the main text or in text boxes;
- profiles and examples of Canadian social welfare programs, services, and organizations;
- a section in each chapter (in Part III) on social work practice in a social welfare context;
- chapter summaries;
- boldfaced key terms in the text and at the end of each chapter, with their page references;
- a glossary of key terms to familiarize readers with words and phrases specific to the social welfare field; and
- a thorough index to help the reader find information quickly and easily.

INSTRUCTOR'S RESOURCES

An important objective of the fourth edition of *Social Welfare in Canadian Society* is to create a comprehensive teaching package that includes a text (to meet the learning needs of students) and an Instructor's Manual (to help educators teach their courses more effectively). The Instructor's Manual includes the following features:

- ideas for in-class activities to facilitate student learning, to stimulate critical thinking and analysis of the text material, and to help students apply social welfare theory;
- suggestions for student assignments to increase students' awareness of social welfare issues, improve research skills, and enhance written and verbal communication;

- recommended readings, which can be used as (a) supplementary readings for the course, (b) sources of information for lecture preparation, and (c) resources for student assignments;
- websites to facilitate further research on social welfare topics; and
- a test bank—which includes true-or-false, multiple-choice, and short-answer questions—to assist students and instructors at course review and examination time.

ACKNOWLEDGMENTS

No one ever creates a book alone. Many thanks go to those who have supported me through the review, research, and development of this project. Sincere appreciation to

- Paul Wallin, for all the hours at the computer, the typing, the researching, and so much moral support;
- the team at Nelson Education Ltd, with special thanks to Liisa Kelly (Developmental Editor), and Kristiina Paul (Freelance Permissions and Photo Researcher) for being so supportive, informative, and responsive during the most demanding phase of the book's development;
- my writing pals, Michael Hamer and Christine Fraser-Brisebois, for their words of encouragement;
- Don C. McGowan, for inspiring me to write, and to appreciate Canada's rich history;
- the staff at the Vancouver Island Regional Library, for helping me with my ILLs;
- the review panel participants for providing me with excellent suggestions on how to improve the fourth edition: Eleanor Wint, University of Northern B.C.; Mike Devine, Memorial University; Dan Andreae, University of Waterloo; Gail Zuk, University of Calgary; and Mary Lou Karley, King's College University; and
- the reviewers of the previous editions for their feedback and direction. Reviewers of the third edition include Ken Barter, Memorial University of Newfoundland; Les Jerome, University of Calgary; Neil McMahon, Mohawk College; and Margaret Wright, University of British Columbia. Reviewers of the second edition include Brian Dwyer, Sheridan College; Luke Fusco, Wilfrid Laurier University; and Paul MacIsaac, Georgian College. Reviewers of the first edition

include Phil Durrant, Niagara College; Arvey Hanowski, University of Regina; Emmett Hogan, Mount Royal College; Cheryl Hebert, Memorial University; Mac Davis, Humber College; and Rory Mahood, Cariboo College.

I hope that the recent revisions to this text meet the needs and expectations of students and instructors, and that these changes enhance the reader's understanding and appreciation of our social welfare system.

—Rosalie Chappell

ABOUT THE AUTHOR

Rosalie Chappell received her Bachelor of Social Work and Master of Social Work degrees from the University of Calgary. She has taught social work and social service work in British Columbia and Alberta at the University-College of the Fraser Valley, Open Learning Agency, Malaspina University-College, North Island College, and Red Deer College. Besides teaching, Rosalie has worked as a clinical social worker, supervisor, consultant, and program evaluator in a diverse range of public- and private-sector organizations, including family counselling agencies, community corrections, alcohol and drug treatment centres, and extended care.

SOCIAL WELFARE IN CANADA

An Overview

CHAPTER

The Nature of Canadian Social Welfare

OBJECTIVES

Social welfare focuses on meeting human needs and enhancing individual and collective well-being. This chapter will explore:

- definitions of social welfare;

- how individual and social well-being are measured;

- the primary functions of social welfare;

- social welfare programs and services;

- the influence of political ideology on social welfare; and

- approaches to social welfare provision.

INTRODUCTION

Undeniably, the "social safety net" we built over the past several decades helped make Canada one of the world's most successful countries, rich in prosperity and opportunity. Programs such as unemployment insurance, social assistance and social services, child benefits, universal pensions and a national network of widely accessible colleges and universities have made

our nation a beacon of civilized values. (Human
Resources Development Canada, 1994a)

Social welfare is a key consideration in a caring, benevolent, and civilized
society. Social welfare shapes our quality of life, our interactions with one
another, and the way we cope with life's challenges and transitions.
Underlying social welfare are core Canadian values, such as compassion and
collective responsibility, and a fundamental belief in the social equality of all
people.

Despite its importance, social welfare is a highly abstract term with no
single, exhaustive, universally agreed upon definition. The use of the term
came into vogue in Canada during the late nineteenth and early twentieth centuries when industrialization, urbanization, and an influx of immigrants were
transforming city life. These events demanded the redefinition of social values,
and more effective ways of helping the poor and disadvantaged (Hareven,
1969). People began to treat the vulnerable members of society with more
fairness, respect, and compassion, and to take responsibility for each other.
The time was right for a new language to reflect the spirit of social reform:
thus, the old-fashioned word "charity" was replaced by "social welfare," a term
that signifies a formal, organized, and governmental approach to ensuring a
basic standard of living for all (Leiby, 1977; Rice & Prince, 2000).

Over time, **social welfare** has come to mean various things. As a *concept*,
social welfare refers to a society in which people enjoy a state of well-being,
health, happiness, and prosperity—in other words, a society that is "faring
well." From the perspective of a *field* or *discipline*, social welfare involves the
study of how a society enhances the well-being of its members. Social welfare
can also be understood as a *system* with a specific function in society. In
Canada, the social welfare system comprises policies and programs designed
to help individuals, families, and communities meet their social and economic
needs. Appendix A lists many of these policies and programs.

THE SCOPE AND PURPOSE OF SOCIAL WELFARE

MEASURING SOCIAL WELL-BEING

The abstract nature of social welfare makes it difficult to say with any certainty
whether society is "faring well" or not. For example, is society only doing well
if it has zero poverty? Is society still doing well if it has a moderate amount of

poverty? What is "moderate"? For that matter, what is "poverty"? From a *subjective* view, how well a society is doing is open to interpretation, which is shaped by people's values, cultural norms, and beliefs about wellness and such constructs as "healthy lifestyles." While subjective assessments of well-being are useful, governments require more *objective* measures before they will direct precious resources (such as time, energy, and taxpayers' money) toward improving people's well-being.

There are various ways to objectively measure social well-being. One measurement tool is the Government of Canada's Indicators of Well-Being in Canada (IWC). The IWC suggests that there are ten broad domains of individual and social well-being: learning, work, financial security, environment, security, health, leisure, social participation, family life, and housing (see Exhibit 1.1). Each domain uses certain indicators (characteristics or changes) related to a person's status, life events, and key influences to measure aspects of well-being. Of the ten domains, those most likely to be addressed by the social welfare system are work, financial security, social participation, family life, and housing; the remaining five domains are the primary focus of other systems, such as health care, education, recreation and leisure, and criminal justice.

THE FUNCTIONS OF SOCIAL WELFARE

Meeting Human Needs

For a society to fare well, its members must be physically, socially, psychologically, financially, and materially healthy. To achieve health in these life areas, people's needs must be adequately met. A human **need** is a necessary condition or requirement of human development that, if not met, will result in serious physical, psychological, or social harm. The diversity of human beings is such that it is impossible to list all possible needs that arise for people over a lifetime. A variety of models nevertheless attempt to outline the range of human needs; Abraham Maslow's hierarchy of needs is one of the best known of these models. Originally, Maslow argued that a person must first meet basic survival and security needs before trying to meet "higher-order" needs related to social interaction, self-esteem, and self-actualization. In later works, Maslow acknowledged that the meeting of human needs is not necessarily in a fixed order; thus, people may be motivated to meet higher-order needs before they have fully satisfied those lower down on the pyramid (Ashley, 2000). Exhibit 1.2 illustrates the different levels of human needs as identified by Maslow: basic needs are found at the bottom of the pyramid, with

EXHIBIT 1.1

INDICATORS* OF WELL-BEING IN CANADA

DOMAIN	STATUS INDICATORS	LIFE EVENTS	KEY INFLUENCES

LEARNING	Educational attainment
	Job-related training
	Adult literacy
	Adult numeracy
	Student literacy
	Student numeracy
	College and trade
	  participation
	University participation
		School drop-outs	Computer access in
			  schools

WORK	Employment rate Weekly earnings Weekly hours worked	Strikes and lockouts Unemployment duration Unemployment rate Work-related injuries	Unionization rates
FINANCIAL SECURITY	Standard of living Family income Retirement income Low-income incidence Low-income persistence Net worth (wealth)	Personal bankruptcies	Income distribution
ENVIRONMENT	Air quality Greenhouse gases Freshwater quality and use		Transportation

SECURITY	Crime rates
	Victims of property crime
	Victims of violent crime
			Perceptions of local
			  police
			Perceptions of personal
			  safety

HEALTH	Life expectancy at birth Self-rated health Self-rated mental health Infant mortality Low birth weight	Mortality from leading diseases	Smoking Obesity Physical activity Regular medical doctor Patient satisfaction
LEISURE	Total leisure time Active leisure time Passive leisure time		
SOCIAL PARTICIPATION	Participation in political activities Participation in social activities Charitable donations Volunteering		Sense of belonging Social networks Trust in others

Continued

| FAMILY LIFE | | Marriage
Age of mother at
  childbirth
Divorce
Young adults living with
  their parent(s) | |
| HOUSING | Housing need | | Housing starts
Rental vacancy rates
Homeless shelters and
  beds |

Status indicators reflect conditions or progress in major life areas, such as education, employment, and health.

Life events are major events that impact well-being, and involve a change or transition from one stage of life to another, such as getting married, changing jobs, or experiencing a major illness.

Key influences refer to individual and societal resources required for well-being, and people's access to, availability of, and maintenance of those resources.

Source: Adapted from Human Resources and Social Development Canada (2008), "Indicators of Well-Being in Canada." Retrieved August 24, 2008, from www4.hrsdc.gc.ca/home.jsp?lang=en.

higher-order needs listed successively up the hierarchy. Most of the needs listed in Maslow's hierarchy are addressed to some extent by Canada's social welfare system.

Which Needs?

In Canada, most people meet their needs—such as the need for food, shelter, safety, and affection—through interactions with informal support systems like family and friends, and through formal institutions like the workplace and the church. When these traditional supports fail to adequately meet people's needs, social welfare programs may be called upon to intervene. Thus, a primary function of the social welfare system is to

- provide the basic necessities to people who cannot sufficiently provide for themselves;

- help people to meet a variety of social needs, such as the need to belong and participate in society;

- enable people to carry out important social roles such as parent or wage-earner;

EXHIBIT 1.2

MASLOW'S HIERARCHY OF NEEDS

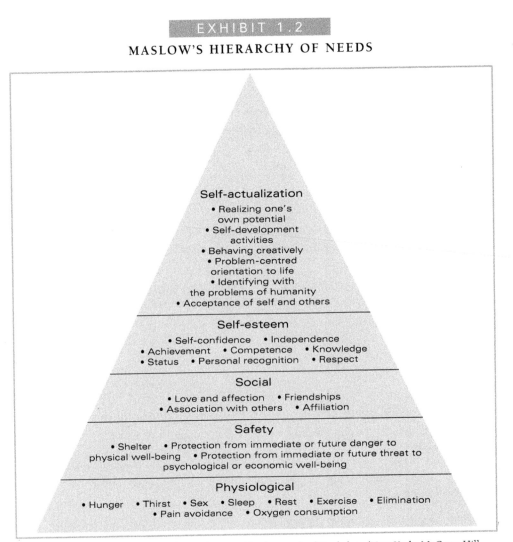

Self-actualization
- Realizing one's own potential
- Self-development activities
- Behaving creatively
- Problem-centred orientation to life
- Identifying with the problems of humanity
- Acceptance of self and others

Self-esteem
- Self-confidence • Independence
- Achievement • Competence • Knowledge
- Status • Personal recognition • Respect

Social
- Love and affection • Friendships
- Association with others • Affiliation

Safety
- Shelter • Protection from immediate or future danger to physical well-being • Protection from immediate or future threat to psychological or economic well-being

Physiological
- Hunger • Thirst • Sex • Sleep • Rest • Exercise • Elimination
- Pain avoidance • Oxygen consumption

Source: Adapted from A. Haber and R. P. Runyon, *Fundamentals of Psychology* (New York: McGraw-Hill, 1983), 304. Copyright 1983. Reproduced with permission of The McGraw-Hill Companies, Inc.

- ensure that resources and opportunities are accessible so that people can meet their needs and support their families; and

- address "special needs" related to substance abuse, mental disorders, and other conditions that inhibit normal human development.

Some social welfare programs (such as child welfare services) may also serve a social control function by curbing unacceptable behaviour (such as the abuse of children) that interferes with the safety or development needs of others (Dobelstein, 1978).

Whose Needs?

While basic needs are common to all humans, how a particular culture chooses to satisfy those needs can vary. The determination of whose needs should be met by public (government) resources is the responsibility of elected officials who must act in the best interests of citizens, and target public assistance to those who really need it. As the Office of the Auditor-General of Canada (2006) notes: "Demands on government are unlimited, but the resources available to meet them are not. Governments must therefore ... [decide] how much they can afford to spend, what to spend it on, and how to get the most for the money spent."

Even in good economic times, Canadian governments tend to limit the help they give to the most vulnerable members of society who, for whatever reason, cannot fully meet their needs (CASW, 2008). At various points in Canada's history, governments have deemed certain groups "vulnerable" and worthy of government assistance; these groups include children living in poverty, Aboriginal peoples, seniors, the unemployed, people with disabilities, recent immigrants, and women.

Security Needs

The Industrial Revolution made it clear that local charities and churches were ill-equipped to meet the needs of a modern industrial society. It nevertheless took the widespread economic and social disruption of the Great Depression to convince Canadians that government intervention was needed during hard economic times. Following the Second World War, Canadian governments responded to "modern problems" by creating a wide range of income security programs, social services, and health care services designed to protect people from the risks inherent in a market economy. In other words, governments set out to ensure a certain level of **social security**.

Since the 1980s, Canadians have witnessed significant changes in their social and economic lives as a result of three economic recessions (in the 1980s, 1990s, and early 2000s), and the acceleration of **globalization** (see Appendix B for an overview of globalization). Shifts and downturns in the economy often bring unemployment, interrupted earnings, and a heightened sense of vulnerability; these changes can also impact people's perceptions of security. Whereas social security used to imply *protection* from the risks of modern life, the term more currently refers to people's **capacity** to change in response to those risks (Banting, 2006).

In the new global economy, the accumulation of assets or **capital** is recognized as key to a person's ability to adapt to change and, ultimately, to the achievement of security. There are various types of capital; however, the social welfare system is primarily concerned with human capital and social capital. *Human* capital may be understood as the skills, capabilities, knowledge, and other personal assets that people use to earn a living, cope with life's problems and challenges, and achieve self-reliance. *Social* capital refers to the social supports, networks, and contacts that people rely upon for emotional support, help in accessing resources, and generally participating in society.

Discussion Questions

The Scope and Purpose of Social Welfare

1. Everyone has their own interpretation of well-being. How do you define well-being?
2. In your opinion, what conditions, resources, or activities are key to a person's (or society's) well-being?
3. Why is it important (or not) for our politicians and governments to be concerned with people's well-being?

SOCIAL WELFARE PROGRAMS AND SERVICES

A wide range of government-sponsored services and programs make up Canada's social welfare system. A **social welfare program** may be conceptualized as a set of projects or activities that aim to meet a public need. Many programs have a service component. Services typically involve direct, face-to-face assistance to people in need; this assistance includes counselling, peer support, information-giving, and advocacy. Many programs focus on social research, policy analysis, program development, or an other activity that enhances social welfare provision but does not offer direct client services.

The boundaries between social welfare and other **social programs** are not always clear; one reason for this is because social welfare services often complement other types of services. For example, it is common for social welfare services and health services to be provided under the same roof, or be linked administratively, as in the case of the Yukon Government's Department of Health and Social Services. Despite these points of overlap, the social welfare system has its own distinct mandate, goals, and objectives. Social welfare programs and services can be classified into two broad categories: (1) income security programs; and (2) social services. Each category is described below.

INCOME SECURITY PROGRAMS

Income security programs provide financial aid to replace or supplement a person's income during times of unemployment due to, for instance, pregnancy, old age, sickness, or disability. These programs attempt to ensure that all Canadians live above a reasonable standard of living, otherwise known as a **social minimum**. The four main types of income security programs are as follows:

- **Targeted cash transfers** are benefits that government "transfers" to individuals whose income or assets fall below a certain level. Targeted cash transfers include the Guaranteed Income Supplement, **social assistance** (commonly called "welfare"), and disability pensions for people with severe disabilities.

- **Universal cash transfers** are provided to all persons, regardless of financial status or need, who meet a basic requirement such as age or residency. The Universal ChildCare Benefit, for example, gives a monthly payment of $100 to all Canadian children under the age of six years, irrespective of the family's financial circumstances.

- **Contributory programs** (also called *social insurance*) are forced savings plans that require working individuals to contribute to a program, which then compensates them when they are not working. Benefits from these programs are based on the claimant's contributions, and are only available to those who maintain a strong connection to the labour force. Employment Insurance, Workers' Compensation, and the Canada and Quebec Pension Plans are examples of contributory programs.

- **Tax credits** are determined through income reported on an individual's tax returns. Canada's progressive tax system allows individuals with low and modest incomes to pay proportionately less income tax. As income rises, benefits are gradually phased out. Examples of this type of program are the Canada Child Tax Benefit and the Goods and Services Tax/Harmonized Sales Tax Credit. Governments have come to prefer using the tax system for assisting "at risk" groups.

SOCIAL SERVICES

Canada's **social services** are non-income benefits designed to improve the living conditions of individuals, families, and communities. These services fulfil several important functions:

- They provide people with goods and services that aim to meet basic social, material, and emotional needs.

- They provide support and opportunities to help people resolve problems of daily living.
- They provide protection to vulnerable members of society, such as children.
- They attempt to prevent individual and social problems, such as drug abuse and suicide.
- They intervene in people's problems so as to lessen their negative effects.

There is an increasing demand for social services in Canada, fuelled in part by an aging population, which drives the need for home support and other seniors' programs. Changes in family composition—including a rise in single mother families, and families with two income-earners—are also creating more demand for family-oriented services, such as childcare.

Because the provinces and territories are primarily responsible for developing their own social services, the type and range of services across jurisdictions will vary. However, most provinces/territories offer social services for specific populations, such as children and youth, parents, seniors, and people with disabilities. In many cases, these services complement or replace the support and care that one's family or other informal support system might normally provide.

The social services are sometimes referred to as **transfers-in-kind**, since they are funded (or transferred) by government to individuals or families in the form of direct services. Depending on their philosophy, some governments prefer to offer a social service, instead of a cash benefit, to meet an identified need. Between 2004 and 2006, the debate as to which type of benefit—service or cash—would best serve Canadian families played out at the federal level. There, liberal politicians wanted to meet the nation's need for childcare by establishing an extensive system of government-regulated childcare spaces; in contrast, conservative politicians preferred to give cash to families so they could purchase the type of childcare best suited to their needs. There are pros and cons to each type of provision: services tend to be used when they are made available, and are therefore likely to meet an identified need; this strategy, however, offers service users little choice in the type of service they receive. The provision of cash, on the other hand, allows people to choose the type of service they want; but because there is no stipulation on how the cash is spent, there is a chance it will not be used for its intended purpose—so the need may go unmet.

PROGRAM ELIGIBILITY

Various systems have been developed at the federal, provincial/territorial, and municipal levels of government to determine **program eligibility**—that is, criteria that, when met, allow a person to participate in, or potentially benefit from, a publicly-sponsored program. In Canada, the issue of program eligibility is largely resolved through two broad classifications of programs, *targeted* and *universal*.

Targeted Programs

Targeted programs are limited to narrowly defined segments of the population who are considered vulnerable or "at risk" for a certain social and/or

EXHIBIT 1.3

THAT AWKWARD AGE

"He's at that awkward age ... too young for old age security, too old for Opportunities for Youth, too late for family allowance, too conventional for Canada Council or local initiative programs, too poor for tax loopholes, too rich for subsidized housing. ..."

Source: Len Norris, "That Awkward Age" (1990). Reprinted by permission.

economic hardship. Groups for whom there is a high risk of poverty, for instance, include lone parents with children, people with work-limiting physical and/or mental disabilities, unattached middle-aged individuals, recent immigrants, and Aboriginal Canadians living off-reserve (HRSDC, 2006a). Social assistance, child tax credits, and subsidized benefits such as housing and childcare are some of the programs that target specific groups.

Three types of financial tests are used by Canadian governments to determine eligibility for targeted income security programs:

- **Income tests** determine eligibility on the basis of the applicant's income and generally ignore individual needs or other assets. Since the late 1980s, income tests have been a common method for ensuring that only low- or modest-income earners receive benefits. Old Age Security is an example of an income-tested program; recipients earning over $64,000 a year receive a reduced benefit rate, and those with annual incomes over $105,000 are ineligible (Service Canada, 2008a).

- **Needs tests** are used to assess an applicant's needs and to determine whether his or her income is sufficient to meet those needs. Provincial social assistance programs tend to use fairly elaborate needs tests: an inventory of the applicant's fixed and liquid assets is made, all sources of household income are identified, and the total needs of the household are determined. If the household's assessed needs are greater than its resources, the applicant is deemed eligible for assistance (NCW, 2006a).

- **Means tests** base eligibility on an applicant's income and assets but virtually ignore personal needs. Although commonly used in the past, means testing is no longer popular since it requires an in-depth—and seemingly intrusive—inquiry into an applicant's finances, living arrangements, and other potential sources of support (or means).

In recent decades, government cutbacks to social spending have led to tighter restrictions on who can use social welfare programs; as a result, government assistance is available to an increasingly smaller segment of Canadians. Employment Insurance is an example of an income security program that has severely tightened its eligibility criteria over the years. During the 1990s, legislative changes made to this program led to a sharp drop in the proportion of unemployed Canadian workers eligible for benefits: from 74 percent in 1990 to only 36 percent in 2004 (Townson & Hayes, 2007).

Most social services have also become less accessible over the years. To deal with funding shortfalls, **social agencies** use various strategies to restrict access to services. For instance, some organizations charge a user fee to clients who can afford it, while others limit program participation by increasing the number of criteria that clients have to meet. It is not uncommon for governments to set strict limitations on the services that they fund. The federally funded Nobody's Perfect program, for example, is only open to parents with children five years of age or younger. In addition to the age restriction, priority is given to "parents who are young, single, socially or geographically isolated or who have low income or limited formal education" (Public Health Agency of Canada, 2003).

Universal Programs

Universal programs are comprehensive in the sense that they are available to broad segments of the population, such as all children under the age of six, or all adults over the age of sixty-five. The notion of universality is based on the belief that benefits should be available as a matter of a citizen's rights rather than economic need or risk. Since need or risk are not factors of eligibility, applicants for these programs are not required to undergo a needs, income, or means test; however, they must meet basic criteria, often related to age and/or residency. Canada's first universal program, Family Allowances, was introduced in 1945 and provided a monthly cash benefit to all Canadian families—rich or poor—that had children.

EXHIBIT 1.4

An Inuit mother and children sign for a Family Allowance cheque at the Royal Canadian Mounted Police headquarters in Coppermine, Northwest Territories (circa 1949–1950).

Source: Library and Archives Canada. Richard Harrington/Richard Harrington fonds/PA-129879. © Library and Archives Canada. Reproduced with the permission of Library and Archives Canada.

Every beneficiary of a universal program receives an equal quality of service or amount of money (a flat rate); as a result, no one in the population is identified as being "in need." Findlay (1983, p. 18) sees certain advantages to this approach: "universality avoids divisions among those who are entitled and those who are not: it eliminates a two-tier system that results in 'second-class' citizens and 'second-class' services for the less influential." Thus, universality is seen as a way to minimize the labelling, stigmatization, or segregation of disadvantaged individuals or groups in society (Jewell, 2005). On a more practical level, universal programs may be more cost-effective than targeted programs, since they do not require an assessment of individual needs and are therefore relatively simple to administer.

While universality in public health care and public education is generally supported in Canada, universality in income security programs has lost its popularity. The critics of universality argue that giving financial assistance to people who do not need it is a waste of taxpayer's money (Canadian Economy Online, 2007). The gradual elimination of universal income security programs began in the late 1980s when the federal government "clawed back" (recovered) payments made to high-income earners receiving Family Allowances and Old Age Security benefits.

Some Canadian governments are showing a greater interest in a contemporary (and European) version of universality, called **progressive universalism**. This type of approach gives a benefit to all persons that meet the basic criteria, with a larger proportion of benefit given to those who need it most. Quebec's early childhood education and care, for example, reflects a progressive universalist approach; in that province, parents who can afford it pay a daily fee of $7 for childcare services, while families with young children on social assistance receive the same quality of services for free (Quebec, 2007).

Some programs are touted as universal, but because of their structural design they end up benefiting some recipients more than others. The federally funded Universal ChildCare Benefit (UCCB) is one of these "in name only" universal programs. Although the program gives $1,200 per year to each Canadian child under six, the benefit is taxable, which means that a portion of it may have to be paid back in tax. A study by policy analyst Ken Battle (2006) found that, depending on the household's income tax bracket and whether the family received other cash transfers or tax credits, a child might receive anywhere from $460 to $1200 per year after taxes. The "universal" structure of the UCCB is in sharp contrast to that of Family Allowances which, from 1945 to 1973, provided tax-free benefits to families with children.

Discussion Questions

Social Welfare Programs and Services

1. Identify some of the social welfare programs and services in your community. Which program area do they fit best: income security or social service?
2. Are the programs you identified provided on a targeted or universal basis? What are some of the criteria used by the targeted programs to determine eligibility?

SOCIAL WELFARE PROVISION: IDEOLOGY AND APPROACHES

POLITICAL IDEOLOGY

Canadians rely primarily on the marketplace, and the law of supply and demand, to provide the goods and services necessary for their well-being. However, because of fluctuations in and the unpredictability of the market, Canadian governments are reluctant to leave the meeting of social welfare needs entirely up to individuals. As a result, governments have assumed a certain level of responsibility for public health care, education, and many social welfare programs that are considered key to the well-being of the nation (Jenson, 2004a).

Despite government's willingness to assume some responsibility for social welfare, there is no clear-cut method for determining which human issues should be considered **private troubles**, and which should be addressed as **public issues**. The private and public can be understood in the following way:

> If a problem can be resolved without making demands on the people that are not immediately affected, then it is private in nature. ... Human acts have consequences on others, and some of these are perceived to create needs to the extent that relief is sought. If the transaction has a broad effect, it is public. (Reyes, 2001)

In Canada, private troubles, such as marital disagreements and emotional upsets, are generally left to individuals to deal with. Public issues, on the other hand, refer to needs and conditions that, if left unaddressed, may hinder large segments of the population from functioning properly, or participating fully in society. Public issues are also known as **social problems**—such as poverty, unemployment, and child abuse—because they negatively affect society as a whole. Sometimes, private troubles become public issues; for example, marital disagreements that escalate to domestic violence leave the private realm and become a public concern (Wharf, 2007).

The degree to which government takes responsibility for social well-being keeps shifting. Those shifts reflect changes in the nation's values, priorities, and goals; the relative importance of programs; and predominant political ideologies. A **political ideology** is a set of beliefs that shape people's views of society, how that society should function, and what should be done to achieve the "ideal" society. Canada's social welfare system is not the product of any one political ideology; rather, that system reflects various ideologies that have risen in response to social, economic, and political developments throughout history. However, three "classic" political ideologies—**conservatism**, **social democracy**, and **liberalism**—have predominated in the shaping of people's views of "need" and the extent to which they think government should help people meet their needs. Each ideology is briefly reviewed below and summarized in Exhibit 1.5.

It should be noted that the ideologies discussed here are reflected in the platforms of the three main Canadian political parties—the Conservative Party, the Liberal Party, and the New Democratic Party; that said, their respective platforms rarely reflect any one particular ideological stance.

CONSERVATISM

Although not entirely opposed to change, conservatism supports traditional values and social roles, and moral (religious) standards. Individualism is important in terms of economic advancement—that is, people are encouraged to compete, work hard, and accumulate wealth and property. In addition to gainful employment, conservatives believe that one's self, the family, the church, and other nongovernment social supports should be a person's main defence against want and need.

Conservatives tend to believe that many people are poor because they made poor choices, they lack self-initiative, or they simply do not want to work (Morel, 2002). Conservatives nevertheless recognize that some people

EXHIBIT 1.5

POLITICAL IDEOLOGIES: A COMPARATIVE VIEW

	CONSERVATISM	SOCIAL DEMOCRACY	LIBERALISM
BASIC VALUES	Moralism Family, church, tradition Class, privilege	Collectivism Fellowship Equality Cooperation	Individualism Self-interest Self-reliance Competition
KEY TO PROSPERITY AND WELL-BEING	Work ("Any job is a good job") Saving Investing	Working together Pooling society's resources and sharing the wealth	Knowledge, education, training Securing a "good" job to ensure self-reliance
ROLE OF GOVERNMENT	Maintain social order Strengthen family Defend role of church and charities Protect interests of business	Regulate the means of production Create equal conditions Ensure social welfare Protect rights of workers/unions	Enable economic progress Create equal opportunity through legislation Defend individual rights and freedoms Protect private property
TAXATION AND REDISTRIBUTION	No or low taxation Whoever earns the money should enjoy it	Heavy taxation Redistribute the wealth from rich to poor	Moderate taxation Give "reasonable" share of wealth to selected groups
CAUSE OF POVERTY	Personal failure, bad choices; unfortunate circumstances	Unequal distribution of wealth and power in capitalist system	Structural flaws in capitalist system
VIEW OF PEOPLE WHO ARE POOR	"Deserving" "Undeserving" (are lazy, immoral, lack resourcefulness)	"Trapped" in a subordinate position to the wealthy and powerful	Lack skills and/or opportunities to achieve self-sufficiency Are a drain on economy
INDIVIDUAL RESPONSIBILITY	Obey laws, work hard, fulfil duties	Share, cooperate, avoid excess	Take initiative, be self-reliant, participate in society
APPROACH TO SOCIAL WELFARE	Residual (government help is a last resort)	Institutional (government help is a citizen's right)	Social investment (government help is a long-term investment)

Source: Adapted from J. Pollard, "Ideology, Social Policy and Home-Based ChildCare," 1991, Table 1 (pp. 104–7) in I. Kyle, M. Friendly, and L. Schmidt (Eds.), *Proceedings from the ChildCare Policy and Research Symposium*, Occasional Paper No. 2, pp. 101–12. Retrieved March 18, 2004, from Childcare Resource and Research Unit, Centre for Urban and Community Studies, University of Toronto, www.childcarecanada.org/pubs/op2/op2.pdf; "Analysis—Conventional Viewpoints," Political Identities: Discussion Series, *Lakewood: The Thinking City*, August 7, 2002. Retrieved December 1, 2008, from Lakewood Public Library Online, www.lkwdpl.org/thinkingcity/august7.html.

are unfortunate victims of circumstance; children who are poor, for example, are likely to be perceived as "innocent victims of parental improvidence and/or ineptness" (Ismael, 2006, p. 5).

For conservatives, the most desirable government is the one that regulates, controls, or intervenes in the market the least. It is for this reason that conservative governments are sometimes referred to as being *laissez-faire* (a French term meaning "to leave alone"). **Laissez-faire governments** expect the market, private enterprise, and the law of supply and demand to provide people with the income and other resources they need to meet all human needs (Philipps, 1997). Conservatives see government as having a primarily protective role: to secure the country by maintaining the military, and to uphold law and order by maintaining police forces. With so few responsibilities, governments are expected to keep their administrations as small and as non-bureaucratic as possible.

According to conservative thought, people's problems are largely personal and private, and best resolved by individual effort rather than government intervention (Wharf, 2007). Conservatives generally view state intrusion in people's private lives as being detrimental because it restricts individual freedoms, and undermines people's inherent sense of self-initiative and responsibility (International Federation of Social Workers, 2005). Social welfare programs, in particular, are believed to foster a dependency on the state, and to "weaken moral fibre" (Galper, 1975, p. 3).

Although the term *neoliberalism* suggests it might be a form of liberalism, it is really a contemporary form of conservatism. Neoliberalism is highly compatible with globalization and, because of this, it is considered the "dominant global ideology" (Cronin, 2006). What makes neoliberalism new ("neo") is its global rather than national perspective; the use of the word "liberal" is in reference to *liberation* from government.

At the heart of neoliberalism is the support for capitalism, free trade, and market expansion. According to neoliberals, government intervention and regulation hinder a country's ability to successfully compete in international markets; this is because, in a global economy, capital or wealth must be allowed to flow freely across boundaries, and transnational corporations must be able to set up shop anywhere in the world with little government interference (Philipps, 1997; Teeple, 2000). Neoliberals argue that, if government would stop interfering in the market (by, for example, taxing the rich and giving to the poor), then the market would be able to fully function, economic growth and prosperity would follow, and there would be enough wealth for all to enjoy.

SOCIAL DEMOCRACY

Since the term *socialism* was coined in the early nineteenth century, two main camps have evolved: (1) the revolutionary or communist camp, which advocates a primarily government-owned and -operated economy; and (2) the evolutionary or social democratic camp, which supports an economy in which there is a mix of public and private enterprise. Social democracy, which tends to oppose the extreme of communism, gained more support in Canada than its communist counterpart. This section therefore discusses socialism from a social democratic point of view.

Traditionally, social democracy rejects the competitive values of capitalism, individualism, and private enterprise. Instead of personal competition, social democrats advocate fellowship and cooperation among citizens. Solidarity is important to social democrats, who prefer to work toward collective rather than individual goals and who frequently use collective action, such as labour strikes, to do so. Egalitarianism—that is, equal power and advantage among citizens—is also considered a worthy goal (Spicker, 2008).

Social democrats challenge the conservative notion that poverty is the result of an individual's shortcomings; instead, they see poverty as a consequence of capitalism and the unequal distribution of wealth and power. From a social democratic viewpoint, the rich inherit riches while the poor inherit poverty, which traps the poor in a subordinate position to the rich (George & Wilding, 1985).

While conservatives view government intervention as a threat to individual freedom, social democrats are willing to give up some freedom if it means that everyone—not just the rich—can benefit from a country's wealth. Thus, social democrats encourage government to use its taxation and other powers to equalize social and economic conditions, a goal that they believe is achieved through an extensive system of universal health, education, and social welfare programs available to all citizens.

LIBERALISM

In many respects, liberalism is similar to conservatism in terms of supporting individualism and competitive private enterprise. However, Canada's brand of liberalism is traditionally linked to efforts to "humanize" capitalist values, and thus strike a balance between economic goals and human development. Unlike conservatives, who tend to cling to tradition, liberals support people's rights to individuality, freedom of self-expression, and lifestyle choice.

Liberals tend to view poverty and other social problems not as a result of individual shortcomings, but as conditions resulting from flaws in the capitalist system. Although liberals promote economic progress, they also see progress as a potential source of hardship. Liberals therefore question the ability of the market alone to meet the full range of human needs in modern society.

Liberals expect government to promote capitalism and economic growth while, at the same time, ensuring individual rights, social justice, and equal opportunity (Brown, 2004). According to liberals, if the market fails to meet people's needs, then government should provide a **social safety net**—that is, a limited range of publicly funded (usually targeted) programs. Liberals tend to favour programs that help people develop the skills and knowledge they need to obtain self-sufficiency; many of those programs focus on job creation, and aid people in the search for "good" (well-paying and secure) jobs.

APPROACHES TO SOCIAL WELFARE PROVISION

A study of social welfare as a field or discipline is likely to reveal what Jacqueline Ismael (1985, p. xi) refers to as a "maze of programs" and a "hodge-podge pattern of service provision"—in other words, there is a great deal of inconsistency in the provision of social welfare in Canada. Gerald Boychuk (2004) explains that, over the course of developing Canada's social welfare system, new approaches or "logics" to helping have been introduced; the old approaches, however, have not necessarily been discarded. The result is a mix of old and new approaches, many of which contradict each other in their design, philosophy, and delivery. Despite the variation, three main approaches to social welfare provision can be identified: the **residual approach**; the **institutional approach**; and the **social investment approach**.

The main political parties in Canada tend to favour one approach over another: for example, conservatives generally support the residual approach; social democrats have traditionally leaned toward an institutional approach; and liberals tend to support a social investment approach. It is nevertheless common for political parties to pick and choose from all three approaches, depending on the presenting issue, party priorities, political climate, and public pressure.

Residual Approach to Social Welfare

The word *residual* refers to "remains" or something "left over." Thus, a residual approach to social welfare assumes that, although economic, social, and other systems meet people's needs most of the time, there will

EXHIBIT 1.6

A residual approach to social welfare does not recognize able-bodied men as "vulnerable" members of society, or as a high priority for government assistance.

Source: Denis Pepin/Shutterstock.

be some outstanding human needs that government must address (Dobelstein, 2003). Residualists see government assistance as a last resort for those who have exhausted all possible help from family, church, and other private resources, and who can demonstrate true need. Assuming that the demand for government aid will always exceed supply, the residual approach uses certain strategies to either deter people who are not truly needy from seeking public assistance, or to make the conditions of receiving benefits so adverse that people seek alternate (nongovernment) forms of assistance. Thus, this approach ensures that any help given is targeted (available to a select few), meagre (to discourage people from preferring government benefits over gainful employment), and short-term (terminated as soon as the individual being helped can once again be self-reliant) (Raphael, 2006; Handel, 1982).

Stigmatization is one of the strategies used by residualists to limit the use of government assistance to those who really need it. The stigmatization of the poor dates back to Canada's early settlement period, when the poor were classified as being either "deserving" or "undeserving" of public aid. The **deserving poor** were sick, aged, disabled, or otherwise incapable of supporting themselves through work and therefore worthy of public aid. In contrast, the **undeserving poor** were able-bodied unemployed adults who were capable of working and paying their own way; this group either received no government assistance or got what was considered second-class help. Today, these residual attitudes are reflected in our culture's stereotypes of the poor. People on social assistance, for example, are often assumed to be "lazy, unwilling to work, and lacking in self-discipline" (Handel, 1982, p. 4). These sentiments are reflected in the comments made by some of the country's top political leaders. Former Prime Minister Jean Chrétien, for example, suggested that people on welfare sit at home, drinking beer (Chrétien says, 1994). Former Calgary mayor and Alberta premier Ralph Klein gained notoriety for having referred to unemployed migrants as "Eastern bums and creeps." It may be difficult to see how stigmatization can be helpful to people who are struggling to make ends meet. However, the original intent of this strategy was to discourage dependency on government, a condition that residualists consider a hindrance to proper human development.

Institutional Approach to Social Welfare

The institutional approach maintains that social welfare is a primary institution of society (similar to religion, government, and education) and therefore has a normal, legitimate, and necessary function in a civilized, modern society (Wilensky & Lebeaux, 1965). Governments that adopt an institutional approach to social welfare do not require people to pay full market prices for goods and services that are essential for well-being. This rights-based view— which is closely aligned with a social democratic ideology—assumes that every citizen, not just people in need, is entitled to a minimum level of food, shelter, clothing, and security (Davies, McMullin, Avison, & Cassidy, 2001). Because citizens are entitled to social welfare programs, there is no stigma attached to receiving government assistance.

Welfare states (sometimes called "social welfare states") embody the values and principles of an institutional approach. A welfare state refers to an industrial capitalist nation whose government uses its power to intervene in the workings of the market to correct **income inequality**, a problem reflected in capitalist systems as a gap between the incomes of the very rich and the incomes of the very poor. To equalize incomes, welfare states follow the principles of **Keynesian economics**. According to Keynesian theory, government can stabilize society by taking a portion of income (in the form of taxation) from high- and moderate-income earners and giving it to low-income earners. This **income redistribution** enables low-income individuals and families to spend more which, in turn, can stimulate the economy (Bellemare, 1993; Mishra, 1981). Welfare states also aim to

1. provide a minimum income to all citizens;

2. protect people from economic insecurity arising from old age, unemployment, sickness, and other contingencies; and

3. provide all citizens with a range of social services (Briggs, 1961).

Following the Second World War, Canadian governments adopted several principles of Keynesian economics, and steadily assumed many responsibilities for social welfare that private charitable organizations had long taken on. The years 1963 to 1973 saw the greatest expansion of social welfare programs; by the early 1980s, these programs represented close to 14 percent of gross domestic product (Drover, 1983). With the introduction of universal health care, unemployment insurance, the Old Age Security pension, and the Canada/Quebec Pension Plans, Canada was well on its way to becoming a welfare state. However, unlike some European nations, Canada did not fully support the establishment (or expense) of an extensive range of income security and social service programs required to reach welfare state status. Thus,

EXHIBIT 1.7

Government-subsidized childcare services are supported by both the institutional and social investment approaches to social welfare.

Source: Patrick Clark/Photodisc/Getty Images.

Canada is not so much a welfare state as a country that offers minimum protection by government, through a limited range of programs, for designated "at-risk" segments of the population.

Social Investment Approach to Social Welfare

Most Canadian governments see the market as the primary source of well-being. However, governments also recognize the need for innovative strategies to address the challenges associated with globalization and other socio economic shifts. Since the mid-1990s, Canadian governments have considered the social investment approach to social welfare as a viable alternative to residual and institutional approaches and well suited to addressing modern problems (Dobrowolsky, 2003). Unlike the institutional approach—which tends to provide support after a problem (such as job loss) has been identified—the social investment approach takes a proactive stance, before problems arise. **Social inclusion** is a central theme in the social investment approach. Initiatives that promote social inclusion not only aim to remove barriers to participation in society, but recognize and value the contributions of all individuals and groups.

Governments that prefer a social investment approach favour programs that promise to yield long-term benefits. Preschool-age children—who are the country's future—are a primary focus. Social welfare programs that invest in young Canadians include the National Child Benefit and a wide range of early childhood development, early learning, and childcare programs. Young working-age adults are another focus of social investment initiatives. Instead of providing cash benefits to the able-bodied unemployed, the social investment approach attempts to help adults form a long-term attachment to the workforce. Programs designed to achieve this objective include welfare-to-work initiatives, employment counselling, and work incentives such as government wage subsidies. According to the social investment approach, work is "the primary tool in the struggle against poverty and unemployment" (Dufour & Morrison, 2005, p. 8).

Social investment strategies aim to enhance social and economic progress, and foster self-sufficiency; to achieve these goals, governments assist individuals, families, and communities in the building of capital. The capital accumulated by individuals and families can be earmarked for certain activities, such as education or retirement, and organized into various types of "personal development accounts." Among the federally sponsored programs available to help people build human capital are

- subsidized postsecondary training and education (to learn employable skills);

- the Canada Learning Bond and *learn$ave* (to help low-income Canadians save for educational purposes);
- the federal Tax-Free Savings Account (to accumulate funds to cover costs related to job loss, retirement, illness, and other contingencies); and
- registered retirement savings plans (to help people save for retirement).

Many social investment initiatives aim to help people develop social networks, social bonds, and social connections—otherwise known as social capital. Among the government-supported programs that focus on strengthening people's social networks are

- family resource centres (for example, Family Place);
- childcare and early learning programs;
- immigrant settlement programs; and
- youth engagement programs.

Common to many social investment strategies is an emphasis on contributory programs. Social investors believe that people who form a strong attachment to the labour force—and subsequently gain the financial means to contribute to their own savings or personal development accounts—are likely to achieve self-sufficiency and be free to make their own choices in life.

Discussion Questions

Social Welfare Provision: Ideology and Approaches

1. How might political ideology (such as conservatism, social democracy, or liberalism) influence a government's actions to alleviate poverty?

2. Which social welfare programs or services in your community reflect a residual, institutional, or social investment approach? Does one particular approach predominate in your community's services?

SUMMARY

Introduction

Social welfare implies a formal, organized, and governmental approach to ensuring a basic standard of living. Social welfare can refer to a concept, a field, or a discipline. The primary function of social welfare is to help individuals, families, and communities meet their social and economic needs.

I. The Scope and Purpose of Social Welfare

Individual and social well-being can be viewed subjectively or objectively. The Indicators of Well-Being in Canada tool is one objective measurement method. To achieve well-being, people's needs must be met; many needs listed in Maslow's hierarchy are addressed by the social welfare system. The social welfare system intervenes when traditional support systems break down, and focuses mainly on meeting basic needs, especially among vulnerable members of society. Social security refers to people's capacity to change in response to social risks, and may be strengthened by the building of human and social capital.

II. Social Welfare Programs and Services

Income security programs provide targeted cash transfers, universal cash transfers, contributory programs, and tax credits. Social services offer goods, services, support, and opportunities; some services protect vulnerable members of society, and others address broader social problems. The demand for social services is growing, and such services vary in design across jurisdictions. Social welfare programs may be targeted or universal, but all require a test to determine program eligibility. While universalism has potential benefits, it is no longer popular in a social welfare context. Overall, most programs are becoming more targeted and less accessible.

III. Social Welfare Provision: Ideology and Approaches

Conservatism, social democracy, and liberalism are political ideologies that influence people's view of "need" and determine which human issues government should treat as "private troubles" or "public issues." The level of responsibility that governments assume for social welfare shifts over time. There are three main approaches to social welfare provision in Canada: the residual approach, the institutional approach, and the social investment approach.

Key Terms

For definitions of the key terms, consult the Glossary on page 413 at the end of the book.

social welfare, p. 4
need, p. 5
social security, p. 9
globalization, p. 9
capacity, p. 9
capital, p. 9
social welfare program, p. 10
social program, p. 10
income security program, p. 11

social minimum, p. 11
targeted cash transfer, p. 11
social assistance, p. 11
universal cash transfer, p. 11
contributory program, p. 11
tax credit, p. 11
social service, p. 11
transfer-in-kind, p. 12

program eligibility, p. 13
targeted program, p. 13
income test, p. 14
needs test, p. 14
means test, p. 14
social agency, p. 14
universal program, p. 15
progressive universalism, p. 16
private trouble, p. 17
public issue, p. 17

social problem, p. 18
political ideology, p. 18
conservatism, p. 18
social democracy, p. 18
liberalism, p. 18
laissez-faire government,
  p. 20
neoliberalism, p. 20

social safety net, p. 22
residual approach, p. 22
institutional approach,
  p. 22
social investment approach,
  p. 22
deserving poor, p. 24
undeserving poor, p. 24

welfare state, p. 24
income inequality, p. 24
Keynesian economics,
  p. 24
income redistribution,
  p. 24
social inclusion, p. 26

CHAPTER 2

Social Welfare Policy

OBJECTIVES

Policy provides the direction and structure to social welfare programs and services. This chapter will explore:

- the definition and goals of social welfare policy;
- the identification of problems to be addressed through policy;
- problem analysis;
- policy consultation and review;
- the selection, authorization, and transition of policy;
- policy implementation; and
- policy analysis.

INTRODUCTION

> Indeed, policy making is a spicy endeavour which happens in an environment that is as much a chaotic marketplace as a planned system. (Dr. Wendy Watson-Wright, Senior Director General, Health Canada, 2001)

Policies can be found in almost every aspect of our lives. Personal policies are typically unwritten rules that we set for ourselves, such as "I don't eat after 8 p.m.," or "I don't participate in gossip." Many parents have policies on what they will or will not allow their children to do. Policies are found in all formal institutions, such as schools ("No talking in class"), and the workplace ("No smoking on the premises"). Policies are also central to government decision making and intervention. There are many types of government or **public policies**; however, it is **social policy** that is most concerned with the development and implementation of social programs, such as social welfare, health care, and postsecondary education. These policies affect all Canadians, since they "determine who pays for and who benefits from government

STAGES OF SOCIAL WELFARE POLICY DEVELOPMENT

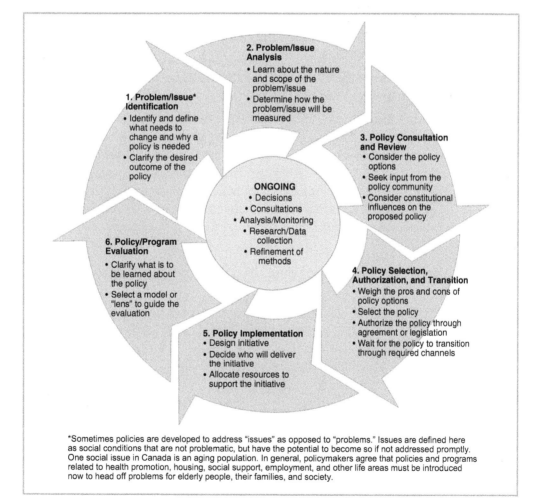

*Sometimes policies are developed to address "issues" as opposed to "problems." Issues are defined here as social conditions that are not problematic, but have the potential to become so if not addressed promptly. One social issue in Canada is an aging population. In general, policymakers agree that policies and programs related to health promotion, housing, social support, employment, and other life areas must be introduced now to head off problems for elderly people, their families, and society.

Source: Rosalie Chappell.

spending, how well or poorly people live, the nature of their relationships to each other, the overall quality of life, and the nation's commitment to social justice" (Abramovitz, 2004, p. 19).

Social welfare policy is a subset of social policy that provides the structure of most income security programs and social services. Working alongside economic policy, social welfare policy aims to

- strengthen job security and labour market supports, such as employment insurance and pension contributions;
- provide opportunities for training and skill development;
- motivate workers to work, and to save for the future;
- redistribute income to minimize the number of people living on a low income;
- create acceptable standards of living and working so as to attract foreign investment; and
- enhance the quality of life for individuals, families, and communities (Conference Board of Canada, 2000).

To understand social welfare programs, one must be familiar with their related policies and the process by which they are created. There is no official or preferred method of policy development in Canada; however, the stages model is widely used (Fafard, 2008). Any number of stages may take place over the course of policy development; Exhibit 2.1 summarizes six generic stages and their respective tasks. Note that certain activities, such as decision making and consultation, take place throughout the policy development process.

STAGE 1: PROBLEM IDENTIFICATION

In stage 1, **social policymakers**—that is, elected government officials who make the laws, legislation, and policies related to social programs—have to identify the problem for which a policy is needed. Policymakers also have to clarify what conditions need to change to address the problem, and what they hope to accomplish by creating a policy.

FROM SOCIAL CONDITIONS TO SOCIAL PROBLEMS

People are subject to a number of social conditions that may strain their ability to meet personal needs. These conditions include feeling lonely, being abused, gambling and not having a job. Although social conditions are not problematic in and of themselves, they may produce **social problems** (also called social risks). For social *conditions* to be considered social *problems*, they must create some measurable degree of economic or social hardship, psychological or physical injury, or other negative consequence. Most social problems are recognized by a large segment of the population who want to see a situation changed, and spark some kind of collective response aimed at correcting the situation (Thompson, Howard, & Jin, 2001; Henslin, 2003).

Certain social conditions are generally accepted as social problems, while others are not. In Canada, there is a general consensus that crime, child poverty, racism, homelessness, violence against women, and drug addiction are major social problems. These problems are recognized by policymakers as "public issues" that should be addressed by government. Other social conditions such as bisexuality, abortion, and divorce are seen as social problems by a smaller number of Canadians, and are subsequently not high priorities for social policymakers.

EXHIBIT 2.2

Homelessness is a major social problem in Canada, especially in large urban centres.

Source: Dainis Derics/Shutterstock.

CHANGING PERCEPTIONS OF SOCIAL PROBLEMS

The perception of social problems changes over time as a result of social, economic, political, cultural, and other influences. What is currently viewed as a social problem might have been considered socially acceptable in the past. A case in point is **racism**. During the first half of the twentieth century, the Government of Canada enacted racist immigration laws to limit the numbers of so-called "undesirables"—including people of Chinese origin, Jewish people, and black Americans—from entering the country. Today, racism and discrimination are not tolerated in Canada, as evidenced by the number of anti-discriminatory and anti-hate laws, and policies that promote multiculturalism, diversity, and social inclusion. As Canadian culture continues to change, so too do people's views of social conditions and problems, and their expectations of government policy. Thus, social policy tends to reflect the values of the nation at any given time.

It is not unusual for changing economic or social conditions to create new social problems, or exacerbate existing ones. In recent decades, globalization and a shift from an industrial to a postindustrial era have been associated with a wide range of social problems, including **social exclusion**. Socially excluded people tend to feel "left out" of society and the social, economic, political, cultural, or other benefits that society has to offer. Social exclusion can be traced to shifts in the labour market, the subsequent rise in low-paid, part-time, and insecure jobs, and the resulting strain on people's ability to support themselves and their families. A lack of sufficient income naturally puts individuals and families at a high risk of **poverty**. Living in poverty can raise the risk of additional challenges such as health problems, poor housing, and welfare dependency—all conditions that can create further barriers to inclusion in society (Galabuzi & Labonte, 2002). People living in poverty are at such a high risk of social exclusion that some policymakers treat "social exclusion" and "poverty" as synonymous, since each condition can cause the other, and both conditions relate to "lack" (Voyer, 2005).

Discussion Questions

▓ **Stage 1: Problem Identification**

1. Why do you think it might be important for economic policy and social welfare policy to work in conjunction with one another?

2. What types of social conditions may Canadians have accepted in the past, but now see as social problems?

▐ STAGE 2: PROBLEM ANALYSIS

In stage 2, policymakers must learn about the nature and prevalence of problems impacting society. This stage also requires policymakers to find ways to define and measure the existence of social problems.

LEARNING ABOUT SOCIAL PROBLEMS

A growing body of empirical research—otherwise known as **social knowledge**—helps policymakers learn about society's conditions and problems. There are many sources of social knowledge. At the government level are departments (such as the federal government's Policy Research Initiative) that conduct a wide range of research on social issues. In the private sector, the research studies undertaken by research institutes and think tanks provide invaluable insight into social trends, conditions, and problems. Professionals in the helping fields, such as social workers, psychologists, and psychiatrists, contribute to social knowledge in various ways. One contribution is made through **practice knowledge**; this information consists of evidence about what appears to help or hinder human progress, based on professionals' observations and direct service to **clients**. Finally, social knowledge has been enriched over several decades by a number of academic disciplines, including sociology, economics, and anthropology. Each discipline applies its own particular theoretical "lens" to the study of society's problems and their impact on people's health and well-being.

Depending on the nature of the information needed, social scientists use various **data collection tools** to gather information on social conditions and problems; those tools include surveys, interviews, and focus groups. Among those tools, **longitudinal surveys** are one of the most useful in the social welfare field. This type of survey follows the progress of the same group of people over a period of time; thus, the survey is able to reveal the types of *events* in people's lives (for instance, job loss or divorce); the time it takes for people to make *transitions* through life (for example, from losing a job to finding new employment); and the *influences* (such as the economy) on those events and transitions. In short, longitudinal surveys identify how changes and emerging patterns in the general population might create either social well-being or problems (Canadian Institutes of Health Research, 2008).

Ironically, the more we learn about social problems, the less we might understand them. Denis Saint-Martin (2004, p. 7) explains: "Nowadays, social problems are viewed as wicked not necessarily because they are, in themselves, more complex but because we, as societies, have accumulated more knowledge about such problems." Social knowledge has called attention to the complex, multidimensional aspects of problems, and how these problems can compound and exacerbate each other. Poverty, for example, used to be viewed quite simply: thirty years ago, poverty implied a lack of money. Today, poverty is understood from a much broader perspective, one that recognizes not only a lack of income, but also a lack of power, political "voice," and inclusion, participation, and opportunity in society (Osberg, 2007).

DEFINING AND MEASURING SOCIAL PROBLEMS

Once a social condition has been identified, it must be defined and measured. The definition and measurement of social problems is a highly complex process, largely because everyone involved in the process has his or her own perception of the problem, its cause, impact, and solution. Nevertheless, a general consensus on definitions and measurements must be reached before policymakers can design policies to effectively address the problem.

One of the first tasks in defining a social problem is giving it a name, such as "violence against women." A more difficult task is identifying the essential qualities or meaning of the problem—in other words, defining what "violence against women" is. The way in which a social problem is defined can vary broadly within and across countries, depending on many factors, including the values and culture of those observing the particular problem, and the objectives of the researchers studying the problem. However, from time to time, a consensus on definitions can be reached. For example, in 1993, when the international community (including Canada) signed the United Nations Declaration on the Elimination of Violence Against Women, the member countries agreed that the term "violence against women" means: "any act of gender-based violence that results in, or is likely to result in, physical, sexual or psychological harm or suffering to women, including threats of such acts, coercion or arbitrary deprivation of liberty, whether occurring in public or in private life" (United Nations, 1993).

Social and economic **indicators** help us to measure the existence of social problems. Indicators are bits of data or statistical measures that represent the various aspects of a social problem, and therefore help us to understand problems in concrete, observable, and objective ways. Some indicators serve to quantify such things as how many or how often people may be affected by a problem. Other indicators give us clues as to how a problem impacts people, or why it might exist. The role of indicators is illustrated in the Government of Canada's measurement of "violence against women." In this case, the phenomenon of "violence against women" is measured by the following set of indicators:

- the impact of the violence on women;
- the risk factors that might increase the likelihood of violence;
- responses by the community to the violence; and
- the use of victim services (Johnson, 2006).

While indicators can make definitions of social problems more complicated, they can also help to illustrate how a problem manifests itself in society and how it might change over time. Indicators are also useful for identifying emerging trends. For example, by tracking the risk factors associated with violence against women over a period of time, social scientists have discovered that being young puts a woman at a higher risk of abuse than being old (Federal-Provincial-Territorial Ministers Responsible for the Status of Women, 2002). Clearly, the type of information derived from indicators can help policymakers target their policies and programs to certain populations in potentially harmful circumstances.

At times, policymakers fail to agree on what a social problem "looks like," how it manifests itself, and how it should be defined or measured. Poverty is a case in point. Unlike the United States, Canada has no single, official set of indicators to measure poverty; rather, governments and groups in the private sector have developed various sets of indicators (or indices) to measure levels of "deprivation." The Government of Canada has developed three indices for this purpose: the Low-Income Cut-Offs (**LICOs**), the Low Income Measure, and the Market Basket Measure. The lack of consensus on what poverty is, and how to measure it, has made it difficult to determine the prevalence of poverty in Canada and to deal effectively with the problem. In early 2008, the federal government assigned a parliamentary committee to study poverty and to consider the possibility of a national poverty reduction strategy. One of the first tasks for the committee is to settle on a definition of poverty, and to figure out how to measure the phenomenon of "being poor."

Discussion Questions

Stage 2: Problem Analysis

1. Identify two or three major social problems in Canada. What are some of the indicators you might use to measure the problem?

2. We often hear or read about social problems through television, the Internet, newspapers, and other mainstream media. Identify some of the pros and cons of relying on these sources of information to teach us about social problems.

STAGE 3: POLICY CONSULTATION AND REVIEW

Stage 3 of policy development requires policymakers to consider various issues. For example, they must determine what the new policy would try to achieve— that is, the policy might aim to *increase* employment, or *decrease* child poverty. Policymakers must also consider the types of policies (such as cash benefits, or social services) that are likely to produce the desired outcomes.

To help with these types of decisions, policymakers often consult with a wide range of individuals, organizations, and agencies from both inside and outside government. Together, these individuals and groups form Canada's **policy community**. Exhibit 2.3 provides a graphic illustration of this community, which is depicted as several concentric rings and overlapping systems.

EXHIBIT 2.3
THE POLICY COMMUNITY

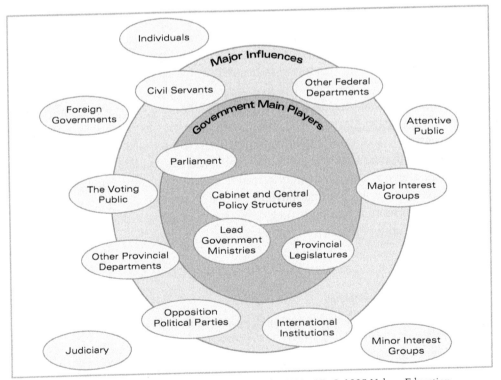

Source: From Whittington/Williams, *Canadian Politics in the 1990s*, 1E. © 1995 Nelson Education Ltd. Reproduced by permission. www.cengage.com/permissions.

At the centre of the action are the government bodies that are ultimately responsible for setting policy. The next ring includes major groups that influence the nature and content of social policy decisions. In the outermost ring are the individuals and groups that clarify, interpret, or shape the public's understanding of policy. Each participant in the policy community interacts with and influences the others, yet no single entity dominates the policy-making process (Pross, 1995). The policy community is key to the policy-making process. Paul Pross (1986, p. 107) writes: "Without the policy community's special capabilities for studying alternative courses of action, for debating their rival merits, and for securing administrative arrangements for implementation, governments would have great difficulty discerning and choosing between policy options."

This section considers the roles and issues of both government and non-governmental participants in the policymaking process.

GOVERNMENT PARTICIPANTS

The Constitution and Cost-Sharing Arrangements

To appreciate how the different levels of government work together on policy matters, it is important to consider the role of Canada's constitution, and the division of governmental power. Canada is a federal state—that is, a country that divides legislative power between a central or federal government, and regional (provincial and territorial) governments. This arrangement allows the federal government to look at overall Canadian values and objectives, while regional governments deal with local needs unique to their area.

In Canada, federalism originated with the British North America Act of 1867, which apportioned powers between the federal and provincial governments and gave each level its own sources of revenue and the authority to pass certain laws. At the time of confederation, social welfare matters seemed insignificant and potentially inexpensive, since Canada had a relatively small, rural, and self-sufficient population, and most personal difficulties encountered by citizens were adequately addressed by family, neighbours, religious charities, or, in extreme cases, by municipal governments. Government responsibility for social welfare seemed unnecessary at the time, and was therefore delegated to the provincial rather than federal level of government.

In the early twentieth century, the social and economic problems created by industrialization, urbanization, and immigration increased the need for an expanded social welfare system. Social programs were nevertheless costly and it was not long before the provinces realized they could not afford them.

The federal government, on the other hand, had broad taxation powers, and the ability to redistribute resources across the nation. Thus, the federal government gradually assumed a greater responsibility for social policy and programs in order to correct what would become known as a **vertical fiscal imbalance**—that is, the disparity between the federal government's ability and that of lower levels of government to raise money.

The vertical fiscal imbalance in the area of social welfare has been addressed through formal cost-sharing arrangements between the federal and provincial/territorial governments. An early example of cost-sharing occurred during the economic depression of the 1930s in the provision of "unemployment relief" (benefits and work projects for the unemployed). At the time, the provinces were constitutionally responsible for employment matters; however, as the costs of assisting a growing number of unemployed Canadians skyrocketed, the federal government bore more of the expense and responsibility for unemployment.

More modern cost-sharing arrangements include the Canada Assistance Plan (CAP) (1966–1996), followed by the Canada Health and Social Transfer (1996–2004). Since 2004, the Canada Social Transfer (CST) has been the primary cost-sharing arrangement for social welfare programming. About 75 percent of the CST currently finances social assistance and social services across Canada, while the remaining 25 percent funds postsecondary education. Under the CST, each province and territory receives an equal per capita payment (AUCC, 2007). In the fiscal year 2009–10, the federal government will transfer almost $11 billion in CST payments to the regional governments (Department of Finance Canada, 2009).

Regional Differences

Federal involvement in social welfare matters has ensured a more consistent and equitable provision of programs across the country. This involvement has nevertheless created tension between federal and regional levels of government. One source of conflict is the federal government's control over matters (such as social welfare) that constitutionally are a provincial/territorial domain. Although the regional governments welcome federal financial support, they have always asserted their constitutional right to design and deliver social programs as they see fit. Moreover, it is important for the provinces and territories to retain their own identities, which are reflected in part as locally developed (as opposed to federally imposed) social welfare policies and programs. A number of factors shape regional identity and create differences in how each region sets its priorities and implements its policies. Some of these differences are described below.

Heritage

Many regional differences are rooted in the traditions brought to Canada by the early European settlers. Ontario, for example, originally based its approach to social welfare on English civil law, which favoured the delivery of social services by private charities or churches (Splane, 1965). In contrast, British Columbia was essentially built by government, which led to government's domination in social welfare matters in that province.

Economic Capacity

Simply put, some provinces and territories are richer than others, mainly because some jurisdictions have more resources and/or a larger tax base to generate greater revenues. The disparity of wealth across the provinces and territories is referred to as a **horizontal fiscal imbalance**. To help correct this imbalance, the federal government created the Equalization program, and Territorial Formula Financing (TFF). Under the Equalization program, the federal government gives additional funding to the less prosperous provinces so that they can implement social programs that are of similar quality to those in wealthier provinces. In 2009–10, a total of $14.2 billion in equalization payments will be transferred to six "have-not" provinces: Quebec, Manitoba, Prince Edward Island, Nova Scotia, New Brunswick, and, for the first time in history, Ontario (Department of Finance Canada, 2008a; Webb, 2008). The TFF transfers extra funding to the three territorial governments in recognition of the higher costs of providing public services in the North. In 2008–9, the three territories received payments totalling over $2.3 billion (Department of Finance Canada, 2008a).

Despite attempts to distribute the nation's wealth fairly across the regions, disparities in wealth still exist. Moreover, the various jurisdictions cannot seem to agree on how equalization payments should be calculated to ensure fairness. Meanwhile, the poorer areas of the country (historically the Atlantic provinces) may not be able to provide the same range and quality of social welfare programs as those found in wealthier jurisdictions.

Ideological Views

Social policies in the various regions of Canada reflect not only the social problems in each region but also general attitudes toward people in need and how to help them. In Quebec, for instance, social welfare has traditionally played an important role in preserving the province's unique culture. Even in tough economic times, Quebec has been a staunch supporter of social welfare programs; the result has been one of the most highly developed social welfare systems in the country (Meinhard & Foster, 2002). In contrast, Alberta's approach to social welfare is much more residual. Alberta's wealth and financial ability allow for a wide range of public programs, yet that province pays, for example, some of the lowest social assistance rates in the country (NCW, 2006a).

Intergovernmental Cooperation

Federalism is often criticized for inhibiting social policy and the development of social welfare programs. Since political power is dispersed across the country and among different levels of government, a consensus on policy decisions can be difficult, if not impossible. Over time, the federal and regional governments have made concessions in order to achieve common social objectives.

In recent years, Canada has moved toward what Denis Saint-Martin (2004, p. 31) refers to as "collaborative governance," a new approach to intergovernmental relations in which social policies and programs evolve from partnerships between the federal, provincial, and territorial levels of government. This type of governance is based, in part, on a problem-solving approach that the federal government calls "doing what works for Canadians;" the separate levels of government are expected to put their differences aside in the interest of all Canadians. The Social Union, formed in 1999, is an example of this type of intergovernmental collaboration (see Exhibit 2.4 for more information on Canada's Social Union).

EXHIBIT 2.4

CANADA'S SOCIAL UNION FRAMEWORK AGREEMENT (1999)

Under Canada's Social Union Framework Agreement (SUFA), and within their respective constitutional jurisdictions and powers, the governments agree to the following principles and actions.

PRINCIPLES
- Treat Canadians fairly, equitably, and with dignity.
- Ensure equal opportunity and respect rights.
- Ensure access to social programs and help people in need.
- Respect the principles of medicare.
- Promote participation in social and economic life.
- Seek Canadians' input on social policy matters.
- Ensure adequate, affordable, stable, and sustainable funding for social programs.
- Ensure that this agreement is in accord with Aboriginal treaties or other rights.

Continued

MOBILITY

- Ensure free movement across the country and access to opportunities.
- Remove unreasonable residency-based policies or practices that inhibit access to social programs.

ACCOUNTABILITY AND TRANSPARENCY

- Be accountable to Canadians for social programs, and act in a transparent fashion.

GOVERNMENTS WORKING TOGETHER

- Work and plan together, identify priorities, and share information.
- Consult before introducing new social initiatives that may impact another government.
- Allow all provinces/territories to participate in new Canada-wide initiatives.
- Work with Aboriginal peoples to find practical solutions to their pressing needs.

FEDERAL SPENDING POWER

- The federal government will notify the provinces/territories before making major changes to social transfers, or introducing new national initiatives, and will introduce new initiatives only if most provinces/territories agree.
- Each province and territory will design its own social programs to suit regional needs; can reinvest any federal funds that it doesn't need (due to existing programming) in a related program area; and will receive federal funding if it is accountable, and participates according to mutual agreements.
- Both levels of government will agree on an accountability framework for new social initiatives.

DISPUTE AVOIDANCE AND RESOLUTION

- Work together to avoid and resolve intergovernmental disputes.
- Evaluate the Framework Agreement three years after its implementation.

*Although the Province of Quebec supports many of the principles of social policy renewal, it chooses not to participate in the Social Union, since the Union represents federal intrusion into provincial jurisdiction.

Source: Excerpted and adapted from Government of Canada. (1999). *A framework to improve the Social Union for Canadians: An agreement between the Government of Canada and the Governments of the Provinces and Territories.* Retrieved December 7, 2008, from www.scics.gc.ca/cinfo99/80003701_e.html. Reproduced with the permission of the Minister of Public Works and Government Services Canada, 2009.

NONGOVERNMENTAL PARTICIPANTS

Citizens

Since 1968 and Pierre Trudeau's call for "participatory democracy," governments have encouraged the Canadian public to speak out about social concerns, voice their opinions about policy decisions that affect them, and take responsibility for social and economic changes in their communities. According to the Canadian Council on Social Development (CCSD, 1969, p. 16), this type of **citizen participation** is not only an essential ingredient in an equitable society, but also offers potential benefits:

> Social policies and programs are intended to meet the needs and serve the interests of the individual citizen, living in community with his fellow man. The citizen therefore has a legitimate interest in the objectives, content and effects of these policies and programs; their planning and their adaptation to changing circumstances will benefit from his active involvement. He himself will also benefit.

In recent decades, policymaking models have emphasized an interactive dialogue between citizens and government decision makers. Citizens can consult with government officials in a variety of ways—for example, by attending legislative hearings or public meetings, or participating in "roundtables" (that is, a group of people exchanging views on selected topics).

Ideally, public forums give both citizens and government officials the opportunity to engage in dialogue that is meaningful, deliberative, and interactive. However, as Susan Phillips (2001, pp. 10–11) observes, the consultation process is flawed because "government usually determines who is invited, there are few opportunities for a real exchange of views and genuine dialogue, and participants receive limited information on how the results are used." Despite potential flaws, the consultation process is something that Canadians generally support. A study by researcher Mary Pat MacKinnon (2004, p. 10) found that, in general, Canadians want to be more involved in the democratic process (beyond voting), and seek "more meaningful opportunities to connect with decision-makers on issues that affect their collective quality of life."

Interest Groups

The social policies that become laws and legislation are often shaped by the efforts of interest groups (also called pressure or lobby groups). **Interest groups** are organized collectives that form to support specific causes, and try to influence government policies for the benefit of their own members or on behalf of the general public. In Canada, there are five broad categories of interest groups (with examples):

- business associations (Canadian Manufacturers and Exporters);
- labour groups (Canadian Labour Congress);
- professional associations (Canadian Association of Social Workers);
- research institutes (Caledon Institute of Social Policy); and
- advocacy groups and advisory councils (National Council on Welfare).

In the early 1990s, a panel created by the Conference Board of Canada concluded that interest groups are vital to a democratic society: "The only legitimate way for government to develop policy is by accepting, even seeking, information and views from those affected and the public at large. Lobbyists present competing views, supply otherwise unavailable information, propose solutions, provide unique insight and counsel so government can assess the implications of proposed policy" (cited in Overton, 1991, p. 18).

In the political arena, interest groups compete with one another for public recognition and government dollars. Thorburn (2008) observes that interest groups that successfully influence social policy decisions are typically "well financed, cohesive and stable, and their leaders, many of whom are former politicians, tend to represent causes which are favourably regarded by politicians and civil servants." Success also hinges on an interest group's ability to gain access to Cabinet ministers and to appear legitimate. Joanne Byfield (2003) suggests that interest groups that are financially supported by the federal government tend to have far more influence than public opinion in shaping public policy.

Interest groups use a variety of strategies to pressure governments to change existing policies, create new policies, or lend more support to specific causes. Radical strategies include public rallies, protest fasts or marches, strikes, boycotts, and sit-ins; more traditional strategies include collective bargaining, polling, holding public information sessions, directly contacting policymakers, participating in government consultation processes (such as roundtables), financing elections, and publicizing issues and concerns through various

EXHIBIT 2.5

Some interest groups try to influence government policies by staging public rallies or demonstrations.

Source: © Shaun Cunningham/Alamy.

media. Representatives of some interest groups may also be invited by a government committee to give an opinion or provide information on a particular issue. An example of this occurred in 2008, when some of Canada's most prominent interest groups (including the National Council of Welfare, the Canadian Council on Social Development, and the Canadian Association of Social Workers) were invited by the Standing Committee on Human Resources, Social Development and the Status of Persons with Disabilities to give their input on a national poverty-reduction plan for Canada (Canadian CED Network, 2008).

International Bodies

References to terms like the *global economy* and *global village* reflect the interdependence of nations around the world in political, economic, social, and cultural matters. Canada is an active member of a number of international organizations, including the United Nations, the Organisation for Economic and Cooperative Development (OECD), the World Trade Organization

(WTO), and the North Atlantic Treaty Organization (NATO). Many of Canada's partners in the global community (such as the OECD) promote the economic integration of nations through international trade and relations; others (such as the United Nations) focus more on social development and human rights. While all nations set their own domestic policies, these policies are open to scrutiny by the global community and, at times, need to be modified to conform to international standards and practices.

One of Canada's most significant social welfare reforms involved a shift from "passive" to "active" income-security policies—a direct result of the OECD's influence. Traditionally, Canada's unemployment insurance and social assistance programs were based on **passive policies**—that is, they did not require beneficiaries of government assistance to work or train in exchange for benefits. Passive programming is compatible with an institutional approach to social welfare, whereby those who meet certain eligibility criteria are entitled to benefits, simply by virtue of being a citizen. Beginning in the early 1990s, the OECD pressured Canada and other member countries to "activate" their income-security policies and require people on Employment Insurance and social assistance to participate in work experience or training programs; specific populations were targeted for those programs, including lone parents (mostly mothers), youth, and chronically-unemployed adults (White, 2003). The idea behind **active policies** is to strengthen people's attachment to the paid labour force, to help unemployed workers gain the knowledge and skills they need to quickly enter or re-enter the work force, and to discourage dependency on the state.

Canada's commitment to human rights is reflected in a number of United Nations' treaties, all of which Canada has ratified and implemented to varying degrees. These treaties influence the direction of Canada's social policies because they require a conformity to international agreements. In recent years, Canada has been criticized for failing to comply with certain obligations under international human rights law, specifically the United Nations' International Covenant on Economic, Cultural and Social Rights (ICECSR). The ICECSR outlines fifteen socioeconomic rights, which include the right to quality health care, income security, and factors related to an adequate standard of living such as food and housing. Some critics attribute many of Canada's social problems—such as growing rates of poverty, homelessness, and hunger—to its failure to incorporate many of the ICECSR rights into domestic legislation, policies, and practices (Poverty and Human Rights Centre, 2007; Ontario Human Rights Commission, 2007). The international community, along with many Canadians, continues to pressure the federal government to meet its international human rights obligations through social policies.

Stage 3: Policy Consultation and Review

1. Identify the unique features (for example, politics, the economy, heritage/ethnic diversity, and social conditions) in your province/territory or community that you think should be considered by policymakers when developing social welfare policies for your area.

2. In what types of activities have you participated for the purpose of influencing in government policy? Do you believe that your efforts were effective? Give reasons for why you think they were or were not effective.

IV STAGE 4: POLICY SELECTION, AUTHORIZATION, AND TRANSITION

Stage 4 of the policymaking process requires policymakers to choose one type of policy over another; once the policy has been selected, it must be authorized by government either through legislation or mutual agreement. The policy then moves through a formal period of transition.

POLICY SELECTION

Even after extensive consultation on policy options, it is not uncommon for policymakers to disagree on which type or "mix" of policy is likely to achieve the desired outcomes. In general, conservative policymakers tend to favour policies that give tax breaks rather than social services to people in need. In contrast, liberal policymakers tend to support policies that provide a mix of cash benefits and services; for example, a policy to assist unemployed workers may have an income-security component (such as Employment Insurance benefits), as well as a social service component (such as the provision of employment counselling).

The wrangling among politicians as to which type of policy is best has delayed the eradication of many social problems in Canada, including child poverty and homelessness. However, most policymakers, regardless of their political stripe, are likely to agree that the most desirable policy is that which benefits the most people, negatively affects the fewest people, produces the most benefits in the shortest period of time, and costs the least (Torjman, 2005).

EXHIBIT 2.6

Historically, politicians have disagreed on what policies are likely to eliminate child poverty. Meanwhile, many Canadian children go without adequate food, shelter, and other basic necessities of life.

Source: © iStockphoto.com/EyeJoy.

AUTHORIZING SOCIAL POLICY

Once a policy is selected, it must be officially authorized or sanctioned. While some policies may be passed into law (or legislated), others may be written up as a course of action, a set of principles, or a mutual agreement, all of which do not require legislation.

Agreements

The Social Union Framework Agreement (SUFA) represents one of the most significant written agreements in Canada. Signed in 1999 by representatives of the federal, provincial (except Quebec), and territorial governments, this intergovernmental agreement outlines the mutually agreed-upon principles and commitments for pan-Canadian social welfare developments.

Agreements are useful for clarifying the roles, obligations, and intentions of a working relationship, but they are not always legally binding. Moreover, many agreements lack enforceable sanctions if a member does not comply with the conditions laid out in the agreement (Addario, 2001). Thus, written agreements tend to be treated as "soft" laws (Eliadis, 2006). The Social Union Framework Agreement, for example, is generally viewed as a politically motivated document of good faith. According to policy analyst Harvey Lazar (2000, p. 7), SUFA is "more about process—about how governments should relate to one another and to their citizens in the making of social policy—than it is about substantive new social policy commitments."

Legislation

Social policy is often the product of a complicated process of enacting laws or legislation. In its initial state, a social policy is introduced as a proposal or **bill**, of which there are two types: (1) public bills, which involve matters of law and have a broad application (such as the nation or a province); and (2) private bills, which grant powers, privileges, or exemptions to individuals, groups, or corporations (Parliament of Canada, 2006). At the federal level, bills are given three readings by both the House of Commons and the Senate; if the bill passes in both houses, it is approved by the governor general and becomes a law (also called an act or statute). When bills are approved at the provincial level, they are signed by the province's lieutenant-governor and passed as law.

The legislative process involves a great deal of debate and review among governmental departments, committees, and legislators, to ensure that bills receive proper scrutiny before they are either rejected or passed into law. See Exhibit 2.7 for details on federal procedures.

POLICY TRANSITION

In terms of legislated policy, it is not uncommon for several months or years to pass between the proposal of a bill and its enactment. Several factors may slow a bill's progress through the legislative process. For instance, Canadian law provides for several "opposition days" to allow the official Opposition to criticize and debate the details of a proposed bill.) Sometimes the government deliberately delays a bill's enactment so that the public has adequate time to consider the content and the direction of the proposed policy. As a result of these types of delays, new social policies and programs may well be outdated by the time they are legally sanctioned.

THE LEGISLATIVE PROCESS AT THE FEDERAL LEVEL

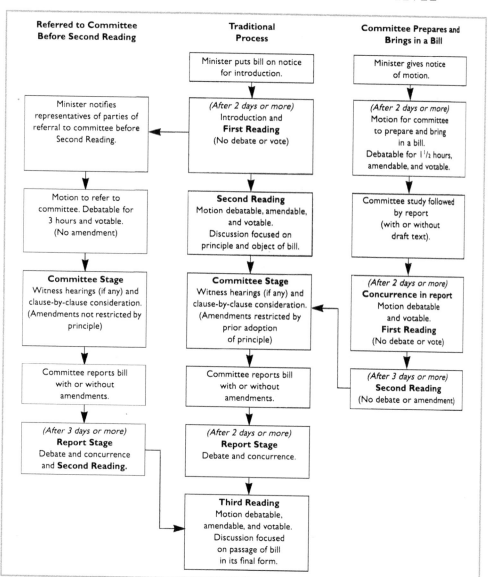

Referred to Committee Before Second Reading

Minister notifies representatives of parties of referral to committee before Second Reading.

Motion to refer to committee. Debatable for 3 hours and votable. (No amendment)

Committee Stage
Witness hearings (if any) and clause-by-clause consideration. (Amendments not restricted by principle)

Committee reports bill with or without amendments.

(After 3 days or more)
Report Stage
Debate and concurrence and **Second Reading.**

Traditional Process

Minister puts bill on notice for introduction.

(After 2 days or more)
Introduction and
First Reading
(No debate or vote)

Second Reading
Motion debatable, amendable, and votable. Discussion focused on principle and object of bill.

Committee Stage
Witness hearings (if any) and clause-by-clause consideration. (Amendments restricted by prior adoption of principle)

Committee reports bill with or without amendments.

(After 2 days or more)
Report Stage
Debate and concurrence.

Third Reading
Motion debatable, amendable, and votable. Discussion focused on passage of bill in its final form.

Committee Prepares and Brings in a Bill

Minister gives notice of motion.

(After 2 days or more)
Motion for committee to prepare and bring in a bill. Debatable for 1½ hours, amendable, and votable.

Committee study followed by report (with or without draft text).

(After 2 days or more)
Concurrence in report
Motion debatable and votable.
First Reading
(No debate or vote)

(After 3 days or more)
Second Reading
(No debate or amendment)

Source: *House of Commons Procedure and Practice* by Robert Marleau and Camille Montpetit, 2000 edition, Stages in the Legislative Process, Figure 16.1—The Three Options of the Legislative Process. © The House of Commons. Reprinted by permission.

Discussion Questions

■ **Stage 4: Policy Selection, Authorization, and Transition**

1. What are the potential pros and cons of (a) legislating policy, and (b) authorizing policy through agreement?

2. In your opinion, what are some of the possible advantages or disadvantages of delaying policy during the transition phase?

ⱽ STAGE 5: POLICY IMPLEMENTATION

In stage 5, policies are implemented or put into action. In a social welfare context, policy implementation is achieved through the development and eventual delivery of an income security program, a social service, or an other type of initiative aimed at enhancing well-being.

In Canada, policymakers must adhere to certain principles when developing social welfare initiatives. For example, initiatives must be

- sustainable (capable of surviving over time, using a "reasonable" number of resources);

- inclusive (foster participation in society);

- responsive (adapt to changing times and circumstances); and

- accessible (capable of being reached and used by Canadians) (Stewart, 2002).

It is not always clear whether policies are indeed sustainable, inclusive, responsive, or accessible until the policy is evaluated or analyzed. At that point, the policy or the program may need to be revised so that certain principles can be applied.

Once an initiative has been transformed from a policy to a program or service, government must decide who (such as a government department or a private nonprofit organization) will deliver the initiative, and what types of resources (such as money, staff, or equipment) will be needed to support the delivery of the initiative.

A primary focus of this book is on the implementation of social welfare policy. Each chapter gives examples of "policy in action," and how those policies (through programs and services) attempt to enhance the social welfare of Canadians.

Discussion Questions

■ **Stage 5: Policy Implementation**

1. Social welfare programs must be designed to be sustainable, inclusive, responsive, and accessible. What other principles (or standards) should social welfare programs adhere to?

2. Social welfare programs and services are policies "in action." Identify three social welfare programs/services in your community; for each initiative, try to determine what its underlying policy is trying to achieve (for example, some policies try to increase employment, while others try to reduce homelessness).

VI STAGE 6: POLICY AND PROGRAM REVIEW

Stage 6 of the policy development process involves the analysis of a policy or program to determine whether it is being carried out the way that it was intended, or whether it is achieving what it set out to achieve. Analysts must first decide what they hope to learn from their study, and then select a model or framework to guide their review. From time to time, a policy analysis or review will reveal flaws in the policy that make it necessary to amend or replace the policy, or, in extreme cases, repeal the policy altogether.

MODELS OF ANALYSIS AND EVALUATION

Whether conducted during or at the end of the policy development process, a formal review can help to identify which areas of the policy/program are doing well, and which areas might need improvement. A wide range of **policy analysis** and **program evaluation** models exist to structure and focus a policy/program review. These models include a cost-benefit evaluation (looks at the relationship between a policy/program's results and its costs); a needs assessment (determines whether an existing or a new policy/program is needed); and an outcome measurement (assesses whether the policy/program has achieved the desired outcomes or results). Two generic models—a logic model, and a process model—are briefly described below.

A Logic Model

A **logic model** identifies the connections between the activities of a policy/program and the achievement of its goals. This model assumes that successful policies/programs are the result of a series of "if-then" relationships: if *inputs* are invested, then certain *activities* can take place; if these activities are carried out successfully, then one can expect specific *outputs* and *outcomes* (Innovation Network Inc., 2005). These various components are summarized below:

- *Inputs* are the resources that are invested in an initiative, and include money, staff, equipment, time, expertise, and physical facilities.

- *Activities* (or processes) refer to how inputs are utilized; for example, resources may be used to provide staff training, improve service delivery, recruit volunteers, or promote services.

- *Outputs* are the goods or services produced by the policy or program, such as the development of written materials for clients, the number of clients served, and the types of services provided.

- *Outcomes* are the ultimate effects or benefits of the policy/program in relation to the goals set; for instance, at the end of a program, clients may report improved health or higher day-to-day functioning (Policy Research Initiative, 2004; O'Connor, 2005).

There are many advantages to analyzing the content of a policy or program. For instance, the study of discrete parts can help to reveal what happens at each stage of policy development or implementation, and how those parts relate to each other. This type of review can also be useful for identifying gaps or inefficiencies in program resources or activities.

A Process Model

While a logic model focuses on the *content* of a policy, a **process model** emphasizes the *process* by which policy is created and implemented. Process models assume that policies and their related programs evolve from sequential stages or steps (for example, Exhibit 2.1 illustrates six possible stages of social welfare policy development). One or more of these stages may be the subject of analysis.

A process model can help to explain what a policy/program does, how it does it, and how those processes relate to the final results. An explanatory approach may seek answers to the following questions:

- How is the problem understood, interpreted, or defined?

- What are the political processes that shaped the policy?

- Who are the main stakeholders of the policy—that is, who is most interested in, or impacted by, the policy?

- Who has influence on the types of solutions that are considered? For example, have policymakers sought the public's input and/or consulted with experts?

- Which type of organization—such as a government agency or a non-profit organization—is responsible for delivering and managing the program?
- Is the program achieving its goals, objectives, and intended outcomes?

Various strategies, such as a literature review or surveys, can be used to gather information about a policy/program's process. One cannot expect a single strategy to answer all questions about a policy's development process simply because the process itself is so complex (Westhues, 2002). Thus, several different strategies may need to be used, depending on what one hopes to learn about the policy/program.

ANALYSIS THROUGH "LENSES"

One way to analyze a policy/program is through a particular "lens." These frames of reference allow for the scrutiny of a policy/program to see if certain principles, standards, or values are being adhered to. Examples of Canadian-based analysis frameworks are provided below.

A Social Work Lens

The Canadian Association of Social Workers (CASW, 2003a) uses a social work lens to analyze the extent to which federal social policies reflect social work values and principles. According to that association, policies should, among other things, reflect dignity and respect for people, equality, and equity; be comprehensive; have constitutional integrity; and engage members of the policy community in the development of programs and services.

A Gender-Based Lens

Status of Women Canada developed the Gender-Based Analysis framework as a way to assess federal policies in terms of gender equality. This framework is applied across federal departments for the purpose of eliminating gender discrimination from federal policies and legislation, and for designing new policies that are gender-free (Status of Women Canada, 1998).

A Life-Course Lens

Traditionally, social welfare policy has been based on the life-cycle model, which focuses on the standard stages of life such as infancy, childhood, youth, adulthood, and old age. Those life stages, however, do not reflect reality as closely as they once did. Today, most people engage in activities independent of their age or stage of life; for example, it is common for people to attend college or vocational school at any time in their life, not just in early adulthood, which used to be the norm (Voyer, 2005).

The Policy Research Initiative (2004) of the Government of Canada is in the process of developing a life-course approach to social policy analysis. This model is based on new, emerging information about how people transition from one life phase to another (for instance, from marriage to divorce); what types of choices they make during these transitions (which impact later life experiences); and what types of resources they need to successfully make life transitions. Using a life-course lens to analyze social policy, analysts will be able to ensure that the policy focuses on individuals, rather than predetermined (and often stereotyped) groups of people such as "youth" or "the elderly." The life-course lens can also help to critique policy in terms of its ability to respond to people's experiences over the lifespan Policy Research Initiative.

An Inclusion Lens

The Public Health Agency of Canada (Atlantic Region) uses an inclusion lens to help governments, nongovernment organizations, and community groups "to analyze the conditions that exclude people, communities, and populations from participating in the social and economic benefits of society" (Shookner, 2002, p. 2). Exhibit 2.8 outlines eight dimensions in which exclusion or inclusion can be observed. For each dimension, there are elements of exclusion and inclusion that should be considered when analyzing a policy, program, or practice. Among the key questions to ask when using an inclusion lens are

- Who is being excluded (or included), and from what?
- How is exclusion (or inclusion) manifested?
- Who benefits from the exclusion (or inclusion)?

AMENDING, REPLACING, OR REPEALING POLICY

No policy is immune to change or abolition. Indeed, Canada's political history is rich with examples of policies that have been introduced, then later deemed as inadequate, and subsequently amended, replaced, or repealed. One example is the Unemployment Insurance (UI) Act. A review of that Act in 1971 prompted a series of amendments that introduced more restrictive eligibility criteria, shorter benefit periods, and higher premium rates. After it

EXHIBIT 2.8

POLICY ANALYSIS: AN INCLUSION LENS

ELEMENTS OF EXCLUSION	DIMENSIONS	ELEMENTS OF INC
Disadvantage, fear of differences, intolerance, gender stereotyping, historic oppression, cultural deprivation	CULTURAL	**Valuing contributions** of women and men to society, recognition of differences, valuing diversity, positive identity, anti-racist education
Poverty, unemployment, non-standard employment, inadequate income for basic needs, participation in society, stigma, embarrassment, inequality, income disparities, deprivation, insecurity, devaluation of caregiving, illiteracy, lack of educational access	ECONOMIC	**Adequate income** for basic needs and participation in society, poverty eradication, employment, capability for personal development, personal security, sustainable development, reducing disparities, value and support caregiving
Disability, restrictions based on limitations, overwork, time stress, undervaluing of assets available	FUNCTIONAL	**Ability to participate**, opportunities for personal development, valued social roles, recognizing competence
Marginalization, silencing, barriers to participation, institutional dependency, no room for choice, not involved in decision making	PARTICIPATORY	**Empowerment**, freedom to choose, contribution to community, access to programs, resources and capacity to support participation, involved in decision making, social action
Barriers to movement, restricted access to public spaces, social distancing, unfriendly/unhealthy environments, lack of transportation, unsustainable environments	PHYSICAL	**Access** to public places and community resources, physical proximity and opportunities for interaction, healthy/supportive environments, access to transportation, sustainability
Denial of human rights, restrictive policies and legislation, blaming the victims, short-term view, one-dimensional, restricting eligibility for programs, lack of transparency in decision making	POLITICAL	**Affirmation of human rights**, enabling policies and legislation, social protection for vulnerable groups, removing systemic barriers, will to take action, long-term view, multi-dimensional, citizen participation, transparent decision making
Isolation, segregation, distancing, competitiveness, violence and abuse, fear, shame	RELATIONAL	**Belonging**, social proximity, respect, recognition, cooperation, solidarity, family support, access to resources

Continued

Discrimination, racism, sexism, homophobia, restrictions on eligibility, no access to programs, barriers to access, withholding information, departmental silos, government jurisdictions, secretive/restricted communications, rigid boundaries	STRUCTURAL	Entitlements, access to programs, transparent pathways to access, affirmative action, community capacity building, interdepartmental links, intergovernmental links, accountability, open channels of communication, options for change, flexibility

Source: *An Inclusion Lens: Workbook for Looking at Social and Economic Exclusion and Inclusion*, Public Health Agency of Canada, (2008, June). Reproduced with the permission of the Minister of Public Works and Government Services Canada, 2009.

underwent another major review in 1994, the UI Act was seen to be so inefficient that it was replaced by the Employment Insurance Act of 1996.

Sometimes policies are introduced, and even legislated, and then later declared illegal or "unconstitutional." Many Canadians have had the courage to challenge certain public policies in the courts, claiming that such policies violate their rights under the Canadian Charter of Rights and Freedoms. Alleged Charter violations often relate to the interpretation of sections 7 and 15 of the Charter:

- *Section 7.* "Everyone has the right to life, liberty and security of the person and the right not to be deprived thereof except in accordance with the principles of fundamental justice."

- *Section 15.* "Every individual is equal before and under the law and has the right to the equal protection and equal benefit of the law without discrimination and, in particular, without discrimination based on race, national or ethnic origin, colour, religion, sex, age or mental or physical **disability**."

There have been a number of victories for citizens whose claims relate to section 15 of the Charter. Many of those victories have involved violations of disability rights, and discrimination on the basis of race, sex, or poverty status.

Since the Charter was enacted in 1982, the courts have struggled with the interpretation of the word "security" in section 7. Specifically, the courts have considered whether certain social problems such as poverty could be interpreted as a threat to an individual's security. The courts have also raised the possibility that "security" might include *economic* security and therefore guarantee a person's right to adequate food, housing, clothing, and income-security benefits. In general, Canadian courts have concluded that, while security is a worthy social goal, government is not responsible for ensuring it

(Buckley, 2005). In 2008, the Supreme Court of British Columbia went one step further on the security issue. That court ruled that, while government (in this case a municipal government) may not be responsible for a person's security, it must not impede a person's right to seek his or her own security; in this particular case, security referred to shelter. Exhibit 2.9 provides more details on this landmark case.

EXHIBIT 2.9

VICTORIA'S ANTI-CAMPING BYLAWS RULED UNCONSTITUTIONAL

In 2005, about seventy homeless people could not find beds in local shelters so they set up tents in Cridge Park, a Victoria public park. Law officials ordered the campers to remove their tents because they violated the City's anti-camping bylaws, which prohibited "temporary abodes" in public parks.

When the campers refused to leave, the City took legal action to evict them. In response to the City's actions, nine homeless people challenged the constitutionality of the anti-camping bylaws.

In her 2008 ruling on the case, B.C. Supreme Court Justice Carol Ross concluded that, due to the insufficient capacity of local shelters, "a significant number of people in the City of Victoria have no choice but to sleep outside in the City's parks or streets." Expert witnesses in the case noted that tents were more likely than blankets or sleeping bags to provide sufficient protection from the elements.

The B.C. Supreme Court ruled that the City of Victoria's bylaws that prohibited the erection of temporary shelters on public property violated "[section] 7 of the Canadian Charter of Rights and Freedoms in that they deprive homeless people of life, liberty and security of the person in a manner not in accordance with the principles of fundamental justice."

The Court added that Victoria's anti-camping bylaws "impose upon those homeless persons, who are among the most vulnerable and marginalized of the City's residents, significant and potentially severe additional health risks. In addition, sleep and shelter are necessary preconditions to any kind of security, liberty or human flourishing."

Victoria City Council announced that it will appeal the court's decision that allows people to erect temporary shelters in public places. In the interim, the Council has passed a new bylaw that will respect the court's decision, and yet limit the erection of temporary shelters to homeless people only, in certain areas, and during specific times.

Source: Canadian Legal Information Institute, *Victoria (City) v. Adams, 2008 BCSC 1363*, October 14, 2008. Retrieved November 22, 2008, from www.canlii.org/en/bc/bcsc/doc/2008/2008bcsc1363/2008bcsc1363.html; City of Victoria, "City Will Appeal BC Supreme Court Decision," media release, October 16, 2008. Retrieved December 14, 2008, from http://www.victoria.ca/cityhall/pdfs/pr_08/081016a_pr.pdf.

Discussion Questions

Stage 6: Policy and Program Review

1. Identify a social welfare policy or program in your community. If you were to launch a process evaluation of those policies/programs, what types of things would you want to learn about?

2. Identify an income-security program and a social service program in your community. For each program, try to identify the human need that it is trying to meet, or the social problem that it is attempting to solve. In your opinion, are those policies effective—why or why not?

3. Do you think that social policies should ensure that people have access to the basic necessities of life, such as food and shelter? Give a rationale for your answer.

SUMMARY

Introduction

Social welfare policy is interrelated with economic policy and provides the structure for most income security programs and social services. The stages model is a popular method of policy development in Canada.

I. Stage 1: Problem Identification

Social problems are conditions that create a negative consequence for a large segment of the population. The perception of social problems changes over time, as do the types of social risks that confront people. Globalization and the shift to a postindustrial era has created new risks. Social exclusion is a social problem that has sparked a renewed interest in the study of poverty.

II. Stage 2: Problem Analysis

Several groups contribute to social knowledge, including government, private research institutes, academic disciplines, and professionals. Increased knowledge about social problems uncovers their complexities. Various data collection tools are used to gather information on social conditions and problems. Social and economic indicators describe social problems in concrete terms. There may be multiple sets of indicators for a single social problem; for example, several different indices are used to measure poverty.

III. Stage 3: Policy Consultation and Review

Government and nongovernment participants make up Canada's policy community. *Government participants* are influenced by federalism and the division of powers. The provinces/territories are constitutionally responsible for social policy and programs; over time, the federal government has assumed some responsibility as well—a situation that has created tension between the two levels of government. *Nongovernmental participants* try to influence Canada's policies through citizen participation, interest group activities, and international agreements.

IV. Stage 4: Policy Selection, Authorization, and Transition

Policymakers often disagree as to which type of policy is likely to achieve the desired results. Once a policy is selected, it must be authorized either through legislation or written agreement. The legislative process is complex and can delay the enactment of social welfare policies.

V. Stage 5: Policy Implementation

Policy implementation is achieved through the development and delivery of income security programs and/or social services. Policymakers must adhere to certain principles when designing programs, and allocate resources to the service delivery organization.

VI. Stage 6: Policy and Program Review

Many models are available to guide the review of policies and their related programs, including the logic model and the process model. Some policies/programs are analyzed through a particular "lens" or frame of reference. It is not uncommon for a policy to be analyzed or reviewed and found to be flawed in some way; the policy may subsequently be amended, replaced, or repealed. Occasionally, public policies have been challenged in courts of law on the basis that they violate people's constitutional rights.

Key Terms

For definitions of the key terms, consult the Glossary on page 413 at the end of the book.

public policy, p. 31
social policy, p. 31
social welfare policy, p. 32
social policymaker, p. 32
social problem, p. 33
racism, p. 34
social exclusion, p. 34
poverty, p. 34
social knowledge, p. 35
practice knowledge, p. 35

client, p. 35
data collection tool, p. 35
longitudinal survey, p. 35
indicator, p. 36
LICO, p. 37
policy community, p. 38
vertical fiscal imbalance, p. 40
horizontal fiscal imbalance, p. 41

citizen participation, p. 44
interest group, p. 45
passive policy, p. 47
active policy, p. 47
bill, p. 50
policy analysis, p. 53
program evaluation, p. 53
logic model, p. 53
process model, p. 54
disability, p. 58

CHAPTER 3

Historical Foundations

OBJECTIVES

Canada's social welfare system expanded over several decades until the mid-1970s. This chapter will explore:

- the early phase of social welfare development (from colonial times to Confederation);

- the transitional phase (from Confederation to the Second World War); and

- the interventionist phase (from the Second World War to the mid-1970s).

INTRODUCTION

> Histories of welfare states are much more than collections of facts and chronologies of programs. They are also compilations of human memories and myths, of political conflict and struggle, of compassion and sharing, and of aspirations and achievements. They are the stories of community members coming together to protect themselves or organizing and encouraging their governments to create security against unforeseen misfortune. And they can teach us so much. (James Rice and Michael Prince, 2000, p. 34)

Canada's social welfare system is not the product of any one period or circumstance in history. Rather, social welfare policies and programs have been introduced and revised at different times and in response to various human needs and social problems. For the most part, the level of social provision reached at any given time in history has depended on public demand, the political and economic climate of the day, and government priorities.

While compassion and generosity have long been cherished Canadian values, a residualist philosophy has dominated social welfare provision. Early settlers expected to either support themselves through work or, if in need, turn to **family**, neighbours, the church, or charitable organizations. It was not until the aftermath of the Great Depression and the social and economic disruption it caused that Canadians seriously considered government in the role of "social manager" (Heclo, 1981).

THE EARLY PHASE (COLONIAL TIMES TO CONFEDERATION)

MAIN THEMES OF THE PERIOD

This period is characterized by self-sufficiency and minimal government involvement in people's welfare. The early immigrants to Canada received food, clothing, work tools, and land grants from government and private sources; however, for the most part, Canadians relied upon themselves to work hard and care for themselves and their dependants. The basic necessities were obtained primarily through self-employment (mostly farming). Asking for charity—even from the churches—was generally discouraged, and recipients of "handouts" were often made to feel like personal failures. With few exceptions (mainly in New France), Canada's early European settlers took a residual approach to social welfare (Guest, 2008a).

SOCIAL WELFARE IN NEW FRANCE

Settlers in New France were helped in a number of ways. Guided by the belief that government is responsible for its citizens, the Government of France funded a variety of educational, health, and other services to those who settled in New France (Meinhard & Foster, 2002). Many private charitable organizations were available as well, which gave housing and education to poor children, care to sick and elderly people, and refuge to the so-called "lunatic."

Charity given to able-bodied poor people was usually based on the condition that they would work hard to become productive members of society (Olasky, 1992). Some organizations, such as Quebec City's general hospital and the Congregation of Notre Dame, offered skills training to help settlers find or create work. The French settlers valued work and self-sufficiency and had little tolerance for begging. As early as 1674, a Royal Decree passed by France prohibited begging by able-bodied persons in Montreal; by 1676, vagrants and beggars were banned from the city unless they had special permission from a parish priest to stay (Myers, 1914).

When the British conquered New France in 1759, the social welfare supports established by the French government disintegrated, causing great hardship (Martin, 1985). Under British military rule until the Royal Proclamation of 1763, the care of the poor was assigned to individuals and religious groups. The Roman Catholic Church assumed the giving of charity as a moral responsibility and as a good deed leading to salvation. Bellamy (1965, p. 36) describes the Roman Catholic Church as being well suited to the role of charity provider: "Long experience in ministering to the weak and suffering, backed by a strong administrative organization, dedicated personnel and wealthy patrons, and its own abundant material resources fitted the Church well for meeting the temporal needs of the people no less than the spiritual needs."

The number of French charities, largely staffed by volunteers, grew during the nineteenth century. These volunteers ran soup kitchens and clothing depots, delivered food and fuel, collected and distributed donations of furniture, visited the sick and infirm, and helped out-of-work people find jobs. Many religious societies, such as the Society of Saint Vincent de Paul, were concentrated in the larger centres of Quebec City and Montreal. These societies provided basic necessities to those in need, regardless of religious affiliation, and advocated for improvements in living conditions for disadvantaged people (Lautenschlager, 1992).

SOCIAL WELFARE AND THE PROTESTANT WORK ETHIC

The Protestant Reformation in sixteenth-century Europe brought the belief that success at work, in the form of profits and wealth, was evidence of godly living, virtue, and God's grace. This new understanding of salvation and work—indeed, the creation of a "work ethic"—accompanied an emerging view of **poverty** as a sign of a sinful life and divine retribution. While many Protestants from Britain helped to relieve the poor from hardship, they did so in the belief that one must work in this world to be saved in the next. Thus, help to the poor "was often accompanied by unsolicited and often irrelevant advice on how the poor might regain God's grace through the exercise of ... thrift, hard work, self-help, and self-discipline" (Guest, 1997, p. 18).

Over time in Canada, the religious references in programs for the poor would gradually diminish. However, the **Protestant work ethic** would become a core value underlying many later social welfare programs, such as work camps during the Great Depression and, more recently, welfare-to-work programs.

POOR LAW PRINCIPLES AND PUBLIC RELIEF

Many of the principles underlying Canada's current social welfare system have their origins in a series of British parliamentary acts collectively called the **English Poor Laws**, the first of which was passed in 1601. Although the poor laws were meant to deal with poverty in England, they influenced how the British colonies viewed and treated the poor. Not all British colonies adopted poor law principles. Nova Scotia and New Brunswick enacted poor laws in 1763 and 1786 respectively; in so doing, the colonial governments (or parishes) in those areas assumed a public responsibility and expense of providing relief to destitute settlers. Newfoundland and Prince Edward Island never endorsed poor law practices to any real extent; rather, they encouraged their poor to rely on family, friends, and charities rather than on government. Since work was plentiful in Upper Canada (now Ontario), that colony rejected the notion of government intervention to help the poor, including poor law legislation (Guest, 2008a).

While the adoption of poor law practices varied across colonial settlements, the basic principles of those laws influenced the provision of **public relief** (an early term for social assistance or "welfare") in many parishes. Some of the basic poor law principles include the following:

- Public relief should be *residual*. Only after all private sources of help (friends, family, neighbours, charities) were exhausted did people have the right to seek help from the government.

- Public relief should be ***categorical***. Governments categorized people in need as being either "deserving" or "undeserving" of public assistance. The deserving poor (or "impotent poor") included elderly, sick, or disabled adults, orphaned children, and others who could not support themselves through paid employment. The undeserving poor included able-bodied adults who could not find work, as well as vagrants or beggars who were capable of, yet unwilling, to work.

- Public relief should be *conditional*. Recipients of public relief were expected to compensate society for any benefits they received. For example, poverty-stricken parents were given public relief on the condition that they not abandon their children.

- Public relief amounts should be calculated according to the **principle of less eligibility**. To discourage people from seeking or becoming dependent on government, benefits were to be minimal and less than the wage of the lowest-paid workers in a settlement (Rice & Prince, 2000).

Parish officials relied upon classifications of the poor as deserving or undeserving to determine whether a person should receive outdoor or indoor relief. **Outdoor relief** consisted of cash and other direct assistance that was provided outside of institutions to people who were deemed deserving and incapable of working. That relief was typically sporadic and meagre. Historical documents reveal that many "deserving" seniors had to resort to begging to supplement what little relief they received from local government (CMCC, 2008).

Indoor relief was provided in institutions, such as workhouses and poorhouses. The **workhouses** (or houses of industry) were for able-bodied unemployed adults who were expected to learn good work habits and pay for their keep through labour (Guest, 1980). (See Exhibit 3.1 for a profile of houses of industry and refuge in Ontario.) Separate **poorhouses** were established to confine various groups of poor people—the old and sick, for example, and orphaned children. However, to keep poor law taxes down, parish authorities sometimes herded all poor people into the same facility; thus, poorhouses became catchall institutions for anyone who was destitute (Guest, 1980). In general, poorhouses and workhouses were unappealing even to the most desperate individuals. Dennis Guest (2008a) notes that in the larger towns, the reputation of these establishments "was so fearsome that only those facing starvation would seek such help."

The parishes dealt with poverty and other social problems in their own unique ways. For example, in some of the smaller towns, poorhouses or workhouses were too expensive to build or maintain. As an alternative, settlement officials, such as those in New Brunswick, auctioned off the poor to work for local families. Some of the larger settlements built a variety of institutions to manage various "problem" populations. Orphanages and insane asylums were established in populated areas and were eventually deemed worthy of public support and given government grants. Asylums were also built to house immigrant women and children who had become widows or orphans during the voyage from Europe (Guest, 1997; Taylor, 1969).

EXHIBIT 3.1

THE HOUSES OF INDUSTRY AND REFUGE IN ONTARIO

The House of Industry and Refuge in Berlin (later Kitchener), Ontario, opened in 1869.
Source: © Doon Heritage Crossroads, Regional Municipality of Waterloo, Kitchener, Ontario.

Beginning in the mid-1800s, counties in Ontario followed the British lead and established institutions for the poor and needy. These institutions—called Houses of Industry and Refuge—were regulated under municipal law. Officers of the law were allowed to commit individuals to the institutions, where they were "diligently employed" either indoors or on adjoining farmlands.

In 1868, Norfolk County became the first county in Ontario to establish a house of refuge for the "elderly, orphaned, indigent and lunatic." Provincial legislation soon followed, which required all Ontario counties to establish similar institutions. Several institutions were created, including the Toronto Home for Incurables; the Hamilton Asylum; industrial schools in Victoria, St. John's and Alexandra; orphanages in Berlin, St. Agatha, and Wellesley; and the Coombe Home for children in Hespeler.

Waterloo County's House of Industry and Refuge, which opened in 1869, was built on a 141-acre farm. After visiting the Waterloo poorhouse in 1871, Reeve William Jaffray of Berlin County told his fellow councillors about the way "the charity of the County" was helping "the poverty-stricken of the land." Jaffray hoped that other institutions in Ontario would follow Waterloo's example and give more specialized care to the blind, the deaf, the "inebriate," and other needy souls.

New ideas about poverty and the treatment of poor people, and the financial security provided by Mother's Allowances (1920), Old Age Pensions (1927), and Family Allowances (1944), caused the demand for large institutions to dwindle. Many of the houses of refuge and industry were either demolished, or sold and converted into other operations.

Continued

Source: E. Hardin, "Regional History: Peace & Prosperity: Waterloo County 1853–1972," 2004, Regional Municipality of Waterloo website. Retrieved November 15, 2008, from www.region. waterloo.on.ca/web/region.nsf/0/63C468981ACA86E385256E0500504073?OpenDocument. Cottonwood Mansion Preservation Foundation (Selkirk, ON), newsletter, April 22, 2008, p. 4. Retrieved November 15, 2008, from http://linetap.com/cottonwoodmansion/May-08.pdf.

Despite the laws that enabled colonial governments to provide relief to the needy, a residual approach to social needs and problems predominated, and parish officials offered benefits only in cases of extreme emergency. The Protestant work ethic legitimated this approach, and curbed any notion of relieving "destitution at the expense of the incentive to work" (Romanyshyn, 1971, p. 5). Rice and Prince (2000, p. 36) point out that the term "'relief,' appropriately described social welfare in this early stage because it implied the state's limited acceptance of a 'public' responsibility for the care of those who were unable to care for themselves." Families were expected to care for their own members and, in the eighteenth century, some governments began imposing fines on those who failed to do so (Morel, 2002).

CONFEDERATION

The passage of the British North America (BNA) Act in 1867 united New Brunswick, Nova Scotia, Ontario, and Quebec into the Dominion of Canada, and divided legislative responsibilities under the confederation between the federal and regional governments. The provinces were given responsibility for "hospitals, asylums, charities and eleemosynary [alms-giving] institutions" which, for the most part, summed up the extent of social programs in populated areas. Since social welfare was considered a private and local matter, many provinces (largely those in central and eastern Canada) delegated their social welfare functions to municipal governments (Guest, 2008a). The BNA Act gave the federal government a minor role in the health and welfare of Canadians, and did little to increase the amount of federal revenue flowing to social welfare causes.

Discussion Questions

▓ **The Early Phase (Colonial Times to Confederation)**

1. Canada's pioneers took a predominantly residual approach to social welfare. Putting yourself in the shoes of a person living in this early period, give reasons why a residual approach may have seemed to be appropriate (and even helpful) for the times.

2. Identify the possible pros and cons of making "public relief" residual, conditional, categorical, and according to the principle of less eligibility.

▌ THE TRANSITIONAL PHASE (CONFEDERATION TO SECOND WORLD WAR)

MAIN THEMES OF THE PERIOD

The transitional phase is characterized by the rapidly changing social welfare needs of Canadians. Industrialization was drawing many rural dwellers into urban centres and, at the same time, the farming economy was giving way to one based on cash. As a result of these changes, family roles shifted: men became the primary wage earners, while women and children became their dependants." If the head of the household fell ill, was injured at work, lost his job, or died, the entire family's financial security was jeopardized (Bellemare, 1993). Urbanization, and related problems such as poverty, crime, and social fragmentation, threatened the stability of growing cities. Despite these pressing social problems, governments staunchly defended residualism, and continued to restrict assistance to the poor or those at immediate risk of becoming poor (Guest, 1997). By the end of the transitional phase, however, Canadian governments had assumed more responsibility for social welfare provision, a move that signalled the beginning of a philosophical shift from private troubles to collective responsibility (Meinhard & Foster, 2002).

SOCIAL MOVEMENTS AND CHANGING ATTITUDES

Industrialization and its associated problems prompted an increase in social consciousness and a feeling of mutual responsibility for one's fellow human beings. As they learned more about the underlying causes of social problems, Canadians began questioning the prevailing belief that poverty and other social ills were the result of individual shortcomings. A number of **social movements**—such as those related to labour reform, child welfare, and women's rights—took firm root during this period. Social reformers (or activists) called attention to the inability of families, charities, churches, and local governments to adequately meet the needs of a modern industrial society. Those reformers also pressured governments to take a more active role in the social and economic lives of citizens (Bellemare, 1993). During this period, a growing interest in social democracy, and the rise of political parties such as the Cooperative Commonwealth Federation (CCF), advanced the notion of **social citizenship**—that is, a right to minimum levels of health and well-being. Some of the highlights of the major social movements of this era are reviewed below.

The Labour Movement and Workers' Compensation

Industrialization created a number of problems for labourers in the mining, fishing, construction, and manufacturing sectors. These workers were being pressured to put in long hours for low pay, often in unpleasant or dangerous conditions. Mounting dissatisfaction among workers resulted in sporadic protests and eventually unions were formed as a means to demand higher standards of living, income security programs, and better wages with paid overtime. By the 1870s, trade unions were gaining collective bargaining power and becoming a powerful political force (Carniol, 1990; Forsey, 1974).

During the early years of industrialization, primitive and dangerous machines were causing frequent work-related accidents and injuries. Neither workers nor employers had financial protection when accidents occurred. For instance, in the late 1800s and early 1900s a worker could sue his employer over an on-the-job injury. If the company lost, the court made it pay the injured worker. If the damages awarded were considerable, the company was often forced to declare bankruptcy and shut down, which hardly benefited the injured worker (McGilly, 1998).

Many trade unions drew public attention to the increasing number of industrial accidents and the shortcomings of the compensation system, and pressured governments to improve the situation for workers. Although Quebec had a form of workers' compensation since 1908, Canada's first comprehensive and compulsory plan was the Ontario Workmen's Compensation Act of 1914. Under this act, all major Ontario employers contributed to the compensation fund; in the event of a work-related accident, a worker or his family could apply for compensation from the fund. The Ontario act was seen across North America as highly advanced legislation for its time. The act also started a workers' compensation movement; by 1920, every province except Prince Edward Island had similar legislation (Guest, 1997; Moscovitch & Drover, 1987).

Improving Conditions for Women and Children

As the pace of industrialization accelerated, families grew more economically insecure. Dependent women and children were vulnerable when a male breadwinner was injured, deserted the family, or died. Divorce was becoming more common, and women who had to work were often forced to leave their children unattended. These conditions triggered a change in attitude toward women, children, and the role of government in family life (Strong-Boag, 1979); these conditions also added fuel to the fire of social change.

The Child Welfare Movement

Canada's child welfare movement gained momentum in the late 1800s when John Joseph Kelso, a reporter for the Toronto Globe, wrote a series of articles about the neglect and abuse of children in Toronto. These articles spurred a public outcry that led to the passage of the 1888 Act for the Protection and Reformation of Neglected Children in Ontario. Later, Ontario's legislature passed the 1893 Act for the Prevention of Cruelty and Better Protection of Children. Considered the first comprehensive piece of legislation in North America to protect children, the new act placed Canada at the forefront of child welfare legislation. The act promoted nonprofit children's aid societies in Ontario and the placement of neglected, abused, and dependent children in foster homes rather than institutions. Superintendents were appointed to monitor the foster homes to ensure an adequate level of care for the children (Guest, 1997). Ontario's act also prompted other jurisdictions across Canada to introduce and enforce child welfare legislation.

The First Wave of the Women's Rights Movement

During the late nineteenth and early twentieth centuries, the women's rights movement focused primarily on improving social and economic conditions for women and children. At that time, women's issues were largely lent credibility through affiliation with the church. Christie and Gauvreau (1996, p. 108) observe: "Under the impress of Christian thought, even the most 'radical social teachings,' which in any other venue would have been perceived as a threat to the social order, were deemed legitimate forms of social amelioration because they were conducted within the respectable avenues of church reform." Women's church associations led to the establishment of national organizations such as the Young Women's Christian Association (YWCA) and the Woman's Christian Temperance Union.

Women were also advocating for extended legal and political rights, such as the right to vote and to run for political office. Although women were not well represented in political parties, they exerted considerable influence on social change through pressure groups such as the National Council of Women (see Exhibit 3.2). By the 1920s, women's groups and early feminists like Emily Murphy and Nellie McClung were making headway in a number of social causes such as mother's pensions, the minimum wage, prison reform, and medical care for women and children (Christie & Gauvreau, 1996).

EXHIBIT 3.2

THE NATIONAL COUNCIL OF WOMEN OF CANADA

The National Council of Women of Canada (NCWC) was founded in 1893, during a time when women were beginning to organize themselves for community action. Many women, looking beyond the charitable societies, garden clubs, cultural clubs, and missionary societies to which they belonged, saw the need for societal reform, better education for women, and women's suffrage (the right to vote). These women realized that they would be much more effective if they spoke with a united voice.

Members of the NCWC can be proud for many achievements, including the following:

- In the late 1800s, the NCWC focused on improving the conditions for female prisoners, female factory workers, and female immigrants. Through its efforts, for example, the NCWC helped to bring about the appointment of women matrons in prisons.
- The NCWC was instrumental in the federal government's enactment of the Act to Confer the Electoral Franchise upon Women in 1918, legislation that gave white Canadian women the right to vote in federal elections.
- The "persons case" was taken to Canada's highest court of appeal, and resulted in the 1929 declaration that women were indeed "persons" and therefore eligible to be appointed to the Senate of Canada. Three of the five women involved in this famous case were active participants in the NCWC.
- The NCWC has played an active role in promoting child welfare, including the prevention of child abuse, the education of children, the provision of quality childcare, and the formation of Children's Aid Societies.
- The NCWC has consulted with governments on a variety of work-related issues. These efforts have contributed to legislation aimed at improving women's working conditions, pay equity, and access to health insurance and pension plans.

As one of Canada's oldest women's organizations, the NCWC continues to work toward its vision of "a vibrant, pro-active, credible Council of Women reflecting the diversity of society, encouraging informed political decision making and public attitudes for the well being of society, through research, education, consultation and cooperation."

Source: National Council of Women of Canada. (2002). Website. Retrieved November 15, 2008, from www.ncwc.ca/aboutUs_history.html, www.ncwc.ca/aboutUs_achievements.html, and www.ncwc.ca/aboutUs.html.

THE FIRST WORLD WAR: CANADA'S FIRST PENSIONS AND ALLOWANCES

The First World War was a stark reminder of the vulnerability of the family unit. The considerable loss of life on the battlefields led to concerns about the growing number of fatherless families. At the same time, a high infant-mortality rate was seen as affecting the ability of families to replenish "the stock of healthy males" (Moscovitch & Drover, 1987, p. 24).

The federal government established a variety of charities to aid Canadian soldiers overseas and to provide relief to soldiers' families. A more organized system of relief was established when the government introduced two schemes for veterans' pensions: the Soldier Settlement, which provided unemployed soldiers with financial assistance and a parcel of farm land; and the Employment Service of Canada, which helped veterans to find jobs. Also, financial assistance was made available to the families of soldiers who had been lost or killed in combat. These systems marked a new direction in social policy, as government accepted greater responsibility for social welfare needs (Struthers, 1983; Guest, 1997).

The war's social and political impact stimulated an interest in legislated income security for mothers and their children. In Canada, the traditional practice of placing abandoned or poor children in institutions or foster homes was giving way to a more enlightened approach, under which children were kept in the home whenever possible. This change meant that mothers required additional support to raise healthy children. In 1916, Manitoba legislated the first mothers' allowance. This provided a small but certain income to all women with dependants, and established the government's role as the provider of income security and protector of minimum social standards. Soon after Manitoba took the lead, mothers' allowances were established in Saskatchewan (1917), Alberta (1919), and Ontario and British Columbia (1920) (Guest, 1997; 2008a).

INCOME SECURITY FOR ELDERLY CANADIANS

During the early twentieth century, many Canadians expressed concerns about the ability of the elderly to provide for themselves and about the capacity of poor families to care for their aging parents. Many older Canadians were applying for public relief, but it was not until several provinces complained about the rising costs of relief that a federal old-age pension scheme was seriously considered (McGilly, 1998).

The Old Age Pensions Act of 1927 established pensions as a right for all seniors, the first federal long-term commitment to social security. At that time, the pension was highly restrictive; to collect pension benefits, Canadians had to be seventy or older—a remarkably high age requirement compared to that in other advanced countries. Moreover, the means test for assessing eligibility was strict and humiliating; clearly, policymakers were reluctant to abandon their poor law attitudes (Guest, 2008a).

RISING UNEMPLOYMENT IN THE "DIRTY THIRTIES"

Various factors triggered the Great Depression in Canada, including the 1929 stock market crash in the United States and Europe's slow postwar economic recovery. Severe economic problems in these countries drastically reduced the demand for Canada's primary products. This hurt Canada's entire economy, which relied heavily on the exporting of raw materials and semi-processed goods. Unemployment rates soared from 3 percent in 1929, to 27 percent in 1933, especially among unskilled labourers and workers in the export industries (Horn, 1984).

High unemployment created a number of social and health problems. For example, by the time the Depression ended in 1939, almost one-third of Canadians were too poor to buy adequate amounts of nutritious food. On top of this, slum conditions had developed in the larger cities. In 1934, the Lieutenant-Governor's Committee on Housing Conditions in Toronto reported that "there are thousands of families living in houses which are unsanitary, verminous and grossly overcrowded" (Cassidy, 1943, pp. 57–58). Similar concerns were voiced by investigators in Montreal, Vancouver, Winnipeg, and other Canadian cities.

Unlike the United States and Britain, Canada was unprepared for the widespread needs created by the Depression. With no unemployment insurance system, those who lost their jobs sought help wherever it was available. Private charitable organizations, such as the Canadian Welfare Council and the Federation of Jewish Philanthropies, were involved in fundraising campaigns to help the unemployed, but had little impact on the problem of mass unemployment and widespread need (Bellamy, 1965).

Most provinces provided some form of public relief to the poor and unemployed. This was usually administered by municipalities, and was available in two forms. **Direct relief** was given in the form of cash, vouchers, or as tangible goods like food, fuel, and clothing. **Indirect relief** was provided through government-funded work projects, which were designed to get the unemployed back to work. These public work projects were nevertheless poorly planned and expensive. Meanwhile, the number of Canadians depending on public relief continued to grow, reaching 1.5 million people in

1933, and 2 million in 1934 (Horn, 1984). Many municipal governments soon found it impossible to cover the growing costs of public relief and other social services. The financial strain forced some of the poorer provinces and municipalities into bankruptcy, and ultimately caused the public to question the government's legitimacy (McGilly, 1998).

As the economic depression wore on, the federal government grew concerned about the growing number of unemployed, transient, and homeless able-bodied men. To quell the simmering threat of social anarchy and widespread revolt, the government set up work camps in remote regions of the country where these men could work building railway lines, clearing forests, or constructing bridges. By many accounts, these camps resembled nineteenth-century workhouses (Yalnizyan, 1994; McGilly, 1998).

While government struggled with the financial strain of relief programs, tension continued to rise among the unemployed. Before long, vast numbers of unemployed men organized protests against government and the unemployment crisis. The On to Ottawa Trek of 1935 was possibly the largest and most famous protest of the Depression years. About 4,000 men from work camps across the country boarded trains and headed to Ottawa to protest unemployment, poor wages, and unacceptable conditions in the work camps (Carniol, 2005; Yalnizyan, 1994). Exhibit 3.3 profiles that famous trek.

A NEW APPROACH TO A GROWING PROBLEM: UNEMPLOYMENT INSURANCE

Although public relief was a provincial responsibility, the federal government began sharing the costs of direct relief programs with the provincial governments during the Great Depression. With its broad taxation powers and greater capacity to borrow, the federal government had richer sources of revenue and was in a position to equalize economic conditions across the provinces, some of which were more severely affected than others by the economic downturn (McGilly, 1998). The federal involvement in public relief was intended to be temporary. Nonetheless, by the time the cost-sharing program was terminated in 1941, the federal government had assumed 40 percent of the total costs of public relief, totalling about $1 billion (Bellamy, 1965).

By the end of the Great Depression, Canadians were beginning to question whether unemployment did in fact represent the personal failure of individuals. As Armine Yalnizyan (1994, p. 31) points out: "The shiver of universal risk had swept over everyone, and people started demanding protections by pooling that risk across society, and not just at the traditional

ON TO OTTAWA

Boarding the trains for Ottawa, 1935.
Source: Courtesy On to Ottawa Historical Society.

During the Great Depression (1929–1939), thousands of young unemployed single men found employment in the work camps set up in British Columbia. However, by April 1935, they were fed up with labouring for six and a half days a week for 20 cents a day. The workers abandoned the camps and congregated in Vancouver, where they went on strike for two months. During that time, the men tried to achieve union wages, but were unsuccessful. They decided to take their case to Ottawa; this journey became known as the On To Ottawa Trek.

Leaving Vancouver on June 3, 1935, the workers "rode the rods" (on and in railway freight cars) as far as Regina, where they were stopped by the RCMP. On July 1, the strike was broken in a police-inspired riot and its leaders were arrested.

In a federal election a few months later, the Conservative government of Prime Minister R.B. "Iron Heel" Bennett was defeated. The new Liberal government abolished the work camps.

Source: On to Ottawa Historical Society. (2002). On to Ottawa Trek. Retrieved October 19, 2008, from http://www.ontoottawa.ca/index1.html. Used by permission.

levels of municipalities and provinces." Greater pressure was being placed on governments to provide a minimum of assistance with respect to income, nutrition, health, housing, and education.

Although the Second World War ended widespread unemployment created by the Great Depression, government officials worried that unemployment would again be a problem with the mass reintegration of soldiers at war's end. To minimize the threat, Prime Minister Mackenzie King introduced a comprehensive unemployment insurance scheme. Since unemployment was a provincial responsibility, King had to seek a constitutional amendment from the British government; this amendment was granted and, in 1940, Canada's Unemployment Insurance Act was passed. Except for veterans' pensions during the First World War, Unemployment Insurance was Canada's first large-scale income security program. During the plan's first year, almost 4.6 million Canadians—including dependants—benefitted from unemployment insurance (Guest, 1997).

Discussion Questions

■ **The Transitional Phase (Confederation to Second World War)**

1. This phase is marked by social unrest, social movements, and citizens demanding more from government in terms of quality of life and social well-being. Compare that era to today, in terms of how you see citizens trying to make their voices heard, and government's response to public demands.

2. Many of the public programs introduced during this phase were focused on improving the income security of Canadians. Identify the main income security programs developed during this era. What historical events warranted the establishment of these particular programs?

THE INTERVENTIONIST PHASE (SECOND WORLD WAR TO MID-1970s)

MAIN THEMES OF THE PERIOD

From the beginning of the Second World War until the mid-1970s, Canadians encouraged governments to raise living standards through an extensive system of public programs. New social attitudes also prompted a growing interest in social equality, human rights, social citizenship, and the social stability that a **welfare state** promised. This era of strong economic growth, high employment, and rising government revenues enabled governments to spend more on social programs and to assume much of the responsibility that had been held by private charities. During this period, Canada established a range of universal programs designed to protect its citizens from the insecurities of an industrial economy and to help them to participate in modern society (Banting, 1987). The building of a publicly sanctioned system of supports represented a shift from a residual to a more institutional approach to well-being, "with government being the predominant force of social welfare" (Meinhard & Foster, 2002, p. 3).

THE MARSH REPORT ON SOCIAL SECURITY

The end of the Second World War marked an economic turning point for Canada. The social and economic damage incurred by the Great Depression made it clear that capitalism alone could not meet everyone's needs. Politicians generally agreed that only through ongoing state intervention in the economy, could the benefits of capitalism be enjoyed by all Canadians. Without that intervention, politicians believed, "inequality would deepen and instability would result" (Broadbent, 2001, p. 6). To determine what interventions were needed, the federal government set up several committees to assess the postwar needs of Canadians.

The committees produced a flurry of reports outlining potential postwar programs. Perhaps the best known among the documents concerned with social policy was the *Report on Social Security for Canada* (commonly known as the Marsh Report). Released in 1943, the Marsh Report was influenced by, and contained many principles from, the famous Beveridge Report that came out of Great Britain in 1942. Leonard Marsh, a prominent social researcher, professor, and author, outlined a comprehensive **social security** plan for postwar Canada. According to Marsh, this plan was long overdue, considering the progress already made in other countries (see Exhibit 3.4).

The Marsh Report underscored the notion that economic and social risks were part of modern industrial life, and that they could be minimized by publicly supported benefits from cradle to grave (Maioni, 2004). Central to Marsh's vision of social security for Canadians was full employment at a living wage, supplemented by employment skills training and job placement services. Marsh proposed that employment risks could be minimized by social insurance programs to replace earnings lost due to unemployment, retirement, accident, disability, illness, death, or maternity. Social assistance would serve as a program of last resort for the small segment of the population who were in need, unable to work, and had no income (Battle, Mendelson, & Torjman, 2006). Marsh (1975) believed that other social security and human welfare needs could be covered by three main programs: (1) children's

EXHIBIT 3.4
MARSH SAYS CANADA'S SOCIAL SERVICES LAG

Marsh Says Canada's Social Services Lag

WINNIPEG, May 16 (CP), ---Dr. Leonard Marsh, of Ottawa, research advisor of the advisory committee on reconstruction, in an interview today named Great Britain, New Zealand and Russia as the countries with the most complete social legislation.

Dr. Marsh, author of the Marsh Report on Social Security, said Russia had the most comprehensive training and educational services of any country today.

"As far as English-speaking countries are concerned, Canada seems to be lagging behind. We lack health insurance, widows' and orphans' pensions, and sickness benefits. Our one redeeming quality is our excellent unemployment insurance."

A delegate to the Canadian Conference on Social Work here, Dr. Marsh emphasized the need for a national health insurance scheme and children's allowances.

Source: "Marsh Says Canada's Social Services Lag," *Victoria Daily Colonist*, May 17, 1944, p. 7. Reprinted by kind permission of the Times Colonist, Victoria.

allowances to help with the additional costs of raising a child; (2) national health insurance to provide health services; and (3) a contributory old-age pension scheme.

A primary principle underpinning Marsh's social security proposal was the **social minimum**, which Marsh (1950, p. 35) defined as "the realization that in a civilized society, there is a certain minimum of conditions without which 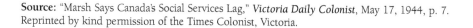 health, decency, happiness, and a 'chance in life' are impossible." According to Marsh, social security programs were the means to establish a social minimum.

Historian Michael Bliss (1975, p. ix) hailed the Marsh Report as the "most important single document in the history of the development of the welfare state in Canada." Despite its apparent significance, Marsh's plan for a comprehensive and coordinated social security system only got as far as being reviewed by the Parliamentary Committee on Social Security in 1943. Some members of that committee feared that the economy could not support

Marsh's plan; others maintained that poverty was the responsibility of individuals and families, not government. The plan was also criticized for recommending that the federal government assume a greater role in providing social security to Canadians, a role that the provinces were constitutionally entitled to. Marsh's report was therefore never tabled in the House of Commons. Even so, the document provided the structural framework for many of Canada's future health and social welfare programs (CMCC, 2002a; Guest, 1997).

FAMILY ALLOWANCE ACT OF 1944

According to Marsh (1975, p. 197), the purpose of family allowance legislation was to ensure a minimum income level for families and, in so doing, make a "direct attack on poverty where it is bound up with the strain imposed by a large family on a small income." Family Allowances were also seen as a solution to the growing problems of poor nutrition and high infant mortality revealed by Depression-era and wartime studies.

Even though its enactment required a constitutional amendment, the Family Allowances Act was passed in 1944. This federally administered allowance was Canada's first universal social welfare program, and was sent to all Canadian families that had dependants under sixteen. In its first year (1945), the program cost taxpayers about $250 million, which was until then the most spent on any social program in Canada (Bellamy, 1965; Guest, 2008b).

SOLIDIFYING CANADA'S RETIREMENT INCOME SYSTEM

The Old Age Pensions Act of 1927 had been criticized for many years because of its stigmatizing means test and inadequate benefits. In 1951, that act was replaced by two new pension plans: Old Age Security (OAS), which provided universal benefits and was fully funded and administered by the federal government, and Old Age Assistance, a means-tested scheme that was cost-shared by the provincial and federal governments and administered by the provinces (Guest, 1997).

In 1965, the Canada Pension Plan (CPP) and its counterpart, the Quebec Pension Plan (QPP), were introduced. These plans provided a first line of defence for paid workers and their families who suffered a loss of income due to retirement, disability, or death. The CPP/QPP was available to 92 percent of the paid labour force when it was first implemented; however, it was expected to be most beneficial to the many workers who did not have access to employer-sponsored pension schemes. The CPP and QPP were different in some ways; both had similar eligibility criteria and benefit levels, and both were compulsory social insurance schemes that required all workers between 18 and 70 to make contributions as long as they were working.

Although the CPP/QPP has many unique features, its historical significance lies in the fact that it was the first income security program to be fully indexed—in other words, benefits increased automatically as the cost of living rose. Prior to the CPP/QPP, any increases in benefits for income security programs (such as Old Age Security) had to be authorized by Parliament or the provincial legislatures.

The introduction of Old Age Security, Old Age Assistance, and the CPP/QPP underscored the federal government's newly accepted responsibility for the security of elderly Canadians. These plans also took the retirement income system one step closer to ensuring a social minimum for seniors (Guest, 1997; Oderkirk, 1996).

CANADA ASSISTANCE PLAN OF 1966

Before 1966, the funding arrangement for provincial/territorial social welfare programs was highly problematic. For one thing, the federal funds to the provinces and territories were categorical—that is, the funds could only be used for specific purposes. For example, Old Age Assistance was limited to people aged 65 to 69; Blind Persons' Allowances were only for those deemed legally blind; and Disabled Persons' Allowances could only be used by people who were totally or permanently disabled. Many people in need, such as abused women, did not fit into any specific category or meet a program's criteria and therefore were left without adequate support. John E. Osborne (1986, p. 58) suggests that the "tight and inflexible" eligibility criteria for many programs "were intended to assure the public that only 'legitimately' needy and 'deserving' poor people qualified; but they also meant that many equally needy poor were denied benefits." To correct this and other problems, the federal government introduced the Canada Assistance Plan (CAP) in 1966.

Under CAP, the provinces and territories were required to meet certain national standards but were allowed considerable leeway in designing and administering social welfare programs. Meanwhile, the federal government paid half the costs. Social assistance recipients received financial aid to meet basic living needs, including food, clothing, and shelter; in some cases, assistance was also available for transportation, day care, and uninsured health needs such as dental and eye care. Under CAP's original provisions, social services were classified as **welfare services**, and were part of an overall strategy to eradicate the causes of poverty, child neglect, and dependence on social assistance, while softening the effects of these problems. Welfare services included protection services for children, rehabilitation programs for people with disabilities, home support for seniors, employment programs, community development services, and **childcare** (HRDC, 1994b).

The introduction of CAP resulted in an increase in federal aid, allowing the provinces and territories to expand, integrate, and improve their respective social welfare programs. In this way, Canada could establish its social safety net, and ensure a minimum standard of living for low-income groups, regardless of why they needed help (HRDC, 1994b).

POVERTY AND THE NOTION OF GUARANTEED INCOME

Several events during the early 1960s motivated Prime Minister Lester B. Pearson to introduce a plan to eliminate poverty in Canada. These events included an increasing awareness of poverty, the American government's declaration of a war on poverty in the United States, and the development of new methods for measuring poverty (Johnson, 1987). The prime minister's announcement paved the way for several studies on poverty. One, by the Economic Council of Canada (1968, p. 1), concluded

> Poverty in Canada is real. Its numbers are not in the thousands, but the millions. There is more of it than our society can tolerate, more than the economy can afford, and far more than existing measures and efforts can cope with. Its persistence, at a time when the bulk of Canadians enjoy one of the highest standards of living in the world, is a disgrace.

Also in 1968, the Senate Committee on Poverty was appointed to look at the extent of poverty in Canada and to recommend policy changes. Two findings of the inquiry were of particular concern to the committee: the high number of children who were growing up in poverty and the approximately two million **working poor** (people who maintain regular employment but remain poor). The committee's report called attention to poverty as a growing social problem, provided insight into the causes of poverty, and suggested the establishment of a social minimum.

Policy experts agreed that, in order to establish a social minimum, the entire income security system would have to be overhauled; this would involve scrapping a number of existing poverty-oriented programs and introducing a federally funded and administered **guaranteed annual income**

(GAI). A GAI suggests that all citizens have the right to a minimum income as the result of either paid work or government subsidies. Under a GAI scheme, Canadians would be assured a minimum income based on marital status, number of children, financial resources, age, and geographic location (Guest, 1997; 2008a).

The Canadian government flirted with the idea of a GAI, but a nationwide plan never materialized. However, several provinces implemented variations of a GAI for seniors who were already receiving the federally funded Old Age Security and Guaranteed Income Supplement. For example, Ontario in 1974 introduced the Guaranteed Annual Income System (GAINS) to ensure a basic income for residents 65 and older; the benefit was calculated as the amount needed to raise a recipient's income above the poverty line.

SOCIAL MOVEMENTS: SHAKING ESTABLISHED FOUNDATIONS

By the 1960s, Canada and other Western countries were witnessing a flurry of new social movements that significantly challenged the *status quo*. These included the "second wave" of the women's movement, the environmental movement, the gay rights movement, and the peace movement. Although concerned with changing government policies and practices, these social movements were perhaps most intent on changing those social values that ultimately oppressed, demoralized, or marginalized people (M. Smith, 2004; Howlett, 1992).

Among the many social movements of the time, the women's liberation (or feminist) movement was especially effective in influencing social policy. Declaring that "the personal is political," women politicized a variety of issues, such as family violence, that were traditionally regarded as "private troubles" rather than "public issues" (M. Smith, 2004). The women's movement had two keys goals: (1) to achieve social justice for women in all areas of human endeavour, including the media, law, education, religion, and science; and (2) to break down established patriarchal power structures that oppressed and controlled women (Eichler & Lavigne, 2008; Armitage, 2003).

The Royal Commission on the Status of Women (RCSW), federally appointed in 1967, was one of the driving forces behind Canada's women's movement. Not only did the commission establish an agenda of issues and strategies for improving conditions for women, but it also identified government as the most suitable system for addressing equality and equity concerns. As a result of the RCSW's efforts, a number of bureaus for women—including the Canadian Advisory Council on the Status of Women—were established at various levels of government. The RCSW also contributed to the formation or consolidation of women's organizations in the private sector.

THE EARLY 1970s: A TIME FOR REVIEW

The Income Security Review of 1970

An increasing concern for rising poverty rates and a growing uneasiness with the costs of social welfare programs sparked a renewed interest in reviewing Canada's income security programs. In 1970, the federal government published *Income Security for Canadians*, a report that outlined how income security programs should be more targeted, to give Canadians with the lowest incomes "the greatest concentration of available resources" (Government of Canada, 1970, p. 1). Among its many recommendations, the report called for the elimination of universality as it applied to Family Allowances and Old Age Security. This proposal drew a mixed reaction in the House of Commons. Owing to the lengthy debates on the proposed reforms and an impending federal election in 1972, the federal government decided to temporarily shelve its proposed revisions to income security programs (Guest, 1997; CMCC, 2002b).

The Social Security Review (1973–1976)

In 1973, the federal government under Prime Minister Pierre Elliott Trudeau launched a joint federal/provincial/territorial review of Canada's social welfare system. A few months later, the federal government issued its report, *Working Paper on Social Security in Canada*, which outlined some of the broad policy areas to consider when planning for a more effective social welfare system. For example, the federal government wanted to focus on finding ways to deal with the problem of low or inconsistent earnings among Canadian workers, and on developing a more universal system of social services (Guest, 1997).

The energy crisis of 1973, rising unemployment rates, high inflation, and general economic decline severely strained government revenues. By the end of 1975, many reforms initiated by the social security review were either axed or severely cut back in an attempt by federal and regional governments to contain public spending. Despite these curtailments, the review paved the way for certain income security programs, including Saskatchewan's Family Income Plan (1974), the federal Refundable Child Tax Credit (1978), and Manitoba's Income

EXHIBIT 3.5

As Prime Minister of Canada (1968-1979; 1980-1984), Pierre Elliott Trudeau was committed to creating a more humane, caring, and "just society"—a society free of poverty and one in which all Canadians could enjoy equal opportunity.

Source: Library and Archives Canada/Credit: Duncan Cameron/Canada. Office of the Prime Minister collection/C-046600. © Government of Canada. Reproduced with the permission of the Minister of Public Works and Government Services Canada (2008).

Support Program (1980). In addition, the review prompted the federal government to triple Family Allowance benefits (from an average of $7.21 to $20 a month per child) and to index those benefits to the consumer price index.

Shifting of the Tide

In a climate of rising inflation and unemployment rates, Canadians began questioning the costs of the social welfare system. Many Canadians were also criticizing social welfare programs for being of poor quality and for doing little to solve social problems. Furthermore, there were concerns that more and more Canadians were coming to rely on social assistance (Heclo, 1981; Rice & Prince, 2000).

In the years following the social security review, Canada's social welfare system underwent considerable downsizing as many programs and services were reduced, frozen, or eliminated. Any ambition that Canada may have had in becoming a full-fledged welfare state vanished. By the mid-1970s, at the peak of social welfare development, Canada had a network of programs that provided partial income security to working people, and more extensive support to those outside the labour market, such as seniors and children (Ross, 1987). Despite this limited protection, the income redistribution required to provide programs and services advanced equality for all Canadians. Edward Broadbent (2001, p. 6)—the former leader of the New Democratic Party of Canada—believes that this redistribution had "the dual results of increasing the real freedom of millions of human beings to the highest level in history and of reducing internal conflict to its lowest level in this century."

Discussion Questions

The Interventionist Phase (Second World War to Mid-1970s)

1. Many modern-day social welfare programs were established during this era. Why do you think the decades from the end of the Second World War to the mid-1970s were particularly receptive to greater government responsibility for social welfare? Consider what might have been happening in the political, social, economic, and cultural environment to support a more institutional approach to social welfare.

2. How might the social movements of the 1960s and 1970s have influenced the expansion of Canada's social welfare system?

SUMMARY

Introduction

Canada's social welfare system has evolved over several decades in response to public demand, politics, and government priorities. A residual approach dominated early social welfare provision until after the Great Depression, when Canadians recognized a social role for government.

I. The Early Phase (Colonial Times to Confederation)

French and British immigrants had their own unique methods of caring for the poor, the sick, and the needy. The Roman Catholic Church and secular charities helped the early French settlers. In the British settlements, the Protestant work ethic and the English Poor Laws guided the provision of public relief. Although the British North America Act assigned responsibility for social welfare to the provinces, there was little interest in or need for a social welfare system.

II. The Transitional Phase (Confederation to Second World War)

Urbanization and its related problems threatened the stability of growing Canadian cities. Industrialization sparked labour reform and workers' compensation legislation. The introduction of veterans' pensions indicated a greater government intervention in social welfare matters. Conditions for women, children, and seniors improved as a result of mothers' allowances, child welfare legislation, and old-age pensions. During the Great Depression, severe economic and social problems, along with ineffective public programs, spurred the federal government to introduce unemployment insurance in 1940. Despite the hardship of the times, governments staunchly defended residualism.

III. The Interventionist Phase (Second World War to Mid-1970s)

By the end of the Second World War, Canadians wanted a higher standard of living. The Marsh Report outlined a comprehensive social security plan, and promoted the concepts of a social minimum and family allowances. Income security for seniors improved with the passage of various pension plans. During the 1960s, an expansion of social welfare programs became possible under CAP, and the war on poverty brought a renewed interest in a guaranteed annual income. Many social movements signalled a greater acceptance of collective responsibility. By the early 1970s, Canadians were concerned about the economy and the growing costs of social welfare. The federal government tried to review those programs, but politics and economic problems were greater priorities. Any notion of Canada becoming a full-fledged welfare state was discarded.

Key Terms

For definitions of the key terms, consult the Glossary on page 413 at the end of the book.

family, p. 63
poverty, p. 64
Protestant work ethic, p. 65
English Poor Laws, p. 65
public relief, p. 65
categorical, p. 65
principle of less eligibility, p. 66
outdoor relief, p. 66

indoor relief, p. 66
workhouse, p. 66
poorhouse, p. 66
social movement, p. 69
social citizenship, p. 69
direct relief, p. 74
indirect relief, p. 74
welfare state, p. 77

social security, p. 78
social minimum, p. 79
indexed, p. 81
welfare service, p. 81
childcare, p. 82
working poor, p. 82
guaranteed annual income, p. 82

4

Social Welfare in an Age of Economic Uncertainty

OBJECTIVES

The era from the mid-1970s to present day is characterized by welfare state retrenchment, review, reform, and a general uncertainty for the direction of social welfare in Canada. This chapter will explore:

- the issues of deficit, debt, and Canada's fiscal crisis;
- welfare state retrenchment during the Mulroney and Chrétien years;
- social welfare reforms;
- the impact of fiscal restraint on Canadians; and
- social investment and fiscalization strategies.

INTRODUCTION

The social welfare structure so laboriously and painstakingly erected in Canada over the past forty years has clearly outlived its usefulness. The social scientists who have studied it, the bureaucrats who have administered it, and the poor who have experienced it are of one mind that in today's swiftly changing world the [social] welfare system is a hopeless failure. The matter is not

even controversial. But what is to take its place?
(*Report of the Special Senate Committee on Poverty*, 1971, p. vii)

Following the economic boom of the 1960s, Canada's economic performance—like that in other industrial countries such as Britain and the United States—began to slow. Unemployment, inflation, and interest rates inched their way upward, and government revenues and household incomes started a downward slide.

At first, Western nations believed that the economic downturn was temporary, so rather than raise taxes or cut public programs, they chose to borrow money. Reduced government revenues, plus interest payments on the borrowed money, made it increasingly difficult for governments to balance their annual budgets. As a result, countries began incurring yearly **budget deficits** (that is, their spending exceeded their income); those deficits accumulated

EXHIBIT 4.1

THE NATIONAL DEFICIT

Source: Reprinted courtesy of the artist, Bob Bierman.

over the years, creating huge **public debt**. Eventually, the Western world realized that the economic decline that began in the 1970s was not temporary; rather, it was part of a long-term trend associated with globalization and a shift from an industrial to a postindustrial era.

Politicians, business groups, and economists around the world warned that Western countries were headed for a **fiscal crisis**, which would soon make it difficult to finance health and other social programs needed by an aging population. In response to these and similar warnings, governments began to shift their priorities away from social development to getting their fiscal house in order. Canada chose to curb its deficit by drastically cutting public spending; this meant that many public programs, including those for social welfare, faced termination, cutbacks, or replacement.

What began as a gradual reduction in social expenditures in the 1970s escalated into a steady erosion of social programs in the 1980s, and a near-dismantling of Canada's social welfare system during the 1990s. Thus, **welfare state retrenchment** characterized the course of social welfare in Canada for almost three decades. This chapter chronicles the main events of that period—an era that reflects what Rice and Prince (2000, p. 84) refer to as a "crisis of the welfare state." Concluding the chapter is a look at selected political and economic developments impacting social welfare today.

WELFARE STATE RETRENCHMENT: THE MULRONEY AND CHRÉTIEN YEARS

A PROGRESSIVE CONSERVATIVE GOVERNMENT

When Brian Mulroney and the Progressive Conservatives (PCs) formed a federal government in 1984, Canada was still recovering from the global recession of 1981 to 1983. Unemployment was widespread, inflation was soaring, and the federal deficit was over $32 billion. After years of deficit spending under a Liberal government, Canadians were hoping that the PCs would reverse the rise in public debt and annual deficits, and kick-start the economy.

Since the Second World War, federal governments had largely supported Keynesian economics, which promoted the redistribution of wealth and the use of the tax system to shift income away from high—and moderate-income earners toward those with low incomes. The PCs brought a new approach to economics called **monetarism**, an economic philosophy that called for debt reduction, reduced public spending, and minimal government intervention (CMCC, 2002b). Such an approach, the Conservatives promised, would curtail the economic problems created by a burgeoning public debt, and eventually restore Canada's economy (Finn, 1985). Conservatives also believed that the making and spending of money in a free market economy would meet human needs more effectively than income redistribution.

The Macdonald Commission and Social Welfare Reforms

In 1985, the Royal Commission on the Economic Union and Development Prospects for Canada (commonly known as the Macdonald Commission) criticized Canada's income security system for being unfair, ineffective, and overly complex; for creating disincentives to work; and for being unsustainable in times of economic downturns and changing demographics (such as an aging population). The commission recommended that a guaranteed annual income (GAI) scheme be implemented as a means to strengthen the income security system. To free up revenues for this, the commission suggested that various income security programs be eliminated, including the Guaranteed Income Supplement, child tax credits, and family allowances (Royal Commission on the Economic Union, 1985).

The PC government took the commission's advice and either scrapped or reduced many social welfare programs; however, it failed to replace them with a GAI. As a result, the income security system was weakened, and many needy Canadians were left with even less financial assistance. The PCs also made significant changes to some of Canada's most revered programs:

- *Old Age Security (OAS).* In its 1989 budget speech, the PC government announced that benefits from OAS would be "clawed back." The introduction of **clawbacks** meant that Canadian seniors with high annual incomes would have to repay part or all of the OAS benefits they received each year.

- *Family Allowance.* In 1989, the federal government began to claw back family allowance benefits from high-income-earning families. Then, in 1993, the Family Allowance Act was scrapped altogether and replaced by the Child Tax Benefit, which was restricted to low- and moderate-income families.

- *Unemployment Insurance (UI).* In 1990 the federal government stopped financing UI, requiring higher premiums from employers and workers. Other amendments resulted in more restrictive eligibility criteria, shortened benefit periods, and harsher penalties for those who quit their jobs.

- *Canada Assistance Plan (CAP).* An act of Parliament in 1991 (Bill C-69) put a "cap" on CAP by requiring the wealthiest provinces (at that time Alberta, Ontario, and British Columbia) to pay for any CAP programs whose costs increased 5 percent or more. This change served as a disincentive to provinces to develop social welfare programs beyond a certain level.

The Legacy of the Progressive Conservative Government

Throughout their years in power (1984 to 1993), the PCs' approach to social welfare was in stark contrast to the liberal approach that Canadians had supported in the postwar era. Beginning in 1984, the PCs steadily chipped away at the social safety net. When the economic recession hit Canada in the early 1990s, the PCs decided that rising unemployment, high inflation, and skyrocketing deficits could be partially contained by further cutting what they saw as costly and overgenerous social welfare programs. These changes substantially altered social welfare provision in Canada.

The PCs were careful not to slash social expenditures too blatantly; instead, they adopted what Grattan Gray (1990, p. 17) describes as "social policy by stealth," whereby social programs were cut incrementally—in fact, almost invisibly—through clawbacks, reduced transfers to the provinces, and other cost-saving strategies. Because individual cuts were hard to identify, it was difficult to track the changes in social program funding from year to year.

Although the PCs reduced many long-established social welfare programs, they also contributed to the development of others; for example, they enriched the refundable Child Tax Credit and Spouses' Allowance, increased assistance to people with disabilities, and launched the Family Violence Initiative. Battle and Torjman (2001, p. 22) observe that despite these advances, the drastic changes made by the PCs to Canada's social welfare system "built a momentum that prepared the way for even more radical changes by the Liberals in the 1990s and into the new century. The Conservatives proved that the universalist welfare state was no longer a 'sacred trust,' if it ever had been."

A NEW LIBERAL DIRECTION

The Liberals won the federal election in 1993, and returned to power with a history of generally supporting welfare state principles. Indeed, Liberal governments had introduced some of Canada's key social policies, including the Old Age Pension (in 1927), Unemployment Insurance (in 1940), and CAP (in 1966). In 1993, however, the Liberals recognized the need for new strategies to confront the challenges of a much different economic and political climate from when they last held office in the early 1980s. From an economic stand-point, Canadians were beginning to feel the effects of globalization and new technologies. According to the Economic Council of Canada (1990), one of these effects was the polarization of employment: "good jobs" were perma-nent, full-time positions with benefits; "bad jobs" included low-paying, part-time, and temporary positions. The impact of the changing labour market was widespread; polls taken during the mid-1990s reported that over 40 percent of working-age adults were living "outside the mainstream society and at the margins of the economy ..." (Ekos Research Associates, 1995, p. 3).

Although Canadian liberals had traditionally been *social* liberals who sup-ported social program spending and Keynesian economics, the Liberals under Jean Chrétien promoted themselves as **business** liberals who believed that fiscal responsibility (for example, balanced budgets) and a strong economy would provide the necessary resources for meeting many social welfare needs (Pal, 1998). The new Liberal Government of Canada still promoted traditional liberal goals, such as the pursuit of individual freedom and self-development;

EXHIBIT 4.2

Prime Minister Jean Chrétien (in office from 1993 to 2003) is well known for eliminating the federal deficit, and for endorsing massive cuts to social welfare funding.

Source: Steve Liss/Contributor/Time & Life Pictures/Getty Images.

however, they favoured a businesslike (more neoliberal) approach to reaching those goals. Chrétien's goal was to merge economic and social policy for the purpose of strengthening the market economy, expanding job opportunities, and helping people to find and keep jobs—the key factors, he believed, in the achievement of social security (HRDC, 1994a).

One task facing the new federal government was to stop increasing the national debt, which by 1993 had reached about $510 billion (Paquet & Shepherd, 1996). In 1994, it launched a general program review with the goal of finding ways to cut costs and deliver federal programs and services in the most efficient way possible. Following the program review, the federal government introduced the 1995 budget, which set out a plan for downsizing its departments and cutting spending. The plan included a reduction of $7 billion over a two-year period in transfer payments to the provinces for health, postsecondary education, and social welfare.

Many Canadians expressed concern about the budget's impact on social programs and people's lives. The National Council of Welfare (NCW, 1995, p. 1), for example, maintained that the proposed changes "marked a giant step backward in Canadian social policy. Followed through to its most likely conclusion, it would dismantle a nation-wide system of welfare and social services that took a generation to build. Sadly, the policies of the 1990s would take us back to the 1950s."

Finance Minister Paul Martin defended the budget's position on government spending by insisting that a less drastic budget would slow Canada's economic recovery and ultimately produce higher interest rates, a drop in the value of the dollar, and a loss of confidence in Canada's economy among business and consumers. Canadians were also told that this time of restraint would allow important social programs such as health and pensions to be sustainable for future generations when an aging population would need them most. Martin summed up his position by stating that "there are times in the progress of a people when fundamental challenges must be faced, fundamental choices made—a new course charted. For Canada, this is one of those times" (Department of Finance Canada, 1995, preface).

Discussion Questions

Welfare State Retrenchment: The Mulroney and Chrétien Years

1. Based on what you know about globalization, shifts in Canada's sociodemographic makeup, and other social, economic, political, and cultural events, explain why Canadian governments might have seen no other choice but to severely restrain public spending during the 1980s and 1990s.

2. Which type of political ideology (conservatism, liberalism, or social democracy) predominated in the federal government's approach to social welfare from 1984 to 1995? Give reasons for your answer.

▍ SOCIAL WELFARE REFORMS

FEDERAL-LEVEL COST-SAVING STRATEGIES

The federal government used various strategies to reduce its expenses. Although it was not a new strategy, decentralization began to be used to a far greater extent. **Decentralization** involves one level of government transferring or *devolving* some or all of its functions, decision-making authority, and/or assets either to a lower level of government or to the private sector. By transferring a portion of, or the entire program or function, the federal government could also transfer many related costs.

In addition to offloading many of its responsibilities, the federal government looked for ways to cut the direct costs of programs—social welfare programs became a prime target. For many years, CAP had been the vehicle by which the federal government transferred funds to the provinces and territories for social welfare programs. In 1996, the federal government eliminated CAP and combined its transfers for health, postsecondary education, and social welfare into one funding arrangement called the Canada Health and Social Transfer (CHST).

The shift to the CHST had significant implications for the funding, development, and delivery of social welfare programs across Canada. First, the CHST proved to be a far less generous funding arrangement than CAP. Under CAP, the federal government was obligated to pay half the costs of social welfare programs, whatever those costs might be. In contrast, the CHST allowed the federal government to give the regional governments an equal amount of federal dollars on a per capita basis, without considering the actual program costs. For provinces and territories that had built extensive and/or costly programs, the shift to the CHST meant a substantial reduction in federal funding.

Second, under the CHST, the regional governments received a lump sum or **block fund**, which could be divided among health, social welfare, and postsecondary education in whatever way they chose. This theoretically meant that the entire block fund could be allocated to health and postsecondary education (traditionally the most popular programs), with nothing for social welfare. (In 2003/04, the federal government would split the CHST into two separate funding streams: the Canada Health Transfer [CHT] would support health care, whereas the Canada Social Transfer [CST] would finance postsecondary education and social welfare programs. Still, there would be no stipulations under the CST as to how the regional governments should divide the funds between postsecondary education and social welfare.)

Third, federal transfers for all social programs shrank considerably when the CHST was introduced (Exhibit 4.3 illustrates the funding changes for social welfare, health, and postsecondary education programs). Most provinces and territories responded to the funding shortfall by transferring money from their budgets for social welfare and postsecondary education to their healthcare budgets. This shift of funds from one social program to another was contrary to the recommendations made by the Romanow

EXHIBIT 4.3

CHANGES IN FEDERAL TRANSFERS: 1993 TO 2000

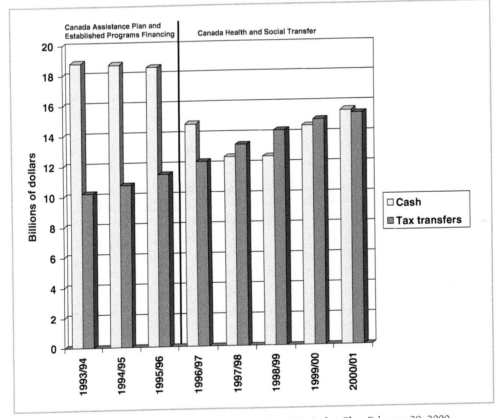

Source: Adapted from Department of Finance Canada, *Budget 2000: Budget Plan*, February 28, 2000, Table 6.2. Retrieved October 2, 2008, from http://www.fin.gc.ca/budget00/bp/bpch6_1-eng.asp.

Commission in its review of Canada's healthcare system in 2002; the Commission emphasized that when "addressing the apparent deficit in health funding, [the] deficit should not be passed on to post-secondary education and social assistance" (Romanow, 2002, p. 69).

AN EROSION IN NATIONAL STANDARDS

The CHST (and later the CST) was far less conditional than CAP, which had required the provinces and territories to adhere to certain national standards for social assistance. Under CAP, the regional governments were expected to

- provide social assistance to every person in need, regardless of the cause of need;
- take a person's basic requirements into account when setting social assistance rates;
- provide an appeal mechanism for people to challenge decisions affecting their entitlement to social assistance;
- allow social assistance to anyone regardless of how long they had lived in the province (known as the residency requirement); and
- not require people to work or volunteer as a condition of receiving assistance (Charter Committee on Poverty Issues, 1998).

In some ways, the regional governments welcomed the elimination of CAP. They had long wanted more autonomy in social programming, and the conditional nature of CAP was contrary to their constitutional right to deliver social welfare programs. With the exception of the residency requirement, the CHST allowed the provinces and territories to determine their own standards for social services and social assistance, including eligibility criteria and benefit rates.

REFORMS AT THE REGIONAL LEVEL

Although **social welfare reform** was an ongoing process for the regional governments, the dramatic changes of the mid-1990s presented an entirely new set of challenges. Many regions were struggling with their own deficits and rising debt, and others were still trying to recover from the impact of the federal government's cap on CAP. It was during this period of economic turmoil that the federal government hit the regions with the dramatic reductions in transfer payments under the new CHST. These reductions forced the regional governments to take a hard look at their programs and budgets, and to determine how they would manage to meet a growing need for social programs with significantly fewer resources.

Each province and territory approached program reform in its own way. For example, New Brunswick realized that social welfare reform was critical to the province's economic survival; reform in wealthy Alberta was shaped more by an ideological preference for small government and limited social spending than by financial necessity; Ontario chose to keep running up annual deficits so that it could cut personal income taxes; and Quebec was caught up in separatist issues and began its program reforms much later than other provinces. Whatever the route chosen, program reform across Canada during the 1990s virtually redefined the role of government and social welfare provision (Evans, 2003).

One of the greatest challenges for the provincial and territorial governments was how to cut social spending while still retaining a core network of programs and services. Like the federal government, the provinces and

EXHIBIT 4.4

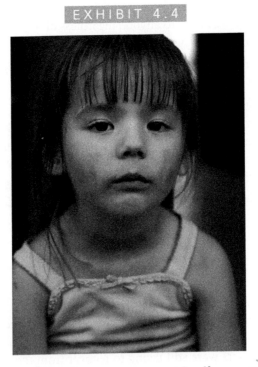

During the late 1990s, all levels of governments cut social welfare programs to some extent, leaving many already disadvantaged children in even greater need.

Source: jmatzick/Shutterstock.

territories decided to decentralize many of their responsibilities. In 1995, for example, Alberta was able to cut social welfare costs by shifting the responsibility for childcare services to a number of community groups and businesses (Hayden, 1997). That same year, Ontario began offloading many provincial social welfare responsibilities to local governments; these responsibilities were nevertheless accompanied by severe funding cuts (for example, between 1996 and 1998, the province cut its transfer funds to municipalities by almost 43 percent) (Dunlop, 2006).

SOCIAL ASSISTANCE UNDER ATTACK

In most jurisdictions, **social assistance** became a principal target for extensive program reform. Although there were many reasons for singling out social assistance programs, the attack was fuelled by neoliberal beliefs that welfare trapped people in long-term dependence on government; welfare was therefore seen as a problem, not a solution, for needy Canadians (Greenwood, 2005). Since the CHST allowed the provinces and territories to develop most of their own standards for social assistance, the regions could take whatever steps they deemed necessary to control their social spending. The phrase "race to the bottom" refers to the successive cuts most jurisdictions made to their social assistance programs: one province slashed its welfare benefits to motivate welfare recipients to seek more generous provision elsewhere; this put pressure on the more supportive provinces to cut their own welfare benefit rates in order to discourage an influx of people seeking assistance (LeRoy & Clemens, 2003). Reductions to welfare benefits continued through the 1990s; by 2002, rates were so low that anyone relying solely on social assistance would most certainly live in **poverty** (NCW, 2003b).

Under the CHST and Canada's adoption of "active" policies, the provinces and territories were allowed to require welfare recipients to work or train in exchange for benefits. Government-sponsored employment programs—generically referred to as **welfare-to-work programs** (or "workfare")—sprang up across Canada, all aimed at getting able-bodied (employable) welfare recipients off assistance and into employment. In 1996, Ontario was the first province to introduce welfare-to-work legislation through its Ontario Works program. Others soon followed, including Manitoba's Employment and Income Assistance Program and Nova Scotia's Employment Support Services.

Fiscal pressures prompted some provinces to restrict welfare eligibility in an attempt to contain the costs of social assistance. Alberta regularly turned away applicants for social assistance on the basis that they had not fully exhausted all other means of support. In 1996, British Columbia started refusing welfare to anyone under the age of 25, preferring instead to offer a means-tested living allowance to young adults who participated in employment programs. Later, in 2001, BC became the first province in Canada to announce its plan to put a time limit on welfare eligibility, a move that would prevent employable recipients from collecting welfare for more than 24 out of every 60 months. Due to a public outcry, the BC Government cancelled its plan to impose welfare time limits, but it did manage to implement other rules to restrict welfare eligibility, including the requirement that welfare applicants had to have two years of financial independence before they could collect welfare (Wallace & Richards, 2008).

The various strategies used by the provinces proved to be successful in reducing the number of people on welfare. However, not all provinces tracked the progress of people who left welfare to know what happened to them. Moreover, studies have indicated that, while many people who left welfare eventually found work, they did not find work that paid well enough to lift

EXHIBIT 4.5

FALLING NUMBERS OF PEOPLE ON WELFARE: 1995 TO 2000

	1995	2000	% CHANGE
ALBERTA	113,200	64,800	−43
ONTARIO	1,344,600	802,000	−40
YUKON	2,100	1,400	−33
PRINCE EDWARD ISLAND	12,400	8,400	−32
BRITISH COLUMBIA	374,300	262,400	−30
NOVA SCOTIA	104,000	73,700	−29
MANITOBA	85,200	63,300	−26
QUEBEC	802,200	618,900	−23
SASKATCHEWAN	82,200	63,800	−22
NEWFOUNDLAND AND LABRADOR	71,300	59,400	−17
NEW BRUNSWICK	67,400	56,300	−16
NORTHWEST TERRITORIES AND NUNAVUT	12,000	10,700	−11

Source: Adapted from National Council of Welfare, "Welfare Incomes 2005: Factsheet #9: Number of People on Welfare," October 2006. Retrieved November 24, 2008, from www.ncwcnbes.net/documents/researchpublications/ResearchProjects/WelfareIncomes/2005 Report_Summer2006/Factsheets/Factsheet09ENG.pdf. Reproduced with the permission of the Minister of Public Works and Government Services Canada, 2008.

them or their families out of poverty (Canadian CED Network, 2003). See Exhibit 4.5 for an illustration of the falling numbers of welfare recipients between 1995 and 2000.

Discussion Questions

■ **Social Welfare Reforms**

1. From what you know about federal–provincial–territorial relations, give reasons why relaxing national standards in social welfare programs might be viewed positively by the different levels of government.
2. Identify what you see as being the pros and cons of decentralization.
3. Do the regional reforms to social assistance reflect a residual, institutional, or social investment approach to social welfare? Give reasons for your answer.

▥ REVIEWING THE IMPACT OF FISCAL RESTRAINT

THE WAR ON DEFICIT SPENDING: CRITICAL VIEWS

There is much evidence to suggest that Canada's poor economic performance from the 1970s to late 1990s was more to blame for the fiscal crisis than social spending. However, social programs bore the brunt of fiscal restraint during Canada's deficit-fighting years. Canadian governments rationalized their drastic cuts as being necessary to eliminate deficits, and to get their fiscal house in order. Those governments promised that, once they restored fiscal balance, they would begin paying down their respective debts—eventually, money would be freed up to reinvest in high-priority programs.

Some critics suggest that governments exploited the fiscal crisis to achieve their own political—largely neoliberal—objectives. From the perspective of journalist Linda McQuaig (1995, p. 9), the deficit became "a key tool for picking away at what many in the elite consider to be our overly generous social welfare system and government policies dedicated to pampering the undeserving, at the expense of the deserving (such as those in the elite)." Edward Broadbent (2001, p. 7) adds that governments in Canada and other Western nations used deficit fighting as justification to abandon their responsibility to ensure equality. He writes: "For the first time in half a century, heads of democratic governments began to use industrial, taxation, and social policy initiatives not as a means of promoting equality but as necessary political instruments to re-establish the complete dominance of the market in civil society." Despite these and other criticisms, many Canadian governments achieved significant fiscal goals.

In its 1998 budget, the federal government announced that, for the first time in 28 years, Canada's budget was balanced. By 2000 the federal government had struck its third consecutive balanced budget; strong economic growth had created almost 1.5 million (mostly full-time) jobs in four years; the national unemployment rate was 6.8 percent, its lowest level in 24 years; and for the third straight year, Canada was leading the Group of Seven (G-7) countries in job creation (Department of Finance Canada, 2000). There was every indication that Canada's fiscal prudence in the 1990s was paying off.

There was also good news from the regional governments. The combined provincial/territorial deficit in 2001–02 was a more "manageable" $22 billion, down from $58.7 billion in 1993–94. Some provinces, including Saskatchewan and Alberta, had been operating on balanced budgets since 1994–95 (Department of Finance Canada, 2003b).

ECONOMIC VERSUS SOCIAL PAY-OFFS

As Canadians ushered in a new millennium, the fiscal crisis appeared to be over. However, many Canadians were asking whether the economic victory was worth the social cost. According to the National Anti-Poverty Organization (2003), the country's economic and fiscal success toward the end of the 1990s failed to translate "into prosperity or even an adequate standard of living" for almost five million Canadians. This **social deficit**—that is, continued hardship and unmet human potential—was reflected in statistics such as the following:

- From 1990 to 2000, the number of Canadians living in poverty rose from 4.39 to 4.72 million (or 16.2 percent of Canadians).

- In 1999, 18.7 percent of children (1.1 million) lived in poverty, compared to 15.2 percent in 1989.

- Between 1989 and 2000, the number of food bank visits doubled (NCW, 2003a; National Anti-Poverty Organization, 2003).

During the deficit-fighting years, federal spending dropped to levels not seen since the 1930s (Osberg, 2004). Federal transfers to the provinces and territories under the CHST were drastically reduced: by the end of the 2001 fiscal year, federal CHST payments were $3.2 billion lower than in 1994–95, which meant fewer supports for Canada's most disadvantaged citizens (St-Hilaire, 2002). (Exhibit 4.6 details the impact of the shift to the CHST on Canadian women).

EXHIBIT 4.6

FROM CAP TO THE CHST: WHAT IT MEANS FOR WOMEN

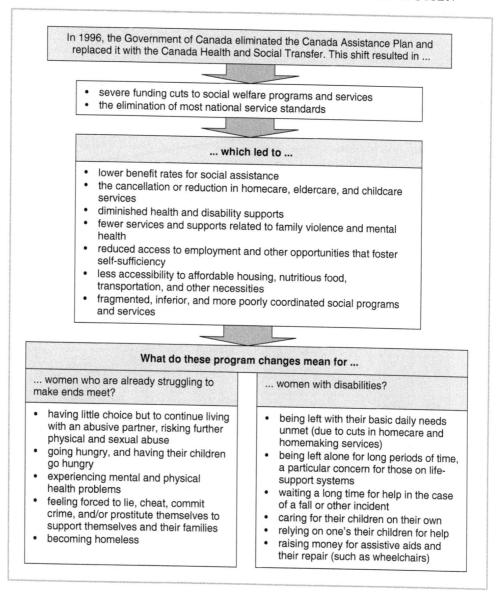

In 1996, the Government of Canada eliminated the Canada Assistance Plan and replaced it with the Canada Health and Social Transfer. This shift resulted in ...

- severe funding cuts to social welfare programs and services
- the elimination of most national service standards

... which led to ...

- lower benefit rates for social assistance
- the cancellation or reduction in homecare, eldercare, and childcare services
- diminished health and disability supports
- fewer services and supports related to family violence and mental health
- reduced access to employment and other opportunities that foster self-sufficiency
- less accessibility to affordable housing, nutritious food, transportation, and other necessities
- fragmented, inferior, and more poorly coordinated social programs and services

What do these program changes mean for ...

... women who are already struggling to make ends meet?	... women with disabilities?
<ul><li>having little choice but to continue living with an abusive partner, risking further physical and sexual abuse</li><li>going hungry, and having their children go hungry</li><li>experiencing mental and physical health problems</li><li>feeling forced to lie, cheat, commit crime, and/or prostitute themselves to support themselves and their families</li><li>becoming homeless</li></ul>	<ul><li>being left with their basic daily needs unmet (due to cuts in homecare and homemaking services)</li><li>being left alone for long periods of time, a particular concern for those on life-support systems</li><li>waiting a long time for help in the case of a fall or other incident</li><li>caring for their children on their own</li><li>relying on one's their children for help</li><li>raising money for assistive aids and their repair (such as wheelchairs)</li></ul>

Source: M. Morris, C. Watters, V. Dawson, C. Martin, C. Nicholson, L. Martin, M. Owen, K. Sehgal, and S. Torres, with, J. Charlebois *Integrating the Voices of Low-Income Women into Policy Discussions on the Canada Social Transfer*, August 2007. Retrieved November 22, 2008, from Canadian Research Institute for the Advancement of Women website, www.criaw-icref.ca/CST_FINAL_REPORT.pdf. S. Masuda, *The Impact of Block Funding on Women with Disabilities*, March 1998. Retrieved November 22, 2008, from Status of Women Canada website, http://dsp-psd.pwgsc.gc.ca/Collection/SW21-29-1998E.pdf.

Some observers charged that, in their zeal to eradicate deficits, Canadian governments cut social welfare programs to the point of marginalizing certain segments of the population (mainly the already poor and disadvantaged) from mainstream society. At the core of this social exclusion was the denial of participation in society, including access to important economic, social, political, and other resources (Galabuzi & Labonte, 2002). Others saw the inequitable distribution of resources in terms of a social injustice, and a violation of people's rights, that was primarily directed at poor and disadvantaged citizens. Shillington (2000) uses the example of the replacement of CAP with the CHST to illustrate this injustice: not only was funding slashed to programs for low-income groups, but most national standards for social assistance were eliminated, enabling the provinces and territories to blatantly deny welfare to people in need.

By 2003, it was clear that economic growth alone could not be expected to ensure the well-being of Canada's most vulnerable citizens (NCW, 2003a). After assessing the results of the deficit-fighting years, policy analyst Katherine

EXHIBIT 4.7

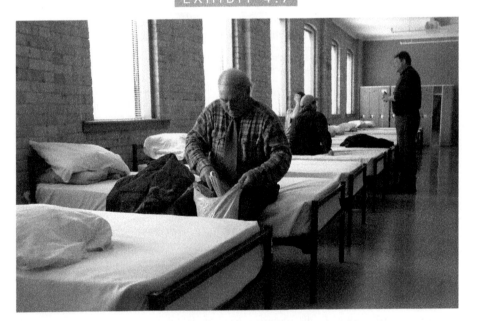

Along with a rising rate of homelessness comes a growing demand for emergency shelters.

Source: The Salvation Army—Ontario Central East Division and Element 80.

Scott (2005, p. 27) concluded: "One can debate at length the merits of fiscal retrenchment in Canada in the 1990s, and there are reasonable differences regarding the extent to which federal and provincial public social spending on income transfers and social services had to be cut, and at what pace, in order to balance government budgets. However, there can be little doubt that the major restructuring of the welfare state has had deep implications for social well-being."

The impact of social spending cuts on Canadians did not go unnoticed in the international community. In 1998, a submission to the United Nations (UN) by the Charter Committee on Poverty Issues reprimanded Canada for its rising poverty rates (especially among children, lone-parent families, and Aboriginal peoples), for the growing number of food banks, and for increasing rates of homelessness. Between 1993 and 2003, Canada fell from first to eighth place on the UN's list of the most desirable places to live in the world. The Organization for Economic Co-operation and Development (OECD, 1997, p. 3) voiced its own concerns when it urged countries (including Canada) to consider the "longer-term societal implications"—such as conditions that exacerbate poverty and weaken social cohesion—that were related to years of deficit fighting and economic restructuring.

Discussion Questions

Reviewing the Impact of Fiscal Restraint

1. Some people think that governments should run on balanced budgets; others believe that deficits (and subsequent debt) are acceptable if it means that social standards and quality of life remain high. Where do you stand on this issue? Give reasons for your position.

2. Explain what is meant by a "social deficit."

IV FROM SOCIAL REINVESTMENT TO FISCALIZATION

A TURNAROUND FOR THE LIBERALS

In 1998, the federal government announced that Canada had entered a phase of **budgetary surpluses**. The Department of Finance Canada (2008b) defines a surplus as "the amount by which government revenue exceeds budgetary spending" (for many of us, a budget surplus is the amount of money that is left over from a paycheque after all the bills have been paid). With its fiscal house in order, the federal government began investing its surplus funds in areas that had been neglected during the deficit-fighting years. Between the fiscal years 1999–2000 and 2004–05, federal expenditures grew steadily from $162 billion to $210 billion (Office of the Auditor General of Canada, 2006).

Andrew Jackson (2003) dubbed the 2003 federal budget as the "U-Turn Budget," because it represented a sharp reversal in Liberal priorities, from fiscal restraint to major social spending. For 2003–04, more than $2 billion was committed to child benefits (including childcare and early learning), initiatives to combat homelessness, and projects to increase affordable housing (Department of Finance Canada, 2003a). By all accounts, the 2003 budget commitments had the potential to reverse Canada's social deficit (Citizens for Public Justice, 2003).

In the federal election in June 2004, the Liberals won under Prime Minister Martin, but with only a minority government. In 2005, the Liberal government set forth its budget, which committed over $75 billion over ten years to "establish a solid base for the Government's commitment to strengthen and secure Canada's social foundations." Significant investments were earmarked for, among other things, early learning and childcare, seniors' programs, Aboriginal communities, and tax relief for people with disabilities (Department of Finance Canada, 2005). The promise of increased funding met favour with the regional governments, especially since some of them were still trying to balance their own budgets. The federal budget passed in May 2005, but before many of these plans could be implemented, the Liberal government was defeated.

THE CONSERVATIVE APPROACH

In the 2006 federal election, Canadians elected the reconfigured Conservative Party of Canada and Stephen Harper became Canada's new prime minister. The Conservatives came to power promising to "Stand Up for Canada" which, according to the prime minister, meant fighting crime, cutting taxes, increasing government accountability, reducing healthcare wait times, and meeting the childcare needs of families with young children.

In general, the Conservatives do not support the practice of directly spending public funds on social welfare programs and services. Rather, they prefer to achieve social goals through **fiscalization**, a process aimed at lowering tax rates and providing tax credits, exemptions, and other types of tax relief. The Canadian Association of Social Workers (CASW, 2008) explains the rationale behind fiscalization: "Tax relief, according to the Conservatives, is part and parcel of sound fiscal management. Better, it seems, to put money into the hands of individuals by not taxing them than to transfer funds from one group of taxpayers to another through program expenditures." This approach determines eligibility for benefits, not by need or disadvantage (as it is done in a welfare state), but by a person's taxable income. Since 2004, the Conservatives have either promised (during election campaigns) or implemented tax schemes to address a number of identified social problems. For example, to address a lack of affordable housing units, the Conservatives have offered tax credits to private-sector housing developers to build or modify affordable rental units for low-income earners. Similarly, to meet a growing need for childcare, the federal government has offered tax credits to employers who create childcare spaces in the workplace.

Fiscalization has its advantages and disadvantages. Proponents of fiscalization maintain that not only is the use of the tax system an effective way of helping the poor, but also it rewards labour market participation since tax benefits are only possible if one earns taxable income. The practice also avoids stigmatizing the poor, since the "giving" of benefits is done privately through the tax system (Brodie & Bakker, 2007). Opponents of fiscalization point out that a potential problem with tax relief measures is the possibility that the tax benefit would not be used in the way that it was intended. The Canada Child Tax Benefit (CCTB), for example, aims to improve conditions for Canada's poorest children; however, there is no way of knowing whether that tax measure actually helps children. Another problem is that, on the surface, tax relief schemes may sound generous when actually they offer little help to the poorest of Canadians. According to Armine Yalnizyan (2005), 32 percent of Canadians who file tax forms earn so little they do not pay taxes; subsequently, they do not benefit from tax relief schemes. In her analysis of the Canada Child Tax Benefit, Sharon Manson Singer (2007) found that "[e]ighty-five cents a day is the sum total of the change in a family's bottom line and no change at all for Canada's lowest income families. ... The Child Tax Credit will help more than 1.2 million parents, and will cost taxpayers $1.4 billion dollars in 2007–08. *That's $1.4 billion to put 85 cents a day in a parent's pocket*" (italics in original).

Some so-called "solutions" to problems can actually penalize low-income families. The Universal ChildCare Benefit (UCCB), for example, pays $100 per month to each child under the age of six. Those payments are not only taxable, but they can push a family into a higher tax bracket. For many low-income families, being in a higher tax bracket means losing their eligibility for other tax breaks. Social policy analysts Battle, Torjman, and Mendelson (2006, p. 1) found that the UCCB's tax structure allows many middle-income families to keep a greater proportion of the benefit than lower-income families, making the UCCB "deeply flawed ..., paying net payments that are unfair and irrational."

ARE TAX CUTS THE ANSWER?

According to the Conservative Government of Canada, "[t]axes in Canada are way too high" (Department of Finance Canada, 2007, p. 12). High taxes are believed to create a variety of problems, such as making it difficult for working Canadians to make ends meet, discouraging foreign investment, and reducing Canada's ability to compete for business in the global market (Jiwani, 2000). Beginning in 2007, the Conservative government launched its five-year plan to lower overall taxes by $60 billion. That would bring the total tax cuts implemented by the Conservatives since being elected to almost $190 billion (Department of Finance Canada, 2007). These tax cuts follow on the heels of the former Liberal government's regime, which reduced taxes by $152 billion between 1997 and 2004 (Yalnizyan, 2005).

Some social and economic analysts argue that taxes in Canada are not too high. In fact, Canada's tax levels, compared with those of Sweden, Norway, Denmark, and Finland, for example, are relatively low. Studies suggest that, contrary to popular belief, high taxation does not automatically inhibit economic progress, nor do low taxes naturally attract investment (Weiss, 1998).

Many people who value social progress advocate for a healthy level of taxation. According to American jurist Justice Oliver Wendell Holmes (1927), "[t]axes are what we pay for civilized society." Social policy expert Marvyn Novick (2007, p. 7) adds: "If communities of inclusion and opportunity are what Canadians want, then we have to be willing to create a better balance between money in our pockets and money we pool together for what we value in common." Brooks and Hwong (2006, p. 7) caution against Canada's falling taxation rates, and conclude that "[t]ax cuts are disastrous for the well-being of a nation's citizens." Many of Canada's major social welfare programs are supported by taxes; for example, both the Canada/Quebec Pension Plans and the Old Age Security are tax-funded. Canadian economist Jim Stanford (2005, p. 19) reminds us that two-thirds of elderly Canadians rely primarily on those public pensions and, without those pensions, thousands of "retired Canadians would fall deep into poverty."

SOCIAL WELFARE IN A GLOBAL ECONOMIC MELTDOWN

When the federal Conservatives were elected in 2006, they showed little interest in repairing or rebuilding Canada's social welfare system. When Canada slid into a global economic recession in late 2008, their interest in strengthening social welfare programs sank even lower. Of more concern to the Conservatives was how to remain in power and how to save a failing economy. The Conservatives eventually yielded to domestic and international pressure to introduce Keynesian measures that would stimulate the economy—in other words, to give large amounts of federal money to Canadians to encourage them to spend, rather than save, their money.

In January 2009, the federal government announced its Economic Action Plan, which included an economic stimulus package of tax cuts and public spending worth $40 billion over two years. Most of the benefits in the budget were targeted to middle-class Canadians, a group that the federal government heavily relied on to continue working and paying income tax. Modest provisions were also included in the budget for unemployed and low-income Canadians, including

- an increase in the amount that low-income families could earn and still receive the Canada Child Tax Benefit;

- investments for First Nations communities to improve infrastructure, social housing, employment programs, and child and family services on reserves;

- an additional five weeks of benefits under Employment Insurance (EI), and expanded training programs for all Canadians (whether on EI or not); and

- funding to update existing government-subsidized housing units, provide housing for low-income seniors, and build social housing for people with disabilities.

The federal government anticipated that the combination of high unemployment, falling government revenues (due to shrinking tax revenues), and the cost of its elaborate stimulus package would require both severe program cuts in low-priority programs and a return to deficit spending—something not seen at the federal level since 1996–97. In January 2009, the federal government estimated that its deficit for the fiscal year 2009–10 would reach $34 billion; four months later, the government announced that the deficit for the year would soar closer to $50 billion—the largest deficit in Canadian history. Running a deficit was contrary to conservative principles, and would reverse much of the fiscal progress that Canada had achieved over the past twenty years. However, most countries around the world—including Canada—eventually accepted that a Keynesian approach, with aggressive spending incentives, was their only hope to kick-start a rapidly deteriorating world economy. Of course, there were no guarantees that such an approach would achieve that goal.

For some time, economists predicted that Ontario would be the region hardest hit during the recession due to massive job losses in that province's manufacturing sector. However, as 2008 came to a close, economists forecast that all regions across Canada would experience some degree of economic slowdown and higher unemployment rates. Indeed, the number of unemployed workers on EI began to rise sharply in November 2008, and continued to climb well into 2009. The jurisdictions experiencing the largest increases of regular EI beneficiaries (compared with the previous year) were Ontario, British Columbia, Alberta, Saskatchewan, Nunavut, and the Yukon. By early 2009, most regional and municipal governments were bracing themselves for a fiscal squeeze as a result of higher unemployment, lower government revenues, and increasing demand for social welfare programs. The costs of social welfare programs were expected to skyrocket, creating a need to run deficits. Governments also considered that they might have to raise taxes to cover the burgeoning costs—a move that could spell political death for a party in power.

Canada's economic recession has raised concerns for the many nonprofit organizations that provide social services, such as emergency shelters, food banks, and outreach for low-income seniors. These organizations are beginning to experience an economic squeeze of their own due to cutbacks in government funding and declines in charitable donations (Financial crisis creating, 2008). The impacts of the global economic recession, particularly for Canada's most disadvantaged citizens, have yet to be determined.

Discussion Questions

From Social Reinvestment to Fiscalization

1. There is much debate on the merits of using the tax system to meet people's social welfare needs. Identify what you see as the possible pros and cons of such an approach.

2. In 2009, the federal government introduced an economic stimulus package to urge Canadians to continue spending, despite an economic recession its economy. How might such a strategy benefit the country's poorest citizens, if at all?

SUMMARY

Introduction

As the economy slowed during the early 1970s, the federal and regional governments began to borrow money rather than cut programs or raise taxes. As a result, governments incurred annual budget deficits, and ran up huge public debts. Realizing that deficit spending was unsustainable, governments planned to drastically cut public spending in an attempt to balance their budgets.

I. Welfare State Retrenchment: The Mulroney and Chrétien Years

The Progressive Conservatives overhauled Old Age Security, Unemployment Insurance, CAP, and Family Allowances; many other funding cuts were gradual and subtle. A new Liberal government in 1993 recommended strategies to confront the challenges of a new global economy. In 1995, the Liberals announced major spending cuts, rationalizing that, if Canadians cut back then, they could make social programs sustainable in the future.

II. Social Welfare Reforms

To reduce expenses, the federal government decentralized many programs, and replaced CAP with the CHST. The CHST was less generous than CAP, but gave the provinces/territories more discretion in how they designed and delivered social welfare programs. To deal with fewer funds, the regional governments slashed welfare benefit rates, and required welfare recipients to work or train in exchange for benefits. These strategies worked to move large numbers of people off welfare.

III. Reviewing the Impact of Fiscal Restraint

In 1998, the federal government balanced its budget, and Canada was in an economic boom. Many Canadians questioned whether the economic victory was worth the social deficit. Certain segments of the population were living in hardship, had been marginalized, and benefited little from the stronger economy. Between 1993 and 2003, Canada fell from first to eighth place on the UN's list of the most desirable places to live in the world.

IV. From Social Reinvestment to Fiscalization

With its fiscal house in order, and growing budget surpluses, the Liberal's 2003 budget called for a reinvestment of funds in areas that had been neglected during the deficit-fighting years. Before the reinvestment plan could be fully implemented, the Liberals lost the 2006 federal election. The Conservative Party came to power with plans to achieve social goals through fiscalization. Social advocates questioned whether that strategy would help the poor, or sustain social welfare programs. In 2008, Canada entered a global economic recession; in response, the federal government returned to deficit spending and unprecedented public spending.

Key Terms

For definitions of the key terms, consult the Glossary on page 413 at the end of the book.

budget deficit, p. 89
public debt, p. 90
fiscal crisis, p. 90
welfare state
    retrenchment, p. 90
monetarism, p. 90
clawback, p. 91

decentralization, p. 95
block fund, p. 95
social welfare reform,
    p. 97
social assistance,
    p. 99
poverty, p. 99

welfare-to-work
    program, p. 99
social deficit,
    p. 102
budgetary surplus, p.
    105
fiscalization, p. 106

THE SERVICE DELIVERY SYSTEM

CHAPTER 5

Service Sectors

OBJECTIVES

Three service sectors are responsible for delivering social welfare programs to Canadians. This chapter will explore:

- the concept of a mixed economy of welfare;

- characteristics of the public, commercial, and voluntary sectors;

- new directions in service delivery, based on an Alternative Service Delivery model;

- the implications of new service delivery requirements for the voluntary sector; and

- an emerging fourth sector (the social economy).

INTRODUCTION

There is now an increasingly common awareness that a healthy Canada depends on the best possible collaboration between all three sectors of society. We need all sectors to be vibrant, strong and effective: [t]o share their views; [t]o be more and more involved in contributing to the decision-making processes; [t]o address the major challenges facing all Canadians and that can help to ensure that Canada's values are

reflected in world affairs. (Mel Cappe, Former Clerk of
the Privy Council, February 6, 2002)

During the period between the Second World War and the mid-1970s,
Canadians generally supported liberal governments that provided a balance between the interests of individuals and the interests of society
Jenson, 2004b. To strike that balance, these governments assumed a certain level of responsibility for the delivery of those programs. Canadian
governments have nevertheless been reluctant to monopolize the delivery
of those programs, preferring instead that businesses and charitable (nonprofit) organizations play a primary role in that respect. What has evolved
in Canada, then, is a **mixed economy of welfare**—that is, various service
delivery systems, all of which focus on the enhancement of well-being,
that are organized, funded, and managed in their own distinct ways (Rice
& Prince, 2000).

The "welfare mix" reflects a loosely defined division of labour between
two broad service sectors: the public and the private. The **private sector** can
be further broken down into the commercial and voluntary sectors. Thus,
there are three broad service sectors:

- The **public sector** includes all programs and services that are funded
  by tax revenues and administered and delivered by some level of government, be it federal, provincial, territorial, or municipal.

- The **commercial sector** is profit-motivated, and sells services to consumers for full market price.

- The **voluntary sector**—also called the charitable, independent, or
  "third" sector—comprises nongovernmental agencies and organizations
  that fulfil a social purpose and deliver programs on a nonprofit basis.

Because of their many valuable contributions to Canada's development,
these three service sectors have been dubbed the "three pillars" of Canadian
society and economy (Liberal Party of Canada, 1997).

Although the three sectors tend to be viewed as discrete entities, there is
considerable overlap between them. Katherine Scott (Scott, 2003a, p. 8)
describes the boundaries of the three as "'fuzzy'—if not downright porous."
These boundaries lack clear definition for the following main reasons:

- government and private-sector agencies often work together on, or
  share the costs of, joint projects;

- the activities, functions, and roles of private and public organizations
  are often similar, making it difficult to discern which sector does
  what; and

- while governments tend to participate at some level in the provision of social welfare—whether through regulation, planning, or funding—they are constantly adjusting their degree of involvement in service delivery, which affects the scope of programs delivered by the private sector.

Over the past decade, the boundaries of the three sectors have been undergoing significant realignment, creating what Hrab (2004, p. 3) refers to as "a new era with respect to the delivery of public services." This chapter reviews the roles of each service sector pertaining to social welfare provision, and explores the specific impact of recent role changes on voluntary social agencies and their capacity to serve.

SERVICE SECTORS: PUBLIC, COMMERCIAL, AND VOLUNTARY DOMAINS

THE PUBLIC SECTOR

Canadians have come to expect governments to protect them from certain risks inherent in modern society—risks such as poverty, unemployment, disability, and illness. Today's broad range of social welfare programs is the government's response to those expectations.

Constitutionally, the responsibility for social welfare lies with the provincial and territorial governments. However, over time, social welfare has become a shared responsibility among the federal, provincial/territorial, and municipal or local levels of government. Income security programs and social services are referred to as **public programs** because they "belong" to the public: that is, the public pays for these programs mainly through taxes, and the public expects elected government officials to be accountable for how those programs are developed, managed, and delivered. Government controls most aspects of income security programs, from policy development to implementation. Although many social services today are delivered by organizations in the private sector, certain social services are fully controlled by government, and delivered directly by government workers (or civil servants). Examples of social welfare services delivered at each level of government are given below.

Federal Government

This level of government directly delivers social services, such as mental health services, to identified federal "client groups," which include First Nations and Inuit peoples, federal offenders, the Canadian forces, veterans, members of the Royal Canadian Mounted Police, recent immigrants and refugees, and federal public service employees. In addition, the federal government directly delivers several national income security programs, including Old Age Security, the Canada Pension Plan, and the Canada Child Tax Benefit. Although many departments at the federal level deliver programs related to social welfare, Human Resources and Skills Development Canada is considered the main "social welfare department."

Provincial/Territorial Government

This level of government directly delivers social welfare programs that are legislated, that need to be delivered in a consistent manner across communities, and/or that require a certain level of enforcement (August, 2006). Social assistance is an example of a legislated income security program that is delivered by government workers in every province and territory. Many provincial/territorial governments also legislate and directly deliver child welfare, adult protection, and mental health services. Most regional governments have entire ministries devoted to the delivery of social services, such as Nova Scotia's Department of Community Services, and Saskatchewan's Ministry of Social Services.

Municipal/Local Government

Canada has never had an established pattern for the delivery of social welfare services at the municipal level. However, since the 1970s—and to a heightened degree since the 1990s—provincial/territorial governments have been devolving responsibilities to the municipalities. Today, many municipalities directly deliver programs that relate to, for example, social housing, social assistance, or childcare (Richmond & Shields, 2003). In many cases, those programs are a segment of a larger provincial/territorial program (for instance, the childcare component of child protection services).

THE COMMERCIAL SECTOR

The term *social welfare* implies a collective, public responsibility for well-being and is therefore associated with state (government) intervention that is not profit-motivated. Thus, the commercial sector is not considered part of the social welfare system. Businesses nevertheless offer a wide range of

EXHIBIT 5.1

GOVERNMENT ASSISTANCE

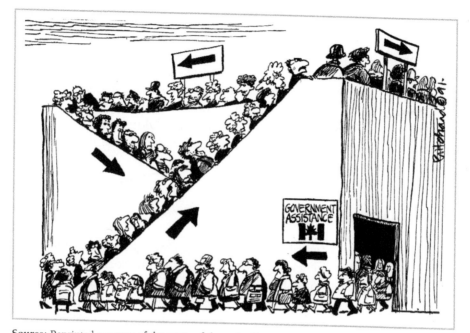

Source: Reprinted courtesy of the estate of the artist, Denny Pritchard.

helping services aimed at enhancing personal well-being. These services include private childcare, addiction treatment, and personal counselling, all of which are available for a fee.

There are various ways of paying for commercial services. In many cases, a business may charge the consumer a flat rate for services rendered. Other services may be offered according to a sliding fee scale, whereby the fee is adjusted according to the client's financial means; this practice is most common when government subsidizes the costs of services for low-income clients. People who pay out of pocket for services—for example, at a private addiction treatment centre—may be reimbursed for service costs if they are covered under an extended health insurance program or other compensatory program such as workers' compensation.

It has never been easier for business to sell helping services on Canadian markets, thanks to an expansion of government-issued licences and privatization policies that encourage free enterprise. Private helping services are also legitimated by a growing number of Canadians who welcome the innovative ideas associated with business, can afford to purchase services, and generally support private (nongovernment) services. Moreover, the many trade agreements, such as NAFTA, struck between Canada and its international neighbours make it relatively easy for private enterprises to cross borders and offer specialized services for a profit.

More and more businesses are leaning toward **corporate social responsibility**, a concept whereby a company engages in activities that are important not only for the good of the company but also for the good of society (Industry Canada, 2006a). Donating a portion of company profits to a children's charity, for example, may not only benefit children in need, but also attract shareholders and customers, boost staff morale, raise the company's image, and ultimately increase profits.

THE VOLUNTARY SECTOR

The voluntary sector comprises a broad spectrum of organizations, otherwise known as voluntary agencies, charitable or nonprofit societies, and nongovernmental organizations (NGOs). These organizations are highly diverse, ranging in size, cause, and activities. While many voluntary organizations are related to such areas as sports, the environment, and the arts, 12 percent of all voluntary organizations focus on meeting human need through the provision of social services. Among these **voluntary social agencies** are relatively small, community-based groups such as family service societies and large, national organizations such as the National Action Committee on the Status of Women. Most voluntary social agencies are

- organized (they have some internal organizational structure);
- nongovernmental (they are structurally separate from government institutions);
- nonprofit (they use any profits to improve the agency, not to benefit the agency owners or directors);
- self-governing (they are independent from other institutions and regulate their own operations); and
- volunteer-friendly (they involve volunteers to some degree in agency activities or management (Saunders, 2004).

Over 19,000 voluntary social agencies exist in Canada, and employ almost 300,000 people. In addition to paid staff, approximately 1.8 million Canadians (mostly women) volunteer their time for these agencies (Barr, Brownlee, Lasby, & Gumulka, 2005).

Catholic Family Services is one of the many voluntary social agencies across Canada that aims to meet human need through the provision of social services.

Source: © Kristiina Paul.

In general, voluntary social agencies perform three main functions:

1. They "*do good works*," which may be understood in terms of delivering tangibles (for example, food, clothing, or shelter) and/ or intangibles (such as counselling or support services) to a community.

2. They *advocate* by, for instance, educating the public about an issue or social problem, or lobbying for change in laws or policies to improve the conditions of a particular client group.

3. They *mediate*, often by bringing together individuals or groups in a community for the purpose of finding solutions or compromises to common problems (Evans & Shields, 2006).

In many respects, voluntary social agencies complement the work performed by government: while government responds to national or regional concerns such as child poverty and homelessness, agencies in the voluntary sector apply their knowledge and expertise at the community level (Voluntary Sector Steering Group, 2002). In 1999, the Government of Canada formally recognized the voluntary sector as playing "an increasingly critical and complex role in helping to achieve the goals important to Canadians and ensure a high quality of life. It has become a vital third pillar in Canadian society, working alongside the public and [commercial] ... sectors to make Canada a more humane, caring and prosperous nation" (Privy Council Office, 1999, p. 1).

While most voluntary social agencies rely on diverse funding sources (see Exhibit 5.3), government is the largest source of funding, providing about 66

EXHIBIT 5.3

DIVERSE FUNDING SOURCES: SOCIAL SERVICES*
IN THE VOLUNTARY SECTOR

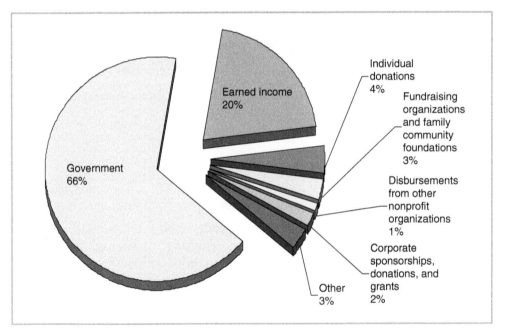

*Statistics Canada defines "social services" as nongovernmental "organizations and institutions providing social services to a community or target population"

Note: The percentage breakdown does not add up to 100 due to rounding.

Source: Adapted from Statistics Canada, "Cornerstones of Community: Highlights of the National Survey of Nonprofit and Voluntary Organizations," Catalogue No. 61–533-XIE, September 2004, revised edition June 2005.

percent of all agency revenue; the bulk of this public funding comes from the provincial/territorial governments. The second-largest source of income is agency-generated earnings derived from, for example, bake sales and raffles.

Discussion Questions

■ **Service Sectors: Public, Commercial, and Voluntary Domains**

1. Identify the various social welfare or "helping" programs in your community (or specific geographic area). In which service sector (public, commercial, or voluntary) does each program best fit? What criteria did you use to categorize each program?

2. What do you see as the pros and cons of each service sector, in terms of how it might manage or deliver social welfare programs?

▓ NEW DIRECTIONS IN SERVICE DELIVERY

CHANGING VIEWS ON GOVERNMENT AND GOVERNANCE

By the 1980s, government departments had evolved into large, bureaucratic systems that were criticized for being expensive, wasteful, rigid, remote, impersonal, and unresponsive to the public's needs. Governments were also blamed for failing to control their spending and balance their budgets. In the 1990s, it became clear that most governments could not effectively address the social and economic problems created by globalization, including massive job losses due to the shift from a manufacturing to a knowledge-based economy (Richmond & Shields, 2003). Neoliberals saw these and other developments as proof that traditional government approaches in general, and Keynesian economics in particular, were no longer effective. Neoliberals argued that monetarism—with its emphasis on controlled public spending, low taxes, and smaller (and more efficient) government systems—was a more suitable approach in a global economy (Shields, 2003). For neoliberals, cutting public programs just made sense.

Fewer public programs, however, is not what Canadians wanted in the 1990s. The demand for public services was, in fact, increasing as a result of an aging population, changing family structure and roles, growing poverty and homelessness, and ongoing job losses (Cooper & Bartlett, 2008). Canadian governments found themselves in a dilemma: How could they meet the social welfare needs of Canadians while, at the same time, reducing public spending and taxes? To address this problem, the federal, provincial, and territorial governments began looking into new methods of governance.

While *government* is generally concerned with the administrative, and decision-making functions of running a country (or a region), *governance* focuses on the innovative ways that public services might be delivered (Saint-Martin, 2004). New approaches to **governance** require a "reinvention" of government roles, and a shift from a "rowing" to a "steering" capacity. When a government "rows," it delivers public programs directly; in contrast, a government that "steers" relies on nongovernment groups to deliver public programs, while monitoring the service delivery process to ensure that quality standards are met (Hrab, 2004).

To shift to a "rowing" capacity, Canadian governments had to enlist the participation and cooperation of nongovernment organizations, and to convince them of the benefits of assuming more service delivery responsibilities. Governments touted the idea of **intersectoral collaboration** as an effective way for agencies from the three sectors to meet their objectives; through collaboration, for example, agencies might save money by pooling their resources, or solve complex social problems by sharing expertise and knowledge (Torjman, 2007a). To facilitate intersectoral collaboration, governments needed a new set of guidelines. Those guidelines would be realized in an Alternative Service Delivery framework.

ALTERNATIVE SERVICE DELIVERY

Part of the Government of Canada's program review in the mid-1990s focused on evaluating all federal programs and services to see which could be devolved to lower levels of government, reduced in size and cost, or transferred to the private sector. This evaluation eventually led to the development of an **Alternative Service Delivery** (ASD) framework. Although the notion of ASD originated at the federal level, it quickly caught on in many provinces, territories, and municipalities across Canada.

The ASD framework offers suggestions as to how governments might reorganize their departments or agencies, or coordinate efforts within a government or among different levels of government. Furthermore, ASD recommends various strategies or working relationships that public and private sector organizations might form to meet service delivery objectives (Treasury Board of Canada Secretariat, 2002). There is a wide variety of ASD strategies; most of these can be conceptualized as falling somewhere along a continuum between the public sector at one end, and the private sector at the other. Exhibit 5.4 suggests that four broad types of collaborative relationships, each with its own roles and accountability, make up the public–private continuum; examples of ASD strategies are given, and placed at their approximate positions on the continuum.

ALTERNATIVE SERVICE DELIVERY (ASD)

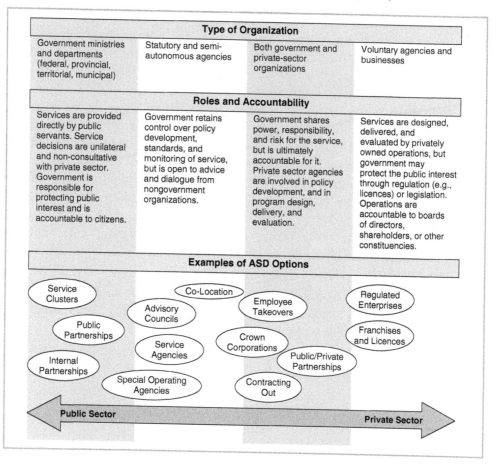

Type of Organization			
Government ministries and departments (federal, provincial, territorial, municipal)	Statutory and semi-autonomous agencies	Both government and private-sector organizations	Voluntary agencies and businesses

Roles and Accountability			
Services are provided directly by public servants. Service decisions are unilateral and non-consultative with private sector. Government is responsible for protecting public interest and is accountable to citizens.	Government retains control over policy development, standards, and monitoring of service, but is open to advice and dialogue from nongovernment organizations.	Government shares power, responsibility, and risk for the service, but is ultimately accountable for it. Private sector agencies are involved in policy development, and in program design, delivery, and evaluation.	Services are designed, delivered, and evaluated by privately owned operations, but government may protect the public interest through regulation (e.g., licences) or legislation. Operations are accountable to boards of directors, shareholders, or other constituencies.

Examples of ASD Options

Service Clusters

Co-Location

Employee Takeovers

Regulated Enterprises

Public Partnerships

Advisory Councils

Service Agencies

Crown Corporations

Franchises and Licences

Internal Partnerships

Public/Private Partnerships

Special Operating Agencies

Contracting Out

◄ **Public Sector**

Private Sector ►

CONTRACTING–OUT

Governments base their choice of ASD strategy on certain criteria, such as the costs of delivery, the public's needs and concerns, and the degree of control that government wants to retain over that service (Hrab, 2004). For the most part, the federal and regional governments continue to exercise full control over income security programs; in contrast, governments tend to see most social services as prime candidates for **privatization**. The main strategy used to deliver social services in Canada's private sector is **contracting-out** (also called *outsourcing* or *purchase-of-service contracting*). In short, contracting-out "occurs when the government purchases services under contract from a private actor [for a specified period] but remains accountable for the delivery of the services" (Panel on the Role of Government, 2004, p. 52).

The value of competition is central to the notion of contracting-out. Competition is an integral part of government's "business model," and is seen as a way to keep the costs of services down, keep service quality up, and generally make service delivery more efficient (Antony et al., 2007). Thus, any individual or organization in the private sector wishing to deliver a service using public funds must compete for those funds. The competitive bidding process typically begins with a government agency inviting the private sector to submit a proposal that outlines the applicant's plan for meeting service delivery requirements; "[p]roposals are then evaluated to ensure they deliver value for money for taxpayers and protect the public interest" (Partnerships British Columbia, 2003, p. 4).

The introduction of ASD in general, and contracting-out in particular, is significant for the delivery of Canadian social services in three main ways. This new approach

1. represents a shift in government's priorities from an emphasis on equity to a focus on efficiency in the distribution of public services and resources (Evans, Richmond, & Shields, 2005);

2. reflects government's preference for a business (or market) model over a welfare state model (Ilcan & Basok, 2004); and

3. promotes the privatization or "marketization" of social welfare programs, and a shift from a public to a private responsibility for well-being.

PRIVATIZATION: ISSUES AND CONCERNS

Since the 1990s, when governments were enthusiastically pursuing ASD strategies, Canadians have voiced their concerns about the offloading of public programs onto the private sector. Many of those concerns relate to the potential impact of privatization on Canada's cherished social programs. There is a fear that private organizations generally have lower service standards than government (White, 2003). There are also issues raised about **accountability**, which refers to the "obligation to explain how a responsibility for an assigned task has been carried out" (McFarlane & Roach, 1999, p. 8). By nature, private organizations are free agents, operating at arm's length from government and without any electoral responsibility or accountability. The issue here is that, while government can be made accountable to the public for its expenditures and practices, private operations may not be to the same extent (Ilcan & Basok, 2004).

Canadians have also been concerned about the privatization of social welfare if it means that businesses are able to compete for and win social service contracts. The prospect of for-profit groups delivering public services tends to strike a chord of public disapproval (Hrab, 2004). Three key beliefs fuel that disapproval:

1. Business is known for pursuing profit, not the public good. As long as the service makes a profit, the company will provide it; once a better rate of return is found elsewhere, the owners will drop the program and go elsewhere, leaving communities without needed services (Quarter, 1992).

2. The idea of large companies using public funds to profit from people's problems runs counter to the core values of the welfare state, such as compassion and "the alleviation of human suffering" (Sauber, 1983, p. 26).

3. There is doubt whether business can adequately serve the most vulnerable and marginalized members of society. The perception is that "[w]hen for-profit corporate entities win a contract, the tendency is for them to seek out the easiest-to-serve clients for quick and favourable results, and ignore the most vulnerable or hard-to-serve clients, who require more staff time and face greater challenges" (Ahmed, 2006, p. 19).

Exhibit 5.5 illustrates the resistance that some childcare advocates in British Columbia feel toward corporate-owned childcare services.

In general, Canadians have expressed more confidence in voluntary organizations than in businesses to deliver public social services. Studies conducted over the past twenty years suggest that Canadians perceive the voluntary sector as

- meeting special needs that governments do not offer or businesses fail to satisfy, and therefore filling service gaps in communities (Evans & Shields, 2006);

- being more trustworthy than government and less likely than business to "engage in opportunistic behaviour" (Hrab, 2004, p. 12);

- being dedicated to their communities, understanding local needs, and personalizing the provision of services more than government; and

- being less bureaucratic than government or large businesses, and therefore "being more flexible and responsive" to local needs (Eakin, 2007, p. 3).

EXHIBIT 5.5

COMMERCIAL CHILDCARE IN B.C.: AN APPEAL TO PARENTS

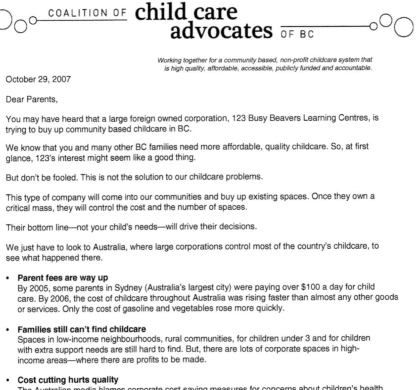

COALITION OF **child care advocates** OF BC

*Working together for a community based, non-profit childcare system that
is high quality, affordable, accessible, publicly funded and accountable.*

October 29, 2007

Dear Parents,

You may have heard that a large foreign owned corporation, 123 Busy Beavers Learning Centres, is trying to buy up community based childcare in BC.

We know that you and many other BC families need more affordable, quality childcare. So, at first glance, 123's interest might seem like a good thing.

But don't be fooled. This is not the solution to our childcare problems.

This type of company will come into our communities and buy up existing spaces. Once they own a critical mass, they will control the cost and the number of spaces.

Their bottom line—not your child's needs—will drive their decisions.

We just have to look to Australia, where large corporations control most of the country's childcare, to see what happened there.

- **Parent fees are way up**
  By 2005, some parents in Sydney (Australia's largest city) were paying over $100 a day for child care. By 2006, the cost of childcare throughout Australia was rising faster than almost any other goods or services. Only the cost of gasoline and vegetables rose more quickly.

- **Families still can't find childcare**
  Spaces in low-income neighbourhoods, rural communities, for children under 3 and for children with extra support needs are still hard to find. But, there are lots of corporate spaces in high-income areas—where there are profits to be made.

- **Cost cutting hurts quality**
  The Australian media blames corporate cost saving measures for concerns about children's health and safety. In a recent survey, 21% of Australian corporate chain workers said they would not send their children to the centre where they worked because of quality concerns!

- **Taxpayers are subsidizing corporate profits**
  Government spending on Australian childcare is up. But, most of it goes into shareholders pockets. At least 40% of the revenue earned by Australia's largest childcare company comes from government subsidies! Profits for this and other corporations are booming.

And, we worry about how much say you, as a parent, will have in your child's care when the owners of the daycare live offshore. Will they want to hear about your child's needs? Or, will the interests of their shareholders come first?

The trust between you and those who care for your children is the heart and soul of community childcare. That's why community owned and controlled childcare is the best option for BC's children.

Let's keep it that way.

There are real solutions to BC's childcare problems. Our government has the money to build an affordable, quality space for every child if they want to. Let's make sure they put your child's needs ahead of foreign shareholder profits!

For more information about how to say NO to foreign controlled childcare, go to www.cccabc.bc.ca.

Source: Coalition of Child Care Advocates of BC. (2007). Letter to parents, October 29, 2007. Retrieved November 23, 2008, from www.cccabc.bc.ca/act/actions/2007/NFS/cccabc_letter_parents_oct07.pdf. Reprinted by permission of the Coalition of Child Care Advocates of BC, www.cccabc.bc.ca.

According to the federal government, "[b]y its very nature and particularly because of its connection to communities, the voluntary sector brings a special perspective and considerable value to its activities" (Voluntary Sector Initiative, 2002, p. 6). The voluntary sector also has a long history of providing social services on behalf of government. Clearly, it has been the voluntary sector—not commercial enterprise—that has predominated in the traditional provision of social welfare programs in Canada.

As it turns out, businesses are not generally attracted to government contracts to deliver social services, since those contracts rarely offer much potential for profit making. Even when a business bids on a social service contract, the government may award the contract to a voluntary organization if that organization is likely to meet the government objectives for the right price.

Discussion Questions

New Directions in Service Delivery

1. What is your opinion about government's decision to "steer," not "row," the delivery of social services? Do you think that government should be more or less involved in the direct delivery of social services? Give reasons for your answers.

2. What are your personal concerns (if any) about privatization? In what ways might privatization benefit social service provision in Canada?

FORGING A NEW PUBLIC–VOLUNTARY RELATIONSHIP

Many social policy analysts suggest that the introduction of the government's new business approach has not only degraded the public–voluntary relationship, but has actually transformed voluntary social agencies (see Exhibit 5.6). The new contracting system, in particular, has created a number of challenges for voluntary agencies. Some of those challenges and their impact on service delivery are discussed in the following section.

NEW FUNDING MECHANISMS

Governments' new business approach has fundamentally changed the way that social services are financed. In the past, governments primarily gave grants to voluntary agencies. Agencies could apply these lump sums to any

EXHIBIT 5.6

THE TRANSFORMATION OF VOLUNTARY SOCIAL AGENCIES

VOLUNTARY SOCIAL AGENCIES USED TO...	VOLUNTARY SOCIAL AGENCIES MUST NOW...
focus primarily on the organization and its clients.	focus primarily on the needs of the market.
be largely accountable to service users (clients).	be largely accountable to the taxpayer (through government).
be autonomous and independent.	collaborate (and even merge) with other agencies to share resources.
receive most of their funding from government.	diversify their funding sources or match government contributions with nongovernment funding.
rely on government to provide "core" funding.	be satisfied with project-based funding from government.
expect government grants.	compete for government contracts.
fundraise for special projects.	fundraise to survive.
run programs on long-term and stable government funding.	run programs on short-term and unpredictable government funding.
freely adapt their programs to meet client and community needs.	deliver programs according to government specifications.
fill gaps in government services.	replace government as primary service provider.
freely advocate on behalf of clients and society.	limit advocacy to 10% of resources or less (if a registered charity).
strive to achieve philanthropic goals.	strive to become more businesslike, entrepreneurial, and market-oriented.

Source: Rosalie Chappell.

aspect of their operations, without having to report on how they spent the money. Voluntary agencies generally appreciated the flexibility of grants, since the money could be used for ongoing expenses, such as rent, utilities, and retaining staff, or for whatever priority the agency had at any given time.

Neoliberal governments, on the other hand, view grants as a form of "government charity," and against the competitive spirit of a business approach (Brock, Brook, Elliott, & LaForest, 2003, p. 21). Beginning in the early 1990s, governments began to phase out the regular use of grants in favour of contracts; this meant a shift away from core funding to project-based funding:

- **Core funding** is money that can be applied to an agency's "core" activities, such as administration (for instance, bookkeeping and reception), operational costs (for example, rent and building maintenance), agency promotion, and ongoing programs.
- **Project funding** is money earmarked for a specific project or program. It is often short-term, lasting only as long as the initiative, and cannot be used to cover costs that are not directly related to the initiative (Calgary Chamber of Voluntary Organizations, 2006).

In the past, government funding to voluntary agencies was long-term and stable, which enabled those agencies to build infrastructures that could support ongoing activities in the community (Evans, Richmond, & Shields, 2005). The shift to project funding has changed all that. For one thing, the short-term nature of project funding requires some agencies to constantly develop and disassemble programs (Eakin & Richmond, 2006). Project funding can also be unpredictable; government funders, for example, can be slow to approve or reject contracts, delaying program startup until funding can be confirmed. Another problem is that project funding may not cover the full costs of service delivery. In her study of community service organizations in Ontario, Eakin (2007) found that agencies delivered an average of $1.14 worth of service for every $1 of government funding.

In addition to project-based funding, governments have introduced other funding conditions. One condition requires contracted agencies to diversify their funding sources: that is, to seek funding not just from government, but from private sources as well. In some cases, government will not even fund a project unless the recipient agency can match the government's contribution with funding from a private source (Eakin, 2001). Some voluntary agencies have diversified their funding by imposing user fees on clients; this practice is nevertheless controversial, because it implies that access to goods and services is based on people's ability to pay rather than on need, and runs counter to welfare state principles (Jiwani, 2000). Other agencies have engaged in entrepreneurial ventures by, for example, holding bake sales, rummage sales, or raffles. A number of agencies approach corporations for donations, or apply to private foundations for financial backing. Unfortunately, voluntary social agencies have not been very successful when it comes to obtaining funding from nongovernmental sources.

EXHIBIT 5.7

There is ongoing pressure on voluntary agencies to raise their own funds through entrepreneurial activities. Car washes are one option.

Source: © 2009 Jupiterimages Corporation.

In fact, only one percent of voluntary agency funding in Canada comes from corporate donations, and only 7 percent from individual donations (Hamdad & Joyal, 2007).

ADMINISTRATIVE OVERLOAD

To ease the public's concerns about privatization, federal and regional governments have assumed a tighter control of how contracted agencies spend public funds. For the most part, this control is exercised through contracts that specify how funding should be spent, how the service is to be delivered and monitored, what the service results and performance requirements should be, and how agencies are expected to report on progress and outcomes. Contracted agencies are also obliged to participate in regular government audits, and to undergo ongoing program evaluations in order to ensure their efforts are producing the desired results for clients—in other words, to justify the use of public funds. These and other demands by government funders have drastically altered the nature of voluntary agency activities which, in the past, focused more on service delivery than on tasks related to accountability, funding, or administration (Evans, Richmond, & Shields, 2005).

Many voluntary social agencies have found that administrative staff workloads are increasing because of the disproportionate amount of time devoted to finding, securing, and maintaining funds. The bidding procedure for government contracts is especially time-consuming, since it often requires agency staff to complete long and detailed proposals, outlining how they would deliver the service on behalf of government (Scott, 2003a). Obtaining private funds to match government contributions can be another onerous task, increasing the existing administrative burden (Evans, Richmond, & Shields, 2005).

In addition to funding-related tasks, voluntary agencies are required to complete "complex, time-consuming, and very detailed accountability reporting systems and controls," albeit with reduced government funds to cover these accountability duties (Eakin, 2007, p. 1). Accountability requirements are particularly time-consuming for agencies with multiple funders, since every funder has its own reporting system, forms, timelines, and audits (Scott, 2003b). In her study of community service agencies, Eakin (2007) found that many senior managers had to drop important responsibilities such as staff development and program management to free up time to meet the varied reporting demands of funders.

ADVOCACY "CHILL"

One of the most important roles of voluntary social agencies is **advocacy**. The type of advocacy an agency performs depends largely on the presenting issue and the organization's purpose. Many agencies advocate on behalf of individual clients, while others advocate on behalf of society in general, raising public awareness of conditions that foster injustice and inequality. Regardless of the form of advocacy taken, all advocacy efforts have the potential to enhance social welfare to some degree.

Following the Second World War, it was common for Canadian governments to fund the advocacy efforts of a wide range of voluntary organizations that represented minority groups; this public support, write Evans and Shields (2006, p. 4), helped to foster social inclusion and broaden "the democratic experience." Over the years, government has withdrawn much of its support for advocacy and has stopped funding many advocacy groups. In 2002, the federal government introduced the "10 Percent Rule" under the Income Tax

Act to prohibit registered charities from devoting any more than 10 percent of their resources to advocacy. In addition, registered charities were told to refrain from engaging in certain "political activities," such as supporting (or opposing) a political party or a candidate running for public office.

The new rules around advocacy and political activity have made it difficult for some voluntary agencies to fulfil their advocacy role. These rules have also increased anxiety among voluntary sector staff and volunteers. Reports suggest that some organizations are afraid of inadvertently devoting more than 10 percent of their resources to advocacy and subsequently contravening the Income Tax Act; others fear that their advocacy activities may be construed by government as "political activities" or as criticism of the government. In any case, there is concern that advocacy activities may somehow jeopardize government funding and/or charitable status. Rektor (2002) finds that voluntary agencies are dealing with these fears in various ways: some are choosing not to advocate on any issue, while others err on the side of caution and speak out less than they are legally entitled to. The term **advocacy chill** refers to the reluctance among the voluntary agencies to negotiate on behalf of their clients (Evans, Richmond, & Shields, 2005). According to Richmond and Shields (2003), the reluctance to advocate dulls the political sword that voluntary agencies have long carried when it comes to representing vulnerable groups and bringing about political and social change.

LOSS OF AUTONOMY AND IDENTITY

A number of social researchers write about the transformation taking place in the character of voluntary agencies; for the most part, that transformation is attributed to the new public–voluntary relationship, and by the pressure on agencies to become more businesslike. The public–voluntary relationship was formed in the spirit of a "collaborative partnership," which, as Evans and Shields (2006, p. 13) explain, implies "joint decision-making in addition to the sharing of human, financial and informational resources." Critics of public–voluntary agreements suggest that while government appears content to share the work, it is unwilling to share decision-making power. The more government takes control over voluntary agencies—through such mechanisms as contract funding and strict accountability procedures—the less autonomous those agencies may be. There is also a common belief that, as the voluntary sector replaces government as a primary provider of social welfare, that sector will morph into a "shadow state" with no real identity of its own.

Evans, Richmond, and Shields (2005, p. 93) believe that the emphasis on business practices and entrepreneurism may be pushing voluntary agencies away from their original philanthropic goals toward a "new market-based managerialism" in which agencies are "servants to contracts controlled by state funders." In this process, voluntary agencies may be restructured to cater more to the needs of the market, rather than the people they are supposed to be serving. The move to a more businesslike or "bottom line" approach may ultimately create more efficient service delivery; however, as Jiwani (2000) points out, efficiency is no guarantee for empathy, a caring approach, or a high-quality service.

Another threat to agency autonomy and identity is related to an agency's mission. Voluntary social agencies are often referred to as "mission-based organizations," because they are motivated by a certain social cause. However, according to the National Survey of Nonprofit and Voluntary Organizations, most nonprofit organizations are struggling to fulfil their missions (Hall et al., 2005). In many cases, those struggles are linked to the new contracting system. With government cutbacks and the shift to contract funding, some agencies find themselves competing not only for fewer government contracts, but for contracts that narrowly define the services the agency can offer. Those contract conditions may not be compatible with an agency's mission; subsequently, agencies run the risk of drifting away from their original mission in the pursuit of badly needed funds (Eakin & Richmond, 2006). The sacrifice of an agency's mission for government dollars can create a number of potential problems, such as increased stress among staff and the loss of the agency's autonomy. Agencies that lose sight of their mission may also lose touch with the needs of their communities; when this happens, agencies "risk eroding their base of legitimacy and credibility" (Scott, 2003a, p. 11).

GOVERNMENT SUPPORT OF THE VOLUNTARY SECTOR

In the early 1990s, Canadian governments increased their devolution of service delivery functions to the private sector and, in doing so, expanded the number of public–voluntary contracts to unprecedented levels (Voluntary Sector Initiative, 2004). The heavier workload came with considerably fewer resources than in the past; as a result, the capacity of many voluntary agencies was strained as they tried to meet the diverse expectations of funders, clients, and communities.

In 1995, the Government of Canada supported the formation of the Voluntary Sector Roundtable (VSR) to see what could be done to strengthen both the voluntary sector's capacity to deliver services and the federal–voluntary working relationship. Three major initiatives came out of the work of the Roundtable: the Panel on Accountability and Governance in the Voluntary Sector

(1997–1998); the Working Together: A Government of Canada/Voluntary Sector Joint Initiative (1999); and the Voluntary Sector Initiative (2000–2005). A great deal of research, reports, guidelines, and new projects were generated from those initiatives, including the development of an *Accord Between the Government of Canada and the Voluntary Sector*.

In addition to federal actions, the provinces and territories have introduced their own initiatives to help the voluntary sector build its capacity to serve communities. Today, there are organizations in most regions dedicated to strengthening the voluntary sector, including the Alberta Nonprofit/Voluntary Sector Initiative; the Manitoba Voluntary Sector Initiative; and Ontario's Voluntary Sector Relations Unit.

Despite government support, conditions in voluntary social agencies have generally worsened over the years. Researchers Eakin and Richmond (2006, p. 5) report that "[b]y every measure, in every study, community-based service providers are faring poorly. They have serious financing problems, reduced organizational capacity, staff and volunteer recruitment and retention problems. They struggle to meet reporting requirements, juggle short-term contracts, and improvise essential services in the face of the continual decline of necessary resources." Other studies suggest that front-line workers, managers, and volunteers are burning out under the heavy workload; meanwhile, the demand for social services keeps growing.

Governments continue their efforts to support the voluntary sector. For example, in 2007 and 2008, the federal government launched a review of its system of grants and contributions, and of the administrative requirements imposed on voluntary agencies, and promised to modify certain policies and practices to ease the burden on contracted agencies (Treasury Board of Canada Secretariat, 2007; Canada Revenue Agency, 2008). The impact of these and other efforts is yet to be determined. What does seem to be clear is that, in order for the voluntary sector to become sustainable and help communities to solve local problems, governments' funding and accountability requirements must be adjusted (Eakin, 2007).

Discussion Questions

■ **Forging a New Public–Voluntary Relationship**

1. Pretend that you have been hired as a consultant to review the problems facing the voluntary sector, and to consider how the voluntary–public relationship might be strengthened. What would you recommend to improve the relationship? What might voluntary agencies do to improve things? What changes should government make?

2. Identify the potential pros and cons of the shift to contract funding for: (a) government; (b) voluntary agencies; and (c) service users (clients).

IV AN EMERGING FOURTH SECTOR: THE SOCIAL ECONOMY

Although the public, commercial, and voluntary sectors are the predominant service delivery systems, it appears that a fourth sector—called the **social economy**—is emerging. The Government of Canada defines the social economy as a grass-roots sector that is entrepreneurial and yet nonprofit in nature. This sector "seeks to enhance the social, economic, and environmental conditions of communities, often with a focus on their disadvantaged members" (HRSDC, 2005a).

Organizations that belong to the social economy are generically referred to as **social economy enterprises** (SEEs). SEEs are run like businesses, and tend to rely upon both paid staff (who are often former clients) and volunteers. It is common for SEEs to draw from a wide range of funding sources, such as revenue from selling items or performing a service, as well as government funding and private donations. Any profits made from the operation are either invested back into the organization to develop programs or used to meet other identified social needs in the community (HRSDC, 2005a).

Most SEEs come up with innovative ways to use their resources. A SEE soup kitchen, for example, might receive food donations from local supermarkets, use that food to make meals, and then sell those meals at a low cost to people in need (Policy Research Initiative, 2005). Some SEEs run second-hand stores to fund their social service programs; others manage housing and consumer cooperatives. There are a wide range of entrepreneurial possibilities. Exhibit 5.8 profiles the Women in Need Society, a SEE in Calgary that finds innovative ways to raise money, provide employment to people in the community, and help women in low-income situations.

Studies show that the social economy is growing in Canada, and accounts for about 2.5 percent of Canada's gross domestic product (Policy Research Initiative, 2005). Quebec leads the way in supporting the development of the social economy. In that province, an estimated 6,200 SEEs employ a total of 65,000 people and sell more than $4 billion in goods and services (HRSDC, 2005a).

Discussion Questions

An Emerging Fourth Sector: The Social Economy

1. Identify the characteristics of the social economy that makes this sector distinctly different from the public, commercial, and voluntary sectors. In what ways is the social economy similar to the other three sectors?

2. Which of the four sectors do you believe has the greatest potential for lifting people out of poverty? Give reasons for your answer.

AGENCY PROFILE: WOMEN IN NEED SOCIETY (WINS)

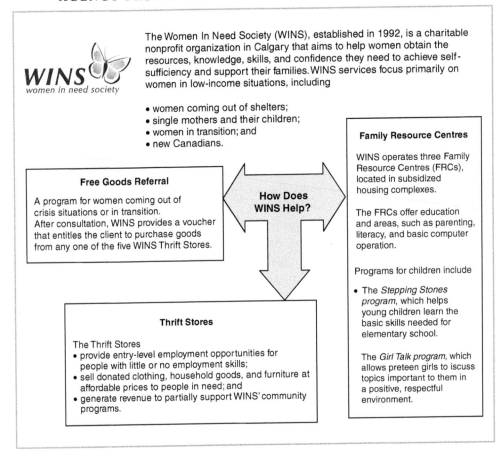

WINS
women in need society

The Women In Need Society (WINS), established in 1992, is a charitable nonprofit organization in Calgary that aims to help women obtain the resources, knowledge, skills, and confidence they need to achieve self-sufficiency and support their families. WINS services focus primarily on women in low-income situations, including

- women coming out of shelters;
- single mothers and their children;
- women in transition; and
- new Canadians.

How Does WINS Help?

Free Goods Referral

A program for women coming out of crisis situations or in transition. After consultation, WINS provides a voucher that entitles the client to purchase goods from any one of the five WINS Thrift Stores.

Family Resource Centres

WINS operates three Family Resource Centres (FRCs), located in subsidized housing complexes.

The FRCs offer education and areas, such as parenting, literacy, and basic computer operation.

Programs for children include

- The *Stepping Stones program*, which helps young children learn the basic skills needed for elementary school.

The *Girl Talk program*, which allows preteen girls to iscuss topics important to them in a positive, respectful environment.

Thrift Stores

The Thrift Stores
- provide entry-level employment opportunities for people with little or no employment skills;
- sell donated clothing, household goods, and furniture at affordable prices to people in need; and
- generate revenue to partially support WINS' community programs.

Source: Excerpted and adapted from Women in Need Society (WINS). (2008). Website. Retrieved November 22, 2008, from www.womeninneed.net and www.womeninneed.net/index.php?page=4.

SUMMARY

Introduction

The public, commercial, and voluntary sectors make up Canada's mixed economy of welfare. In recent years, the boundaries between the sectors have been undergoing significant realignment, heralding a new era in the delivery of public social welfare services.

I. Service Sectors: Public, Commercial, and Voluntary Domains

Each level of government in the *public sector* delivers its own mix of income security programs and social services. The federal government is responsible for certain "client groups," and for pan-Canadian programs; regional governments are likely to deliver legislated social services; and the municipalities tend to deliver components of larger provincial programs. The *commercial sector* is not part of the social welfare system; this sector sells private helping services for a fee. The *voluntary sector* delivers a wide range of social services; in general, voluntary-sector agencies "do good works," advocate, and mediate.

II. New Directions in Service Delivery

During the 1980s, public criticism and the rise of neoliberalism fostered efforts to shrink the size and power of government. To meet the demand for services, governments devolved many service-delivery responsibilities to the private sector; the Alternative Service Delivery framework provided options for new working relationships. Contracting-out has become the main strategy for delivering social services in the private sector. Overall, Canadians have been more concerned about the delivery of social services by businesses than by voluntary agencies.

III. Forging a New Public–Voluntary Relationship

Government's new business approach has transformed voluntary social agencies, especially in terms of financial instability and administrative overload. Other problems encountered by voluntary agencies include advocacy restrictions, and a threat to agency identity and autonomy. The establishment of the Voluntary Sector Roundtable and other government initiatives aimed to strengthen the capacity of the voluntary sector, and to improve public–voluntary relationships. Despite these efforts, the conditions in many voluntary agencies have worsened.

IV. An Emerging Fourth Sector: The Social Economy

The social economy is growing in Canada, accounting for about 2.5 percent of Canada's gross domestic product. Social economy enterprises are entrepreneurial yet nonprofit, are run like businesses, draw from a variety of funding sources, and rely on both paid staff (often former clients) and volunteers.

Key Terms

For definitions of the key terms, consult the Glossary on page 413 at the end of the book.

mixed economy of
  welfare, p. 116
private sector, p. 116
public sector, p. 116
commercial sector,
  p. 116
voluntary sector,
  p. 116
public program,
  p. 117

corporate social
  responsibility, p. 120
voluntary social agency,
  p. 120
governance, p. 124
intersectoral
  collaboration, p. 124
Alternative Service
  Delivery, p. 124
privatization, p. 125

contracting-out, p. 125
accountability, p. 126
core funding, p. 131
project funding,
  p. 131
advocacy, p. 133
advocacy chill, p. 134
social economy, p. 137
social economy
  enterprise, p. 137

CHAPTER

Social Agencies

OBJECTIVES

Social agencies are responsible for delivering a wide range of social welfare resources to people in need. This chapter will explore:

- the definition and main characteristics of social agencies;
- community-based residential and nonresidential organizations;
- the internal structures and functions of social agencies; and
- the primary features of organic organizational structures.

INTRODUCTION

> Organisations are of two kinds, those which aim at getting something done, and those which aim at preventing something from being done. (Bertrand Russell, British philosopher and advocate for social reform, 1952, p. 51)

Social agencies are formally structured organizations that fulfil a variety of functions: they provide goods, services, and financial assistance to people in need; engage local community members in local projects; and mobilize resources to address community problems (Jaco & Pierce, 2005). All social agencies operate on a nonprofit basis and are found in both the public and voluntary sectors. **Voluntary social agencies** are nonprofit organizations in the private sector, and include family service bureaus, immigrant settlement agencies, and women's shelters. These agencies may be either sectarian (religious) or secular (nonreligious); 72 percent of voluntary social agencies are registered charities (Barr, Brownlee, Lasby, & Gumulka, 2005). **Public social agencies** are government departments and divisions, and include social assistance offices and, in most jurisdictions, child protection units.

Although social agencies vary in terms of tasks, administration, organizational structure, goals, and mandate, most agencies share the following basic functions (with examples):

- service delivery (assessing client needs and providing services and/or material resources to clients);

- administration (guiding agency activities by developing and revising policies and procedures);

- funding (securing funding and following budgets);

- accountability (ensuring the quality of service and evaluating the effectiveness of programs);

- recruitment (hiring and supervising staff and volunteers); and

- public relations (fostering and maintaining positive relationships with the community).

The way an agency carries out its functions and activities depends largely on whom it serves, what it intends to accomplish, and how its programs are designed. An agency's activities are usually targeted toward a certain population, such as families with children, people with disabilities, or seniors. Those activities are planned with a specific goal in mind; for example, a program that helps parents learn nonviolent methods of disciplining a child (activity) may aim to prevent child abuse (the goal).

The types of goods or services a social agency delivers are usually determined by the identified needs of people living in a community. For example, an area that has a high rate of teen moms typically has a need for childcare and young parent programs that are located near the high school. How successful agencies are at meeting local needs depends on several external factors, including community and political support and funding availability. Moreover, the effectiveness of programs and services is often a function of several internal factors, such as the setting in which services are delivered, the agency's strategic and operational plans, and organizational structure. This chapter looks at some of these factors.

EXHIBIT 6.1

The existence of soup kitchens and other emergency food programs reflects the needs of many Canadian communities.

Source: © Jim West/Alamy.

COMMUNITY-BASED SOCIAL AGENCIES

Most Canadian social agencies plan and deliver their programs according to a **community-based model**. Community-based services tend to focus on client strengths (rather than detriments), encourage people to make decisions about their own well-being, and recognize the value of natural supports (such as family and friends) in people's lives. Agencies that adopt a community-based approach typically strive to be responsive to changing community needs, and are flexible in matching services to people's needs and preferences. Those services are likely to be comprehensive (offering a broad continuum of services from a wide variety of service providers), and outreach-oriented (to help people when and wherever they need it). Community-based services are often the result of local support and collaboration, and tend to be are integrated with other local organizations and groups (Standing Senate Committee on Social Affairs, Science and Technology, 2006a). Features of the community-based approach can be found in both public and voluntary agencies, and in residential and nonresidential settings alike.

RESIDENTIAL CENTRES

The majority of **residential centres** provide living quarters, meals, and other services for people who require round-the-clock care. The type of residential centre that exists in a given community is determined by the needs of its residents. Some common types are

- long-term-care facilities or nursing homes for seniors;
- shelters for transient people;
- assessment or treatment centres for children or youth with emotional or behavioural disorders;
- group homes for people with developmental delays;
- rehabilitation centres for children and youth with physical disabilities;
- care centres for people with psychiatric disabilities;
- inpatient addiction treatment centres; and
- transition houses for abused women and their children.

In 2007, there were over 4,500 residential centres in Canada that were funded, licensed, or approved by provincial/territorial departments of health and/or social services. Almost 238,000 Canadians live in residential centres; most of these individuals are elderly or have a **mental health problem** (Statistics Canada, 2008f).

Although residential centres are sometimes called "institutions," they are nothing like the poorhouses, workhouses, or insane asylums of the nineteenth and early twentieth centuries. Those institutions placed more importance on rules and procedures than on the residents' needs, and residents were usually discouraged from accessing alternative services if they disagreed with what the institution had to offer. In contrast, modern residential centres make a conscious effort to integrate the principles of community-based practice into their services and help their residents retain ties to natural supports and other resources in the community. Moreover, the residential centres of today try to avoid appearing "institutional"; for example, these centres may locate themselves in residential neighbourhoods, and strive to make the building, residents' rooms, and gathering places (such as dining rooms) as natural and homey as possible.

Obviously, not everyone who is in need or faces a problem requires residential services. This type of intervention is most appropriate when an individual requires a type of assessment (such as for psychiatric purposes) that cannot reasonably be done in the person's home. People who exhibit violent or

EXHIBIT 6.2

Lunatic asylums, such as this one in Toronto in 1867, were some of Canada's first "residential centres."

Source: Copyright © Toronto Public Library.

inappropriate behaviour, or need supervision or stabilization beyond what family or a nonresidential service provider can give, may also be suited to residential care. Residential services are also appropriate for those who need specialized treatment, such as intensive drug rehabilitation. Whatever the reason for the placement, individuals living in residential settings must have regularly scheduled reviews to adjust the level of care as needed, and to ensure that the services are meeting the client's needs and goals (Conceptual Framework Subcommittee of the Residential Services Advisory Committee, 2002).

There are mixed opinions on the future use of residential services in Canada. Some observers predict that, because the population is both growing and aging, the demand for residential services will naturally increase. To manage that demand, residential-care facilities may turn to strategies designed to "ration" services; for instance, long-term care centres may choose to create longer wait lists, or tighten their admission criteria to exclude people needing intensive care (Sudbury & Rook, 2003). Other observers suggest that, although the number of seniors is increasing and people are living longer, seniors tend to be healthier than those of previous generations and may need less residential care. Moreover, the principle of **aging in place** is driving the creation of innovative housing options designed to help elderly persons live at home longer.

NONRESIDENTIAL CENTRES

Nonresidential centres normally provide services on a drop-in, appointment, or outreach basis. They cater to those who can look after many of their own needs, who require only short-term help, and who do not pose a threat to themselves or to the rest of society. It is common to find a continuum of services in nonresidential centres. This is the case with "one-stop" or **multiservice centres**, which offer a variety of social services under one roof, allowing people to obtain a wide range of support at one location. Services in these centres may

- be aimed at a particular group (for example, a centre may target children and families, and provide a comprehensive set of services such as family counselling, parent education, support for teen moms, and childcare); and/or
- serve a variety of populations (for example, people with disabilities, victims of abuse, immigrants, and homeless people) and age groups (such as infants, teens, and seniors).

One Toronto study suggests that social agencies that are actively expanding their range of services, and becoming multiservice centres, may be doing so in response to a greater demand for services and more complex needs among their clientele. There is also the possibility that, by stretching their mandates and offering a wider range of services agencies may be able to tap into a greater number of funding sources (Toronto Community and Neighbourhood Services, 2004).

Nonresidential centres try to deliver their services in a flexible and user-friendly manner and provide a variety of options in the way people can participate. *Drop-in centres*, for example, usually offer loosely scheduled programs that can be accessed at any time during service hours. Telephone services offer support and anonymity and—in the case of crisis lines—are available around the clock. *Outreach services* are provided "outside the office," in the clients' natural environment. There are various forms of outreach. For example, *in-home services* are provided to people in their homes, whereas *street outreach* seeks out and helps people living on the street, especially in urban centres. *Online support* is offered through the Internet; chat rooms, discussion forums, and e-mail can be used to facilitate services such as information sharing, peer support, and professional counselling.

SYSTEM OF CARE

In general, residential and nonresidential centres differ in the range and intensity of services they offer, and in the ways they deliver those services; that said, no type is inherently more effective than any other. Each has strengths to offer the community; working in tandem, these centres can form a solid base of community support and care. The term *system of care* refers to the mix of service components that, when offered in a coordinated and integrated fashion, is responsive to the varying levels and changing needs of clients (Conceptual Framework Subcommittee of the Residential Services Advisory Committee, 2002). Exhibit 6.3 offers a conceptualization of a system of care for children and youth; this system includes both residential and nonresidential services, as well as informal support systems such as families and self-help groups. The arrows in the Exhibit indicate the movement the child or youth might make from one type of service to another to meet his or her needs or circumstances at any given time.

Discussion Questions

Community-Based Social Agencies

1. Identify the potential advantages and disadvantages of services provided in (a) a residential setting and (b) a nonresidential setting. How might the combination of both types of services benefit clients?

2. What types of residential and nonresidential centres exist in your community? Is there a predominance of one type of centre (for example, are there more nonresidential than residential centres)? Why might a community favour the establishment of one type of centre over another?

AGENCY SYSTEMS: INTERNAL STRUCTURES AND FUNCTIONS

Before a social agency can deliver services, it must develop a solid internal structure upon which to base its work. An agency's strategic and operational frameworks provide this structure. A **strategic framework** describes the

EXHIBIT 6.3

SYSTEM OF CARE FOR CHILDREN AND YOUTH

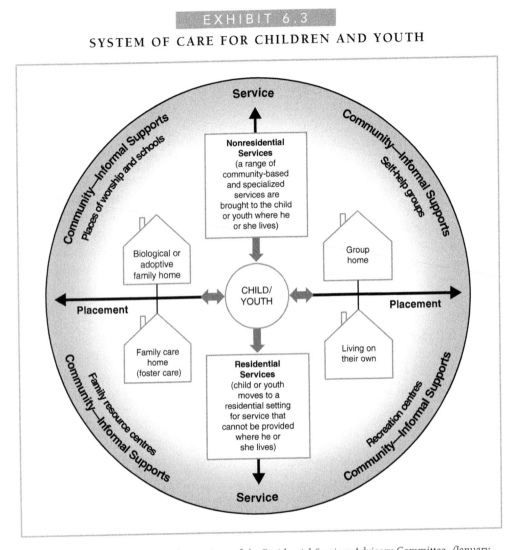

Source: Conceptual Framework Subcommittee of the Residential Services Advisory Committee, (January 2000). *Working with Community to Support Children, Youth and Families:* Page 9. [online]. Available: http://www.mcf.gov.bc.ca/change/pdfs/working_with_community.pdf [March 13, 2004]. Copyright © Province of British Columbia. All rights reserved. Reprinted with permission of British Columbia. www.ipp.gov.bc.ca.

agency's priorities, and how the agency intends to achieve its ultimate goal, mission, and vision. In contrast, an agency's **operational framework** is a practical plan for two main levels of internal activities: **direct services** involve face-to-face interactions between front-line workers and clients; and **indirect services** are conducted off the front line, and include administration, program planning and evaluation, and the development of policies and procedures. This section explores some of the components of strategic and operational frameworks and their implications for service delivery.

A STRATEGIC FRAMEWORK

Understanding Community Conditions

A sound strategic framework is based on a good understanding of the community in which the agency functions. Many agencies conduct an **environmental scan** to learn about local social and economic conditions (for example, persistently high unemployment) that may influence the community's needs. Such knowledge will also inform the agency about its potential ability to meet local needs over the long term—in other words, its potential for sustainability. In order to be sustainable, an agency must

- have adequate opportunities to do its work;
- be able to attract and retain competent staff;
- obtain sufficient funding and other resources;
- demonstrate its achievements in order to attract future funding; and
- gain support from the community (Shapiro, 2008).

One way to assess an agency's potential sustainability is through the application of a SWOT analysis. This type of assessment considers a community's strengths, weaknesses, opportunities, and threats. Such information can help an agency take advantage of the strengths and opportunities, and minimize the weaknesses and threats.

Assessing Community Needs

A **community needs assessment** is one tool that social agencies may use to gather information and "paint" a picture of local needs. That information might be gleaned from a variety of sources, including documents (such as community profiles or census data), direct observation, interviews, and focus groups. Members of the community, and professionals who work in health and social service agencies, are often excellent sources of information about perceived community needs.

Through community needs assessments, agencies may be able to clarify the types of services that a certain group needs (for example, local youth might need specialized employment programs), and how that group might benefit from a new program. A community needs assessment can also be useful for determining how a new program might be designed and delivered (in a group setting, for instance, or through outreach), and for identifying the resources (such as funding or facilities) needed to provide the service. Finally, an assessment of community needs may ascertain whether a proposed program will likely be used by the target population (Jill Florence Lackey and Associates, 2004). Many social agencies are able to accurately assess a community's needs, and offer services that are well-used by local residents. The offering of services, however, does not guarantee their use. Exhibit 6.4 points out potential barriers to help-seeking that agencies need to consider when planning new programs.

Establishing the Agency's Direction

A strategic framework typically describes what the agency hopes to achieve and how. Most social agencies develop a **vision statement** that articulates the agency's image of an ideal community. For example, the Faye Peterson Transition House (2008) envisions a world in which "[e]very Woman, youth and [child] live[s] in a safe, inclusive community free of violence, racism and oppression. Women are equal, independent and fully participatory members of society."

While an agency's vision gives it something to strive for, its mission clarifies what it intends to achieve. Every social agency has a **mission statement** that describes what the organization is, what it does, and to whom the programs are targeted. Family Services of Greater Vancouver (2008), for instance, has the following mission: "We are a not-for-profit organization dedicated to strengthening people, families, and communities [what it is]. We provide a diverse range of professional support and counselling services [what it does] to those who are experiencing challenges in their lives [who the programs are for]."

An **agency's goal** states in realistic terms what the organization plans to do in the long-term to achieve its vision and mission. For example, if the agency's mission is to alleviate homelessness, the overall goal might be to provide housing options for homeless people in the community. According to the Treasury Board of Canada (2008), goals must be compatible with the organization's vision and mission; be consistent with information derived from the environmental scan; be appropriate to community needs; provide a clear direction and scope for the agency's programs; and be relevant over the long term.

Underlying an agency's vision, mission, and goals is a set of values—or acceptable standards—that govern how the agency conducts itself when carrying out its work (Treasury Board of Canada, 2008). When articulated, **value statements** reflect the social agency's core ideology. Family Services of

EXHIBIT 6.4

IF WE "BUILD IT," WILL THEY COME?

Social agencies are created, and a wide variety of services for individuals, families, and groups exist. But not everyone who needs help seeks it. Why? Below are some theories on the barriers to help-seeking.

Researchers Kessler, Brown, and Broman (1981) propose that voluntary help-seeking occurs in three stages. An individual

1. recognizes that he or she has a problem;
2. decides to seek outside help; and
3. contacts a social agency or professional helper.

Real or perceived barriers to help-seeking can arise at any of these stages. The most common barrier is an individual's **denial that a problem exists**.

Age can influence a person's willingness to seek help. Common barriers for youth include a lack of knowledge about available sources of help, concerns about confidentiality, and doubt that professionals will understand or help them. Elderly people tend to resist outside help because they are afraid of losing independence by, for example, being "committed" to an institution.

A study by Poole and Isaac (2001) identifies several reasons why women with addictions might not seek treatment. In addition to denial of the problem by self, family, or friends, there is

- **fear** of stigmatization, guilt, and shame;
- **worry** about their children and their care;
- a perception that helping professionals are **poorly trained**;
- **attitudes** among professionals that women are "sicker" and less likely to recover than men;
- **scarcity of residential programs** that can take woman with their children; and
- **lack of transportation** to and from addictions services.

The BC Partners for Mental Health and Addictions reports that about one in five British Columbians has a mental disorder or addiction, but two-thirds of them will not seek help. Many people with mental health concerns are **afraid of being labelled** "crazy," "mentally defective," "incurable," or some other stigmatizing term, or are **concerned about what others might think**.

Source: R. Kessler, R. Brown, and C. Broman, "Sex Differences in Psychiatric Help-Seeking: Evidence from Four Large-Scale Surveys," *Journal of Health and Social Behavior* 22(1) (March 1981): 49–64. Retrieved November 22, 2008, from, and cited in, Centre for Suicide Prevention, "Barriers to Help-Seeking," *SIEC Alert* 35 (May 1999), www.suicideinfo.ca/csp/assets/alert35.pdf. N. Poole and B. Isaac, *Apprehensions: Barriers to Treatment for Substance-Using Mothers*, 2001. Retrieved November 22, 2008, from British Columbia Centre of Excellence for Women's Health, www.bccewh.bc.ca/publications-resources/documents/apprehensions.pdf. BC Partners for Mental Health and Addictions, *Stigma and Discrimination Around Mental Disorders and Addictions*, 2006. Retrieved November 22, 2008, from www.heretohelp.bc.ca/sites/default/files/images/ 32_stigma.pdf.

Greater Vancouver (2008) has a clearly defined set of values: quality (of programs and services); respect (for all individuals); possibility (a belief in people's ability to overcome challenges); diversity (recognition of and respect for differences); and accountability (for responsibly managing resources). Organizational values are reflected in every aspect of an agency's operations, including its programs and administration.

AN OPERATIONAL FRAMEWORK: DIRECT SERVICES

An operational framework outlines the types of services that an agency will deliver. Most social agencies offer direct services that are preventive in nature—that is, they either try to prevent the emergence of human problems or try to lessen the negative effects of problems once they have arisen. Typically, agency services operate at one or more of the following three levels:

- **Primary prevention** activities aim to prevent the development of personal and social problems by educating people, providing information, or promoting certain practices. They are usually targeted at large segments of "healthy" populations for the purpose of maintaining or enhancing well-being. Alcohol and drug education for pre-teens is a well-known primary prevention initiative.

- **Secondary prevention** activities (or "early intervention") address problems in the early stages of development before they have become serious or chronic. This level of prevention involves controlling or changing the conditions that are creating the problem. Respite services, for example, can help family caregivers to reduce stress related to caregiving and subsequently prevent burnout.

- **Tertiary prevention** activities (or "treatment") aim to reduce the negative effects of problems—such as disability and dependence—that have become chronic or complex. Social welfare programs in this category include child protection services, family therapy, and residential care for youth with emotional disorders. Tertiary prevention programs are often mandatory and sanctioned by law. For example, child protection workers have the legal authority to intervene in a family's affairs if child neglect or abuse is suspected.

Tertiary prevention has long been the main focus of direct services. In recent years, however, social programmers have shown a greater interest in primary prevention because it is generally agreed that it is easier, less expensive, and more humane to improve the lives of people before, rather than after, problems develop. Furthermore, the direct benefits of treating chronic problems are not easily identified or measured, whereas a growing number of studies point to the effectiveness of primary prevention programs. Findings such as these have prompted many Canadian municipalities to direct their resources to building healthy communities; by meeting local needs, municipalities hope to curb crime, homelessness, and other social problems before they occur.

AN OPERATIONAL FRAMEWORK: INDIRECT SERVICES

Administration

An agency's **administration** is primarily concerned with the exercise of authority (power) and decision making. The *governance level* of an agency is ultimately responsible and accountable for the organization and the work it does in the community. In the voluntary sector, social agencies are usually governed by a board of directors or trustees; in the public sector, governance is the responsibility of a first minister and his or her senior staff. Among other things, this level of administration must carve out a niche for the agency in the community, develop a positive public image, and ensure that the agency is accountable to its **stakeholders**—that is, the staff, volunteers, funders, locals, and others who have a vested interest in the agency's activities and achievements.

Activities at the *management level* involve the delegation of tasks, the organization of people, and the allocation of resources needed to complete the work. At this level, agency managers and supervisors obtain and allocate resources, design programs, recruit staff, and coordinate their duties. A primary activity at this level is finding effective ways to achieve the agency's goals. This usually involves providing training and professional development opportunities for staff, monitoring the effectiveness of programs, and ensuring that programs are responsive to the changing needs of the community (Institute on Governance, 2008a; 2008b).

In theory, the governance and management levels are distinct with regard to the types of knowledge and skills required; in reality, it is not uncommon for the roles and responsibilities of the two levels to overlap so that common goals can be met. The Institute on Governance (2008b) cautions against letting the lines between levels become too blurred or confused: "In the non-profit sector, the primary charge of boards is the governance role but their responsibilities might often cross over into the management and work roles of the organization. Senior management is almost always heavily involved in the governance role. The real danger is not the mixing of these roles, but unclear definition of responsibilities and lost lines of accountability."

EXHIBIT 6.5

Most voluntary agencies are governed by a volunteer board of directors, which is accountable to the local community, funders, staff, and other agency stakeholders.

Source: © 2009 Jupiterimages Corporation.

Program Planning

Program planning involves a series of decisions related to how the agency's programs will be designed, run, and delivered to clients. There are various program-planning models available to social agencies, each with a different focus and set of procedures. However, a generic program-planning process may involve six key steps:

1. Determine how people in the planning process will work together, make decisions, and move through the planning stages.

2. Confirm whether the program development plan should be carried out and, if so, in what manner.

3. Set goals and objectives, and define the target population (that is, the potential client group).

4. Design program strategies and activities.

5. Identify indicators of success (in other words, how will program planners know that the program is achieving its objectives?).

6. Review the viability of the proposed program and determine whether it can be easily evaluated.

These steps do not always progress in a neat, tidy, or chronological order. As new information comes in and fresh challenges arise, the activities for one step may have to be undertaken earlier or later in the process (THCU, 2001).

To assess the feasibility of a program plan before a long-term investment is made, some agencies run new programs on a "pilot" basis. During this trial period, a program's expenditures can be monitored, and program activities can be observed and critiqued to ensure that the program goals and objectives are being achieved. Any shortcomings in the program can be modified during this pilot phase.

Program Evaluation

Social agencies use various tools to evaluate their programs and services. **Program evaluation** can be understood "as the process in which services and programs are examined to determine whether they are needed and used, how well they are run, whether they meet their stated objective, and whether they are worth the cost" (McDonald, 2005, p. 307). Various types of program evaluation are available; however, most social welfare programs today undergo **outcome evaluations**. These types of evaluations focus on the results of programs, and seek to identify how program activities have improved the behaviour, skills, attitudes, or knowledge of program participants (Canadian Outcomes Research Institute, 2007).

Program funders have taken a particular fancy to outcome evaluations since they are likely to tell them whether their dollars are producing expected results. In a national survey of the evaluation practices of Canada's voluntary sector, 89 percent of funders that required program evaluation in funded agencies wanted information about client outcomes (Hall, Phillips, Meillat, & Pickering, 2003). Outcome evaluations are also used to assess the effectiveness of government programs. For example, federal government departments that are responsible for programs funded under the Social Union Framework Agreement are required to "measure and monitor the outcomes of programs and report publicly on a regular basis on program performance" (Treasury Board of Canada, 2000).

Outcomes can also be useful to agencies: knowing how (or if) programs benefit clients is useful for improving existing programs, or developing new ones. The ability to demonstrate positive outcomes may also lend credibility to an agency, not to mention increase an agency's chances of continued funding. Unfortunately, program evaluation has both limitations and challenges. One limitation is that evaluators often have a difficult time proving that the improved well-being of program participants is the result of the program and not some other influence in participants' lives (Herman & Renz, 1998). Also, many social agencies find that outcome evaluation is an expensive, complicated, and time-consuming process that requires a certain expertise not always available in-house (Hall et al., 2003).

Policies and Procedures

All social agencies—whether large government bureaucracies or small voluntary agencies—operate according to fixed rules, otherwise known as **policies and procedures**. Typically, an agency has policies that outline how it intends to reach its long- and short-term goals. Procedures naturally flow from policy, and describe the activities and resources that will be applied to meet policy requirements (Huebner, 1999).

Social agencies that provide direct client services usually have policies and procedures that outline the structure and process of programs and how clients are expected to enter, participate in, and exit from programs. The rules that govern the stages of programs are often referred to as *intake*, *participation*, and *termination* policies:

- An intake policy outlines the criteria (such as age or income level) a person has to meet to be allowed into a program.

- A participation policy clarifies what a participant has to do (for example, follow rules of conduct or attend regularly) to continue in a program.

- A termination policy states when (such as a certain point in time, or when a goal has been reached) a program participant can be expected to exit a program.

Program policies and procedures fulfil a number of functions: they help agency staff organize their work; they prevent chaos and confusion; and they ensure that in view of limited resources only people who qualify for services are allowed to use them. Despite their usefulness, agency policies and procedures can create a number of challenges for clients. In extreme cases, the rules and regulations governing so-called "helping services" can contribute to tragic outcomes (see Exhibit 6.6).

EXHIBIT 6.6

WHEN RULES MATTER MORE THAN PEOPLE: THE CASE OF KIMBERLY ROGERS

In April 2001, Kimberly Rogers was convicted of welfare fraud for receiving over $13,000 in social assistance at the same time she was attending school and collecting student loans. (She earned a diploma in social services at Cambrian College.) The penalty for the fraud conviction was harsh:

- a six-month sentence of house arrest;
- permission to leave her apartment for only three hours a week;
- a requirement to repay over $13,000 to the Ontario government;
- 18 months' probation;
- loss of the right to have part of her student loan forgiven; and
- loss of welfare benefits for three months.

At the time of her conviction, Kimberly was five months pregnant.

In May 2001, Rogers launched a case against Ontario Works under Canada's Charter of Rights and Freedoms on the following grounds:

- cruel and unusual punishment (for cutting her off welfare in addition to a house arrest);
- violation of the Charter's guarantees to life, liberty and security of the person; and
- violation of Canada's international covenants for depriving a pregnant woman and her unborn baby of basic sustenance.

The Ontario Superior Court of Justice granted a temporary injunction reinstating Kimberly's welfare benefits. Even so, Kimberly could not support herself: under Ontario Works Benefits, she received $468 a month, but her rent was $450 a month, leaving her with $18 a month to buy food and other necessities.

Kimberly was alone, pregnant, and broke. On August 11, 2001, Kimberly Rogers—eight months pregnant and confined to her apartment under house arrest—was found dead in her apartment.

Source: Excerpted and adapted from the Committee to Remember Kimberly Rogers, (2003, September). *Justice with Dignity* (brochure). Retrieved December 9, 2008, from DisAbled Women's Network (DAWN) Ontario, http://dawn.thot.net/Kimberly_Rogers/overview.html.

Program Profile: Applying for Welfare in Ontario

The policies and procedures of Canada's **social assistance** programs can hardly be described as "user-friendly." Indeed, those policies and procedures can cause considerable anxiety and stress for clients, and even prevent people who are in legitimate need from seeking help. A number of studies have examined welfare systems, and their impact on service users. The following section highlights the findings from studies of the welfare application process in Ontario. Keep in mind that Ontario's system is not unique to that province; most welfare systems in Canada are characterized by complex rules and requirements.

In 1997, in response to concerns about rising caseloads and the costs of social assistance, the Government of Ontario overhauled its social assistance system; the result was Ontario Works, and a new Service Delivery Model (SDM). The SDM promised to improve the methods used to verify people's eligibility for welfare. It was expected that, by screening out ineligible applicants sooner in the intake process, the government could save money as well as direct welfare resources more expediently to those who were eligible.

The SDM requires welfare applicants to participate in a two-step application process: a preliminary telephone assessment and a face-to-face verification interview. Step One requires welfare applicants to call one of the province's Intake Screening Units; during that call, applicants are given information about social assistance and application procedures, and are asked about their employment and financial situation. A study by Herd, Mitchell, and Lightman (2005) found the telephone assessment process to be problematic for welfare applicants in several respects. For instance, some applicants complained of being put on hold for long periods of time, waiting to speak to an intake worker; others remarked on interviews that lasted up to one and one half hours. The researchers of the study concluded that the telephone application system erected several potential barriers to welfare, including the following:

- The telephone intake system is not user-friendly for applicants with poor English skills, physical and/or mental disabilities, or low educational attainment.

- People who do not have a telephone are at a disadvantage.

- Every telephone call is recorded, which may deter applicants from providing sensitive information needed for the application.

Applicants who manage to pass the initial telephone assessment are referred to a local Ontario Works office for Step Two of the application process—another interview and further processing. This stage aims to verify an applicant's eligibility for welfare, and may include multiple appointments, participation in an employment information session, the completion and signing of forms, and a review of documents. To satisfy the income verification portion of the application, applicants are required to supply various documents, including "support court orders, divorce settlements, affidavits, cheque stubs, bank records, appeal letters from other income sources, tax slips from Revenue Canada, Income Tax assessments, childcare receipts, pay stubs, sponsorship agreements or payments, student loan assessments, fire insurance settlement documents, and any other verification as applicable" (Herd, Mitchell, & Lightman, 2005, p. 4). While recognizing that the documents may help to screen out welfare applicants who are ineligible for assistance, the researchers point out the potential impact of the system's emphasis on paperwork and documentation: that is, people who are in legitimate need, and may in fact meet the eligibility criteria for welfare, may either be discouraged from applying or drop out before the application can be completed.

In addition to restricting access to welfare, administrative changes to Ontario Works have introduced strategies to pressure welfare recipients to leave the system as soon as possible. The establishment of the system's Consolidated Verification Process requires that welfare cases be regularly reviewed, and that welfare recipients be carefully monitored, especially if those individuals have been labelled by the authorities as being likely to commit welfare fraud. To keep close tabs on recipients, welfare workers can demand additional documentation from clients, and can suspend or cancel benefit cheques if clients do not comply. The welfare recipients in Herd, Mitchell, and Lightman's (2005, p. 4) study found the monitoring procedures to be "intrusive" and "dominated by suspicion and a mentality of policing."

Discussion Questions

Agency Systems: Internal Structures and Functions

1. If a community needs assessment was being conducted in your community, and you were asked to give your opinion on what new service(s) might be needed, how would you respond? What makes you think that the service(s) you identified might be needed?

2. List some of the social services or income security programs in your community. Which level of prevention (primary, secondary, or tertiary) does each service/program provide?

3. Certain social welfare programs—such as social assistance—are governed by complex policies and procedures that can frustrate clients, and even discourage them from seeking help. What are some of the reasons why social agencies might be reluctant to eliminate or simplify these complex rules?

■ ORGANIC MODELS OF ORGANIZATION

For much of the twentieth century, the **bureaucratic model of organization** was praised for its reliability and predictability. Bureaucracies came to be known as "well-oiled machines" that efficiently achieved their goals through the application of

- specialization (clear divisions of labour);
- formalization (work is done according to set job descriptions);
- departmentalization (activities are grouped according to function);
- a clear chain of command (usually flowing vertically from "top" or upper management to "bottom" or front line);
- centralization (decision making is concentrated at a single point in the organization); and
- a hierarchical structure (people and activities are grouped into a pyramid-shaped hierarchy, with several front-line workers at the lower layer, one or more levels of middle management, and upper management at the top).

All organizations are bureaucratic to some extent. However, governments, hospitals, public school systems, universities, and many large corporations are common examples of large bureaucracies.

Support for the bureaucratic model began to wane in the late 1970s, when governments were struggling with a weakened economy and high operating costs. Big bureaucracies were also being criticized for being too slow, inflexible, and inefficient, and having too many complex procedures, otherwise known as "bureaucratic red tape." By the 1990s, rapidly expanding workloads, and the changing needs of service users, funders, and governing bodies, required new organizational structures, ones that allowed workers to respond quickly to change. This need was met by **organic models of organization**. The reference to "organic" implies that organizations are like living organisms, capable of adapting to an ever-changing environment. There are many variations of organic models; however, most emphasize "flat" hierarchical structures, flexibility, diversity, innovation, and cooperative ways of working.

FLAT HIERARCHICAL STRUCTURES

The organizational structures of large bureaucracies tend to be "tall," with several vertical layers or departments. At the top of the hierarchy is an individual or a group that oversees and sets policies for an agency's general operations;

people at this level usually hold the most decision-making power in an organization. Below the top level are various levels of subordinates. There may be one or more tiers of middle managers who are responsible for the different divisions in an agency (for example, a division for seniors' programs, a child and youth division, and so on). At the next level down are any number of offices or programs, each with its own department head (another level of middle management) who supervises staff and oversees the day-to-day operations. At the lowest level of the hierarchy are the front-line workers and support staff, who carry out the program activities, tasks, and services. Each department tends to have a narrow span of control—that is, a small number of subordinates per manager.

When compared to government, voluntary social agencies tend to have relatively **flat hierarchical structures**, with fewer layers of middle management (see Exhibit 6.7 for a comparative view of tall and flat organizational structures).

During the 1980s and 1990s, Canadian governments tried to reduce the costs of the public service by reducing middle management, amalgamating departments, and otherwise flattening the hierarchy. With a reduction in the number of supervisors, front-line government workers were expected to develop a broader (less specialized) range of skills, and to take on more tasks, responsibilities, and general workload; at the same time, the remaining managers were assigned larger numbers of staff to supervise.

There are potential advantages and disadvantages to flatter organizational structures. A possible advantage is that, with few or no levels of middle management, there is opportunity for more contact, and even shared decision making, between front-line workers and upper management. Moreover, managers in flat organizations can usually approve changes more quickly because decisions do not need to travel through so many departments. One possible disadvantage is the difficulty in recruiting workers who are skilled in several areas of expertise; furthermore, a small number of managers may find it difficult to supervise a relatively large group of staff.

FLEXIBILITY

Flexibility is central to a social agency's ability to adapt to changes in funding, workload, or community needs. Organic organizations are well suited to change because of their relatively informal and decentralized structures. These types of organizations also tend to recruit workers who have broad or generic skill sets, and can perform a wide variety of duties. Staff are usually expected to multitask, multiskill, and wear multiple "hats" (for example, counsellors may double as supervisors). A team with a diverse skill base is particularly useful in agencies that carry several service contracts, or have a

EXHIBIT 6.7

EXAMPLES OF TALL AND FLAT HIERARCHIES

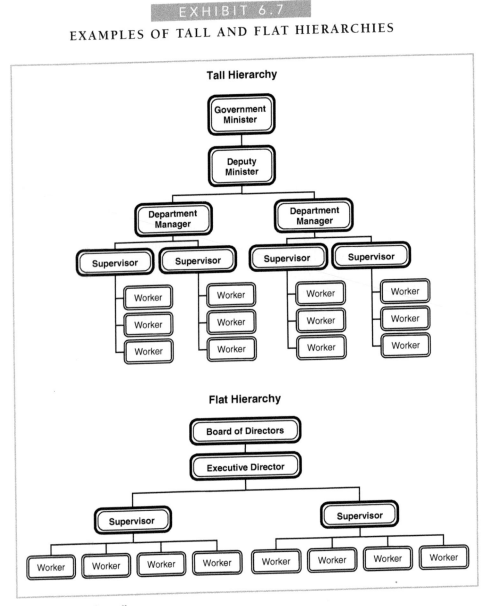

Source: Rosalie Chappell.

broad client base. Even workers whose work is limited to the front line are likely to need a wide range of helping skills, including counselling, teaching, mediation, group work, and family intervention (Hiscott, 2002).

While agencies have to be flexible to the demands of the work environment, they also have to be willing to respond to the needs of workers. Due to shifts in government policy, many social agencies now operate on short-term contracts, and cannot offer workers any more than temporary, part-time, or contract positions. As a result, many people in the social welfare field have to take on several different jobs (or contracts), or work for more than one employer, in order to earn a decent income. Other workers may not want full-time permanent employment, and seek only temporary work. In either case, organizations must be open to negotiating "creative" schedules and work conditions that meet the needs of both staff and agencies.

Flexible social agencies tend to recognize the importance of a healthy work–life balance—that is, a balance between personal, family, and work responsibilities—and try to help staff achieve a balance. There are benefits of a work–life balance for both employers and employees, including less stress for workers, increased job satisfaction, and fewer sick days (HRSDC, 2005b). Exhibit 6.8 illustrates some of the employment policies, programs, and practices a "flexible organization" might offer.

DIVERSITY

One of the effects of globalization and other socioeconomic changes taking place is increasing **diversity** in the workforce. In general, Canadian workers are becoming "increasingly multi-ethnic, multilingual, and multi-religious" (Sykes, 2008, p. 5). Workers are of all ages, abilities, and sexual orientations; they have a range of education; and they come from different ethnic backgrounds.

While some people may view diversity or "differentness" as a source of conflict, most organizations recognize its potential benefits. A diverse team in a social agency, for instance, is likely to be representative of a local community; subsequently, people in need may find it easier to approach an agency where all the staff look, act, and think a little differently (Bredin Institute, 2006). Moreover, staff with different backgrounds and skills can enhance creativity and innovation in the workplace. Canadian Heritage (2004) suggests that, not only does diversity enrich cultural expression, but it tends to make "daily life more varied and interesting."

Studies suggest that, despite the potential advantages of diversity in the workplace and the increasing diversity of many Canadian communities, many voluntary agencies are far from diverse. For example, in London, Ontario's Voluntary Sector Employment and Training Needs Study (Daya, El-Hourani, & De Long, 2004), researchers found that most organizations rarely recruited individuals of diverse backgrounds as employees or volunteers (especially on boards of directors). Another Canadian study—which looked at paid employment in the voluntary/nonprofit sector—found that, with the exception of organizations that provided immigrant services, organizations did not reflect the cultural diversity of their communities, especially in health and social service agencies in large cities (HR Council for the Voluntary and Non-Profit Sector, 2008).

EXHIBIT 6.8

STRIKING A WORK–LIFE BALANCE: OPTIONS AND EXAMPLES

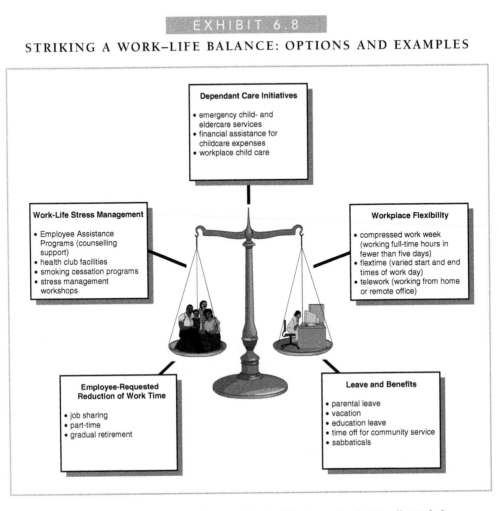

Source: Human Resources and Social Development Canada, "Creating a Family-Friendly Workplace (Culture Change)," 2005. Retrieved October 23, 2008, from www.hrsdc.gc.ca/eng/ lp/spila/wlb/imt/08family_friendly.shtml. Human Resources and Social Development Canada, "Workplace Programs, Policies and Practices," 2007. Retrieved October 23, 2008, from www.hrsdc.gc.ca/eng/lp/spila/wlb/11programs_policies_practices.shtml.

INNOVATION

A rapidly changing society requires innovative strategies for dealing with those changes. In a social welfare context, innovation refers to the development and implementation of new ideas toward the improvement of a policy, program, service, practice, or structure (ARRIPS, 2002). Innovation is particularly important to the delivery of social welfare programs; social agencies are forever seeking more creative and effective ways to help people and to connect people with the resources that they need.

Innovative ideas at the agency level are often referred to as **best practices**—simply put, these are strategies or approaches that people perceive as working well, and would recommend to others. Best practices are sometimes identified through rigorous program evaluation, but much of the time they are discovered by trial and error. Each level of a social agency is likely to have its own collection of best practices; for example, on the front line, there might be preferred methods of assessing client needs; supervisors might use mainly "tried and true" team-building techniques; and boards of directors might have favourite fundraising strategies.

COOPERATION

Since the late 1970s, organizations have been de-emphasizing masculine values that encourage competition and an authoritarian way of working, and emphasizing feminine values, such as power sharing, group consensus, and a democratic approach to decision making. A more cooperative way of working together is found both within and among social agencies:

- *Intra*-**agency cooperation** focuses on empowering workers and the people who use services, and on promoting an environment of co-operation and inclusion in the workplace. In social agencies, workers and clients are often included in various aspects of the organization's operations; for example, staff might be invited to join the agency's planning or advisory committee, and former clients might serve on a board of directors.

- *Inter*-**agency cooperation** involves two or more organizations working together. A variety of terms—such as *strategic alliances*, *collaborations*, and *partnerships*—are used to describe inter-agency relationships; each type of working relationship has a slightly different purpose, structure, and process, as is illustrated in Exhibit 6.9.

Clearly, there are many potential benefits to working cooperatively. In terms of inter-agency cooperation, working together on community projects often involves a pooling of money and other resources, making team efforts more efficient than individual ones. Inter-agency coordination may lead to more streamlined client referral systems, shared locations, improved communication and information sharing, and integrated service delivery (Thomas & Skage, 1998). There is also a belief that pervasive and complex social problems are best addressed when people unite, identify and interpret the issues, share their expertise and views, and work together toward solutions (Government of Canada, 2004c). While teamwork might have its advantages,

EXHIBIT 6.9

LEVELS OF MUTUAL RELATIONSHIPS

LEVELS	PURPOSE	STRUCTURE	PROCESS
NETWORKING (E.G., NATIONAL YOUTH HOMELESSNESS NETWORK)	To foster dialogue and a common understanding To provide a clearing-house for information To create a base of support	Nonhierarchical Informal/flexible links Loosely defined roles Community action is primary link among members	Low-key leadership Minimal decision making Little conflict Informal communication
ALLIANCE (E.G., NATIONAL CHILDREN'S ALLIANCE)	To match needs and coordinate activities To limit the duplication of services To ensure tasks are completed	Core group acts as communication hub Semiformal links Roles somewhat defined Members act in advisory capacity Group raises funds	Facilitative leaders Complex decision making Little conflict Formal communication within core group
PARTNERSHIP (E.G., AFFORDABLE HOUSING PROGRAM)	To share resources to address common issues To pool resources to create something new	Clearly defined roles Formal links Group generates new resources and a joint budget	Leadership is autonomous Group decision making among core members Communication is frequent and clear
COALITION (E.G., COALITION AGAINST FAMILY VIOLENCE IN NORTHWEST TERRITORIES)	To share ideas To draw resources from existing systems To commit to project for at least three years	Roles, time, and commitment are defined Links are formal and clarified in writing Group generates new resources and a joint budget	Shared leadership Formal and group decision making Communication is frequent and prioritized
COLLABORATION (E.G., AN ACCORD BETWEEN THE GOVERNMENT OF CANADA AND THE VOLUNTARY SECTOR)	To achieve a shared vision To build an interdependent system to address issues and opportunities	Formal roles, time commitment, and evaluation Formal links Written work assignments	Strong leadership Consensus model of decision making High trust level among members High productivity Ideas and decisions equally shared Highly developed communication

Source: Adapted from Teresa Hogue (Chandler Center for Community Leadership), *Community Based Collaboration: Community Wellness Multiplied*, 1994. Retrieved May 14, 2009, from National Network for Collaboration website, http://crs.uvm.edu/nnco/collab/wellness.html.

it can also present challenges. For example, it takes time to establish good working relationships, and to make decisions through consensus—time that is often in short supply in the helping field. Moreover, inter-agency work often requires well-developed organization and coordination skills—skills that not all workers bring to the job (Community Social Planning Council of Toronto and Family Service Association of Toronto, 2006).

Discussion Questions

Organic Models of Organization

1. Identify two or three social agencies in your community (or selected geographic area). In what ways are those agencies flexible, diverse, and innovative?

2. Identify a social agency in your community that appears to have a "tall" organizational structure, and one that has a "flat" structure. How might the organizational structure of each agency impact the way that it serves the public?

3. In what ways might social agencies improve intra-agency and inter-agency cooperation?

SUMMARY

Introduction

Social agencies include voluntary agencies and government departments. The way an agency carries out its functions and activities depends on whom it serves, what it intends to accomplish, and how its programs are designed. The type of goods or services an agency offers is largely shaped by local needs.

I. Community-Based Social Agencies

Social welfare programs in residential and nonresidential settings are delivered according to a community-based model. Residential centres provide round-the-clock care, while nonresidential centres provide services on a drop-in, appointment, or outreach basis. Many nonresidential centres (such as multiservice centres) offer a continuum of service. A system of care, when well coordinated, can respond to the varied and changing needs of clients.

II. Agency Systems: Internal Structures and Functions

Social agencies need a solid internal structure upon which to base their work. A strategic framework articulates an agency's priorities and how it intends to achieve its goals; a strategic plan is based on an understanding of the community, and clarifies the agency's direction through vision, mission, goals, and value statements. An operational framework provides a plan for the provision of direct services (primary, secondary, and tertiary prevention) and indirect services (administration, program planning, and program evaluation). Policies and procedures can help agencies organize their work; however, those rules can cause problems for clients and needlessly limit access to services.

III. Organic Models of Organization

Organic organizational models provide an alternative to the bureaucratic model. Organic models are known for their adaptability to changes in the environment, their emphasis on "flat" hierarchical structures, and their promotion of flexibility, diversity, innovation, and cooperative ways of working.

Key Terms

For definitions of the key terms, consult the Glossary on page 413 at the end of the book.

social agency, p. 141
voluntary social agency, p. 142
public social agency, p. 142
community-based model, p. 143
residential centre, p. 144
mental health problem, p. 144
aging in place, p. 146
nonresidential centre, p. 146
multiservice centre, p. 146
system of care, p. 147
strategic framework, p. 147
operational framework, p. 148

direct service, p. 148
indirect service, p. 148
environmental scan, p. 149
community needs assessment, p. 149
vision statement, p. 150
mission statement, p. 150
agency goal, p. 150
value statement, p. 150
primary prevention, p. 152
secondary prevention, p. 152
tertiary prevention, p. 152
administration, p. 153
stakeholder, p. 153
program planning, p. 154

program evaluation, p. 155
outcome evaluation, p. 155
policies and procedures, p. 156
social assistance, p. 157
bureaucratic model of organization, p. 160
organic model of organization, p. 160
flat hierarchical structure, p. 161
diversity, p. 163
best practices, p. 165
intra-agency cooperation, p. 165
inter-agency cooperation, p. 165

Service Providers

OBJECTIVES

The responsibility for social welfare provision is shared by professional and nonprofessional helpers. This chapter explores some of the helping approaches, issues, and challenges related to service provision among:

- social workers;
- social service workers;
- agency volunteers;
- self-help groups; and
- unpaid caregivers.

INTRODUCTION

> At the center of the universe is a loving heart that continues to beat and that wants the best for every person. Anything we can do to help foster the intellect and spirit and emotional growth of our fellow human beings, that is our job. Those of us who have this particular vision must continue against all odds. Life is for service. (Fred Rogers, host of TV's *Mister Rogers' Neighborhood*, 2001)

Before the expansion of the welfare state, volunteers provided the bulk of help to people in need. In fact, volunteers established some of Canada's first social welfare institutions including orphanages and homes for the aged. During the

1950s and 1960s, the growth of the welfare state encouraged the establishment of formal programs and services and the hiring of professional helpers such as social workers and psychologists. By the 1970s, formally trained helpers had largely displaced volunteers "who, by implication, could not provide adequate service" (Chappell, 1999). This view of volunteers began to change in the 1980s when governments started cutting back on social welfare spending. Governments assumed that any service gaps resulting from the cuts would be filled by volunteers and self-help groups, and that families would take more responsibility for the care of their members (Jiwani, 2000).

Today, professional helpers are still in demand; however, nonprofessionals provide a considerable share of support to people in need. Thus, social welfare provision has become the responsibility of two broad helper groups:

- **Professional helpers** are paid to provide services, and bring a recognized knowledge base, training, and relevant experience to the helping process. Social workers, social service workers, and other professional helpers use planned, systematic, measurable, and otherwise "scientific" methods and processes when working with clients. Often, practice is guided by a code of ethics specific to a profession.

- **Nonprofessional helpers** include "lay" helpers, volunteers, self-help groups, family caregivers, peer counsellors, friends, and other "informal" helpers, all of whom help others without expecting a payment in return. Although many nonprofessional helpers have received training in basic helping techniques, this group is recognized for its use of natural helping skills.

A mix of professional and nonprofessional help can offer a wide range of service options: for example, a parent in conflict with a teen may seek assistance from a social worker, attend a self-help group for parents, and learn about other community resources through a volunteer information line. At first glance, different types of helpers seem to naturally complement each other. Historically, however, there has been tension between professional and nonprofessional groups. Some of that tension relates to the issue of "expertise": professional helpers may see themselves as "experts" with "scientific" solutions to human problems; at the same time, natural helpers may view themselves as "experts" because of their own struggles in life, and having "been there." According to Frank Riessman (1999), the squabbling over whose expertise is better must be resolved if professional and nonprofessional helpers are to work together.

There are points at which professional and nonprofessional helpers come together on behalf of people in need. One point of contact is **care team** meetings, which are often formed to coordinate services for clients who have a variety of needs, or are connected to several different agencies. It is common

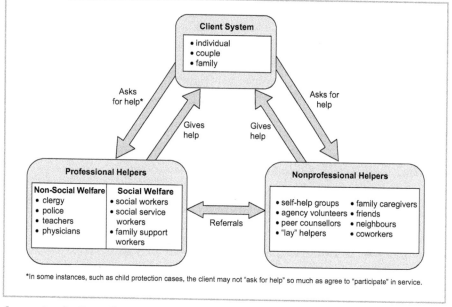

EXHIBIT 7.1

LINKS AMONG PROFESSIONAL AND NONPROFESSIONAL HELPERS

*In some instances, such as child protection cases, the client may not "ask for help" so much as agree to "participate" in service.

Source: Rosalie Chappell.

for clients to invite a volunteer (such as a sponsor from a twelve-step self-help program), a family member, or a friend to care team meetings for moral support or practical assistance (such as help with language translation). Exhibit 7.1 illustrates possible linkages, points of contact, and reciprocal give and take between professional and nonprofessional helping systems.

PROFESSIONAL HELPERS

SOCIAL WORKERS

During the nineteenth century, **social workers** began taking a compassionate and empathic approach to the problem of poverty, as opposed to the punitive approach associated with the poor laws. Through social reform movements, social workers educated the public about poverty and its related problems, and lobbied for legislation to improve living standards for people in need (CASW, 2000). Social workers also worked directly with people who were disadvantaged, providing material aid and counselling that aimed to not only meet their basic physical needs, but also empower them. These efforts established a long-standing association between social workers and the social welfare system, and continues to influence the development and delivery of income security programs and social services. Social workers make up the largest single occupational group in Canada's social welfare system, accounting for about 30 percent of workers (Stephenson, Rondeau, Michaud, & Fiddler, 2000).

Social workers are employed in a wide range of settings, including hospitals, voluntary agencies, religious organizations, employee assistance offices, Aboriginal band councils, and private practice. Most social workers in Canada (71 percent) work in healthcare and community service agencies. Certain trends, such as an aging population with its need for more services and an above-average rate of retiring social workers, are expected to increase the need for social workers in the future (Service Canada, 2007a).

Social Work Values and Knowledge

The **social work** profession is based on altruistic, humanitarian, and egalitarian ideals, all of which shape its philosophy as well as its service goals and interventions. Underlying social work's philosophy are a number of core values, including respect for persons, social justice, and service to humanity. A fundamental belief in confidentiality, integrity, and competence guides professional practice (CASW, 2005).

Social work knowledge derives both from inside the social work profession and from other disciplines. Knowledge produced within the profession is based upon the shared experience of workers, individual professional experiences, and applied research. Knowledge is also gathered from other disciplines such as psychology, psychiatry, education, and public health, and from many academic fields, including sociology, philosophy, economics, and law. This "cross-pollination" of various fields gives social work a highly **interdisciplinary knowledge base** (Johnson, McClelland, & Austin, 2000).

Social Work Practice

Social work's **scope of practice** outlines the types of functions and activities that are appropriate for social workers to engage in. The primary domain of practice centres on the relationship between individuals and their environment, otherwise known as **person-in-environment**. The CASW (2000) describes the two components of this perspective: "*Person* refers to developmental and social functioning abilities in the context of environmental influences. The concept of *environment* in social work includes factors in society that enhance or impede the development of individual social well-being" (italics added). To work from a person-in-environment perspective, social workers must learn about (1) a client's personal level of functioning; (2) how that functioning may be affected by external forces, such as work or the economy; and (3) how a client interacts with her or his environment (McMahon, 1994). This approach acknowledges the complexity of interactions between people and their environment, and recognizes that people both shape and are shaped by their environment (International Federation of Social Workers, 2000).

The person-in-environment perspective requires social workers to take a **multilevel approach to practice**. At the *micro* level, social workers aim to help individuals, families, and small groups enhance their social well-being; this may be achieved through a variety of methods, including one-to-one, family, or group counselling. At the *mezzo* level, social workers seek to improve conditions within and among social welfare organizations; this may involve advocating for new programs. The *macro* level of practice looks at broader social problems and political issues, and may involve seeking change in legislation or social policy. What social workers actually do at each level depends largely on the setting in which they work, and on what they are trying to achieve. Most social work activities, however, require some degree of skill in assessment, intervention, and evaluation.

EXHIBIT 7.2

Many social workers work with their clients on a one-to-one basis.

Source: © iStockphoto.com/killerb10.

Social Work Education

In most provinces, a minimum of a Bachelor of Social Work degree is required for entry into the social work profession. People who have completed a B.S.W. may continue on in their education to obtain a graduate degree (Master of Social Work), or a postgraduate degree (Doctor of Social Work, or Ph.D.). It is normally at the graduate and postgraduate education levels that students specialize in a particular field of practice.

Ideally, the structure and content of social work education are shaped by the context in which practice takes place. However, as Gilles Rondeau (2001) points out, a rapidly changing political, economic, and social climate and the restructuring of service delivery systems have created challenges for social work education. One challenge involves keeping courses and programs relevant to changing human needs and problems. In particular, social workers must learn how to

- address client needs that are becoming increasingly complex as a result of persistent poverty and chronic unemployment;

- meet rising demands for services in a climate of shrinking social welfare resources;

- provide effective service in an environment in which social problems, such as family violence and substance abuse, are becoming more pervasive; and

- take the kind of social action that can change current political and economic systems.

To meet the needs of a more culturally diverse society, social work education programs also need to find ways to attract a greater number of visible-minority and Aboriginal social workers to the profession (Durst, 2006).

Regulation of Social Work

The regulation of social work practice in Canada is highly complex. Each province has legislation and a professional association to govern social work practice; the associations in nine of those provinces and the territories form a federation under the Canadian Association of Social Workers (CASW). The CASW plays a leadership role in advancing the social work profession in Canada, and sets national standards and guidelines for social work practice. These standards include a Code of Ethics, which "sets forth values and principles to guide social workers' professional conduct" (CASW, 2005, p. 2).

In addition to having professional associations, Ontario and Alberta each have a "college of social work." (In this context, colleges are governing bodies, not educational institutions.) While associations and colleges share many of the same values and principles, each regulatory body has its own mission: professional associations tend to represent the interests of the social work profession, while colleges aim to protect the public from unqualified or incompetent practitioners (OCSWSSW, 2003).

Legislation and regulation in each province and territory define the limits of what social workers can and cannot do. These limitations are articulated in various documents such as codes of ethics, scope of practice statements, and documents that specify the qualifications (such as educational achievement) that social workers must have to practise the profession. Social workers who join a regulatory body in their region become "registered," "certified," or "licensed" (depending on the jurisdiction); these social workers are expected to practise in accordance with the standards set by their profession, and to be accountable to their clients, their profession, and society (CASW, 2003b; MacDonald & Adachi, 2001). Legislation in each jurisdiction protects the use of the titles "social worker" and "registered social worker;" these designations can only be used by those who meet certain professional standards.

Professional Identity

Social work is similar to other helping **professions** (such as nursing, policing, and psychology) in that it possesses a code of ethics, it has the means to regulate and enforce standards of behaviour among its members, and it has developed a theoretical body of knowledge that guides practice (Cross, 1985). For much of the twentieth century, social work was distinguished from other helping professions by "a distinct set of professional skills, based on an identified knowledge base, provided through formal education, and refined through years of practice with others in the profession" (Stephenson, Rondeau, Michaud, & Fiddler, 2000, p. 5). (See Exhibit 7.3 for some of the commonalities and distinctions between social work, psychology, and psychiatry.)

Since the early 1980s, changes in social and economic policies—largely enforced by neoliberal governments—have made it more difficult to discern what is and is not social work. This loss of professional identity can be observed in a variety of ways, including the following:

- To save money, primary healthcare centres (such as hospitals) have grouped workers from various disciplines under generic titles such as "healthcare professionals." In these types of settings, social workers may be supervised by non-social-workers who do not recognize or encourage the use of skills that are specific to the social work profession (Fildes & Cooper, 2003).

EXHIBIT 7.3

A COMPARISON OF THREE HELPING PROFESSIONS

	SOCIAL WORK	PSYCHOLOGY	PSYCHIATRY
PRIMARY FOCUS OF HELP	Interactions between people and their social environment	Individual thoughts, feelings, and behaviour	Thought processes and brain functioning
GENERAL AIM OF PRACTICE	To help people develop and use personal and community resources to solve problems	To help people understand, explain, and change their behaviour	To help people prevent or manage mental illness or behavioural disorders
ASSESSMENT/DIAG-NOSTIC TOOLS	Psychosocial history taking; client interviews; observation	Diagnostic tests (IQ, personality, etc.); interviews; observation	Medical exam; *Diagnostic and Statistical Manual*; interviews; observation
PRACTICE METHODS (EXAMPLES)	Individual counselling; marital/family therapy; group work; advocacy; community practice	Individual counselling; marital/family therapy; group work; consultation	Prescribe psychotropic medication; biological treatments; psychotherapy
SPECIALIZATIONS (EXAMPLES)	Clinical (counselling); child welfare; gerontology; school; family services	Clinical; counselling; develo3p2.254pmental; school; forensic; sports	Child and adolescent; geriatric; forensic; liaison; addictions
EDUCATION LEVELS	B.S.W., M.S.W., D.S.W., Ph.D.	B.A. or B.Sc., M.A., Ph.D.	Medical degree plus minimum five years' psychiatric training
PROFESSIONAL ASSOCIATIONS AND REGULATORY BODIES	Canadian Association of Social Workers; College of Social Workers (Ontario and Alberta)	Canadian Psychological Association; College of Psychologists	Canadian Psychiatric Association; Royal College of Physicians and Surgeons of Canada

Source: Rosalie Chappell.

- In an attempt to keep costs down and meet service demands, social agencies are hiring greater numbers of helpers with fewer credentials, or with little or no social work training. Although non-social-workers may meet the demands of the job, their predominance can weaken social work's presence in the social welfare field.

Social work's identity has been gaining redefinition over the past few years in part because of the legislation or regulation of **restricted practice activities**—that is, practices that can be carried out only by certain occupational groups or by designated professionals within those groups. Restricted practice activities for social workers vary from province to province; however, those most likely to "belong" to social work include child welfare, clinical social work, and family mediation (CASW, 2000).

Social work's identity is also being clarified through stricter registration rules. A case in point is in Alberta, where they are limiting access to social work registration. For many years, the Alberta College of Social Workers (ACSW) allowed people with a two-year diploma in social work to become registered social workers; in 2003, the ACSW decided to allow only those with a minimum B.S.W. degree to become a Registered Social Worker. As regulations and legislation help clarify social work's professional boundaries, we can expect the lines between social work and other professions to crystallize as well.

SOCIAL SERVICE WORKERS

The expansion of the social welfare system in the 1950s and 1960s led to an increased demand for service providers and, subsequently, to the development of college-level social work programs. Today, close to seventy certificate or diploma programs across Canada offer basic social work training. Most college-level programs combine classroom work with practical experience, and tailor their curricula to the needs of the job market (Lecomte, 2005). Typically, students are trained as generalist social workers, and are introduced to basic social work methods, values, and ethics. Graduates of these programs are most commonly known as **social service workers** or human service workers, but other titles—such as community support worker or family support worker— may apply. Since people in this group have a lower level of social work education than a bachelor's degree, they are sometimes referred to as *paraprofessionals* (Stephenson, Rondeau, Michaud, & Fiddler, 2000).

Social service workers are employed by many of the same types of agencies as social workers, however, most find work in the voluntary rather than the public sector. Social service workers are often assigned a variety of duties, including

- preparing intake reports;
- referring clients to community resources;
- providing crisis intervention;
- leading client groups, such as life skills workshops;
- coordinating and supervising volunteers; and
- participating in the admission of clients to appropriate programs (Service Canada, 2007b).

Although social service workers and social workers perform similar tasks, the former tend to have fewer responsibilities and less discretionary power. It is not uncommon for a social service worker to serve as a caseworker under the supervision of a social worker.

In 2004, there were 86,500 social service workers employed in Canada, representing a 60 percent increase since 1997. Industry sources suggest that a growing number of people who have problems related to old age, disability, homelessness, or addiction will drive the need for social service workers in coming years. An expansion of social services for Aboriginal people (especially youth) is already opening up new job prospects for social service workers (BC Work Futures, 2005).

There is no uniform regulation of social service workers in Canada. Ontario is one of the few provinces that has completed a regulatory process to oversee social service practice. The Ontario College of Social Workers and Social Service Workers (OCSWSSW) has created a number of frameworks to guide social service practice; one framework is a scope of practice for social service workers who are members of the OCSWSSW. Exhibit 7.4 summarizes the scope of practice for social service workers and social workers in Ontario.

REWARDS AND CHALLENGES FOR PROFESSIONAL HELPERS

Some Canadian studies have found that working conditions for social workers and social service workers are characterized by work overload, job insecurity, lower pay and fewer benefits than other occupations, stress and burnout, work–life conflict, and a general dissatisfaction with work (CASW, 2004; Evans, Richmond, & Shields, 2005). Other studies emphasize the rewards of social service. For example, many people enter the social welfare field because they are committed to a cause, and they see social service as an important and meaningful endeavour; these workers report being generally satisfied with their jobs (Saunders, 2004). Others are attracted to the field because of the flexible work schedules, a culture that promotes teamwork, and a highly dynamic work environment that provides stimulating challenges and opportunities (Ahmed, 2006).

Some analysts question whether the rewards of social service are enough to compensate for low wages and poor working conditions, or to keep qualified helpers committed to the field over the long term. Ron Saunders (2004, p. 48) predicts a looming crisis within the social welfare

EXHIBIT 7.4

SCOPE OF PRACTICE IN ONTARIO: SOCIAL WORK AND SOCIAL SERVICE WORK

According to the Ontario College of Social Workers and Social Service Workers (OCSWSSW), "the scope of practice of the profession of social work [and social service work] means the assessment, ... treatment and evaluation of individual, interpersonal and societal problems through the use of ... knowledge, skills, interventions and strategies, to assist individuals, dyads, families, groups, organizations and communities to achieve optimum psychosocial and social functioning." The scope of practice of social work also includes diagnostic services.

AREA OF FOCUS	TASK OR FUNCTION
WORKER AND CLIENT ACTIVITIES	• Assessment • Diagnosis (not applicable to social service workers) • Treatment • Evaluation (These activities are carried out within a worker/client relationship.)
HUMAN SERVICE PROGRAMS	• Program development • Management • Administration • Service delivery • Evaluation (These tasks may be completed in collaboration with other professionals.)
PROFESSIONAL SUPERVISION OF ...	• Peers • Students • Other supervisees
CONSULTATION SERVICES PROVIDED TO ...	• Peers or professionals from other disciplines in relation to the worker and client activities listed above
SOCIAL POLICYMAKING	• Development • Promotion • Implementation • Evaluation (These tasks aim to improve social conditions and equality.)
RESEARCH OR EDUCATIONAL SERVICES RELATED TO ...	• Worker and client activities • Human service programs • Professional supervision • Consultation services • Social policymaking • Other activities recognized by the OCSWSSW

Source: Excerpted and adapted from Ontario College of Social Workers and Social Service Workers, *Standards of Practice Handbook* (2000), pp. 1–2. Retrieved May 31, 2009, from http://206.221.245.198/sections/pdf/1.6B%20code%20of%20ethics%20english.pdf.

field: the "dissatisfaction with earnings in the non-profit sector rises with age, suggesting that employees in the sector eventually reach a point where the gap between the intrinsic rewards of working in the sector (fulfilling a valued mission) and the extrinsic rewards (pay, job security) becomes a problem for them. Since the paid workforce in the sector is older, on average, than that of the for-profit sector, this issue may become more acute in the coming years."

A Labour Force Study of paid employment in Canada's voluntary/non-profit organizations suggests that a new generation of workers may be attracted to the social welfare field because of its challenging and rewarding work. On the other hand, the field's overemphasis on paperwork and other administrative duties may not appeal to many young people (Human Resources Council for the Voluntary & Non-Profit Sector, 2008). Retaining staff in social agencies (especially in the voluntary sector) is expected to become more challenging as time goes on. A migration of qualified workers out of social service to higher paying jobs in other fields is already under way (Canada West Foundation, 2000).

Discussion Questions

Professional Helpers

1. In your opinion, what client situations, problems, or needs might best be addressed by (a) a social worker and (b) a social service worker? Give a rationale for your answers.
2. What types of knowledge or skills should be taught at the postsecondary level to prepare students for making a difference in today's world?
3. If applicable, identify what attracts you to a career in the social welfare field.

AGENCY VOLUNTEERS

Approximately 11 percent of Canadian adults—mostly middle-aged women—donate their time to voluntary social agencies (Hall, Lasby, Gumulka, & Tryon, 2006; McClintock, 2004). These **agency volunteers** may perform any number of duties, including mentoring or teaching clients; delivering or serving food to clients; driving clients to appointments and community activities; supporting people in distress (such as on crisis phone lines); and giving information and support to people in need (Sperling & Lasby, 2007).

The integration of volunteers in social agencies is becoming more common in Canada. Professionals and volunteers work side by side in a wide

EXHIBIT 7.5

The financial survival of many food banks and other social agencies depends heavily on volunteer labour.

Source: THE CANADIAN PRESS/Toronto Star—Colin McConnell.

range of organizations and on behalf of various groups, including recent immigrants, children and families, and victims of crime. In these days of government cutbacks and growing demand for services, many social agencies have become so reliant on volunteers that they could not survive without them (Ahmed, 2006). Studies show believe that, overall, volunteers feel welcomed and valued in their placements, and belive that their contributions are appreciated by agency staff (Evertman, 2002).

BENEFITS OF VOLUNTEERING

Among other things, volunteers are valued for their use of **natural helping skills** in their interactions with social agency clients. In a study by Patterson, Memmott, Brennan, and Germain (1992), respondents reported that the most helpful volunteers were the ones who provided humour, exchanged personal experiences, shared material resources; reached out to others; and followed up after problems were resolved. Emotional support—expressed through listening, encouraging, empathizing, showing concern, and the like—is another important component of natural helping (Gottlieb, 1983). Helpful people are also those who assist others to clarify needs and to problem-solve, and who provide suggestions and information. According to Romeder (1990), helping efforts are most effective when the person being helped feels understood and accepted.

Volunteers are recognized for bringing additional benefits to organizations. For example, organizations report that because volunteers have *chosen* to serve an agency for no material gain, they lend credibility to the agency. Volunteers also bring a vitality to their work as well as knowledge, focus, objectivity, and specialized skills. Agencies often rely on volunteers for their objective views on agency operations, and for their constructive feedback and ideas on how to improve existing programs or procedures (Muegge & Ross, 1996).

MANDATORY VOLUNTEERS

Volunteer Canada (2006, p. 17) defines volunteering as "the offering of time, energy and skills of *one's own free will*" (italics added). Thus, forcing someone to volunteer runs contrary to the definition and spirit of volunteering. Since the late 1990s, however, it has become more common for people to volunteer because they are required to. These **mandatory volunteers**—known in some circles as *voluntolds*—account for over 7 percent of Canadian volunteers, and include high school students who must volunteer in order to graduate; people sentenced by the courts to complete community service orders; and recipients of social assistance, who agree to volunteer in exchange for welfare benefits (Hall, Lasby, Gumulka, & Tryon, 2006).

Many organizations promote the potential benefits of mandatory community service. Government social assistance programs, for example, see volunteering as way for welfare-to-work recipients "to contribute to their communities, learn basic work and life skills, gain experience and make contacts for future employment" (District of Nipissing Social Services, 2008). Skeptics doubt that mandatory volunteering fosters people's loyalty to a cause. Research shows that people required to do volunteer work typically find it unfulfilling, which may turn them off from volunteering in the future

(Hall, McKechnie, Davidman, & Leslie, 2001). By trying to accommodate unwilling volunteers, voluntary agencies may use up resources that could go to supporting volunteers who really want to help (Richmond & Shields, 2003). Moreover, the short-term nature and restricted hours of availability that characterize mandatory volunteering are not always compatible with agency needs. A high turnover among mandatory volunteers is also common: since most volunteers leave the agency once they have fulfilled their mandatory commitment, agencies are often in a perpetual state of volunteer recruitment, orientation, and training (Toronto Community and Neighbourhood Services, 2004).

GOVERNMENT SUPPORT OF VOLUNTEERISM

Since 1977, the Government of Canada has promoted volunteerism through Volunteer Canada. It was nevertheless the United Nations' proclamation of the International Year of Volunteers in 2001 that made government recognize "the critical role played by volunteers and voluntary organizations in society" (Volunteer Canada, 2001). Governments are particularly aware of the economic value of volunteerism: it is estimated that the approximately one billion hours of volunteer work annually performed by Canadians is the equivalent of 549,000 full-time jobs (Hall, McKechnie, Davidman, & Leslie, 2001). Thus, volunteers are increasingly seen as possible solutions to the rising costs of social welfare and other public programs.

In 2002, the Government of Canada introduced the Canada Volunteerism Initiative (CVI) to promote the participation of Canadians in society. Under this initiative, volunteer centres opened in every province and territory; national volunteer centres were established to promote volunteerism; and a number of how-to documents were produced to help voluntary agencies learn the "science" of managing volunteers (Volunteer Canada, 2004). Evaluation reports suggest that the strategies developed under the CVI have been highly successful in terms of helping organizations recruit, manage, and recognize volunteers more effectively (Volunteer Canada, 2008).

CHALLENGES FOR VOLUNTEERS AND AGENCIES

In 2006, the federal government cancelled the Canada Volunteerism Initiative (and $9.7 million going to that program) on the basis that the initiative did not "meet the priorities of the federal government or Canadians" (Treasury

Board of Canada Secretariat, 2006). The government's move caught many Canadians off guard, especially in light of government's urging for nonprofit organizations to extend their reliance on volunteers (Linda Graff and Associates Inc., 2006). Clearly, organizations that utilize volunteers require some level of funding to recruit, train, supervise, motivate, and adequately recognize volunteers. To compensate for the federal government's withdrawal of funding, many provinces and the territories stepped in to support voluntary agencies and volunteerism. The Government of Nova Scotia (2006), for example, appointed a Minister of Volunteerism and, in so doing, made a commitment to work with the voluntary sector to increase the number of volunteers needed to ensure the quality of nonprofit service.

Despite provincial/territorial support of volunteerism, a number of voluntary agencies struggle to recruit and retain volunteers. In 1997, over 31 percent of Canadians volunteered for a charitable or nonprofit organization (including social agencies); by 2000, the rate had dropped to 27 percent (Hall et al., 2003). Declining volunteer rates are attributed to a variety of developments, including lower interest in volunteering among youth, time and energy constraints among working adults, and changing priorities for women, who have always volunteered at higher rates than men.

Fewer volunteers are doing more of the work: about one-quarter of all volunteers in Canada contribute three-quarters of all volunteer hours (Hall, Lasby, Gumulka, & Tryon, 2006). These core groups of volunteers, who donate the bulk of volunteer support, are at high risk of burnout—women are particularly vulnerable because they tend to be already overextended, yet feel obligated to contribute even more (Mailloux, Horak, & Godin, 2002). Social agencies may find themselves in a bind: they need volunteers to meet increasing service demands, and yet are reluctant to overwork existing volunteers for fear that they will burn out. A possible solution is to limit the range of services offered to clients; this prospect is nevertheless an undesirable one for most social agencies because of the growing demand for social services.

Discussion Questions

Agency Volunteers

1. In your opinion, what are the top three things that a nonprofit organization should or should not do to show its volunteers that they are valued and needed?

2. In what situations (if any) might a client benefit more from the services provided by a volunteer as opposed to a professional? Give reasons for your answer.

▥ SELF-HELP GROUPS

Self-help groups (or mutual aid groups) are defined as networks of individuals who meet to share common experiences, situations, or problems (Self-Help Resource Centre, 2008b). Members in these groups connect on the basis "that all members are equal—all are experts on their own lives, no one knows more than anyone else and no one has all the answers" (Standing Senate Committee on Social Affairs, Science & Technology, 2006a, p. 234). Although professionals do not lead self-help groups, they may be invited to meetings to provide information on medical, legal, or other matters. See Exhibit 7.6 for a comparison of self-help, support, and therapy groups.

There is a self-help group for practically every human issue imaginable, including bereavement, addiction, disability, parenting, relationships, and employment. Depending on its purpose, a self-help group may focus on problem solving (such as Al-Anon), self-development (for example, Parents Supporting Parents), or consciousness raising (including Senior Power of Regina). These various groups can be roughly classified into four broad types:

1. traditional *face-to-face groups* (whose members meet in person), which are voluntary, free, and autonomous;

2. *support groups*, which receive assistance from an organization such as free meeting space, and are facilitated by trained volunteers;

3. *transition groups*, which are initially led by professionals or educators, and later by the members themselves; and

4. *online groups*, which connect people through newsgroups, e-mail discussion groups, live chat groups, and discussion forums (Self-Help Resource Centre, 2008b; You're not alone, 1997).

THE BENEFITS OF SELF-HELP

Research suggests a strong link between social support (such as that derived from membership in a self-help group) and improvements in many aspects of well-being. Social support is believed to increase a person's ability to ward off disease, maintain good health, recover from illness, and cope with serious injury. Health Canada suggests that the support provided by self-help groups may enhance well-being and subsequently reduce the need for hospitalization

EXHIBIT 7.6

MAKING DISTINCTIONS: SELF-HELP, SUPPORT, AND THERAPY GROUPS

SELF-HELP/MUTUAL AID	SUPPORT	THERAPY
Primary goal is to effect personal change through helper therapy principle.	Primary goal is to provide support and information.	Primary goal is to effect personal change through therapeutic methods based on human behaviour theory and professional methods.
Interactions among members are de-emphasized and not focused on as a therapeutic device.	Focus is on support and comfort.	Focus is on the assumption that cure or change is based on reworking relationships in the group.
Helping methods are specific to the group ideology and based on successful strategies developed through shared information, feelings, and experiences among members with a common issue.	Helping methods are based on shared information, feelings, and experiences among members of a formal agency or organization.	Helping methods are based on specific ideology of the therapist. The focus is on relationships established among members with the help of a professional therapist. Members often have various issues.
Emphasizes that all members are both helpers and helpees.	Support group leader may share personal issues or experiences.	Emphasizes psychological distance between professional and members.
No fee or minimal contribution.	Set fee or membership.	Payment for professional service.
Common issue is the reason for the group's existence, and members come from all walks of life.	Members share a common concern.	Members generally have different backgrounds and different issues.
Admits anyone who qualifies.	Membership is determined by the organization and/or group leader.	Membership is determined by a professional.
Rarely depends on outside organizational support except from its own members and nationally run federations.	Organizational support for the group is provided by paid staff.	Participants may meet in an agency or private settings, which may be subject to regulations and codes of conduct.
Meetings are structured and task-oriented.	Meetings are relatively unstructured.	Meeting structure is based on therapeutic techniques of psychotherapist or counsellor.

Source: Adapted from *Self-Help Mutual Aid and Professionals: A Practical Alliance*, Self-Help/Mutual Aid Workshop Series Manuals (Vancouver: Self-Help Resource Association of B.C., 2004), p. 2. Retrieved March 18, 2004, from www.vcn.bc.ca/shra/publication/resources/pdf/pdf%20forms/SelfhelpMutualAid ProfessionalsAPracticalAlliance-original.pdf.

and other publicly funded services (Health Systems Research Unit, 1997). Both the Canadian Medical Association and the Ontario Medical Association have recognized self-help as an important adjunct to professional health services (Self-Help Connection, 2006).

Another benefit of self-help is derived from the sharing of knowledge, skills, and resources among group members, a process that can empower people to solve their own problems. People who attend self-help groups can also expand their social support networks (and social capital), reduce feelings of isolation or loneliness, and enhance their sense of belonging (Self-Help Connection, 2006).

A great deal of benefit can be derived from helping others. One benefit, advanced by self-help expert Frank Riessman, is identified in the helper therapy principle: "By being the helper as well as the receiver of help, a self-help group participant acquires the enhanced self-esteem and feeling of worth that comes with being important to others. The experiential knowledge, gained from coping with a common problem, is valued, just as credentials and technical expertise are valued in a professional helping situation" (Pape, 1990, p. 5).

GOVERNMENT SUPPORT OF SELF-HELP

A variety of factors are increasing the need for self-help groups, including an aging population, a growing number of people requiring healthcare and mental health services, shrinking social welfare budgets, and a diminished capacity among professionals to meet service demands. Since the late 1990s, governments and professional associations have been actively seeking the assistance of self-help groups to meet many health, social, and emotional needs of Canadians. Self-help groups are identified as being particularly powerful sources of support for persons with a **mental health problem** and/or an addiction (Standing Senate Committee on Social Affairs, Science & Technology, 2006a).

Self-help groups in Canada have a long history but, unlike many professionals in the social welfare field, they have survived with little or no government funding. In its study of supports for people with mental illness, the Standing Senate Committee on Social Affairs, Science and Technology (2006a) recognized the financial difficulties facing many self-help organizations, and which weaken their capacity to support members with mental health problems. In 2006, the Committee urged the federal government to establish ongoing funding to existing groups and create a network of self-help initiatives across the country, for people with mental health needs. The following year, the federal government provided funding to establish and support a Canadian Mental Health Commission, which is mandated to lead the development of a national mental health strategy. An important component of that strategy will be the strengthening of self-help, support, and peer groups for people with a mental illness or addiction.

SELF-HELPERS AND PROFESSIONALS

Romeder (1990, p. vi) envisions how professionals and self-helpers might work together: "Professionals who understand self-help can properly refer people to self-help groups, and self-helpers who understand when professional guidance is needed can suggest it to their group members, so that people get the help that is most appropriate for them. A partnership between traditional professional care and the self-help movement can provide a superior service." Traditionally, professional helpers and self-helpers have kept their distance from each other. In their study of partnerships between health professionals and self-help groups, Banks, Crossman, Poel, and Stewart (1997) found that the two camps generally agreed on their respective roles and what constitutes a positive working relationship, but differed over principles. Professionals, for example, placed more importance than self-helpers on group leadership and on clarifying roles and goals. In contrast, self-helpers placed more emphasis on group organization, on providing outreach to group members, and on nurturing helpful relationships.

Widespread recognition of self-help as a viable health promotion strategy has sparked a greater interest among professional helpers to include self-help groups in their work with clients. In recent years, a variety of how-to guides have been published that aim to enhance professional/self-help relations. One of those guides, published by the Self-Help Resource Centre (2008a), suggests that professional helpers might benefit from visiting a self-help group meeting to find out what takes place, or attending a meeting as a consultant or guest speaker. To improve self-help/professional relations, agency workers might post a group's brochure on the office notice board, or donate the use of office equipment or other resource. Professionals might also network with local self-help centres to keep abreast of self-help initiatives in the community.

Discussion Questions

■ **Self-Help Groups**

1. List the various self-help groups in your community (or selected geographic area). For each group listed, identify whether it meets the criteria for a face-to-face group, support group, or transition group.

2. This section looks primarily at how professionals might promote and support self-help groups. What are some of the ways in which self-help groups might promote and support professional help?

IV UNPAID CAREGIVERS

As governments cut back on social welfare programs, informal support systems are expected to assume a greater responsibility for the care of dependent children and adults. **Unpaid caregivers**—which include spouses, other relatives, friends, and neighbours—provide 70 percent of necessary care to older, chronically ill, and disabled Canadians. That care is given in private homes and in institutions (Special Senate Committee on Aging, 2009). A study by Hollander, Liu, and Chappell (2009) estimated the economic contribution of unpaid Canadian caregivers to be at least $26 billion in 2009.

An aging population is a primary factor driving the need for the care of seniors with chronic health problems. Between 1996 and 2006, the percentage of Canadians who spent unpaid time caring for older relatives, friends, and neighbours increased from 16.5 to 18.4 (Statistics Canada, 2008a). The 2007 General Social Survey found that 22 percent of middle-aged women, and 19 percent of middle-aged men, care for an elderly person; however, it is women who perform the most intensive caregiving tasks, such as cooking, cleaning, bathing, and dressing. One in four caregivers are seniors (Special Senate Committee on Aging, 2009).

Many caregivers belong to what is known as the **sandwich generation**—a group caring for both dependent children and older relatives. According to the 2002 General Social Survey, about 27 percent of Canadians between 45 and 64 belong to the sandwich generation (Williams, 2005).

EXHIBIT 7.7

Caring for aging relatives, friends, and neighbours is a growing trend in Canada. Women are more likely than men to be primary caregivers.

Source: Orange Line Media/Shutterstock.

THE IMPACT OF FAMILY CAREGIVING

Reports show that many Canadians care for their elderly spouses, parents, or other relatives "because there is no one else available or because there is a lack of home care services" (Special Senate Committee on Aging, 2008, p. 41). Despite this apparent sense of obligation to caregive, most caregivers recognize the benefits of helping. A study by Stobert and Cranswick (2004) found that up to 90 percent of caregivers reported that their relationship with the care recipient had strengthened through the helping process, and that caregiving was a way to pay back what they had received from others along the way. Another study found that 54 percent of caregivers were coping "very well" with their responsibilities (Cranswick & Dosman, 2008).

A small percentage of caregivers report having difficulties in the caregiving role (Cranswick & Dosman, 2008). The term *caregiver burden* refers to the potential negative consequences of caring for another person for an extended period of time. Stobert and Cranswick's (2004) study found that middle-aged caregivers had to rearrange social activities and plans for holidays in order to meet their caregiving obligations; some caregivers incurred extra expenses, and others had to change their work schedules, including reducing their hours of work. Caregivers also reported physical complaints: among caregivers aged 65 and over, 13 percent of women and 7 percent of men reported sleep disturbances, and 16 percent of women and 7 percent of men reported various health problems. Robert Dobie of the National Advisory Council of Aging identifies the potential impact of caregiving stress on both those who give care, and those who receive it:

> The added responsibility of informal caregiving can lead to physical and mental exhaustion and have a detrimental effect on the health of caregivers. Lack of formal supports can lead to burn out, causing caregivers to withdraw from caregiving. This, in turn, can lead to higher rates of institutionalization for seniors. (Robert Dobie, cited in Special Senate Committee on Aging, 2009, p. 118)

CARE FOR THE CAREGIVER

Caregivers rely on a variety of supports when trying to strike a balance between care responsibilities and work, or when they can no longer cope with caregiving on their own. According to the 2007 General Social Survey, caregivers relied on their children (to help with such things as household chores), a spouse (to modify personal and work arrangements), extended family, and friends or neighbours. Twelve percent of caregivers seek support from a government program, such as respite (Cranswick & Dosman, 2008). **Respite services** give caregivers a break from their caregiving duties by providing day care to elderly people, by temporarily placing seniors in residential settings, or by assigning home support workers to help with housework, meal preparation, and other household tasks.

Professional helpers play an important role in the support of family caregivers. According to the Victorian Order of Nurses (VON Canada, 2004), agency workers can not only encourage unpaid caregivers to take regular breaks from caregiving responsibilities, but can also help caregivers plan for those breaks. To effectively plan, professionals have to understand the caregiving situation, the relationship between the caregiver and the care recipient, and the types of support already available from family, friends, and others. Moreover, professionals should understand what respite means to the caregiver, and what the caregiver hopes to gain from respite. This knowledge can be used to individualize respite care for unpaid caregivers; for example, some caregivers may need as little as information about community resources, while other caregivers may need to get away for a vacation.

GOVERNMENT SUPPORT OF CAREGIVERS

By the end of the 1990s, it was clear that, despite various supports in place for caregivers, Canada's system of community care with its overreliance on informal caregiving was unsustainable. A number of reports identified the need for a more organized, coordinated, and comprehensive eldercare strategy—one that would involve various levels of government, the private sector, families, and community groups, and that would meet the caregiving needs of a growing number of old people. Although the federal government shied away from introducing a comprehensive, nationwide system of elder care, it recognized the potential financial burden of caregiving in 1998 when it introduced a tax credit for caregivers. In 2004, the federal government committed $1 billion over five years to assist family caregivers of seniors and people with disabilities (Liberal Party of Canada, 2004).

In 2006, the Special Senate Committee on Aging was created to review government programs and services for seniors. After the second phase of its review, the committee recommended that government should do more to support unpaid caregivers, especially those trying to juggle caregiving and paid employment. In its 2008 report, the committee recommended actions that included

- giving caregivers more information on how to care for themselves;
- establishing a national respite program;
- expanding the Compassionate Care Benefit under the Employment Insurance program to make it more flexible and available to people needing time off work to caregive; and
- adjusting the Canada Pension Plan to enable caregivers to temporarily leave the workforce without losing CPP entitlements (Special Senate Committee on Aging, 2008).

In 2009, the Special Senate Committee on Aging wrapped up its review of public programs and services for seniors. By that time, the federal government had made little progress in terms of giving additional support to unpaid caregivers. In its final report, the committee reaches a dismal conclusion: "The current supports for caregivers are insufficient, and Canadians are forced to choose between keeping their jobs and caring for the ones they love" (Special Senate Committee on Aging, 2009, p. 8).

FUTURE CONSIDERATIONS

Caregiving impacts many systems, including those who provide and receive care, other family members, friends, and governments. An aging population will only increase the impact of caregiving on Canadians. For example, population projections show that by 2056, the proportion of seniors will have more than doubled, a situation that will require more younger adults to care for older relatives (Cranswick & Dosman, 2008). Many families, however, will not be prepared to take on additional caregiving responsibilities. This is particularly true for small families (such as those headed by a lone parent), financially insecure families, and unstable or dysfunctional families (CPRN, 2005).

Discussion Questions

■ **Unpaid Caregivers**

1. Envision the type of care you would like to receive when you are elderly. What role, if any, would you want your family, friends, or other informal supports to play in your caregiving scheme?

2. What are some strategies unpaid caregivers might use to minimize the risks of long-term caregiving?

SUMMARY

■ **Introduction**

The responsibility for social welfare provision is shared by professional and non-professional helpers. Cutbacks to social welfare programs make it important for professionals and volunteers, self-help groups, and unpaid caregivers to work together on behalf of people in need. Care team meetings provide a point of contact for these helpers.

■ **I. Professional Helpers**

Social work is the predominant occupation in the social welfare field. Social work practice is based on humanitarian ideals, a set of core values and beliefs, and an interdisciplinary knowledge base; the focus is on the person-in-environment.

Social workers can train at the undergraduate, graduate, and postgraduate levels. A challenge for social work education is to remain relevant to changing human needs. Legislation and regulation define the social work profession. Social service workers perform basic social work duties, mainly in voluntary agencies. Few provinces regulate social service practice. Poor working conditions are discouraging people from entering and staying in the social welfare field, which may contribute to a future shortage of social workers and social service workers.

II. Agency Volunteers

About 11 percent of adults volunteer for voluntary social agencies. Generally, volunteers feel valued and appreciated by staff. Volunteers use their natural helping skills with clients, and benefit agencies in many ways. Mandatory volunteers are required to perform community service; there are pros and cons of this type of volunteering. Government recognizes the economic value of volunteering, and promotes volunteerism through initiatives at both the federal and regional levels. The declining number of volunteers and volunteer burnout are among the concerns facing agencies that rely on volunteers.

III. Self-Help Groups

A wide variety of self-help groups exist; most groups can be classified as face-to-face groups, support groups, transition groups, or online groups. Research confirms a link between social support (such as that found in self-help groups) and many aspects of well-being. The need for self-help groups continues to grow, especially among people with a mental health problem or addiction. While professional helpers and self-helpers have traditionally worked independently from each other, they are learning to work together on behalf of people in need.

IV. Unpaid Caregivers

Government cutbacks, an aging population, and other factors are increasing the need for unpaid caregivers. Most caregivers recognize the benefits of helping; a small percentage experience caregiver burden. Caregivers receive help from family and friends, as well as from government support such as respite services. Agency workers can encourage caregivers to practise self-care, such as taking planned breaks. Canada's overreliance on informal caregiving is impractical in the long run, and a more comprehensive eldercare system is needed.

Key Terms

For definitions of the key terms, consult the Glossary on page 413 at the end of the book.

professional helper, p. 170

nonprofessional helper, p. 170

care team, p. 170

social worker, p. 171

social work, p. 172

interdisciplinary knowledge base, p. 172

scope of practice, p. 172

person-in-environment, p. 172

multilevel approach to practice, p. 173

profession, p. 175

restricted practice activity, p. 176

social service worker, p. 177

agency volunteer, p. 180

natural helping skill, p. 181

mandatory volunteer, p. 182

self-help group, p. 185

mental health problem, p. 187

unpaid caregiver, p. 189

sandwich generation, p. 189

caregiver burden, p. 190

respite service, p. 191

CHAPTER

Promoting Change in Micro, Mezzo, and Macro Systems

OBJECTIVES

Social welfare initiatives aim to change those elements that inhibit the meeting of human needs. This chapter explores the strategies used to promote change at the:

- micro level of society (individuals, families, and small groups);
- mezzo level of society (organizations); and
- macro level of society (communities).

INTRODUCTION

> Change is inevitable in a progressive society. Change is constant. (Benjamin Disraeli, British Prime Minister, October 29, 1867)

Change is constant in the social welfare field. Some change is spontaneous, acting in random and unpredictable ways. Spontaneous change can happen quickly, such as helping clients cope with unexpected personal crises, or aiding a community to deal with a natural disaster. Spontaneous change may also occur slowly over a longer period of time, such as when a community's economic base shifts over several decades. Unlike spontaneous change, planned change is predictable, controllable, and carried out with a conscious intent. In a social welfare context, planned change applies a scientific method with a specific set of procedures to modify a situation, condition, or state of being for the purpose of helping people meet their needs.

For the **planned change process** to be successful, five elements must exist. First, there must be a *target of change*—that is, a person, organization, or other entity that is expected to change. Second, planned change requires a *change agent*, which is a person or team who is responsible for carrying out the plan. A third element—the *method of change*—comprises specific interventions, strategies, or approaches, and a clear plan of action for creating the change. Fourth, planned change involves a *beneficiary of change*, an identifiable individual or group who is expected to benefit from the change effort. The beneficiaries of change in many social welfare policies and programs are the most vulnerable members of society, such as children living in poverty or women living in abusive situations. The beneficiary and the target of change are often one and the same; job readiness programs for youth, for instance, not only attempt to "change" young people through skills development, but are also expected to benefit youth in terms of future employment. Fifth, the *context of change* must be identified; this is the setting in which the planned change effort takes place. These settings may be found at the micro, mezzo, or macro levels of society:

- At the **micro level**, social welfare programs target individuals, families, and small groups to help them develop their *capacity* for self-sufficiency.

- At the **mezzo level**, organizations take steps to change themselves to increase their *capacity* for serving clients more effectively.

- At the **macro level**, change is directed at large segments of the population (such as communities) so they may have a greater *capacity* for meeting their own needs.

The word **capacity** is emphasized above to highlight the importance of this concept in the planned change process. There is a general consensus in the social welfare field that well-being is largely a function of a system's capacity or capability to perform certain roles (such as the role of parent) or produce something worthwhile (such as a sufficient income). Thus, a primary focus of the planned change process is on enabling individuals, families, small groups, organizations, and communities to build capacity by developing skills, accumulating knowledge, making social connections, creating or accessing opportunities, and obtaining needed resources (Frank & Smith, 1999).

EXHIBIT 8.1
ELEMENTS OF PLANNED CHANGE

	MICRO LEVEL	MEZZO LEVEL	MACRO LEVEL
TARGETS OF CHANGE (EXAMPLES)	Small groups Individuals Families	Social agencies Churches Workplaces Businesses Schools	Social values and attitudes Political systems Community Economy Laws and legislation
METHODS OF CHANGE (EXAMPLES)	Individual counselling Family services Social group work	Staff training Team building Structural social work	Community development Social planning Social action
AGENTS OF CHANGE (EXAMPLES)	Social workers Social service workers	Management Workers/staff "Steering committees"	Grassroots organizations Social activists Community developers Social planners
BENEFICIARIES OF CHANGE (EXAMPLES)	Individuals Families	Service users Service providers Community	Community General society

Source: Rosalie Chappell.

Exhibit 8.1 provides a graphical illustration of how the three levels of society may be linked, and gives examples of possible targets and beneficiaries of change, change agents, and methods of change for each level.

CHANGE AT THE MICRO LEVEL: INDIVIDUALS, FAMILIES, AND GROUPS

Social welfare programs that focus on micro-level change aim to help individuals, families, or small groups obtain the basic necessities for proper human development, social functioning, and self-sufficiency. One advantage of such programs is that they target relatively small systems, which makes it more likely that identified needs will be met. A potential disadvantage of such a narrow focus is that even after a person's needs are met, the social or environmental conditions that created those needs may remain. For example, a food bank may provide visitors with food on any given day, but food banks can hardly be expected to change a society that allows its members to go hungry. In this case, certain elements in the environment—such as new legislation that raises minimum wage or welfare rates—are needed for people to be able to purchase food. Despite their limitations, programs that attempt to change micro-level systems are necessary, and they are the main focus of many social agencies.

PROGRAMS FOR INDIVIDUALS

Most social agencies that provide direct client services have programs for individuals. Examples include mental health counselling, settlement programs for recent immigrants, and employment services for women. These programs and services are justified by the belief that communities suffer—as does society as a whole—when individual needs are not met. Social workers and other professional helpers also recognize that providing services on a one-on-one basis is an effective way to help people change their behaviour, learn new coping strategies, and either change or adapt to their environment (Fischer, 1978).

Each individual who seeks help from a social agency has a unique set of needs, issues, and concerns. That said, most requests for service by individuals relate to one or more of the following areas:

- *Interpersonal conflict* involves disagreement between two or more people who recognize that a problem exists. Examples: marital discord, parent–teen conflict.

- *Dissatisfaction in social relations* refers to a lack or an excess that a person perceives as being damaging to a relationship. Examples: loss of sexual desire in a marriage, spending too much time away from family.

- *Problems with formal organizations* relates to a discrepancy between what an individual wants and what an organization does. Examples: getting arrested, getting fired.

- *Difficulties in role performance* means having trouble carrying out a particular social role. Examples: parental neglect of a child, a student skipping school.

- *Decision problems* reflect uncertainty around taking a particular course of action. Examples: deciding to leave a spouse, choosing a new career.

- *Reactive emotional distress* refers to challenges in dealing with difficult feelings. Examples: coping with grief and loss, learning to manage anger.

- *Inadequate resources* is a lack of the basic necessities of life. Examples: living in poverty, homelessness (Epstein, 1980).

Programs that are designed for individuals are rooted in the **social case-work** approach, which evolved in the late 1800s as an outgrowth of the organized charity movement. That movement recognized the shortcomings of providing haphazard and inconsistent help to the poor, and called for a more coordinated approach to helping. Originally, the casework method was used by "friendly visitors"—volunteer social workers who visited the poor and provided friendship and support rather than financial relief. After the First World War, a growing body of research paved the way for more professional, systematic, and scientific approaches to change. It was no longer enough for social workers to simply "mean well"; they were now required to have formal training in the social sciences, to draw from recognized bodies of practice models when helping others, and to conduct a thorough and systematic exploration of the individual's social environment, using formal interviewing skills and strict assessment procedures (Johnson, McClelland, & Austin, 2000).

Depending on their particular discipline, service providers in the social welfare field may draw from a variety of casework models to help individuals achieve their goals. The recent popularity of **brief therapies** is compatible with

EXHIBIT 8.2

Family casework focuses on helping all members of a family reach their specific goals.

Source: Bruce Ayres/Stone/Getty Images.

a rapidly changing political and economic environment that values efficiency and results. Brief therapies emphasize specific, measurable, and short-term goals. Unlike many traditional therapies—such as psychoanalysis—brief therapies tend to focus on the client's present and future (rather than on the past), and help clients build on their strengths (rather than dwell on personal deficits).

FAMILY SERVICES

The family is considered the basic unit of social organization and plays an indispensable role in the economic, physical, and emotional lives of individuals and society. Canadian governments recognize the autonomy and privacy of families and, with the exception of child protection laws (and adult protection laws in some provinces), are reluctant to intervene in the private realm of family. Governments nevertheless provide a wide range of support to help families carry out their basic roles and functions.

Modern-day family needs and challenges are diverse and often complex. However, most families approach social agencies in the wake of one or more of the following events:

- An addition to the family, be it through marriage, remarriage, birth, adoption, fostering, an adult child moving back home, or an elderly relative being taken in.

- The separation or loss of a family member through divorce, marital separation, death (including suicide), incarceration, institutionalization, or a child leaving home.

- Dysfunctional behaviour, such as addiction, delinquency, domestic violence, or child abuse.

- A change in status or role, which can be the result of job loss, retirement, children growing up and leaving home, or a developmental crisis (Janzen & Harris, 1997).

Not all families seek services voluntarily. In the case of child protection matters, for example, families can be compelled to accept services or risk having their children legally apprehended and placed in alternative care.

In the 1920s and 1930s, **family casework** emerged as a scientific approach to helping families. The "science" included a thorough assessment (or "investigation") of a family's problems and a detailed plan for how the family would go about adjusting to their social environment (Scott, 2004). When providing services, early family caseworkers chose interventions that were likely "to reinforce and strengthen the endangered family, by drawing in the community's resources, not only in material relief, but in character and spiritual strength as well" (McGill University, 1931). Family services quickly became accepted as a form of support from which all families—not just poor families—might benefit from time to time.

Today, a number of nonresidential programs are available to support and strengthen families. These programs each take their own unique approach to helping and are provided by practitioners from various disciplines, including social work and psychology. Below are some of the types of family services offered in Canada:

- *Family support and resource programs* generally focus on helping families access resources and learn problem-solving skills so that the members can fulfil their respective social roles (such as parent, student, or provider).

- *Family therapy* aims to restructure family dynamics and communication patterns, or to alter dysfunctional behaviour patterns.

- *Family preservation* is intensive intervention that often takes place in the family home, and aims to improve family functioning, especially in terms of caring for children.

- *Family reunification* helps separated families reunite and learn new ways of coping so they can stay together.

- *Family group decision making* involves the family, its closest supports, and a professional facilitator, who work together to resolve family problems (such as violence against a spouse or a child) (Conceptual Framework Subcommittee of the Residential Services Advisory Committee, 2002).

SOCIAL GROUP WORK

Some social agencies provide group programs as a more affordable and less time-consuming alternative to individual services. In addition to these practical advantages, **social group work** can often help clients meet certain goals more effectively than one-on-one sessions. For example, the face-to-face interactions inherent in small groups can increase the emotional maturity of members. Some people find that relationships formed within the group can complement outside relationships. Group experience can also help members prepare for more active participation in society by encouraging them to try out new behaviours and interaction skills in a relatively safe and controlled environment and receive feedback from fellow members before applying those skills in the "real" world (Coyle, 1959).

Social groups usually have three to ten members who share common goals, needs, or lifestyles related to a particular theme. That theme may be explored through

- socialization groups (such as anger management groups for adolescent boys);
- support groups (such as parent groups that focus on parent–teen interactions);
- personal growth groups (such as marriage enrichment groups);
- educational skill-enhancement groups (such as life skills groups for people with severe disabilities); and/or
- therapy groups (such as those focused on issues related to schizophrenia, manic depression, or other psychiatric disorders).

Each type of group requires its own set of interventions to help members achieve emotional, physical, learning, or social goals. In turn, group facilitators must have a solid understanding and expertise related to group process and dynamics, stages of group development, group facilitation and leadership, and dealing with resistance.

It is not uncommon for clients to attend a group (where interpersonal difficulties may be addressed) in conjunction with individual counselling (where personal issues may be explored).

THE ROLE OF SOCIAL WORKERS IN MICRO-LEVEL CHANGE

Social casework, family casework, and social group work are three approaches that social workers use to encourage people to become empowered—that is, to help people "identify and use their own problem solving skills in order to improve their life situations" (CASW, 2000). Choosing which approach to apply often depends on the size of the client system (for example, whether it is an individual or a family), the presenting need or problem, and the social worker's professional role in the change process. Although the approaches vary in the way they help people, there are certain generic steps that are common to any planned change in a micro system. These steps are as follows:

1. Identify the need for change.
2. Establish a working relationship.
3. Clarify (assess) the client's needs or concerns.
4. Set goals for change, and identify indicators of success.
5. Develop an "action plan," which specifies who will do what, when, where, and how.

6. Implement the plan.

7. Monitor the effectiveness of the plan, and modify strategies as necessary to achieve the goal.

8. Evaluate the intervention to determine its effectiveness.

9. Terminate the working relationship.

The planned change process does not always evolve in a linear fashion; as client needs or goals arise, certain phases may be repeated or deferred. Similarly, at some point in the helping process, it may seem reasonable to shift direction, which may mean modifying, or even reworking, the plan. In any case, the planned change process must be a cooperative team effort, with the change agent and client working together toward a goal, and each fulfilling her or his role in the various stages of change.

Discussion Questions

■ **Change at the Micro Level: Individuals, Families, and Groups**

1. What are the main strengths and weaknesses of (a) individual services; (b) family services; and (c) social group work?

2. Identify the organizations in your community (or selected geographic area) that offer individual, family, or group services. Are there any gaps in these services in your area? What types of services, if any, are needed to fill those service gaps?

CHANGE AT THE MEZZO LEVEL: ORGANIZATIONS

Most social agencies run smoothly and when problems or issues arise, they make the necessary adjustments and move on. Some situations may nevertheless threaten the stability or even survival of the organization; to deal with these situations, the organization may need to undergo a significant restructuring of one or more aspects of its operation. Major changes that occur within social agencies do so at the mezzo level of society and are generically referred to as **organizational change**.

IDENTIFYING THE NEED FOR CHANGE

Organizational change begins with someone recognizing the signs that something in the agency is not working as well as it could. Any stakeholder may call attention to an agency's "symptoms." In many cases, social agencies actively seek feedback from clients as to the strengths and weaknesses of service delivery; this information is often obtained through client satisfaction questionnaires. Stakeholders external to an agency may also notice when something in the organization needs improvement. Funders, for example, may detect inefficiencies in an agency's financial reporting system, or professionals in the community may find that an agency's intake or referral system is not as streamlined as it should be. Management is likely to notice when the agency's resources are not used the way they were intended. Agency staff tend to speak out on issues directly affecting clients, such as program facilities that are too noisy or offer inadequate space.

PREPARING FOR CHANGE

What Will Change Look Like?

In addition to identifying what needs to change, it is important to clarify the organization's vision of success—that is, what will the result of change "look" or "feel" like? (OHCC, 2004). Some organizations, for example, envision themselves as being more inclusive, family-friendly, or gender-equitable. Whatever vision the agency has of itself will eventually need to be translated into concrete goals; these goals will help the agency recognize when it has become what it set out to be. Exhibit 8.3 describes how one social agency strove to become anti-racist.

EXHIBIT 8.3

AGENCY PROFILE: ORGANIZATIONAL CHANGE AT THE CHILDREN'S AID SOCIETY OF HAMILTON

In 2001, the Children's Aid Society of Hamilton (CAS) embarked on an Anti-Racism Multicultural Organizational Change Initiative to respond more effectively to the ethnic, racial, religious, and cultural diversity of the Hamilton area. The initiative aims to identify and remove barriers to CAS services and to enhance the quality of those services.

Before developing a change plan, the CAS surveyed over 700 staff, volunteers, and other agency stakeholders, and conducted a community needs assessment. The findings from those surveys formed the basis of a change plan. Five areas of CAS were targeted for change: Data Collection and Information Systems; Human Resources; Training; Services and Programs; and Communications and Community Linkages. An action plan was developed for each area.

Continued

Many goals have already been achieved. For example:

- Staff, managers, and foster parents have received cultural competency and anti-racism training.
- The CAS has shared the Implementation Plan and "lessons learned" about the change process with other organizations.
- The CAS has introduced outreach strategies to build bridges with community members and to educate the community about child protection legislation and CAS programs.

The CAS welcomes feedback from service users and community partners for the purpose of monitoring and evaluating the Implementation Plan.

The process of anti-racism organizational change is an exciting, albeit daunting endeavour. The process takes time, commitment, patience, dedication, and long-term vision. The CAS acknowledges that this is a learning process that requires ongoing support from staff and the community.

Source: Excerpted and adapted from the Children's Aid Society of Hamilton. (2008). "Anti-Racism Organizational Change Initiative." Retrieved December 14, 2008, from http://www.hamiltoncas.com/multicult/multicult.html. Used by permission.

Knowledge-Building

An important step in the preparatory stage of change is building knowledge about one's own organization in order to gain a clear picture of what needs to change. This can involve an assessment of the strengths and weaknesses of an agency's major systems, including its strategic and operational plans, financial performance and costs, policies and procedures, human resource management, and/or programming (Rogers & Fong, 2000). A wide range of tools and strategies, such as program evaluations and internal audits, can give agencies this type of information. Many organizations find it helpful to apply a certain "lens" when scrutinizing their operations. For example, an agency that wants to become more inclusive might use an "inclusion lens" (mentioned in Chapter 2).

Preparing for organizational change not only requires a sound knowledge of one's workplace, but of the environment in which the organization functions. Before restructuring, an agency will want to know whether its changes are likely to reflect the community it serves. This information can be gathered by environmental scans and community needs assessments.

Committing to Change

For organizational change to be successful, the individuals at all levels of the organization—such as the board, management, staff, and volunteers—must commit to the change. Successful change also requires change agents who can guide the organization and its members through the process. These change agents should have credibility in the organization and be able to make sound decisions, effectively problem-solve, and appropriately plan the change process.

The change agents—who are often agency managers—may form a steering committee to plan and implement the change process. Ideally, a steering committee is representative of the entire agency, and therefore includes a mix of staff, volunteers, managers, and other stakeholders, such as local residents (OHCC, 2004).

One of the first tasks of the steering committee is to develop an action plan, which serves as a guide to the organizational change process. A good action plan reflects the vision of change and the change goals, and describes specific steps and activities of the change process. The plan also identifies who is responsible for which task, when each task will be completed, and what resources (such as money and equipment) are needed to successfully carry out the plan.

IMPLEMENTING CHANGE

According to Brewster and colleagues (2002), organizational change has to occur simultaneously at two levels. At the individual level, staff, volunteers, and others in the agency learn new skills, attitudes, and/or behaviours; at the operational level, various systems in an agency are improved. Each level of change requires help from the other: for individuals to change, the system must provide a supportive environment; for a system to change, the staff and others must be willing to embrace the agency's new policies, procedures, and/or practices.

Individual Change

Training is a key strategy for facilitating individual change. A variety of training kits have been developed to increase awareness, improve skills, or change behaviour in Canadian workplaces. For example, the Manitoba Civil Service Commission uses a number of training modules to help government workers understand workplace discrimination and harassment, and to suggest what they can do to develop a healthy work environment. Those training modules include *Cultural Diversity*; *Communicating with Aboriginal People*; and *Building a Respectful Workplace* (Canadian Heritage, 2008).

An effective training package will have the following elements:

- a thorough *needs assessment*, to ensure that training is relevant to the needs and expectations of the participants;

- clear *goals and objectives*, to guide the training and to articulate what the training aims to achieve;

- training *information*, which describes the rationale for training, the training schedule, the content and methods of training sessions, and the expectations of the trainers and management; and

- an *evaluation plan*, to measure the outcomes of training and to identify what is required in order to improve future training sessions (Brewster, Buckley, Cox, & Griep, 2002).

EXHIBIT 8.4

Staff training is a key component of organizational change.

Source: © iStockphoto.com/track5.

While training is a useful way to help staff and others learn about, adjust to, and eventually accept workplace change, it has its limitations. Block (1996) suggests that, in addition to training, the change agents must provide a safe forum for stakeholders to ask questions about the proposed changes; voice their reactions and concerns about the changes; discuss their needs, wants, and expectations about the proposed changes; and understand the options they have for how they might adapt to the changes.

When an organization decides it needs to undergo major change, it is normal for stakeholders to support the proposed changes on one level, and yet feel some resistance as well. Fuchs (2004) writes: "Change, by nature, intrudes on people's 'comfort zones,' so many equate it with pain, whether or not they think it will result in improvements." To prevent or reduce resistance, staff must be encouraged to engage in, take ownership for, and shape the change efforts; for example, staff might be asked to design a segment of the change plan or lead a training session.

Systemic Change

When change is systemic, it impacts all aspects or levels of a system or structure. Normally, **systemic change** involves the modification of an agency's policies, procedures, and practices. The systemic change that many voluntary social agencies have undergone in recent years has been in direct response to new funding arrangements with governments. In her study of over 100 voluntary and nonprofit organizations across Canada, Katherine Scott (2003b) found that two-thirds of respondents changed their programs and services, modified or adopted new methods of program evaluation and accountability reporting, and/or changed their organizational structure and processes, in order to pursue new funding opportunities. Funding shortages have also led to major restructuring, especially at the program level. For example, some agencies have had to narrow their client focus (such as limiting the age range or type of need of people they served); others have shifted their priorities to only the most needy clients or those in severe crisis (Reed & Howe, 2000).

EVALUATING CHANGE

An agency that invests in major organizational change will want to know if its efforts paid off—in other words, did the agency achieve its goals and vision of success? Two types of evaluation may be applied to determine the effectiveness of change: (1) **formative evaluation** usually occurs during the change process, and is mainly concerned with whether the action plan is working and what, if anything, in the plan needs modification; and (2) **summative evaluation** measures the end results of the change effort.

A formative evaluation involves monitoring the change process and introducing specific "tests" at certain points. For example, if the agency is trying to improve its reporting procedures, and the staff are taking a series of training sessions to learn the new routine, a monitoring plan might include the following:

1. immediately after each training session, staff are asked to complete an exit questionnaire, which assesses how well they understand the new reporting procedures;

2. three months after training, staff are given a follow-up assessment, which indicates whether the new reporting procedures are being implemented correctly; and

3. over the long term, staff attend refresher courses to reinforce the new reporting system (Canadian International Development Agency, 2006).

Summative evaluation occurs at the end of a change campaign, and measures whether the organization has reached its goals. Some organizations find it useful to apply various types of methods, and a mix of qualitative and quantitative measures, to assess the results of change. **Qualitative measures**, such as job satisfaction questionnaires, provide information about individuals' subjective experiences with the changes. **Quantitative measures** focus on aspects that can be counted or quantified in some way such as staff turnover rates or service utilization statistics (OHCC, 2004).

A SOCIAL WORK APPROACH TO ORGANIZATIONAL CHANGE

While many traditional social work approaches focus on changing the client (for example, through casework or group work), a number of approaches target social agencies, and try to make them more responsive to people's needs. **Structural social work** is one among many of the anti-oppressive approaches taken by social workers to change the organizations that employ them. A proponent of the structural model, Robert Mullaly (1997) contends that to change a social agency from within, social workers have to radicalize and democratize the agency. *Radicalizing* an agency involves confronting agency policies and procedures (such as discriminatory intake procedures) that negatively affect clients, and working to ensure that clients can access the full range of available services. *Democratizing* the agency involves taking steps to make the organization less bureaucratic and hierarchical, and more democratic and inclusive. This process may include helping clients become more involved in the agency's decision-making process (for example, by encouraging them to serve on the board of directors) and replacing boss–subordinate relationships with ones that are more nearly equal (perhaps by *consulting with* instead of *reporting to* supervisors).

Discussion Questions

▓ **Change at the Mezzo Level: Organizations**

1. Have you ever worked in an organization that underwent major restructuring? If so, what were some of the positive aspects of the change process? What were the negative aspects of change?

2. The section on training gives an example of how staff might be engaged in the organization's change process. How else might staff be engaged in, shape, or take ownership of the change process?

▥ CHANGE AT THE MACRO LEVEL: COMMUNITIES

CANADA'S COMMUNITY AGENDA

While social welfare programs and agencies do what they can to help people meet individual needs, their success often depends upon the functioning of systems at the macro level of society. Macro systems may be understood as the largest structures and systems of society, and include communities, a society's norms and values, a culture's traditions and customs, government policies and practices, and economic processes. These structures tend to be complex, well established, and supported by the *status quo*. Even so, these structures are not immune to change; if they fail to meet people's expectations, or if they hinder access to resources or opportunities needed for well-being, they may be challenged and changed. Perhaps more than any other macro system, communities have become prime candidates for change in recent years.

Studies indicate that many Canadian communities are struggling: not only do they lack the capacity to address the economic, health, and social problems they face, but also they are in a state of "decline" or "breakdown" (Hughes & Stone, 2004). Declining conditions are particularly worrisome for Canada's large urban centres, where poverty, crime, and other social problems are concentrating in certain neighbourhoods and threatening the stability and social cohesion of whole cities. Major change in those communities is inevitable if they want to not only survive, but to thrive.

Although each community has its own needs and challenges, they share the common goal to improve their quality of life (Tamarack Institute for Community Engagement, 2006). This "community agenda" revolves around the concept of **resilience**, which Sladowski and Hayes (2007, p. 2) define as "the capacity to mobilize resources in order to maintain quality of life in the face of change." To build resilience, communities must develop resources related to the following areas or "clusters:"

- *sustenance*, which focuses on basic necessities such as affordable housing and adequate income to achieve physical and emotional well-being;
- *adaptation*, which is concerned with developing ways to cope with stress and building capacities related to empathy and problem solving;
- *engagement*, which refers to actively participating in society; and
- *opportunity*, which involves skill development and the creation of economic opportunities in order to work and thrive in the labour market (Torjman, 2007b).

Each cluster comprises a set of actions that foster the development of personal capacity and community infrastructure. To build personal capacity, people need opportunities to enhance skills, abilities, and assets. An investment in community infrastructure requires resources to expand the range of amenities and supports that enhance well-being. Both capacity and community building involve a broad spectrum of participants, including individuals, groups, and organizations in the public, commercial, and voluntary sectors (Cooper & Bartlett, 2008). See Exhibit 8.5 for a graphical illustration of how the four clusters relate to each other and to the central theme of resilience.

EXHIBIT 8.5

THE COMMUNITIES AGENDA

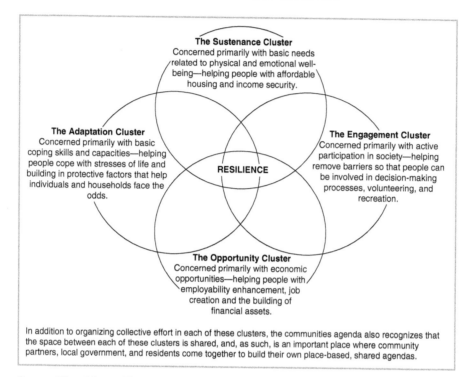

The Sustenance Cluster
Concerned primarily with basic needs related to physical and emotional well-being—helping people with affordable housing and income security.

The Adaptation Cluster
Concerned primarily with basic coping skills and capacities—helping people cope with stresses of life and building in protective factors that help individuals and households face the odds.

RESILIENCE

The Engagement Cluster
Concerned primarily with active participation in society—helping remove barriers so that people can be involved in decision-making processes, volunteering, and recreation.

The Opportunity Cluster
Concerned primarily with economic opportunities—helping people with employability enhancement, job creation and the building of financial assets.

In addition to organizing collective effort in each of these clusters, the communities agenda also recognizes that the space between each of these clusters is shared, and, as such, is an important place where community partners, local government, and residents come together to build their own place-based, shared agendas.

Source: "Shared Space: The Communities Agenda," Sherri Torjman, Vice-President, Caledon Institute of Social Policy, 2007. This book can be purchased by contacting Caledon Institute of Social Policy directly at: caledon@caledonist.org.

MODELS OF COMMUNITY CHANGE

A number of models have been developed to guide change at the community level. These models, however, are rarely implemented in their "pure" form; rather, community change agents tend to borrow ideas and strategies from various change models, and then tailor change efforts to the needs of the community. Many community change efforts nevertheless draw from the principles and practices of three classic approaches: community (or locality) development; social planning; and social action. The goals, assumptions, strategies, and other characteristics of each of these models are reviewed below and compared in Exhibit 8.6.

THREE APPROACHES TO COMMUNITY CHANGE

CHARACTERISTIC	COMMUNITY DEVELOPMENT MODEL	SOCIAL PLANNING MODEL	SOCIAL ACTION MODEL
Goals	Self-help; improve community living; emphasis on process goals	Using problem-solving approach to resolve community problems; emphasis on task goals	Shifting of power relationships and resources to an oppressed group; basic institutional change; emphasis on task and process goals
Assumptions concerning community	Everyone wants community living to improve and is willing to contribute to the improvement.	Social problems in the community can be resolved through the efforts of planning experts.	The community has a power structure and one or more oppressed groups; social injustice is a major problem.
Basic change strategy	Broad cross-section of people involved in identifying and solving their problems	Experts using fact gathering and the problem-solving approach	Members of oppressed groups organizing to take action against the power structure, which is the enemy
Characteristic change tactics and techniques	Consensus: communication among community groups and interests; group discussion	Consensus or conflict	Conflict or contest: confrontation, direct action, negotiation
Practitioner roles	Catalyst; facilitator; coordinator; teacher of problem-solving skills	Expert planner; fact gatherer; analyst; program developer and implementer	Activist; advocate; agitator; broker; negotiator; partisan
Views about power structure	Members of power structure as collaborators in a common venture	Power structure as employers and sponsors	Power structure as external target of action, oppressors to be coerced or overturned
Views about client population	Citizens	Consumers	Victims
Views about client role	Participants in a problem-solving process	Consumers or recipients	Employers, constituents

Source: From C. Zastrow, *Introduction to Social Work and Social Welfare: Empowering People*, 9th ed. © 2008 Wadsworth, a part of Cengage Learning, Inc. Reproduced by permission. www.cengage.com/permissions.

In the following discussion, *community* is defined as a town, city, neighbourhood, region, or other geographic location.

Community Development

Community development is based on the assumption that local problems are best resolved by the efforts of local residents. This approach to change originated in settlement houses such as the one Sarah Libby Carson opened in Toronto in 1899. With the "aim of bridging the gulf between rich and poor," community development programs gave local residents an opportunity to learn from their educated middle-class "peers" about social problems and how to resolve them (Bruce, 1966, p. 143). During the expansionary years of Canada's welfare state, governments took over many community development responsibilities and, with a bureaucratic "top-down" approach, decided what communities needed and how those needs would be met. As voluntary-sector agencies became more prominent, a "bottom-up" **grassroots approach** to community development began to flourish. A grassroots approach relies on citizen participation to drive community development: citizens are encouraged to identify and articulate their goals, design their own methods of change, and pool their resources in the problem-solving process (Halseth & Booth, 1998).

Over time, as government leaders adopted a more consensus-oriented way of connecting with citizens, top-down and bottom-up approaches began to converge. The result is a more cooperative working relationship between government and communities. Community projects—such as creating opportunities for rural youth and improving access to government services in remote areas—are the result of joint efforts between community groups and government. As with all community development efforts, these projects aim not to challenge or reform established social structures, but to work with existing structures to improve community conditions.

The term *comprehensive community initiative* (CCI) refers to a "new and improved" version of community development. While every CCI is unique, they are all

- community-driven, meaning that local citizens identify their own issues and concerns, set their priorities, and choose the strategies they think will best achieve their goals;
- supportive of partnering, collaboration, and the participation of people of diverse backgrounds;

- asset-based, and therefore build on a community's strengths by expanding local resources and opportunities; and

- aware of the limitations of local change, and therefore seek change in the broader social and economic systems in order to improve the quality of life for all (Smith & Torjman, 2004).

CCIs reject the tradition of tackling complex issues such as poverty, unemployment, health, homelessness, and crime in isolation from one another. Instead, CCIs assume that all problems affecting neighbourhoods are interrelated, and therefore require several interrelated solutions. Certain types of CCIs—including community economic development and **social economy enterprises**—try to lift people out of poverty by combining economic activities (such as local job creation), community cooperation and participation (such as local ideas and networking), and social structures (such as social welfare, health, and education) (Ameyaw & Simpson, 1994). Together, these multilevel solutions aim to strengthen the local economy, infrastructure, and services.

Social Planning

Rather than seeking radical or fundamental change, **social planning** seeks community change through a rational, formal, and technical problem-solving procedure led by expert (professional) planners. Change is based more on facts, statistics, and other objective data than on community participation; however, social planners often seek the opinions of community members about proposed initiatives. Social planning is committed to social development in a variety of areas, including health, safety, economic security, and education; the focus of planning is often on renewal and the design of new towns, neighbourhoods, or housing projects. A key objective of these initiatives is to improve the general functioning of residents by meeting a wide range of needs through the provision of goods and services. The plan for a new apartment block for seniors, for instance, may include an onsite pharmacy, special safety and security options, and facilities for recreation and social events. Social planning also strives to increase social capital by integrating or grouping services together (as in the case of multiservice centres) to enhance social support, connections, and interaction.

Community change often begins with a formal community assessment strategy to identify local needs. Social planners consider the alternatives for meeting the identified needs, and then set objectives for new programs, services, or facilities. The next steps involve developing an action plan, implementing that plan, and formally evaluating the results of their efforts. A version of this step-by-step process was used by the Edmonton Social Planning Council (ESPC, 2008) to address the city's affordable-housing shortage. The Council held two public forums to assess the impact of rent increases and low vacancy rates in Edmonton. After reviewing the information generated from the forums, the Council produced a final report that outlined their recommendations. The Alberta government responded to the report by targeting funds to help renters find or keep their housing. In 2008, the ESPC launched a survey (evaluation) to find out if the housing situation had indeed changed for renters.

In Canada, social planning originated in the late 1800s with the organized charity movement and subsequent establishment of Charity Organization Societies. These societies set out to coordinate and integrate services so that people could access social services more easily. The social planning movement gained momentum during the 1950s, 1960s, and early 1970s in response to continued economic growth and the rapid expansion of social programs. During this time, social planning councils emerged to identify social issues, needs, and resources; conduct research on those issues; help organizations set up new services; and perform other community planning activities (Social Planning Council of Metropolitan Toronto, 1997; Ginsler, 1988).

During the economic downturn in the 1980s, some councils, especially in large cities, were able to obtain healthy budgets, qualified staff, and other resources to continue serving their communities. Other councils struggled to survive as a result of insufficient funds, lack of personnel, or poor support from their communities. Many financially strapped councils could no longer afford staff, and were eventually transformed into committees of volunteers (Ginsler, 1988).

Social Action

Social action is based on the assumption that there are disadvantaged or oppressed groups in society who have to be organized in order to demand justice from the larger society. Social activists may choose to either join forces with these disadvantaged groups or act on their behalf. In either case, social action is a collective effort that attempts to convince those holding power (such as politicians) to reform unjust policies, practices, or systems. Unlike community development, social action does not require a consensus for change within the community. Indeed, social action may take place even when a majority of the community denies that a problem exists.

Social activists use a variety of strategies to promote their cause, gain support, and bring about positive change. These include *collaboration* strategies (such as lobbying), *campaign* strategies (such as petitions), and *contest* strategies (such as demonstrations). Today's social activists are also likely to use *advocacy*, and to engage in *policy dialogue* to influence politicians.

EXHIBIT 8.7

Participating in a protest rally or march is a way to take social action, and to influence reform in a government policy, practice, or system.

Source: CP PHOTO/Winnipeg Free Press/Wayne Glowacki.

Social action in Canada originated in the settlement movement of the late 1880s. While the organized charity movement focused on helping people adjust to existing social conditions, reformists from the settlement houses fought for societal change. Settlement houses were located in the poorest sections of town, which meant that settlement workers quickly became aware of the poverty and social dislocation created by industrialization and urbanization. These workers rejected the prevailing *laissez-faire* philosophy, and strove to correct social inequities and injustices for disadvantaged groups (Burghardt, 1987).

In the early twentieth century, poor work conditions became catalysts for social action. For instance, during the Winnipeg General Strike of 1919, almost 30,000 workers went on strike. This protest, which called attention to poor wages, deplorable working conditions, and other labour-related problems, sparked the formation of a number of social action organizations. One of those organizations was Winnipeg's Community Welfare Council, a social action group devoted to community awareness on social issues. Over time, other organizations would emerge that would fight for better conditions for children, women, labourers, Aboriginal peoples, persons with disabilities, gay men and lesbians, and low-income groups.

Many contemporary social activists rely on the collective efforts of average citizens to achieve their goals. This grassroots approach is obvious when members of a community come together because of a common concern, and go on to establish an organization or group committed to addressing that concern. These organizations tend to be independent, community-based operations that are not affiliated with governments, and whose members advocate on their own or another group's behalf. There are many examples of these grassroots organizations in Canada, including

- Mothers Against Drunk Driving (MADD), founded by mothers whose children had been killed by impaired drivers;
- DisAbled Women's Network (DAWN) of Ontario, founded by women with disabilities to promote the inclusion and equality of women and girls with disabilities; and
- National Anti-Poverty Organization (NAPO), founded to eliminate poverty in Canada and serve as watchdogs for inequities in the social welfare system.

COMMUNITY PRACTICE

By virtue of their training and knowledge base, social workers can make effective community organizers (CASW, 1998). For example, they tend to have good listening and communication skills, understand how systems work, and be comfortable working with both individuals and groups. Social workers who engage in **community practice** do so with the "belief that people acting together have a great capacity to improve their own circumstances, as they have first-hand knowledge of the situation and what needs to happen to change things for the better" (Hall, 2007). The process of community practice involves the organization of citizens around certain issues, problems, or unmet needs; the development of strategies for change; and the provision of relevant information to community groups.

Depending on the type of community organization being undertaken, social workers fulfil various roles:

- *Community development.* As *brokers*, social workers help individuals and groups connect with needed programs and services in the community. Since a main focus of community development is problem solving, social workers may also act as *enablers* by teaching community members effective problem-solving skills.

- *Social planning.* In a social planning capacity, social workers may be employed to develop action plans, collect and analyze data on local issues and concerns, and share research findings with social planning councils, government departments, and others. Social workers may also be instrumental in connecting with, generating interest among, and motivating local groups to participate in the planning process.

- *Social action.* Until the professionalization of social work in the early twentieth century, all social workers were social activists: "Whether through visits to the poor and homeless, demonstrations in the streets, or surveys to expose shocking conditions, the first social workers were crusaders whose full-time occupation was social action" (Thursz, 1977, p. 1274). Today's social workers may assume the role of *activist* (seek change in social or political power structures to improve conditions for a disadvantaged group); *advocate* (speak or act on behalf of a client to achieve certain goals); or *initiator* (call attention to problems or injustices that need correction) (Zastrow, 2008).

Discussion Questions

Change at the Macro Level: Communities

1. Have you ever lived in a community in which community development, social planning, or social action took place? If so, describe the sequence of events, the types of actions people took to create change, and the outcomes of that change process. What were some of the positive impacts of the change? What were some of the negative impacts?

2. Which of the three community change approaches (or strategies from one or more approaches) might be most effective for reducing poverty? Give reasons for your answer.

SUMMARY

Introduction

Planned change applies a scientific method to changing conditions so that people can meet their needs. Central to the planned change process is a target of change, one or more change agents, methods of change, and an identified beneficiary of change. In terms of context, planned change can take place at the micro, mezzo, or macro levels of society. Capacity building is a key element of planned change.

I. Change at the Micro Level: Individuals, Families, and Groups

Micro-level change focuses on helping individuals, families, or small groups. Social casework models (such as brief therapies) are designed to help individuals. Family services are available to support and strengthen the family unit. In some respects, social group work may be more effective than one-on-one sessions. A social worker's choice of social casework, family casework, and/or social group work depends on factors such as the presenting need or problem.

II. Change at the Mezzo Level: Organizations

Organizational change begins with recognizing the need for change. To change, agencies must have a vision of success, be committed to change, and prepare for change by learning about the organization and the community. Change agents, and a steering committee, can guide the organization through the change process. The actual change occurs at an individual level and a systemic level. Formative and summative evaluations are used to determine the effectiveness of change. Structural social work is an approach taken by social workers to improve the organizations that employ them.

III. Change at the Macro Level: Communities

Many Canadian communities are facing declining conditions. Canada's "community agenda" aims to improve the quality of life in communities; resilience is a primary goal of that agenda. Most community change reflects the principles and practices of community development, social planning, and/or social action. Community practice is a field of social work that involves organizing citizens, developing strategies for change, and providing information to community groups.

Key Terms

For definitions of the key terms, consult the Glossary on page 413 at the end of the book.

planned change process, p. 197

micro level (of society), p. 197

mezzo level (of society), p. 197

macro level (of society), p. 197

capacity, p. 197

social casework, p. 200

brief therapy, p. 200

family casework, p. 201

social group work, p. 202

organizational change, p. 204

systemic change, p. 209

formative evaluation, p. 210

summative evaluation, p. 210

qualitative measure, p. 210

quantitative measure, p. 210

structural social work, p. 210

resilience, p. 212

community development, p. 215

grassroots approach, p. 215

comprehensive community initiative, p. 215

social economy enterprise, p. 216

social planning, p. 216

social action, p. 217

community practice, p. 219

PART 3

MEETING THE NEEDS OF CANADIANS THROUGH PROGRAMS AND SERVICES

The Social Welfare of Low-Income Groups

OBJECTIVES

Poverty, unemployment, and their associated challenges inhibit the well-being of individuals and families. This chapter will explore:

- poverty in Canada;

- the impact of poverty;

- organized approaches to poverty and unemployment; and

- issues related to working with low-income and marginalized groups.

INTRODUCTION

Poverty is to be without sufficient money, but it is also to have little hope for better things. It is a feeling that one is unable to control one's destiny, that one is powerless in a society that respects power. The poor have very limited access to means of making known their situation and their needs. To be poor is to feel apathy, alienation from society, entrapment, hopelessness and to believe that whatever you do will not turn out successfully. (Royal Commission on the Status of Women of Canada, 1977, p. 311).

Canada is often praised for its healthy and stable economy, and for having one of the world's highest per capita levels of economic productivity. Despite this, the nation's wealth fails to trickle down to all Canadians, many of whom can barely make ends meet. Among those struggling financially are working poor individuals who, despite having full-time jobs, do not earn enough to adequately support themselves or their families. A growing number of individuals—many of them children—visit food banks daily and rely on the good will of charities for clothing, shelter, and other basics. Studies show that poverty is even a concern for middle-class Canadians; a 2006 survey by Environics found that close to half of all Canadians believed they were just one or two missed paycheques away from destitution (Laird, 2007).

Canadian governments spend billions of dollars annually to enhance the financial security of citizens; most of those efforts are made through employment programs, tax credits, cash transfers (such as Old Age Security), and government-subsidized social services such as childcare. Although these programs provide some level of economic security, they fail to prevent or reduce poverty for many Canadians. Reports indicate that Canada has both the financial means and social knowledge to eradicate poverty. However, as some analysts suggest, Canada has been lacking the political will to make the elimination of poverty a national priority. As Alain Noel (2006) observes, policymakers have traditionally treated poverty "as a relatively minor or residual preoccupation" and as a normal outcome of economic progress.

There is evidence to suggest that the traditional *laissez-faire* attitude toward poverty is gradually changing; poverty reduction has recently become a global concern, and one that many nations see as a precursor to social and economic well-being. In Canada, the anti-poverty agenda is driven by the collaborative efforts among individuals, community groups, businesses, voluntary agencies, and some governments who are determined to find lasting solutions to poverty (Policy Research Initiative, 2008).

POVERTY IN CANADA

DEFINING AND MEASURING POVERTY

There is no single official or universally accepted definition of **poverty**: every country has a different view of poverty and, even within the same country, people's views of poverty change over time. In Canada, a variety of poverty definitions exist. Most definitions relate poverty to a certain level of income; Michaud, Cotton, and Bishop (2004, p. 6), for example, define poverty as "a

EXHIBIT 9.1

Poverty is a reality for a growing number of Canadians.

Source: Aaron Kohr/Shutterstock.

subsistence standard of living with an income that is not sufficient to purchase the bare necessities." Some poverty definitions equate poverty with **social exclusion**—that is, poverty exists when a person is unable, or is denied the opportunity, to fully engage in society, or meet society's expectations in terms of roles, relationships, and participation (Townsend, 1993). Other definitions emphasize the powerlessness of being poor, being "voiceless" and dependent on others for resources. This chapter uses the term *poverty* in reference to low income and its associated conditions and challenges.

Despite the lack of an official definition of poverty, Canada has developed various methods to measure conditions of deprivation. Three of those measuring tools—all developed by the Government of Canada—are described below. (*Note:* Each tool defines "family" as one or more persons.)

- *Low-Income Cut-Offs* (**LICOs**). A LICO identifies a minimum level of income required for a family to purchase food, shelter, and other basics. A family that spends 20 percent or more than the average household on basic necessities is said to be living in low income (Exhibit 9.2

illustrates the 35 low-income cut-offs in Canada). Since the LICOs are adjusted from time to time, they reflect changes in the economy and the amount of money people presumably need to enjoy a reasonable standard of living in Canada.

- *Low-Income Measure (LIM)*. The LIM estimates the proportion of a selected geographic area that has substantially less income than the rest of the area. Low-income families are defined as those whose incomes are less than half the median family income in the area (income is adjusted according to family size). The LIM is often used at the international level to compare family income between countries.

- *The Market-Basket Measure (MBM)*. The MBM estimates the costs of basic necessities such as food, shelter, and transportation, and then compares those costs to a family's disposable income. Low-income households are those with a lower level of income than the cost of the basket. Often used in conjunction with the LICOs and LIM, the MBM is useful for identifying regional variations in the cost of living and people's purchasing power across Canada.

EXHIBIT 9.2

LOW-INCOME CUT-OFFS (LICOS): AFTER-TAX, 2007

| FAMILY SIZE | POPULATION OF COMMUNITY | | | | |
	RURAL (FARM AND NON-FARM)	UNDER 30,000	30,000 TO 99,999	100,000 TO 499,999	500,000 OR MORE
1	11,745	13,441	14,994	15,184	17,954
2	14,295	16,360	18,250	18,480	21,851
3	17,800	20,370	22,725	23,011	27,210
4	22,206	25,414	28,352	28,709	33,946
5	25,287	28,940	32,285	32,691	38,655
6	28,044	32,095	35,805	36,255	42,869
7+	30,801	35,250	39,324	39,819	47,084

Source: Adapted from Statistics Canada, "Low Income Cut-Offs for 2007 and Low Income Measures for 2006," Catalogue No. 61-533-XIE, Statistics Canada Income Research Paper Series, Catalogue No. 75F0002M—No. 004, ISSN 1707–2840.

Although the LICOs were originally designed to measure *low income*, as opposed to *poverty*, many analysts refer to them collectively as Canada's "poverty line." Moreover, the LICOs have become the most widely used measures of poverty in Canada. The LICOs are useful for a number of purposes, including their ability to report on **poverty rates** (the percentage of low-income Canadians), and the **depth of poverty** (how far incomes are below the low-income cut-off lines). According to the LICOs, almost 15 percent of Canadians are poor. As for the depth of poverty, the LICOs show that those who live in the deepest poverty are two-parent families under the age of 65; on average, these families require an additional $10,400 per year to raise their income above the low income cut-off (NCW, 2007a).

WHO IS POOR IN CANADA?

Certain populations in Canada are at higher risk of poverty than others. This is true for single adults under age 65 (especially young adults); people with disabilities; recent immigrants and refugees; and Aboriginal peoples. Many Canadians living in poverty are the **working poor**—people who earn more than half their income from employment, and yet do not earn enough to stay out of poverty (NCW, 2007b). Many of these individuals work for minimum wage, or are stuck in part-time or **non-standard jobs** (temporary, contract, or seasonal jobs). A total of 1.5 million Canadians belong to working poor families (CCPA, 2006).

The term *feminization of poverty* calls attention to the fact that women are more likely than men to be poor, regardless of the woman's age, income, family status, ethnicity, or other characteristic (SPRC, 2006). Among women, lone mothers are at highest risk (49 percent are poor), followed by unattached women under 65 (43 percent are poor) (NCW, 2006b). Aboriginal women are twice as likely as non-Aboriginal women to be poor (Cornish, 2008).

One of Canada's greatest concerns is the persistently high rate of poverty among children. Almost one child out of every nine lives in poverty. Forty percent of poor children live in lone-mother families (Campaign 2000, 2008). Other children at high risk of poverty are those with disabilities, and children living in recent immigrant, visible minority, and Aboriginal families.

Exhibit 9.3 provides additional facts about poverty in Canada.

EXHIBIT 9.3
POVERTY FACTS

POVERTY SNAPSHOT
- Number of people living in poverty in Canada: 4.8 million (based on before-tax LICOs)
- Percentage of Canadians living in poverty: 15.5% (1994: 18.6%; 1984: 18.7%)
- Family type with highest poverty rate: lone-parent mothers (47.1%)
- Family type with lowest poverty rate: senior couples (4.8%)
- Number of children living in poverty: 2 million (17.7% of all Canadian children)
- Age group most likely to be poor: children (17.7%)
- Age group least likely to be poor: seniors (14%)

DEPTH OF POVERTY
- Families farthest below the poverty line: two-parent families ($10,400 below)
- Families closest to the poverty line: single senior women ($3,200 below)

WOMEN
- Number of years since 1980 when women's poverty rates were lower than men's: 0
- Percentage of women living in poverty: 16.6% (compared to 14.4% of men)
- Senior women are more likely to be poor than senior men (17.8% versus 9.3%)

WORKING FOR PAY, BUT STILL POOR
- Families that receive more than half of family income from employment: 48% of poor families; 62% of poor singles
- Major income earner working full-time, all year: 5.1% of poor families; 13% of poor singles
- Percentage of food-bank clients whose primary source of income is from employment: 13.5%*

SOCIAL ASSISTANCE
Percentage of poor families relying primarily on welfare:
- Two-parent families: 8%
- Working-age couples without children: 20%
- Working-age single people: 24%
- Lone-parent mothers: 24%

INCOME INEQUALITY
- Share of total after-tax income:
  - By the richest 20 percent of family units: 44%
  - By the poorest 20 percent: 4.6%

Continued

- Increase in after-tax incomes since 1980:
  - By the richest 20 percent of family units: +17.4%
  - By the poorest 20 percent: +4.3%

*Canadian Association of Food Banks, *Hungercount 2007* (2007), p. 2. Retrieved November 22, 2008, from www.cafb-acba.ca/documents/HungerCount2007.pdf.

Source: National Council of Welfare, *Poverty Profile 2004* (2007). Retrieved November 22, 2008, from www.ncw-cnbes.net/en/research/povertyprofile/webonly2004.html.

CONTRIBUTING FACTORS TO POVERTY

Poverty is a complex and multidimensional social problem, with many inter-related contributing factors. In a market economy like Canada's, one of the most critical determinants of poverty is the ability of people to work and to earn enough money to support themselves and their families. Although most Canadians earn a sufficient income, many others face ongoing hardship. Some of those barriers to adequate income are described below.

Unemployment

By the end of 2008, 6.6 percent of working-age Canadians who were actively looking for and were available for work could not find it (Statistics Canada, 2009a). In March 2009, Canada's **unemployment rate** reached 8 percent (the highest level in seven years); economists predicted that unemployment rates would continue to rise as a result of the economic recession (Canada to be hit, 2008). Groups most likely to be unemployed during the recession are youth aged 15 to 24, and men aged 25 to 54 (Statistics Canada, 2009b). Other groups at high risk of, unemployment are Aboriginal peoples, recent immigrants, and people with disabilities. Some parts of the country, such as the Atlantic provinces, have historically higher unemployment rates.

Underemployment

When people are **underemployed**, it usually means that they are not working as much as they could or want to, or are overqualified for the job they have. Many Canadians seek full-time work, but can only find part-time or non-standard employment (Almey, 2007). Full-time jobs are disappearing in Canada. In 2008 alone, 71,000 full-time jobs were lost, while 36,000 part-time jobs were created (Statistics Canada, 2009a). Underemployed workers often have to either juggle several part-time jobs or seek financial help from welfare departments to make ends meet.

Rising Costs Versus Low Wages

The costs of basic necessities—especially housing—continue to rise in Canada. For example, in 2000, a family of four living in Vancouver required a minimum income of $27,670 to purchase a basic level of food, shelter, transportation, and clothing; by 2006, that same family needed $31,175 (HRSDC, 2008). Since the mid-1970s, levels of minimum wages (which are set by the provinces) have not kept up with the rising cost of living. Saunders (2005) estimates that one in six full-time workers in Canada are in jobs that pay less than ten dollars an hour. Two-thirds of these workers are women; other groups who are likely to work for minimum wage include Aboriginal people, recent immigrants, and people with disabilities (Murray & Mackenzie, 2007).

Government Policies

For almost three decades, governments have been steadily reducing funds to social assistance, Employment Insurance, and other social welfare programs, leaving many Canadians struggling to get by. Governments are often blamed for keeping minimum wages low, allowing part-time jobs to replace full-time positions, and for doing little to stem the tide of a growing population of working poor. Some policy analysts believe that Canadian governments have contributed to both the current homeless crisis and the problem of hunger through inadequate social policies, and their failure to redistribute income from the rich to the poor (Laird, 2007; National Food Security Assembly, 2005). Many of the factors that put women at a higher risk of poverty than men are attributed to public policies that do not support the varied roles of women in society (see Exhibit 9.4).

Discussion Questions

■ **Poverty in Canada**

1. Many definitions of poverty exist. How would you define poverty? What indicators provide evidence that poverty exists in your community?

2. This section has explored some of the reasons why women are at high risk of poverty. Identify the possible reasons why the risk of poverty is also high among (a) people with disabilities; (b) Aboriginal people; and (c) recent immigrants.

3. What are the main contributing factors to poverty in Canada?

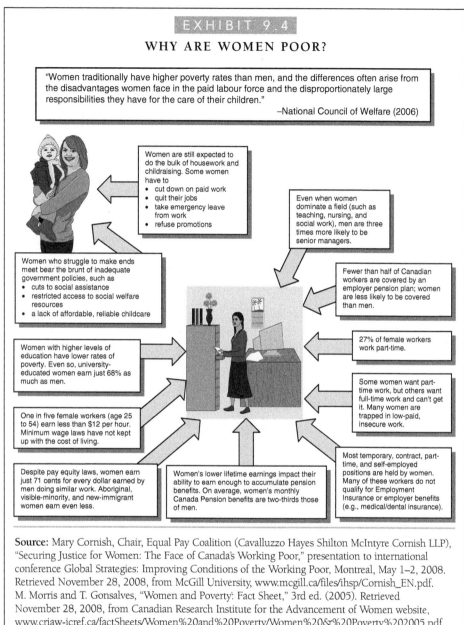

EXHIBIT 9.4

WHY ARE WOMEN POOR?

"Women traditionally have higher poverty rates than men, and the differences often arise from the disadvantages women face in the paid labour force and the disproportionately large responsibilities they have for the care of their children."

–National Council of Welfare (2006)

Women are still expected to do the bulk of housework and childraising. Some women have to
- cut down on paid work
- quit their jobs
- take emergency leave from work
- refuse promotions

Even when women dominate a field (such as teaching, nursing, and social work), men are three times more likely to be senior managers.

Women who struggle to make ends meet bear the brunt of inadequate government policies, such as
- cuts to social assistance
- restricted access to social welfare resources
- a lack of affordable, reliable childcare

Fewer than half of Canadian workers are covered by an employer pension plan; women are less likely to be covered than men.

Women with higher levels of education have lower rates of poverty. Even so, university-educated women earn just 68% as much as men.

27% of female workers work part-time.

Some women want part-time work, but others want full-time work and can't get it. Many women are trapped in low-paid, insecure work.

One in five female workers (age 25 to 54) earn less than $12 per hour. Minimum wage laws have not kept up with the cost of living.

Despite pay equity laws, women earn just 71 cents for every dollar earned by men doing similar work. Aboriginal, visible-minority, and new-immigrant women earn even less.

Women's lower lifetime earnings impact their ability to earn enough to accumulate pension benefits. On average, women's monthly Canada Pension benefits are two-thirds those of men.

Most temporary, contract, part-time, and self-employed positions are held by women. Many of these workers do not qualify for Employment Insurance or employer benefits (e.g., medical/dental insurance).

Source: Mary Cornish, Chair, Equal Pay Coalition (Cavalluzzo Hayes Shilton McIntyre Cornish LLP), "Securing Justice for Women: The Face of Canada's Working Poor," presentation to international conference Global Strategies: Improving Conditions of the Working Poor, Montreal, May 1–2, 2008. Retrieved November 28, 2008, from McGill University, www.mcgill.ca/files/ihsp/Cornish_EN.pdf. M. Morris and T. Gonsalves, "Women and Poverty: Fact Sheet," 3rd ed. (2005). Retrieved November 28, 2008, from Canadian Research Institute for the Advancement of Women website, www.criaw-icref.ca/factSheets/Women%20and%20Poverty/Women%20&%20Poverty%202005.pdf. National Council of Welfare, "Women and Poverty" (July 2006). Retrieved November 28, 2008, from www.ncwcnbes.net/documents/researchpublications/ResearchProjects/PovertyProfile/2002–03Report_Summer2006/FactSheets/WomenandPoverty.pdf. Statistics Canada, Social and Aboriginal Statistics Division, "Women in Canada: A Gender-Based Statistical Report," 5th ed., Catalogue No. 89–503-XPE (Ottawa: March 2006). Retrieved November 28, 2008, from www.statcan.ca/english/freepub/89–503-XIE/0010589–503-XIE.pdf. Statistics Canada, "Earnings and Incomes of Canadians over the Past quarter Century: 2006 Census," Catalogue No. 97–563-X (Ottawa: May 2008). Retrieved November 28, 2008, from www12.statcan.ca/english/census06/analysis/income/pdf/97–563-XIE2006001.pdf. Canadian Labour Congress, "Women in the Workforce: Still a Long Way from Equality" (Ottawa: May 5, 2008). Retrieved November 28, 2008, from http://canadianlabour.ca/sites/clc/files/omensequalityreportEn.pdf.

▥ THE IMPACT OF POVERTY

Persistent poverty can impact people in various ways and on many different levels. The effects of poverty on child development, physical and mental health, crime, family violence, and other problems are well documented. The negative consequences of poverty on child development are of particular concern, not only because of the injustice of exposing children to hardship and deprivation, but also because the harmful effects of poverty can carry into adulthood, and compromise a person's ability to hold down a job, earn a sufficient income, and otherwise participate fully in social and economic life.

Exhibit 9.5 highlights some of the negative consequences of poverty and the cyclical nature of the poverty experience. The top section of the chart centres around two main consequences of poverty:

- *Poor housing.* People who are poor often live in rundown or unsafe neighbourhoods, which are geographically isolated from recreation centres, libraries, early learning programs, job opportunities, and other resources.

- *Poor food.* People who are poor often lack the means to buy fresh or nutritious food; poor diets are associated with such problems as poor pre- and postnatal care, low birth weight, and general physical weakness.

The consequences of inferior housing conditions and inadequate food on human health are varied and numerous. Research has found that inadequate housing tends to be related to certain health problems, such as asthma and bedwetting in children; poor nutrition tends to be linked to ailments such as anaemia and chronic back problems in women.

The middle section of Exhibit 9.5 highlights some of the potential effects of poor housing, poor food, and poor health. For children, difficulties in functioning may manifest themselves as delays in cognitive, social, and physical *development*, which may, in turn, lead to learning problems and to involvement in high-risk behaviours. For adults, functioning difficulties may negatively impact *work* and the ability to earn a living. Poverty conditions are also associated with high levels of stress and other *psychological* problems, which can contribute to interpersonal or family conflicts, including family violence. Finally, difficulties in personal functioning and the fulfilment of important responsibilities and social roles— be it in school, work, or other life areas—may lead to *social exclusion* and marginalization.

EXHIBIT 9.5

THE PRICE OF POVERTY

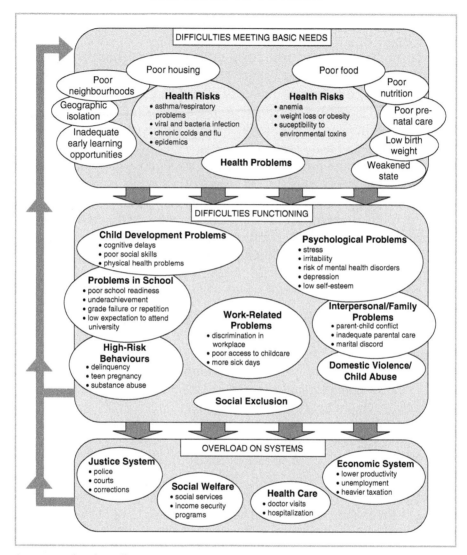

Source: Rosalie Chappell.

When individuals suffer from the repercussions of poverty, everyone ultimately suffers. Neighbourhood decay, an eroding sense of community, rising crime rates, and other poverty-related problems impact the quality of life for everyone, not just those who are poor. Poverty is also costly in economic terms: people living in poverty typically need more services, which means that more public resources must be used to support social welfare, health care, justice, and other systems (as depicted in the bottom section of Exhibit 9.5).

The impacts of poverty tend to occur in a circular fashion—that is, not only can poverty contribute to a variety of problems, but also those problems can converge to create even more hardship and deprivation. For example, a person living in poverty might experience health problems; those health problems might, in turn, interfere with the person's ability to learn and to get an education, or to find and keep a job; that lack of education or work experience might hinder the person from finding a good job and making a decent wage, which can then lead to further poverty. The circular pattern of poverty is suggested by the upward arrows in Exhibit 9.5. At times, social welfare, health, and other systems are able to interrupt the poverty cycle. However, those systems often lack the resources to effectively address the complex problems created by chronic or long-term poverty.

POOR HOUSING—A PRODUCT OF POVERTY

Canadians have witnessed a dramatic rise in the cost of housing in recent years and, as a result, are spending a greater proportion of their income on shelter. The term **unaffordable housing** means that shelter costs more than 30 percent of a household's before-tax income (CMHC, 2007). In 2007, less than 1 percent of new homes were considered to be affordable, compared to over 10 percent in the early 1980s (Shapcott, 2008).

While many Canadian homeowners can hardly keep up with large mortgages and declining incomes, those who rent also face affordability challenges. Since the 1990s, when changes in government legislation relaxed the rent controls in several large cities, rents have been rising, and subsequently making it more difficult for low-income renters to find affordable housing. One Canadian study found that between 1991 and 2001, the proportion of renter households that spent over 30 percent of their income on shelter increased from 35 percent to 41 percent. More than 20 percent of the households in the study were paying at least half of their income on rent, leaving them with little money for much else including the meeting of children's nutritional and educational needs (Federation of Canadian Municipalities, 2009). In addition to high rents, there are fewer rental units available; in some major cities, such as Vancouver, Victoria, and Montreal, the apartment vacancy rate persistently remains under two percent (Laird, 2007).

When housing is unaffordable, homelessness becomes a real possibility. Homelessness is becoming an increasingly visible social problem in Canada, especially in large urban centres such as Vancouver, Montreal, and Toronto. Over the years, the definition of homelessness has expanded; today, most policymakers refer to homelessness as being either *absolute* or *relative*:

- **absolute homelessness** is present when a person lacks physical shelter and has to sleep in places not intended for human habitation, such as the streets, vehicles, and abandoned buildings;

- **relative homelessness** is present when a person has physical shelter, but that shelter is temporary, unsafe, unaffordable, provides inadequate protection from the elements, lacks access to clean water and sanitation, or otherwise fails to meet basic standards of health and safety (Hwang, 2001).

EXHIBIT 9.6

The rising cost of housing in Canada increases the risk of homelessness.

Source: Kuzma/Shutterstock.

The extent of homelessness in Canada is difficult to assess, but social advocates estimate that as many as 300,000 Canadians have no fixed address. Stereotypes would have us believe that the majority of the homeless population are older single men who have a mental illness or an addiction problem. While many of those individuals are homeless, so too are growing numbers of women, families with children, students, and recent immigrants (Laird, 2007). Many others are considered at risk of homelessness because they are living in unstable conditions and may be forced to suddenly leave their home; women living in physically and/or sexually abusive situations are included in this group. Families with children living in unaffordable housing are also at a high risk of eviction (Campaign 2000, 2002).

POVERTY AND FOOD INSECURITY

At one time, the notion that anyone in Canada might go hungry was beyond comprehension. It was during the 1980s, with the emergence of food banks and children's meal programs in schools, that food insecurity became recognized as a social problem (McIntyre, 2003). The term *food insecurity* refers to "the inability to obtain sufficient, nutritious, personally acceptable food through normal food channels or the uncertainty that one will be able to do so" (Davis & Tarasuk, 1994, p. 51). A variety of factors may contribute to food insecurity, but it is most closely linked with poverty and the unaffordability of a healthy diet (National Food Security Assembly, 2005).

According to the Canadian Community Health Survey (CCHS), 9 percent of adults, and over 5 percent of children, are food-insecure. Among the households with children, the issue of food insecurity is greatest among lone-mother families (one-quarter of whom report food insecurity). Findings also show that close to half of all low-income households, almost 60 percent of all welfare recipients, and over a third of Aboriginal households living off-reserve are food-insecure (Health Canada, 2007a).

One yardstick for measuring food insecurity is the number of people using emergency food programs. Many of these programs are grassroots community-action food projects, such as soup kitchens, community gardens, and food box programs. Food banks are the most common type of community-based food program in Canada. Over a one-month period in 2008, over 700,000 people visited food banks in Canada; 37 percent of those visitors were children (Food Banks Canada, 2008). The number of employed people who use food banks is on the rise: in 2008, over 14 percent of food bank users were employed, compared to about 12 percent in 2002. The provinces with the greatest food bank usage are Ontario, Quebec, and British Columbia.

Discussion Questions

The Impact of Poverty

1. Poverty can have both immediate and long-term consequences for children. What are some of those consequences, and how might they affect a child's future functioning as an adult?

2. Poverty is considered to be both a cause and an effect of human hardship. How might Canada's social welfare, health, and other systems do a better job at interrupting the poverty cycle?

ORGANIZED APPROACHES TO POVERTY AND UNEMPLOYMENT

CHANGING ATTITUDES AND APPROACHES

From Passive to Active Policies

During the economic downturn in the early 1970s, many unemployed Canadians turned to social assistance (SA) and/or Unemployment Insurance (UI). Before long, governments began to see those programs as too costly, inefficient, and ineffective (Battle, 2001). The ineffectiveness of SA and UI was largely attributed to their **passive policies**, which supported the giving of "unconditional" benefits and generally left it up to employable recipients to find their way into—or back into—the workforce. By the 1990s, governments had condemned these passive programs not only for failing to move people off public assistance, but also for fostering dependency on government programs.

Beginning in the mid-1990s, Canadian governments introduced **active policies** to SA and UI by requiring beneficiaries of those programs to work, volunteer, retrain, or otherwise engage in work-related activity in exchange for benefits. To facilitate this process, the federal government introduced large-scale training and skills development programs to provide the tools people needed to find employment. Neoliberal governments touted these active programs as a way to foster self-sufficiency; reinforce the intrinsic values of work, discipline, and productivity; and help people gain the confidence and skills they needed to successfully compete in the workforce. According to neoliberal attitudes, any job—regardless of pay or conditions—was better than government assistance, and had far more potential for lifting people out of poverty (SRDC, 2005).

Those with more social democratic leanings call attention to the detriments of active programming. Some observers see the shift to active participation as a reflection of society's residual attitudes that consider able-bodied people to be "undeserving" of government assistance (Brodie, 1994). Other critics recognize that, although active programs may move adults off public programs into jobs, many of those jobs are only part-time and/or pay poverty wages. Thus, the transition from income security programs to employment may serve to increase the working poor population—a situation that benefits neither poor working families nor society (Williams, 2006).

Social Investment Through Asset-Based Policies

During the 1990s, the emergence of new economic and social theories pointed to the role of assets in individual and social well-being. In a social welfare context, assets refer to resources, advantages, and capacities that enable people to achieve financial security and independence (Policy Research Initiative, 2003). There are various types of assets, including (with examples)

- human capital (employment; education);
- social capital (social networks; business connections);
- physical capital (a car; house; furniture); and
- financial capital (savings; a retirement pension) (Robson, 2006).

Assets are critical to the achievement of self-sufficiency. Financial assets, for instance, can enable people to start a business, or buy a home; they can also provide a "cushion" to soften the blow of job loss or other interruption of income, and ultimately give a person a sense of control over his or her life and future (Jackson, 2004). "Softer" assets, such as social capital, can strengthen a person's connections in a community, as well as boost self-esteem, self-confidence, and resilience to change (Williams, 2006).

Not surprisingly, low-income earners tend to be limited in their ability to build financial and physical capital, because the accumulation of those assets requires a certain level of pre-tax income. Some social welfare policies, such as social assistance, actually discourage people from accumulating savings (Policy Research Initiative, 2003). The result is that low-income people often live hand to mouth, with few reserves for emergencies that arise and little prospect of ever improving their economic situation. To reverse this process, the Government of Canada has been experimenting with **asset-based social**

policies as a possible solution to persistent low-income. Some of those experiments involve **individual development accounts** (IDAs). Individuals who participate in an IDA program save whatever they can from their earnings; in turn, the government matches that amount. Thus, government and low-income earners work together to help individuals build assets, which the participant can one day draw from to, for instance, attend college or buy a home (Seguin, 2009). The Canada Learning Bond and projects under *learn*$ave are examples of IDAs designed to enable low-income Canadians to increase their human capital through postsecondary education.

In addition to promoting self-sufficiency, asset-based policies encourage habits of saving, and try to help people gain an understanding of finances. However, not all individuals or families have an interest in or the ability to save. It may also be too much to ask of people living in poverty—who may be dealing with poverty-related conditions, such as poor health, low self-esteem, and stressful living conditions—to also concentrate on saving enough money for future reference (Canadian Centre for Community Renewal, 2003). Asset-based policies are therefore considered by Canadian governments as one of the many options to help people improve their financial security and quality of life.

Ideally, a mix of benefits—such as income security programs, labour programs, tax relief, asset-building initiatives, housing supports, and childcare—should be available to meet the diverse needs of low-income Canadians (Queen's International Institute on Social Policy, 2007). Some of the more traditional benefits available to vulnerable or high-risk populations are offered through Employment Insurance, social assistance, child benefits, housing programs, and food programs. These programs are briefly reviewed below.

Employment Insurance

Between the time it was enacted in 1940 and the mid-1970s, Canada's Unemployment Insurance (UI) program was considered a cornerstone of the social welfare system. However, by the mid-1970s, questions about the cost of the UI system versus its effectiveness led to a series of amendments. Finally, in 1996, the UI Act was replaced by the Employment Insurance (EI) Act (the name change was intended to emphasize employment and de-emphasize unemployment). The new EI Act narrowed the eligibility criteria for benefits, reduced the benefit rates, and shortened the period one could draw benefits. Many workers, especially those in part-time or non-standard jobs, were suddenly disqualified from EI benefits. By 2007, only 40 percent of all Canadian workers were eligible for EI benefits, compared to 57 percent in 1993 (Campaign 2000, 2007).

As well as changing eligibility criteria, EI adopted an active approach to income-security. EI requires most people receiving benefits to demonstrate that they are actively participating in efforts to improve their employment prospects. Among the more recent activation strategies are Community Employment Innovation Projects (CEIPs). CEIPs are usually found in communities that have high levels of chronic unemployment. In exchange for their EI benefits, unemployed locals are paid to participate on community projects that offer long periods of employment and give workers a chance to gain work experience, expand their job contacts, and build new skills (Gyarmati, Raaf, Palameta, Nicholson, & Hui, 2008).

Beginning in 1996, the federal and provincial/territorial governments entered into a variety of labour market agreements to give the individual regions more control over their employment development programs. In general, the agreements enable each province and territory to develop their local and regional labour markets, remove barriers to employment, make training more accessible, and create job opportunities for unemployed workers. Certain types of agreements—the Labour Market Development Agreements (LMDAs)—is funded by the Employment Insurance account. In addition to EI insurance benefits, the LMDAs provide two broad types of resources:

- Employment Benefits aim to help individuals find and keep jobs, and include targeted wage subsidies, skills development, work experience, and self-employment assistance; and

- Support Measures provide financial assistance to organizations and businesses to offer employment services (such as employment counselling); to communities to help them adjust to labour market restructuring; and to research groups to engage in innovation projects aimed at improving employment.

Evaluations conducted on employment benefits and support measures show mixed results, depending on whether participants were active or former recipients of EI insurance benefits. For example, in 2008, skills development appeared to be the most effective strategy for increasing earnings for active EI claimants. However, for former EI claimants, targeted wage subsidies proved to be most effective for increasing employment and earnings (HRSDC, 2009d).

Social Assistance

Social assistance or "welfare" has always been considered the income program of last resort because it is reserved for people who are unemployed, have no savings, have exhausted all other avenues of support, and can prove they are in need. With the introduction of the Canada Assistance Plan in 1966, the provinces and territories were able to expand their respective welfare systems, and create more sophisticated systems of eligibility, benefit rates, appeal procedures, and monitoring. What evolved were 13 different social assistance programs across Canada, with names such as Ontario Works, BC Employment and Assistance, and Nova Scotia's Employment Support and Income Assistance Program.

During the deficit-fighting years of the 1990s, most regional governments made sweeping changes to their social assistance programs, including a drastic reduction in welfare incomes. By 2005, welfare incomes had fallen below 1986 levels, and most of those incomes were well below the low-income cut-offs (NCW, 2006c). The provinces and territories claim that lower welfare benefits can be an incentive to motivate able-bodied welfare recipients to choose work over welfare. Policy expert Sid Frankel (2005, p. 3) disagrees: he believes that lowering welfare benefits to encourage work "may actually hamper transition from welfare to work through forcing recipients to focus on the privations of daily life, eroding their confidence and dissipating (or at least not building) an asset base which is helpful in obtaining and maintaining labour market attachment." The impact of lower welfare incomes continues to be felt at many different levels, including the need for more homeless shelters and food banks.

In addition to slashing welfare incomes in the 1990s, most provinces and territories created welfare-to-work (or "workfare") programs to "activate" their welfare clients. A central component to **welfare-to-work programs** are action plans, which identify what clients have to do in exchange for benefits. Some clients, for example, are required to participate in training programs, while others have to follow a specific job search strategy. Failure to follow through on an action plan can result in a reduction, suspension, or termination of welfare benefits.

Since the mid-1990s, the number of people on welfare has been falling steadily. According to the National Council of Welfare (NCW, 2006d), the number of people on welfare (excluding First Nations) fell from over 3 million to 1.6 million. Those in support of welfare-to-work programs accredit the falling numbers on welfare to the success of those programs, claiming that people have left welfare for work. In 2000, the National Welfare to Work Study found that welfare-to-work programs had done little more than shift people from welfare into the growing ranks of the working poor and, in so doing, draw a discrete veil over the problem of poverty (HRDC, 2000). In their study of welfare-leavers across Canada, Frenette and Picot (2003) found that within a year of getting off welfare, more than one-third had returned; within five years, one-half had returned.

In recent years, some provinces/territories have rejected the punitive and coercive approaches associated with welfare-to-work programs, and have adopted the use of incentives to motivate welfare recipients to find work. Some regions encourage recipients to work by subsidizing work-related expenses, such as childcare. In other regions, where wages are lower than welfare benefits recipients may receive a combination of wages and a top-up of benefits. One of the most generous incentive programs is in Quebec, where a bonus ranging from $500 to $2,900 is paid to welfare recipients who get a job (Quebec wants, 2008).

Child Benefits

Child benefits reflect the general belief that families with children face heavier financial burdens than single people or childless couples with similar incomes. A number of child benefit schemes in Canada have been introduced, revised, and scrapped over the years. The current scheme is the National Child Benefit (NCB), introduced in 1998. All provinces and territories participate in the NCB except Quebec, which has chosen to develop its own family and child support programs.

One of the primary goals of the NCB is to prevent and reduce the depth of child poverty in Canada. The NCB works toward this goal by providing support to families with children through two federally administered programs:

- *Canada Child Tax Benefit (CCTB)*. This is an income-tested monthly payment available to low- and middle-income families with children under 18; about 82 percent of Canadian families with children receive this benefit.

- *National Child Benefit Supplement*. This is used to top up the monthly CCTB payments for Canada's lowest-income families with children; about 40 percent of Canadian families with children receive the supplement (Federal-Provincial-Territorial Ministers Responsible for Social Services, 2008).

Another function of the NCB is to lower the **welfare wall** for families on social assistance. This "wall" refers to factors that make staying on welfare more financially attractive than employment. Many families find that when they leave welfare for a job (especially a job that does not come with benefits), they lose access to many subsidized welfare services, as well as medical, dental, and prescription drug benefits. At the same time, employment brings work-related expenses such as transportation, work clothes, childcare, and income taxes. Thus, some families are financially worse off employed than they are on welfare. Through the NCB, families can receive the child benefits, as well as many welfare benefits and services even after the parents leave social assistance for paid employment (Government of Canada, 2006c). It is hoped that, by making it easier for parents to support their children while working, the NCB will help to strengthen parents' attachment to the workforce (Jenson, 2003).

Evaluation reports indicate that the NCB makes a positive difference in the economic lives of low-income families with children, and that without the NCB as many as 12 percent of families would have slipped into poverty (Federal-Provincial-Territorial Ministers Responsible for Social Services, 2008). Despite some progress, the NCB has not been found to reduce child poverty to any real extent. Indeed, child poverty rates in 2008 were not much lower than those in 1989, when the House of Commons pledged to eliminate child poverty by the year 2000 (Campaign 2000, 2008).

Housing Programs

While Canada has been cutting back its **government-assisted housing programs** over the years, help with shelter is still available for low- and moderate-income Canadians. That help includes

- public housing (government-owned rental units that are rented for a proportion of the tenant's income);
- nonprofit housing (rental units that are owned and operated by non-profit housing corporations);
- shelter allowances (financial assistance that pays a portion of the rent for people on welfare);
- rent supplements (financial assistance that pays a portion of the rent in a public, nonprofit housing, or private-sector unit); and
- portable housing allowances (financial assistance that enables tenants to remain where they are or to move to another rental unit) (Canadian Federation of Apartment Associations, 2006).

In addition to the above measures is the Affordable Housing Program (AHP), which began in 2001 as a national, cost-shared housing initiative between the federal and regional governments. Under the AHP, financial assistance is available for building new low-cost housing units, and for low-income homeowners, landlords, and rooming house owners to bring existing dwellings up to acceptable living standards.

Canada has sponsored two national initiatives aimed at reducing homelessness. The National Homelessness Initiative (NHI) was launched in 1999 to build and renovate emergency shelters for homeless people and to create a range of services, such as street outreach, meal programs, and food banks to assist homeless people. In 2007, the NHI was replaced by the Homelessness Partnering Strategy (HPS). The main objective of the HPS is to move homeless people out of emergency shelters into transitional or permanent housing, which is seen as a first step to self-sufficiency. The HPS also offers homeless people a continuum of services provided by health, social welfare, mental health, and other systems.

The Government of Canada is providing almost $270 million over two years to the HPS, to support projects that aim to prevent or reduce homelessness. Housing advocates generally agree that the federal government's contribution is grossly inadequate to meet the housing needs of low-income Canadians. Emergency shelters, in particular, are a poor substitute for proper housing. Although government-assisted housing programs exist across Canada, there are not enough to meet the demand. In 2006 in British Columbia, for example, approximately 11,000 people were on the waiting list for subsidized housing (Laird, 2007).

Food Programs

Over time, Canadian governments have assumed a greater role in ensuring food security. In 1998, the Government of Canada introduced the National Action Plan for Food Security to improve the diets of high-risk populations (such as low-income pregnant women), and to provide healthy meals to vulnerable groups (such as school-age children and elderly people). Health divisions in most regional governments support initiatives aimed at improving access to local nutritious food, enhancing community capacity to address food security issues, and generally creating food systems that are reliable and sustainable (VIHA, 2009). At the municipal level, some governments have adopted food charters to support community economic development, agricultural land use, and emergency food distribution (City of Vancouver, 2007).

Despite government efforts, health educator Lynn McIntyre (2003, p. 47) sees Canada's response to food insecurity as being largely ad hoc, with a primarily local rather than national scope. According to McIntyre, food security initiatives in Canada have focused mainly on

- providing free or subsidized food (for example, school-based meal programs, food banks, and soup kitchens);
- improving food preparation and grocery shopping skills (for example, community kitchens and targeted nutrition education programs); and
- promoting alternative methods of obtaining food (for example, farmers' markets, community gardens, and food box programs).

EXHIBIT 9.7

An unacceptable number of visitors to Canada's food banks are children.

Source: © Noel Chenier.

Many food programs, such as food banks and community kitchens, continue to rely heavily on the generosity of the general public to donate food, and on volunteers to manage and distribute food to those in need. These approaches are generally viewed as inadequate for addressing the growing problem of food insecurity in Canada. Food banks, for example, are not reliable sources of food, simply because they rarely have enough food to meet the demand, and food donations tend to be inconsistent.

POVERTY REDUCTION PLANS

The term *poverty reduction* refers to a process by which not only the symptoms, but also the root causes of poverty are addressed (Tamarack Institute for Community Engagement, 2009). Unlike many European countries (such as the United Kingdom and Ireland), Canada has no comprehensive national poverty reduction plan. There is nevertheless progress being made at the provincial level. In 2002, Quebec became the first province to introduce a poverty reduction plan, and it is the only province that enforces its plan through legislation. Since Quebec took the lead, Newfoundland and Labrador (see Exhibit 9.8), Nova Scotia, Ontario, Manitoba, New Brunswick, and British Columbia have either put poverty reduction strategies in place, or are in the process of doing so. Although the details of each poverty-reduction plan are unique, all the provincial plans share common elements. For example, each plan makes poverty a government responsibility and its eradication a focal point of economic development. These plans also provide a balance between helping employable people find jobs and ensuring that those who cannot work, or have specific needs, receive adequate financial assistance and other supports. Another important aspect of the provincial plans is their focus on improving access to a wide range of supports, including childcare services, health care, affordable housing, income security, education and training, and jobs that pay a living wage. Finally, all the current plans are established for the long term, are supported by ongoing human and financial resources, and have built-in mechanisms to measure progress, report to the public, and coordinate efforts among partners (Collin, 2007).

For several years, the National Council of Welfare and other anti-poverty advocates have been calling upon the Government of Canada to develop and implement a national poverty reduction strategy. Reports from federally appointed committees—the House of Commons Standing Committee on Finance in 2006 and the Standing Senate Committee on Human Rights in 2007—emphasize the role the federal government might play in the fight against poverty, especially among children. During 2007 and 2008, the federal government appointed three more committees to study various aspects of poverty and homelessness. Each committee is expected to produce reports that outline their research findings and recommendations for how the Government of Canada might address poverty and its related problems. Those recommendations will be of particular importance in the context of a global economic recession, which began in 2008.

In the meantime, the federal government participates in a wide range of projects aimed at reducing poverty in Canada. Many of those projects fit under the broad umbrella of **comprehensive community initiatives** (CCIs). Vibrant Communities is a type of CCI that adapts a variety of poverty-reduction strategies to the specific needs of communities. To reduce poverty in communities, projects under the Vibrant Communities initiative focus on the building of local economic and social assets; partnerships among government and nongovernment groups is an important aspect of these projects, as is the sharing of best practices across communities (Tamarack Institute for Community Engagement, 2007).

EXHIBIT 9.8

NEWFOUNDLAND AND LABRADOR'S POVERTY REDUCTION STRATEGY

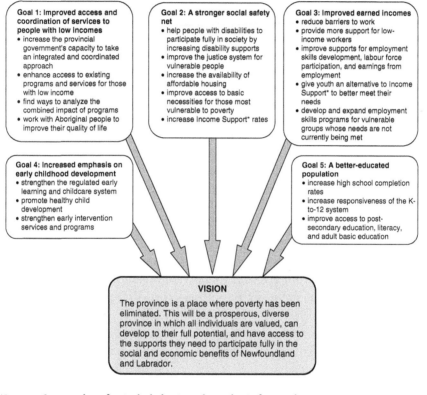

Newfoundland and Labrador's Poverty Reduction Strategy aims to prevent, reduce, and alleviate poverty. The Strategy's goals and objectives for the 2006–2010 period are as follows:

Goal 1: Improved access and coordination of services to people with low incomes
- increase the provincial government's capacity to take an integrated and coordinated approach
- enhance access to existing programs and services for those with low income
- find ways to analyze the combined impact of programs
- work with Aboriginal people to improve their quality of life

Goal 2: A stronger social safety net
- help people with disabilities to participate fully in society by increasing disability supports
- improve the justice system for vulnerable people
- increase the availability of affordable housing
- improve access to basic necessities for those most vulnerable to poverty
- increase Income Support* rates

Goal 3: Improved earned incomes
- reduce barriers to work
- provide more support for low-income workers
- improve supports for employment skills development, labour force participation, and earnings from employment
- give youth an alternative to Income Support* to better meet their needs
- develop and expand employment skills programs for vulnerable groups whose needs are not currently being met

Goal 4: Increased emphasis on early childhood development
- strengthen the regulated early learning and childcare system
- promote healthy child development
- strengthen early intervention services and programs

Goal 5: A better-educated population
- increase high school completion rates
- increase responsiveness of the K-to-12 system
- improve access to post-secondary education, literacy, and adult basic education

VISION

The province is a place where poverty has been eliminated. This will be a prosperous, diverse province in which all individuals are valued, can develop to their full potential, and have access to the supports they need to participate fully in the social and economic benefits of Newfoundland and Labrador.

*Income Support benefits include basic and non-basic financial supports.

- *Basic benefits* include family and individual benefit (to assist with expenses such as food, clothing, personal care, household maintenance and utilities); and shelter (including rent and mortgage).

- *Non-basic benefits* include municipal tax payments; eye exams and prescription glasses; medical transportation; private childcare (related to employment or training); and expenses for burials. The eligibility for non-basic benefits may vary according to personal circumstances.

Source: Adapted from Government of Newfoundland and Labrador. (2006). *Reducing Poverty: An Action Plan for Newfoundland and Labrador*. Retrieved October 27, 2008, from http://www.hrle. gov.nl.ca/hrle/poverty/poverty-reduction-strategy.pdf. Used by permission.

Discussion Questions

■ **Organized Approaches to Poverty and Unemployment**

1. What are some of the potential pros and cons of passive and active policies?

2. In your opinion, how realistic are asset-based social policies for low-income earners? Identify some of the possible advantages and disadvantages of asset-based policies and programs in the fight against poverty.

3. If you were a government policymaker, how would you go about lowering the "welfare wall" for families on social assistance? (Consider various incentives to encourage parents to choose work over welfare.)

IV WORKING WITH LOW-INCOME AND MARGINALIZED GROUPS

Traditionally, social workers have aimed to help people cope with the effects of poverty and improve their life circumstances. They have also rallied to many poverty-related causes and advocated on behalf of low-income individuals and groups. Social workers, more than any other professional group, have the training and education to help individuals become self-sufficient. Moreover, social workers assume a professional obligation to advocate for the most vulnerable members of society, and to urge governments to move poverty to the top of their political agendas (CASW & NASW, 2008).

One of the challenges in working with poor and disadvantaged groups is learning to appreciate the complexities of living in hardship. Poverty represents a lack of income, but it is also a condition characterized by social isolation, discrimination, poor housing, and limited access to recreation, transportation, and childcare. Jones and colleagues (2002, p. 3) suggest that some of these problems may be exacerbated by well-meaning social workers and other professionals; for example, welfare workers may feel pressured by their employer to move their clients into work or training and, in so doing, create "a complex juggling of work and domestic responsibilities for those with children." In turn, clients may experience stress, marital discord, and difficulties in parenting. Through careful observation and active listening and by maintaining a person-in-environment perspective, practitioners may help families identify, describe, and address the various pressures they feel.

Charles Zastrow (2008) points out that to leave welfare, one must be motivated to take the necessary steps to improve one's circumstances.

However, ongoing economic pressures and past failures to leave welfare may be discouraging and sap an individual's motivation to change. To help discouraged or unmotivated people, practitioners must be encouraging—that is, they must be accepting, sensitive, empathic, nonjudgmental, and genuinely interested in their clients. Workers also need to help their clients find creative ways to learn new skills, behaviours, and roles. Finally, workers should recognize and call attention to signs of progress and convey a sense of confidence in their clients' ability to succeed.

SUMMARY

Introduction

Canada has one of the most robust economies in the world, and yet many citizens do not share in the nation's wealth. Despite government spending to improve the financial security of citizens, low income remains a problem. Historically, policymakers have treated poverty as a low priority. In recent years, governments and others have been taking more aggressive steps to reducing poverty in Canada.

I. Poverty in Canada

Several definitions and measurements of poverty exist, but most relate poverty to a certain level of income. LICOs are erroneously considered Canada's "poverty lines." Populations that are at high risk of poverty include women, single adults, people with disabilities, recent immigrants, refugees, and Aboriginal people. Canada has many working poor families and unacceptable levels of child poverty. Barriers exist that prevent people from earning adequate income; these barriers include unemployment, underemployment, rising costs of living, low wages, and weak government policies.

II. The Impact of Poverty

Persistent poverty can impact people in various ways; the negative effects of poverty on children is a main concern. Inadequate housing and food, and poor health, are linked to poverty, and can impair a person's level of functioning in major life areas. Poverty may lead to the social exclusion of certain groups, and create economic and social problems for mainstream society. Moreover, poverty can cause individual and social problems; those problems may, in turn, contribute to more hardship. Social welfare and other systems often lack the resources to effectively address poverty. Canadians are spending a greater proportion of their income on shelter: housing is becoming more unaffordable, and growing numbers of Canadians are at risk of homelessness. Food insecurity is another potential consequence of poverty, as is evidenced by the emergence of food banks and other emergency food programs.

III. Organized Approaches to Poverty and Unemployment

Active policies require recipients of SA and EI to engage in work-related activities in exchange for benefits. There is much debate over the merits of active policies. Governments are experimenting with asset-based policies to help people achieve financial security. Ideally, a mix of benefits should be available to meet the diverse needs of low-income Canadians. Many targeted programs aim to improve the financial situation of vulnerable Canadians, including Employment Insurance, social assistance, the National Child Benefit, housing programs, and food programs. Unlike the federal government, some provinces have established poverty reduction plans. In response to urgings from anti-poverty advocates, the federal government has appointed several committees to study poverty and homelessness.

IV. Working with Low-Income and Marginalized Groups

Traditionally, social workers have focused on helping people cope with poverty conditions. To be effective, practitioners have to try to understand people's experiences of poverty and the complexities of living in hardship. Equally important is for professionals to understand the pressures people face when moving from income security programs to independence, and to encourage and support clients in their efforts to change.

Key Terms

For definitions of the key terms, consult the Glossary on page 413 at the end of the book.

poverty, p. 226
social exclusion, p. 227
LICO, p. 227
poverty rate, p. 229
depth of poverty, p. 229
working poor, p. 229
non-standard job,
 p. 229
feminization of poverty,
 p. 229
unemployment rate,
 p. 231
underemployed, p. 231

unaffordable housing,
 p. 236
absolute homelessness,
 p. 237
relative homelessness,
 p. 237
food insecurity, p. 238
passive policy, p. 239
active policy, p. 239
asset-based social policy,
 p. 240
individual development
 account, p. 241

social assistance,
 p. 242
welfare-to-work
 program, p. 243
welfare wall, p. 244
government-assisted
 housing program,
 p. 245
poverty reduction,
 p. 247
comprehensive
 community initiative,
 p. 248

CHAPTER 10

The Social Welfare of Children and Their Families

OBJECTIVES

The social welfare of children and their families is central to the well-being of society. This chapter will explore:

- the developmental needs of children and youth;
- the impact of family type on child and youth development;
- family violence (related to spousal abuse and child abuse); and
- working with families with children.

INTRODUCTION

> The true measure of a nation's standing is how well it attends to its children—their health and safety, their material security, their education and socialization, and their sense of being loved, valued, and included in the families and societies into which they are born. (UNICEF, 2007, p. 1)

In proclaiming 1994 the International Year of the Family (IYF), the United Nations was calling attention to the importance of the **family** in society. As sociologist Reginald Bibby (2005) points out, families are key to individual and social well-being, a primary source of support and stability, and the foundation of communities. Families are also the "basic social unit of production and consumption" and are therefore key to a country's economic development (United Nations, 1996). Families with children play a particularly important role by supplying the nation's future adults, workers, and parents. Katherine Scott (2008, p. 1) reminds us that "[w]hat happens to children affects us all. If our children do not thrive, our societies will not thrive."

Studies confirm that, in general, Canadian children are doing well: most are born healthy and live in caring families and supportive communities. However, many children are growing up in poverty and deprivation, live in abusive situations, or lack adequate adult supervision or positive role models—conditions that can put a child's physical, social, cognitive, and behavioural development at risk (Boys and Girls Clubs of Canada, 2008).

Parents are the primary caregivers, and are ultimately responsible for their children's well-being. Canadian governments nevertheless assume a collective responsibility for the welfare of children. The Government of Canada (2004a, p. 5) articulates its obligation to children: "The role of government and society with respect to children is to provide the legislative and policy framework, the institutional and organizational structures, the fiscal and other supports and services to enable families to ensure their children's healthy development. However, if families are unable to care for their children, then governments and society have a responsibility to provide support and ensure that they are cared for and protected." Government responsibility for young Canadians is reflected in public programs—such as universal health care, public education, and city recreation programs—that aim to help children grow up happy, healthy, and active. In addition to these mainstream programs, there are child protection services, family-support programs, early learning opportunities, and other social welfare initiatives for children and families needing extra support. Many of these programs are part of Canada's national action plan for children (see Exhibit 10.1 for that plan's main goals, related priorities, and national initiatives).

Despite Canada's official commitment to children, many child advocates argue that Canadian governments are not doing enough for families raising children. Part of the problem may be what Omidvar and Richmond (2003) see as an inconsistent approach to children's needs and issues: "Children have risen to the top of government agendas at various times over the past decade, only to fall again whenever there is an economic downturn, a budget deficit, a federal–provincial relations crisis or ... a concern over terrorism and national

EXHIBIT 10.1

A CANADA FIT FOR CHILDREN

Vision			
Children have the opportunity to be fully prepared to live a responsible life in a free society, in a spirit of understanding, peace, dignity, tolerance, equality, and solidarity.			
Goals			
To support families and strengthen communities	To promote healthy lives	To protect from harm	To promote education and learning
Priorities for Action			
1. Child- and family-friendly policies 2. Early learning and child care 3. Poverty 4. Separation and divorce 5. Social inclusion and diversity 6. Aboriginal children 7. Inclusion and support of children with disabilities 8. Poverty and sustainable development (international level)	1. Healthy, active living 2. Effective parenting 3. Mental health 4. Immunization 5. Physical environment and prevention of injuries 6. Sexual/reproductive health 7. Tobacco, alcohol, drug abuse, and addictions 8. Aboriginal children's health 9. Paediatric health care and research 10. Health services in official language minority communities	1. Child maltreatment 2. Out-of-home care and adoption 3. Violence, bullying, and other forms of intimidation 4. Youth justice 5. Violent and harmful content in the media 6. Immigrant, refugee, and asylum-seeking children 7. Sexual exploitation and trafficking	1. Quality learning 2. Arts and culture 3. Human rights education and global citizenship 4. Canadian culture and national identity 5. Environment learning and sustainability 6. Literacy 7. Trained and professional educators 8. Education for all children
National Initiatives to Meet Goals (examples)			
• Universal Child Care Benefit • Canada Child Tax Benefit • Employment Insurance (maternity and parental benefits) • Understanding the Early Years Initiative • Child-Centred Family Justice Strategy • Federal Strategy on Early Childhood Development for Aboriginal Children • Assisted Living Program (First Nations) • First Nations National Child Benefit Reinvestment Initiative	• Registered Disability Savings Plan • Mental Health Commission • Autism Spectrum Disorders Initiative • Prenatal healthcare services for Aboriginal people • Centres of Excellence for Children's Well-Being • Pan-Canadian Fetal Alcohol Spectrum Disorder Initiative • Canada's Physical Activity and Food Guides	• Support for multifaceted response to combat child sexual exploitation and human trafficking • Youth Justice initiatives • Laws and programs to address violence, bullying, and other forms of intimidation • Family Violence Initiative • Family Violence Prevention Program (First Nations) • National Clearinghouse on Family Violence	• Canada Education Savings Program • Family Literacy Initiative • New Paths Initiative (First Nations) • Teacher Recruitment and Retention Initiative • Special Education Program • Parental and Community Engagement Strategy • National Child Day (educational materials)

Source: Information from Government of Canada, "'Plus 5' Review of the 2002 Special Session on Children and World Fit for Children Plan of Action: Response by Canada" (Ottawa: 2007). Retrieved November 27, 2008, from UNICEF, www.unicef.org/worldfitforchildren/files/Canada_WFFC5_Report_Eng.pdf; Government of Canada, "A Canada Fit for Children: Canada's Plan of Action in Response to the May 2002 United Nations Special Session on Children" (Ottawa: April 2004). Retrieved November 27, 2008, from www.hrsdc.gc.ca/eng/cs/sp/sdc/socpol/publications/2002–002483/canadafite.pdf.

security." Quebec is the only jurisdiction in Canada—in fact, in all of North America—where a comprehensive **family policy** and related programs and services have been developed to meet the full range of needs of families with children. Nevertheless, other provinces and territories are making strides to improve their provision of support to children, youth, and families.

MEETING THE DEVELOPMENTAL NEEDS OF CHILDREN AND YOUTH

A FOCUS ON YOUNG CHILDREN

Over the next few decades, as baby boomers retire (and if birth rates remain low), Canada's workforce is expected to shrink; the effect will be a proportionately small workforce supporting a comparatively large group of dependants (mostly children and seniors). In the early 1990s, policymakers decided that the best way to offset this demographic shift was to increase the productivity of what would eventually be a much smaller workforce. Research confirms that the first five years of a child's life is critical to how well he or she does in school, copes with life's challenges, and wards off chronic disease in his or her adult years (Government of Canada, 1999a). Thus, to ensure that future workers are healthy, well-functioning, and productive, policymakers have shifted their attention to the needs of young children, and developed policies to ensure that children get a good start in life.

A National Children's Agenda

One of the earliest policy priorities of Canada's Social Union was to address the needs of children prenatal to age six who were living in or at risk for poverty. In 1999, the members of the Social Union launched the National Children's Agenda (NCA), a comprehensive and long-term plan that articulates a shared vision for children across the levels of government and First Nations communities. Initiatives under the NCA aim to enhance children's lives by improving physical and emotional health, personal safety and security, learning, and social engagement and responsibility.

Over the last decade, the NCA has generated a number of landmark research projects such as the National Longitudinal Survey of Children and Youth (which studies the influential factors on child development from birth to early adulthood) and the Understanding the Early Years initiative (which assesses the needs of young children and their families, and applies that knowledge to the development of community programs). The NCA has also supported the development of various health and social welfare programs, such as the National Child Benefit, the Early Childhood Development Initiative, and the Multilateral Framework on Early Learning and ChildCare. The National Child Benefit was discussed in Chapter 9; the other two programs are briefly described below.

- In 2000, the federal government launched the Early Childhood Development (ECD) Initiative to enable the provinces and territories to develop their own ECD programs. (The federal government struck a separate ECD arrangement with First Nations and other Aboriginal groups.) ECD programs aim to help children reach their full potential by ensuring that they are physically and emotionally healthy, safe, prepared for school, and socially engaged (HRSDC, 2007). Each region determines its own mix of early childhood development programs, in accordance with the region's identified needs and priorities. One group's vision of ECD programs in British Columbia is featured in Exhibit 10.2.

- In 2003, the federal and regional governments agreed on a Multilateral Framework on Early Learning and ChildCare (ELCC). Under this agreement, the federal government transferred funds to the provinces and territories to design, implement, and regulate ELCC programs in childcare centres, preschools, nursery schools, and other formal settings (Government of Canada, 2003a).

The Issue of Childcare

Studies have long confirmed the potential of quality **childcare** to enhance the physical, social, emotional, and cognitive development of young children; to prepare children for school and adulthood; and to enable parents, especially those with lower incomes, to go to work or school. Canadian families rely on various sources to meet their childcare needs, including private daycare centres and informal sources such as family and paid sitters. In Canada, most (79 percent) centre-based childcare services are private nonprofit operations; all centre-based services are required to meet provincial/territorial regulations (Childcare Resource and Research Unit, 2007). Despite government childcare initiatives, there are never enough childcare spaces to meet the demand. One study found that, in 2006, just over 19 percent of children aged five and under had access to regulated childcare (Ballantyne, 2008).

For several years, childcare advocates have been lobbied the federal government for a national childcare program, which would expand the number of regulated and affordable childcare spaces, and standardize the quality of service, teacher/staff training, wages, and program monitoring across the country (Childcare Resource and Research Unit, 2007). Although Canada came close to

EARLY CHILDHOOD DEVELOPMENT: A FRAMEWORK FOR ACTION

First Call BC Child and Youth Advocacy Coalition proposes a province-wide framework for action for early childhood development, "within which communities can determine, develop and deliver the ECD supports and services that are needed by their young children and families" (p. 8).

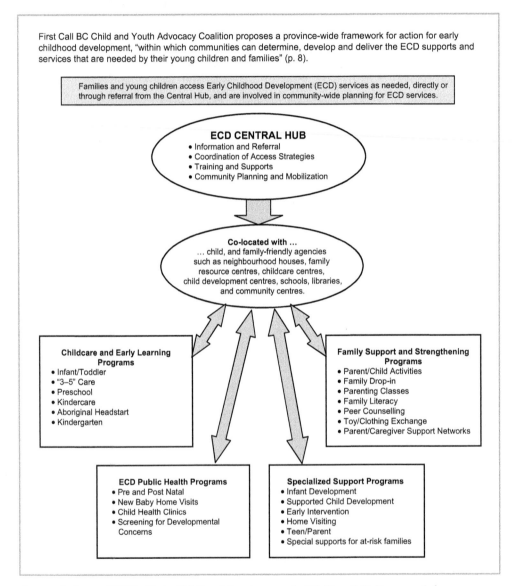

Source: P. Coates. (2008). "Early Childhood Development in BC: First Call's Framework for Action," (Appendix 1, p. 18). Retrieved November 22, 2008, from First Call: BC Child and Youth Advocacy Coalition, http://www.firstcallbc.org/pdfs/EarlyChildhood/ 1-framework%202008.pdf. Used by permission.

establishing a national childcare program under Prime Minister Paul Martin, that idea was quashed when the Conservative Party came to power in 2006. The new federal government promptly cancelled the ELCC agreements it had with nine provinces. After experimenting with various childcare policies, the federal government's role in childcare is currently limited to providing the Universal ChildCare Benefit (UCCB) to every child under six and funding childcare programs for Aboriginal peoples, military families, and other federal "client" groups. The regional governments are primarily responsible for developing and implementing their own childcare programs, with limited financial support from Ottawa through the Canada Social Transfer.

Most reports suggest that Canada is in the midst of a "childcare crisis." A poll conducted by Environics Research Group (2008) found that 77 percent of Canadians believe that the lack of affordable childcare is a serious problem in Canada. Another poll found that Canadians generally support a national childcare system that would provide quality and affordable childcare to all families (Environics Research Group, 2006), and that a national system is preferred to monthly UCCB cheques (see Exhibit 10.3). A UNICEF study compared the childcare services in 25 developed countries, and ranked Canada last not only for failing to properly address its childcare needs, but for neglecting to establish a national plan that would give priority to disadvantaged children (Canada tied, 2008).

THE NEEDS OF OLDER CHILDREN AND YOUTH

Mental Health

The needs of young children currently dominate family policy agendas, yet many older children also need support. Children in middle childhood (age six to twelve) face challenges related to entering the school system, choosing friends, and taking greater risks (Hanvey, 2002). As children enter adolescence (age thirteen to eighteen), they must deal with issues relating to rapid growth and development while learning the life skills they will need as adults. Today's youth must also make decisions about drug and alcohol use, sexual relations, and other activities that have implications for their health and welfare and may have long-term consequences.

The way young people meet the challenges of growing up is influenced by their state of mental health. **Mental health** is defined by the Public Health Agency of Canada (2002) as a person's capacity to think, feel, and behave in ways that enhance the quality and enjoyment of life, and having the skills to effectively deal with life's challenges. A person's self-esteem, coping skills, choice of friends, and general well-being are common indicators of mental health.

EXHIBIT 10.3

MOST CANADIANS PREFER CHILDCARE SERVICES
TO CHEQUES: POLL

A poll reveals Canadians prefer a national child care system to the Harper government's $100 monthly cheque by a ratio of 2 to 1.

The Harper government established its "Universal ChildCare Benefit" when they cancelled the Liberal's plans for a national early childhood education and childcare program.

Almost twice as many Canadians said that setting up the national early childhood education and childcare program is preferable (58%) to a monthly allowance of $100.00 (31%).

"The demand for a system of childcare services has not subsided but in fact has significantly increased since 2006," said Paul Moist.

Support is particularly high in the Atlantic with 63% in favour of a national child-care system and 30% preferring the $100 monthly allowance. The results are comparable in Quebec—64% to 31%, and Ontario 62% to 27%.

"Centres are closing and staff shortages are rampant. If families are lucky enough to find a childcare space, fees are between $600 and $1,500/month," added Martha Friendly, a Toronto-based policy researcher who has been tracking Canadian childcare for 30 years.

According to a 2006 OECD report, Canada had the lowest public investment and service access rates, and among the highest parent fees.

Nanos Research conducted a random telephone survey of 1,201 Canadians from October 4 to October 6, 2008. The margin of accuracy for a sample of 1,201 is +/− 2.8%, 19 times out of 20.

Source: Canadian Union of Public Employees (CUPE). (2008, October 9). "Most Prefer Child Care to Cheques: Poll". Retrieved November 23, 2008, from http://cupe.ca/child-care/Canadians-prefer-chi. Used by permission.

It is not always clear when a young person is experiencing a **mental health problem**, since many "strange" behaviours may be attributed to normal hormonal changes in puberty, "self-expression," or healthy rebelliousness. There are nevertheless signs that a mental health problem may exist, including unexplained fears, declining school performance, and involvement in alcohol and drug abuse, violence, sexual acting-out, or other high-risk behaviour (U of C Faculty of Social Work, 2007). The cause of mental health problems may be located in either a person's biology or environment or in both. Biological sources of mental health disorders include chemical imbalances and head injuries; environmental causes may be anything from being bullied at school, to witnessing violence in the home, to feeling pressured to get good grades. Like most human conditions, mental health problems occur along a continuum, ranging from mild (for example, feeling "stressed out") to serious (for example, feeling suicidal).

The prevalence of mental health problems among young Canadians is unknown. Ontario, however, estimates that, in that province, one out of five young people suffer from a serious mental health problem (Offord Centre for Child Studies, 2008). Studies suggest that disorders such as depression and anxiety are becoming more common among children and youth. A particularly disturbing trend is Canada's rising youth suicide rate, which is about three times higher than that of the general population (Leitch, 2007) and the third-highest in the world (Wilkerson & Guscott, 2005).

If left untreated, mental health problems may affect a young person's ability to succeed in school, make friends, and problem-solve; later, as an adult, the individual may experience difficulties working, earning a living, and forming meaningful relationships. Mental health problems not only take a personal toll, but also can mean a loss for society in terms of social participation and economic productivity (Offord Centre for Child Studies, 2006).

A wide range of nonresidential programs are available in Canada to assess and treat mental health problems in young people. Among those programs are

- assessment services, to diagnose developmental disorders or delays, learning disabilities, attention deficit disorders, and other functional difficulties;

- individual and family counselling, to address grief and loss, anxiety, depression, eating disorders, and other issues;

- support and educational groups, to enable children or teens to meet, share experiences, and learn about such topics as anger management, self-esteem, and parental divorce or separation;

- creative therapy, to help young people deal with sexual abuse or other traumatic experiences through art, play, dance, or other expression; and

- crisis intervention, to respond to children and youth in distress or emergency situations.

There are also residential programs for children and youth who are experiencing more severe emotional, social, and/or behavioural problems. One such program is the Woodlands Residential Treatment Program in Waterloo, Ontario; this centre provides a wide range of services for twelve-to-sixteen-year-olds, including emotional management, life skills training, and peer relationship building (Lutherwood, 2009).

A Focus on Youth: A Growing Priority

A globalized world has not only created new opportunities for youth, but has also increased the pressure on youth to prepare for a competitive and rapidly changing labour market. This new reality has prompted governments to rethink their perspectives on youth, and to develop policies and programs—often with input from youth—to give this population adequate support, guidance, and opportunities (Hay, 2008). The content and scope of youth-oriented policies vary considerably across Canada, but most can be grouped according to three broad categories:

- *Population-based youth policies* identify specific, desired outcomes for youth (for example, it is desirable that youth be "employable" or "healthy").

- *Targeted policies for youth subgroups* focus either on a single facet of youth development such as socialization, or on the needs of a specific subpopulation of youth such as those living in disadvantaged circumstances.

- *Targeted policies for individual youth* address personal issues within a therapeutic setting, such as a counselling centre (Jeffrey, 2008).

Each type of youth policy is based on a particular set of theoretical perspectives about youth, their needs, and how those needs might best be met. Many youth policies maintain that youth benefit most from recognizing and building on their strengths, skills, or assets, rather than dwelling on their shortcomings; other youth policies emphasize the development of **resilence** so that youth are better able to manage or cope with change, adversity, or stress (Jeffrey, 2008). A number of youth policies and programs in Canada take a **youth engagement approach**, which asserts that youth benefit from participating in meaningful activities, having a voice in matters that affect them, and sharing power with adults. This type of approach is often used to reduce the marginalization of youth (such as visible minority groups from poor neighbourhoods), or to minimize risk-taking behaviours (such as drug use or criminal activity). According to the Centre of Excellence for Youth Engagement (2007), "[t]hrough engagement, youth gain a sense of **empowerment** as individuals and make healthy connections with others, which is associated with reduction of risk behaviours and increased participation in positive activities." There are many youth engagement programs across Canada, and each one offers its own mix of opportunities. One example is HeartWood (2009)—a centre for community youth development in Nova Scotia—where youth may participate in wilderness adventures, learn leadership skills, and provide peer support, mentoring, and community service.

EXHIBIT 10.4

Engaging in wilderness adventures can help youth learn new skills, interact positively with others, and gain a sense of empowerment.

Source: © Lespalenik/Dreamstime.com.

PARENT SUPPORT PROGRAMS

Although a child's development may be hindered by risk factors such as poverty, research suggests that parenting is a more powerful influence than risk factors on a child's development (Statistics Canada, 1997). All parents experience difficulties from time to time when supervising, instructing, or disciplining children. However, more severe parenting problems, such as over-controlling behaviour, harsh discipline, and a lack of responsiveness or warmth, can lead to the development of childhood disorders (Government of Canada, 2006d). According to Stevenson (1999, pp. 3–4), children who exhibit conduct disorders are 36 times more likely to have parents who use "ineffective, aversive, inconsistent or negative disciplining most of the time." Research has also found that "non-positive parenting can lead to signs of vulnerability such as poorer school outcomes"

(Government of Canada, 2003b, p. 24). Contrary to popular belief, non-positive parenting is not confined to poor families. One study found that, while 37 percent of Canadian children who show signs of vulnerability live in the poorest families, over 24 percent are from the nation's wealthiest families (Willms, 2007).

A variety of parent support programs exist across Canada to help parents learn the skills, obtain the information, and access the resources they need to raise happy and healthy children. Among those programs is Health Canada's Nobody's Perfect Parenting Program; offered nationwide since 1987, this program provides education and support to parents of preschool children. Another parenting program, COPE (Community Parent Education Program), teaches parents a variety of techniques to respond to children who have challenging behaviours. Many parent-support programs are the creation of community or grassroots (nongovernment) efforts. British Columbia's Parents Together, for example, is a self-help group that was established by parents for parents experiencing conflict with their teens.

Discussion Questions

Meeting the Developmental Needs of Children and Youth

1. This section identified some of the economic reasons why early childhood development is a priority for government policy. What are some other reasons why resources should be directed to very young children?

2. Based on your observations or experience, what are some of the pressures on parents today that make it tough to raise healthy children?

THE IMPACT OF FAMILY TYPE ON CHILD AND YOUTH DEVELOPMENT

There is no ideal family type—each family has its own strengths and weaknesses, and offers different opportunities and challenges to its members. In recent years, family type has been the subject of research studies in Canada and other countries. Many of those studies have compared the well-being and development of children living in various types of families (Ross, Roberts, & Scott, 1998). This section briefly explores three family types and their influences on the well-being of children and youth: lone-parent families, blended families, and divorced families.

LONE-PARENT FAMILIES

Increases in marital separation and out-of-union births are driving up the proportion of families that are headed by a lone parent. In 2006, almost 16 percent of families (one out of four families with children) were **lone-parent families** (HRSDC, 2009b). Over two million Canadian children now live in families with one parent (Bonnell, 2007). Although most lone-parent families are headed by women, the rate of families headed by a lone father is on the rise. Between 2001 and 2006, the proportion of lone-father families increased almost 15 percent, an increase attributed to divorce-court decisions to grant the custody of children to fathers (Milan, Vézina, & Wells, 2007).

The family's income level is a main determinant of a child's experience in a lone-parent family. In general, lone-parent families are more likely than two-parent families to live in poverty, especially if headed by a woman (Ambert, 2006). In 2005, the median annual household income for lone-parent families in Canada was $30,000, compared to almost $68,000 for two-parent families (Bonnell, 2007). Among lone-parent families, young mothers are especially vulnerable to economic challenges. These women often lack education, job skills, work experience, affordable childcare, and child support; as a consequence, it may be difficult for them to keep themselves and their families out of poverty (Milan, 2000). The negative consequences of poverty on children are wide ranging, and include developmental delays and problems in school.

Even if poverty is not an issue, children living in lone-parent families are at a higher risk of behavioural and academic problems than their peers in two-parent families. Children of lone parents, for example, are more likely to be aggressive and/or hyperactive, to fail grades, or to drop out of high school. When older, individuals from lone-parent families are more likely to become a teen parent, achieve less education, be unemployed, have a criminal record, and experience marital problems (Ambert, 2006).

An abundance of research emphasizes the deficits rather than the assets of lone-parent families. Canadian research nevertheless concludes that "while lone-parent children are at higher risk for certain poor developmental outcomes compared to other children, the clear majority grow up healthy" (Ross, Roberts, & Scott, 1998). The differences in child outcomes in lone- and two-parent families may be a function not so much of family type as of a cluster of factors—such as low income, depression, and lack of social support—that are commonly experienced by lone (mostly female) parents (HRDC, 1999a). Child and family experts also remind us that raising a child is simply a greater challenge for one parent than two. Two parents are able to share the supervision, instruction, and disciplining of a child; in turn, a child with two parents has a better chance of receiving emotional support when needed and spending time with a parent. Moreover, two parents have the potential for two incomes, and a pooling of resources, which lessens the chance of poverty (Ambert, 2006).

The rising number of lone-parent families is creating a demand for specialized services. For example, the Single Parent Association of Newfoundland (SPAN, 2009) operates a one-parent resource centre where lone parents can obtain information and referrals specific to lone-parenthood, as well as access crisis intervention services, food, and clothing. This organization also receives government grants to help lone parents on welfare gain financial independence through part-time employment programs.

BLENDED FAMILIES

Since the 1970s, rising divorce rates have increased the number of people available to remarry (Milan, 2000). It is not uncommon for one or both partners to bring a child from a previous union into the new family—a situation that creates a stepfamily or **blended family**. This type of family may consist of only the mother's children (the most common), or only the father's children. In most (80 percent) blended families, the couple has at least one child together (HRSDC, 2009b). Blended families represent under 12 percent of Canadian couples with children (Juby, 2003); however, statistics suggest that this family type will soon outnumber the traditional nuclear family (Ontario Stepfamily Association, 2009).

Life in a blended family can be challenging in a variety of ways. The beginning stages of forming a stepfamily can be particularly stressful, especially if both partners have one or more children from a previous union. One challenge for couples may be trying to simultaneously bond with each other and one or more stepchildren. Stepfamily life may also be complicated by unresolved conflicts between the divorced parents and their former partners, or when the children move back and forth between parental households. For many blended families, the greatest challenge is dealing with the conflicts that arise between its members—for instance, between two stepsiblings, or between a stepparent and stepchild. It is not uncommon for marital problems to stem from conflict with a stepchild, or from disagreement on parenting styles in dealing with that conflict (Preece, 2003).

Most parents and their children are able to bond early in the child's life. In stepfamilies, this early childhood bonding experience is usually lacking, which may partially explain why stepparent–stepchild relationships tend to be vulnerable to stress within the family (Preece, 2003). The conflict is not

EXHIBIT 10.5

Since the 1970s, higher rates of divorce and remarriage have made "blended" families a more common family type in Canada.

Source: Andi Berger/Shutterstock.

restricted to just stepparent–stepchild relationships. One study found that 44 percent of ten- and eleven-year-old children in blended families had trouble getting along with their natural parent (Milan, 2000).

In response to the unique situation of blended families, a number of social agencies offer information and support that is specific to stepfamily issues and needs. Booklets such as *The Art of Living Better in a Recombined Family* (from the Quebec government) and *Building Your Stepfamily: A Blueprint for Success* (from the BC Council for Families) offer a number of tips and insights into how to make stepfamilies work. A growing source of information for stepfamilies is the Internet. The Ontario Stepfamily Association's website, for instance, offers suggestions and advice for stepparents, stepchildren, and the extended stepfamily. A number of voluntary agencies across Canada provide services specifically for blended families. Among these agencies is the Stepfamily Foundation of Alberta, which offers peer support, support groups, courses, and referrals to legal, mediation, and other stepfamily-oriented community services.

DIVORCED FAMILIES

With more relaxed divorce laws and social attitudes toward divorce, divorce has become an acceptable option for people in unhappy marriages. Between 2001 and 2005, two million Canadians ended a marriage or common-law relationship (Statistics Canada, 2007a). Most couples who break up do so because of conflicting values and interests, physical or emotional abuse, substance abuse, infidelity, and/or career-related differences (Bibby, 2005).

Nearly half of all divorces in Canada involve dependent children (Statistics Canada, 2005). In the Future Families Project, Reginald Bibby (2005) found that, although couples believed they made the right decision to divorce, most acknowledged that the divorce was hard on their children. It is normal for children whose parents are divorcing to "feel vulnerable and alone, depressed and highly stressed" (Calgary Counselling Centre, 2004). Children from divorced families also tend to show higher levels of antisocial behaviour—such as aggression and criminal behaviour—than children from intact families (Statistics Canada, 2005).

Research studies have found that parental conflict related to a relationship breakdown is potentially more harmful to children than the actual separation. In many cases, the negative effects on children can be reduced if conflict between partners is kept to a minimum, if there is good communication between the parents and the children, and if parents make the effort to ensure that the child's relationship with both parents is close and secure (Horner, 2002).

Since the 1970s, programs have emerged to help children and their parents cope with the challenges of separation and divorce. Most of these programs tend to fit within one or more of the following categories:

- *Child-focused programs* are typically education or therapy groups that try to help children understand and cope with divorce. The Government of Manitoba (2009), for example, offers programs that give children of divorce "a chance to work through their questions, concerns and anxieties with other children their own age."

- *Parent-focused programs* try to help children by helping their parents deal with divorce issues. For instance, workshops at Family Service Toronto (2008) offer practical information and support to parents who are considering, or going through, a separation or divorce.

- *Counselling* provides one-to-one support to parents and children affected by divorce. This type of support is offered by many voluntary agencies across Canada, including the Children of Divorce program at the Calgary Counselling Centre.

Most divorce group programs for children are available through family courts, government, family service agencies in the voluntary sector, or church-related organizations. The negative effects of divorce on children are often noticeable in the school setting in terms of academic problems—thus, many schools in Canada have established programs to help children cope with their parents' divorce (Government of BC, 2003).

Discussion Questions

▥ The Impact of Family Type on Child and Youth Development

1. What do you think is the ideal family type (if any) for children? Give reasons for your answer.

2. Every family type has potential strengths and weaknesses. Identify what you believe may be the strengths of (a) lone-parent families; (b) blended families; and (c) divorced families.

▥ FAMILY VIOLENCE

Family violence is a social problem in Canada that has far-reaching social, economic, justice, and health consequences (Health Canada, 2002). In Canada, family violence is understood as the abuse of power within "relationships of kinship, intimacy, dependency or trust" (National Clearinghouse on Family Violence, 2006). Family violence includes a wide range of behaviours such as physical assault, emotional abuse, neglect, sexual assault, financial exploitation, stalking, and witnessing violence within the family.

Every child exposed to family violence will respond differently, depending on his or her age, the severity and frequency of the conflict, and other factors. However, most children experience some level of emotional, social, and/or behavioural difficulty (Peterborough County, City Health Unit, 2008). Two types of family violence—spousal abuse and child abuse—may be particularly hard on a child's well-being.

SPOUSAL ABUSE

Spousal abuse (or partner abuse) affects Canadians from all walks of life, backgrounds, cultures, and income levels. This type of abuse is committed by one marital, common-law, or same-sex partner against the other, and includes a broad range of behaviours, including physical abuse, sexual assault or exploitation, emotional abuse, criminal harassment or stalking, economic or financial abuse, and spiritual abuse. According to the 2004 General Social Survey on Victimization, about 7 percent of women and 6 percent of men are abused by a current or a former spouse or common-law partner. The evidence indicates that woman abuse by a male partner is the most frequent and severe form of spousal abuse. Furthermore, female victims are more likely than male victims to incur physical injuries, require medical attention, suffer emotional consequences such as depression or anxiety attacks, and fear for their safety (Mihorean, 2005).

Spousal abuse is a complex social problem, with no single, definitive "cause"; however, certain factors raise the risk of this type of abuse occurring. Just being a woman increases the risk of spousal abuse because of the power imbalances between men and women in society. Women at the highest risk of abuse are those who are Aboriginal, have a disability, live in poverty, or are geographically or socially isolated from the larger society (Department of Justice Canada, 2006a).

Abuse can potentially create problems in all aspects of an abused person's life, including physical and mental health and the ability to work, parent, and fulfil other important roles. One of the greatest concerns about spousal abuse is its immediate and long-term harm to children. Studies show that children who witness (see or hear) violence in the home are more likely than other children to experience depression, fear, anxiety, or other difficult emotion. Academic difficulties are common among child witnesses to violence, as are behavioural problems, including hyperactivity, aggression, and delinquency (Department of Justice Canada, 2006a). Research suggests that male children who witness their father's abuse of a woman are three times more likely to grow up and abuse their own partner (AuCoin, 2005). Children witness 37 percent of all reported cases of spousal abuse in non-Aboriginal households, and 50 percent of reported cases in Aboriginal households (Quennell, 2007).

Canada's Family Violence Initiative supports the development and provision of many services for abused women and their children. Among these resources, shelters are a primary support. Shelters include transition houses (emergency, short-stay housing); "second-stage" housing (longer-term housing in conjunction with support services); and safe homes (short-term emergency housing in private homes) (National Clearinghouse on Family Violence, 2008). In 2006, there were over 500 shelters in Canada (Taylor-Butts, 2007).

A number of programs across Canada are designed specifically to assist children who have been exposed to violence by one parent against the other. For example, the Children Who Witness Abuse program in British Columbia offers one-on-one counselling, educational presentations, and group support. These services may be provided in a variety of settings, including schools, women's shelters, and family service agencies.

CHILD ABUSE

Exposing children to violence is one form of **child abuse**; children may also endure physical abuse, sexual abuse and exploitation, emotional abuse, and neglect. In Canada, the most frequent type of child abuse is neglect. The maltreatment of children usually occurs while the child is in the care of someone they trust and depend on, such as a parent, caregiver, or teacher. Child abuse can also occur in any type of setting, including the child's home, school, childcare centre, or on the Internet. Any child is vulnerable to abuse to some extent; however, children at highest risk are those who are marginalized due to having a disability or living in a low-income, Aboriginal, or racial/ethnic minority family (Department of Justice Canada, 2006b).

The impact of abuse on children depends on many factors, including the length of time over which the abuse occurs, the child's developmental level, and the relationship between the child and the abuser (Meston, 1993). However, any problems created by abuse are likely to manifest themselves in one or more of the following areas (with examples):

- psychological (nightmares, depression, anxiety);
- physical (failure to thrive, psychosomatic complaints, overall poor health);
- behavioural (poor socialization, eating disorders, drug abuse, self-destructive or suicidal behaviour);
- academic (poor grades, suspensions, grade repetition);
- sexual (promiscuity, dissatisfaction with sex in adulthood);
- interpersonal (insecure attachments to caregivers, difficulty in making friends, fear of intimacy);
- self-perceptual (low self-esteem, inaccurate body image, confused sense of identity);
- spiritual (general loss of faith, lack of spirit or enthusiasm for life); and/or
- subsequent violence in adulthood (abuse of own children, perpetration of violence against partner) (Latimer, 1998; Taylor-Butts, 2007).

The negative effects of mistreatment during childhood can have long-term consequences; as adults, victims of abuse may experience difficulty working, earning a sufficient income, forming meaningful relationships, and participating fully in society. Child mistreatment also has its social and economic costs; one study estimates that child abuse costs $15 billion a year in Canada for health care, social welfare services, and lost productivity by parents (Johnson, 2006).

Because child abuse tends to remain hidden and denied, it is difficult to estimate the prevalence of this problem. Much of what we know about reported cases of child abuse in Canada comes from two main sources of information: the Canadian Incidence Study of Reported Child Abuse and Neglect (CIS) and the Incident-Based Uniform Crime Reporting (UCR) survey. According to the CIS, in 2003, there were over 235,000 reports of child maltreatment investigations, and

EXHIBIT 10.6

Historically, child neglect is the most common form of child abuse in Canada, and can affect physical, emotional, and cognitive development.

Source: John Joseph Kelso/Library and Archives Canada/PA-118221.

nearly half of those were substantiated by child welfare authorities (Trocmé et al., 2005). The UCR survey reveals that, in 2006, a total of 622 out of every 100,000 young Canadians were victims of physical or sexual violence (Ogrodnik, 2008).

CHILD PROTECTION SERVICES

The Canadian Constitution and laws give the state the authority to protect the best interests of children and youth. This authority—or *parens patriae* ("father of the people")—allows each province and territory to develop their own **child welfare system** for abused or neglected children and their families.

All child welfare systems across Canada are similar in the sense that they investigate reports of alleged maltreatment, offer support services to families with children, and provide various care options for at-risk children. Despite these similarities, child protection measures vary across jurisdictional boundaries in many ways. For example, each province and territory has its own ideas about the state's role in family life, what factors constitute "risk" to children, and how child abuse/neglect should be defined. There are also differences in the ways in which child welfare services are delivered: some regional governments provide direct child welfare services, while others contract them out to a mandated children's aid society. Disparity also exists among the types of abuse that child welfare workers must investigate, their investigation procedures, and the criteria they apply when deciding whether to remove a child from the home. Further variation is found in First Nations communities. In some cases, child welfare services are provided by self-governed Indian bands that are funded by the federal government under the Indian Act; other First Nations communities are served by Aboriginal family service agencies that work within a province's or territory's child welfare laws and provide services to Aboriginal families both on- and off-reserve (Trocmé et al., 2005).

Historically, Canada's child protection systems have been criticized for being either too intrusive into the lives of families (the large-scale removal of Aboriginal children from their homes illustrates this point), or too lax in the attention to high-risk children. Researchers continue to search for more effective ways of protecting children. One group of researchers suggests that a better system would be focused on the primary prevention of harm to children, rather than on reacting to child maltreatment after it occurs (MacDonald, 2004). A model developed by Butchart and Harvey (2006) suggests that three levels of prevention might effectively address the problem of child abuse:

- The *societal and community level* focuses on raising public awareness about child abuse and neglect, changing social norms and attitudes about abuse, and reforming macro-level systems (such as political and economic systems) to provide greater protection and security to children and their families.

- The *relationship level* is mostly concerned with interrupting abuse or neglect at the earliest stage possible; typically, initiatives at this level target high-risk populations.

- The *individual or micro level* aims to help children and their caregivers prevent abuse through increased knowledge, healthy habits, and awareness.

Exhibit 10.7 provides a graphical illustration of the three interrelated levels of prevention, and gives examples of strategies or interventions at each level.

EXHIBIT 10.7

CHILD MALTREATMENT: THREE LEVELS OF PREVENTION

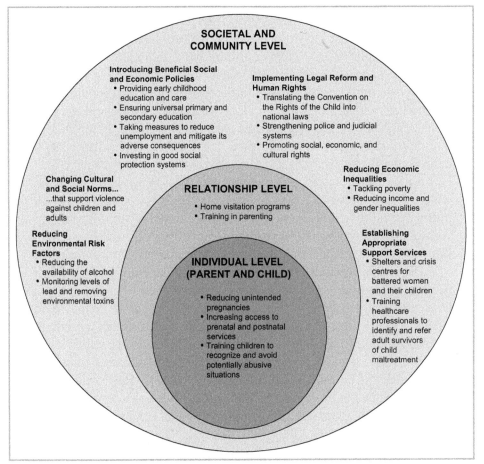

Source: Adapted from Alexander Butchart and Alison Phinney Harvey for the World Health Organization and International Society for Prevention of Child Abuse and Neglect. "Preventing Child Maltreatment: A Guide to Taking Action and Generating Evidence," (tab. 3.1, p. 35).
© World Health Organization 2006. Retrieved December 10, 2008, from http://whqlibdoc.who.int/publications/2006/9241594365_eng.pdf.

CHILDREN IN CARE

Children who come under the protection of a provincial or territorial child welfare system are referred to as **children in care**. There are an estimated 80,000 children and youth in care in Canada, an increase of 60 percent since 2002 (National Youth in Care Network, 2007). The rise in the number of children placed in care in recent decades has been attributed to the higher number of reported incidences of neglect and abuse and more aggressive approaches taken to eradicate child abuse (Farris-Manning & Zandstra, 2003).

Intervention in a family's life on behalf of a child can take many different forms. The child welfare agency may become involved in situations in which a family is having difficulties (for example, a parent is abusing alcohol) and additional supports are required to provide for the child's care or supervision. In other cases, the child welfare worker and parent/caregiver may draw up an agreement that outlines what the parent(s) must do (for example, take a parenting course) to retain custody of their child(ren). In cases of abuse or extreme neglect, the child may be removed from the family home and placed in alternative care (J.N. Mukongolo & Associates, 2007). Depending on the resources available in the community, a child may be placed in

- a foster home (the home of a family other than the child's own);
- a group home (a private or government community-based facility run by professional staff);
- an institutional home (a facility that provides more structure, supervision, and support than foster homes or group homes);
- a mental health centre (a residential facility for youth at risk of harming themselves); or
- a custody facility (residential care for a child or youth at risk of running away or physically harming someone) (National Youth in Care Network, 1998).

Research suggests that the benefits for children living in foster or family-based care are greater than those offered by group or institutional care. This has led to a trend toward kinship care (which places the child in a foster home with relatives) and guardianship care (which places the child with a family who is known to the child) (Farris-Manning & Zandstra, 2003).

Discussion Questions

■ **Family Violence**

1. It is often difficult for victims of family violence to talk about their abusive experiences. Identify some of the personal qualities (for example, empathy) that professional helpers should demonstrate when lending support to victims of abuse.

2. Envision the "perfect" child welfare system. What types of services might a child welfare worker provide in this ideal system? How might those services help?

IV WORKING WITH FAMILIES WITH CHILDREN

Working with families is an important activity in social welfare programs and a primary focus for many social workers. There are a number of rewards associated with helping families meet their basic needs, effectively problem-solve, and reach their goals. There are also many challenges. Social workers, for example, have to constantly hone their assessment and intervention skills in order to help families deal with the rapidly changing social, economic, and political environment.

Many social workers take a strengths-based approach to family service, in which more emphasis is put on a family's strengths (such as the ability to show affection to its members) than its deficits. Empowerment plays an important role in the focus on strengths. When social workers engage in empowering activities with families, they are essentially helping family members help themselves and—ultimately—manage their own lives. Empowerment can be observed when a family is able to (1) identify its needs and know how to meet those needs; (2) advocate on its own behalf so that necessary resources can be accessed; and (3) give input into the programs and policies that directly affect the family.

Empowered families are knowledgeable about the services available to them. Social workers can provide these services directly, or they can help families learn about and connect with appropriate community resources. As cuts to social welfare programs make services unavailable, unaffordable, or unsuitable, many families may need to do more, such as minding children in the home rather than taking them to day care. This will require front-line workers to help families discover their own *internal* strategies for meeting needs and resolving problems, as opposed to relying on *external*, government-sponsored supports.

Another way social workers might help families is by providing information about child development, and what parents might do to support their child's development. In the role of "coach," social workers can encourage parents to listen to and talk with their children; to show love, support, and affection; and to help their children or teens make decisions and solve problems. Social workers can provide practical support as well; for example, parents may need help planning for spending time with their children or budgeting for purchases, such as music lessons or hockey equipment. Finally, social workers can help parents recognize their own strengths, intuitive abilities, and successes as caregivers.

SUMMARY

Introduction

Families with children supply the nation's future adults, workers, and parents. Most Canadian children are doing well, yet many live in disadvantaged circumstances. Although parents are the primary caregivers, government assumes a responsibility for children's well-being. Canada has a wide range of social welfare programs for children and families; many of these programs are included in the national action plan for children. In general, the development of these programs has not been consistent, and they tend to be poorly coordinated.

I. Meeting the Developmental Needs of Children and Youth

Policymakers aim to help children get a good start in life through early-learning and childcare programs. Canada is not meeting current childcare demands, and may be experiencing a childcare crisis. Mental health is an important factor in how young people deal with challenges. Serious mental health problems among young people are increasing, and suicide is a particular concern. Mental health programs are offered by residential and nonresidential centres. Youth have become a recent priority for governments; many policies and programs take a youth engagement approach. Parenting problems may contribute to childhood disorders; however, parent support programs are available to give parents the resources they need to effectively raise their children.

II. The Impact of Family Type on Child and Youth Development

Most lone-parent families are headed by women. The family's income level is likely to shape a child's experience in a lone-parent family. Children in lone-parent families are at high risk for behavioural and academic problems. The greatest challenge for many stepfamilies is dealing with conflicts between their members. It is not unusual for stepparent–stepchild relationships to be vulnerable to family stress. Nearly half of all divorces in Canada involve dependent children. Parental conflict related to a relationship breakdown is potentially more harmful to children than the actual separation. A range of specialized services is available to give information and support to lone-parent families, stepfamilies, and divorced families.

III. Family Violence

Although anyone may suffer abuse, certain factors (such as being a woman) can increase the likelihood of being abused by a spouse/partner. Spousal abuse has many potential negative consequences for those being abused, and for children who witness it. A variety of support services are available in Canada for abused women and their children; shelters are a primary support. Various forms of child abuse exist, all of which can have far-reaching effects on children. The prevalence of child abuse in Canada is unknown; however, statistics are collected on reported cases. Child welfare systems vary across the country, and offer a range of care options for children at risk.

IV. Working with Families with Children

Family practice is the focus for many social agencies and workers. It is important for workers to continually refine their skills to help families deal with a rapidly changing environment. Empowerment is a central theme in family services. To help families cope with cuts to services, social workers engage families in activities that promote internal and empowering solutions. Social workers may provide information about child development, and assist parents in activities that support their child's development.

Key Terms

For definitions of the key terms, consult the Glossary on page 413 at the end of the book.

family, p. 254
family policy, p. 256
childcare, p. 257
mental health, p. 259
mental health problem, p. 260
resilience, p. 262

youth engagement approach, p. 262
empowerment, p. 262
lone-parent family, p. 265
blended family, p. 266

family violence, p. 269
spousal abuse, p. 270
child abuse, p. 271
child welfare system, p. 273
children in care, p. 275

CHAPTER 11

Social Welfare and Older Canadians

OBJECTIVES

The social welfare of older Canadians is becoming an increasingly critical issue in the context of an aging population. This chapter will explore:

- the organized approaches to aging in Canada;

- issues related to the health, wellness, and security of seniors;

- the ways in which older people are cared for and supported;

- work and participation among seniors; and

- social work practice with elderly populations.

INTRODUCTION

[Seniors are] a rich and vibrant part of our country. As we increasingly draw on seniors to meet labour force requirements strained by decades of low fertility, our society has new motivation to value seniors as contributing members of society, and not as burdens to be problematized. At the same time, it is necessary to provide the services and supports which will allow seniors to live with dignity. (Special Senate Committee on Aging, 2007, p. 1)

Canada, like other Western industrialized countries, has an aging population, which means that the proportion of older people in the population is increasing. According to the 2006 Census, one out of seven Canadians is 65 years or older. The fastest-growing group of seniors are those aged 80 and over. Experts forecast that, if the current aging trend continues, more than one in four Canadians will be over age 65 by 2031 (McLachlin, 2008).

Population aging is the result of a combination of factors. Increased longevity is one factor: Canadians are living longer due to new medical technologies, improvements in health care and nutrition, better methods of controlling infectious diseases, and healthier lifestyle choices. Today, the average woman can expect to live over 82 years, and the average man to almost 78 years. Another contributor to population aging is low birth rate. Since the end of the Second World War, families have been getting smaller; on average, Canadian women now have 1.5 children (in contrast to 2.2 children in 1981) (Statistics Canada, 2007d).

Over the past twenty years, there has been ongoing debate among policymakers, social analysts, economists, and others about the implications of an aging population. Many who see this demographic shift as a potential problem stress that the proportion of dependent people (mostly children and retired seniors) may soon surpass the proportion of working-age adults. Statistics support this trend; for example, in 2005, there were approximately 44 dependent people per 100 working-age people; by 2056, that rate is expected to reach 69 to 100 (Bélanger, Martel, & Malenfant, 2005). Canada's shrinking workforce is the result of two main factors: (1) the **baby boomers**—who currently represent one-third of the population—are beginning to retire and leave the workforce; and (2) there are proportionately fewer people entering the workforce. (The dominance of the baby boom generation is reflected in the bulge found in the population pyramid in Exhibit 11.1.) The shifting dependant-to-worker ratio raises a number of concerns. One is that a greater share of resources (such as health care, social services, public pensions, and housing) will be consumed by a growing number of retired or "noncontributing" members of society. Another concern is that a relatively small workforce will have to support a rather large group of dependants—a burden that is both unreasonable and unsustainable.

Although population aging will undoubtedly create challenges, not everyone accepts the doom-and-gloom predictions of an "age quake." After studying population aging from various angles, the Special Senate Committee on Aging (2007) concludes that, while the retirement of the baby boomers is likely to impact the labour market, that turn of events does not necessarily imply an erosion of Canada's standard of living, nor the collapse of public

EXHIBIT 11.1

CANADA'S AGING POPULATION

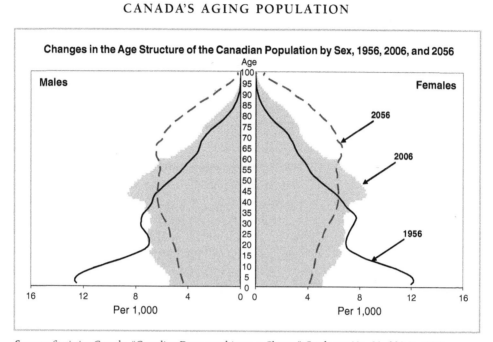

Changes in the Age Structure of the Canadian Population by Sex, 1956, 2006, and 2056

Source: Statistics Canada, "Canadian Demographics at a Glance," Catalogue No. 91–003-X, ISSN 1916–1832. January 2008.

programs. Moreover, a number of social analysts "argue that Canada is well-equipped to face this social and demographic phenomenon—and that people shouldn't worry that much about the growing percentage of seniors in the population" (Turcotte & Schellenberg, 2007, p.7). One way Canadian governments have been trying to "equip" the nation for a growing number of older people is by promoting **active aging**—that is, optimizing opportunities that enhance people's quality of life from birth to death. By creating a generally healthy population, Canada expects to reduce the demand on health, social welfare, pensions, and other resources that could easily be depleted by a large population of dependent old people. For many seniors, active aging means remaining healthy and independent and engaged in meaningful activities related to work, education, recreation, and volunteering (Special Senate Committee on Aging, 2007). This chapter explores some of the challenges and opportunities related to active aging.

In the discussion that follows, the terms *senior, older person,* and *elderly person* are used interchangeably to refer to those aged 65 or over.

▌ ORGANIZED APPROACHES TO AGING

THE ROLE OF RESEARCH

While everyone agrees that an aging population will bring both challenges and opportunities, relatively little is known about the potential impact this demographic shift will have on individuals, families, communities, and the nation as a whole. As the Special Senate Committee on Aging (2007) points out, this lack of knowledge has made it difficult for policymakers to anticipate the needs and issues of future seniors. This situation is gradually changing as Canada continues to build social knowledge related to aging and late adulthood. One of the most comprehensive studies on aging in the world is the Canadian Longitudinal Study on Aging (CLSA, 2009). This national study, launched in 2008, will track the biological, psychological, social, economic, and other aspects of approximately 50,000 Canadian men and women between the ages of 45 and 85 over a twenty-year period. Among other things, the CLSA aims to identify the components of "successful aging" and to try to determine what factors contribute to disease or disability as people age.

The recent spotlight on aging is helping to dispel some of the myths associated with old age (see Exhibit 11.2), and to expose the prevalence of **ageism** in society. Ageism is defined as "discrimination based on age, especially prejudice against older people" (Edwards & Mawani, 2006). In Western cultures, in which youth tends to be more valued than old age, ageism is reflected in social attitudes that portray older people as being useless, stupid, or a burden on family and society (WHO, 2007). These attitudes can lead to the discriminatory treatment of old people. Over the years, Canadian governments have been applying a "discrimination lens" to policy analysis, in an effort to make public policies less ageist. One result of these analyses is the realization that the age-based eligibility criteria for the public care of seniors is discriminatory. More progressive social policies are now defining "old age" not by an arbitrary number of years but by level of need or functioning. The shift away from chronological age as an eligibility criteria makes sense when considering the aging process among certain groups; for instance, the health and social conditions of an average 55-year-old First Nations person is equivalent to that of a 65-year-old non-Aboriginal senior (Special Senate Committee on Aging, 2007).

Another important research discovery relates to the diversity of seniors. As Dobie (2006) points out, the seniors of today hardly fit the stereotype of "a monolithic group of poor, frail, sick or dependent persons." Rather, seniors represent a highly diverse group: they live in every region of Canada; some

EXHIBIT 11.2

MYTHS AND FACTS ABOUT OLDER CANADIANS

MYTH	FACT
Intellectual functioning decreases as we age.	Current research does not support the notion that intellectual functioning declines after middle age.
Most older people lose interest in, or a capacity for sexual relations.	Research suggests that the normal aging process alone does not directly impact sexuality.
Age affects older adults' ability to drive safely.	Statistically, healthy older adults are the safest of all age groups on the road.
The majority of older adults live in institutions.	According to Statistics Canada, only 3.4 percent of seniors lived in nursing homes or other homes for the aged in 2004–2005.*
Older people cannot expect to successfully learn new technologies.	Older adults are one of the fastest-growing groups purchasing and learning to use computers and computer-related products and services.
Developing dementia is a normal part of aging.	While age raises the risk for dementia, most people do not develop dementia as they age.
Older people are more likely to be depressed than younger people.	According to Statistics Canada, younger people are more likely to report feeling sad or depressed than older age groups.
It is becoming less likely for an older people to be employed.	Over the last decade, the number of employed older adults has increased.
Older adults are more likely to be victims of crime than younger people.	According to the 2004 General Social Survey (GSS), only 10% of seniors are victims as against 31% of non-seniors.
Older people are more likely to commit suicide than younger people.	Overall, Canadian seniors are less likely than younger adults to commit suicide.
Older people have little influence on our government.	According to Statistics Canada, older adults are more likely to consistently vote in all elections, at all levels of government, than younger persons.
Most older adults live alone.	Most older adults live with a spouse, with children or grandchildren, or in a collective dwelling.
Most older adults are preoccupied with death.	In general, older adults are less anxious about death.
The majority of older adults are poor.	Most older adults do not live in poverty.

*Statistics Canada, "Residential Care Facilities: 2004/2005," *The Daily*, May 30, 2007. Retrieved December 1, 2008, from www.statcan.gc.ca/daily-quotidien/070530/dq070530d-eng.htm.

Source: Adapted from Ontario Seniors' Secretariat, *Aging Quiz*. © Queen's Printer for Ontario, 2007. Reproduced with permission.

were born here, others immigrated here; they have different interests and backgrounds, and participate at different levels; some are gay or lesbian, most are heterosexual; some live alone, others with a partner or adult child. The experience of being older is also changing: today's seniors are more financially secure, better educated, more active, and more technologically savvy than those of previous generations (Turcotte & Schellenberg, 2007).

EXHIBIT 11.3

In general, today's seniors are healthier and more physically active than those of previous generations.

Source: © iStockphoto.com/McIninch.

Research is providing insight into the different stages of late adulthood. Old age used to encompass a relatively short period of a person's life: an average man born in 1945, for example, could expect to be a senior from the age of 65 (when he retired) to 68 (when he died) (Bothwell, Drummond, & English, 1989). Since people are living much longer these days, the senior years encompass a longer period of time. Three broad categories of old age are now recognized:

- the "young old" (age 65 to 75) are generally healthy, fit, and financially well off;

- the "middle old" (age 75 to 85) tend to have less money and fewer resources, and are starting to slow down; and

- the "frail old" (age 85 and older) are likely to have a number of health and social needs (Special Senate Committee on Aging, 2008).

There are also attitudinal differences among the three groups. An Ekos Research Associates (2007) poll found that seniors of different ages had contrasting opinions on volunteerism, political activism, health care, and citizenship. The various differences between the three subgroups of seniors have implications for the design and delivery of social welfare, health, and other public programs.

THE INTERNATIONAL PLAN OF ACTION ON AGEING

In 1982, the United Nations introduced the first international strategy—the Vienna International Plan of Action on Ageing—for governments around the world to use as a guide when developing policies and programs related to aging. Twenty years later, the UN released its revised International Plan of Action on Ageing (also known as the Madrid Plan) to reframe aging more as a "milestone of human progress" than a "challenge" (Zelenev, 2008). While the Madrid Plan recognizes key principles and priorities, it encourages each country to adapt the priorities to its own circumstances (United Nations, 2006).

Canada's rendition of the Madrid Plan focuses on the enhancement of health and well-being over the life course, the promotion of independent living, and the expansion of opportunities for the participation of older persons in society (Edwards & Mawani, 2006). Although the initiatives under Canada's plan are highly varied, most are based on one or more of the following concepts:

- *Inclusivity*. Initiatives target all seniors, including those who are at risk and those who are healthy and active.

- *Healthy aging*. Initiatives promote behaviours, habits, and choices that enhance the physical, mental, spiritual, and social well-being of people of any age over the entire life course.

- *Population health*. Initiatives reflect the belief that factors such as income, housing, social support, education, and transportation are powerful determinants of overall health.

- *Aging in place*. Initiatives focus on ensuring that resources are in place to meet people's needs as they grow older so that they can continue to live in their own homes for as long as possible.

- *Social justice*. Initiatives are based on the core belief that every person, regardless of age, is entitled to security, autonomy, and dignity, protection from discrimination and abuse, and appropriate care and services (McLachlin, 2008).

These concepts form the foundation of social welfare programs and services for seniors at the federal, regional, and local levels.

FEDERAL AND REGIONAL INITIATIVES

The responsibility for the health and social welfare of older Canadians is shared among the federal, provincial, and territorial governments.

Policies and programs that have a national scope—such as Falls-Prevention Initiatives, and the Canadian Diabetes Strategy—are the concern of the federal government. Aging and seniors' issues fit within the mandates of a number of federal departments and agencies; however, the Department of Human Resources and Skills Development Canada (HRSDC) is the main department responsible for the well-being of seniors. In addition, the federal government has appointed individuals and groups to address specific issues related to aging and seniors. These appointees include the following:

- a Seniors Secretariat within the HRSDC to provide a focal point for federal departments that serve senior populations;

- a Secretary of State for Seniors to assist the Minister of HRSDC in carrying out his or her responsibilities and acts as an advocate for Canadian seniors;

- the National Seniors Council (which replaces the National Advisory Council on Aging) to advise the federal government on issues and opportunities related to the well-being of Canada's seniors; and

- the Special Senate Committee on Aging to conduct a large-scale review of issues, policies, and programs related to seniors.

Every provincial and territorial government has a department whose general purpose is to improve the quality of life for seniors. Many of those departments have established frameworks to guide the development of seniors-related policies and programs in their regions. For example, a Strategy for Positive Aging in Nova Scotia has been developed by the provincial government's Department of Seniors. In addition, several regional jurisdictions have appointed independent councils to advise government on seniors' issues; for instance, the New Brunswick Advisory Council on Seniors advises the provincial Minister of Health on matters relating to seniors in the region.

In 1996, the Federal-Provincial-Territorial Ministers Responsible for Seniors introduced the National Framework on Aging (NFA), a conceptual framework that outlines an overall vision for policies and programs for seniors in Canada. The NFA also identifies five principles—dignity, independence, participation, fairness, and security—that policymakers should follow when developing policy and programs for seniors.

In 2005, the Ministers Responsible for Seniors articulated their priorities for action in the document *Planning for Canada's Aging Population: A Framework*; one year later, the ministers proposed a new vision, areas of focus, and strategies to promote healthy aging in Canada. The various components of Canada's framework on aging are outlined in Exhibit 11.4.

VOLUNTARY AND LOCAL INITIATIVES

The extent to which seniors are aging well is perhaps most noticeable at the community level, where many of the efforts made by government, voluntary organizations, seniors' groups, and others are directed. Voluntary agencies— often in the form of councils, associations, networks, or committees—play a particularly important role in the lives of seniors. Organizations that provide seniors' programs often focus on a specific aspect of senior life, such as housing. Other organizations have broader mandates; the Saskatoon Council on Aging (2008), for example, offers programs for seniors that are educational (such as computer classes), social (such as drop-in programs), and health-related (such as blood pressure clinics). Although the mandates of voluntary groups may vary, most of them support seniors in their efforts to live independently, to carry out daily activities in a normal community context, and to make decisions about their own lives.

Many initiatives for seniors focus on the creation of supportive environments where older people can live well and remain active. Towns, cities, and

EXHIBIT 11.4

HEALTHY AGING IN CANADA: A FRAMEWORK FOR ACTION

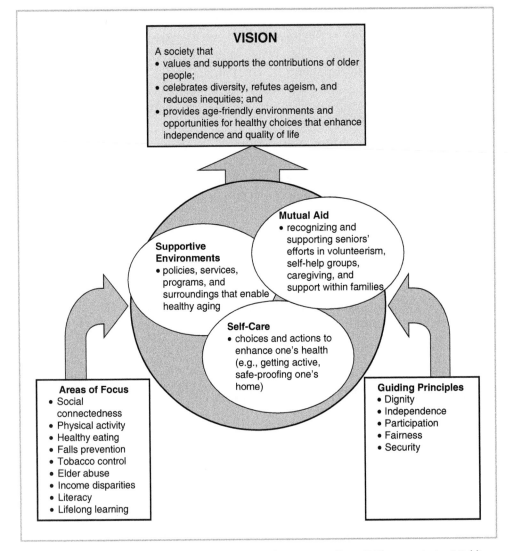

VISION

A society that
- values and supports the contributions of older people;
- celebrates diversity, refutes ageism, and reduces inequities; and
- provides age-friendly environments and opportunities for healthy choices that enhance independence and quality of life

Mutual Aid
- recognizing and supporting seniors' efforts in volunteerism, self-help groups, caregiving, and support within families

Supportive Environments
- policies, services, programs, and surroundings that enable healthy aging

Self-Care
- choices and actions to enhance one's health (e.g., getting active, safe-proofing one's home)

Areas of Focus
- Social connectedness
- Physical activity
- Healthy eating
- Falls prevention
- Tobacco control
- Elder abuse
- Income disparities
- Literacy
- Lifelong learning

Guiding Principles
- Dignity
- Independence
- Participation
- Fairness
- Security

Source: "Healthy Aging in Canada: A New Vision, a Vital Investment: From Evidence to Action," Public Health Agency of Canada (2006). Adapted and Reproduced with the permission of the Minister of Public Works and Government Services Canada, 2009.

villages that are supportive of seniors are often referred to as **age-friendly communities**. While each locality will be age-friendly in its own unique way, they are all likely to

- recognize seniors for their capabilities and resources;
- be responsive to the needs and preferences of seniors;

- respect seniors' decisions and lifestyle choices;
- protect the vulnerable members of the senior population; and
- promote the inclusion of and contributions by seniors in community life (WHO, 2007).

EXHIBIT 11.5

AN AGE-FRIENDLY COMMUNITY

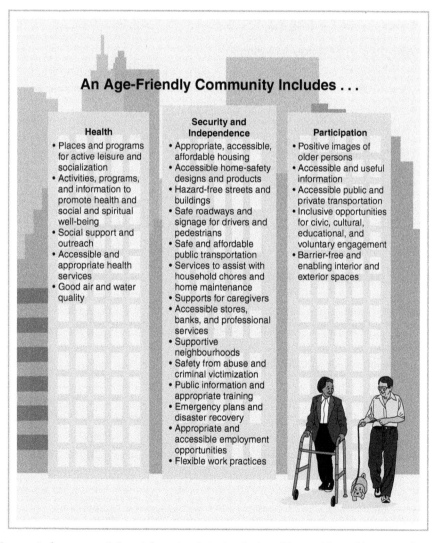

An Age-Friendly Community Includes . . .

Health
- Places and programs for active leisure and socialization
- Activities, programs, and information to promote health and social and spiritual well-being
- Social support and outreach
- Accessible and appropriate health services
- Good air and water quality

Security and Independence
- Appropriate, accessible, affordable housing
- Accessible home-safety designs and products
- Hazard-free streets and buildings
- Safe roadways and signage for drivers and pedestrians
- Safe and affordable public transportation
- Services to assist with household chores and home maintenance
- Supports for caregivers
- Accessible stores, banks, and professional services
- Supportive neighbourhoods
- Safety from abuse and criminal victimization
- Public information and appropriate training
- Emergency plans and disaster recovery
- Appropriate and accessible employment opportunities
- Flexible work practices

Participation
- Positive images of older persons
- Accessible and useful information
- Accessible public and private transportation
- Inclusive opportunities for civic, cultural, educational, and voluntary engagement
- Barrier-free and enabling interior and exterior spaces

Source: Author-generated chart, information derived and adapted from Public Health Agency of Canada, Division of Aging and Seniors. (2006). Brochure. World Health Organization: Global Age-Friendly Cities Project. Retrieved November 8, 2008, from http://www.phac-aspc.gc.ca/seniors-aines/pubs/age_friendly/pdf/age_friendly_e.pdf.

Very often, age-friendly communities include seniors in the planning, development, and evaluation of aging-related policies, programs, and practices (Edwards & Mawani, 2006).

Age-friendly communities are not only those that benefit older people. Indeed, environments supportive of seniors tend to be good for everyone's quality of life. Exhibit 11.5 identifies some of the features of an age-friendly community, in terms of health, security and independence, and participation.

Discussion Questions

▪ Organized Approaches to Aging

1. How might ageism negatively impact the lives of seniors and society in general? What are some of the strategies that individuals, organizations, and communities might use to combat ageism?

2. Identify some of the organized initiatives in your community that are aimed at benefiting seniors. From your perspective, how are those initiatives improving the lives of seniors and/or the community in general?

THE HEALTH, WELLNESS, AND SECURITY OF SENIORS

PHYSICAL HEALTH AND ACTIVITY

According to one study, as many as 37 percent of Canadian seniors consider their health to be good (Turcotte & Schellenberg, 2007). Even so, 81 percent of Canadian seniors reports a chronic health problem—such as diabetes, hearing problems, or injuries from falls—that restricts daily activities (Edwards & Mawani, 2006).

Older people are at higher risk of disability than younger groups. Mobility disabilities (such as difficulty walking or standing for long periods) are the most common type of disability among seniors; in 2006, mobility problems limited the daily activities of 43 percent of seniors (Statistics Canada, 2007b). Women are more likely than men to have mobility problems. Chronic health conditions and disabilities increase the need for caregivers or technical aids, such as walkers and wheelchairs, and subsequently threaten an older person's ability to remain independent and active.

According to the 2005 Canadian Community Health Survey, most seniors do not get enough physical exercise (Statistics Canada, 2006c).

To address this issue, a number of voluntary seniors' groups, extended care centres, and other organizations offer exercise classes, walking programs, and other activities to keep seniors active. A growing number of programs—such as the Senior Fitness Instructors Course—are designed to train fitness leaders to help seniors meet their physical activity needs.

MENTAL HEALTH

Mental health problems are not an inevitable part of aging; however, it is estimated that between 17 and 30 percent of Canadian seniors experience one or more mental health problems (United Way of Guelph, 2006). Depression affects as many as one out of five seniors (Gordon, 2000). Depression is associated with the challenges that come with aging, including physical ailments, chronic pain, cognitive and sensory impairments, and a sense of loss related to events such as forced retirement, declining physical abilities, and the death of a spouse (Special Senate Committee on Aging, 2008). Suicide is a possible outcome of severe depression: men over 85 years of age have the highest suicide rate in Canada (Statistics Canada, 2008g).

Dementia—which involves a loss of memory and cognitive ability—is the most common mental health problem among seniors. The Canadian Study of Health and Aging (2002) estimates that 8 percent of seniors suffer from some form of dementia; this figure is expected to more than double by 2021 (Conn, 2003). Although several types of dementias exist, Alzheimer's disease affects the majority (64 percent) of Canadians with a dementia disorder (Alzheimer Society of Canada, 2005).

By helping older people to improve their coping skills, self-esteem, and social support systems, mental health programs aim to prevent or at least delay the onset of mental disorders and placement in long-term care. Many mental health programs recognize the link between an individual's personal attributes and the quality of his or her social environment. Programs that take a **psychosocial approach** tend to focus simultaneously on enhancing older people's cognitive, emotional, and spiritual life while strengthening external support systems, such as those related to income security, health care, and housing.

INCOME SECURITY

Most older Canadians rely on the **retirement income system** for financial support after they leave the workforce. This system was established with two goals in mind: "to ensure that elderly people have incomes high enough to allow them to live in dignity no matter what their circumstances were during their working years; [and] to maintain a reasonable relationship between income before and after retirement so that old age does not bring a drastic reduction in a person's standard of living" (NCW, 1999, p. 1). Canada's retirement income system is built on three main tiers:

- *Old Age Security (OAS).* This program offers four types of benefits: (1) a retirement pension; (2) a Guaranteed Income Supplement (GIS) for low-income seniors; (3) a spousal allowance; and (4) a survivor's allowance for spouses. Many provinces and territories provide additional benefits and services to those who are eligible for the GIS.

- *The Canada Pension Plan (CPP).* This is a self-supporting contributory program that requires employed people and their employers, and the self-employed, to make regular contributions during the working years. A pension can then be drawn on retirement. Quebec residents draw from their own plan, the Quebec Pension Plan (QPP).

- *Private pension plans and savings.* These options include both self-administered and employer-sponsored registered pension plans (RPPs), registered retirement savings plans (RRSPs), and other private pension plans.

The economic situation of Canadian seniors has been steadily improving over the last few decades: between 1980 and 2003, the proportion of seniors living in poverty fell from 21 percent to 7 percent. Despite these gains, many Canadian seniors live under difficult economic conditions. This is especially true for senior women, Aboriginal people, recent immigrants, visible minorities, people with disabilities, and those living alone (National Advisory Council on Aging, 2005a; 2005b). Fewer than 38 percent of Canadian workers have workplace pensions (Statistics Canada, 2008h), and 29 percent of all Canadians have no retirement savings at all (Statistics Canada, 2006d). Even private-company pension funds cannot guarantee financial security for retirees; for instance, when the economic recession hit in 2008, many pension plans that relied on the stock market witnessed a rapid decline in the value of their investments.

The administrative structure of Canada's retirement income system may actually be creating financial stress for older people. For example, close to 300,000 Canadians receiving OAS are entitled to the GIS and the spousal allowance; however, many of them do not receive those benefits because they do not know about them, the application process is too complicated, or they have been cut off because they failed to renew their application in time (National Advisory Council on Aging, 2005a). In recent years, the federal government has tried to remedy some of these bureaucratic deficiencies by amending the CPP, the OAS, and the GIS so that benefits are more accessible to eligible seniors. Other changes—such as the introduction of pension income splitting—have attempted to raise income levels among seniors (Seniors Canada, 2008).

ELDER ABUSE

Elder abuse is a serious yet underreported social problem. The World Health Organization (WHO, 2002) defines **elder abuse** as "a single or repeated act, or lack of appropriate action—occurring in any relationship where there is an expectation of trust—that causes harm or distress to an older person." Abuse against an elderly person may be physical, emotional or psychological, or financial (the most common). Elder abuse may also be in the form of neglect by a caregiver to meet the basic needs of an older person. Seniors from all walks of life may be affected by elder abuse; however, those at highest risk are usually very old or frail, female, isolated, disabled, dependent on others for care, or have a cognitive impairment. Estimates suggest that elder abuse affects anywhere from 4 to 10 percent of Canadian seniors (National Seniors Council, 2007).

Elder abuse is addressed in a variety of ways in Canada. In addition to criminal laws, some provinces and territories have introduced adult protection legislation that, among other things, provide protocols and investigative procedures for responding to complaints of abuse. The Madrid Plan recognizes elder abuse not just as a legal concern, but as a reflection of a lack of opportunities for older people in society (Zelenev, 2008); in response to this insight, programs are attempting to expand the scope of activities for seniors. The federally funded New Horizons for Seniors Program (NHSP) is one of the most popular strategies in Canada to keep seniors connected to and active within their communities. In addition to funding community-based projects to reduce isolation among seniors, the NHSP sponsors the Elder Abuse Awareness Campaign, an initiative aimed at improving the safety and security of older Canadians (HRSDC, 2008b).

Service responses to elder abuse often occur on the front lines of voluntary social agencies. An interdisciplinary approach is used in many communities to coordinate the efforts of a wide range of professionals in healthcare, social work, legal, and other fields on behalf of at-risk seniors. One community response is made by Family Service Toronto, which has established an elder abuse team to investigate reports of abuse or neglect of older people and to provide support services to elderly victims.

The Health, Wellness, and Security of Seniors

1. What types of activities may help to ward off mental health problems in elderly people?
2. Elder abuse is a disturbing issue in our society. What are some of the ways your community is addressing the problem?

CARING FOR AND SUPPORTING SENIORS

Stereotypes would have us believe that to be old is to be institutionalized. While many seniors live in institutions, most (93 percent) live in their own home, and would like to continue living there. To age in the dwelling of one's choice requires a wide range of supports, services, and housing options. This section looks briefly at selected types of residential care, and the resources designed to facilitate "aging in place," that are available to Canadian seniors.

RESIDENTIAL CARE

Depending on the jurisdiction, **residential centres** for the elderly are referred to as long-term-care homes, nursing homes, residential care facilities, continuing care centres, and similar terms. Regardless of name, these institutions are designated for people who require some level of assistance or service due to a physical or cognitive limitation. The level of care needed may be as little as room and board only, or as much as shelter in combination with meals, round-the-clock nursing services, assistance with daily living activities, administration of medications, and/or therapeutic or rehabilitative services (Caregiver Resource Centre, 2008). About 7 percent of all Canadian seniors live in residential care centres as a result of health problems; this rate rises to 40 percent of seniors over 80 (Dobie, 2006). Senior women are twice as likely as senior men to live in a residential care centre (Statistics Canada, 2007e).

The care needs of older people in residential care are becoming more complex. A primary reason for this is that most people needing long-term care have multiple chronic conditions, and may be in various stages of dementia (Jones, 2007). Increased life expectancy has something to do with this trend. For example, people are living longer, and therefore reaching the point that they develop chronic problems. There are also more individuals with intellectual and developmental disabilities who are living into their advanced years and developing later-onset cognitive impairments that require intensive care

EXHIBIT 11.6

In addition to tending to the basic needs of seniors, many long-term-care centres offer arts, crafts, and other creative opportunities to residents.

Source: DAJ/Getty Images.

(Hirst, 2006). These trends, along with ongoing cutbacks in facility staffing and other resources, are putting greater demands on staff who work in homes for the aged.

INDEPENDENT AND ASSISTED LIVING

Owing to government cuts to residential care, and to new technologies that allow seniors to live independently, fewer seniors are living in institutions than in past decades. Also, there has been a philosophical shift toward the concept of aging in place. These developments are reflected in the variety of housing options now available to seniors: some options are without care, while others offer varying levels of care. Seniors' housing without care include retirement villages (small communities of seniors living in single-family or semidetached homes, apartments, or townhouses), and granny flats (a self-contained unit located on a relative's property, or a self-contained suite in a house). Seniors' housing with care is generically referred to as **supportive housing**. The aim of this type of housing is to help seniors balance independence with specific support. Offering the least amount of support is **congregate housing** (often a private apartment or room within a larger complex, plus meals). The most support is available through **assisted living** facilities (often a private living space and meals, as well as other services such as personal care, laundry, and housekeeping) (Special Senate Committee on Aging, 2007; Canadian Centre for Elder Law Studies, 2005). In Canada, supportive housing may be provided by either government or private-sector organizations.

Adequate and affordable housing is central to everyone's quality of life, but as Montgomery (1977, p. 253) states: "The quality of the housing environment becomes increasingly significant in the lives of many aged families and individuals. And the quality of this [environment] largely determines the extent to which they will retain their independence." While most seniors are well housed, finding affordable housing is a challenge for many seniors; this is especially true for seniors who are Aboriginal, live alone, or live in large cities (Clark, 2005). Some elderly people find that staying in their own house is more affordable than moving to supportive housing. Through the federally funded Residential Rehabilitation Assistance Program, and the Home Adaptations for Seniors' Independence Program low-income seniors can bring their homes up to basic health and safety standards, or modify their houses to enable daily living activities. Home adaptations may include installing a shower seat or grab bars in the bathroom, or building wheelchair ramps or lifts.

HELPING SENIORS

More than a quarter of all Canadian seniors living independently receive help with personal care, housework, yard work, shopping, or other activity because they have a health condition or disability. About three-quarters (72 percent) of seniors receive all or part of help from a spouse, other relative, or friend (Turcotte & Schellenberg, 2007). Many seniors living in residential care facilities also rely on friends and family to provide personal care or other type of assistance.

Most health and social welfare experts agree that, because people are living longer and developing more complex conditions, seniors will not be able to rely on family for all the care they need (Dobie, 2006). This realization, in combination with a growing older population and a general trend away from institutionalization, is increasing the demand for **home and community care** services (Canadian Mental Health Association, 2002). In short, home and community care consists of "programs that enable individuals to receive care at home and/or live as independently as possible in the community" (Premiers' Council on Canadian Health Awareness, 2002, p. 4). These programs include professional services (such as nursing, social work, and occupational therapy); personal care services (such as bathing, grooming, and toileting); and homemaking and home support services (such as laundry services, housecleaning, and meal preparation) (Special Senate Committee on Aging, 2008).

In 2002, the Romanow Commission's study of the future of health care in Canada found home and community care to be one of the fastest-growing segments of the health system, and far more cost-effective than the institutional care of seniors. However, the quality of home and community care services, and the qualifications of those who provide them, is inconsistent across the country. Many Canadians believe that the standardization of service may be achieved through a national homecare program (Special Senate Committee on Aging, 2008). Although the federal government has come close to introducing this type of program in the past, no such initiative is currently being pursued.

SOCIAL CONNECTEDNESS

The ability to connect with others is essential to good physical and mental health in the senior years. Crompton and Kemeny (1999, p. 24) observe that

> some of the health-related effects of aging are buffered when people have someone they can confide in and can count on, and who can give them advice and make them feel loved. Conversely, lack of such support is a powerful risk factor for poor health, perhaps because people have no one to help shield them from the effects of various stressors.

The need for social connectedness is particularly strong among seniors who live alone. Many seniors live with a spouse, a partner, or an adult child; however, more than one-quarter of seniors, primarily women, live alone (Statistics Canada, 2002). While seniors may choose to live alone, this particular living arrangement can lead to loneliness and a subsequent decline in health. About one-half of people aged 80 and older report feeling lonely (Government of Canada, 2006a).

Social connectedness may be thought of in terms of four dimensions: social support, social networks, social engagement, and supportive social environments. Each dimension is briefly described below.

- *Social support* is what people receive from close family, friends, neighbours and others. When seniors feel socially supported, they are likely to feel valued and appreciated, and encouraged to develop the skills and habits they need to live a good life. Friendly visiting programs are among the outreach programs that offer social support to seniors; these programs usually match volunteers with seniors who live alone, or have few friends or no family.

- *Social networks* are interconnected systems of support and information, usually made up of family, friends, and community members. As people age, their social networks tend to shrink as a result of retirement, disability, and the death of peers. With fewer people to rely on, seniors may become vulnerable to social isolation and related problems. A number of volunteer programs and seniors' centres offer programs to help older people expand their network of people they can call when they need help, information, or someone to talk to.

- *Social engagement* refers to the active involvement in one's community, and the relationships formed as a result of that involvement. Attendance at religious services and volunteering are two examples of social engagement. Research has found that social engagement through intergenerational activities can enhance the lives of both older persons and young people (see Exhibit 11.7 for an example). By encouraging individuals of various ages to meet, interact with, and learn from each other, intergenerational programs can help people develop more-open and less-biased perceptions of each other.

- *Supportive social environments* enable seniors to foster social support, develop social networks, and become socially engaged. Supportive social environments include age-friendly communities that promote a wide range of resources and opportunities for seniors, including employment, volunteering, recreation, lifelong learning, and civic participation (Edwards & Mawani, 2006).

AGENCY PROFILE: AN INTERGENERATIONAL PROGRAM

LINKages Society of Alberta is a community-based registered charity that offers intergenerational programs that connect young people with seniors who reside in care facilities.

LINKages recognizes the value of creating caring relationships between youth and seniors, especially in light of an aging population, and a society that sometimes isolates older and younger generations from each other.

LINKages' intergenerational programs aim to

- build bridges between the generations;
- reduce negative attitudes and dispel myths about seniors;
- promote a greater understanding and respect for generations; and
- enhance the personal benefits of volunteering.

The youth and seniors are selected for the programs in collaboration with schools, communities, and care facilities. Youth volunteers participate in training and orientation sessions to learn about seniors' health issues, care facility policies, and procedures, and to clarify individual expectations.

In the Junior High Program, the students visit the seniors twice a week during the lunch hour. The visits take place in a central area and are supervised by LINKages staff. Many of the visits involve planned activities, such as games, crafts, reading, storytelling, talent shows, movies, and helping seniors write their biographies.

Because the volunteer students in the Senior High Program are usually more experienced, they require less supervision. However, LINKages staff are available to provide information, support, and advice to students as needed. Activities during the visits are designed to enhance student–senior interactions, and students are encouraged to be true companions for their senior.

Source: Excerpted and adapted from LINKages Society of Alberta. (2008). Website. Retrieved November 29, 2008, from http://www.link-ages.ca/index.php?option=com_content&view=article&id=92&Itemid=156, www.link-ages.ca/index.php?option=com_content&view=article&id=81&Itemid=84, www.link-ages.ca/testjoomla/index.php?option=com_content&view=article&id=55&Itemid=29#intro, www.link-ages.ca/index.php?option=com_content&view=article&id=57&Itemid=100, www.link-ages.ca/index.php?option=com_content&view=article&id=58&Itemid=101. LINKages logo courtesy of LINKages Society of Alberta.

Discussion Questions

■ **Caring For and Supporting Seniors**

1. What are some of the trends driving the need for home and community care?

2. Social connectedness may be thought of as having four dimensions: social support, social networks, social engagement, and supportive social environments. Identify the programs or services in your community that target one or more of these dimensions. From your perspective, are there any gaps in programs related to social connectedness and, if so, what types of programs are needed?

IV WORK AND PARTICIPATION

SENIORS AT WORK

Most Canadian seniors are retired; however, a growing number are employed or actively looking for work. Between 2001 and 2005, the percentage of working seniors rose from 6 to 8 percent (Special Senate Committee on Aging, 2007). There are many reasons why older Canadians continue working past the traditional retirement age of 65, including the following:

- Many older people want to work. These seniors remain in the workforce past the traditional retirement age of 65 because they are physically and mentally capable of working, and find work to be self-fulfilling. One study found that the appeal of "freedom 55" is gradually fading as many older Canadians seek opportunities to continue contributing to society through work (Expert Panel on Older Workers, 2008).

- Some older Canadians need to keep working. In most cases, this "need" is financial, especially if the individual is ineligible for CPP or private pension benefits. This is especially true for recent immigrants and single women (Special Senate Committee on Aging, 2008).

- A growing number of retirees are returning to work. An older person may take an initial retirement, and then look for a "bridge job" to help ease the transition between full-time work and full-time retirement. Bridge jobs are usually part-time, and pursued more out of choice than financial necessity (Héber & Luong, 2008).

- Some workers have to retire for reasons beyond their control. Workers in this situation may have been laid off due to company downsizing, or were already unemployed when they turned 65, or worked for an employer that had a **mandatory retirement policy**. In general, involuntary retirement is associated with less enjoyment of the retirement years (Turcotte & Schellenberg, 2007).

For the most part, mandatory retirement policies have been phased out in Canada. However, in some occupations such as firefighting, physical abilities are required, and workers can be forced to retire at a specific age. Moreover, some jurisdictions—for instance, New Brunswick—allow private companies to implement mandatory retirement under the provisions of their pension or retirement plans. With few exceptions, mandatory retirement policies have little to offer in a country whose population is aging, and where more workers are needed to fill jobs (McLachlin, 2008). Other strategies—such as workplace flexibility policies and phased retirement—are nevertheless needed to encourage a higher labour market participation among old workers.

VOLUNTEERING

In addition to helping to improve the lives of others, volunteering can benefit the volunteers themselves. Some find that volunteering helps them make a smooth transition from work to retirement by providing a sense of purpose, self-worth, and identity, as well as opportunities to use their skills (Special Senate Committee on Aging, 2007). A number of studies have associated volunteering with good physical and mental health. The likelihood of volunteering declines with age; even so, 32 percent of seniors volunteer for an organization, and each of those seniors contributes, on average, 245 hours a year (the most of any age group) (Hall, Lasby, Gumulka, & Tryon, 2006).

Shrinking government funding and the increasing demand for services are leading some social agencies to recruit more volunteer service providers. Older people in general, and baby boomers in particular, are being targeted as prime candidates to provide many of the services once delivered by professional helpers. Bowen and McKechnie (2001, p. 5) point out that "we need to keep our eyes firmly fixed on the future aspirations and abilities of the country's Baby Boomers so that as they begin to think about retirement and leave the workforce, volunteering and community service will be a real and viable option on their menu of possibilities."

POLITICAL ACTIVISM AND CONSULTATION

For many senior citizens, active participation in society means taking political action. As Turcotte and Schellenberg (2007) note: "By taking part in the political debate, seniors can bring to the attention of public officials issues important to their well-being and to their communities. By exercising their right to vote, they may induce political parties to consider their needs in the formulation of social programs." As a rule, though seniors do not engage in radical political activity (such as boycotts or sit-ins) as much as younger people, they rarely hesitate to voice their dissatisfaction with government policy. In 1985, the largest seniors' protest in Canadian history took place in response to the federal government's proposal to de-index pension payments. The collective action of seniors forced the government to scrap the de-indexation plan. Another successful protest led by seniors took place in 1997 (see Exhibit 11.8).

Much of seniors' political clout is exercised within organizations that are established by seniors, and run by seniors for seniors. The Manitoba Society of Seniors and the Saskatchewan Seniors Mechanism are two examples of voluntary groups that represent and advocate on behalf of seniors in their

EXHIBIT 11.8

March 1997: About 150 senior citizens march on Parliament Hill to protest against the Federal Drug Patent Bill—a piece of legislation that would substantially drive up the cost of prescription drugs. The federal government was pressured to amend the bill.

Source: CP PHOTO.

respective provinces. Not only do these groups advise local and provincial governments on matters that concern seniors, but they work to enhance the image of seniors and their quality of life.

Seniors want to be consulted on matters that affect them and future generations; they also want "to make significant and lasting contributions to their communities and to Canadian society" (Government of Canada, 2000). Seniors, however, have historically had difficulty "getting the ear of government" (Spencer, 2003). In recent years, Canadian governments have been making a greater effort to include seniors in public consultations and policy-making processes. In 1998, for example, the federal government established the Canada Coordinating Committee to consult with seniors on a variety of issues, including seniors' housing and health and the role of seniors in society. Later, in 2003, the members of the Liberal Task Force on Seniors made a point of including seniors in their study of social and economic issues related to aging. The prime minister's appointment of a Seniors Secretariat in 2005 was, among other things, an attempt to give Canadian seniors a stronger voice in the issues, decisions, and policies that affect them. A number of provinces (including Ontario, Manitoba, and Prince Edward Island) have also appointed seniors secretariats to help seniors advance their causes.

Discussion Questions

■ **Work and Participation**

1. Identify what you see as the possible pros and cons of mandatory retirement.

2. The likelihood of volunteering decreases with age, yet nonprofit organizations are needing volunteers more than ever. What might organizations do to attract and retain more senior volunteers?

▓ SOCIAL WORK PRACTICE WITH ELDERLY POPULATIONS

In many ways, social work practice is the same with elderly clients as with other populations. However, as Steven Hick (2004) points out, gerontological social work requires "specialized knowledge of health care issues, poverty, housing and mental health, including knowledge of the ageing process and the issues surrounding Alzheimer's disease. Since a large proportion of the elderly population are women, social work with older adults is often considered a women's issue." Professionals with expertise in both social welfare and health services can assist in specialized areas such as elder abuse, substance abuse, and mental health.

Gerontological social workers require a wide range of skills to effectively help older clients. For example, assessment skills are needed to identify an individual's needs, strengths, and resources. Moreover, workers should be well versed in how to plan, implement, and evaluate programs for elderly people. Social workers who serve older populations should be able to work with families as well as multidisciplinary or inter-agency teams. These and other skills may be used by gerontological social workers in one or more of the following service areas:

- *individual and family counselling*—assessing the needs and strengths of elderly clients and their families, and linking clients with resources to meet those needs;

- *adult day programs*—providing outreach, supportive services, group work, and care-planning services in structured day program settings;

- *adult protective services*—assessing factors that may put elderly clients at risk of abuse or neglect, and developing, implementing, and monitoring plans to ensure clients' safety and security;

- *respite services*—recruiting and training respite care workers and identifying families in need of this service; and

- *hospital or nursing home care*—assessing social needs, providing counselling and support services, advocating on behalf of elderly clients and their families, and participating in program, care, and/or discharge-planning (Zastrow, 2008).

The demand for gerontological social work and social services is growing as the population ages, and as people live longer with a serious health problem or disability. Currently, in Canada, there is a shortage of trained gerontologists (Special Senate Committee on Aging, 2008). This situation is gradually changing with the introduction of college-based gerontology programs, such as the Social Service Worker Gerontology diploma program at the Ontario Colleges of Applied Arts and Technology.

SUMMARY

Introduction

Canada, like other Western industrialized countries, has an aging population. While some social analysts emphasize the potential problems of an aging population, others emphasize the potential benefits. To prepare the nation for an older population, Canadian governments have introduced policies and programs that promote active aging.

I. Organized Approaches to Aging

Canada's social knowledge on aging and late adulthood is expanding. Research is helping to expose the impact of ageism, redefine "old age," recognize the diversity of seniors, and realize subgroups of seniors. Canada's version of the Madrid Plan focuses on health and well-being over the life course, independent living, and opportunities for older persons. The responsibility for the well-being of older Canadians is shared by the different levels of government. The National Framework on Aging guides aging-related initiatives. Resources and opportunities for seniors are visible at the local level where voluntary agencies, governments, and others work together to create age-friendly communities.

II. The Health, Wellness, and Security of Seniors

The majority of seniors live with a chronic health problem; older people are at a high risk of disability. Depression and dementia are the most common mental health problems among seniors. Most older Canadians rely on the retirement income system; this system is built on three main tiers. While the economic situation of seniors has improved over the years, many Canadian seniors struggle financially. The federal government is trying to streamline certain income programs to make them more accessible. Elder abuse is a serious social problem, which is addressed through laws, adult protection legislation, voluntary sector programs, and policies that expand opportunities for older people.

III. Caring For and Supporting Seniors

Residential care is available for people with a physical or cognitive limitation. The care needs of older people are becoming more complex. Fewer seniors are living in institutions thanks to an expanding range of housing options, including supportive housing. Finding affordable housing can be a challenge for seniors; programs are available to help low-income seniors stay in their own homes. Many seniors rely on others—such as family and friends—for help with daily activities. Although home and community care services are available, they lack standardization and regulation. Social connectedness can be achieved through social support, social networks, social engagement, and supportive social environments.

IV. Work and Participation

For a variety of reasons, a growing number of seniors keep working after the traditional retirement age of 65. With some exceptions, mandatory retirement policies have been phased out in Canada, and workplace strategies are now needed to attract workers. Almost one-third of seniors volunteer for an organization; baby-boomer retirees are targeted as potential volunteers. Seniors are politically active in various ways: some seniors belong to organizations that advocate on behalf of seniors; others engage in public policy consultations and policymaking processes.

V. Social Work Practice with Elderly Populations

Gerontological social work requires advanced assessment and intervention skills, as well as specialized knowledge of seniors' issues. Social workers must also be able to plan, implement, and evaluate programs for seniors, work with families, and participate in multidisciplinary teams. Seniors may be supported through a variety of services, including adult day programs. The demand for gerontological social work is growing as the population ages, and as healthcare resources shrink.

Key Terms

For definitions of the key terms, consult the Glossary on page 413 at the end of the book.

population aging, p. 280
baby boomer, p. 280
active aging, p. 281
ageism, p. 282
aging in place, p. 286
age-friendly community, p. 288
mental health problem, p. 291

psychosocial approach, p. 291
retirement income system, p. 291
elder abuse, p. 293
residental centre, p. 294
supportive housing, p. 296

congregate housing, p. 296
assisted living, p. 296
home and community care, p. 297
social connectedness, p. 298
mandatory retirement policy, p. 300

CHAPTER 12

Aboriginal Canadians and the Social Welfare System

OBJECTIVES

Aboriginal systems of helping and healing are emerging and evolving alongside mainstream social welfare approaches. This chapter will explore:

- the historical foundations of Canada's "Indian policy;"

- attempts to "bridge the divide" between Canadian governments and Aboriginal peoples;

- healing and wellness in Aboriginal communities;

- issues and challenges for First Nations on reserves, Aboriginals living off a reserve, and Aboriginal children; and

- social work with Aboriginal peoples.

INTRODUCTION

We owe the Aboriginal peoples a debt that is four centuries old. It is their turn to become full partners in developing an even greater Canada. And the reconciliation required may be less a matter of legal texts than of attitudes of the heart. (Romeo LeBlanc, Governor-General of Canada, 1996)

Long before the arrival of European settlers, the Aboriginal population comprised several separate nations, each with its own culture, language, and system of government. Today, Canada's Aboriginal population is still far from homogeneous: the Inuit, Métis, and First Nations all have their own needs, issues, and traditions. According to the 2006 Census, 4 percent of Canadians identify themselves as an Aboriginal person. This group includes 700,000 First Nations peoples, 390,000 Métis, and almost 50,000 Inuit (Statistics Canada, 2008b). (For definitions of terms related to these groups, see Exhibit 12.1.)

EXHIBIT 12.1

DEFINITIONS OF TERMS

Aboriginal peoples are the descendants of the original inhabitants of North America. The Canadian Constitution recognizes three groups of Aboriginal people: Indians, Métis, and Inuit.

Indian collectively describes all the indigenous people in Canada who are not Métis or Inuit. There are three categories of Indians in Canada: Status Indians, Non-Status Indians, and Treaty Indians.

- *Status Indians* are people who are entitled to have their names included on the Indian Register, an official list maintained by the federal government. Certain criteria determine who can be registered as a Status Indian. Only Status Indians are recognized as Indians under the Indian Act, which defines an Indian as "a person who, pursuant to this Act, is registered as an Indian or is entitled to be registered as an Indian." Status Indians are entitled to certain rights and benefits under the law.

- *Non-Status Indians* are people who consider themselves Indians or members of a First Nation but whom the Government of Canada does not recognize as Indians under the Indian Act, either because they are unable to prove their status or have lost their status rights. Many Indian people in Canada, especially women, lost their Indian status through discriminatory practices in the past. Non-Status Indians are not entitled to the same rights and benefits available to Status Indians.

- *Treaty Indians* are Status Indians who belong to a First Nation that signed a treaty with the Crown.

First Nations peoples—a term often used in place of "Indians"—refers to both Status and Non-Status Indian peoples in Canada.

Métis are people of mixed First Nations and European ancestry; they identify themselves as distinct from Inuit and First Nations people.

Inuit people inhabit the northern regions of Canada, principally Nunavut, the Northwest Territories, and the northern parts of Labrador and Quebec. Inuit are not covered by the Indian Act.

A **band** is a group of First Nations people for whom lands have been set apart or whose money is held by the Crown. Many bands prefer to be known as "First Nations."

Continued

A **reserve** (or reservation) is a tract of land owned by the Government of Canada, and set apart for the use and benefit of a First Nations band. Many First Nations have replaced the term *reserve* with *First Nations community*. The terms *on-reserve* and *off-reserve* refer respectively to people or things (such as services) that are part of, or separate from, a First Nations community. Inuit and Métis have never lived on reserves.

Source: *Words First: An Evolving Terminology Relating to Aboriginal Peoples in Canada*, Ottawa, Indian and Northern Affairs Canada, 2002. Reproduced with the permission of the Minister of Public Works and Government Services Canada, 2009.

In recent decades, Aboriginal peoples have seen progress in many life areas such as health, housing, economic development, and educational attainment. This has resulted in a demographic shift within the Aboriginal community, with a significant growth rate. The population boom shows an increase in young Aboriginals—today, over 68 percent are First Nations people under the age of 35. There is also an increase in elderly Aboriginal people as they live longer than ever before (Assembly of First Nations, 2007). Although government interventions have contributed to Aboriginal health and well-being, much of the progress in these areas is attributed to the strength, courage, and determination of Aboriginal peoples. These qualities have created what Esquimaux and Smolewski (2004) refer to as a "renaissance of traditional Aboriginal values and mores," as Aboriginal peoples reclaim their traditional languages and practices and find effective ways to work on long-standing issues.

Despite some positive trends, studies confirm that Aboriginal peoples are more socially, economically, and environmentally disadvantaged than non-Aboriginal Canadians. In its 2004 Speech from the Throne, the Government of Canada (2004b) acknowledged that "Aboriginal Canadians have not fully shared in our nation's good fortune. While some progress has been made, the conditions in far too many Aboriginal communities can only be described as shameful." These conditions include

- more than half of all Aboriginal children live in poverty;
- Aboriginal people are three times more likely than other Canadians to be unemployed;
- over one-quarter of Aboriginal adults have less than Grade 9 education;
- almost one-third of Aboriginal adults have a disability (twice the national rate);
- on average, First Nations and Inuit people live five to ten years less than other Canadians;

- the suicide rate among First Nations youth is seven times higher than that among non-Aboriginal youth (the Inuit rate is eleven times higher); and

- Aboriginal women are three times more likely than other women to be victims of spousal abuse (Statistics Canada, 2006a; Chansonneuve, 2005; Subcommittee on Population Health, 2008).

A growing number of social analysts attribute the social, health, and economic challenges facing Aboriginal groups to a history of repressive control by government, the ineffectiveness of mainstream social welfare programs, and a loss of social and economic autonomy (Carniol, 2000).

HISTORICAL FOUNDATIONS OF CANADA'S "INDIAN POLICY"

EARLY ABORIGINAL–GOVERNMENT RELATIONS

King George III of England signed a Royal Proclamation in 1763 to protect Aboriginal groups from being exploited by the European settlers and colonial officials in Canada. The Proclamation recognized Aboriginals as autonomous and self-governing groups within the colonial system, and deserving of their own lands separate from the colonial settlements. Despite this status, Aboriginal peoples were generally viewed by the Canadian settlers as being inferior, uncivilized, and incompetent. Colonial governments used these racist perceptions to justify the creation of "Indian policies" to control Aboriginals (Rice & Snyder, 2008). Assuming a paternal role in Aboriginal affairs, the Canadian government looked upon Aboriginal peoples as being in need of "protection from vices" and "instruction in peaceful occupations" (Scott, 1914). Years later, a Royal Commission on Aboriginal Peoples would describe the apparent "protection" of indigenous people as a form of domination and "a code word implying encouragement to stop being Aboriginal and merge into the settler society" (RCAP, 1996a).

AN ASSIMILATION PLAN

In 1844, the British government transferred the management of Aboriginal affairs to the Province of Canada, where white Indian Department superintendents or agents would supervise the natives (later to be known as First Nations) who lived on land reservations. By that time, the colonial governments no longer saw Aboriginal groups as autonomous nations, but as British subjects whose best chance at survival was as members of the dominant white society. The colonial governments took it upon themselves to prepare the natives for **assimilation**—that is, "to remake the Indian people in the image of European manners and values, [and] to move them into the mainstream of Canadian life" (Historical review, 1975). "Indians" were defined as being Aboriginal by birth, blood, or adoption, a member of a band, and/or married to an Aboriginal person.

The assimilation process required Indians to learn English and convert to Christianity—tasks facilitated by the schools and churches established on the reserves. To become "civilized" and "normalized," the Indians were expected to learn farming techniques and other European occupations, as well as adopt Euro-Canadian values, behaviours, and institutions. Colonial officials aided this process by systematically weakening band leadership, destroying Indian trading patterns, and banning religious ceremonies and other traditional practices (History of the Indian Act, 1978; Taylor, 2009). The assimilation strategies played out on land reservations (or reserves), which were considered "temporary laboratories for a program of forced culture change" (History of the Indian Act, 1978). Once the Aboriginal way of life was wiped out, the colonial governments planned to dismantle the reserves; similarly, the Indian status would be used to protect the natives only until they acquired European habits of self-reliance (Henderson, 2009). The colonial governments expected that, before long, the Aboriginals would abandon their traditional ways, join the dominant society, and pass along their new values and customs to their children (Rice & Snyder, 2008).

ENFRANCHISEMENT

The passage of the Gradual Civilization Act in 1857 marked Canada's formal commitment to the process of assimilation. This statute introduced the concept of **enfranchisement**—a process that gave members of First Nations the opportunity to surrender their special Indian status and lands and become full-fledged citizens of the white colony. Citizenship came with the right to vote, an honour the government felt would appeal to the natives (Makarenko, 2008).

By the time the British North America Act was passed in 1867, few Indians had chosen to be enfranchised. Under the new Dominion government, the responsibility for Aboriginal peoples was divided between two levels of government: the federal government took responsibility for Status Indians and reserves; the responsibility for all Non-Status Indians was assigned to the provinces. Determined to assimilate the Aboriginal peoples into the Christian and Euro-centric society, the Government of Canada passed a compulsory enfranchisement provision in 1869. Under this new act, a Status Indian woman who married a Non-Status man automatically lost her status, and any children born into the marriage were denied Indian status (Makarenko, 2008).

The passage of the first Indian Act in 1876 reinforced the government's goal of assimilation. Through the Indian Act, efforts would "be made to aid the Red man in lifting himself out of his condition of tutelage and dependence, and ... through education and every other means, to prepare him for a higher civilization by encouraging him to assume the privileges and responsibilities of full citizenship" (RCAP, 1996b).

THE ROLE OF RESIDENTIAL SCHOOLS

A more aggressive approach to assimilation came in 1879, when Prime Minister John A. Macdonald introduced a system of houses of industry— or **residential schools**—for Aboriginal children. These schools were government-funded, and run by Roman Catholic, United, Anglican, and Presbyterian churches. To prepare children for life in mainstream Canadian society, the government removed Aboriginal children from the "uncivilizing influences" of their families and communities, placed them in boarding schools, and taught them Euro-Canadian values and customs (Jacobs, Storey, & Poirier, 1992).

One Aboriginal group describes the "civilizing" strategies used at the schools: "Students were discouraged from speaking their first language or practising native traditions. If they were caught, they would experience severe punishment. ... All correspondence from the children was written in English, which many parents couldn't read. Brothers and sisters at the same school rarely saw each other, as all activities were segregated by gender" (Indian residential schools, 2008). Children were taught to be ashamed of their heritage, and to reject everything Indian, including their families and spiritual beliefs (Chansonneuve, 2005).

Attendance at residential schools was mandatory, with Indian agents enforcing the rule. At the peak of the residential school system in 1931, there were about eighty residential schools, located in every territory and in most provinces. Between 1883 and 1996 when the last school closed, almost 150,000 First Nations, Métis, and Inuit children had attended the schools (Indian residential schools, 2008).

EXHIBIT 12.2

Children in class at the residential school on Stoney Reserve, Morley, Alberta (circa 1949–1950).

Source: Glenbow Archives Na-5719–4.

Discussion Questions

▨ **Historical Foundations of Canada's "Indian Policy"**

1. *Racism* is a belief that race determines a person's (or a people's) traits or capabilities. Identify the ways in which Canada's colonial government demonstrated racism in its treatment of Aboriginal peoples.

2. Describe how the concepts and practices of "assimilation" and "enfranchisement" are related.

▥ BRIDGING THE DIVIDE: ATTEMPTS AT REFORM

A SHIFTING BALANCE OF POWER

By the Second World War, the federal government controlled most aspects of life on reserves. However, assimilation efforts had largely failed. Isolationist policies such as the residential schools and the system of reserves had worked at cross-purposes to the goal of assimilation (Hick, 1998). Moreover, instead of facilitating assimilation into mainstream society, the Indian Act had mainly served to disempower Indians and keep them in a state of dependency. The Indian people nevertheless held steadfast to their original status as a distinct nation with a legal right to land, culture, and self-government (Historical review, 1975).

As poverty, addiction, violence, and social disorganization worsened among indigenous peoples, Aboriginal leaders came forward to demand change and to defend their people's rights. In particular, Aboriginal peoples wanted the federal government to end its enfranchisement policies, relax its grip on Aboriginal affairs, and honour its own treaties. The Indian Act was amended in 1951 to lift the ban on potlatches, powwows, and other traditional ceremonies. However, the clauses in the act relating to enfranchisement and Indian status remained intact (INAC, 1990; Ward, 2002).

In 1969, in its Statement of the Government of Canada on Indian Policy (also known as the White Paper), the federal government recognized "that the separate legal status of Indians and the policies which have flowed from it have kept the Indian people apart from and behind other Canadians. The Indian people have not been full citizens of the communities and provinces in which they live and have not enjoyed the equality and benefits that such participation offers" (Clément, 2008). To correct injustices made in the past, the federal government agreed to abolish the Indian Act, relinquish its responsibility for Status Indians, and give First Nations communities more control over their lands. In exchange, Status Indians would abandon their special status and achieve equal footing with non-Aboriginal Canadians (INAC, 1990).

Most First Nations rejected the government's proposal on the basis that it represented another attempt by the federal government to assimilate them into the dominant society, and that the loss of special status under the Indian Act signalled the loss of rights for all Aboriginal Canadians. Such opposition to the White Paper led to the federal government's abandonment of the scheme in 1971.

AN ABORIGINAL PEOPLES MOVEMENT

The 1969 White Paper sparked dialogue and protest not only among First Nations, but among all Aboriginal peoples across Canada; the proposed policy also served as a catalyst for a nationwide Aboriginal rights movement (RCAP, 1996a). Canada's Aboriginal peoples began to formally organize themselves, hoping that organization might be a way to protect their common interests and rights, publicly promote their cause, and ultimately help them reclaim their rights. Although many Aboriginal-controlled groups were formed during that time (and since), five specific groups became collectively known as Canada's **National Aboriginal Organizations** (NAOs). Those five groups are known today as

- the Assembly of First Nations (representing First Nations citizens in Canada);

- the Congress of Aboriginal Peoples (representing off-reserve Aboriginal people);

- the Métis National Council (representing Métis people in Canada and internationally);

- the Inuit Tapiriit Kanatami of Canada (representing the four Inuit regions of Nunatsiavut in Labrador, Nunavik in northern Quebec, Nunavut, and the Inuvialuit Settlement Region in the Northwest Territories); and

- the Native Women's Association of Canada (representing Aboriginal women)

The achievements of Aboriginal organizations on behalf of First Nations, Métis, and Inuit peoples have been nothing short of remarkable (Abele, 2004). A major achievement involved the entrenchment of Aboriginal rights in the Constitution Act of 1982. The legal recognition of Aboriginal rights and title has helped to advance native causes, bring native rights to the forefront of Canadian political agendas, and pave the way for further reforms in Aboriginal policy. One significant reform occurred in 1985, when the Government of Canada amended the Indian Act to guarantee the equal treatment of Aboriginal men and women, to restore status and band membership rights to First Nations, and to abolish enfranchisement policies.

THE 1990S: FORGING NEW PARTNERSHIPS

The 1990s were characterized by governments' determination to eliminate budget deficits. Despite that single-minded goal, Canadian governments could not ignore the growing influence of Aboriginal affairs in the social, economic, legal, and political aspects of society. That influence was bolstered by a number of international developments, beginning with the United Nations' proclamation of 1993 as the International Year of the World's Indigenous People and the period 1995 to 2004 as the International Decade of the World's Indigenous People. (A Second International Decade of the World' Indigenous People would commence in 2005.) Not only did the various international designations highlight the challenges faced by Aboriginal, peoples, they also drew attention to the value of traditional cultures, and the role of indigenous people in society (United Nations, 2002). This international spotlight also motivated governments around the world—including Canada—to address the deplorable conditions in which many Aboriginal people live, and to forge new mutual relations to improve those conditions. Aboriginal peoples achieved several milestones during the 1990s, advancing them in their political and social aspirations. Four of those milestones are summarized below.

- In 1991, the Government of Canada appointed a Royal Commission on Aboriginal Peoples (RCAP) to review Aboriginal–government relations and the role of Indian, Inuit, and Métis people in society. In 1996, the commission released its final report, making 440 recommendations for resolving a broad range of Aboriginal issues.

- In 1995, the Government of Canada released its Inherent Rights Policy, which recognized Aboriginal peoples' right to **self-government**. Under self-government agreements, Aboriginal communities would assume greater responsibility and control over their internal affairs, and yet remain citizens of Canada, have the same rights and legal responsibilities as other Canadians, and work within the existing Canadian political and parliamentary structures. (By the end of 2008, 17 self-government agreements involving 36 Aboriginal groups would be completed) (INAC, 2008a).

- In 1998, the Government of Canada made a commitment to work with Aboriginal peoples, other levels of government, and the private sector to improve the living conditions of Canada's Aboriginal peoples. To formalize this commitment, the federal government launched Gathering Strength: Canada's Aboriginal Action Plan. To begin the reform process, the Government of Canada issued a Statement of Reconciliation, a formal apology that acknowledged government's unjust treatment of Aboriginal peoples in the past.

- The Social Union Framework Agreement (SUFA) ensures that Canadian "governments will work with the Aboriginal peoples of Canada to find practical solutions to address their pressing needs" (Government of Canada, 1999b). In late 1999, the Federal-Provincial-Territorial Council on Social Policy Renewal met with the Ministers Responsible for Aboriginal Affairs and NAO leaders to negotiate how the NAOs might implement the principles and obligations underlying SUFA (Government of Canada, 1999c).

EXHIBIT 12.3

Politicians and indigenous groups work together on a variety of issues related to the social welfare of Aboriginal peoples. Above, in July 2006, B.C.'s Premier Gordon Campbell (right) and Minister of Aboriginal Affairs are greeted by Haida Gwaii hereditary chiefs upon arrival at Second Beach in Skidegate, located in B.C.'s Queen Charlotte Islands.

Source: CP PHOTO/Richard Lam.

THE KELOWNA ACCORD

Beginning in 2004, the federal government under Prime Minister Paul Martin initiated a process aimed at raising the standard of living for Aboriginal peoples to that of non-Aboriginal Canadians within a ten-year period. That process, which was endorsed by Aboriginal, provincial, territorial, and federal leaders, culminated in the Kelowna Accord, a comprehensive agreement to guide a new Aboriginal–government relationship and to develop a full range of economic, health, education, and housing initiatives. The Government of Canada pledged over $5 billion over five years to support the initiatives, which would be implemented on reserves and in urban centres (Patterson, 2006).

Before the Kelowna Accord could be implemented, the Conservatives won the 2006 federal election. Although it promised to meet the targets of the Kelowna deal, the new government allocated just over $1 billion over four years to improve conditions for Aboriginal Canadians. Overall, Aboriginal and other analysts consider that amount of funding to be far below that proposed by the former Liberal government, and grossly inadequate to reach the Accord's goals (Undoing the Kelowna, 2006).

TAKING STOCK

Despite their differences and issues, Canadian governments and Aboriginal groups have worked together on the development of numerous policies and programs to address poverty, addictions, and other challenges facing indigenous peoples. How the Aboriginal-focused policies and programs are designed and delivered today is in sharp contrast to how they were forty years ago. For example:

- A full range of social and health programs are now available to all Aboriginal groups (First Nations, Métis, and Inuit peoples), not just to those with Indian status.

- Band councils and self-governments on reserves have assumed responsibility for most of the administration of on-reserve health, education, and social welfare programs.

- Aboriginal-controlled agencies and staff now manage most social services, education, economic, and other supports developed for Aboriginal people living off reserves.

- NAOs now play a central advisory role in federal policy development. Experts have also established national organizations to advise on policies related to Aboriginal child welfare, health, mental health, and women's issues (Abele, 2004).

Although Aboriginal peoples are included to a far greater extent in the policy development and decision-making process, the federal government retains a significant degree of control over the funding and administration of Aboriginal programs. SUFA, for example, intended to give Aboriginal organizations more authority over the development of their social welfare programs. However, in a formal review of SUFA in 2003, the NAOs criticized SUFA for (among other things) excluding Aboriginal groups from intergovernmental dialogues on social policies and programs, and failing to recognize them as full-fledged partners in the development of SUFA initiatives (Federal-Provincial-Territorial Ministerial Council on Social Policy Renewal, 2003).

Ongoing government control is seen by many as a continuation of colonial attitudes, which served to disempower and exploit Aboriginal peoples (Rice & Snyder, 2008). This sentiment is reflected in the statements made by Aboriginal leaders. For example, Chief Lawrence Joseph of the Federation of Saskatchewan Indians referred to the 2008 federal budget as a "tool of oppression" that offered little hope to Aboriginal peoples in terms of economic self-sufficiency (KAIROS, 2008).

Discussion Questions

▣ Bridging the Divide: Attempts at Reform

1. Many Aboriginal organizations gained political momentum in the late 1960s and early 1970s. From what you have learned in previous chapters, describe the social and political changes occurring during those decades that would have supported an Aboriginal human rights movement.

2. In your opinion, should Canadian governments control any aspect of Aboriginal life? If yes, what aspects should governments control, and why?

▣ HEALING AND WELLNESS IN ABORIGINAL COMMUNITIES

COLONIZATION AND THE RESIDENTIAL SCHOOL SYSTEM

The imposition of the Indian Act, enfranchisement laws, residential schools, and other "Indian" policies were intended not only to "civilize" Aboriginal peoples, but also to colonize them. Emma LaRoque (1994) defines **colonization** as a "process of encroachment and subsequent subjugation of Aboriginal peoples since the arrival of Europeans. From the Aboriginal perspective, it refers to loss of lands, resources, and self-direction and to the severe disturbance of cultural ways and values." Colonization reflects a sense of racial superiority, whereby a dominant group (in this case, Euro-Canadians) portrays an allegedly "weaker" group as having "something wrong with them" (Foucault, 1965, p. 7). Rice and Snyder (2008) point out that the myths about the incompetence and racial inferiority of indigenous peoples have persisted through the years; today, those myths continue to reinforce negative and potentially harmful stereotypes of Canada's Aboriginal peoples.

One of the key mechanisms used to colonize Aboriginal peoples was the residential school system, which taught students to reject their traditional ways and to feel ashamed of their native heritage. Many of the students were also physically and sexually abused by school officials, with traumatic effects that linger to this day. An estimated one-third of all Aboriginal people now living have been negatively impacted by the residential school system (Standing Senate Committee on Social Affairs, Science and Technology, 2006b).

Psychiatrist Charles R. Brasfield (2001) suggests that although many of the effects of residential schools resemble post-traumatic stress syndrome, they also have a distinct cultural component. For this reason, the term **residential school syndrome** has been coined to describe the cluster of symptoms specific to the problems created by Indian residential schools. These symptoms include distressing memories or dreams of life at the school; sleeping disorders; anger management problems; and avoidance of people, places, and events that bring back memories of the school. A number of former students also encounter difficulties expressing love to or communicating with their children, resulting in an intergenerational impact from the school system (Government of Canada, 2003c).

It is generally accepted that many present-day social and economic problems facing Aboriginal people are the symptoms of unresolved grief and historical trauma caused by long-term colonization processes (Chansonneuve, 2005). The legacy of residential schools, in particular, lives on in the form of mental health disorders, suicide, addictions, family violence, and chronic unemployment. These symptoms are interconnected, since they tend to share common causes and consequences. Moreover, the impact of these symptoms typically goes well beyond the individual. Addiction, for instance, can take a heavy toll on an individual's health, as well as on his or her family's well-being; addiction can also lead to such problems as accidents, violence, and criminal activity, and therefore puts a community's safety and resources at risk. As conditions worsen, alcohol and drugs may be abused to a greater extent as a way to self-medicate, to cope with stress, or to manage difficult feelings; however, this abuse may only serve to exacerbate existing problems (Standing Senate Committee on Social Affairs, Science and Technology, 2006b).

TRADITIONAL VERSUS MAINSTREAM APPROACHES TO HELPING

In their efforts to cope with the impact of unresolved grief and trauma, many Aboriginal people have turned to social welfare and other mainstream programs. However, those programs have not always been helpful. Many reasons are cited for that failure. Some theorists point out that mainstream interventions are generally incompatible with Aboriginal cultural values and beliefs and insensitive to the realities and needs of Aboriginal peoples (Kirmayer,

Brass, & Tait, 2000). In one study, Aboriginal people reported that the main reasons they avoided using mainstream services were "racism; women's fear of losing children; fear of re-victimization by institutions; fear of not being understood; not culturally relevant; lack of follow-up; fragmentation of services; lack of resources; ineffective communication; and jurisdictional disputes" (Chartrand & McKay, 2006).

Many **mainstream approaches** to helping are based on the medical model, and tend to view human disorders as discrete entities that can be "fixed" or treated through medication, psychotherapy, or other conventional intervention. These approaches typically focus more on the individual rather than on his or her environment and the interaction between the two. Mainstream services are often designed to treat a specific problem, such as addiction or family violence, and ignore other concerns. Moreover, these services tend to function independently from each other; thus, people with multiple problems and needs must seek help from multiple service providers.

Over the past two decades, a number of traditional (or Aboriginal) approaches to helping and healing have emerged across Canada. In contrast to mainstream interventions, **traditional approaches** are based on the concept of balance and a **holistic view** that recognizes the interconnectedness between the individual, the family, nature, and the community, and the relationship between the physical, psychological, social, and spiritual aspects of the individual (Svenson & Lafontaine, 1999). From a traditional perspective, a person's "problems in living" represent an imbalance in need of adjustment or **healing**. For Aboriginal Canadians, the healing process goes beyond the restoration of balance in an individual's life: rather, healing involves a "societal recovery from the lasting effects of oppression and systemic racism experienced over generations" (Hylton, 2002, p. 5). Moreover, healing strategies tend to address human problems—such as addictions, poverty, and family violence—simultaneously in recognition of their overlapping causes and effects.

Traditional Aboriginal healing practices are considered to be outside the mainstream social welfare system, although they are sometimes used in conjunction with mainstream services. Thus, Aboriginal peoples can now choose between a broad range of mainstream programs (such as psychotherapy) and programs based on traditional practices (such as the Medicine Wheel)—or utilize both as needed.

HEALING STRATEGIES AND INITIATIVES

Government-funded healing initiatives during the 1980s focused on the pervasive problems of alcoholism and drug abuse in First Nations communities. However, it was soon recognized that other social problems, such as those relating to residential schools, family relationships, and mental health, were serious and widespread in First Nations communities and needed to be made priorities for healing initiatives.

To help Aboriginal peoples deal with the adverse effects of the residential school system, the federal government introduced the Aboriginal Healing Strategy in 1997. Part of this strategy involved the establishment of the Aboriginal Healing Foundation (AHF) in 1998, a nonprofit, nongovernmental corporation run by Aboriginal people. The foundation funds community-based traditional healing projects that address the historic trauma of abuse suffered in residential schools; by 2009, over 1,300 funding grants had been given to support such projects (Aboriginal Healing Foundation, 2002).

All AHF healing projects—which include healing circles and leadership training for healers—are developed, delivered, and managed by native groups and organizations. Projects are also tailored to the needs of Aboriginal peoples and communities; are based on traditional Aboriginal values, principles, and practices; and take place in culturally relevant settings. Although individuals are active in their own healing, the process is guided by Elders, skilled healers, and others who are well respected in the community. An individual's "personal problems" are placed within a social and historical context (which serves to reduce self-blame and denial), and cultural interventions (such as traditional ceremonies) are used to promote collective healing and a sense of belonging (Aboriginal Healing Foundation, 2008).

Many traditional healing programs exist in Canada. One of the more established programs is in the Ojibway community of Hollow Water, Manitoba. There, the Community Holistic Circle Healing (CHCH) program uses a thirteen-step process to address sexual abuse (and related issues such as addiction). The steps can take several years to complete, and focus on educating people about the seriousness of the violence, changing people's attitudes toward abuse, preventing further incidents of abuse in the community, and helping people heal. A variety of people can take part in the process, including the survivor of the offence, the offender, family members, and provincial justice system workers. A program evaluation conducted by the Public Safety and Emergency Preparedness Canada (2003, p. 2) found that CHCH had reduced the community's reliance on mainstream resources and could prove to "be a cost-effective alternative to the [mainstream] criminal justice process."

Systems and strategies continue to be developed in response to Aboriginal concerns. For example, researchers Michael Bopp, Judie Bopp, and Phil Lane have created a generic community response system to address domestic violence in Aboriginal communities. Exhibit 12.4 depicts that system's nine interrelated interventions which, together, aim to prevent and reduce incidents of domestic violence in Aboriginal communities.

A COMMUNITY RESPONSE TO ABORIGINAL DOMESTIC VIOLENCE

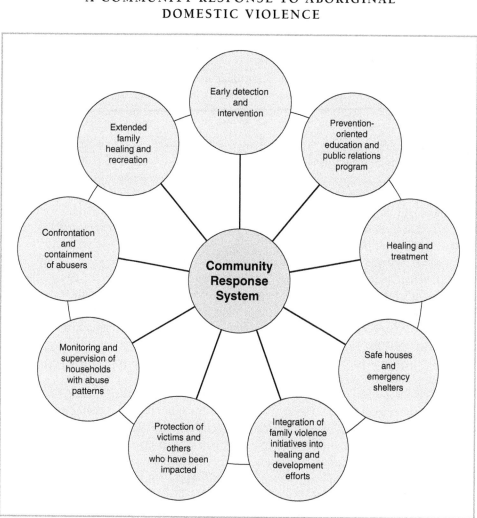

Source: Adapted from M. Bopp, J. Bopp, and P. Lane, Four Worlds Centre for Development Learning. (2003). *Aboriginal Domestic Violence in Canada.* (fig. 3, p. 87). Retrieved November 27, 2008, from Aboriginal Healing Foundation, http://www.ahf.ca/pages/download/28_38. Used by permission of the Aboriginal Healing Foundation.

INDIAN RESIDENTIAL SCHOOLS SETTLEMENT AGREEMENT

While healing programs address the therapeutic needs of residential school survivors, compensation fulfils a legal responsibility. In 2007, the Government of Canada agreed to compensate Aboriginal peoples for their loss of culture and

EXHIBIT 12.5

STATEMENT OF APOLOGY BY PRIME MINISTER STEPHEN HARPER

Mr. Speaker, I stand before you today to offer an apology to former students of Indian residential schools.

The treatment of children in Indian residential schools is a sad chapter in our history. In the 1870s, the federal government, partly in order to meet its obligations to educate Aboriginal children, began to play a role in the development and administration of these schools.

Two primary objectives of the residential schools system were to remove and isolate children from the influence of their home, families, traditions and cultures, and to assimilate them into the dominant culture. These objectives were based on the assumption that Aboriginal cultures and spiritual beliefs were inferior and unequal. Indeed, some sought, as it was infamously said, "to kill the Indian in the child." Today, we recognize that this policy of assimilation was wrong, has caused great harm, and has no place in our country.

Most schools were operated as "joint ventures" with Anglican, Catholic, Presbyterian and United churches. The Government of Canada built an educational system in which very young children were often forcibly removed from their homes, often taken far from their communities. Many were inadequately fed, clothed and housed. All were deprived of the care and nurturing of their parents, grandparents and communities. First Nations, Inuit and Métis languages and cultural practices were prohibited in these schools. Tragically, some of these children died while attending residential schools and others never returned home.

The government now recognizes that the consequences of the Indian residential schools policy were profoundly negative and that this policy has had a lasting and damaging impact on Aboriginal culture, heritage and language. While some former students have spoken positively about their experiences at residential schools, these stories are far overshadowed by tragic accounts of the emotional, physical and sexual abuse and neglect of helpless children, and their separation from powerless families and communities.

The legacy of Indian residential schools has contributed to social problems that continue to exist in many communities today. It has taken extraordinary courage for the thousands of survivors that have come forward to speak publicly about the abuse they suffered. It is a testament to their resilience as individuals and to the strength of their cultures.

Regrettably, many former students are not with us today and died never having received a full apology from the Government of Canada. The government recognizes that the absence of an apology has been an impediment to healing and reconciliation. Therefore, on behalf of the Government of Canada and all Canadians, I stand before you, in this chamber, so vital, so central to our life as a country, to apologize to

Continued

Aboriginal Peoples for the role that Canada played in the Indian residential schools system.

To the approximately 80,000 living former students, and all family members and communities, the Government of Canada now recognizes that it was wrong to forcibly remove children from their homes and we apologize for having done this. We now recognize that it was wrong to separate children from rich and vibrant cultures and traditions, that it created a void in many lives and communities, and we apologize for having done this. We now recognize that, in separating children from their families, we undermined the ability of many to adequately parent their own children and sowed the seeds for generations to follow, and we apologize for having done this. We now recognize that, far too often, these institutions gave rise to abuse or neglect and were inadequately controlled, and we apologize for failing to protect you.

Not only did you suffer these abuses as children, but as you became parents, you were powerless to protect your own children from suffering the same experience, and for this we are sorry. The burden of this experience has been on your shoulders for far too long. The burden is properly ours as a government, and as a country. There is no place in Canada for the attitudes that inspired the Indian residential schools system to ever prevail again.

You have been working on recovering from this experience for a long time and in a very real sense, we are now joining you on this journey. The Government of Canada sincerely apologizes and asks the forgiveness of the Aboriginal Peoples of this country for failing them so profoundly.

We are sorry.

In moving towards healing, reconciliation and resolution of the sad legacy of Indian residential schools, the implementation of the Indian Residential Schools Settlement agreement began on September 19, 2007. Years of work by survivors, communities, and Aboriginal organizations culminated in an agreement that gives us a new beginning and an opportunity to move forward together in partnership. A cornerstone of the settlement agreement is the Indian Residential Schools Truth and Reconciliation Commission.

This commission represents a unique opportunity to educate all Canadians on the Indian residential schools system. It will be a positive step in forging a new relationship between Aboriginal Peoples and other Canadians, a relationship based on the knowledge of our shared history, a respect for each other and a desire to move forward with a renewed understanding that strong families, strong communities, and vibrant cultures and traditions will contribute to a stronger Canada for all of us.

Source: Video—Indian Residential Schools Statement of Apology—Prime Minister Stephen Harper—2008, http://www.ainc-inac.gc.ca/ai/rqpi/apo/pmsh-eng.asp. Reproduced with the permission of the Minister of Public Works and Government Services, 2009, and courtesy of the Privy Council Office.

language as a result of the residential schools. The settlement includes a lump-sum payment to all former students; a system through which former students can seek further compensation for the abuse they suffered; a Truth and Reconciliation Commission to educate the public on the impact of residential schools; funds to commemorate the legacy of the schools; and additional funds to the Aboriginal Healing Foundation (Government of Canada, 2006b). Chief Phil Fontaine (2005) of the Assembly of First Nations observes that "[w]hile no amount of money will ever heal the emotional scars, this settlement package will contribute to the journey on the path to healing—not only for all residential school survivors, but for their children and grandchildren."

As a separate gesture, Prime Minister Stephen Harper made a Statement of Apology to former students of Indian Residential Schools, on behalf of the Government of Canada (INAC, 2008b) (see Exhibit 12.5).

Discussion Questions

■ **Healing and Wellness in Aboriginal Communities**

1. Identify some of the ways in which the residential schools have impacted former students. How might those impacts have an intergenerational effect on families?

2. In your opinion, what are some of the potential benefits (or detriments) of a holistic approach to helping?

IV ISSUES AND CHALLENGES FOR SELECTED GROUPS

FIRST NATIONS AND THE ISSUE OF RESERVES

The ultimate goal for many First Nations communities is to be self-governed, with full authority and control over the design, administration, and delivery of on-reserve programs and services. As these communities evolve toward self-government, they share with government many of the responsibilities for the management and delivery of on-reserve programs and services.

Some observers question whether reserves are supportive environments for First Nations. There is considerable historical baggage associated with reserves, which were once considered "places of confinement" and "laboratories" of assimilation experiments. Many reserves are also geographically isolated and struggling economically, socially, and culturally (Standing Senate Committee on Social Affairs, Science and Technology, 2006b). According to the Community Well-Being Index—which measures the quality of education, employment, income, and housing in Canadian communities—only one First Nations community rates in the top 100 Canadian communities, while 92 place in the 100 worst communities in Canada (INAC, 2008e).

Joseph Quesnel (2008) suggests that, while Aboriginal people living off reserves may have their difficulties, they may be in a favourable position to access opportunities and succeed in mainstream society. On the other hand, new sources of economic development may be the answer for First Nations communities. As a result of treaty settlements, First Nations are gaining more control over their land and resources, and making their own decisions on how to use their resources to achieve their objectives. These economic developments may not only yield sufficient revenue to improve individual communities but also empower them as a people.

Today, a number of economic development opportunities and supports are available to First Nations. For example, under the federally sponsored Community Economic Development Program, First Nations can access funds to help plan and develop projects, find financial backing, and implement projects that will create jobs and establish businesses on-reserve. In 2008, the federal government committed to developing a new federal framework to enhance Aboriginal economic development. To begin the framework development process, Indian and Northern Affairs Canada has sought input from both economic development experts and the general public (INAC, 2008c).

First Nations peoples are also forming partnerships with business. For example, in 2009, businessman and former prime minister Paul Martin created a $50 million equity fund called Capital for Aboriginal Prosperity and Entrepreneurship (CAPE). That fund will be used to invest in existing Aboriginal companies such as manufacturing, fish farming, and food processing, as well as to finance in business training for managers of those companies. CAPE is a social economy enterprise that is expected to provide both a financial return for Martin, and a social economy return for Aboriginal peoples and other Canadians. From Martin, point of view, Aboriginal communities want to be economically independent; CAPE is expected to help First Nations reach that goal (Cowan, 2009).

To guide the development and delivery of economic and social initiatives for First Nations peoples, the Assembly of First Nations has proposed a First Nations Wholistic Policy and Planning Model (see Exhibit 12.6). At the core of the framework is the community, the context of all initiatives. Moving out from the centre, each ring represents a domain that is central to policy and planning processes. Those domains are the individual (represented in the Medicine Wheel); the four cycles of the lifespan; key components of governance; fourteen determinants of health; and the three elements of social capital (relations within and outside the community).

EXHIBIT 12.6

FIRST NATIONS WHOLISTIC POLICY AND PLANNING MODEL

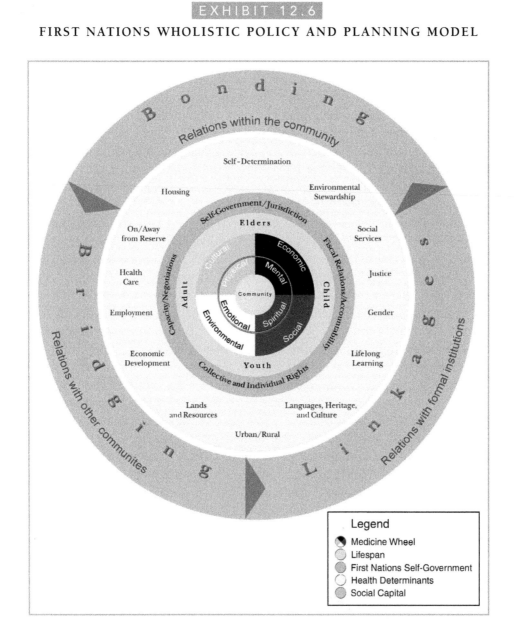

Source: Assembly of First Nations. (2007, May). *Sustaining the Caregiving Cycle: First Nations People and Aging: A Report from the Assembly of First Nations to the Special Senate Committee on Aging,* (Figure 1, p.8). Retrieved November 10, 2008, from http://www.afn.ca/misc/SCC.pdf.

MEETING THE NEEDS OF URBAN ABORIGINAL PEOPLE

According to the 2006 Census, 54 percent of Aboriginal peoples live in urban centres, a 50 percent increase from 1996 (Statistics Canada, 2008b). Many Aboriginals have found that living in a city allows them better access to well-paying jobs and educational opportunities than living on-reserve. Moving to the city may also be an opportunity to escape the social problems—such as alcoholism and suicide—that characterize many reserves (Quesnel, 2008). Studies nevertheless show that city life is not positive for all Aboriginal people; many face barriers to quality education, employment, and housing, and child poverty is common.

The development of programs for urban Aboriginal peoples has been inconsistent and largely uncoordinated. However, one type of urban-based resource—Native Friendship Centres—have become popular multipurpose centres for Aboriginal people living in cities. These centres offer an alternative to mainstream social agencies in their provision of family, employment, and educational counselling, as well as early childhood development programs. Friendship centres have also been instrumental in the establishment of other organizations, such as women's shelters, soup kitchens, and housing corporations (Lowe, 2007).

In 1998, the federal government introduced the Urban Aboriginal Strategy (UAS) to improve the coordination of Aboriginal policies and programs in urban centres, as well as make initiatives more responsive to local Aboriginal needs and priorities. A primary aim of the UAS is to increase Aboriginal self-reliance and life choices for Aboriginal women, children, and families living in cities by helping them to improve their employment and life skills (INAC, 2009a).

ABORIGINAL CHILDREN

Conditions have been improving for Aboriginal children in recent years; however, many fall behind other young Canadians in terms of physical and mental health, educational attainment, and employment prospects. This is especially true for Status Indian and Inuit children (Townsend & Werwick, 2008). Aboriginal children are also overrepresented in foster care and criminal justice systems, as victims of abuse, and in poverty statistics (NCW, 2007c). Some observers attribute these inequities to disputes among different levels of government and Aboriginal organizations over which authority should control what program. While the leaders squabble over program responsibility, many health, social welfare, and educational services for Aboriginal children are

EXHIBIT 12.7

A wide range of federally funded programs focus on improving the quality of life and future prospects for Aboriginal children.

Source: Paul Austring Photography/First Light/Getty Images.

either delayed or disrupted. The collective failure of governments and Aboriginal authorities to improve conditions for children has implications for the future. Children who do not have a good start in life are likely to enter adulthood with fewer resources than other Canadians, and face considerable disadvantage in postsecondary training, in the labour market, and when starting their own families (O'Sullivan, 2006).

Community programs that support Aboriginal young people and their families are critical to the well-being of all Aboriginal peoples. Many of these programs—created by Aboriginal individuals, families, organizations, and communities—are currently available, and offer "hope for future generations" (NCW, 2007c). This section looks at some of those programs.

Programs for Young Children

In 1997, representatives of the NAOs and the federal, provincial, and territorial governments began developing a long-term action plan known as the National Children's Agenda (NCA). Under the NCA, the Federal Strategy on Early Childhood Development for First Nations and Other Aboriginal

Children was created to meet the specific needs of young Aboriginal children who live on- and off-reserve. The Strategy allows Aboriginal communities and organizations to enhance and expand existing programs for preschool children for the purpose of improving their health and social well-being. A wide range of programs are supported by the Strategy, including the following:

- Aboriginal Head Start programs aim to prepare young children for school by providing "a positive sense of themselves, a desire for learning, and opportunities to develop fully" (INAC, 2008d). Head Start programs promote Aboriginal cultures and languages, health and nutrition, and parental involvement. Head Start programs are offered on- and off-reserve, and are available to First Nations, Inuit, and Métis preschool children and their families.

- The First Nations and Inuit Child Care Initiative ensures that childcare programs in First Nations and Inuit communities reflect local needs and cultures, and create more effective and affordable childcare spaces so that parents of young children can work or attend school. The initiative also offers after-school care for older children (HRSDC, 2009a).

- The First Nations' National Child Benefit Reinvestment (NCBR) initiative is an on-reserve counterpart to provincial/territorial programs. Under the NCBR, the savings derived from unused portions of social assistance are reinvested in culturally relevant, community-based projects (such as meal programs) aimed at reducing the negative effects of Aboriginal child poverty (INAC, 2009b).

- Brighter Futures is a community-based health promotion program for First Nations on-reserve and Inuit communities; its counterpart, the Community Action Plan for Children, is for Métis, Inuit, and off-reserve First Nations families. Each of these initiatives supports a wide range of culturally sensitive programs and services to help parents increase their awareness and understanding of health-related issues and to develop healthy habits. The program is made up of five components: early childhood development, parenting, mental health, healthy babies, and injury prevention (Health Canada, 2007b).

Child Welfare Services

Before Europeans settled in Canada, Aboriginal communities successfully used traditional methods to care for and protect their children. When mainstream child welfare systems were established in the late nineteenth century, social workers imposed their own strategies of child protection on Aboriginal

ABORIGINAL CHILDREN IN CARE BY PROVINCE AND TERRITORY

	PERCENT OF ALL CHILDREN (0–14) WHO ARE ABORIGINAL*	NUMBER OF CHILDREN IN CARE			
		TOTAL	ABORIGINAL	% IN CARE WHO ARE ABORIGINAL	DATE
NEWFOUNDLAND AND LABRADOR	6%				
PRINCE EDWARD ISLAND	2%				
NOVA SCOTIA	3%	2,000	310	16%	2006
NEW BRUNSWICK**	4%	1,445	191	13%	September 30, 2006**
QUEBEC	2%	11,135			March 31, 2006
ONTARIO	2%	19,035			March 31, 2006
MANITOBA	23%	6,629	5,627	85%	March 31, 2006
SASKATCHEWAN	25%	3,050	2,135	70%	2005
ALBERTA	9%	8,565	4,880	57%	March 2006
BRITISH COLUMBIA	7%	9,157	4,542	50%	March 2006
YUKON***	33%	252			September 2006
NORTHWEST TERRITORIES	63%				
NUNAVUT	95%	311	311	100%	October 2006

Continued

*"Statistics Canada, "Population Reporting an Aboriginal Identity, by Age Group, by Province and Territory" (table), *2001 Census Summary Tables*. Retrieved July 4, 2007, from www.statcan.ca/l01/cst01/demo40a.htm?sdi=aboriginal%20identity.

**New Brunswick: Data includes 178 First Nations children on-reserve served by First Nations Child and Family Services Agencies as of July 2007.

***Yukon: An estimate from the Grand Chief of the Council of Yukon First Nations put the share of First Nations children in care at over 80 percent (*CBC News*, "CYFN Withdraws from Children's Act Review," March 24, 2006.)

Source: National Council of Welfare. (2007, Fall). *First Nations, Métis and Inuit Children and Youth: Time to Act* (tab. 7.1, p. 86). Retrieved November 23, 2008, from http://www.ncwcnbes.net/documents/researchpublications/ResearchProjects/FirstNationsMetisInuitChildrenAndYouth/2007Report-TimeToAct/ReportENG.pdf. Reproduced with the permission of the Minister of Public Works and Government Services, Canada, 2008.

peoples. For decades, Aboriginal children were commonly apprehended and placed in non-native foster care. This practice culminated in what is known as the "sixties scoop"—a massive apprehension of Aboriginal children that began in the 1960s (Johnston, 1983). By the early 1980s, Aboriginal children were overrepresented in the child welfare system; in Saskatchewan, for example, 63 percent of all children in care were Aboriginal. Those systems continue to remove Aboriginal children from their families at disproportionate rates (see Exhibit 12.8). Recent reports estimate that 38 percent of children in care across Canada are Aboriginal; yet Aboriginal children represent only 5 percent of all children (Blackstock, Prakash, Loxley, & Wien, 2005).

Aboriginal children who are apprehended and placed in foster care outside of their communities are at risk of losing their language, culture, and sense of Aboriginal identity and belonging. Needless to say, this approach to child welfare is associated with widespread family breakdown and a general lack of cohesion in Aboriginal communities. Reports also indicate that Aboriginal "graduates of the child welfare system make up a disproportionate number of street kids and commercially exploited youth in the sex trade in Canadian cities" (Castellano, 2002, pp. 19–20). Not surprisingly many Aboriginal communities view mainstream child welfare systems more as colonization devices than as methods to protect children (Blackstock et al., 2006).

Since 1990, the federally funded First Nations Child and Family Services program has allowed First Nations to develop their own child welfare services for registered children living on reserves. These services are designed according to provincial/territorial child welfare guidelines. Although First Nations services vary from region to region, they all try to address child welfare issues on the reserve, place native children in Aboriginal homes, and employ child welfare workers who are Aboriginal and familiar with First Nations culture

(Durst, 2002). Today, over 110 Aboriginal child and family service agencies exist in Canada; the majority of these serve members of First Nations living on reserves (CWLC, 2007). The Aboriginal Justice Inquiry/Child Welfare Initiative (AJICWI) in Manitoba is a unique system that gives control over the delivery of child protection services to both Métis and First Nations peoples. Under that system, First Nations authorities can serve First Nations families living either on or off a reserve (MacDonald, 2005).

With the exception of Manitoba's system, the protection of Aboriginal children living off-reserve in Canada falls within the mandate of mainstream provincial/territorial child welfare systems (CWLC, 2007).

Discussion Questions

Issues and Challenges for Selected Groups

1. There is a question whether reserves offer the optimal environment for First Nations. From your observations and knowledge of reserves, what might be some of the pros and cons of reserves for the social and economic development of First Nations peoples?

2. What are some of the potential risks or losses related to the placement of Aboriginal children in non-Aboriginal foster care?

V SOCIAL WORK WITH ABORIGINAL PEOPLES

Aboriginal people often associate mainstream social workers with the operation of residential schools, and the mass apprehension of Aboriginal children during the "sixties scoop." These associations have not only eroded the relationship between mainstream social workers and Aboriginal people, but also fuelled the demand for Aboriginal social workers. Today, a wide range of opportunities exist in Aboriginal-controlled programs and systems (including self-governed communities) for Aboriginal social workers and other types of helpers (Stephenson, Rondeau, Michaud, & Fiddler, 2000).

The growing demand for Aboriginal social workers has led to an expansion of Aboriginal-controlled social work education programs. These programs specifically prepare social workers for service in Aboriginal communities. An example of this type of program is the School of Indian Social Work at the First Nations University of Canada. There, social work courses are based on First Nations culture, philosophy, and values, and students are given the opportunity to learn through interactions with First Nations individuals, families, and communities. To ensure that training reflects a First Nations approach, the program includes both Elders and traditional First Nations educators in curriculum development (First Nations University of Canada, 2009).

Some experts believe that non-Aboriginal workers may be effective helpers if they first receive **cross-cultural training**. Such training might include

- an orientation to traditional Aboriginal approaches to helping;
- awareness of the effects of the colonization process;
- recognition of the importance of Aboriginal identity or consciousness;
- appreciation of the value of cultural knowledge and traditions in promoting healing and empowerment; and
- an understanding of various avenues of Aboriginal self-expression (McKenzie & Morrissette, 2003).

At the community development level, social workers may be able to support Aboriginal peoples in their progress toward self-determination and self-government. Mawhiney and Hardy (2005, p. 129) point out that those goals "are consistent with the [social work] profession's ideological position of respecting self-determination and cultural diversity, advocating against oppression and inequity, and promoting non-discriminatory practice."

SUMMARY

Introduction

Four percent of Canadians are Aboriginal. The Aboriginal population is growing rapidly, and Aboriginal peoples are reclaiming their traditional languages and practices. Despite much progress, Aboriginal peoples are generally more disadvantaged than other Canadians. Those disadvantages are associated with historic repression by government, the ineffectiveness of mainstream programs, and a loss of autonomy.

I. Historical Foundations of Canada's "Indian Policy"

Colonial governments set out to assimilate natives into mainstream society through enfranchisement policies, which included the first Indian Act of 1876. A more aggressive approach to assimilation came in the form of residential schools, where children were taught to reject their Indian heritage, families, and communities.

II. Bridging the Divide: Attempts at Reform

Efforts to assimilate and enfranchise Aboriginal peoples generally failed. As conditions worsened for Aboriginal people, they demanded change; that assertion resulted in an Aboriginal rights movement, and the formation of several NAOs. Aboriginal peoples made significant political advances during the 1990s; however, a later change in government decreased the potential of the Kelowna Accord. Overall, the policy and program development process has improved for Aboriginal peoples, but the federal government still controls many Aboriginal affairs.

III. Healing and Wellness in Aboriginal Communities

Many of the social and economic problems facing Aboriginal peoples are attributed to colonization and the residential school system. Mainstream social welfare programs are available to Aboriginal people; however, those programs are not always responsive to Aboriginal circumstances. Traditional approaches to healing are available under the Aboriginal Healing Strategy; healing services are delivered by Aboriginal organizations. The federal government agreed to compensate Aboriginal peoples for their losses incurred at residential schools, and a Statement of Apology has been made.

IV. Issues and Challenges for Selected Groups

First Nations are gaining more control over their resources and activities, and their communities are bolstered by economic development initiatives. City dwelling offers both benefits and challenges to Aboriginal people; support is available to urban dwellers through Native Friendship Centres and initiatives such as the Urban Aboriginal Strategy. Although conditions for Aboriginal children are improving, many still live in disadvantaged or deprived circumstances. The National Children's Agenda and other initiatives support young children and their families. Many Aboriginal communities are developing their own child welfare services; however, child protection off-reserve is mainly controlled by provincial/territorial authorities.

V. Social Work with Aboriginal Peoples

There is a growing demand for Aboriginal social workers and, in turn, a demand for Aboriginal-focused social work programs. Non-Aboriginal service providers may be effective helpers with cross-cultural training. At the community development level, social workers may support Aboriginal peoples in their progress toward self-determination and self-government.

Key Terms

For definitions of the key terms, consult the Glossary on page 413 at the end of the book.

Aboriginal peoples, p. 308
Indian, p. 308
First Nations people, p. 308
Métis, p. 308
Inuit, p. 308
band, p. 308
reserve, p. 309

assimilation, p. 311
enfranchisement, p. 311
residential school, p. 312
National Aboriginal Organization, p. 315
self-government, p. 316
colonization, p. 319
residential school syndrome, p. 320

mainstream approach (to helping), p. 321
traditional approach (to helping), p. 321
holistic view, p. 321
healing, p. 321
cross-cultural traning p. 335

CHAPTER 13

The Social Welfare of Recent Immigrants

OBJECTIVES

The social welfare of recent immigrants is dependent on their integration into Canadian society. This chapter will explore:

- the historical highlights of Canada's immigration policy;

- acclimatization (stage one of the settlement process);

- adaptation (stage two of the settlement process); and

- issues related to social workers and settlement practice.

INTRODUCTION

Canada's history is replete with stories of people seeking a new life for themselves and their families. As a country populated to a very large extent by immigrants and their descendants, that experience is deeply rooted in our national consciousness. Canadian values have been influenced by the need to welcome and integrate people from many cultures, religions, languages and national experiences. (Citizenship and Immigration Canada, 1998, p. 1)

Canada is a country of **immigrants**. According to the 2006 census, almost 20 percent of Canadians are foreign-born (Chui, Tran, & Maheux, 2007). Most recent immigrants are from China, followed by India, the Philippines, and Pakistan (see Exhibit 13.1). As a result, the majority of newcomers to Canada

EXHIBIT 13.1

TOP 10 COUNTRIES OF BIRTH OF RECENT IMMIGRANTS (1981–2006)

ORDER	2006 CENSUS	2001 CENSUS	1996 CENSUS	1991 CENSUS	1981 CENSUS
1	People's Republic of China	People's Republic of China	Hong Kong	Hong Kong	United Kingdom
2	India	India	People's Republic of China	Poland	Viet Nam
3	Philippines	Philippines	India	People's Republic of China	United States of America
4	Pakistan	Pakistan	Philippines	India	India
5	United States of America	Hong Kong	Sri Lanka	Philippines	Philippines
6	South Korea	Iran	Poland	United Kingdom	Jamaica
7	Romania	Taiwan	Taiwan	Viet Nam	Hong Kong
8	Iran	United States of America	Viet Nam	United States of America	Portugal
9	United Kingdom	South Korea	United States of America	Lebanon	Taiwan
10	Colombia	Sri Lanka	United Kingdom	Portugal	People's Republic of China

Note: *Recent immigrants* refers to landed immigrants who arrived in Canada within five years prior to a given census.

Source: Statistics Canada, *Immigration in Canada: A Portrait of the Foreign-Born Population, 2006 Census*, Catalogue No. 97–557-XIE, ISBN 978-0-662-47177-6, December 2007.

are **visible minorities**—that is, individuals, other than Aboriginal persons, who are non-white or non-Caucasian. Between 1981 and 2001, the proportion of Canadians belonging to a visible-minority group rose from 5 to 13 percent. It is projected that, in a few years, one in five Canadians will belong to a visible-minority group (Statistics Canada, 2008e).

There are many benefits of immigration for Canada. Ethnic foods, art, music, and literature enrich the country's social and cultural life. In economic terms, immigrants are recognized for bringing capital, initiative, and expertise to the labour force. Perhaps most importantly, immigrants are helping to offset Canada's declining birth rate and aging population. Over the coming years, Canada will need to admit greater numbers of immigrants to fill the labour shortages created by the retiring baby boomers; the contributions made by immigrant workers—through labour and taxation—will support health care, social welfare, and other vital services in the coming years.

By and large, recent immigrants are positive about living in Canada, and are adapting well to their new homeland. However, a growing number of recent immigrants face serious disadvantages, especially in the labour market where unemployment and underemployment is common. Researcher Geneviève Bouchard (2007) reports that the economic conditions among newcomers is worsening over time, especially among visible minorities.

Studies indicate that Canadians are generally supportive of immigrants and the immigration process. Many Canadians are nevertheless concerned that local, regional, and federal governments are not doing enough to help recent immigrants settle into, participate in, and contribute to society. Howard Duncan (2007) from the Metropolis Project believes that Canadians are uncomfortable with letting immigrants struggle on their own as "segregated and economically polarized populations," a traditional practice that must change "not only to achieve a stronger measure of social justice but to prevent social instability."

Canada's social welfare system is responsible for facilitating the **settlement process**. Although this process is different for everyone, it typically involves three stages:

- *Acclimatization* marks the period when newcomers deal with their immediate basic needs after moving here; finding a place to live, learning the local language, and enrolling children in school are some of the initial tasks.

- *Adaptation* is a period when newcomers learn to function more independently, are able to access services on their own, are making friends and cultivating employment contacts, and are setting personal goals (Canadian Council for Refugees, 1998; Goss Gilroy Inc., 2000).

- *Integration* is the ultimate goal of the settlement process. Integration is synonymous with **social inclusion**, a process that is characterized by a sense of belonging, acceptance, and recognition. According to Omidvar and Richmond (2003), "For immigrants and refugees, social inclusion would be represented by the realization of full and equal participation in the economic, social, cultural and political dimensions of life in their new country. In a simple but useful sense, therefore, social inclusion for immigrants and refugees can be seen as the dismantling of barriers that lead to exclusion in all these domains."

Social welfare programs—and, in particular, settlement programs—are primarily concerned with helping **recent immigrants** successfully carry out the tasks related to acclimatization and adaptation. During these two stages, governments and others must work to reduce barriers that prevent the full integration or inclusion of newcomers into Canadian society. This chapter explores some of the issues and interventions related to the acclimatization and adaptation stages; first, however, is a brief account of Canada's immigration policy.

CANADA'S IMMIGRATION POLICY: HISTORICAL HIGHLIGHTS

RACIST BEGINNINGS

Although Canada has always considered immigrants and refugees from around the world, its immigration policies have clearly indicated which individuals "deserve" to be admitted to Canada. These same policies also reflect the country's attitudes toward people of various nationalities, races, and colours. During the eighteenth and nineteenth centuries, Canada welcomed newcomers who would develop the vast and sparsely populated land and help build the national railways. By relaxing immigration restrictions and offering free land, the federal government was able to attract large numbers of immigrants to Canada. In those early years, Canada's immigration policy stated a preference for white people (mostly from Britain, Europe, and the United States). That policy tightened even more with the Canadian Immigration Acts of 1906 and 1910, which intended to keep out poor, sick, or "immoral" applicants. Asian immigrants in particular were unwelcome in Canada. To ensure Anglo-Saxon supremacy, the Canadian government kept the entry of Asians into Canada to a minimum by imposing a head tax on Chinese immigrants and by being highly selective with regard to Japanese and East Indian immigrants (CIC, 1995). (For a closer look at the Chinese head tax, see Exhibit 13.2.)

EXHIBIT 13.2

THE CHINESE HEAD TAX: FROM RACISM TO REDRESS

THE RACIST YEARS

- *1881–1885.* Canada recruits over 15,000 people from China to help build the Canadian Pacific Railway. Once the railway is completed, Chinese labourers are no longer needed or wanted. The Government of Canada imposes a $50 head tax on immigrants of Chinese origin.

- *1900–1903.* The head tax has not deterred Chinese people from immigrating to Canada. The federal government raises the tax to $100 in 1900, and to $500 in 1903.

- *1923.* By now, about 81,000 Chinese immigrants have paid the head tax, raising $23 million in revenue for Canadian governments. Although the tax is profitable, Chinese immigrants are seen as competition for white labour. The federal government passes the Chinese Immigration Act (nicknamed the "Exclusion Act"), which severely restricts people of Chinese origin from entering Canada. Many family members still in China are prohibited from joining their loved ones in Canada.

- *1947.* Since 1923, fewer than 50 Chinese immigrants have been admitted to Canada. The Government of Canada repeals the Chinese Immigration Act. People of Chinese origin are allowed to become Canadian citizens and to vote. The entry of Chinese immigrants is still restricted, but within a broader category relating to persons of "Asiatic race."

SEEKING REDRESS

- *2000.* The Chinese Canadian National Council (CCNC) launches a class-action lawsuit against the Government of Canada, claiming that the Chinese head tax violated, among other things, the Canadian Charter of Rights and Freedoms. The CCNC loses the case.

- *2006.* Prime Minister Stephen Harper apologizes to Chinese-Canadians for the head tax imposed on Chinese immigrants, and promises to give a "gift" of $20,000 to each head tax payer (or widow).

- *2008.* The federal government has made over $12 million in payments to Chinese-Canadians.

Source: Citizenship and Immigration Canada, "85th Anniversary of the Chinese Immigration Act," October 29, 2008. Retrieved May 18, 2009, from CIC website, http://www.cic.gc.ca/multi/mpa-ahm/85-eng.asp. Chinese Canadian National Council, (2005). "Head Tax Redress Campaign: Chinese Head Tax and Exclusion Act: CCNC and the Redress Campaign." Retrieved November 27, 2008, from CCNC website, www.ccnc.ca/sectionEntry.php?entryID=10&type=Advocacy.

Immigration peaked between 1904 and 1913, when two-and-a-half million people moved to Canada, and then slowed considerably during the Great Depression. At the end of the Second World War, Canada revised its immigration policies to accept a greater number of immigrants and to consider more immigrants from non-white countries. There were several reasons for Canada's more open-door policy, including the following:

- Canada's economic needs had changed—the country needed skilled, well-educated immigrants who could work with new technologies.
- Jobs were plentiful and Canadians no longer perceived immigrants as competitors for jobs.
- Canadians were better educated, more worldly, less prejudiced, and more open to other cultures.
- Canadians were showing more interested in challenging **racism** and pursuing human rights and the humane treatment of others.
- Minority groups were becoming more organized and gaining political power.
- An anti-communist sentiment motivated Canadians to give asylum to people fleeing communist countries.
- A declining birth rate and labour shortages forced Canada to consider admitting immigrants from non-European countries (Belanger, 2006).

Despite more enlightened postwar views surrounding immigration, Prime Minister Mackenzie King emphasized that immigration policies would still be used as a tool to maintain a predominantly white society. King's position reflected a general attitude among Canadians that non-white people were unsuitable candidates for immigration because of their presumed inability to fit into a predominantly Euro-Canadian society (Stasiulis & Abu-Laban, 2004). The new Immigration Act of 1953 reflected these racist views by making it more difficult for people from less-favoured nations to become Canadian citizens (CIC, 1995).

The 1960s were marked by the recognition of universal human rights and more inclusive legislation. The Canadian Bill of Rights, proclaimed in 1960, prohibited discrimination by the federal government on the basis of race, colour, gender, or ethnic origin. In 1967, the federal government amended Canada's Immigration Act to bring it into line with the bill of rights—no longer could the acceptance of immigrants be based on discriminatory criteria such as ethnic origin or race. Instead, applicants would be assessed according to a points system, which awarded so many points for education, occupation, age, knowledge of English or French, employment opportunities in Canada, and other objective criteria. The lifting of discriminatory immigration criteria drastically altered Canada's ethnic profile. Before the points system was introduced, people from Asia represented just 3 percent of all immigrants; by the 1970s, 33 percent of immigrants were from Asia (Statistics Canada, 2003a).

A growing acceptance of cultural diversity, and the passage of Canada's new Multicultural Policy of 1971, paved the way for a new Immigration Act in 1976. This act favoured newcomers who were entrepreneurs, investors, and others who could contribute to Canada's economy. The Act made new demands on the federal government. For one thing, the government had to do more to help newcomers adapt to Canadian life, to reunite families, and to assist in the resettlement of refugees. In addition, the new act required the federal government to project desired immigration quotas for one-to-three-year periods. Initially, the quotas were used to anticipate the number of workers needed to fill Canadian jobs; later, the quotas became a tool for increasing the population, which was declining as a result of low birth rates (Chinook Multimedia Inc., 2000).

Exhibit 13.3 illustrates the wide variation in immigration levels, as well as immigration rates, from 1900 to 2006.

EXHIBIT 13.3

NUMBER OF IMMIGRANTS AND IMMIGRATION RATE IN CANADA (1900–2006)

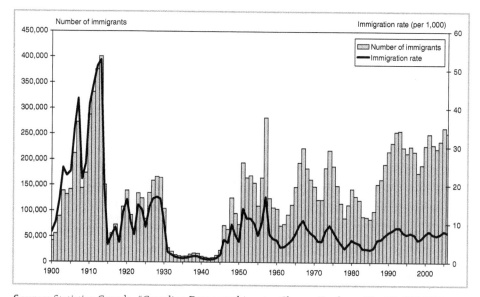

Source: Statistics Canada, "Canadian Demographics at a Glance, Catalogue No. 91–003-XIE, ISSN 1916–1832. January 2008.

IMMIGRATION PROBLEMS AND REFORMS

During the 1980s, cracks in the Immigration Act began to emerge. One problem was that Canada needed skilled and educated workers; however, the immigration quotas were mainly being filled by unskilled extended family members sponsored by immigrants in Canada (Heritage Community Foundation, 2005). Immigration was also becoming a burden on social programs: new immigrants were expected to assume responsibility for supporting the family members they sponsored, yet many of these sponsors were reneging on their support agreements, costing taxpayers millions of dollars in welfare benefits (CIC, 1995). Moreover, immigration procedures had become too complicated and were being applied inconsistently across Canada; globalization and changes in the labour market had rendered the immigrant selection process outdated; and existing legislation was ill equipped to deal with the growing number of illegal aliens entering Canada. By 1985, public approval of immigration programs had dropped to a new low.

To address the many problems related to immigration, the federal government amended the Immigration Act in 1997. Immigrants' applications were now divided into three classes: an economic class (which included skilled workers and business immigrants); a family class; and a refugee class. The new act put more emphasis on selecting independent immigrants who would bring skills, education, experience, and other assets to Canada's labour force. Further reforms came in 2000, when the Liberal government proposed to replace the twenty-year-old immigration act with new legislation that would "curb criminal abuse of the immigration and refugee systems" and expand "policies to attract the world's best and brightest to Canada" (CIC, 2000). A few months later, following the 9/11 attacks in the United States, Canada introduced its Immigration and Refugee Protection Act (IRPA) to try to keep out those who posed a threat to national security, yet admit those who could make important contributions to Canadian society.

The past few years have witnessed a greater preference for immigrants likely to meet the country's economic goals than for immigrants in the family reunification category. In 2006, over half of all immigrants plus their spouses, partners, and dependants were admitted under the economic class of the immigration policy. Most of these immigrants were selected because they were considered most "likely to stimulate the economy or integrate into the labour market given their age, education level and knowledge of Canada's official languages" (Statistics Canada, 2008c).

In 2008, the federal government amended the Immigration and Refugee Protection Act to make it more responsive to Canada's labour-market needs, and to reduce the backlog and wait times for those wanting to move here (Kenny, 2008). Today, people can immigrate to Canada by way of four categories:

- Experience Class, for temporary foreign workers and international students with Canadian degrees and work experience;

- Federal Skilled Worker Class, for workers with recent work experience in an occupation in high demand in Canada;

- Business Class, for experienced business people to own and manage businesses; and

- Family Class, for sponsored spouses, dependent children, parents, or grandparents of permanent residents or citizens (Chui, 2003).

Discussion Questions

▣ **Canada's Immigration Policy: Historical Highlights**

1. In your opinion, how might the racist immigration policies of Canada's past influence people's current attitudes toward immigrants?

2. What are some of the reasons why Canadians became more open-minded about non-white immigrants after the Second World War?

3. Do you believe that Canadians today are more or less accepting of non-white immigrants? Give reasons for your answer.

▣ STAGE I OF THE SETTLEMENT PROCESS: ACCLIMATIZATION

For the federal government, the goal of the **acclimatization stage of settlement** is twofold. One goal is to help newcomers complete a variety of basic settlement tasks with the support of programs and services. A second goal is to garner public support for the immigration process itself—support that is considered key to immigrants' economic success and inclusion in Canadian society (Omidvar & Richmond, 2003).

SETTLEMENT PROGRAMS

Since 1948, Canada has offered a variety of **settlement programs** to help immigrants and refugees get a good start in their new life in Canada. For the most part, settlement programs are delivered by service providers in voluntary social agencies, otherwise known as **immigration service agencies** (ISAs).

Usually, these agencies are stationed in communities with concentrated immigrant populations. The Ottawa Community Immigrant Services Organization (OCISO, 2007) is one example of an ISA. With other community partners, this organization provides newly arrived immigrants with culturally and linguistically appropriate programs, and supports community-based initiatives that aim to facilitate the integration of newcomers into the community.

Although Citizenship and Immigration Canada (CIC) is ultimately responsible for settlement policies and programs, certain provinces have entered into agreements with the federal government to gain more control over the design, management, and delivery of settlement programs in their jurisdictions. The first intergovernmental agreement was reached in 1991, when the Canada–Quebec Accord gave Quebec control of its own settlement programs, including reception services, and language training. In return, the federal government provides funding for those programs (CIC, 2007a).

While settling in a new country is bound to produce some challenges, most newcomers face similar barriers during their first six months in Canada. According to the Longitudinal Survey of Immigrants to Canada, the most common barriers are

- finding employment (due to a lack of "Canadian experience, difficulty transferring foreign qualifications, and language");
- accessing training (due to "language barriers, high costs and course availability");
- finding housing (due to the "high cost of housing and not having a credit history"); and
- accessing healthcare services (due to "waiting lists, costs and language barriers") (Fellegi, 2006).

To reduce these and other barriers during the initial settlement process, the federal government recently allocated a total of $1.3 billion over five years to allow ISAs to expand their services (CIC, 2007a). This funding will enrich the three core settlement programs offered under Citizenship and Immigration Canada: the Immigrant Settlement and Adaptation Program, Language Instruction for Newcomers to Canada, and the Host Program. These programs are briefly reviewed below.

Immigration Settlement and Adaptation Program (ISAP)

ISAP was established in 1974 to provide essential services to newcomers, and to improve settlement services across Canada. In terms of indirect services, ISAP funds projects designed to enhance service delivery to newcomers, educate the public about settlement, share information on settlement activities, and train settlement program staff. ISAP also funds "service-bridging" initiatives, such as Ontario's Settlement Workers in Schools program; this program connects (or "bridges") recent immigrant families to resources in the school system and community for the purpose of fostering student achievement (Ontario Council of Agencies Serving Immigrants, 2007).

ISAP is perhaps best known for its wide range of direct services available to newcomers, including

- *assessment and referral* activities, which determine newcomers' needs, resources, and barriers, and connect them to community resources and services such as health services, legal services, education, and job centres;

- *information and orientation* activities, which provide newcomers with basic information about their rights and responsibilities as Canadian citizens, assist them with the tasks of daily living, and help them learn about their community;

- *interpretation and translation* activities, which provide language interpretation and translate documents and forms required to access medical, legal, education, employment, and other services;

- *counselling*, which provides support and encouragement to newcomers, assists in basic problem solving, and helps newcomers locate more in-depth psychological counselling services if needed; and

- *employment-related services*, which help newcomers connect with job search services and potential employers (CIC, 2005).

Exhibit 13.4 outlines these and related settlement services, along with their objectives and intended beneficiaries.

Host Program

Under the Host Program, organizations and individuals recruit people who are familiar with Canada, train them as volunteers, and then match them with newcomers to Canada. Host services are often provided on a one-on-one or group basis. The Host Program can benefit both newcomers and volunteers. Newcomers learn about Canada, local services and systems, and possible work opportunities; they also get a chance to practise their English or French. Volunteers benefit from making new friends and learning about other cultures. Through newcomer–Canadian connections, the Host Program aims to promote ethnic diversity and social inclusion, enhance cross-cultural awareness, and reduce racial stereotyping. In 2006, almost 5,000 recent immigrants participated in the Host program (CIC, 2007a).

EXHIBIT 13.4

SETTLEMENT SERVICES: EXAMPLES, OBJECTIVES, AND BENEFICIARIES

SPECIFIC SERVICES	SERVICE OBJECTIVES	BENEFICIARIES OF SERVICES
Orientation Language assessment, referral Employment and career counselling, job placement, skills upgrading, certification programs Community, multicultural programs Citizenship programs	Services to help immigrants (individually and as community members) develop the skills and knowledge to participate in society Services to help the host community Services to promote multiculturalism	Immigrants Host community Ethnocultural communities
Advocacy on behalf of immigrants with public institutions, etc. Translation and interpretation Community, volunteer, integration programs	Services to build a bridge between immigrant and society	Immigrant Host community Ethnocultural communities
Family counselling Other counselling and support groups Health programs Mental health services	Services adapted to address the special needs of immigrants	Immigrants
Public education Cross-cultural and anti-racism training for mainstream service providers	Services to help the community adapt to newcomers	Host community Mainstream service organizations

Source: Adapted from *Best Settlement Practices: Settlement Services for Refugees and Immigrants in Canada*, Canadian Council for Refugees, February 1998, http://www.web.ca.ccr/bpfinal.htm. Used by permission of the Canadian Council for Refugees.

Language Programs

Linguistic adaptations are a challenge for many newcomers to Canada. Before 1980, most new immigrants to Canada had a first language of either English or French; today, fewer than 20 percent have this skill (Fellegi, 2006). The ability to communicate effectively with others is essential to a newcomer's full integration into a country's social, economic, and cultural life. Through the

Language Instruction for Newcomers to Canada (LINC) program, adults who are new to Canada receive free basic instruction in English or French. At the same time, the LINC curriculum gives newcomers an opportunity to learn about various aspects of Canadian life. Language instruction is available through colleges, school boards, workplaces, and other organizations (CIC, 2007a). Reports show that within the first two years after arriving in Canada, over one-quarter of immigrants in the family or economic class, and close to half of all refugees, take at least one language course (Schellenberg & Maheux, 2007).

Support for Refugees

Immigrants move to another country by choice; in contrast, **refugees** are forced by the threat of persecution to flee their homeland. Under the UN's Convention Relating to the Status of Refugees (the Geneva Convention) and other international agreements, Canada is obligated to protect legitimate refugees. To qualify as a refugee, people must first meet the criteria for a Convention refugee or a person in need of protection. Canadian officials investigate the refugee's claim and decide whether the applicant meets either the Refugee and Humanitarian Resettlement Program (for people seeking protection from outside Canada), or the In-Canada Asylum Program (for people making refugee protection claims from within Canada) (CIC, 2007b). When compared to other countries, Canada has earned a reputation as a leader in refugee protection. In recent years, Canada has tightened its refugee selection criteria; even so, Canada resettles from 10,000 to 12,000 refugees every year (CIC, 2008). In 2006, that number represented about 13 percent of all newcomers to Canada (Statistics Canada, 2008c).

In addition to personal protection and safety, and the promise of a permanent home, refugees need many of the same supports as other immigrants. Many refugees also have specific needs resulting from persecution in their homeland; for example, a number of refugees are survivors of torture who are dealing with serious physical, psychological, and emotional consequences when they arrive in Canada (Canadian Council for Refugees, 2008). Basic health services are available to refugees, as well as support under ISAP, LINC, and the Host Program. In addition, refugees may be eligible for the Resettlement Assistance Program, which offers help finding accommodation, and financial assistance to purchase clothing, household items, and other basic necessities during the first year in Canada (CIC, 2008).

EXHIBIT 13.5

Poster promotes the Canadian Council for Refugees' 30th anniversary, as well as "30 years of building a home of justice for refugees and immigrants."

Source: Courtesy of Canadian Council for Refugees.

IMMIGRANT SETTLEMENT PATTERNS

Impact on Large Cities

Recent immigrant settlement patterns have largely been an urban phenomenon. Most immigrants (63 percent) settle in Canada's three largest cities of Toronto, Montreal, and Vancouver (Chui, Tran, & Maheux, 2007). According to the Longitudinal Survey of Immigrants to Canada, the choice of which city to settle in is largely determined by the fact that a spouse, partner, or other relative already lives there, or that there are employment prospects (Chui, 2003).

The heavy influx and concentration of immigrants in large cities is creating a number of challenges for those centres, especially in terms of urban development and increasing demand on health, social welfare programs, and other public services such as schools (CIC, 2001). Immigration also shapes the labour market by increasing the number of employed workers and those looking for work, and by making the workforce more culturally and racially diverse. This is certainly the case in Toronto, where over half of recent immigrants are working-age adults (Chui, Tran, & Maheux, 2007).

The federal, regional, and local levels of government have been trying to find ways to disperse immigrants more evenly across the country; such strategies would not only dilute the concentration of newcomers and reduce the strain on resources in large centres, but also fill labour shortages in smaller towns and cities. To help matters, the federal government has removed a cap on how many immigrants a province or territory is allowed to take; this has allowed jurisdictions outside the main settlement areas of Ontario, Quebec, and British Columbia to recruit more immigrants as needed. A number of regions are trying to attract immigrants through elaborate advertising campaigns that promote their rural and smaller centres as desirable places to live, work, and raise a family.

EXHIBIT 13.6

Chinatowns are some of the most colourful and recognizable "ethnic enclaves" in Canada.

Source: © Michael Klinec/Alamy.

Ethnic Enclaves

One of the trends associated with the urbanization of immigration is the phenomenon of **ethnic enclaves**. These enclaves are neighbourhoods where large numbers of the same ethnic or racial group settle and open restaurants, groceries, retail stores, banks, and other businesses. Many examples of ethnic enclaves—such as Little Italy and Chinatown—are found in Canada's large cities. Researchers have identified both pros and cons of ethnic enclaves. On the positive side, the residents in concentrated

EXHIBIT 13.7

ETHNIC ENCLAVES: SOCIAL ADVANTAGES AND DISADVANTAGES

ADVANTAGES	DISADVANTAGES
Create a protected housing sub-market for immigrants of a specific ethnicity.	May constrain immigrants' housing choices.
Provide ease of access to housing for immigrants or ethnics.	Under certain conditions, may "ghettoize" immigrants or minorities.
Sustain "community life" and help foster social networks, neighbourliness, mutual support, and recreation, particularly for stay-at-home women, reducing isolation and facilitating settlement.	May inhibit social mixing with others and participation in the mainstream culture(s).
Promote the viability of community-based facilities, services, and institutions with the concentration of consumers and self-help initiatives (e.g., elder care, daycare centres, religious congregations, mosques, temples).	May isolate children of immigrants, and impede their acculturation to diversity. Identifying immigrants or ethnics with a neighbourhood may lead to stereotyping of those groups and, in extreme cases, make them easy targets for prejudice or violence.
Increase the viability of culturally and linguistically relevant public services (e.g., heritage language ESL classes, cooperative housing, mosques, temples, churches).	May restrict immigrant employment opportunities by limiting their encounters and networking with people of different backgrounds.
Lay basis of ethnic economy and the emergence of ethnic business districts.	May impede the social integration and growth of civic life of the city or society.
Promote cultural and physical diversity of a city's neighbourhoods, create centres of interest and entertainment for the city as a whole.	
Help reduce the suburban monotony and sameness by fostering "cultural landscapes."	

Source: Adapted from Mohammad A. Qadeer. (October 2003). *Ethnic Segregation in a Multicultural City: The Case of Toronto, Canada* (fig. 2, p. 26). CERIS Working Paper No. 28. Joint Centre of Excellence for Research on Immigration and Settlement—Toronto. Retrieved November 29, 2008, from http://ceris. metropolis.net/Virtual%20Library/community/WP28_Qadeer.pdf. Used by permission of the author.

groups can enjoy common interests, form social networks, and participate in various cultural and religious activities. These neighbourhoods can be especially beneficial to immigrant women, many of whom do not speak English or French, and who desire the closeness of family and friends. On the negative side, ethnic enclaves can segregate residents from the mainstream society and, in turn, limit their opportunities to connect with others, learn English or French, find work, or attend school outside the neighbourhood. Perhaps one of the biggest concerns about ethnic enclaves is their potential to concentrate recent immigrants, many of whom are poor, into "enclaves of poverty" or "ghettos"—environments that pose particular risks to the health and well-being of children (Omidvar & Richmond, 2003). Exhibit 13.7 outlines other possible advantages and disadvantages of ethnic enclaves.

Discussion Questions

Stage I of the Settlement Process: Acclimatization

1. What are the three core settlement programs available to newcomers to Canada, and how do their respective services attempt to "acclimatize" newcomers to their new country?

2. From your perspective, what are the potential benefits and detriments of high concentrations of immigrants in Canada's largest cities?

STAGE II OF THE SETTLEMENT PROCESS: ADAPTATION

A variety of factors influence the degree to which newcomers adapt to the Canadian way of life. According to the Canadian Council for Refugees (1998), successful adaptation depends on the extent to which service providers—such as those working in government offices, voluntary agencies, hospitals, schools, and police departments—are able to adjust to the diversity of the populations they serve. Government policies can also impact adaptation; for example, the federal government only offers settlement services such as ISAP to newcomers during the initial period of settlement, leaving many immigrants on their own during the middle (adaptation) and final (integration) stages of settlement. Another influence on the adaptation process is government and public opinion about immigrants. According to the Canadian Council for Refugees (2008, p. 7), "[n]egative comments and portrayals by politicians, in the media or between members of the public are hurtful to refugees and immigrants and undermine their efforts to integrate into Canadian society."

An issue that has recently come to the forefront of studies on immigrant adaptation is the process of **social exclusion**. In a multicultural country like Canada, social exclusion is typically based on a person's racial or cultural attributes. To socially exclude an immigrant is to deprive him or her of the goods, services, and chances in life that are necessary for basic survival and social participation. As Paulo DeCoito (2008) from the Social Planning Council of Peel points out: "What makes social exclusion a major problem at this time is the fact that most of the people being 'excluded' from equal access to the resources and opportunities in Canada tend to be the very people that Canada needs to grow its population and its economy: non-White immigrants from Asia, Africa, Latin America, and the Caribbean."

The **adaptation stage of settlement** requires an effort by both foreign- and native-born individuals: newcomers are encouraged to adapt to Canadian ways without giving up their cultures; at the same time, Canadian-born citizens and organizations are urged to respect the cultural gifts that newcomers bring to this country. This mutual obligation is critical to a socially cohesive society (Dorais, 2002). According to Aycan and Berry (1996), the adaptation stage has three interrelated levels:

- *Psychological adaptation* refers to characteristics that are internal to the individual, such as optimism, a sense of confidence, self-esteem, and life satisfaction.

- *Sociocultural adaptation* refers to the degree to which the individual is able to acquire the skills needed to manage day-to-day activities in a new culture.

- *Economic adaptation* refers to the sense of accomplishment derived from working.

The following section considers these levels of adaptation as they relate to three selected groups: young newcomers, women, and workers.

YOUNG NEWCOMERS

In 2004, about 51,000 immigrants admitted to Canada were under the age of 15. The Canadian Council of Social Development predicts that by the year 2016, one-quarter of Canada's child and youth population will be immigrants (CCSD, 2006). Research tells us that most young immigrants are adapting well to life in Canada. However, as Sarah Crowe (2006) from the National Children's Alliance points out, some newly arrived young immigrants

> ... not only struggle with the usual tensions associated with growing up but also struggle with coming to a new country that can be significantly different from their own. Their families are often poor, have little or no knowledge of English or French especially in the case of refugees, and are often ill prepared for living in Canadian society. Some of these children are illiterate in their own language and have little or no experience of formal schooling.

The language issue is a particularly important point. Kids who do not speak English or French are at high risk of exclusion from educational and social opportunities (Kilbride & Anisef, 2001). It is becoming more common for children and youth to arrive in Canada and not have either English or French as their first language; in 2002, almost three-quarters of all immigrants under the age of 15 were in this situation (Crowe, 2006).

Some young refugees face particular challenges in the adaptation process. Children who have fled war or abuse in their homeland, or who have been separated from their parents, may be under considerable stress when they arrive in Canada. In his study of Canada's boat people, Morton Beiser (1999) found that recent refugee youth were twice as likely as adults 35 and older to suffer from depression; they were especially at risk of suicide.

A growing body of research on the needs and issues of young newcomers is fuelling the expansion of programs and services for this group. Support programs for young immigrants vary across the country since they tend to be tailored to local needs. Examples of these types of support services are the following:

- Winnipeg's Employment Solutions for Immigrant Youth offers a classroom-based program to help immigrant youth find employment in the Manitoba labour market.

- The Central Alberta Refugee Effort offers an Immigrant Youth Program to help young newcomers adapt to their new life in central Alberta.

- The African Child and Youth Program, sponsored by the Immigrant Services Society of British Columbia, provides social, recreational, and academic programs to young people from Africa.

Certain programs for young immigrants are in particularly high demand. There is, for instance, an increasing need for culturally relevant early-learning and childcare programs, especially for low-income visible-minority groups. Also popular are outreach programs, in which workers connect with young newcomers, and help them to transition into school and community activities. Moreover, there is an increasing need for prevention and support programs for youth at risk of gang behaviour, criminal activity, and dropping out of school. Finally, English-as-a-second-language programs are always in demand (Mitchell, 2005).

WOMEN

With the exception of language training, the service needs of recent immigrants are similar to those of the Canadian public; for instance, most people need basic health care, and education for their children. While the *type* of service is not extraordinary to newcomers, the *delivery* of those services has been shown to strongly influence their use of services. How services are delivered is especially important to women immigrants.

Overall, women immigrants are more likely to seek help from agencies that offer culturally sensitive programs—ones that recognize and respect their particular values, beliefs, and norms. In her study of immigrant women in Atlantic Canada, researcher Barbara Cottrell (2008) found that women immigrants seek help if the helper is someone they know or has been referred by someone they trust; knows something about their culture; and is female and from the same country of origin. It is also important to women that helpers speak the same language. However, as Cottrell (2008) points out, some catchment areas—such as the Peel Region in Ontario—have such a multitude of languages and dialects that the provision of same-language services is not always realistic for social agencies.

According to the 2004 General Social Survey on Victimization, about 5 percent of recent immigrant women experience spousal or partner violence; however, this rate is considered to be low due to underreporting (Statistics Canada, 2006b). An immigrant woman may not report an incident of violence for a variety of reasons: for example, she may not understand her legal rights, she may be financially dependent on her husband (who is usually the abuser), or she may be unable to speak French or English (Woodall, 2004). In her survey of front-line service providers, Ekuwa Smith (2004) found that many abused immigrant women were reluctant to seek help because they distrusted the police; were unfamiliar with how the justice, social welfare, and other support systems worked; and doubted that resources would be culturally sensitive to their needs.

Many social agencies in Canada have taken steps to make their operations more culturally sensitive. Some agencies hire workers who represent the racial and ethnic diversity of the population they serve, and ensure that all front-line and office staff receive diversity training. A number of agencies also make a point of regularly reviewing their program standards, policies, and procedures to ensure they are inclusive of immigrants and ethnic minorities (Luther, 2007). Some agencies—such as Immigrant Women Services Ottawa—try to reduce barriers to help-seeking by tailoring all their programs to the needs of immigrant women.

WORKERS

Employment plays an important role in a newcomer's adaptation to a new country and the eventual integration and participation in Canadian society. Aycan and Berry (1996, p. 11) observe that work

> provides purpose to life, it defines status and identity, and enables individuals to establish relationships with others in the society. It is especially the latter function that becomes critical for immigrants, because adaptation is facilitated by social interactions. The more one inter-acts with the groups in the larger society, the faster one acquires skills to manage everyday life.

For working-age immigrants, successful adaptation involves entering the workforce, making enough income to achieve financial independence, and eventually advancing in one's career (Canadian Council for Refugees, 1998).

Well into the 1980s, newcomers to Canada could expect that, after the initial settling-in period, they would be able to find a well-paying job. In those days, immigrant employment participation rates were as high or higher than that of Canadian-born workers, and their earnings were comparable. Today, the fact that 12 percent of working-age immigrants are unemployed suggests that easy access to the labour market may be a thing of the past for new Canadians.

A number of Canadian studies help to identify the barriers to employment for recent immigrants. According to the Longitudinal Survey of Immigrants to Canada, the most serious difficulty newcomers face is tapping into the good jobs. To a lesser extent, immigrant job seekers run into problems when trying to get their educational credentials from abroad recognized in Canada. Newcomers also find that not having Canadian work experience

EXHIBIT 13.8

In 1959, when these Italian immigrants arrived at Pier 21 in Halifax, Canada had plenty of jobs to offer newcomers.

Source: From the Sforza Family Collection of the Pier 21 Society.

hinders employment, as does not being able to speak English or French (Schellenberg & Maheux, 2007). Reports suggest that visible-minority immigrants—especially from black or Asian origins—tend to have more difficulty finding work than non-visible-minority workers (Fellegi, 2006).

The ability of recent immigrants to find good jobs is influenced by ongoing changes in Canada's employment structures. For one thing, labour market restructuring has created greater wage disparities. Even when recent immigrants find full-time work, they earn less than other workers: on average, immigrant men earn only 63 cents (and women earn 56 cents) for every dollar earned by Canadian-born male workers (Chui, Tran, & Maheux, 2007). Reports show that close to 8 percent of recent immigrants are working full-time for poverty wages (Fleury, 2007).

Another consequence of labour market restructuring is the emergence of a knowledge economy, which has transformed the type of worker in demand. Some recent immigrants have found that, between the time they applied to immigrate and the time they actually arrived in Canada, the demand for their particular job skills had declined. In many cases, newcomers have to take whatever job they can find; that job is not always in the same occupational field they were in prior to moving to Canada (Chui, 2003; Schellenberg & Maheux, 2007).

Disadvantages in employment are directly related to high rates of poverty among recent immigrants. In 2004, over 20 percent of recent immigrants of working-age were living in poverty, compared to less than 10 percent of other Canadians (Fleury, 2007). Among the risks of poverty is the hardship suffered by the children of newcomers, in terms of poor health, housing, and education. Another risk of declining employment and rising poverty among recent immigrants is "the potential harm that these problems may bring to race relations and social cohesion" (Reitz, 2003). On a more positive note, it is expected that the aging population will gradually increase the demand for skilled immigrants—especially those with a background in information technology—to fill positions vacated by retiring baby boomers (Statistics Canada, 2003b).

Discussion Questions

■ **Stage II of the Settlement Process: Adaptation**

1. Certain groups—specifically, young newcomers, women, and workers—can face certain challenges during the adaptation stage of settlement. For each group, identify one or more potential challenge related to (1) psychological adaptation; (2) sociocultural adaptation; and (3) economic adaptation.

2. Why might immigrants from visible-minority groups have more difficulty landing jobs in Canada than non-visible-minority job seekers?

IV SOCIAL WORKERS AND SETTLEMENT PRACTICE

Newcomers to Canada, especially those who belong to a visible-minority group, typically struggle with poverty, unemployment, underemployment, and lack of affordable housing. Social workers (or "settlement workers") can provide valuable support and advocacy to these groups. To be effective, settlement workers have to be personally suited to working with immigrants and refugees; that is, they should be sensitive to racism issues and to the impact that professional helpers can have on clients. The Canadian Council for Refugees (2000) adds that professionals engaged in **settlement practice** need to demonstrate certain values (such as respect for the individual, client empowerment, and accountability); professional ethics (including respect for client confidentiality and avoidance of conflicts of interest); and skills (for example, interviewing, case management, and advocacy). Settlement practice also requires a strong grounding in theories and principles relating to the following:

- the settlement process (including the adaptation process, influences on integration, and the effects of settlement on family);
- the immigrant and refugee experience;
- multiculturalism and cultural change;
- human rights and racism;
- global and Canadian influences that shape immigration and settlement; and
- relevant systems (such as the social welfare, health, education, and justice systems).

Social workers can increase their cultural sensitivity by engaging in **cross-cultural training**. This type of training often involves some form of cultural immersion: participants are transported into ethnocultural communities, where they become sensitized to the cultural values of others and, at the same time, arrive at a better understanding of their own cultural values (Herberg & Herberg, 2001). Through cross-cultural training, participants may also "become aware of the existence of their prejudices, stereotypes, and racist behaviours, and of the potential impact of these factors on clients" (Christensen, 1996, p. 148).

Effective cross-cultural training encourages participants to adapt their traditional knowledge frameworks and practice methods to their work with minority clients. For example, social workers might focus less on changing the individual and concentrate more on reducing racist practices in external systems. They might also refine their assessment skills with regard to clients from different ethnic and cultural backgrounds; this includes recognizing the value that each client places on tradition. Herberg and Herberg (2001, p. 173) note that although "some [people] cling to their traditional values ... others abandon many of their original customs and mores, actively rejecting the 'old ways.'" It is therefore crucial for helpers to develop a clear understanding of the client's cultural values and preferences. Unless they can do this, social workers may find it difficult to establish rapport with minority-group clients and help them stay engaged in settlement activities.

A study by Cottrell (2008) found that settlement workers want to respond effectively to the cultural backgrounds of their clients, yet felt they lacked the skills to do so. Those who had completed a social work or similar degree had received some general training in providing culturally competent care; however, they found their training to be fragmented and not entirely relevant to the demands of their jobs. The Canadian Association of Schools of Social Work (CASSW) is working to improve this situation. The CASSW now requires social work curricula to address multiculturalism before they can be accredited (Hanley, 2000).

SUMMARY

Introduction

Canada is a country of immigrants. There are many social, cultural, economic, and demographic benefits of immigration. Most recent immigrants are visible minorities who are likely to face disadvantages, especially in the labour market. The social welfare system is mostly concerned with the stages of acclimatization and adaptation. Integration is synonymous with social inclusion, and is the ultimate goal of settlement.

I. Canada's Immigration Policy: Historical Highlights

Canada's immigration policies were originally racist, and limited the entrance of non-white immigrants to Canada. After the Second World War, Canada became more accepting of immigrants; even so, immigration policies were used to ensure a predominantly white society. In the 1960s, immigration policy became more inclusive. By the 1980s, several problems in the immigration process led to changes in the Immigration Act and a greater emphasis on the admittance of self-sufficient immigrants. The creation of the Immigration and Refugee Protection Act aimed to keep out those who posed a threat to national security. Today, immigration policy favours immigrants who are likely to meet the country's economic goals.

II. Stage I of the Settlement Process: Acclimatization

The primary goals of the acclimatization stage are to help newcomers complete basic settlement tasks, and to garner the public's support for immigration process. To facilitate early settlement, immigration service agencies deliver the ISAP, the Host Program, and the LINC program. Refugees can access these programs as well as the Resettlement Assistance Program. Most immigrants settle in Toronto, Montreal, and Vancouver, centres that are challenged by a heavy influx of immigrants. Governments are searching for ways to disperse immigrants more evenly across the country. There are both pros and cons of ethnic enclaves; the biggest concern is their potential to concentrate large numbers of poor immigrants.

III. Stage II of the Settlement Process: Adaptation

The adaptation stage of settlement requires an effort by both foreign- and native-born individuals. Adaptation occurs on three levels (psychological, sociocultural, and economic), and is influenced by several factors. Social exclusion is typically based on a person's racial and cultural attributes. Many young immigrants face challenges in the adaptation process; not speaking English or French is a particular barrier. A growing number of programs are available for young newcomers. The way that helping services are delivered influences the utilization of those services by women immigrants. These women prefer agencies and programs that are culturally sensitive; many social agencies have tailored their approaches accordingly. Employment plays an important role in the adaptation process. Many immigrants (especially visible minorities) are unemployed, underemployed, or living in poverty. Labour market restructuring contributes to employment problems.

IV. Social Workers and Settlement Practice

In settlement practice, service providers must be personally suited to working with immigrants and refugees; demonstrate certain values, ethics, and skills; and have a relevant knowledge base. Social workers sometimes take cross-cultural training to increase their cultural awareness and sensitivity, to refine their assessment skills, and to adapt their helping strategies to meet the needs of minority clients. Social work education programs do not always prepare students for work with recent immigrants, but the CASSW is making progress in this respect.

Key Terms

For definitions of the key terms, consult the Glossary on page 413 at the end of the book.

immigrant, p. 338
visible minority, p. 339
settlement process, p. 339
acclimatization, p. 339
adaptation, p. 339
integration, p. 340
social inclusion, p. 340
recent immigrant, p. 340

racism, p. 342
acclimatization stage of settlement, p. 345
settlement program, p. 345
immigration service agency, p. 345
refugee, p. 349
ethnic enclave, p. 352

social exclusion, p. 354
adaptation stage of settlement, p. 354
settlement practice, p. 359
cross-cultural training, p. 360

Social Welfare and People with a Disability

OBJECTIVES

The inclusion of persons with disabilities is key to the well-being of all society. This chapter will explore:

- disability in Canada (definitions, types and severity of disability, and disability among selected groups);

- the evolution of Canada's disability policy;

- housing, income, and employment issues for people with disabilities; and

- social work with persons with disabilities.

INTRODUCTION

> Given the challenges facing our communities, it is our shared responsibility to uncover and mobilize the latent capacity of all citizens. People with disabilities, like every citizen, have both the capacity and the responsibility to strengthen our communities. We must ensure that each community member thrives and contributes. (Philia, 1997)

People with physical or mental disabilities have always been part of Canadian society, but they have not always had the same opportunities as those without a disability. For the most part, social attitudes have determined the extent to which people with disabilities are included in society. Those attitudes are also reflected in predominant definitions of disability. For much of history, disability was defined in terms of a person's physical or mental impairments, and how those impairments impacted daily activities. This view led to the development of disability-related interventions that focused on changing or "rehabilitating" people to help them "fit in" and function "normally" in mainstream society. The problem with this approach was that it presumed a standard of normal daily living; in fact, what is "normal" is different for everyone (Rajan, 2004).

Today, **disability** is defined not so much by a person's physical or mental impairments as by the ability (or willingness) of society to accept differences between people. This view assumes that it is social attitudes that must change

EXHIBIT 14.1

People with disabilities are active participants in all aspects of society, including sports.

Source: Muellek/Shutterstock.

to accept all persons, regardless of ability, as participants in society. To reflect this progressive view, policies, programs, and services are starting to focus more on improving **access** to *all* opportunities in society for the benefit of *all* members of society (Rajan, 2004). This particular approach recognizes that people with or without disabilities have similar goals: "to participate as valued, appreciated equals in the social, economic, political and cultural life of the community," and "to be involved in mutually trusting, appreciative and respectful interpersonal relationships at the family, peer and community levels" (Crawford, 2003, p. 5).

DISABILITY IN CANADA

WHAT IS A DISABILITY?

Disability is a complex, multidimensional issue and is therefore difficult to define. This lack of definition is why social work, health, education, and other disciplines so often take different approaches to disability; why programs for people with disabilities vary in design and delivery; and why disability-related programs tend to have different eligibility criteria. Three theories of disability have nevertheless shaped how people understand and define disability, and how governments design disability-related social policies. They are the impairment perspective, the functional limitations perspective, and the ecological perspective.

- From an **impairment perspective**, disability is a biologically based illness, disease, or "problem" that originates in a person's body or mind and that can be "fixed" or cured. This biomedical view of disability is often criticized for its general disregard for the role that social, political, or economic factors can play in the disability experience; for its limited focus on the defective element (impairment) of a person's body or mind; and for its tendency to label people with disabilities as being "defective," "abnormal," and, by implication, "inferior" to non-disabled people.

- While the **functional limitations perspective** supports the notion that disability is biologically based, it also considers the ways disability impacts (or limits) the non-medical aspects of a person's life, such as work and relationships. Moreover, this perspective takes into account how people with disabilities—and others—perceive and react to those limitations. One of the main criticisms of this model is its emphasis on the costs of disability in terms of lost productivity, diminished social role, and other types of disadvantage.

- The **sociopolitical perspective** (also called the *ecological perspective*) emerged in the 1970s, but it was not until the mid-1990s that it gained popularity over the impairment and functional limitations perspectives. Like its predecessors, the sociopolitical perspective assumes that disability is the consequence of an abnormal medical condition and subsequent impairment. However, this perspective also recognizes the connections between impairment, a person's activity limitations, and his or her participation in specific environments such as home, school, and work. According to this perspective, a person's experience of "disablement" is largely the result of the stigmatization, discrimination, and subsequent marginalization of people with disabilities, rather than the physical impairment itself (HRDC, 2003; Bickenbach, 1993).

North American models of disability tend to emphasize the sociopolitical perspective and the role that society plays in "disabling" people by excluding them from participation in mainstream activities. This broader view of disability is reflected in the Government of Canada's definition: "Disability is not defined merely as being the direct result of a health problem or any physical or mental limitation ... [but rather] the result of complex interactions between a health problem or functional limitation and the social, political, cultural, economic, and physical environment. These, in combination with personal factors such as age, gender, and level of education, can result in a disadvantage—that is, a disability" (HRSDC, 2006b).

In 2001, the World Health Organization created the *International Classification of Functioning, Disability and Health* (ICF), to shift the world's focus of disability away from the medical or biological *cause* of disability, to the *impact* of society's response to disability. The ICF goes one step further and "normalizes" disability, suggesting that everyone's health is limited to some degree, and therefore everyone experiences some level of disability. Thus, disability is a universal human experience (WHO, 2009).

TYPES AND SEVERITY OF DISABILITIES

The term *disability* is often used generically to refer to a broad range of conditions, even though there are many specific forms of disability (see Exhibit 14.2). In Canada, what is or is not a disability varies, depending on the criteria of disability-related programs and services. According to the Canada Pension Plan, for example, a disability is a physical and/or mental condition

EXHIBIT 14.2

PREVALENCE OF DISABILITIES IN ADULTS IN CANADA

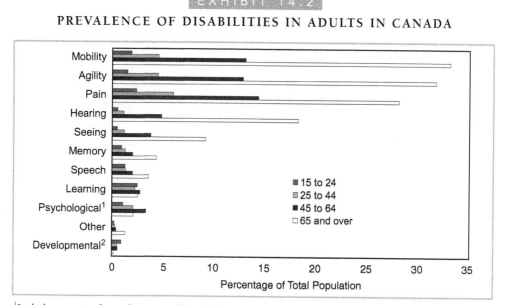

[1]Includes emotional, psychiatric, and alcohol/drug problems.

[2]Use with caution.

Source: Adapted from Statistics Canada, "Participation and Activity Limitation Survey 2006: Analytical Report," Catalogue No. 89–628-XIE, No. 002, ISSN 1915–0466, December 2007.

that is severe (prevents the person from working) and prolonged (likely to be long-term or result in death) (Service Canada, 2008b). For the purpose of determining a person's eligibility for compensation, the Workers' Compensation Board of Saskatchewan (2005) defines disability as "[a]ny restriction or lack of ability to perform an activity in the manner or within the range considered normal for a human being."

According to the 2006 Participation and Activity Limitation Survey (PALS), 14 percent of Canadians have a disability. Seniors have the highest rate of disability of any age group, at 43 percent; this rate is expected to rise as a result of an aging population. Almost 82 percent of adults with disabilities have more than one disability. For example, an elderly person might have difficulty walking (a mobility impairment) and also be suffering from dementia (a psychological disability) (Statistics Canada, 2007b).

Among Canadian adults, 6.6 percent have a severe disability. Because a disability may be caused by several factors, its severity can be highly individual. One person with an intellectual disability, for instance, may have no difficulty performing daily tasks of living, whereas another person with the same diagnosis may experience severe functional limitations. Severe disabilities tend to become more common with age, and can affect various life areas such as mobility, independence, the ability to work, income levels, recreation, and emotional well-being. The diversity in needs and performance levels of people with the same disability "label" presents policymakers with the challenge of planning and developing social policies and programs to meet a wide range of needs (Statistics Canada, 2007b).

DISABILITY IN SELECTED POPULATIONS

Children

According to the 2006 PALS, almost 4 percent of children have a disability. The most common disabilities among children are learning disabilities (69 percent) and chronic health conditions (67 percent) such as asthma, severe allergies, attention deficit disorder, and autism. Fifty-eight percent of children with disabilities have a mild-to-moderate disability; the remaining 42 percent live with a severe disability. Boys are more likely than girls to have a disability. Almost three-quarters of school-age children with disabilities have multiple disabilities (Statistics Canada, 2008d).

Children with special needs used to be placed in large institutions, but today, most live at home with their families. Studies reveal the challenges for parents who care for a child with a disability. For example, parents must coordinate their caregiver responsibilities with other commitments such as work and personal relationships. For most families, it is not the child's disability that poses the greatest challenges, but the severity of that disability. When compared to parents of children with mild-to-moderate disabilities, parents of severely disabled children are less likely to be satisfied with their own health; more likely to experience high levels of stress; and more apt to report that their child's disability impacts their income, work, personal time, and ability to find childcare (Statistics Canada, 2008d).

A wide range of programs and services aim to help children with disabilities live as normal a life as possible. Reports show that schools, recreation centres, and other community organizations have come a long way in including children with disabilities in mainstream activities. Despite progress, barriers still exist for special needs children. Among other things, more can be done to increase the support provided by classroom aides; there is also a need to improve training to staff in social, health, and educational settings so they can respond effectively to children with various types of disabilities (Bendall, 2008).

Aboriginal Peoples

The disability rate among **Aboriginal peoples** is almost twice that of non-Aboriginal Canadians. One study shows that over 31 percent of registered First Nations people has a disability, and many of those disabilities are the result of diabetes (McDonald, 2005b; Government of Canada, 2009). First Nations children are twice as likely as other Canadian children to have a disability. Among First Nations children, the most common disabling conditions are asthma (15 percent) and allergies (12 percent) (First Nations Regional Longitudinal Health Survey, 2005).

Studies conducted a few years ago found a general scarcity of disability-related programs and services on reserves, factors that exacerbated other disadvantages such as isolation, poverty, and unemployment. Those living in northern or remote areas faced the greatest challenges. For example, one report found that poorly maintained roads in rural areas forced some wheelchair users to remain at home, isolated from the rest of the community (Federal-Provincial-Territorial Ministers Responsible for Social Services, 2000a). In response to research findings like these, the Government of Canada and Aboriginal organizations began negotiating agreements aimed at improving conditions for Aboriginal people with disabilities. One of those agreements created the Aboriginal Human Resources Development Strategy in 1999, an initiative designed to increase employment opportunities for disabled Aboriginal people. Other initiatives—such as the Métis National Council Reference Group on Ability Issues—focus on developing culturally sensitive services for specific Aboriginal groups with disabilities.

Women

Canadian women have a higher rate of disability than men, and they also have higher levels of pain and discomfort associated with their disability (Statistics Canada, 2007b). Although women tend to suffer from mild rather than severe disabilities, the resultant activity limitations may be enough to impact day-to-day activities. In particular, cyclical or fluctuating illnesses, such as autoimmune conditions, chronic fatigue syndrome, and depression, together with other illnesses to which women with disabilities are susceptible, can severely affect one's ability to hold down a job (Doe & Kimpson, 1999). Almost three-quarters of working-age women with disabilities are currently unemployed or out of the labour market (Canadian Labour Congress, 2007). Among those who work, the average annual income is only $8,360 (UNPAC, 2006). Social assistance benefits are equally dismal; in New Brunswick, for example, benefits for a single person with a disability are below $7,400 per year (Government of New Brunswick, 2009). McFadyen (2006, p. 1) points out that the inequalities faced by women—related to, for example, caregiving responsibilities, wages, and employment—"is heightened substantially by disability status."

Research at the national and international levels shows that women with disabilities are at a much higher risk of abuse than women without disabilities. In terms of sexual abuse, 83 percent of women with disabilities are likely to be sexually abused; up to 70 percent of girls with intellectual disabilities are likely to be sexually abused before the age of 18 (National Clearinghouse on Family Violence, 2002). Because many women with disabilities have to rely on others for their care and financial security, they may lack control over their personal affairs, such as leaving an abusive marital relationship. Some women may fear that, if they leave, they will be left without any assistance or lose custody of their children (Rajan, 2004).

EXHIBIT 14.3

Many women with disabilities are able to work if given the appropriate workplace supports and accommodations.

Source: Gina Sanders/Shutterstock.

Disability in Canada

1. What are the three theories of disability that have shaped people's understanding and definition of disability? Identify how each theory might influence the way that society treats people with disabilities.

2. Identify some of the main challenges facing children, Aboriginal people, and women because of a disability. What types of additional supports are needed by each group?

CANADA'S DISABILITY POLICY AGENDA

EARLY APPROACHES TO DISABILITY

Beginning in the mid-1800s, people with mental disorders were housed in large institutions, where they were educated, trained, and treated for their disabilities. These individuals were considered inferior to other members of society, and discouraged from re-entering the community (Roeher Institute, 1996). The popularity of eugenics at the turn of the twentieth century was accompanied by the view that people with mental disabilities were a danger not only to themselves but to others. Institutional programs were redesigned for the purpose of protecting mainstream society from people with mental disabilities. Sterilization became a widely accepted method for controlling the "menace of the feeble-minded" (MacMurchy, 1932, p. 36), and for preventing mentally "defective" people from "poisoning" the race (Roeher Institute, 1996, p. 4).

From the 1920s to the 1960s, people with any type of disability were generally considered incompetent, with little or nothing to contribute to society. Most services for this group were provided in institutions, where disability was viewed from a medical (or impairment) perspective and treated as an illness or disease. Treatment was guided by rehabilitation teams consisting of physicians, psychiatrists, medical social workers, and related health professionals (Status of Disabled Persons Secretariat, 1994).

DEINSTITUTIONALIZATION AND THE DISABILITY RIGHTS MOVEMENT

By the mid-twentieth century, Canadians had become critical of the practice of "warehousing" people with disabilities in large government-funded institutions, and of the increasing costs of maintaining those institutions. There was also a general concern that, although the institutions promoted the humane treatment of residents, they actually made residents more passive, dependent, and socially excluded; these conditions reduced the likelihood that the resident would ever return to the community. An emerging body of research revealed that community-based services, and the administration of antipsychotic drugs, may be more humane and just as effective as long-term institutionalization in the treatment of disability (Peters, 2003). Moreover, experts on disability issues promoted new and enlightened ways of thinking about people with disabilities. Sociologist Wolf Wolfensberger, for example, argued that "people with developmental disabilities should live in the most 'normal' settings possible if they were expected to behave normally" (Dawson Creek Society for Community Living, 2006).

Further criticisms of institutionalization came in the 1960s and 1970s, when a growing awareness of human rights fostered the **disability rights movement**. This movement is characterized by a general call for the elimination of socially imposed restrictions on people with disabilities, and for equal access to mainstream resources and opportunities (New Brunswick Association for Community Living, 1992). In short, "people with disabilities want[ed] to be seen as people first, to be treated as individuals, to have opportunities to participate in and contribute to society" (Rogow, 2002, p. 1). Moreover, people with disabilities promoted their role as *consumers* of services rather than as *patients*. These demands, along with government's desires to reduce the costs of disability-related care and treatment, led to **deinstitutionalization**, a process that moves institutionalized people to community settings, and replaces institutional care with community-based programs and services.

Canada's deinstitutionalization process has been driven by several different groups working toward similar ends. The efforts of those groups have led to various social movements, including

- the **community mental health movement**, which advocates for the rights of people with mental illness and a non-institutional approach to their care;

- the **community living movement**, which focuses on the creation of community-based supports and services for people with intellectual disabilities; and

- the **independent living movement**, which calls for programs designed to enable people with a disability to integrate into the community.

These social movements have been instrumental in the large-scale closure of institutions across Canada, and either the reunification of residents with their families or the relocation of residents to community-based settings, such as group homes.

THE DISABILITY COMMUNITY

While deinstitutionalization moved people out of the institutions, it did not guarantee an easy transition to "normal" community living. Indeed, during the early stages of deinstitutionalization, there were few disability-related supports and services, and people with disabilities continued to be isolated and excluded from mainstream activities. Peters (2003) observes: "Because persons with disabilities were relegated to the margins of society, societal norms only reflected characteristics ascribed to 'able-bodiedness.' For example, [buildings were] only constructed for able-bodied persons who could walk, and not for persons who used assistive devices such as wheelchairs." These types of environmental barriers began to break down as families, caregivers, people with disabilities, and other advocates pushed for the development of disability-related programs, services, and accommodations. The result of these efforts was the establishment of a wide range of organizations, often run by individuals with disabilities, designed to improve the living conditions for this group. Together, these organizations and individuals make up what is commonly referred to as the **disability community**.

Disability-related organizations are highly diverse: they may deliver either direct or indirect services, or a combination of both; they may be either national or local in scope; and they may either specialize in a single disability or serve people with any type of disability (HRDC, 2002). Examples of voluntary disability-related organizations are

- the Canadian Association for Community Living, a nationwide, non-profit federation with thirteen provincial and territorial chapters that work on behalf of people with intellectual disabilities;

- the Council of Canadians with Disabilities, which advocates at the national level for the equality and improved status of people with any type of disability;

- the Canadian Mental Health Association, which champions the rights and responsibilities of people with mental health challenges or disabilities and helps them find work, housing, and social support; and

- Independent Living Canada, which coordinates a network of Independent Living Centres that are open to people with any type of disability, that are controlled by people with disabilities, and that tailor their services to local needs.

THE 1980S: A TURNING POINT FOR DISABILITY RIGHTS

Until the 1980s, disability policy in Canada focused on the provision of health, education, and social welfare programs to enable people with disabilities to improve their standard of living and participation in community life. However, many needs—such as the need to use transportation systems and access public buildings—were virtually ignored. Issues related to access gained international attention when the United Nations declared 1981 as the International Year of Disabled Persons, designated an International Day of Disabled Persons, and assigned the decade 1983 to 1992 as the International Decade of Disabled Persons. These actions also heralded "a global commitment to ensure people with disabilities share equally in the full benefits of citizenship" (Dis-IT Research Alliance, 2006a).

In 1981, the Parliamentary Special Committee on the Disabled and the Handicapped released *Obstacles*, a report that called attention to a wide range of physical, attitudinal, and other barriers that prevented people with disabilities from accessing community resources and opportunities. *Obstacles* included several recommendations for disability policies related to such areas as human rights, transportation, and income security; many of these recommendations came from people with disabilities and other members of the disability community. One year following the release of *Obstacles*, the rights of people with disabilities were included in the *Canadian Charter of Rights and Freedoms*. By prohibiting discrimination on the basis of physical or mental disability, the Charter became the first national constitution in the world to recognize people with disabilities (HRDC, 1998).

The work of the Parliamentary Special Committee on the Disabled and Handicapped, along with the lobbying efforts of the disability community, paved the way for a new policy framework to ensure the full citizenship and inclusion of persons with disabilities. The framework reflects a sociopolitical model of disability, which focuses on removing environmental barriers to inclusion, changing societal attitudes toward disability, and recognizing the potential of people with disabilities (Dis-IT Research Alliance, 2006b). During the 1980s, the new framework, backed by human rights legislation, prompted a flurry of reforms aimed at ensuring access for people with disabilities. These reforms included changes to the *National Building Code of Canada*, which made it mandatory for newly constructed public buildings to be barrier free, and modifications to communication systems to allow people with speech or hearing impairments to use telephones and other devices more effectively. Across Canada, municipalities modified their public transit systems to make them wheelchair-accessible, installed visual and auditory traffic control signals, widened sidewalks and gave them curb cuts, and designated handicapped parking spaces—all efforts to facilitate the mobility and access of people with disabilities.

THE 1990S: NEW APPROACHES TO DISABILITY ISSUES

The early 1990s were dominated by efforts to deinstitutionalize people with disabilities and to reintegrate them into communities. In 1991, the Government of Canada introduced the National Strategy for the Integration of Persons with Disabilities; this five-year plan intended to fund projects across Canada aimed at improving access to transportation, education, housing, employment, and communications for people with disabilities. The national strategy was followed by Mainstream 1992, a template to fully integrate Canadians with disabilities into mainstream society.

By the mid-1990s, the federal government realized that more effort was needed to address the personal, day-to-day challenges of living with a disability; to reduce negative attitudes toward disabilities; and to coordinate the confusing array of disability-related public policies and programs (HRDC, 1999b). To gain headway in these areas, the government appointed a Task Force on Disability Issues. The task force's recommendations would eventually lead to increased federal funding to disability-related organizations, and amendments to several pieces of legislation—relating to tax, employment, and justice—to improve the conditions of people with disabilities.

In 1996, the Federal-Provincial-Territorial Ministers Responsible for Social Services identified Canadians with disabilities as a national priority. Two years later, the first ministers released the document *In Unison: A Canadian Approach to Disability Issues*, which outlined their shared vision and goals for the full citizenship for people with disabilities. To respond to the changing needs of people with disabilities, *In Unison* proposed a new approach to disability-related programs and services (see Exhibit 14.4). Under the In Unison initiative, the achievement of full citizenship would be based on the following "building blocks":

- *disability supports* (goods, services, and resources, including technical aids, special equipment, life skills training, and interpreter services);

- *employment* (access to education opportunities and more flexible training programs); and

- *income programs* (income security for the unemployed).

EXHIBIT 14.4

A NEW APPROACH TO DISABILITY ISSUES

OLD . . .   NEW . . .

Recipients ───────────────────▶ Participants

Passive income support ──────────────▶ Active measures to promote
                                                         employment in addition to
                                                         providing necessary income
                                                         support

Dependence ──────────────────▶ Independence

Government responsibility ─────────────▶ Shared responsibility

Labelled as "unemployable" ────────────▶ Identification of work skills

Disincentives to leave income ──────────▶ Incentives to seek employment
support   and volunteer opportunities

Insufficient employment ──────────────▶ Opportunities to develop skills
supports   and experience

Program-centred approach ─────────────▶ Person-centred approach

Insufficient portability of ──────────────▶ Portable benefits and services
benefits and services

Multiple access requirements ───────────▶ Integrated access requirements

Source: *In Unison: A Canadian Approach to Disability Issues*, SP-113-10-98E, Human Resources and Skills Development Canada, 1998. Reproduced with the permission of the Minister of Public Works and Government Services Canada, 2009.

A review of the In Unison initiative in 2000, revealed that, while advances had been made in disability policies, there was room for improvement. For example, disability supports needed to be more accessible, portable, and consistent across the country (Federal-Provincial-Territorial Ministers Responsible for Social Services, 2000b). Some members of the disability community were also critical of governments for not doing enough to help Canadians with disabilities, such as creating accessible buildings and flexible workplaces. Other disability advocates pointed out that since the 1980s, disability issues had been caught in a vicious cycle, whereby the same issues were raised and addressed by similar government responses, but with little effect (see Exhibit 14.5).

EXHIBIT 14.5

THE DISABILITY ISSUES CIRCLE

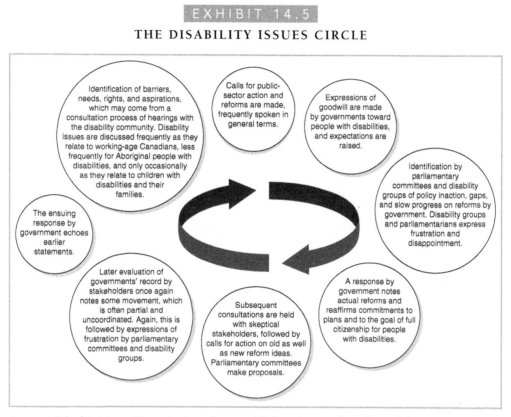

Identification of barriers, needs, rights, and aspirations, which may come from a consultation process of hearings with the disability community. Disability issues are discussed frequently as they relate to working-age Canadians, less frequently for Aboriginal people with disabilities, and only occasionally as they relate to children with disabilities and their families.

Calls for public-sector action and reforms are made, frequently spoken in general terms.

Expressions of goodwill are made by governments toward people with disabilities, and expectations are raised.

Identification by parliamentary committees and disability groups of policy inaction, gaps, and slow progress on reforms by government. Disability groups and parliamentarians express frustration and disappointment.

The ensuing response by government echoes earlier statements.

Later evaluation of governments' record by stakeholders once again notes some movement, which is often partial and uncoordinated. Again, this is followed by expressions of frustration by parliamentary committees and disability groups.

Subsequent consultations are held with skeptical stakeholders, followed by calls for action on old as well as new reform ideas. Parliamentary committees make proposals.

A response by government notes actual reforms and reaffirms commitments to plans and to the goal of full citizenship for people with disabilities.

Source: Michael J. Prince, "Governing in an Integrated Fashion: Lessons from the Disability Domain," Box **23** (Ottawa: Canadian Policy Research Networks, Inc., June 27, 2001), p. 63. Retrieved May 18, 2009, from Canadian Policy Research Networks, Inc., website, www.cprn.org/documents/3662_en.pdf.

THE ISSUE OF ACCESS

To be truly independent, one must have reasonable access to goods, services, and opportunities. The achievement of access varies across the disability community. For many Canadians with disabilities, accessibility is possible through the purchase of technical aids such as a wheelchair or a hearing aid; others require certain services such as home care or tutoring. The way buildings are designed and jobs are structured also has implications for access. Governments have responded to the issue of access in various ways in recent years. Some of those ways are described below.

HUMA and Accessibility Legislation

In 2005, the Standing Committee on Human Resources, Skills Development, Social Development and the Status of Persons with Disabilities (commonly referred to as HUMA) reviewed the federal government's policies and programs relating to persons with disabilities. HUMA's report, *Accessibility for All*, made several recommendations to the Government of Canada to improve the access to programs, services, employment, and other areas for people with disabilities (Government of Canada, 2005). Two years later, the federal government introduced the Enabling Accessibility Fund to help the provinces and territories improve access to physical spaces and public programs by all Canadians, regardless of ability.

Efforts to improve accessibility have also been initiated at the provincial and territorial levels. For example, in 2005, Ontario passed the Accessibility for Ontarians with Disabilities Act to ensure access "to goods, services, facilities, accommodation, employment, buildings, structures and premises." The Act recognizes the importance of collaboration among individuals, communities, and the public and private sectors, in the campaign to remove and prevent barriers to full participation (Government of Ontario, 2008).

A National Disability Act

For many years now, government and members of the disability community have considered the merits of a national disability act. The Council of Canadians with Disabilities suggests that the creation of such an act may lead to more accessible federal transportation and telecommunications systems. Moreover, a national act may spark the development of a disability policy analysis lens for reviewing government policy to ensure that disability—and accessibility—issues are properly addressed. On the other hand, the extent to which a national disability act could address income (such as minimum wage rates) and social services for people with disabilities would be limited since those issues are provincial/territorial responsibilities (D'Aubin, 2006).

In 2006, the federal government (under the Conservatives) promised to "introduce a National Disability Act to promote reasonable access to medical care, medical equipment, education, employment, transportation, and housing for Canadians with disabilities" (HRSDC, 2006c). In 2007, the government announced that it was conducting policy research to develop a proposal for a Canadians with Disabilities Act. To date, there has been no mention of the proposed act in any federal budget (March of Dimes Canada, 2008).

THE UNITED NATIONS CONVENTION ON THE RIGHTS OF PERSONS WITH DISABILITIES

In 2004, when the United Nations drafted its Convention on the Human Rights of Disabled People, it did so in an effort to advance and protect the rights of people with disabilities, to encourage a greater public acceptance of people with disabilities, and to motivate governments around the world to do more to facilitate the full participation of persons with disabilities. In 2006, the United Nations General Assembly adopted the landmark disability convention. Although Canada agrees with the principles of the convention, the federal government cannot ratify the convention without the consent of the provinces and territories. If both levels of government agree, then Canadian governments have both a domestic and an international obligation to remove barriers to full participation for persons with disabilities. As it currently stands, Canada has no legal obligation to comply with the UN disability convention (Kinsella, 2008).

Discussion Questions

▨ **Canada's Disability Policy Agenda**

1. What were some of the main factors and events that led to the disability rights movement? What other social movements were occurring during the 1960s and 1970s that may have lent credibility or support to the rights of people with disabilities?

2. Until the 1980s, disability policy in Canada focused primarily on the improvement of the standard of living and participation in community life for people with disabilities, but ignored many issues related to access. Identify some of the main policies, initiatives, or events that attempted to improve accessibility.

▥ HOUSING, INCOME, AND EMPLOYMENT: KEYS TO FULL PARTICIPATION

HOUSING OPTIONS

Deinstitutionalization, and the movement toward inclusion, independence, and self-determination, have inspired the creation of various living options for people with a disability (Community Living Research Project, 2007). Although health-related institutions are still available for people with severe disabilities, other living arrangements are also available, including

- group homes, where staff provide support to the residents in terms of personal care, meal preparation, and other tasks of daily living;

- cluster housing, which allows individuals to live independently and yet close to each other in communities separated from the general community;

- supported living, whereby an individual lives independently with the assistance of occasional supports;

- semi-independent living, in which individuals enjoy independent living in conjunction with limited weekly services from paid staff;

- family living (or foster care), a situation in which an individual lives with a relative or non-related host family who provides care and support; and

- independent living, in which an individual lives either alone or with a spouse or a roommate in a detached house or apartment (Community Living Research Project, 2007; Roeher Institute, 1996).

Housing reforms have included the development of new housing designs, as well as programs to make independent living a reality for many people with disabilities. Programs such as the federally sponsored Residential

EXHIBIT 14.6

Homes can easily be modified to accommodate the daily living needs of people with disabilities, thereby enhancing independence and self-sufficiency.

Source: Larry Dale Gordon/The Image Bank/Getty Images.

Rehabilitation Assistance Program subsidize the costs of modifying residences to make them safer, healthier, and more accessible and adaptable to the changing functional needs of residents.

THE DISABILITY INCOME SYSTEM

To be able to participate fully in society, one must have adequate income to purchase food, shelter, clothing, transportation, and other basic necessities. For people with disabilities who are unable to earn enough to support themselves, income support is available under the **disability income system**. Four rough categories of income make up this system:

- *Earnings replacement* programs aim to replace income that has been lost as the result of an injury, illness, or disability-related condition (such as AIDS). Included in this category are Employment Insurance, the Canada Pension Plan Disability Program, the Veterans Disability Pension, and private disability insurance.

- *Income support* programs target people with little or no income, and are usually delivered through provincial or territorial social assistance departments.

- *Compensation for loss* is money paid to those who have suffered a loss as a result of a disabling injury or accident. Compensatory programs include workers' compensation, automobile insurance, and some private insurance programs.

- *Compensation for disability-related costs* are benefits to offset the costs of having a disability (for example, the cost of a wheelchair or medication). These benefits are usually provided through provincial social assistance or disability insurance programs (Torjman, 1996).

Although Canada's disability income system supports many people with special needs, it has two main flaws. First, the system is far from being cohesive, comprehensive, coordinated, or easily accessed. Because the various types of income programs have been introduced at different times and by different levels of government, each program has its own rules for administering benefits and for assessing eligibility. There is also a lack of coordination and integration of these programs across governments, and even within single governments. The result is a highly confusing system that persons with disabilities must try to navigate to find the help they need (Stapleton & Tweddle, 2008). Second, even when an income program is accessed, it does not guarantee benefits sufficient to meet a person's needs. People with disabilities who cannot earn an income through work may have little choice but to apply for provincial/territorial social assistance or disability pensions. However, in most jurisdictions, the benefit rates under these programs are below the LICOs, and fail to recognize the extra costs of disability. As a result, having a disability means living in poverty for many Canadians (Council of Canadians with Disabilities, 2009).

In recent years, Canadian governments have introduced measures aimed at improving the financial security of people with disabilities. At the federal level, tax incentives are available to help high-income-earning families secure the long-term financial security of a member with a disability. These measures include the Registered Disability Savings Plan, the Canada Disability Savings Grant, and the Canada Disability Savings Bond (HRSDC, 2009e). Some provinces, through their poverty reduction strategies, aim to improve income supports so that people with disabilities are able to participate fully in society. The Government of Newfoundland and Labrador (2006), for example, plans to work with other governments to pursue a national income support program for persons with disabilities.

WORKING WITH A DISABILITY

The benefits and rewards of working are well documented. One advantage of working is the opportunity to interact with other people, "a vital activity for people with disabilities, many of whom live in loneliness and isolation" (Priest et al., 2008, p. 4). Canadian governments have played a central role in the rehabilitation and employment of people with disabilities, beginning with the first Workmen's Compensation Act of 1914. In 2004, the federal and regional governments developed a Multilateral Framework for Labour Market Agreements to guide intergovernmental partnerships aimed at improving employment among people with disabilities. A variety of programs and services under the framework are available to working-age people with disabilities, including assistive aids, pre-employment training, and postsecondary education (Government of Canada, 2007).

In addition to employment programs under the multilateral framework, several federal initiatives offer specialized employment assistance to people with disabilities. For instance, the Disability Vocational Rehabilitation Program (under the Canada Pension Plan) helps people who receive disability pension benefits return to work. Other initiatives—such as the Opportunities Fund for Persons with Disabilities and the Entrepreneurs with Disabilities Program—provide financial and other support to those looking for work or starting their own business.

With the rising popularity of **social economy enterprises** (SEEs), innovative employment options are opening up for people with disabilities. Through these enterprises, people who might otherwise be classified by government systems as "unemployable" due to a disability are gaining skills and earning a living. In their study of seven SEEs in British Columbia, researchers Priest et al. (2008) found that most successful SEEs incorporate two main strategies:

- *workplace accommodations* include working out flexible work schedules with staff, giving employees adequate breaks, and matching job tasks to individual ability and preference; and

- *social supports* include personal and life skills counselling, job coaching, and referrals to community services such as mental health centres.

In general, the employees in this study were found to enjoy a higher standard of living, greater financial security, improved self-esteem, increased independence, and broadened social networks compared to their unemployed peers. An example of a social economy enterprise in Vancouver is profiled in Exhibit 14.7.

While many Canadians with disabilities want to work, a number of barriers may prevent them from doing so. Studies show that, even in good economic times, people with disabilities tend to have more difficulty finding work than those without disabilities. These potential employees may find themselves in a position of needing workplace accommodations such as modified hours, limited duties, or certain technological supports—requests that employers may not want to fulfil. In a 2006 study, 25 percent of unemployed persons with disabilities believed that they had been refused a job because of their disability (Statistics Canada, 2008e). Barriers to work prevent many people with disabilities from supporting themselves through employment. In 2006, there were 2.5 million working-age Canadians with activity limitations who were potentially able to work; of this group, just over half were employed (Priest et al., 2008).

DISABILITY AND A GROWING NEED FOR FLEXIBLE SYSTEMS

Many people have an **episodic disability** such as HIV, multiple sclerosis, or a mental disorder, which affects them on a sporadic and often unpredictable basis (Stapleton & Tweddle, 2008). Although people with an episodic disability might be able to work, they may find it difficult to work a full work week, or

EXHIBIT 14.7

A SOCIAL ECONOMY ENTERPRISE: SEWING WITH HEART

Sewing with Heart is an innovative social [economy] enterprise, which produces a variety of quality nylon bags handmade by individuals recovering from mental illness.

Sewing with Heart started as a partnership between the Coast Employment Program and the Flag Shop in Vancouver, British Columbia. People with mental illness are given the opportunity to work from their homes, creating retail-worthy products from the Flag Shop's remnants. Participants in the Coast Foundation Employment Programs take the remnants—which are made of colourful, durable nylon fabric—and recycle them into useful and sturdy multi-purpose tote bags. Community-minded businesses sell the bags at a price that provides the workers with a reasonable wage.

Today, Sewing with Heart functions as a "worker co-operative," under the auspices of the Coast Social Enterprise Foundation. The Foundation operates profitable businesses that offer employment opportunities for the recovery of persons with mental illness. Underlying those opportunities is the belief that job creation and improved economic status is key to clients' independence and freedom to make choices.

Those who make the tote bags are self-motivated individuals who want to earn income and develop skills. To qualify for the Sewing with Heart program, individuals must be nineteen years or older, living with a persistent mental illness, and be connected with a mental health care professional (psychiatrist, general practitioner, or mental health team).

Source: Coast Foundation Society. (2008). Website. Retrieved December 10, 2008, from http://coastmentalhealth.com/sewing.html. Used by permission. Logo courtesy of Coast Foundation Society. Used with permission.

even a full day. A major gap in Canada's disability-related policies and programs is the lack of recognition given to people with a disability who can only work part of the time. Traditionally, income and employment programs in Canada have considered a working-age person to be either totally disabled and unemployable, or totally able and employable, with little recognition of anything in between. This has created a situation in which short periods of employment may mean a loss of some or all disability benefits. Thus, some people with a disability may start working, but not be able to continue; meanwhile, their benefits have been cut off. To avoid ending up in this situation, some individuals who are able to work part time don't work at all.

In recent years, Canadian governments have tried to reduce barriers to employment for people with disabilities who can and want to work. These efforts have primarily focused on revising employment and income assistance programs to allow people with a disability to cycle in and out of the workforce as needed (Priest et al., 2008). The federal government, for example, has reformed its Canada Pension Plan Disability Program to ensure a rapid reinstatement of benefits to individuals who try to work but, because of a disability, have to withdraw from the workforce. Government systems are also being reformed to provide alternatives to traditional work structures, such as offering more flexible hours of work.

Discussion Questions

Housing, Income, and Employment: Keys to Full Participation

1. Canada's disability income system is criticized for having two main flaws. Identify these flaws and how they might impact the lives of people with special needs.

2. Social economy enterprises (SEEs) are proving to be a promising avenue of employment for many people with disabilities. What SEEs (if any) are operating in your community, and what types of products or services do they provide? Identify the various ways SEEs might help or hinder the inclusion of people with disabilities in the community.

IV IMPLICATIONS FOR SOCIAL WORK PRACTICE

Over the years, social workers, like other helping professionals, have been modifying their approaches to working with people with disabilities. As part of the transition from institution-based treatment to community-based services, social work practice shifted away from traditional medical models toward social models. As a result, social workers directed their attention to helping clients adjust to community living through strategies such as sheltered workshops and residential group homes. By the 1990s, the focus of services had shifted again, this time toward helping clients achieve independence in mainstream settings.

In many respects, the evolution of social work practice within the disability community parallels the transition from segregation to mainstreaming (see Exhibit 14.8). The **open house concept** emphasizes the full participation of people with disabilities in school, work, social, and other activities, and their enjoyment of the same rights and privileges as Canadians without disabilities. Each component of the open house concept, as it relates to social work practice, is reviewed below.

EXHIBIT 14.8

FROM SEGREGATION TO MAINSTREAMING:
A CONCEPTUAL MODEL

WAREHOUSE ⟶	GREENHOUSE ⟶	OPEN HOUSE
Caring for	Enabling	Accommodating
Protection	Support	Autonomy/empowerment
Labelled permanently incapacitated	Adaptation of individual	Adaptation of social and physical environment
Deemed incompetent	Recognition of capacity	Rights/responsibilities

Source: *In Unison: A Canadian Approach to Disability Issues*, SP-113-10-98E, Human Resources and Skills Development Canada, 1998. Reproduced with the permission of the Minister of Public Works and Government Services Canada, 2009.

ACCOMMODATION

Accommodation involves modifying the environment so that a person with a disability can participate in activities that take place in that environment. Social workers might promote accommodation by helping someone obtain wheelchair access or special computer equipment needed for training or employment. Similarly, social workers can help people with disabilities work with government agencies on improving public transportation or other systems to facilitate better access to work, school, or community activities.

AUTONOMY AND EMPOWERMENT

Although social workers do not directly empower others, they can help people acquire the knowledge and skills they need to enhance their independence and a sense of **empowerment**. Social workers facilitate many activities that are personally empowering, including assertiveness training, life skills training, problem-solving exercises, and peer-leadership training. Workers can also facilitate the empowering process by

- providing adequate information about possible options so that people can make their own informed choices and decisions;
- encouraging people to express their wishes and exercise their right to self-determination;

- acknowledging the capabilities that people have to manage their own lives; and

- helping others advocate for themselves, challenge oppressive labels, and regain control of their lives (Roeher Institute, 1996).

ADAPTATION OF THE SOCIAL AND PHYSICAL ENVIRONMENT

Social workers can help staff in social agencies, educational institutions, and other organizations focus on the problems that reside in their own systems rather than viewing the person with the disability as a "problem to be solved." In addition, social workers can participate in reviews of agency policies, programs, and practices, as well as in modifications of agency systems to make them more inclusive (that is, free of barriers). Many social workers who serve the disability community find that a community development approach is more effective than traditional counselling approaches: "By promoting community development, the focus is shifted away from individuals and placed on strengthening the capacity of communities to be inclusive" (Panitch, 1998, p. 10).

RIGHTS AND RESPONSIBILITIES

Social workers have long called attention to, and demanded changes in, policies and programs that inhibit independent living for people with disabilities. In recent years, however, social workers have shifted much of their attention to helping people with disabilities speak out and assert their rights on their own behalf. One of the underlying themes of the disability movement is the demand for "rights, not charity"; social workers can play an important role in helping people with disabilities gain both control of resources and the right to make decisions that affect their own lives.

S U M M A R Y

Introduction

Changing social attitudes determine the extent to which people with disabilities are included in society. Disability is gradually being redefined as society's failure to accept differences between people, rather than an individual's physical or mental impairment. This view is reflected in policies and programs that aim to eliminate barriers to full inclusion, and to accommodate the diverse needs of all citizens.

I. Disability in Canada

The impairment, functional limitations and sociopolitical perspectives shape people's understanding of disability. There are various ways to define disability; the ICF defines disability in terms of society's response to disability. Canada's definitions are specific to related programs and services (such as pension programs). Seniors have the highest rate of disability of any age group; most adults with disabilities have multiple disabilities. The diversity of needs among the disabled population makes policymaking and program development a challenging endeavour. Certain groups, including children, Aboriginal peoples, and women, face particular challenges as a result of a disability.

II. Canada's Disability Policy Agenda

Changing attitudes and social movements have led to deinstitutionalization and a community-based approach to disability. Various disability-related organizations make up the disability community. Since the early 1980s, the sociopolitical model of disability has gained popularity. The issue of access continues to be a main theme and the focus of many disability-related policies and programs. The In Unison initiative guides the development of further efforts to promote full citizenship for people with disabilities. Policies such as a national disability act and Canada's ratification of the UN's disability convention have yet to be realized.

III. Housing, Income, and Employment: Keys to Full Participation

Deinstitutionalization has helped to expand living options and housing designs for people with disabilities. The disability income system provides financial help; however, the system is seriously flawed. Canadian governments have supported the rehabilitation and employment of people with disabilities through policies and programs. Intergovernmental efforts under the Multilateral Framework for Labour Market Agreements aim to improve employability for people with disabilities; even so, this population faces several barriers to employment. Social enterprises are providing new employment opportunities. More flexible work- and income-related policies and programs are needed to accommodate people whose disability restricts them to part-time work.

IV. Implications for Social Work Practice

Over the years, social workers and other professional helpers have modified their approaches to working with people with disabilities; the focus today is on helping clients achieve independence in mainstream settings. An "open house" approach can be used to help people with disabilities participate fully in society. This approach emphasizes accommodation; autonomy and empowerment; adaptation of the social and physical environment; and rights and responsibilities.

Key Terms

For definitions of the key terms, consult the Glossary on page 413 at the end of the book.

disability, p. 364

access, p. 365

impairment perspective, p. 365

functional limitations perspective, p. 365

sociopolitical perspective, p. 366

Aboriginal peoples, p. 369

disability rights movement, p. 372

deinstitutionalization, p. 372

community mental health movement, p. 372

community living movement, p. 372

independent living movement, p. 372

disability community, p. 373

disability income system, p. 381

social economy enterprise, p. 383

episodic disability, p. 383

open house concept, p. 385

accommodation, p. 386

empowerment, p. 386

A Century of Response: Historical Highlights in Social Welfare and Related Systems

1908 The Juvenile Delinquents Act is passed.

The Annuities Act—precursor of the Old Age Pension Act—is passed by the Canadian government.

1910 The Canadian Immigration Act is amended to keep poor, sick, and "immoral" applicants out of Canada.

1914 The First World War begins.

Parliament creates the Canadian Patriotic Fund to provide financial assistance to the families of soldiers.

Ontario becomes the first province to enact workers' compensation legislation.

1916 Canada's first mothers' allowances are implemented in Manitoba.

1918 The Child Tax Exemption (first federal child-based tax credit) is established.

The Canadian Mental Health Association is founded.

The Canadian National Institute for the Blind opens.

The First World War ends.

1919   The Soldier Settlement Act is passed.

The Winnipeg General Strike takes place.

The Community Welfare Council in Winnipeg becomes one of Canada's first social action groups.

1920   The Returned Soldiers' Insurance Act is passed.

1923   By this year, about 81,000 Chinese immigrants have paid the head tax, raising $23 million in revenue for Canadian governments.

1926   The Canadian Association of Social Workers is founded.

1927   The Old Age Pension Act is passed.

1929   Women become eligible for appointment to the Canadian Senate after they are declared "persons" by the Judicial Committee of the British Privy Council.

1930   The Great Depression begins.

For the first time in history, the federal government funds unemployment relief in municipalities.

The War Veterans Allowance Act is passed.

1931   The number of Indian residential schools peaks (about 80 schools are in operation across Canada).

1932   The Cooperative Commonwealth Federation (CCF) is founded in Calgary.

1935   The On to Ottawa Trek takes place, in which hundreds of unemployed men hop trains in British Columbia and head for Parliament Hill, protesting poor work camp conditions and high unemployment.

William Lyon Mackenzie King is sworn in as prime minister (under a Liberal government).

The Employment and Social Insurance Act is passed (and repealed in 1937).

1937   The Royal Commission on Dominion–Provincial Relations (Rowell-Sirois Commission) is appointed by the federal government.

1938   The Canadian Association of Social Workers develops a code of ethics.

1939   A national Youth Training Act is passed.

The Second World War begins, putting an end to the Great Depression.

1940   The Unemployment Insurance Act is passed.

1942   The *Report of the Inter-Departmental Committee on Social Insurance and Allied Services* (also known as the Beveridge Report) comes out of Great Britain.

1943   Leonard Marsh's *Report on Social Security for Canada* (also known as the Marsh Report) is released.

1944   The Family Allowances Act is passed (program is implemented in 1945).

The National Housing Act is passed.

The Department of National Health and Welfare is established.
The federal Department of Veterans Affairs is established.

1945   The federal Veterans Rehabilitation Act is passed.
The Second World War ends.

1946   The Central Mortgage and Housing Corporation (later renamed Canada Mortgage and Housing Corporation) is established.
The War Veterans Allowance Act is passed (replaces War Veterans Allowance Act of 1930).

1947   Canada's first health insurance program begins in Saskatchewan.
The Government of Canada repeals the Chinese Immigration Act, abolishing the ban on Chinese immigrants from entering Canada.

1948   Lester Pearson is sworn in as prime minister (under a Liberal government).
The federal government implements settlement and integration programs for immigrants.
Canada endorses the United Nations' Universal Declaration of Human Rights.

1951   The Indian Act is amended, which lifts a ban on several traditional ceremonies.
The Old Age Assistance Act is passed.
The Old Age Security Act is enacted.
The Blind Persons Act comes into effect.
Canada's first social work doctorate program is offered at the University of Toronto.
The UN adopts the Convention Related to the Status of Refugees (the Geneva Convention).

1953   The Immigration Act is amended, inviting more immigrants from Caucasian countries.

1954   The Rehabilitation of Disabled Persons Act is passed.

1956   The Unemployment Assistance Act is passed (federal government begins sharing the cost of provincial social assistance).

1957   John Diefenbaker is sworn in as prime minister (under a Progressive Conservative government).
The federal government introduces registered retirement savings plans (RRSPs).

1958   The Canadian Association for Community Living is founded.

1960   Status Indians gain the right to vote in federal elections.

1961   The Vocational Rehabilitation of Disabled Persons Act is passed.
The *Canadian Bill of Rights* becomes law.

1962 Statistics Canada begins collecting data for nearly 100 separate criminal offences in its Uniform Crime Reporting Survey.

1964 The federal Youth Allowances Act is passed.

1965 The Canada and Quebec Pension Plans are introduced.
The International Convention on the Elimination of All Forms of Racial Discrimination is ratified.

1966 The Canada Assistance Plan is initiated.
The Guaranteed Income Supplement is introduced.
The Medical Care Act is passed.
Canada's first Bachelor of Social Work program is offered at the University of Windsor.

1967 The Canadian Association of Schools of Social Work is established.
The Royal Commission on the Status of Women is appointed.
Amendments to the Immigration Act eliminate discriminatory criteria for selecting immigrants.

1968 Pierre Trudeau is sworn in as prime minister (under a Liberal government).
The Senate Committee on Poverty (the Croll Committee) is appointed by the federal government.
The Divorce Act is amended (makes divorce easier to obtain).

1969 The Statement of the Government of Canada on Indian Policy (the "White Paper") is released.
Homosexual acts between consenting adults are decriminalized.

1970 The federal government publishes *Income Security for Canadians*, reviewing Canada's social security system.

1971 The Unemployment Insurance Act is amended, providing easier eligibility and special benefits.
The Senate Committee on Poverty releases its report, *Poverty in Canada*.
Canada introduces a multicultural policy by accepting the recommendations of the Royal Commission on Bilingualism and Biculturalism.
The National Council of Welfare is founded.

1972 The Child Care Expenses Deduction is introduced, providing a tax deduction to families with childcare expenses related to work.

1973 Newfoundland passes the Neglected Adults Welfare Act—the first adult protection legislation in North America.
The federal government launches a social security review with the *Working Paper on Social Security in Canada*.
The Canadian Advisory Council on the Status of Women is established.
The federal Residential Rehabilitation Assistance Program begins.

The Family Allowance benefits are tripled, indexed to the cost of living, and made taxable.

1974   Canada's first large-scale guaranteed annual income experiment, Mincome, is launched in Manitoba.

The federal government appoints a National Advisory Council on Voluntary Action as a first step to improving Government of Canada/Voluntary Sector relations.

The federally funded Immigration Settlement and Adaptation Program (ISAP) begins.

1975   This year is the UN's International Year of Women.

1976   The UN's Decade for Women: Equality, Development and Peace begins.

The Spouse's Allowance is introduced.

A new Immigration Act is passed (and implemented in 1978) to do more to help newcomers settle in Canada.

1977   The federal government initiates the Established Programs Financing (EPF), which puts funding for hospital, medicare, and postsecondary education under one funding formula.

The Canadian Human Rights Act is passed.

Quebec becomes the first province to forbid discrimination on the basis of sexual orientation.

1978   The federal government establishes a Non-Profit Housing Program.

The Refundable Child Tax Credit is introduced (first time the Canadian income tax system is used to deliver benefits to families that do not pay income tax).

An amendment to the Immigration Act allows refugees to apply to Canada as immigrants.

1979   This year is the UN's International Year of the Child.

1980   The International Classification of Impairments, Disabilities, and Handicaps (ICIDH) is released by the World Health Organization.

The Special Committee on the Disabled and the Handicapped is established as a parliamentary task force to evaluate programs for persons with disabilities and to suggest improvements to these programs.

The federal government appoints the National Advisory Council on Aging.

1981   This year is the UN's International Year for Disabled Persons.

The Parliamentary Special Committee on the Disabled and the Handicapped releases its *Obstacles* report.

Canada's first food bank opens in Edmonton.

The federally funded Language Instruction for Newcomers to Canada (LINC) program is introduced.

1982 The *Canadian Charter of Rights and Freedoms* is entrenched in the *Canadian Constitution*.

The National Native Alcohol and Drug Abuse Program is established.

The National Clearinghouse on Family Violence is established.

The UN introduces its first International Plan of Action on Ageing.

1983 The UN declares 1983 to 1992 as the International Decade of Disabled Persons.

1984 Brian Mulroney is sworn in as prime minister (under a Progressive Conservative government).

The Canada Health Act is passed.

The Host Program is established to facilitate the resettlement of refugees (services are extended to immigrants in 1991).

1985 The Royal Commission on the Economic Union and Development Prospects for Canada (Macdonald Commission) releases its final report.

The Indian Act is amended, extending several status and property rights to members of First Nations.

The Status of Disabled Persons Secretariat is appointed to raise awareness of disability issues and support the inclusion of persons with disabilities.

Statistics Canada launches the General Social Survey, which aims to gather information and report on social trends and issues every five years.

Federal and provincial/territorial ministers responsible for social services agree on a strategy to help welfare recipients find and keep jobs.

1986 The first Health and Activity Limitation Survey (HALS) is completed.

The federally funded Child Sexual Abuse Initiative is launched (ends in 1991).

The national Task Force on Child Care recommends a universal system of child care.

1987 The Parliamentary Committee on Human Rights and the Status of Disabled Persons is established.

This year is the UN's International Year of Shelter for the Homeless.

1988 The federally funded Refundable Child Tax Credit is converted to the Non-Refundable Child Tax Credit.

Phase I of the federal Family Violence Initiative is announced.

The Canada–U.S. Free Trade Agreement is ratified.

The federal government launches the Seniors Independence Program.

The Canadian Multiculturalism Act is passed.

The federal government introduces the Women at Risk Program to assist refugee women and their dependants.

1989   The House of Commons resolves to end child poverty by the year 2000 (this goal is never reached).

Clawbacks are introduced into family allowances and Old Age Security, eliminating the universal status of these programs.

The National Survey on Elder Abuse—Canada's first major survey to study elder abuse—is administered.

The Standing Committee on Human Rights and the Status of Disabled Persons is established by the House of Commons to propose, promote, monitor, and assess initiatives toward the integration and equality of persons with disabilities.

1990   The Unemployment Insurance Act is amended (responsibility for funding shifts from the federal government to employers and employees).

The Standing Senate Committee on Aboriginal Peoples is formed to review parliamentary bills on native issues.

The federal government proposes a Native Agenda to settle land claims, improve social and economic conditions on reserves, and enhance Aboriginal–government relations.

The First Nations Child and Family Services program is created, allowing First Nations to develop their own child welfare services for registered Indian children living on reserves.

1991   The Canada–Quebec Accord is signed, giving Quebec control of its own immigrant settlement programs and language training.

Phase II of the federal Family Violence Initiative is announced.

The Royal Commission on Aboriginal Peoples is appointed by the federal government.

The First Nations Child and Family Services program begins.

A funding "cap" is imposed on Canada's wealthiest provinces under the Canada Assistance Plan.

Canada ratifies the UN Convention on the Rights of the Child.

The second Health and Activity Limitation Survey (HALS) is completed.

The National Strategy for the Integration of Persons with Disabilities is introduced.

The Goods and Services Tax (GST) and the GST Tax Credit are introduced.

1992   Mainstream 1992 provides a framework for guiding the full integration of people with disabilities into society.

Canada's *Action Plan for Children* defines key roles for children, parents, and caregivers in the plan's overall agenda and for implementing specific programs.

The Brighter Futures program introduces long-term programs designed to address conditions of risk during early childhood.

1993 Jean Chrétien is sworn in as prime minister (under a Liberal government).

This year is the UN's International Year of the World's Indigenous People.

The findings of the *Violence Against Women Survey*—Canada's first national survey of violence against women—are released.

The federal government replaces Family Allowances with the Canada Child Tax Benefit.

The federal government initiates the Ventures in Independence program for seniors.

The Unemployment Insurance Act is amended (reduces benefits).

The North American Free Trade Agreement (NAFTA) is ratified (comes into effect in 1994).

The UN begins using the Human Development Index to measure social conditions in member countries.

1994 The federal government conducts a general Program Review (the department of Human Resources Development Canada launches its own Social Security Review).

This year is the UN's International Year of the Family.

Community Action Programs for Children (CAPC) are launched under Health Canada's Child Development Initiative.

The National Longitudinal Survey of Children and Youth is launched.

The National Population Health Survey is introduced.

The Settlement Renewal Initiative is launched to devolve responsibility for immigrant settlement to the provinces.

The UN's International Decade of the World's Indigenous People begins.

1995 The Federal-Provincial-Territorial Council on Social Policy Renewal is formed.

The federal New Horizons: Partners in Aging initiative is launched (and is terminated in 1996, then reinstated in 2004).

The federal government introduces the Inherent Rights Policy as a guide to First Nations self-government.

Aboriginal Head Start is introduced.

The First Nations and Inuit Child Care Initiative is launched.

Twelve national organizations form a Voluntary Sector Roundtable to collaborate on common issues and concerns relating to voluntary organizations.

1996 The Federal Task Force on Disability Issues releases its report *Equal Citizenship for Canadians with Disabilities*.

Report of the Royal Commission on Aboriginal Peoples is released.

The Self-Government Negotiations Funding Support program is launched (for First Nations).

The Canada Assistance Plan is replaced by the Canada Health and Social Transfer.

The National Framework on Aging is released.

The new Employment Insurance Act replaces Unemployment Insurance. Labour Market Development Agreements between the federal and regional governments come into force.

Canada's child poverty rate rises to almost 21 percent.

The Canadian Council on Social Development releases *A Statistical Profile of Urban Poverty* and launches the Urban Poverty Project to consider poverty reduction initiatives.

The Federal-Provincial-Territorial Council on Social Policy Renewal meets for the first time, and identifies young children and people with disabilities as national priorities.

The Employability Assistance for People with Disabilities replaces the Vocational Rehabilitation of Disabled Persons Act.

The last Indian residential school is closed.

1997 Phase III of the Family Violence Initiative begins.

Amendments to the Immigration Act create three categories of immigrant applications: an economic class, a family class, and a refugee class.

The Canadian Race Relations Foundation begins operation, dedicated to the elimination of racism in the country.

The federal government establishes the Social Cohesion Network to help clarify the meaning of social cohesion and identify directions for future policy research.

The Federal-Provincial-Territorial Council on Social Policy Renewal agrees to develop a national children's agenda.

Canada's National Survey of Giving, Volunteering and Participating is administered for the first time.

The implementation of welfare-to-work programs in Ontario is made possible by the enactment of the provincial Social Assistance Reform Act.

Canada's first comprehensive family/child policy is introduced in Quebec.

The federal government launches the Aboriginal Healing Strategy.

The National Reinvestment Framework is developed to guide the reinvestment of unused social assistance funds into programs for low-income families with children.

The UN's International Decade for the Eradication of Poverty begins.

The federal government announces that it will establish Centres of Excellence for Children's Well-Being as part of its contribution to the National Children's Agenda.

Funding is made available through the Opportunities Fund for Persons with Disabilities, and the Entrepreneurs with Disabilities Program, to help people with disabilities achieve their employment goals.

1998 The federal government launches Gathering Strength: Canada's Aboriginal Action Plan as a long-term approach to increasing the quality of life for Aboriginal peoples.

The federal government makes a formal apology to Aboriginal peoples in the form of a *Statement of Reconciliation.*

The federal government establishes the Aboriginal Healing Foundation as part of Gathering Strength: Canada's Aboriginal Action Plan.

The federal government introduces the Urban Aboriginal Strategy.

The Canadian Incidence Study of Reported Child Abuse and Neglect becomes the first national study to examine reported child abuse.

The National Child Benefit is introduced (includes the Canada Child Tax Benefit and the National Child Benefit Supplement).

The federal government achieves a balanced budget for the first time in nearly twenty years.

The Canada Pension Plan undergoes drastic changes to make it more sustainable.

Ontario's Social Work and Social Service Work Act is passed.

The Human Resources Strategic Analysis of the Social Work Sector is launched.

The federal government establishes the Canada Coordinating Committee to consult with seniors.

The document *In Unison: A Canadian Approach to Disability Issues* is released as a guide to the full participation of people with disabilities.

Canada releases its National Action Plan for Food Security to improve the diets of high-risk groups.

The federal government launches the Social Development Partnerships program (supports projects that promote the inclusion of people with disabilities).

Family Violence in Canada: A Statistical Profile is released for the first time (and is republished every year after) by the Canadian Centre for Justice Statistics (provides data on the nature and extent of family violence).

The federal government launches the Resettlement Assistance Program, which provides income support and a range of other services to government-assisted refugees.

1999 This year is the UN's International Year of the Older Person.

Ontario becomes the first province to extend to same-sex couples the same rights as those extended to heterosexual common-law couples.

Members of the Federal-Provincial-Territorial Council on Social Policy
Renewal sign the Social Union Framework Agreement (SUFA) and release
the document *A National Children's Agenda: Developing a Shared Vision.*
The first report from the National Welfare to Work Study is released.
The federal government launches Understanding the Early Years,
The federally-funded Aboriginal Human Resources Development
Strategy begins.
The Supporting Communities Partnership Initiative begins, which launches
Phase I of the National Homelessness Initiative.
The Panel on Accountability and Governance in the Voluntary Sector releases
its report, *Building on Strength: Improving Governance and Accountability in
Canada's Voluntary Sector.*
The federal government releases *Future Directions: The Challenges Facing
Persons with Disabilities,* a guide to disability policy reform.
The National Improving the Quality of Life of Canadian Seniors Project is
launched.

2000   Canada's unemployment rate falls to its lowest level in 25 years
(6.8 percent).
The Immigration and Refugee Protection Act is tabled in the House of
Commons.
Phase I of the Voluntary Sector Initiative begins.
The second National Survey of Giving, Volunteering and Participating is
conducted.
The findings of the Strategic Human Resources Analysis of the Social Work
Sector are released in the document *In Critical Demand: Social Work in
Canada.*
The report *In Unison 2000: Persons with Disabilities in Canada* is released
(updates findings from the In Unison initiative launched in 1998).
The Early Childhood Development Agreement is introduced (requires the
federal, provincial, and territorial governments to cost-share early
childhood development programs).
The *learn$ave* project is launched to help low- and modest-income
Canadians save for education.
Maternity and Parental Benefits under Employment Insurance are extended
to 50 weeks.

2001   Canada's Affordable Housing Program is launched.
An Accord Between the Government of Canada and the Voluntary Sector is
released.
This year is the UN's International Year of the Volunteer.
The Aboriginal Peoples Survey is administered for the first time.

The Office of Indian Residential Schools Resolution of Canada is created to resolve claims related to residential schools.

For the first time in Canadian history, the census collects data on same-sex unions.

The national Longitudinal Survey of Immigrants to Canada is launched.

The World Health Organization introduces its International Classification of Functioning, Disability and Health.

The Canada Volunteerism Initiative is launched to encourage volunteerism in voluntary organizations.

The Canadian Study of Health and Aging completes its 10-year national longitudinal study on dementia.

Statistics Canada replaces the Health and Limitations Survey (HALS) with the Participation and Activity Limitation Survey (PALS) to collect information on adults and children who have a disability.

2002 Phase II of the Voluntary Sector Initiative begins, with a focus on developing practical tools and strategies for voluntary agencies and organizations.

Quebec introduces its National Strategy to Combat Poverty and Social Exclusion, the first government-sponsored poverty reduction plan in Canada.

Canada and other nations adopt the United Nations' A World Fit for Children strategy.

The UN develops its second International Plan of Action on Ageing (also known as the Madrid Plan).

The Toronto Declaration on the Global Prevention of Elder Abuse is released.

The Survey of First Nations People Living On-Reserve is administered.

The federal government introduces the First Nations Governance Act (Bill C-7) to the House of Commons in an effort to overhaul the 126-year-old Indian Act.

The Federal Strategy on Early Childhood Development for First Nations and Other Aboriginal Children is introduced.

The Immigration and Refugee Protection Act comes into force.

The Prime Minister's Caucus Task Force on Urban Issues releases its report, *Canada's Urban Strategy—A Vision for the 21st Century*.

The Standing Senate Committee on Social Affairs, Science and Technology releases its final report (the Kirby Report) on Canada's health care system.

The Romanow Commission releases its final report, *Building on Values*: The Future of Health Care in Canada.

The first Canadian Community Health Survey is released.

Vibrant Communities is launched as a national multi-sector collaborative strategy to reduce poverty in Canada.

The overall social costs of substance abuse in Canada (in terms of lost productivity, premature death, and burden on services) is estimated at $40 billion.

2003   The federal budget announces substantial reinvestments in social programs.

Canadian governments agree on a Multilateral Framework on Early Learning and Child Care.

Canada and Mexico collaborate on the creation of a *Guide for the Development of a Comprehensive System of Support to Promote Active Ageing* .

Prime Minister Chrétien appoints a Liberal Caucus Task Force on Seniors.

Paul Martin is sworn in as prime minister (under a Liberal government).

The federal government appoints a Task Force on Active Living and Dignity for Seniors.

The total number of food banks in Canada reaches 639.

The National Homelessness Initiative is extended for another three years.

Manitoba passes the Child and Family Services Authorities Act (gives Métis and First Nations the authority to provide child welfare services in that province).

The federal government introduces the Child Disability Benefit.

Compassionate Care is added as a benefit under Employment Insurance.

The "10 Percent Rule" comes into effect (restricts advocacy by registered charities under the federal Income Tax Act).

Statistics Canada releases results from the first cycle of the Longitudinal Survey of Immigrants to Canada.

2004   The Canada Social Transfer, and the Canada Health Transfer, replace the Canada Health and Social Transfer.

British Columbia becomes the first province to put a time limit on welfare eligibility.

The United Nations drafts the Convention on the Human Rights of Disabled People.

The Multilateral Framework for Labour Market Agreements replaces the Employability Assistance for People with Disabilities initiative.

The federal Child Disability Benefit is implemented.

The Employment Insurance account reports a surplus of nearly $44 billion.

Canada releases *A Canada Fit for Children*, a plan to improve conditions for children.

Prime Minister Paul Martin announces plans to establish a national home care program and a national childcare program if re-elected.

The Vanier Institute of the Family releases *The Future Families Project*, a national survey of Canadian family values and aspirations.

The federal government initiates the Kelowna Accord, an agreement between the Government of Canada, the Provincial Premiers, Territorial Leaders, and the leaders of five national Aboriginal organizations, aimed at improving employment, education, and living conditions for Aboriginal peoples.

2005 The Canada Learning Bond is introduced (to help modest-income families save for their children's postsecondary education).

The federal government passes a law legalizing same-sex unions.

The Ministers Responsible for Seniors releases the document *Planning for Canada's Aging Population: A Framework.*

A Seniors Secretariat is created to coordinate federal programs for seniors.

The Standing Committee on Human Resources, Skills Development, Social Development and the Status of Persons with Disabilities (HUMA) releases their report, *Accessibility for All.*

2006 Steven Harper is sworn in as prime minister (under a Conservative government).

The federal government introduces the Universal Child Care Benefit in lieu of the proposed national childcare program.

The Canada Employment Credit is announced to reduce taxes on work-related expenses.

The federal government announces a Tax Fairness Plan, targeted at seniors.

The federal government cancels the Canada Volunteerism Initiative.

The federal government cancels any agreements made with the provinces under the Multilateral Framework on Early Learning and Child Care.

The Government of Canada makes funds available under the Targeted Initiative for Older Workers.

The Special Senate Committee on Aging is charged with a large-scale review of issues, policies, and programs related to seniors.

The Homelessness Partnering Strategy is announced (begins in 2007).

The United Nations adopts its Convention on the Human Rights of Disabled People.

Statistics Canada administers the Aboriginal Children's Survey as part of the 2006 Census.

The second Aboriginal Peoples Survey is administered.

2007 The federal government introduces a Working Income Tax Benefit to help make work pay for low- and modest-income Canadians.

The Special Senate Committee on Aging releases its first interim report, *Embracing the Challenge of Aging.*

Human Resources and Social Development Canada establishes the Expert Panel on Older Workers to consider the current and future prospects of older workers.

A Secretary of State for Seniors is hired to act as an advocate for Canadian seniors.

The National Seniors Council replaces the National Advisory Council on Aging established in 1980.

The federal government announces the Enabling Accessibility Fund (provides grants to community-based projects to enable Canadians with disabilities to participate in and contribute to their community and the economy).

The federal government announces a Registered Disability Savings Plan, the Canada Disability Savings Grant, and the Canada Disability Savings Bond to help Canadians save for long-term financial security.

The Government of Canada agrees to compensate Aboriginal peoples for their losses incurred from attending residential schools.

2008   The federal government introduces the Tax-Free Savings Account.

The Standing Senate Committee on Social Affairs, Science and Technology is charged with examining social issues in Canada's largest cities.

The Standing Committee on Agriculture and Forestry begins its study on rural poverty.

The House of Commons Standing Committee on Human Resources, Social Development and the Status of Persons with Disabilities (HUMA) begins a feasibility study on a national poverty reduction strategy.

The Canadian Longitudinal Study on Aging begins its pilot study.

The federal New Horizons for Seniors Program launches an Elder Abuse Awareness Campaign.

The federal Home Adaptations for Seniors' Independence program begins.

A UNICEF study rates Canada the worst of 25 countries in providing childcare services.

Prime Minister Harper makes a Statement of Apology to former students of Indian residential schools.

Canada slides into a deep economic recession, the biggest economic decline since the recession of 1991.

2009   Former Prime Minister Paul Martin creates the Capital for Aboriginal Prosperity and Entrepreneurship to back Aboriginal businesses.

In January, Ontario loses 71,000 of the 129,000 jobs lost in Canada due to the economic downturn.

The number of welfare recipients in British Columbia reaches over 32,000 in March—a 47 percent increase since September 2008.

In March, 681,400 Canadian workers are receiving regular Employment Insurance benefits—a 10.6 percent increase from the previous month. The strongest increases are in Alberta and British Columbia.

In March, Canada's unemployment rate reaches 8 percent, the highest rate in seven years.

The federal government releases *Canada's Economic Action Plan (Budget 2009)*, a strategy to stimulate economic growth during a severe economic recession. Under the plan, the government promises to (among other things):

- raise the level at which the National Child Benefit supplement for low-income families and the Canada Child Tax Benefit are phased out;
- provide further tax breaks to low- and middle-income seniors;
- invest in the construction of social housing units for low-income seniors, persons with disabilities, and Aboriginal peoples;
- allow working Canadians to earn more income before paying federal income taxes;
- double the tax relief under the Working Income Tax Benefit to encourage low-income Canadians to find and keep jobs;
- enrich the Aboriginal Skills and Employment Partnership (ASEP) initiative, to create more jobs for Aboriginal Canadians;
- commit $305 million over two years to improve the health outcomes for First Nations and Inuit people;
- extend partnerships with provinces to improve child and family services on reserves; and
- increase for two years all regular Employment Insurance (EI) benefit entitlements by five extra weeks and increase the maximum benefit period to 50 weeks from 45 weeks.

Globalization and Social Welfare

It has been said that arguing against globalization is like arguing against the law of gravity. (UN Secretary-General Kofi Annan, 2002)

GLOBALIZATION: FRIEND OR FOE?

The International Federation of Social Workers (2005) defines **globalization** as "the process by which all peoples and communities come to experience an increasingly common economic, social and cultural environment. By definition, the process affects everybody throughout the world."

Modern-day globalization is the brainchild of several Western nations, who came together shortly after the Second World War to develop a new framework for restructuring economic and political relations. The U.S.-dominated World Bank, the International Monetary Fund, and eventually, the World Trade Organization were created to foster economic development based on the principles of **neoliberalism**. Globalization is synonymous with free trade, unlimited investment, and the spread of capitalism.

In 1995, at the World Summit for Social Development in Copenhagen, nations from around the world recognized the contradictions of globalization:

Globalization ... opens new opportunities for sustained economic growth and development of the world economy, particularly in developing countries. Globalization also permits

> countries to share experiences and to learn from one another's achievements and difficulties, and promotes a cross-fertilization of ideals, cultural values and aspirations. At the same time, the rapid processes of change and adjustment have been accompanied by intensified poverty, unemployment and social disintegration. Threats to human well-being, such as environmental risks, have also been globalized. (United Nations, 1995)

Some of those "threats to human well-being" are briefly described below.

Economic Dependence and Vulnerability

In a global economy, governments tend to relax their duties and tariffs, and encourage the free flow of imports and exports across borders. The easy flow of investment, labour, goods, and services between countries has made most nations economically dependent on each other. Those close economic ties also make trading partners economically vulnerable; a case in point is the collapse of the mortgage market in the United States in 2008, which affected stock markets around the world and triggered a global economic recession.

Loss of Democracy

National governments have become torn between responding to the needs of their own citizens and the needs of the "global community." While becoming less accountable to citizens, governments are becoming more accountable to business (largely **transnational corporations** or TNCs). TNCs control most of the world's trade, and some are reportedly richer than some countries. These corporations have the power to dictate where they do business (usually in countries that offer the least regulation, the most resources, and the biggest tax breaks), and what types of conditions they wish to do business under (sometimes at the expense of the environment and human rights). Democracy is threatened when the welfare of citizens becomes secondary to the profits of business (McDonagh, 2002).

A Blending of Cultures

Groups of people with different ethnic backgrounds, religious beliefs, values, and language are interacting more than ever. Closer cultural contacts can lead to a greater understanding of people, and subsequently more tolerance for each other. However, greater cultural interactions may also produce more tension and conflict. Overall, globalization has made cultures less distinguishable, more homogenous, and—in particular—more "Americanized."

Global Economy: Global Threats

Globalization promotes technologies such as the Internet, wireless telephones, TV satellites, and the rapid transmission of information and ideas around the world. The opening of borders also allows for the easy, and often rapid, infiltration of undesirable elements across borders, which can threaten both personal and national security. Some of those threats are as follows:

- Open trade and transportation allow infectious diseases to spread around the world in record time.
- Terrorists can access countries more easily, and operate in and against several nations simultaneously.
- Transnational businesses can relocate to countries with the weakest environmental laws that allow the cheap extraction of resources and the extreme production of waste, accelerating global warming and affecting the whole world.
- Globalization is associated with rising fuel costs, erratic weather caused by global warming, the increase in crops for biofuels, and the ruination of farm lands from an overuse of pesticides and chemical fertilizers, all of which contribute to a global food crisis.

These threats are most likely to impact the segments of society who are already vulnerable or marginalized, such as those living in poverty. Floods associated with global warming, for example, tend to have the greatest impact on those who live in substandard housing; when disaster strikes, the rich can board up their homes and leave town, while the poor are left behind to cope with the aftermath.

JOBS AND JOB SECURITY

Between the 1970s and the 1990s, globalization shifted Western nations into a postindustrial era. During that period, many resource and manufacturing jobs were relocated to countries with cheap labour and slack regulations. To stay competitive, the industries that remained in Canada adopted technologies such as automation to reduce staff and lower the production of goods and services. This economic shift changed the world of work for Canadians. This section looks at **labour market restructuring** and its impact on the lives of Canadians.

Good Jobs, Bad Jobs

Technology has revolutionized the labour market by automating many labour-intensive tasks. While this has created a demand for highly literate workers with strong computer and other technical skills, it has also created many low-skilled jobs and an increasing disparity between "good" and "bad" jobs.

"Good" jobs are usually full-time, permanent, and well paid, with benefits and opportunities for promotion. These jobs are largely filled by highly skilled, well-educated workers. "Bad" jobs (or "McJobs") are often non-unionized, offer poor pay and working conditions, and provide few (if any) benefits and little chance of advancement. These jobs are usually filled by workers who are unskilled or have little education—often older workers, young people, recent immigrants, visible minorities, and women. Part-time or **non-standard jobs** (for example, temporary, casual, and short-term contract positions) are often considered "bad jobs," especially among those wanting to work full-time. Between 1976 and 2007, the proportion of Canadian workers in part-time positions rose from about 7 percent to 11.5 percent (HRSDC, 2009c). In December 2008, 36,000 part-time jobs were created while 71,000 full-time jobs were lost (Statistics Canada, 2009a).

Down with Manufacturing, Up with Services

Much of the labour-intensive manufacturing that once took place in Canada is now being outsourced or "offshored" to less-developed countries. Between 2002 and 2008 (when a global economic recession began), Canada lost a total of 388,000 manufacturing jobs. The regions hit hardest were Ontario (with a loss of up to one in five manufacturing jobs) and Quebec (which lost one in six manufacturing jobs) (Weir, 2008).

While manufacturing jobs disappear, the number of service jobs continues to rise. By 2005, real estate, healthcare, social welfare, government, and other service sectors employed 78 percent of Canada's labour force (Industry Canada, 2006b). Many service workers, such as lawyers and accountants, are well paid and in high demand. Others, such as retail clerks, cleaners, and food service workers, often work for minimum wage and are more easily replaced; this group includes a high percentage of women (especially visible-minority women).

Unfortunately, Canada has found it difficult to sell its services to the rest of the world. Information, financial, scientific, and other types of services account for only 13 percent of Canada's exports, and there is little indication that global demand for Canadian services will increase anytime soon (Roy, 2001).

Wage Disparity and Income Inequality

The outsourcing of lower-skilled jobs to developing countries is often blamed for falling wages in Canadian industries. The term **income inequality** refers to the difference between the average earnings of the rich and those of the poor. A study by Statistics Canada (2007c) shows that the distribution of wealth in this country has been steadily shifting since 1980. In that year, the difference in income between the poorest fifth of Canadians and the richest fifth was $83,800; by 2005, it had reached $105,400.

A troubling trend is that Canada's income inequality continues to grow even in good economic times, when work is plentiful and unemployment is low. Another disturbing trend is that working families with children are earning a shrinking share of available income, even though they are working harder and longer than ever before (Yalnizyan, 2008).

A STRAIN ON SOCIAL WELFARE PROGRAMS

There is no doubt that labour market restructuring has benefited many Canadians. Many others, however, are at an increasingly high risk of job displacement, unemployment, underemployment, debt overload, bankruptcy, and poverty. Needless to say, a growing number of vulnerable or out-of-work people increases the demand for social welfare programs and services. The resources most in demand include the following:

- Employment Insurance;
- employment and support services (such as employment counselling, and targeted wage subsidy programs);
- social assistance (welfare);
- emergency shelters;
- food banks and other emergency food programs;
- mental health services and crisis intervention services (such as suicide hotlines);

- family services (including services that respond to stress-related problems and domestic violence); and

- child protection services (when parents cannot adequately meet the needs of their children).

Key Terms

For definitions of the key terms, consult the Glossary on page 413 at the end of the book.

globalization, p. 407
neoliberalism, p. 407
transnational corporation, p. 408

labour market restructuring, p. 410
non-standard jobs, p. 410

income inequality, p. 411

GLOSSARY

(Numbers in parentheses refer to the chapter(s) containing the main discussion of the term. Boldfaced terms are found in the glossary.)

A

Aboriginal peoples The descendants of the original inhabitants of North America. The Canadian Constitution recognizes three groups of Aboriginal people: *Indians, Métis,* and *Inuit*. (12)

absolute homelessness A state of living without physical shelter, or living in places not intended for human habitation, such as the streets, vehicles, and abandoned buildings. See also *relative homelessness*. (9)

access The ability and right to enter, use, or take advantage of opportunities, services, or resources. (14)

acclimatization stage of settlement The first stage of the *settlement process,* when *recent immigrants* deal with their immediate basic *needs*, including finding a place to live, learning the local language, and enrolling children in school. See also *adaptation stage of settlement* and *integration*. (13)

accommodation The act of modifying an environment so that a person with a *disability* can participate in activities that take place in that environment. (14)

accountability The demonstration or "proof" of how one uses resources and achieves results; the obligation to account to others; and/or the obligation to answer to, report or explain, or give reasons for one's actions. (5)

active aging Participating in activities that maximize social, physical, and mental well-being throughout one's life. Active aging is seen as a way to ensure a good quality of life in later years and to extend healthy life expectancy. (11)

active policy A government plan of action that guides people toward entering (or re-entering) the workforce, or that gives incentives to beneficiaries who choose work or training in lieu of benefits. See also *passive policy*. (2, 9)

adaptation stage of settlement The second stage of the *settlement process,* when *recent immigrants* learn to function more independently, are able to access services on their own, are making friends and cultivating employment contacts, and are setting personal goals. See also *acclimatization* stage of settlement and *integration*. (13)

administration An organizational activity that involves developing or interpreting *policies and procedures*, planning and managing *direct service* activities, and ensuring that the organization meets its goals and objectives. (6)

advocacy Speaking or acting on behalf of another person or group by, for example, disseminating information in order to influence the opinions of others, and calling for changes in laws, regulations, and government policies. (5)

advocacy chill The reluctance among staff in *voluntary social agencies* to negotiate on behalf of their *clients*, due to a fear of their organization being penalized in terms of losing charitable status or government funding. (5)

age-friendly community A town, city, or village that is supportive of seniors in terms of recognizing their capabilities, responding to their *needs*, respecting their decisions and choices, protecting them, and promoting their inclusion. (11)

ageism Prejudice and discrimination against a person on the basis of age; usually used in reference to elderly people. (11)

agency goal Part of an organization's *strategic framework* that states the concrete steps the organization plans to take over the long-term to achieve its vision and mission. See also *mission statement*, *value statement*, and *vision statement*. (6)

agency volunteer A "natural" or *nonprofessional helper* who donates his or her time and skills without monetary compensation to a *social agency*. (7)

aging in place The act of growing old in the dwelling of one's choice; often refers to aging in one's home rather than in an institution. (6, 11)

Alternative Service Delivery A framework that suggests how governments might reorganize their departments or agencies, coordinate their efforts, and work with all service sectors in the delivery of public programs (5)

asset-based social policy A type of *public policy* that views the accumulation of resources, advantages, and capacities as critical to the achievement of financial security and self-sufficiency; assets include human, social, physical, and financial *capital*. (9)

assimilation A process in which a person, or a group of people, adopts aspects of a dominant culture; this process may or may not be voluntary. (12)

assisted living A living arrangement (often for seniors and people with a *disability*) that offers private living space and meals, as well as other services such as personal care, laundry, and housekeeping. See also *congregate housing* and *supportive housing*. (11)

B

baby boomer A portion of the population that was born in a demographic birth boom between 1947 and 1966. (11)

band A group of *First Nations people* for whom lands have been set apart, or whose money is held by the Crown. Many bands prefer to be known as "First Nations." (12)

best practices Strategies, methods, or approaches that are perceived as working well, and would be recommended to others. Best practices can be discovered through *program evaluation*, observation, trial and error, or other means. (6)

bill A written proposal for a law or piece of legislation that is submitted to a legislature (at either the federal or provincial level) for approval (2)

blended family A family structure where both parents have brought at least one child from a previous union, or there is a mix of at least one child from a previous and the current union. (10)

block fund A lump sum of money given by one level of government to a lower government for a specific purpose; the amount of the fund is usually calculated on a per capita basis. (4)

brief therapy A type of therapeutic intervention that aims toward the achievement of specific, measurable, and short-term goals, emphasizes the *client's* present and future (rather than the past), and focuses on personal strengths rather than deficits. (8)

budget deficit The amount by which government spending exceeds income. See also *budgetary surplus* and *public debt*. (4)

budgetary surplus The amount by which government income exceeds spending. See also *budget deficit* and *public debt*. (4)

bureaucratic model of organization A framework used to structure organizations, characterized by several divisions or departments, specialization, formalization, departmentalization, a clear chain of command, centralization, and a hierarchical structure. See also *organic model of organization*. (6)

C

capacity The means or capabilities (such as people, skills, or resources) required to reach social and economic goals. (1, 8)

capital Various types of wealth that can be applied to improving one's quality of life. Types of capital include human (such as skills and knowledge); social (such as relationships and contacts); physical (such as material goods); natural (such as food and water); and financial (such as income and savings). (1)

caregiver burden The negative physical and psychological consequences of caring for another person for an extended period of time. Caregiver burden tends to have objective consequences (such as physical health complaints) and subjective consequences (such as psychological distress). (7)

care team A group of *professional helpers* and *nonprofessional helpers* that coordinates its efforts on behalf of *clients* who have a variety of *needs* or are connected to several different agencies. (7)

categorical A criteria relating to *public relief* in colonial times. Under the *English Poor Laws*, governments categorized people in need as being either "deserving" or "undeserving" of government assistance. (3)

child abuse An act against a child that harms or threatens that child's well-being. Child abuse includes physical or sexual assault, neglect or abandonment, emotional or psychological mistreatment, and witnessing *family violence*. Also called "child maltreatment." (10)

childcare The act of caring for and supervising children. Non-parental childcare is provided by someone other than an immediate family member, and can take place in a child's home, in another person's home, or in a centre. (3, 10)

children in care Children who come under the protection of a *child welfare system*. These children may continue living in their home under the supervision of a child protection worker, or be placed in alternative care such as a foster home or a group facility. (10)

child welfare system A government program that offers support services to *families* with children, investigates reports of alleged *child abuse* maltreatment, and provides various care options for *children in care*. (10)

citizen participation The active involvement of community members in the planning, development, and/or administration of policies and programs that affect them. (2)

clawback A *public policy* that requires high-income-earning individuals to repay part or all of the cash benefits they receive from an *income security program*. Programs that utilize clawbacks include Employment Insurance and Old Age Security. (4)

client A consumer, participant, or beneficiary of a *social welfare program* or service. (2)

colonization The encroachment upon, and subjugation of, one group by a more powerful group, usually for the purpose of exploiting the less powerful group's resources. The term colonization is often used in reference to the treatment by the Canadian government of *Aboriginal peoples* and their subsequent loss of resources, land, self-determination, family ties, and culture. (12)

commercial sector A subdivision of the *private sector* in which businesses, corporations, and companies deliver programs and services for a profit. See also *public sector* and *voluntary sector*. (5)

community-based model A framework used by *social agencies* that recognizes the importance of responding to community needs, matching services to people's *needs* and preferences, building on local strengths, and offering services in "natural" and "normal" (as opposed to institutional) settings. (6)

community development A community-based process of helping citizens resolve local problems that directly affect them. The aim of community development is not to challenge or reform established social structures, but rather to work with existing structures to increase the problem-solving *capacity* of the community. (8)

community living movement A collective, organized effort aimed at helping people with an intellectual *disability* make a smooth transition from institutional to community-based living. (14)

community mental health movement An organized effort that advocates for the rights of people with a *mental health problem,* and the provision of care in non-institutional approach settings. (14)

community needs assessment An evaluation used to determine the need for a particular program or service in a given community. (6)

community practice A *social work* field that focuses on motivating and helping community members to evaluate, plan, and coordinate their efforts to meet local health, social, and other *needs*. Sometimes referred to as "developmental social work." (8)

comprehensive community initiative A community-based process of helping citizens in a comprehensive way, on the assumption that all problems affecting neighbourhoods are interrelated and therefore require several interrelated solutions. (8, 9)

congregate housing A living arrangement (often for seniors and people with *disabilities*) that provides minimal care. Typically, the housing consists of a private apartment or room within a larger complex and the provision of meals. See also *assisted living* and *supportive housing.* (11)

conservatism A *political ideology* that promotes traditional values, moral (religious) standards, and conformity to the existing social order. Conservatives encourage people to compete, work hard, and accumulate wealth and property, yet maintain close ties to established social institutions, such as the *family* and the church. (1)

contracting-out A process in which the government purchases services from a private company, while remaining accountable for the delivery of those services. Also known as "outsourcing." (5)

contributory program An *income security program* that works as a savings plan, requiring working individuals to contribute to a fund, which then compensates them when they are not working. Government examples are Employment Insurance and the Canada/Quebec Pension Plans. (1)

core funding Income that can be applied to a *social agency*'s basic or "core" activities, such as *administration*, staffing, operational costs, agency promotion, and ongoing programs. (5)

corporate social responsibility An approach taken by businesses to include the public interest in its corporate decision making, thereby garnering the goodwill of the community. (5)

cross-cultural training Education and skill building that helps professional helpers raise their level of cultural sensitivity. (12, 13)

D

data collection tool An instrument used to collect quantitative or qualitative information about social conditions and problems. Examples include statistics, surveys, interviews, and focus groups. (2)

decentralization A process that involves one level of government transferring or "devolving" some or all of its functions, authority, and/or assets either to a lower level of government or to the private sector. (4)

deinstitutionalization A process to move institutionalized people into community settings, and to replace institutional care with community-based programs and services. (14)

depth of poverty A statistic that measures how far an income is below a low-income cut-off line or *LICO*. (9)

deserving poor A social label once applied to people who were sick, aged, disabled, or otherwise incapable of supporting themselves and deemed worthy of *public relief*. The term fell out of popular use by the mid-twentieth century. See also *undeserving poor*. (1)

direct relief Government aid given to the poor in the form of cash; vouchers for basic necessities; or essential resources such as food, fuel, and clothing. See also *indirect relief* and *public relief*. (3)

direct service The delivery of assistance through face-to-face interactions, often by front-line workers. Examples include personal counselling and therapy groups. See also *indirect service*. (6)

disability A physical, mental, or environmental condition that substantially restricts a person's ability to perform tasks that are normal for his or her age. (2, 14)

disability community A collective of people with a *disability*, their *families*, caregivers, advocates, and organizations that serve them. (14)

disability income system A range of income programs for people with a *disability* who are unable to earn enough to support themselves. These programs include earnings replacement, income support, compensation for loss, and compensation for disability-related costs. (14)

disability rights movement A collective, organized, large-scale effort aimed at eliminating socially imposed restrictions on people with a *disability*, ensuring their full citizenship, and creating equal *access* to mainstream resources and opportunities. (14)

diversity A concept that embraces the "differentness" of people and cultures. (6)

E

elder abuse The maltreatment of an older person within a relationship in which there is an expectation of trust (examples: the relationship between spouses, or between parent and child, or between caregiver and care recipient). Types of maltreatment include physical, sexual, or emotional abuse, financial exploitation, and neglect. (11)

empowerment The act of increasing the strength of an individual, *family*, group, organization, or community; gaining personal control, authority, and decision-making power over one's affairs. (10, 14)

enfranchisement A process that gives the rights of citizenship (including the right to vote) to a person or group. (12)

English Poor Laws A series of British parliamentary acts that were initiated by Elizabeth I during the sixteenth and seventeenth centuries; their aim was to reduce *poverty* and begging in England. Many principles of these laws were adopted in early Canadian settlements. (3)

environmental scan A method of assessing a community's social and economic conditions that may influence local needs or impact an organization's ability to meet those needs. (6)

episodic disability A type of *disability* that can affect individuals on a sporadic and often unpredictable basis. Examples include HIV, multiple sclerosis, and mental disorders. (14)

ethnic enclave A neighbourhood or district that retains certain cultural, racial, religious, ancestral, or other distinctions from the larger population. These neighbourhoods are often populated by *immigrant* and *visible-minority* groups. Examples are Chinatown and Little Italy. (13)

F

family A group of people composed of a married couple or a common-law couple, with or without children, or of a lone parent living with at least one child. (3, 10)

family casework A *social work* approach that emerged in the 1920s and 1930s designed to help the entire *family* unit (or several members of the family). (8)

family policy A type of *social policy* used to guide government initiatives for *families* with children. Examples are the National Children's Agenda, and the Family Violence Initiative. (10)

family violence The abuse of power within a *family*, or in relationships of trust or dependency; family violence encompasses a wide range of behaviours, including physical assault, emotional abuse, neglect, sexual assault, financial exploitation, and stalking. (10)

feminization of poverty A view of *poverty* that illustrates the ways women are more likely than men to be poor, regardless of the woman's age, income, family status, ethnicity, or other characteristic. (9)

First Nations peoples A term often used in place of *Indians*, that refers to both Status and Non-Status Indian people. (12)

fiscal crisis The negative economic impact of an accumulation of annual deficits, combined with a growing *public debt*. (4)

fiscalization A process whereby the value of policies and programs is measured not in terms of their actual results, but in view of their impact on budgets. The "fiscalization of social policy" refers to the use of the tax system to achieve social goals. (4)

flat hierarchical structure An organizational structure that has few levels of management; a characteristic of the *organic model of organization*. (6)

food insecurity The state of not having or eating enough nutritious food, going hungry, or worrying about not being able to obtain an adequate amount or quality of food. (9)

formative evaluation An assessment that occurs during a *planned change process*, that focuses on whether an action plan is working and what might need modification in order to reach the desired goal. See also *summative evaluation*. (8)

functional limitations perspective A theory that defines *disability* largely in terms of how it limits a person's activities, as well as how people with a disability and others perceive and react to those limitations. For other perspectives, see *impairment perspective* and *sociopolitical perspective*. (14)

G

globalization "The process by which all peoples and communities come to experience an increasingly common economic, social and cultural environment" (International Federation of Social Workers, 2005). (1, Appendix B)

governance The process used by governments and other organizations to exercise power and authority, manage problems, and deliver programs and services. (5)

government-assisted housing program A government program that provides full or partial subsidies for housing to low-income individuals and *families*. Examples include public housing, nonprofit housing, shelter allowances, rent supplements, and portable housing allowances. (9)

grassroots approach Activities or projects that are started by "average" people rather than by formal systems (such as government or *professions*); considered a "bottom-up" rather than a "top-down" approach to social change. (8)

guaranteed annual income A concept that suggests that all citizens have the right to a minimum income as the result of either paid work or government subsidies. (3)

H

healing In Aboriginal theory, the process of restoring balance or harmony to the overall health and well-being of individuals, *families*, groups, or communities. Within the *traditional approach (to helping)*, healing is a group of ideas, activities, events, initiatives, and relationships that occur at several different levels, from the individual to the inter-tribal. (12)

holistic view Looking at the whole of something rather than just its individual parts; a recognition of the interconnectedness between the individual, the *family*, nature, and the community, and of the balance between the physical, psychological, social, and spiritual aspects of the individual. The holistic view is central to the *traditional approach (to helping)*. (12)

home and community care Programs that provide professional care in a person's home (rather than in a hospital or nursing home), that help people remain independent in their community for as long as possible, and that aim to prevent chronic health problems. (11)

horizontal fiscal imbalance A condition in which a province or territory has more wealth than another province or territory. (2)

I

immigrant A person who was born in another country, has moved to Canada by choice, and has been granted the legal right to live in this country. See also *refugee* and *recent immigrant*. (13)

immigration service agency A *voluntary social agency* that delivers *settlement programs* to *recent immigrants* and *refugees*. (13)

impairment perspective A theory that defines *disability* as a biologically based illness, disease, or "problem" that originates in a person's body or mind, and that can be "fixed" or cured by specific interventions. See also *functional limitations perspective* and *sociopolitical perspective*. (14)

income inequality The unequal distribution of wealth in capitalist systems, characterized as a division between the very rich and the very poor; the inequality is reflected in the average earnings of high-income and low-income groups. Also referred to as "income gap." (1, Appendix B)

income redistribution A strategy that is based on *Keynesian economics*; in practice, governments use the tax system to shift (or redistribute) income away from high- and moderate-income earners toward those with low incomes. (1)

income security program A government-sponsored initiative that provides financial aid to replace or supplement a person's income during times of unemployment. People often receive these benefits because of old age, sickness, or *disability*. (1)

income test A type of financial test used to determine eligibility for an *income security program* or *social service*. Eligibility is based on an applicant's income rather than on personal *needs* or means of earning income. See also *needs test* and *means test*. (1)

independent living movement A philosophy and *social movement* that promotes self-representation for people with a *disability* through political organization. (14)

indexed When an *income security program* is indexed, it does not have to have legislative approval to increase its benefits—rather, the benefits increase automatically as the cost of living rises. (3)

Indian An indigenous person who is not *Métis* or *Inuit*. There are three categories of Indians in Canada: Status Indians, Non-Status Indians, and Treaty Indians. See also *First Nations peoples*. (12)

indicator A statistic or piece of data that measures or "indicates" the existence of something. An indicator can help to illustrate how a social or economic condition manifests itself in society, and how it might change over time. (2)

indirect relief Aid provided through government-funded work projects during the Great Depression, designed to get the unemployed back to work. See also *direct relief*. (3)

indirect service An activity in *social agencies* that does not usually involve personal contact with *clients*, but that can influence the type and quality of *direct services*. Examples include *administration*, *program planning*, and *program evaluation*. See also *direct service*. (6)

individual development account A type of savings account into which both an individual and the government contribute. Thus, government and low-income earners work together to help individuals build assets, which the participant can one day draw from to, for instance, attend college or buy a home. (9)

indoor relief A type of *public relief* provided by colonial governments to people in *need*; the "relief" was in the form of room and board in institutions such as *workhouses* and *poorhouses*. See also *outdoor relief*. (3)

institutional approach The view that *social welfare* is a primary institution of society (similar to religion, government, and education) and therefore has a normal, legitimate, and necessary function in a civilized, modern society. See also *residual approach* and *social investment approach*. (1)

integration The third and ultimate stage of the *settlement process*, when *recent immigrants* achieve a sense of belonging, acceptance, and recognition. Integration is synonymous with *social inclusion*. See also *adaptation stage of settlement* and *acclimatization stage of settlement*. (13)

inter-agency cooperation A management approach in which the members of *social agencies* cooperate and work together to improve a community's programs and services. (6)

interdisciplinary knowledge base A foundation of knowledge that is based on the shared experience and research of people from various *professions*, vocations, or academic fields. (7)

interest group An organized collective that forms to support specific causes, and tries to influence government policy for the benefit of its own members or on behalf of the general public. (2)

intersectoral collaboration A management approach that promotes the cooperation of, and the pooling of resources among, government and non-governmental agencies. (5)

intra-agency cooperation A management approach used by a *social agency* to create an environment of *empowerment* for its workers and *clients*. (6)

Inuit An Aboriginal person who inhabits the northern regions of Canada, principally Nunavut, the Northwest Territories, and the northern parts of Labrador and Quebec. (12)

K

Keynesian economics An economic theory that emphasizes the role of government in stabilizing society by taking a portion of income (in the form of taxation) from high- and moderate-income earners and giving it to low-income earners. The theory goes that cash that is redistributed through *income security programs* enables poorer people to spend more which, in turn, can stimulate the economy. See also *income redistribution*. (1)

L

labour market restructuring Significant shifts in economic conditions, the types of work offered, and the pool of workers available to provide the goods and services that are in demand. (Appendix B)

laissez-faire **government** A government that supports the conservative idea of minimal government, and expects the market, private enterprise, and the law of supply and demand to provide people with the income and other resources they need. The French term means "to leave alone." (1)

liberalism A *political ideology* that emphasizes people's rights to individuality, freedom of self-expression, and lifestyle choice. Liberals tend to view *poverty* and other *social problems* as conditions resulting from flaws in the capitalist system, not as a result of individual shortcomings. (1)

LICOs (Low-Income Cut-Offs) A collection of measurements developed by Statistics Canada that identify the minimum level of income required for a *family* to purchase food, shelter, and other basics in Canada. (2, 9)

logic model A framework that describes the components of a policy or program, and the causal relationships between them. The description reveals a series of "if-then" relationships: if resources are invested in a program, then program activities can take place; if these activities are carried out successfully, then one can expect certain program outputs and outcomes. (2)

lone-parent family A type of family that is headed by one parent of any marital status, with at least one child living in the same dwelling. (10)

longitudinal survey A statistical survey that is administered to a constant group of people several times at regular intervals over a relatively long period of time. Survey results are often used to study developmental trends across the lifespan of certain populations. (2)

M

macro level (of society) The largest structures and systems of society, which include the state (government), communities, societal norms and values, a culture's traditions and customs, and economic processes. These structures and systems tend to be complex and well-established. See also *micro level* and *mezzo level*. (8)

mainstream approach (to helping) A process of helping people that is based on a medical model. This model tends to view human disorders as discrete entities that can be "fixed" or treated through medication, psychotherapy, or other conventional intervention. See also *traditional approach (to helping)*. (12)

mandatory retirement policy A rule or law that requires people to stop working when they reach a certain age. (11)

mandatory volunteer A person who is required to volunteer in order to qualify for another event, such as high school graduation, or meeting the requirements of a court order. This group is also known as "voluntolds." (7)

means test A type of financial test used to determine eligibility for an *income security program* or *social service*. Eligibility is based on an applicant's income and assets but virtually ignores personal *needs*. See also *income test* and *needs test*. (1)

mental health A person's *capacity* to think, feel, and behave in ways that enhance the quality and enjoyment of life and the skills to deal with life's challenges. (10)

mental health problem A psychological (cognitive or emotional) disorder that is characterized by distress or *disability*, and that interferes with a person's ability to complete the daily tasks of living. (6, 7, 10, 11)

Métis A person of mixed First Nation Indian and European ancestry; someone who identifies him- or herself as distinct from *Inuit* and *Indian*. (12)

mezzo level (of society) The segment of society that is made up of organizations, businesses, clubs, associations, and other formal systems that are established for the purpose of achieving an identified goal. See also *micro level* and *macro level*. (8)

micro level (of society) The segment of society that is made up of the smallest units, such as individuals, *families*, and small groups. See also *mezzo level* and *macro level*. (8)

mission statement Part of and organization's a *strategic framework* that describes what the organization is, what it does, to whom its efforts will be targeted, and what it intends to achieve. See also *agency goal*, *value statement*, and *vision statement*. (6)

mixed economy of welfare The provision of *social welfare programs* through various service delivery systems, all of which focus on the provision of well-being, that are organized, funded, and managed in their own distinct ways. (5)

monetarism An economic philosophy that maintains that inflation is caused by an excess amount of money in the economy; thus, monetarists urge governments to avoid dumping money into the economy—in other words, to minimize spending on *public programs* and services. (4)

multilevel approach to practice A *social work* orientation that supports interventions at *micro, mezzo,* and *macro levels* of society. (7)

multiservice centre A combination of supports (such as health care and *social services*) that are offered at one location. (6)

N

National Aboriginal Organization A formal, organized, and recognized group of *Aboriginal people* who engage in activities aimed at protecting their common interests and rights, publicly promoting their cause, and reclaiming their rights. (12)

natural helping skill An ability acquired through personal experience and informal interpersonal interactions rather than formal training. Examples include humour and exchanges of personal experiences. (7)

need A necessary condition or requirement of human development that, if not met, will result in serious physical, psychological, or social harm. (1)

needs test A type of financial test used to determine eligibility for an *income security program* or *social service*. Eligibility is based on an applicant's personal needs and the level of income required to meet those needs. See also *income test* and *means test*. (1)

neoliberalism A contemporary form of *conservatism* that promotes small government, fiscal responsibility, and the role of business in providing a strong economy that will meet *social welfare* needs. Neoliberalism is highly compatible with *globalization* and, because of this, it is considered the "dominant global ideology." (1, Appendix B)

nonprofessional helper A person who helps others without monetary compensation, including natural helpers, informal helpers, "lay" helpers, *agency volunteers*, *self-help groups*, *unpaid caregivers*, and peer counsellors. The term may also apply to paid and formally trained helpers who are not members of a recognized *profession*. See also *professional helper*. (7)

nonresidential centre A *social agency* that provides services on a drop-in, appointment, or outreach basis. These organizations cater to people who do not need to be institutionalized in order to receive services. See also *residential centre*. (6)

non-standard job An employment option that includes part-time, casual, temporary, contract, or seasonal jobs. (9, Appendix B)

O

open house concept An idea that recognizes the value of the full participation of people with a *disability* in school, work, recreation, or other activity, and their enjoyment of the same rights and privileges as people who do not have a disability. (14)

operational framework An internal structure that a *social agency* uses as a practical guide to delivering *direct services* and managing *indirect services*. See also *strategic framework*. (6)

organic model of organization A framework used to structure organizations, and that views organizations as living organisms, capable of adapting to an ever-changing environment. Most organic structures emphasize *flat hierarchical structures*, flexibility, *diversity*, innovation, and cooperative ways of working. See also *bureaucratic model of organization*. (6)

organizational change A fundamental shift in the way an organization operates, usually involving a significant restructuring of one or more of its internal systems; a type of change at the *mezzo level of society*. (8)

outcome evaluation A type of *program evaluation* that assesses the actual achievement of a program rather than its intent, and that identifies changes in behaviour, skills, attitudes, or knowledge of program participants. (6)

outdoor relief A type of *public relief* provided by colonial governments to people in *need*; the "relief" was in the form of cash and other assistance, given directly to people in their own homes. See also *indoor relief*. (3)

P

passive policy A government plan of action that does not require beneficiaries of government assistance to give anything in exchange for benefits. See also *active policy*. (2, 9)

person-in-environment A *social work* perspective that acknowledges the complexity of interactions between people and their environment, and that recognizes that people both shape and are shaped by their environment. (7)

planned change process A step-by-step scientific, methodical approach used in the *social welfare* field to facilitate change in people, organizations, and other systems. The process involves a target of change, a change agent, a method of change, a beneficiary of change, and a context of change. (8)

policies and procedures A set of documents outlining a fixed set of rules used to guide an organization's operations. (6)

policy analysis A systematic examination of a *public policy* for the purpose of learning about the policy. An analysis may, for example, seek to determine how, why, or for whom the policy was developed, and if the policy reflects certain principles or standards. (2)

policy community A loosely defined set of individuals, groups, and organizations from both inside and outside government that influence the development of *public policy*. (2)

political ideology A set of beliefs that shape people's views of society, how that society should function, and what should be done to achieve the "ideal" society. (1)

poorhouse An institutions created in colonial times to "manage" and house the poor and homeless, and to keep them from roaming the streets. Also called "almshouse." (3)

population aging A demographic phenomenon characterized by an increasing number of older people in the population. (11)

poverty (1) A state of living characterized by lack, deprivation, and an inability to obtain the bare necessities. (2) A form of *social exclusion*, in which a person is unable, or is denied the opportunity, to fully engage in society or meet society's expectations in terms of roles, relationships, and participation. (3) A state of being powerless, voiceless, or dependent on others for resources. (2, 3, 4, 9)

poverty rate A statistic that quantifies the percentage of people living in low income in a geographic area. (9)

poverty reduction A process that addresses both the symptoms and the root causes of *poverty*. (9)

practice knowledge A body of information or data, collected by *professional helpers* through observation and the provision of *direct services*, that gives evidence regarding what activities appear to help or hinder *client* progress. (2)

primary prevention Activities usually targeted at large segments of the population that aim to prevent the development of personal and *social problems* through education, the provision of information, or the promotion of certain practices. See also *secondary prevention* and *tertiary prevention*. (6)

principle of less eligibility A guideline established under the *English Poor Laws*, used during colonial times, that required public benefits to be minimal and less than the wage of the lowest-paid workers in a settlement. (3)

private sector A nongovernment component of the economy in which organizations are privately owned and operated. The private sector includes commercial or business (profit-making) operations and voluntary (nonprofit) operations. See also *commercial sector*, *voluntary sector*, and *public sector*. (5)

private trouble A human *need*, condition, or situation that can be resolved by the person who is immediately affected, rather than by government. See also *public issue*. (1)

privatization The transfer of most or all assets or services from a government to an agency in the *private sector*. (5)

process model A framework used to analyze or evaluate a *social welfare program* or a *social policy* that is primarily concerned with how the program or policy is created or implemented. The process model assumes that policy evolves from sequential stages or steps. (2)

profession A vocation based on specialized education that possesses a code of ethics, has the means to regulate and enforce standards of behaviour among its members, and has developed a theoretical body of knowledge that guides practice. The professions include *social work*, nursing, policing, law, and psychology. (7)

professional helper A person paid to provide helping services and to bring a recognized knowledge base, training, and relevant experience to his or her practice. This type of help is often guided by a code of ethics specific to the helper's *profession*. Examples include *social workers*, psychiatrists, and psychologists. In contrast, see *nonprofessional helper*. (7)

program eligibility A set of criteria that, when met, allows a person to participate in, or potentially benefit from, a publicly sponsored program. (1)

program evaluation A process of examining programs and services to determine whether they are needed and used, how effective they are, how well they are run, and/or whether their benefits justify their costs. (2, 6)

program planning A process carried out by *social agencies* to ensure that programs and services are designed to meet the *needs* of *clients* and that they reflect the community's broader goals. Planning involves a series of steps, which include setting goals and objectives, designing programs, and evaluating the plan's viability. (6)

progressive universalism An approach to the provision of income security benefits that supplies benefits to all persons who are eligible, but gives a larger benefit to those who need it most. This is a contemporary (and European) version of a *universal program*. (1)

project funding A source of money that is specified for use in a certain activity or program. It is often short-term, lasting only as long as the initiative, and cannot be used to cover costs not directly related to the initiative. (5)

Protestant work ethic A set of values that promotes thrift, hard work, self-help, and self-discipline as a means to material prosperity and personal salvation. (3)

psychosocial approach A therapeutic way of working that recognizes the importance of the relationship and interactions between a person's psychology and his or her environment. (11)

public debt The accumulated amount of government deficits. See also *budget deficit* and *budgetary surplus*. (4)

public issue A human *need*, condition, or situation that government assumes responsibility for. Many public issues are *social problems* that, if left unaddressed, are likely to negatively impact large segments of the population. In contrast, see *private trouble*. (1)

public policy A plan of action developed by government in response to a particular issue or *need*; this plan gives structure to *public programs*. (2)

public program An activity or project that stems from a *public policy*, is funded by taxpayers, is administered by government, and has a specific purpose, goal, and/or objective. (5)

public relief Government aid provided to people who are unable to support themselves through work or other means. An early term for *social assistance* or "welfare." (3)

public sector The government component of the economy in which programs and services are funded fully by tax revenues. Although a government program/service may be managed or delivered by a *private sector* organization, government remains accountable for that program/service. See also *private sector*, *commercial sector*, and *voluntary sector*. (5)

public social agency A government department or division that provides a *social welfare program*; examples include welfare offices and government-based child protection units. See also *voluntary social agency*. (6)

Q

qualitative measure A method of evaluating or estimating the quality, nature, meaning, or other subjective aspect of a person's experiences as part of a *program evaluation*. See also *quantitative measure*. (8)

quantitative measure A method of counting or quantifying objective data (such as staff turnover rates or service utilization statistics) as part of a *program evaluation*. See also *qualitative measure*. (8)

R

racism Prejudice or discrimination against one or more people based on the belief that race determines certain traits, behaviours, or abilities. (2, 13)

recent immigrant A person who immigrated to Canada within the past ten years. See also *immigrant*. (13)

refugee A person who has been forced to flee persecution in his or her homeland and to take refuge in a foreign country. See also *immigrant*. (13)

relative homelessness A state of living with physical shelter that is temporary, unsafe, unaffordable, inadequate, lacks *access* to clean water and sanitation, or otherwise fails to meet basic standards of health and safety. See also *absolute homelessness*. (9)

reserve A tract of land owned by the Government of Canada, and set apart for the use and benefit of an *Indian* or First Nations *band*. Many First Nations have replaced the term "reserve" with "First Nations community." (12)

residential centre An organization that provides living quarters, meals, and a range of services to people who require round-the-clock care. These facilities were originally called "institutions." See also *nonresidential centre*. (6, 11)

residential school A boarding school that offers students both an education and a place to live. In Canada, the term usually refers to an educational system initiated by the federal government in 1883 to assimilate *Aboriginal peoples* into mainstream society. See also *assimilation*. (12)

residential school syndrome A cluster of psychological, social, physical, and other symptoms experienced by *Aboriginal peoples* who attended *residential schools*. The syndrome does not apply to mainstream residential schools. (12)

residual approach The view that *social welfare programs* should be used sparingly and only as a last resort, when help from one's *family*, church, banks, and other private sources has been exhausted. See also *institutional approach* and *social investment approach*. (1)

resilience The ability to cope effectively with hardship, or to recover quickly from some type of adversity. (8)

respite service A program that gives *unpaid caregivers* a break from their caregiving duties by providing day care or home support to those needing care. (7)

restricted practice activity A task that can be carried out only by certain occupational groups or by designated professionals within those groups. (7)

retirement income system A range of *income security programs* available to people in their senior or retirement years. In Canada, the system comprises three major programs: Old Age Security, the Canada/Quebec Pension Plan, and private pension plans and savings. (11)

S

sandwich generation A segment of the population that is in the role of caregiver to both dependent children and aging relatives. (7)

scope of practice A defined set of functions and activities that limit the range of what *professional helpers* can and cannot do in their provision of service. (7)

secondary prevention Activities that focus on identifying a *social problem* in its early stages of development, and then controlling or changing the conditions that caused it. Also referred to as "early intervention." See also *primary prevention* and *tertiary prevention.* (6)

self-government An arrangement between a government and a group of people that allows the group to govern themselves (usually within the structures of the existing laws). Canadian law allows some *First Nations peoples* to live under this type of arrangement. (12)

self-help group An organized yet nonprofessional network of individuals who provide mutual aid and share common experiences, situations, problems, and strategies. (7)

settlement practice A collection of interventions, values, knowledge, and professional ethics adopted by settlement workers and applied to their work with *recent immigrants* and *refugees.* (13)

settlement process For a *recent immigrant*, the steps taken to become a full-fledged member of a new country or society. This process typically involves three stages: *acclimatization, adaptation*, and *integration.* (13)

settlement program An initiative designed to help *recent immigrants* and *refugees* quickly become established, self-sufficient, and contributing members of Canadian society. Examples include the Immigrant Settlement and Adaptation Program, Language Instruction for Newcomers to Canada, and the Host Program. (13)

social action Collective and coordinated efforts that aim to eliminate a *social problem*, correct an injustice, or meet a human *need*. This approach usually involves influencing those with power (such as politicians) to change certain policies, laws, or procedures, and/or reforming social institutions that are deemed inadequate. (8)

social agency A formally structured organization in the public and voluntary sectors whose main objective is to meet human *needs*. See also *public social agency* and *voluntary social agency*. (1, 6)

social assistance An *income security program* that gives cash to individuals and *families* who, for whatever reasons, are unable to adequately meet their *needs*, and who have exhausted all other means of support. Commonly known as "welfare"; formerly referred to as *public relief*. (1, 4, 6, 9)

social casework A *social work* approach to practice that involves a scientific, step-by-step method to helping individuals. (8)

social citizenship A concept that promotes minimum levels of health, education, and personal well-being as a right by virtue of being a citizen. (3)

social connectedness A term used to describe both the quality and number of connections a person has with other people. Social connectedness includes four dimensions: social support, social networks, social engagement, and supportive social environments. (11)

social deficit A theory that emphasizes an excess of social and economic liabilities—such as hardship, unmet human potential, and limited opportunities—relative to social and economic assets. Governments are often blamed for creating a social deficit by failing to provide adequate *social programs*. (4)

social democracy A *political ideology* that rejects the competitive values of capitalism, individualism, and private enterprise, and encourages fellowship and cooperation among citizens. Social democrats generally encourage government to use its taxation and other powers to equalize social and economic conditions. (1)

social economy "A grass-roots sector that is entrepreneurial and yet nonprofit in nature" and focuses on enhancing "the social, economic, and environmental conditions of communities, often with a focus on their disadvantaged members" (HRSDC, 2005). See also *social economy enterprise*. (5)

social economy enterprise An organization within the *social economy* that is run like a business; is often staffed by a mix of paid employees and volunteers; produces goods and services for the market; and applies its profits toward the achievement of social or environmental goals. (5, 8, 14)

social exclusion A social process whereby large segments of the population are prevented from fully integrating into or participating in society, or feel alienated, marginalized, or unaccepted by the mainstream society. Groups who are likely to experience social exclusion are those who are poor or uneducated. (2, 9, 13)

social group work A *social work* approach directed toward a small group of people who have similar *needs* or lifestyles, who are dealing with a common issue, and/or who are working toward a common goal. (8)

social inclusion A social goal that is achieved when citizens gain full and equal participation in the economic, social, cultural and political dimensions of society. (1, 13)

social investment approach The view that *social welfare programs* should yield long-term benefits. This approach takes a proactive stance, preferring to prevent rather than react to social problems; a focus is on fostering social inclusion and participation. See also *institutional approach* and *residual approach*. (1)

social knowledge A body of information, data, research results, and *practice knowledge* that is used to understand and address social conditions and *social problems*. (2)

social minimum A reasonable standard of living or quality of life that can be subjectively measured by social norms, or objectively measured by the average real gross domestic product (GDP) per person. (1, 3)

social movement An organized, large-scale effort to achieve identified social goals; usually involves a large segment of the population that shares a similar ideology, vision, and objectives. Examples include the labour reform movement, the child welfare movement, and the *disability rights movement*. (3)

social planning A process committed to social development that is based on the notion that community change is best achieved through a rational, formal, and technical problem-solving procedure led by expert (professional) planners. (8)

social policy A plan or guideline developed and used by government to create, maintain, or change living conditions so that they are conducive to people's health and well-being. Examples are *social welfare policy* and healthcare policy. (2)

social policymaker An elected government official who creates the laws, legislation, and policies related to *social programs*. (2)

social problem A condition in society that creates a measurable degree of social hardship, psychological or physical injury, or other negative consequence for a large segment of the population, and that people are concerned about and want changed. Social problems tend to spark some kind of collective response aimed at correcting the situation. Sometimes called "social risk." (1, 2)

social program Systems consisting of services, benefits, or activities that are designed to improve human welfare or meet a social *need*, and that are fully or partially funded by government. Canada has three major social programs: *social welfare*, health care, and postsecondary education. (1)

social safety net An informal term that refers to the collection of publicly funded programs designed to protect people from the negative consequences of natural disasters, personal crises, health problems, and other hardships. Most programs in the "net" are designed to prevent individuals from falling into *poverty* beyond a certain level. (1)

social security A term that refers to the "cradle-to-grave" protection of individuals and families from socially recognized conditions (such as unemployment) that hinder people's ability to meet basic human *needs*. Social security is derived from many different sources, including work, savings, and publicly funded *income security programs*, *social services*, and healthcare services. (1, 3)

social service A non-income and intangible benefit that aims to enhance social functioning and general well-being for individuals, *families*, and small groups. Social services are sometimes called *transfers-in-kind* because they are given to individuals and families in lieu of cash transfer payments. (1)

social service worker A person who has been trained—usually at the college level—as a generalist *social worker*, and has reached a certain level of competence in basic *social work* methods, values, and ethics. Sometimes considered a paraprofessional; also known by other titles, such as "human service worker." (7)

social welfare A concept, field, and/or system that is concerned with individual and collective well-being; that helps people meet their basic social and economic *needs*; and that prevents, reduces, or alleviates *social problems*. (1)

social welfare policy A government's plan or guideline that provides the direction for most *income security programs* and *social services*. Social welfare policy is a type of *public policy* and a subset of *social policy*. (2)

social welfare program A set of projects, activities, or initiatives that aim to enhance the well-being of society and to meet a public *need*. Examples include *income security programs*, *social services*, and social research. Programs may or may not have a service component. (1)

social welfare reform An effort by government to restructure *social welfare policies* and related programs for the purpose of correcting a problem, improving conditions, or restoring a function to an former state. (4)

social work A *profession* dedicated to helping individuals, groups, and communities strengthen their skills, abilities, and *capacity* for the purpose of enhancing well-being. (7)

social worker A person officially recognized by a provincial/territorial social work association or college to practise the *profession* of *social work*. (7)

sociopolitical perspective A theory that accepts *disability* as the consequence of an abnormal medical condition and subsequent impairment; however, the theory also views a person's experience of "disablement" as largely the result of the stigmatization, discrimination, and subsequent marginalization of people with a disability, rather than the physical impairment itself. Also known as the ecological perspective or social perspective. See also *impairment perspective* and *functional limitations perspective*. (14)

spousal abuse A form of *family violence* committed by one marital, common-law, or same-sex partner against the other; includes physical abuse, sexual assault or exploitation, emotional abuse, criminal harassment or stalking, economic or financial abuse, and spiritual abuse. (10)

stakeholder A person who has a vested interest in a *social agency's* activities and achievements; stakeholders include an agency's staff, volunteers, and funders, and members of the local community. (6)

strategic framework An internal structure that a *social agency* uses to describe its priorities and how it plans to achieve its ultimate goal, mission, and vision. See also *operational framework*. (6)

structural social work One of the many anti-oppressive *social work* models that focus on changing the organizations that employ them in order to improve conditions for staff and *clients*. (8)

summative evaluation An assessment that measures the end results of a *planned change process*. See also *formative evaluation*. (8)

supportive housing A living arrangement for seniors or people with a *disability* that includes a private living space combined with a certain level of care; this type of housing is intended to help individuals balance independence with specific support. See also *assisted living* and *congregate housing*. (11)

system of care A mix of services and resources that, when offered in a coordinated and integrated fashion, is responsive to the varying levels and changing *needs* of *clients*. (6)

systemic change An approach to *organizational change* that occurs in all aspects or levels of an organization, usually involving the modification of an agency's policies, procedures, and practices. (8)

T

targeted cash transfer A financial benefit that government "transfers" to individuals whose income or assets fall below a *social minimum*. These benefits include the Guaranteed Income Supplement, *social assistance*, and *disability* pensions. In contrast to *universal cash transfer*. (1)

targeted program An *income security program* or *social service* that is restricted to a certain population considered vulnerable, disadvantaged, or at risk for a certain social or economic hardship. In contrast to *universal program*. (1)

tax credit An amount deducted from a taxpayer's income tax when certain criteria are met; the amount allowed is calculated according to a taxpayer's income level. Examples include the Canada Child Tax Benefit and the Goods and Services Tax/Harmonized Sales Tax Credit. (1)

tertiary prevention Activities that aim to reduce the negative effects of personal or *social problems* that have become chronic or complex; these activities are often legislated. Also known as "treatment." See also *primary prevention* and *secondary prevention*. (6)

traditional approach (to helping) A way of seeing and intervening in personal and *social problems* that is based on Aboriginal theory; a process of *healing* that is shaped by a *holistic view* of human *needs*/problems, and emphasizes the participation of individuals in their own healing process. See also *mainstream approach (to helping)*. (12)

transfer-in-kind A type of benefit that is funded and "transferred" by government to individuals or families in the form of a *social service* or a *direct service*. (1)

transnational corporation A company that manages production or delivers services in more than one country. (Appendix B)

U

unaffordable housing The economic living condition of individuals or *families* who spend more than 30 percent of before-tax household income on shelter. (9)

underemployed People who are not working as much as they could or want to, or whose skills exceed those required for the job they have. (9)

undeserving poor A nineteenth-century social label that refers to able-bodied, unemployed people who are capable of supporting themselves through paid labour and are thus unworthy of government assistance. See also *deserving poor*. (1)

unemployment rate A statistic that reports on the proportion of the workforce that is not working, but is actively looking for and is available for work. (9)

universal cash transfer An *income security program* provided to all persons, regardless of financial status or *need*, who meet a basic requirement such as age or residency. Example: Universal ChildCare Benefit. In contrast to *targeted cash transfer*. (1)

universal program A government benefit available to all Canadians as a matter of right, regardless of economic status or *need*. In contrast to *targeted program*. (1)

unpaid caregiver An adult relative, spouse, friend, neighbour, or other informal helper who provides assistance to an older person (or someone with a chronic health condition) without monetary reimbursement. (7)

V

value statement Part of an organization's *strategic framework* that reflects the organization's core ideology. See also *mission statement*, *agency goal*, and *vision statement*. (6)

vertical fiscal imbalance A term to describe the disparity between the federal government's ability to raise money as compared to that of lower levels of government. See also *horizontal fiscal imbalance*. (2)

visible minority According to Canada's Employment Equity Act, a person, other than a member of the *Aboriginal peoples*, whose race is non-Caucasian or is non-white in colour. (13)

vision statement Part of an organization's *strategic framework* that describes the organization's image of an ideal community, and what the organization intends to achieve. See also *mission statement*, *agency goal*, and *value statement*. (6)

voluntary sector A subdivision of the *private sector* made up of nongovernmental organizations that fulfil a social purpose and deliver programs on a nonprofit basis. Also called the "charitable," "independent," or "third" sector. See also *public sector* and *commercial sector*. (5)

voluntary social agency A *social agency* in the *private sector* that operates on a nonprofit basis, and provides one or more *social services* often on behalf of government; it is common for these agencies to be registered charities. Examples are family service bureaus, *immigration service agencies*, and women's shelters. See also *public social agency*. (5, 6)

W

welfare service The provision of goods and services over and above the financial assistance given to people on *social assistance*. Examples include government-subsidized rehabilitation programs for people with a *disability*, home support for seniors, and *childcare*. (3)

welfare state A nation whose government intervenes in the workings of the market through *income redistribution* for the purpose of correcting the problem of *income inequality*. Sometimes called "social welfare state." Welfare states are compatible with an *institutional approach* to social welfare and *Keynesian economics*. (1, 3)

welfare state retrenchment The efforts of government to curb the costs of *social welfare programs*, often by reducing or eliminating programs, or by replacing "generous" programs with more meagre ones. (4)

welfare-to-work program Provincial/territorial government initiatives designed to move welfare recipients off *social assistance* by making them work or train in exchange for benefits; an example of an *active policy*. Sometimes called "workfare." (4, 9)

welfare wall A characteristic of welfare systems that inadvertently makes *social assistance* more financially attractive than employment. (9)

workhouse In colonial times, an institution built with public funds in which able-bodied unemployed people were expected to learn good work habits and pay for their keep through labour. Also known as "houses of industry." (3)

working poor A portion of the population that earns more than half its income from employment, and yet does not earn enough to stay out of *poverty*. (3, 9)

Y

youth engagement approach A method used to reduce risk-taking behaviours among youth by enabling their participation in meaningful and empowering activities. (10)

REFERENCES

Abele, F. (2004, April). *Urgent need, serious opportunity: Towards a new social model for Canada's Aboriginal peoples.* CPRN Social Architecture Papers, Research Report F39, Family Network. Retrieved March 12, 2009, from www.cprn.com/documents/28340_en.pdf.

Aboriginal Healing Foundation. (2002). *Annual report 2002.* Retrieved March 12, 2009, from www.ahf.ca/pages/download/28_17.

Aboriginal Healing Foundation. (2008). *The Aboriginal Healing Foundation: Summary points of the AHF final report.* Retrieved March 12, 2009, from www.ahf.ca/pages/download/28_13239.

Abramovitz, M. (2004). Definition and functions of social welfare policy: Setting the stage for social change. In J. Blau & M. Abramovitz, *The dynamics of social welfare policy* (pp. 19–55). New York: Oxford University Press.

Addario, L. (2001, June). *Implementing Canada's commitments to women: An agenda for action.* Retrieved February 2, 2004, from Canadian Feminist Alliance for International Action, www.fafia-afai.org/research/hrimple.html.

Ahmed, I. (2006, July). *On the front lines of Toronto's community service sector: Improving working conditions and ensuring quality services.* Retrieved September 18, 2008, from Community Social Planning Council of Toronto and Family Service Association of Toronto, www.socialplanningtoronto.org/CSPCT%20Reports/Front%20Lines%20-%20Community%20Service%20Sector%202006-Online%20PDF.pdf.

Almey, M. (2007, March). *Finding data on women: A guide to major sources at Statistics Canada.* Retrieved February 3, 2009, from http://epe.lac-bac.gc.ca/100/200/301/swc-cfc/finding_data_on_2007-e/SW21-22-2007E.pdf.

Alzheimer Society of Canada. (2005, October). *Key facts about Alzheimer's disease and related dementia: Prevelance figures.* Retrieved February 28, 2009, from www.alzheimer.ca/english/disease/stats-intro.htm.

Ambert, M.A. (2006, March). *One-parent families: Characteristics, causes, consequences, and issues.* Retrieved February 24, 2009, from Vanier Institute of the Family, www.vifamily.ca/library/cft/oneparent.pdf.

Ameyaw, S., & Simpson, P. (1994). *The CED perspective.* Community Economic Development Centre. Burnaby: Simon Fraser University. Retrieved March 7, 2004, from www2.sfu.ca/cedc/resources/online/cedconline/sapsperspect.htm.

Annan, K. (2002). *Secretary General, accepting Moscow award, says strength of Russian spirit "is your country's greatest natural asset."* UN Press Release SG/SM/826205/06/2002. Retrieved January 11, 2009, from www.un.org/News/Press/docs/2002/sgsm8262.doc.htm.

Antony, W., Black, E., Frankel, S., Henley, D., Hudson, P., Land, W., et al. (2007, May). *The state of public services in Manitoba, 2007: Privatization: The public service Trojan horse.* Retrieved August 31, 2008, from Canadian Centre for Policy Alternatives,

www.policyalternatives.ca/documents/Manitoba_Pubs/2007/State_of_Public_
Services_2007.pdf.

Armitage, A. (2003). *Social welfare in Canada* (4th ed.). Don Mills: Oxford University Press.

ARRIPS (Action Research Roundtable on the Innovative Public Service). (2002).
Organizing for deliberate innovation: A toolkit for teams. Retrieved September 1, 2008,
from Canadian Centre for Management Development, www.ccmd-
ccg.gc.ca/Research/publications/pdfs/Inno_e.pdf.

Ashley, N. (2000, Summer). Beyond Maslow: Asset building with people whose basic
needs are not met or who are in crisis. *Heliogram, A Heliotrope Publication: Solutions to
Strengthen People and Communities* 3(1). Retrieved December 27, 2008, from
www.csgv.ca/counselor/assets/BeyondMaslow.pdf.

Assembly of First Nations. (2007, May). *Sustaining the caregiving cycle: First Nations people
and aging: A report from the Assembly of First Nations to the Special Senate Committee on
Aging, May 2007.* Retrieved March 12, 2009, from www.afn.ca/misc/SCC.pdf.

AUCC (Association of Universities and Colleges of Canada). (2007). *Federal budget summary: March 19, 2007.* Retrieved January 26, 2009, from University of Manitoba,
http://umanitoba.ca/dentistry/research/researchPdfs/FederalBudget2007Summary.pdf.

AuCoin, K. (2005). Children and youth as victims of violent crime. *Juristat, Canadian Centre
for Justice Statistics, Catalogue No. 85-002, 25*(1). Retrieved February 24, 2009, from
Statistics Canada, www.statcan.ca/english/freepub/85-002-XIE/0010585-002-XIE.pdf.

August, R. (2006). Community social services. In *The encyclopedia of Saskatchewan.*
Retrieved August 28, 2008, from Canadian Plains Research Center, University of
Regina, http://esask.uregina.ca/entry/community_social_services.html.

Aycan, Z., & Berry, J.W. (1996). *Impact of employment-related experiences on immigrants'
psychological well-being and adaptation to Canada.* Retrieved May 27, 2004, from
www.cpa.ca/cjbsnew/1996/ful_aycan.html.

Ballantyne, M. (2008). Harper and child care. In T. Healey (Ed.), *The Harper Record,*
pp. 339–344. Retrieved February 24, 2009, from www.policyalternatives.ca/doc-
uments/National_Office_Pubs/2008/HarperRecord/Harper_and_Child_Care.pdf.

Banks, S., Crossman, D., Poel, D., & Stewart, M. (1997). Partnerships among health
professionals and self-help group members. *Canadian Journal of Occupational Therapy*
64(3): 259–69. Retrieved February 15, 2004, from www.caot.ca/CJOT/CJOT64/
Banks64_5_259-269.pdf.

Banting, K.G. (1987). Visions of the welfare state. In S.B. Seward (Ed.), *The future of
social welfare systems in Canada and the United Kingdom* (pp. 147–63). Proceedings of
a Canada/UK Colloquium, October 17–18, 1986, Ottawa/Meech Lake. Halifax:
Institute for Research on Public Policy.

Banting, K.G. (2006). Dis-embedding liberalism? The social policy trajectory in
Canada. In D.A. Green & J.R. Kesselman (Eds.), *Dimensions of inequality in
Canada* (pp. 417–52). Vancouver: UBC Press. Retrieved August 23, 2008, from
http://post.queensu.ca/~bantingk/Disembeding%20Liberalism%20.pdf.

Barr, C., Brownlee, B., Lasby, D., & Gumulka, G. (2005). *Understanding the capacity of social services organizations.* A synthesis of findings from the National Survey of Nonprofit and Voluntary Organizations and the National Survey of Giving, Volunteering and Participating. Retrieved August 28, 2008, from Imagine Canada, http://nonprofitscan.imaginecanada.ca/files/en/misc/understanding_capacity_social_services_orgs.pdf.

Battle, K. (2001, September). *Relentless incrementalism: Deconstructing and reconstructing Canadian income security policy.* Retrieved March 1, 2009, from www.caledoninst.org/PDF/894598873.pdf.

Battle, K. (2006, January). *The choice in child care allowance: What you see is not what you get.* Retrieved December 27, 2008, from Caledon Institute of Social Policy, www.caledoninst.org/Publications/PDF/564ENG.pdf.

Battle, K., & Torjman, S. (2001, May). *The post–welfare state in Canada: Income testing and inclusion.* Retrieved August 26, 2008, from Caledon Institute of Social Policy, www.caledoninst.org/PDF/894598814.pdf.

Battle, K., Mendelson, M., & Torjman, S. (2006, June). *Towards a new architecture for Canada's adult benefits.* Ottawa: The Caledon Institute of Social Policy. Retrieved August 26, 2008, from www.caledoninst.org/Publications/PDF/594ENG.pdf.

Battle, K., Torjman, S., & Mendelson, M. (2006, February). *Finding common ground on child care.* Retrieved August 27, 2008, from Caledon Institute of Social Policy, www.caledoninst.org/Publications/PDF/572ENG.pdf.

BC Work Futures. (2005, May). *Community and social service workers (NOC 4212).* Retrieved September 18, 2008, from www.workfutures.bc.ca/profiles/profile.cfm?noc=4212&lang=en&site=graphic).

Beiser, M. (1999). *Strangers at the gate: The 'boat people's' first ten years in Canada.* Toronto: University of Toronto Press.

Bélanger, A., Martel, L., & Malenfant, E.C. (2005, December). *Population projections for Canada, Provinces and Territories: 2005-2031.* Retrieved February 28, 2009, from Statistics Canada, www.statcan.ca/english/freepub/91-520-XIE/0010591-520-XIE.pdf.

Bélanger, C. (2006). *Quebec history: Why did Canadian immigration policy change after 1945?* Retrieved March 11, 2009, from Marianopolis College, http://faculty.marianopolis.edu/c.belanger/QuebecHistory/readings/Whytheimmogrationpolicychanged after1945.html.

Bellamy, D. (1965). Social welfare in Canada. In *Encyclopedia of social work* (15th ed., pp. 36–48). New York: National Association of Social Workers.

Bellemare, D. (1993). The history of economic insecurity. In *Family security in insecure times* (pp. 57–86). Ottawa: National Forum on Family Security.

Bendall, L. (2008). Attitudes towards children with disabilities need improvement, parents say. *CBC News.ca*, May 2, 2008. Retrieved May 29, 2009, from www.cbc.ca/health/story/2008/05/02/fhealth-specialneeds.html.

Bibby, R. (2005). Future families project: A survey of Canadian hopes and dreams. *Transition Magazine, Winter 2004–2005 34*(4). Taking the pulse of Canada's families. Retrieved February 24, 2009, from www.vifamily.ca/library/transition/344/344.html.

Bickenbach, J.E. (1993). *Physical disability and social policy*. Toronto: University of Toronto Press.

Blackstock, C., Cross, T., George, J., Brown, I., & Formsma, J. (2006, March). *Reconciliation in child welfare: Touchstones of hope for indigenous children, youth, and families*. Retrieved March 12, 2009, from www.reconciliationmovement.org/docs/Touchstones_of_Hope.pdf.

Blackstock, C., Prakash, T., Loxley, J., & Wien, F. (2005). *Wen:de: We are coming to the light of day*. Ottawa: First Nations Child and Family Caring Society of Canada. Retrieved March 12, 2009, from www.reconciliationmovement.org/docs/WendeReport.pdf.

Bliss, M. (Ed.). (1975). A preface. In L. Marsh, *Report on social security for Canada* (pp. ix–x). Toronto and Buffalo: University of Toronto Press.

Block, P. (1996). *Stewardship: Choosing service over self interest*. San Francisco: Berrett-Koehler.

Bonnell, G. (2007). Nuclear family in decline: Census. *Toronto Star*, September 12, 2007. Retrieved February 24, 2009, from www.thestar.com/News/Canada/article/255716.

Bothwell, R., Drummond, I.A., & English, J. (1989). *Canada since 1945: Power, politics, and provincialism* (2 ed.). Toronto: University of Toronto Press.

Bouchard, G. (2007, March). *The Canadian immigration system: An overview workshop on German and European migration and immigration policy from a transatlantic perspective: Challenge for the 21st century*. Retrieved March 11, 2009, from Governance Institute for Research on Public Policy, www.irpp.org/miscpubs/archive/bouchard_immig.pdf.

Bowen, P., & McKechnie, A.J. (2001). *Volunteer connections: New strategies for involving older adults*. Retrieved February 28, 2009, from Volunteer Canada, www.volunteer.ca/volunteer/pdf/OlderAdults-Eng.pdf.

Boychuk, G. (2004, January). *The Canadian social model: The logics of policy development*. CPRN Social Architecture Papers, Research Report F/36: Family Network. Retrieved December 27, 2008, from Canadian Policy Research Networks, www.cprn.org/documents/26085_en.pdf.

Boys and Girls Clubs of Canada. (2008, Fall). *Creating positive alternatives for Canadian youth*. Retrieved February 24, 2009, from www.bgccan.com/upload/roots%20of%20youth%20violence_e.pdf.

Brasfield, C.R. (2001, March). Residential School Syndrome. *BC Medical Journal 43*(2): 78–81. Retrieved March 12, 2009, from www.bcmj.org/residential-school-syndrome.

Bredin Institute. (2006). *Cultural diversity in the workplace*. Retrieved September 1, 2008, from www.bredin.ab.ca/ImmigrantServices/Employment%20Preparation/Cultural%20Diversity%20in%20the%20Workplace.aspx.

Brewster, S., Buckley, M., Cox, P., & Griep, L. (2002, April). *Diversity education: A literature review.* Alberta Community Development/Canadian Heritage/ University of Calgary. Retrieved February 14, 2009, from www.plannet.ca/ pdf/derplitr.pdf.

Briggs, A. (1961). The welfare state in historical perspective. *European Journal of Sociology II(2),* 221–58.

Broadbent, E. (2001). Ten propositions about equality and democracy. In E. Broadbent (Ed.), *Democratic equality: What went wrong?* (pp. 3–13). Toronto: University of Toronto Press.

Brock, K., Brook, D., Elliott, J., & LaForest, R. (2003). *Globalization and the voluntary sector in Canada.* An exploratory study by the Public Policy Forum and the Queen's School of Policy Studies. Retrieved August 31, 2008, from www.ppforum.com/ common/assets/publications/en/ow_p_05_05_2003.pdf.

Brodie, J. (1994). *Politics on the boundaries: Restructuring and the Canadian women's movement.* North York, ON: Robarts Centre for Canadian Studies, York University.

Brodie, J., & Bakker, I. (2007, March) *Canada's social policy regime and women: An assessment of the last decade.* Status of Women Canada. Retrieved February 2, 2008, from http://epe.lac-bac.gc.ca/100/200/301/swc-cfc/canadas_social-e/SW21 -156-2007E.pdf.

Brooks, N., & Hwong, T. (2006, December). *The social benefits and economic costs of taxation: A comparison of high- and low-tax countries.* Retrieved August 27, 2008, from Canadian Centre for Policy Alternatives, www.policyalternatives.ca/documents/ National_Office_Pubs/2006/Benefits_and_Costs_of_Taxation.pdf.

Brown, G.S. (2004). *The ideological roots of socialism: A collection of "isms."* Lecture notes: University of Nevada, Las Vegas. Retrieved August 24, 2008, from http://faculty.unlv.edu/gbrown/westernciv/wc201/wciv2c19/wciv2c19lsec2.html.

Bruce, M. (1966). *The coming of the welfare state.* New York: Schocken Books.

Buckley, M. (2005, November). *Litigating section 15: The path to substantive equality in charter adjudication.* Retrieved August 25, 2008, from www.20years.ca/Buckley-Litigating_s_15_Nov_7_2005-withrevs-2.pdf.

Burghardt, S. (1987). Community-based social action. In A. Minahan (Ed.), *Encyclopedia of Social Work* (18th ed., vol. 1, pp. 292–99). Washington, DC: National Association of Social Workers.

Butchart, A., & Harvey, A.P. (2006). *Preventing child maltreatment: A guide to taking action and generating evidence.* World Health Organization and International Society for Prevention of Child Abuse and Neglect. Retrieved December 10, 2008, from http://whqlibdoc.who.int/publications/2006/ 9241594365_eng.pdf.

Byfield, J. (2003, March 3). The charter—A judicial coup d'état. *Citizens Centre REPORT Magazine.* Retrieved August 25, 2008, from http://fathersforlife.org/articles/ report/charter_coup.htm.

Calgary Chamber of Voluntary Organizations. (2006, February). *Financing voluntary and nonprofit organizations in Alberta*: A report on the Alberta Regional Finance Action Group. Retrieved August 31, 2008, from www.ecvo.ca/Regional_Finance_Action_Group_Summary_Report_2006.pdf.

Calgary Counselling Centre. (2004). *Children of divorce program*. Retrieved February 24, 2009, from www.calgarycounselling.com/programs/children_divorce.htm.

Campaign 2000. (2002). *Meeting your MP campaign: Background information.* Retrieved February 3, 2009, from www.campaign2000.ca/act/meetMP2002/meetyourMP background.pdf.

Campaign 2000. (2007). *2007 Report card on child and family poverty in Canada: It takes a nation to raise a generation: Time for a National Poverty Reduction Strategy.* Retrieved February 3, 2009, from www.familyservicetoronto.org/policy/CanadaReportCard 2007Nov15.pdf.

Campaign 2000. (2008). *Family security in insecure times: The case for a poverty reduction strategy for Canada: 2008 Report card on child and family poverty in Canada.* Retrieved February 3, 2009, from www.familyservicetoronto.org/policy/C2000National ReportCardNov2008.pdf.

Canada Revenue Agency. (2008). Small and rural charities: Making a difference for Canadians. Retrieved January 11, 2009, from www.cra-arc.gc.ca/E/pub/tg/rc4457/rc4457-e.pdf.

Canada tied for last in UNICEF child care ranking. (2008). *CTV.ca*, December 11, 2008. Retrieved February 24, 2009, from www.ctv.ca/servlet/ArticleNews/story/CTVNews/20081211/UNICEF_child_081211/20081211?hub=TopStories.

Canada to be hit by recession, 7.5% jobless rate, OECD warns. (2008). *CBC News*, November 25, 2008. Retrieved February 3, 2009, from www.cbc.ca/money/story/2008/11/25/oecd-report.html.

Canada West Foundation. (2000). Building better partnerships: Improving relations between governments and non-profits. *Research Bulletin 5*(September, Calgary). Retrieved September 18, 2008, from Canada West Foundation, www.cwf.ca/V2/files/200008.pdf.

Canadian CED Network. (2003, November 24). *Human capital development in Canada: Closing the gaps.* Retrieved August 26, 2008, from www.ccednet-rcdec.ca/files/human%20capital%20FINAL%20PDF.pdf.

Canadian CED Network. (2008, April). *Poverty hearings have begun: HUMA Committee of Parliament.* April 2008 CCEDNet Newsletter: BC/Yukon. Retrieved August 25, 2008, from www.ccednet-rcdec.ca/?q=en/node/4916.

Canadian Centre for Community Renewal. (2003). *Tools and techniques for community recovery and renewal.* Retrieved March 1, 2009, from www.cedworks.com/files/pdf/free/P203AFG07.pdf.

Canadian Centre for Elder Law Studies. (2005, March). *A legal framework for supportive housing for seniors: Options for Canadian policy makers: Final report.* Retrieved February

28, 2009, from CMHC, ftp://ftp.cmhc-schl.gc.ca/chic-ccdh/Research_Reports-Rapports_de_recherche/eng_unilingual/CHIC%20Legal%20Framework(w).pdf.

Canadian Council for Refugees. (1998, February). *Best settlement practices: Settlement services for refugees and immigrants in Canada.* Retrieved March 11, 2009, from www.ccrweb.ca//bpfina1.htm.

Canadian Council for Refugees. (2000, May). *Canadian national settlement service standards framework.* Retrieved March 11, 2009, from www.ccrweb.ca//standards.PDF.

Canadian Council for Refugees. (2008, September). *State of refugees: An introduction to refugee and immigration issues in Canada.* Retrieved March 11, 2009, from www.ccrweb.ca/documents/state-of-refugees.pdf.

Canadian Economy Online. (2007). *Key economic events, 1944: Family allowance program: Supporting Canadian children.* Retrieved August 23, 2008, from www.canadi-aneconomy.gc.ca/English/economy/1944family.html.

Canadian Federation of Apartment Associations. (2006 March). *Housing programs information sheet.* Retrieved February 3, 2009, from www.cfaa-fcapi.org/pdf/InfoSheeHProgr0603.pdf.

Canadian Heritage. (2004, January 20). *Canadian diversity: Respecting our differences.* Retrieved September 1, 2008, from www.canadianheritage.gc.ca/progs/multi/respect_e.cfm.

Canadian Heritage. (2008, November 29). *Measures adopted by the governments of the provinces: Manitoba.* Retrieved February 14, 2009, from http://pch.gc.ca/pgm/pdp-hrp/docs/convention/p4-MB-eng.cfm.

Canadian Institutes of Health Research. (2008). *Institute of Aging (IA): The Canadian Longitudinal Study on Aging (CLSA).* Retrieved August 24, 2008, from www.cihr-irsc.gc.ca/e/22982.html.

Canadian International Development Agency. (2006). *Voluntary sector: Capacity development strategy.* Retrieved February 14, 2009, from www.acdi-cida.gc.ca/cidaweb/acdicida.nsf/En/NAT-6127358-FLJ.

Canadian Labour Congress. (2007, November 27). *International day of persons with disabilities, December 3, 2007.* Retrieved February 23, 2009, from www3.canadian-labour.ca/en/International_Day_of.

Canadian Mental Health Association. (2002, January). *Seniors' mental health and home care: A national study.* A Report Prepared for the Canadian Mental Health Association. Retrieved May 18, 2004, from www.cmha.ca/english/shmcare/national_report.pdf.

Canadian Outcomes Research Institute (2007) *Solutions: Outcome planning.* Retrieved September 16, 2008, from www.cori.ca/.

Canadian Study of Health and Aging. (2002). *About the study.* Retrieved February 28, 2009, from csha.ca/about_study.asp.

Cappe, M. (2002, February 6). *Leadership forum awards dinner: Remarks by Mr. Mel Cappe to the Arthur Kroeger College of Public Affairs.* Retrieved February 1, 2009, from

Privy Council Office, www.pco-bcp.gc.ca/index.asp?lang=eng&page=clerk-greffier&sub=archives&doc=20020206_kroeger-eng.htm.

Caregiver Resource Centre. (2008). *Housing Options for Seniors*. Retrieved February 28, 2009, from www.dmfseniors.org/caregivers/housing_options.asp.

Carniol, B. (1990). Social work and the labour movement. In B. Wharf (Ed.), *Social work and social change in Canada* (pp. 114–43). Toronto: McClelland and Stewart.

Carniol, B. (2000). *Case critical: Challenging social services in Canada* (4th ed.). Toronto: Between the Lines.

Carniol, B. (2005). *Case critical: Social services and social justice in Canada* (5th ed.). Toronto: Between the Lines.

Cassidy, H.M. (1943). *Social security and reconstruction in Canada*. Toronto: Ryerson Press.

Castellano, M.B. (2002). *Aboriginal family trends: Extended families, nuclear families, families of the heart*. Retrieved March 12, 2009, from Vanier Institute of the Family, www.vifamily.ca/library/cft/aboriginal.pdf.

CASW (Canadian Association of Social Workers). (1998, March). *CASW statement on preventive practices and health promotion* Retrieved February 14, 2009, from www.casw-acts.ca/practice/recpubsart3.html.

CASW (Canadian Association of Social Workers). (2000, March). *CASW national scope of practice statement*. Retrieved February 14, 2009, from www.casw-acts.ca/practice/recpubsart1.html.

CASW (Canadian Association of Social Workers). (2003a, March). *Social policy principles*. Retrieved December 27, 2008, from www.casw-acts.ca/advocacy/socialpolicy_e.pdf.

CASW (Canadian Association of Social Workers). (2003b, August 12). *Regulation of social work in Canada*. Retrieved September 18, 2008, from www.casw-acts.ca/canada/regulation_e.html.

CASW (Canadian Association of Social Workers). (2004, November). *The impacts of working conditions on social workers and their practice: A CASW review of current literature*. Retrieved September 18, 2008, from CASW, www.casw-acts.ca/advocacy/impacts_e.pdf.

CASW (Canadian Association of Social Workers). (2005). *Code of ethics*. Retrieved September 18, 2008, from www.casw-acts.ca/practice/codeofethics_e_000.pdf.

CASW (Canadian Association of Social Workers). (2008). *Tax reduction and minimal government: An evaluation of the 2008 budget*. Retrieved January 3, 2009, from www.casw-acts.ca/advocacy/budget08_e.pdf.

CASW & NASW (Canadian Association of Social Workers and National Association of Social Workers). (2008, October 2). *Putting poverty on the election platform: The time to eradicate poverty is now*. Retrieved February 3, 2009, from www.casw-acts.ca/advocacy/preradication08_e.html.

CCPA (Canadian Centre for Policy Alternatives). (2006). *The growing gap between the rich and the rest of us: Learn more: Do you feel like you're one or two missed paycheques away from hard times?* Retrieved February 3, 2009, from www.growinggap.ca/learn/gap_missed_paycheques.

CCSD (Canadian Council on Social Development). (1969). *Social policies for Canada, part 1.* Ottawa: Author.

CCSD (Canadian Council on Social Development). (2006). *The progress of Canada's children and youth, 2006: Portrait.* Retrieved March 11, 2009, from www.ccsd.ca/pccy/2006/pdf/pccy_portrait.pdf.

Centres of Excellence for Youth Engagement. (2007). *Vision.* Retrieved February 24, 2009, from www.engagementcentre.ca/vision.php.

Chansonneuve, D. (2005). *Reclaiming connections: Understanding residential school trauma among Aboriginal people.* Retrieved March 12, 2009, from Aboriginal Healing Foundation, www.ahf.ca/pages/download/28_101.

Chappell, N. (1999). *Volunteering and healthy aging: What we know.* Canadian Forum on Volunteering. Retrieved September 18, 2008, from http://volunteer.ca/en/volcan/older-adults/canada_adults_report_printable.

Charter Committee on Poverty Issues. (1998, November 13). *Submissions to the committee on economic, social and cultural rights, United Nations.* Retrieved August 26, 2008, from www.equalityrights.org/ngoun98/ccpi.htm.

Chartrand, L., & McKay, C. (2006, January). *A review of research and criminal victimization and First Nations, Métis and Inuit peoples, 1990 to 2001.* Retrieved March 12, 2009, from www.justice.gc.ca/eng/pi/rs/rep-rap/2006/rr06_vic1/rr06_vic1.pdf.

Childcare Resource and Research Unit. (2007). *Trends and analysis 2007: Early childhood education and care in Canada 2006.* Retrieved February 24, 2009, from www.childcarecanada.org/pubs/other/TandA/Trends_Analysis07.pdf.

Chinook Multimedia Inc. (2000). *Immigrant voices: 1967–present: Overview.* Retrieved March 11, 2009, from www.canadianhistory.ca/iv/1967-Present/overview2.html.

Chrétien says he's sorry for remarks. *Calgary Herald*, April 22, 1994, p. A13.

Christensen, C.P. (1996). The impact of racism on the education of social service workers. In C.E. James (Ed.), *Perspectives on racism and the human services sector* (pp. 140–51). Toronto: University of Toronto Press.

Christie, N., & Gauvreau, M. (1996). *A full-orbed Christianity: The Protestant churches and social welfare in Canada 1900–1940.* Montreal: McGill-Queens University Press.

Chui, T. (2003). *Longitudinal survey of immigrants to Canada: Process, progress and prospects.* Retrieved March 11, 2009, from Statistics Canada, http://dsp-psd.tpsgc.gc.ca/Collection/Statcan/89-611-X/89-611-XIE2003001.pdf.

Chui, T., Tran, K., & Maheux, H. (2007). *Immigration in Canada: A portrait of the foreign-born population, 2006 census.* Retrieved March 11, 2009, from Statistics Canada, www12.statcan.ca/english/census06/analysis/immcit/pdf/97-557-XIE2006001.pdf.

CIC (Citizenship and Immigration Canada). (1995, December). *Growing together: A backgrounder on immigration and citizenship: The history of immigration.* Retrieved February 3, 2000, from www.cic.gc.ca/english/pub/grow/grow_00e.html.

CIC (Citizenship and Immigration Canada). (1998). *Building on a strong foundation for the 21st century: New directions for immigration and refugee policy and legislation.* Retrieved March 11, 2009, from http://dsp-psd.pwgsc.gc.ca/Collection/ Ci51-86-1998E.pdf.

CIC (Citizenship and Immigration Canada). (2000, April 6). *Caplan tables new immigration and refugee protection act.* News Release. Retrieved March 11, 2009, from www.immigrationoffice.ca/html/ottawaapril6-_2000_.html.

CIC (Citizenship and Immigration Canada). (2001, May). *Towards a more balanced geographic distribution of immigrants.* Retrieved March 11, 2009, from http://dsp-psd. pwgsc.gc.ca/Collection/Ci51-109-2002E.pdf.

CIC (Citizenship and Immigration Canada). (2005). *Evaluation of the Immigration Settlement and Adaptation Program (ISAP): 1.0 Introduction.* Release. Retrieved March 11, 2009, from www.cic.gc.ca/english/resources/evaluation/ isap/intro.asp#s2.

CIC (Citizenship and Immigration Canada). (2007a). *Annual report to Parliament on immigration, 2007: Section 5: Integrating newcomers.* Retrieved March 11, 2009, from www.cic.gc.ca/english/resources/publications/annual-report2007/section5.asp#1.

CIC (Citizenship and Immigration Canada). (2007b). *Resettlement from outside Canada: Convention refugees abroad class.* Retrieved March 11, 2009, from www.cic.gc.ca/ english/refugees/outside/convention.asp.

CIC (Citizenship and Immigration Canada). (2008). *The refugee system in Canada.* Retrieved March 11, 2009, from www.cic.gc.ca/english/refugees/canada.asp.

Citizens for Public Justice. (2003, September). *Closing the gap: Eliminating the social deficit, creating a stronger Canada.* Submission to the Standing Committee on Finance Pre-Budget Consultations by Citizens for Public Justice, September 2003. Retrieved August 27, 2008, from http://action.web.ca/home/cpj/attach/Closing%20The%20Gap.pdf.

City of Vancouver. (2007). *Vancouver food charter: Context and background: January 2007: As prepared by the Vancouver Food Policy Council.* Retrieved February 3, 2009, from http://vancouver.ca/COMMSVCS/SOCIALPLANNING/initiatives/foodpolicy/tools/ pdf/Van_Food_Charter_Bgrnd.pdf.

Clark, W. (2005). What do seniors spend on housing? *Canadian Social Trends, Autumn 2005* (78): 2-7. Statistics Canada. Retrieved February 28, 2009, from dsp-psd.tpsgc. gc.ca/Collection-R/Statcan/11-008-XIE/0020511-008-XIE.pdf.

Clément, D. (2008). *Canada's rights movement: A history: White paper on Indian policy.* Retrieved March 12, 2009, from www.historyofrights.com/events/white_paper.html.

CLSA (Canadian Longitudinal Study on Aging). (2009). *Understanding the aging process to improve the quality of life of all Canadians.* Retrieved February 28, 2009, from www.clsa-elcv.ca/en/welcome.

CMCC (Canadian Museum of Civilization Corporation). (2002a, September 10). *The history of Canada's public pensions: 1928–1951: Demanding more: Political events.* Retrieved August 26, 2008, from Civilization.ca, www.civilization.ca/hist/pensions/cpp-a28-pe_e.html.

CMCC (Canadian Museum of Civilization Corporation). (2002b, September 10). *The history of Canada's public pensions: 1968–1989: Reaching more Canadians: Political events.* Retrieved August 27, 2008, from Civilization.ca, www.civilization.ca/hist/pensions/cpp-a68-pe_e.html.

CMCC (Canadian Museum of Civilization Corporation). (2008). *The history of Canada's public pensions: 1867–1914: Old age and poverty: Political events.* Retrieved December 31, 2008, from Civilization.ca, www.civilization.ca/cmc/exhibitions/hist/pensions/cpp-a67-pe_e.shtml.

CMHC (Canada Mortgage and Housing Corporation). (2007). *Canadian housing observer, 2007: New housing for a changing world.* Retrieved February 3, 2009, from www.cmhc-schl.gc.ca/odpub/pdf/65704.pdf.

Collin, C. (2007, October 23). *Poverty reduction in Canada: The federal role.* Retrieved February 3, 2009, from www.parl.gc.ca/information/library/PRBpubs/prb0722-e.htm.

Community Living Research Project. (2007, March). *Residential options for adults with developmental disabilities: Quality and cost outcomes: A plain language summary.* Retrieved February 23, 2009, from www.communitylivingbc.ca/what_we_do/innovation/documents/PlainLanguage_residentialalternatives.pdf.

Community Social Planning Council of Toronto and Family Service Association of Toronto. (2006, July). *On the front lines of Toronto's community service sector: Improving working conditions and ensuring quality services.* Retrieved February 5, 2009, from www.familyservicetoronto.org/policy/FrontLines_CommunityServiceSector2006.pdf.

Conceptual Framework Subcommittee of the Residential Services Advisory Committee. (2002, January). *Working with community to support children, youth and families.* Retrieved February 14, 2009, from www.llbc.leg.bc.ca/public/PubDocs/bcdocs/354463/bccfd_working_with_comm_2002.pdf.

Conference Board of Canada. (2000). *Performance and potential 2000–2001: Seeking "Made in Canada" solutions.* Ottawa: Author.

Conn, D.K. (2003, September 19). An overview of common mental disorders among seniors. In National Advisory Council on Aging, *Writings in gerontology: Mental health and aging* (18). Retrieved May 19, 2004, from www.hc-sc.gc.ca/seniors-aines/naca/writings_gerontology/writ18/writ18_2_e.htm.

Cooper, M., & Bartlett, D. (2008). *Toward a new funding framework and priorities for FCSS Phase I: Overview and Recommendations for Phases II and III: Summary.* Retrieved January 11, 2009, from www.calgary.ca/docgallery/bu/cns/fcss/fcss_funding_framework_consultation_paper.pdf.

Cornish, M. (2008). *Securing justice for women: The face of Canada's working poor.* Presentation to international conference: Global strategies: Improving conditions of the working poor (Montreal, May 1–2, 2008). Retrieved November 28, 2008, from McGill University, www.mcgill.ca/files/ihsp/Cornish_EN.pdf.

Cottrell, B. (2008). Providing services to immigrant women in Atlantic Canada. *Our Diverse Cities* 5 (Spring 2008): 133–37. Retrieved March 11, 2009, from Metropolis Canada, http://canada.metropolis.net/pdfs/ODC_spring2008_e.pdf.

Council of Canadians with Disabilities. (2009). *Poverty*. Retrieved February 23, 2009, from www.ccdonline.ca/en/socialpolicy/poverty.

Cowan, J. (2009). Former PM Paul Martin announces $50-million fund for aboriginal enterprises. *National Post*, March 11, 2009. Retrieved March 12, 2009, from www.financialpost.com/scripts/story.html?id=1379101.

Coyle, G.L. (1959). Some basic assumptions about social group work. In M. Murphy (Ed.), *The social group work method in social work education* (Curriculum Study XI, pp. 91–100). New York: Council on Social Work Education.

CPRN (Canadian Policy Research Networks Inc.). (2005). *A healthy balance: Caregiving policy in Canada: Backgrounder*. Retrieved February 15, 2009, from www.cprn.com/documents/40910_en.pdf.

Cranswick, K., & Dosman, D. (2008). *Eldercare: What we know today*. Retrieved May 19, 2009, from www.homecareontario.ca/public/docs/publications/family-caregivers/eldercare-what-we-know-today.pdf.

Crawford, C. (2003, March). *Towards a common approach to thinking about and measuring social inclusion: DRAFT?* Roeher Institute. Retrieved February 23, 2009, from www.ccsd.ca/events/inclusion/papers/crawford.pdf.

Crompton, S., & Kemeny, S. (1999). In sickness and in health: The well-being of married seniors. *Canadian Social Trends, Winter 1999* (55): 22–27. Retrieved February 28, 2009, from dsp-psd.tpsgc.gc.ca/Collection-R/Statcan/11-008-XIE/0039911-008-XIE.pdf.

Cronin, J. (2006). *Neoliberalism and capitalist restructuring*. Retrieved October 31, 2008, from http://alternatives-international.net/article253.html.

Cross, S. (1985, Spring). Professionalism: The occupational hazard of social work, 1920–1960. *The Social Worker* 53(1): 29–33.

Crowe, S. (2006). *Immigrant and refugee children in middle childhood: An overview*. Retrieved March 11, 2009, from National Children's Alliance, www.nationalchildren-salliance.com/nca/pubs/2006/Immigrant%20and%20Refugee%20Children%20in%20their%20Middle%20Years.pdf.

CWLC (Child Welfare League of Canada). (2007). *The welfare of Canadian children: It's our business*. A collection of resource papers for a healthy future for Canadian children and families. Retrieved March 12, 2009, from www.cwlc.ca/files/file/policy/Welfare%20of%20Canadian%20Children%202007.pdf.

D'Aubin, A. (2006). *Newsletter 58: Making the new government aware of disability issues*. Retrieved February 23, 2009, from National Educational Association of Disabled Students, www.neads.ca/en/about/newsletter/article.php?id=101.

Davies, L., McMullin, J.A., Avison, W.R., & Cassidy, G.L. (2001, February). *Social policy, gender inequality and poverty*. Retrieved August 24, 2008, from Status of Women Canada, www.swc-cfc.gc.ca/pubs/pubspr/0662653327/200102_0662653327_e.pdf.

Davis, B., & Tarasuk, V. (1994). Hunger in Canada. *Agriculture and Human Values 11*: 50–57.

Dawson Creek Society for Community Living. (2006). *History of the society*. Retrieved February 23, 2009, from www.dcscl.org/history.html.

Daya, S., El-Hourani, M.H., & De Long, B. (2004, April). *London's voluntary sector: Employment and training needs study.* Pillar - Voluntary Sector Network. Retrieved September 18, 2008, from www.pillarnonprofit.ca/documents/LondonVoluntary-SectorEmploymentTrainingNeedsStudy.pdf.

DeCoito, P. (2008, January). *Social exclusion of minority groups: A conceptual framework.* Social Planning Council of Peel. Retrieved March 11, 2009, from www.spcottawa.on.ca/Documents/Reports/Background/Social_Exclusion_Conceptual_Framework.doc.

Department of Finance Canada. (1995, February 27). *Budget in brief.* Ottawa: Author. Retrieved August 26, 2008, from www.fin.gc.ca/budget95/binb/brief.pdf.

Department of Finance Canada. (2000, October 18). *Economic statement and budget update: Overview.* Retrieved August 27, 2008, from www.fin.gc.ca/ec2000/pdf/overe.pdf.

Department of Finance Canada. (2003a, February 18). *Budget 2003: Overview: Building the Canada we want.* Retrieved August 27, 2008, from www.fin.gc.ca/budget03/PDF/overe.pdf.

Department of Finance Canada. (2003b). *Budget 2003: Annex 5: Fiscal performance of Canada's federal-provincial-territorial government sector.* Retrieved February 4, 2004, from www.fin.gc.ca/budget03/bp/bpa5e.htm.

Department of Finance Canada. (2005). *Budget 2005: Securing our social foundations.* Retrieved August 27, 2008, from www.fin.gc.ca/budget05/pamph/pasoce.htm.

Department of Finance Canada. (2007, March 19). *The budget speech 2007: Aspire to a stronger, safer, better Canada.* The Honourable James M. Flaherty, P.C., M.P. Minister of Finance. Retrieved November 6, 2008, from www.budget.gc.ca/2007/pdf/speeche.pdf.

Department of Finance Canada. (2008a). *Activities and issues: Canada Social Transfer (Federal transfers to provinces and territories, November 2008): Canada Social Transfer.* Retrieved January 26, 2009, from www.fin.gc.ca/fedprov/cst-eng.asp.

Department of Finance Canada. (2008b, April 29). *Glossary: Surplus.* Retrieved August 27, 2008, from www.fin.gc.ca/gloss/gloss-s_e.html.

Department of Finance Canada. (2009). *Canada social transfer.* Retrieved May 26, 2009, from www.fin.gc.ca/fedprov/cst-eng.asp.

Department of Justice Canada. (2006a). *Spousal abuse: A fact sheet from the Department of Justice Canada.* Retrieved February 24, 2009, from www.justice.gc.ca/eng/pi/fv-vf/facts-info/sa-vc.pdf.

Department of Justice Canada. (2006b). *Child abuse: A fact sheet from the Department of Justice Canada*. Retrieved February 24, 2009, from www.justice.gc.ca/eng/pi/fv-vf/facts-info/child-enf.pdf.

Dis-IT Research Alliance. (2006a). *The disability community's perspective on disability-related policy*. Retrieved February 23, 2009, from Disability-Related Policy in Canada, www.disabilitypolicy.ca/policy/overview/community.php.

Dis-IT Research Alliance. (2006b). *A socio-political model of disability*. Retrieved February 23, 2009, from Disability-Related Policy in Canada, www.disabilitypolicy.ca/policy/overview/model.php.

District of Nipissing Social Services. (2008). *Ontario Works*. Retrieved September 18, 2008, from www.dnssab.on.ca/ow.htm.

Dobelstein, A.W. (1978). Introduction: Social resources, human need, and the field of social work. In A. Fink (Ed.), *The field of social work* (7th ed., pp. 3–21). New York: Holt, Rinehart & Winston.

Dobelstein, A.W. (2003). *Social welfare policy and analysis* (3rd ed.). Pacific Grove: Brooks/Cole–Thompson Learning.

Dobie, R. (2006, November 27). *Proceedings of the Special Senate Committee on Aging: Issue 1–Evidence*. Retrieved February 28, 2009, from www.parl.gc.ca/39/1/parlbus/commbus/senate/Com-e/agei-e/01evb-e.htm?Language=E&Parl=39&Ses=1&comm_id=600.

Dobrowolsky, A. (2003). *Fostering social cohesion: Social investment state/civil society inter-actionism: New forms of governance in Britain*. Working Paper #9. Retrieved August 24, 2008, from www.cccg.umontreal.ca/pdf/wp9.pdf.

Doe, T., & Kimpson, S. (1999, March). *Enabling income: CPP disability benefits and women with disabilities*. Ottawa: Status of Women Canada. Retrieved February 23, 2009, from http://dsp-psd.pwgsc.gc.ca/Collection/SW21-38-1999E.pdf.

Dorais, M. (2002, September). Immigration and integration through a social cohesion perspective. *Horizons* 5(2): 4–5. Retrieved March 11, 2009, from www.policyresearch.gc.ca/doclib/HOR_v5n2_e.pdf.

Drover, G. (1983, Winter). Beyond the welfare state: Brief to the Royal Commission on the Economic Union and Development Prospects for Canada. *The Social Worker* 51(4): 141–44.

Dufour, P., & Morrison, I. (2005). The state of the social investment state. *Canadian Journal of Career Development* 4(1): 3–10. Retrieved August 24, 2008, from www.contactpoint.ca/cjcd/v4-n1/article1.pdf.

Duncan, H. (2007, September). Social cohesion. *Metropolis Project Metropolis World Bulletin* 7: 2. Retrieved March 11, 2009, from http://international.metropolis.net/research-policy/World/World_Bulletin_socialcohesion_e.pdf.

Dunlop, J. (2006). Privatization: How government promotes market-based solutions to social problems. *Critical Social Work* 7(2). Retrieved August 26, 2008, from

www.criticalsocialwork.com/units/socialwork/critical.nsf/tovr/CB277191FB4AB6528
5257277002B8598?opendocument&referer.

Durst, D. (2002, October 3). *Self-government and the growth of First Nations child and family services*. Retrieved March 12, 2009, from www.pinkcandyproductions.com/portfolio/conferences/state_of_federation/papers/Durst.pdf.

Durst, D. (2006, June 12). *Social welfare and social work education in Canada: Implications for Canada's north*. International Co-operation in Social Work and Social Policy: June 12–14, 2006, Bodo, Norway. Retrieved September 18, 2008, from www.uarctic.org/Paper_by_Douglas_Durst_WYU7L.pdf.file.

Eakin, L. (2001, September). *An overview of the funding of Canada's voluntary sector*. Voluntary Sector Initiative Working Group on Financing. Retrieved August 31, 2008, from www.vsi-isbc.org/eng/funding/pdf/overview_of_funding.pdf.

Eakin, L. (2007, September). *We can't afford to do business this way: A study of the administrative burden resulting from funder accountability and compliance practices*. Retrieved August 31, 2008, from Wellesley Institute, www.wellesleyinstitute.com/files/cant_do_business_this_way_report_web.pdf.

Eakin, L., & Richmond, T. (2006, November 21). *Community service organizations at risk*. Retrieved August 28, 2008, from LynnEkin.com, http://lynneakin.com/wp-content/uploads/2006/11/community_organizations_at_risk.pdf.

Economic Council of Canada. (1968). *Fifth annual review.* Ottawa: Author.

Economic Council of Canada. (1990). *Good jobs, bad jobs: Employment in the service economy.* Ottawa: Minister of Supply and Services Canada.

Edwards, P. & Mawani, A. (2006, September). *Healthy aging in Canada: A new vision, a vital investment: From evidence to action*. Retrieved February 28, 2009, from Public Health Agency of Canada, www.phac-aspc.gc.ca/seniors-aines/pubs/haging_newvision/pdf/vision-rpt_e.pdf.

Eichler, M., & Lavigne, M. (2008). Women's movement. In *The Canadian encyclopedia, Historica Foundation of Canada*. Retrieved August 27, 2008, from www.thecanadian encyclopedia.com/index.cfm?PgNm=TCE&Params=A1SEC830181.

Ekos Research Associates. (1995). *Rethinking government '94: An overview and synthesis*. Cited in Canadian Policy Research Networks. (1995). Annual Report 94–95 (p. 3). Retrieved August 26, 2008, from www.cprn.org/documents/42066_en.pdf.

Ekos Research Associates. (2007). *The rethinking Canada's aging population: 2007 sudy: Filling critical gaps in our knowledge*. Retrieved February 28, 2009, from www.ekos.com/studies/Aging2007.pdf.

Eliadis, F.P. (2006, July). *Poverty and exclusion: Normative approaches to policy research*. Retrieved December 27, 2008, from Policy Research Initiative, www.policyresearch.gc.ca/doclib/DP_PEX_Norm2_200411_e.pdf.

Environics Research Group. (2006, June). *Canadians' attitudes toward national child care policy*. Prepared for the Child Care Advocacy Association of Canada. Retrieved

February 24, 2009, from www.ccaac.ca/pdf/resources/Reports/Public_Opinion_on_Child_Care_Policy.pdf.

Environics Research Group. (2008, October 8). *Attitudes toward child care.* Retrieved February 24, 2009, from www.ccaac.ca/pdf/resources/polls/2008EnvironicsReport_Attitudes_toward_child_care.pdf.

Epstein, L. (1980). *Helping people: The task-centered approach.* St. Louis: C.V. Mosby.

ESPC (Edmonton Social Planning Council). (2008). *Edmonton renter's survey.* Retrieved February 14, 2009, from www.edmontonsocialplanning.ca/index.php?option=com_content&task=view&id=366&Itemid=1&date=2008-09-01.

Esquimaux, C.C.W., & Smolewski, M. (2004). *Historic trauma and Aboriginal healing.* Retrieved March 12, 2009, from The Aboriginal Healing Foundation, www.ahf.ca/pages/download/28_41.

Evans, B., Richmond, T., & Shields, J. (2005). Structuring neoliberal governance: The nonprofit sector, emerging new modes of control and the marketisation of service delivery. *Policy & Society* 24(1), Lee Kuan Yew School of Public Policy, National University of Singapore. Retrieved August 31, 2008, from www.policyandsociety.org/archive/vol24no1/PS%2024-1%20Evans,%20Richmond%20and%20Shields.pdf.

Evans, B., & Shields, J. (2006). *Neoliberal restructuring and the third sector: Reshaping governance, civil society and local relations.* Working Paper Series Number 13, July 2000. Centre for Voluntary Sector Studies, Ryerson University Faculty of Business. Retrieved August 28, 2008, from www.ryerson.ca/cvss/WP13.pdf.

Evans, G. (2003). *Canada: Administrative and civil service reform.* Senior Consultant, Institute of Public Administration of Canada. Retrieved August 26, 2008, from the World Bank Group, www1.worldbank.org/publicsector/civilservice/rsCanada.pdf.

Evertman, J. (2002, Fall/Winter). A day of fun and feedback. *Communicate* 14(3): 7.

Expert Panel on Older Workers. (2008). *Supporting and engaging older workers in the new economy.* Retrieved February 28, 2009, from www.hrsdc.gc.ca/en/publications_resources/lmp/eow/2008/older_workers_2008.pdf.

Fafard, P. (2008, May). *Evidence and healthy public policy: Insights from health and political sciences.* National Collaborating Centre for Healthy Public Policy. Retrieved August 24 2008, from www.cprn.org/documents/50036_EN.pdf.

Family Service Toronto. (2008). *Families in transition (FIT).* Retrieved February 24, 2009, from www.familyservicetoronto.org/programs/families.html.

Family Services of Greater Vancouver. (2008). *Who we are: Mission/value statement.* Retrieved September 2, 2008, from www.fsgv.ca/mainpages/whoweare/missionvaluestatement.html.

Farris-Manning, C., & Zandstra, M. (2003, April). *Children in care in Canada: A summary of current issues and trends with recommendations for future research.* Child Welfare League of Canada. Retrieved February 24, 2009, from www.nationalchildrensalliance.com/nca/pubs/2003/Children_in_Care_March_2003.pdf.

Faye Peterson Transition House. (2008). *About us.* Retrieved September 2, 2008, from www.fayepeterson.org/index.php?pid=36.

Federal-Provincial-Territorial Ministerial Council on Social Policy Renewal. (2003). *Three year review: Social Union Framework Agreement (SUFA).* Retrieved March 12, 2009, from www.socialunion.gc.ca/sufa/Three_Year_Review/e/tyrsufa.html.

Federal-Provincial-Territorial Ministers Responsible for Social Services. (2000a). *In Unison 2000: Disability supports: Issues and challenges.* Retrieved March 8, 2009, from www.socialunion.gc.ca/In_Unison2000/iu02100e.html.

Federal-Provincial-Territorial Ministers Responsible for Social Services. (2000b). *In Unison 2000: Next steps.* Retrieved February 23, 2009, from www.socialunion.gc.ca/In_Unison2000/iu05000e.html.

Federal-Provincial-Territorial Ministers Responsible for the Status of Women. (2002). *Assessing violence against women: A statistical profile.* Retrieved August 24, 2008, from www.swc-cfc.gc.ca/pubs/0662331664/200212_0662331664_e.pdf.

Federal-Provincial-Territorial Ministers Responsible for Social Services. (2008, January). *The National Child Benefit: Progress report 2006.* Retrieved February 3, 2009, from www.nationalchildbenefit.ca/ncb/Progress_Reports/2006/pdf/ncb_progress_report_2006.pdf.

Federation of Canadian Municipalities. (2009). *Affordable housing and homelessness.* Retrieved February 3, 2009, from www.fcm.ca/english/View.asp?mp=467&x=712.

Felligi, I. (2006). A multicultural profile of Canada. *Transition Magazine 36*(2) (Summer 2006). Retrieved March 11, 2009, from www.vifamily.ca/library/transition/362/362.html.

Fildes, R., & Cooper, B. (2003, November). *Preparing for change: Social work in primary health care.* Retrieved September 18, 2008, from CASW, www.casw-acts.ca/advocacy/primary_health_e.pdf.

Financial crisis creating "perfect storm" for charity organizations: Donations declining as need for help rises, say community groups. (2008). *CBC News, November 10, 2008.* Retrieved February 2, 2008 from www.cbc.ca/canada/story/2008/11/10/charitable-donations.html?ref=rss.

Findlay, P. (1983). Social welfare in Canada: The case for universality. In CASSW *Canadian Social Work Review '83* (pp. 17–24). Ottawa: Canadian Association of Schools of Social Work.

Finn, E. (1985). *The great deficit hoax.* Ottawa: Canadian Centre for Policy Alternatives.

First Nations Regional Longitudinal Health Survey. (2005). *First Nations health survey reveals the "good, the bad, the ugly" about life in First Nations in Canada.* News release, November 15, 2005. Retrieved February 23, 2009, from www.rhs-ers.ca/english/pdf/press_releases/rhs_press_release-nov15-2005-childrens_health.pdf.

First Nations University of Canada. (2009). *School of Indian Social Work (ISW).* Retrieved March 12, 2009, from www.firstnationsuniversity.ca/default.aspx?page=28.

Fischer, J. (1978). *Effective casework practice: An eclectic approach.* New York: McGraw-Hill.

Fleury, D. (2007, July). *A study of poverty and working poverty among recent immigrants to Canada: Final report.* Human Resources and Social Development Canada. Retrieved March 11, 2009, from www.hrsdc.gc.ca/eng/publications_resources/research/categories/inclusion/2007/sp_680_05_07_e/sp_680_05_07e.pdf.

Fontaine, P. (2005, November 23). *Assembly of First Nations National Chief applauds historic reconciliation and compensation agreement as a major victory for residential school survivors.* Retrieved March 12, 2009, from www.afn.ca/article.asp?id=1935.

Food Banks Canada. (2008). *HungerCount 2008: A comprehensive report on hunger and food bank use in Canada.* Retrieved February 3, 2009, from www.cafb-acba.ca/documents/HungerCount_en_fin.pdf.

Forsey, E. (1974). *The Canadian labour movement, 1812–1902.* Historical booklet, No. 27. Ottawa: Canadian Historical Association.

Foucault, M. (1965). *Madness and civilization.* London: Random House.

Frank, F., & Smith, A. (1999). *The community development handbook: A tool to build community capacity: Section I: Understanding the terms.* Human Resources Development Canada. Retrieved February 14, 2009, from www1.servicecanada.gc.ca/eng/epb/sid/cia/comm_deve/SECTIONI.doc.

Frankel, S. (2005, March 31). *Welfare to work: The next generation: Reflections on the symposium.* Retrieved February 3, 2009, from www.envision.ca/pdf/w2w/Papers/SidFrankelReportW2W.pdf.

Frenette, M., & Picot, G. (2003, March). *Life after welfare: The economic well being of welfare leavers in Canada during the 1990s.* Statistics Canada: Analytic Studies: Research Paper Series: Catalogue No. 11F0019MIE: No. 192. Retrieved February 3, 2009, from www.statcan.gc.ca/pub/11f0019m/11f0019m2003192-eng.pdf.

Fuchs, S.E. (2004, March 9). *Organizational change in the Internet era.* Retrieved February 14, 2009, from IBM, www.ibm.com/developerworks/rational/library/3770.html.

Galabuzi, G.E., & Labonte, R. (2002, November). *Social inclusion as a determinant of health.* The Social Determinants of Health Across the Life-Span Conference, Toronto, November 2002. Retrieved August 24, 2008, from the Public Health Agency of Canada, www.phac-aspc.gc.ca/ph-sp/oi-ar/pdf/03_inclusion_e.pdf.

Galper, J.H. (1975). *The politics of social services.* Englewood Cliffs, NJ: Prentice-Hall.

George, V., & Wilding, P. (1985). *Ideology and social welfare.* London and New York: Routledge.

Ginsler, E. (1988, September). Social Planning Councils. *Perception* 2(2): 52–53.

Gordon, M. (2000). Dealing with depression. *Expression Magazine: Newsletter of National Advisory Council on Aging,* 13(3): 1-2. Retrieved February 28, 2009, from dsp-psd.pwgsc.gc.ca/Collection/H71-4-1-13-3E.pdf.

Goss Gilroy Inc. (2000, August). *Evaluation framework for the host program: Citizenship and Immigration Canada.* Cited in Community Bridging Programs Research Project.

March 2003, p. 9. Retrieved March 11, 2009, from www.amssa.org/programs/iicc/CB%20Research%20Report%2031-03-03-%20Web_copy.pdf.

Gottlieb, B.H. (1983). *Social support strategies*. Beverly Hills: Sage.

Government of BC. (2003, March). *Children's programs on divorce and separation: Report*. Ministry of Attorney General Justice Services Branch Family Justice Services Division. Retrieved February 24, 2009, from www.ag.gov.bc.ca/justice-services/publications/fjsd/children/DivorceSeparationPrograms.pdf.

Government of Canada. (1970). *Income security for Canadians*. Ottawa: Department of National Health and Welfare.

Government of Canada. (1999a). *A national children's agenda: Developing a shared vision*. Ottawa: Government of Canada.

Government of Canada. (1999b, February 4). *A framework to improve the Social Union for Canadians: An agreement between the Government of Canada and the governments of the provinces and territories*. Retrieved March 12, 2009, from www.socialunion.gc.ca/news/020499_e.html.

Government of Canada. (1999c, December 16). *Meeting of the Federal-Provincial-Territorial Ministerial Council on Social Policy Renewal*. News Releases. Retrieved March 12, 2009, from www.socialunion.gc.ca/news/161299_e.html.

Government of Canada. (2000). *Canada's participation in the International Year of Older Persons (IYOP)—1999*. Retrieved February 28, 2009, from www.phac-aspc.gc.ca/seniors-aines/iyop_wrapup/english/raising.htm.

Government of Canada. (2003a, March). *Multilateral framework on early learning and child care*. Retrieved February 24, 2009, from www.socialunion.gc.ca/ecd-framework_e.htm.

Government of Canada. (2003, April 4). *Indian Residential Schools Resolution Canada: Frequently asked questions*. Retrieved May 16, 2004, from www.irsr-rqpi.gc.ca/english/news_questions.html.

Government of Canada. (2003b, November). *The well-being of Canada's young children: Government of Canada report 2003*. Retrieved February 24, 2009, from www.socialunion.gc.ca/ecd/2003/RH64-20-2003E.pdf.

Government of Canada. (2004a, April). *A Canada fit for children: Canada's plan of action in response to the May 2002 United Nations special session on children*. Retrieved February 24, 2009, from www.hrsdc.gc.ca/eng/cs/sp/sdc/socpol/publications/2002-002483/canadafite.pdf.

Government of Canada. (2004b, February 2). *Speech from the Throne*. Retrieved March 12, 2009, from www.pco-bcp.gc.ca/index.asp?lang=eng&page=information&sub=publications&doc=sft-ddt/2004_1_e.htm.

Government of Canada. (2004c, January 12). *National Homelessness Initiative: About the initiative*. Retrieved February 10, 2004, from www21.hrdc-drhc.gc.ca/initiative/index_e.asp.

Government of Canada. (2005, October). *Government of Canada response to "Accessibility for All": Eighth report of the Standing Committee on Human Resources, Skills Development, Social Development and the Status of Persons with Disabilities.* Retrieved February 23, 2009, from www.hrsdc.gc.ca/eng/isp/pub/cpp/disability/8threport/8threport.pdf.

Government of Canada. (2006a). *The human face of mental health and mental illness in Canada.* Retrieved March 5, 2009, from www.phac-aspc.gc.ca/publicat/human-humain06/pdf/human_face_e.pdf.

Government of Canada. (2006b, May). Indian residential schools settlement agreement. *Social Policy Digest*, May 2008, pp. 3–4. Retrieved March 12, 2009, from www.first-callbc.org/pdfs/CurrentIssues/service%20canada.pdf.

Government of Canada. (2006c). *National Child Benefit: Progress report 2006* (pamphlet). Retrieved February 3, 2009, from www.nationalchildbenefit.ca/ncb/Progress_Reports/2006/pdf/ncb_pamphlet_2006.pdf.

Government of Canada. (2006d). *The well-being of Canada's young children: Government of Canada report 2006.* Retrieved February 24, 2009, from www.socialunion.gc.ca/well_being/2007/en/well_being.pdf.

Government of Canada. (2007, February 16). *Canada's new government announces $223 million for agreements to assist people with disabilities.* Retrieved February 23, 2009, from www.marketwire.com/press-release/Human-Resources-And-Social-Development-Canada-636037.html.

Government of Canada. (2009). *Persons with disabilities online: Guide to Government of Canada services for people with disabilities and their families.* Retrieved February 23, 2009, from http://pwd-online.ca/pwdc.4nt.2nt@.jsp?lang=eng&geo=5&cid=20.

Government of Manitoba. (2009). *Caught in the middle.* Retrieved February 24, 2009, from Manitoba Family Services and Housing, www.gov.mb.ca/fs/childfam/caught_in_the_middle.html.

Government of New Brunswick. (2009). *Social assistance rate schedules.* Retrieved March 7, 2009, from www.gnb.ca/0017/social_assistance/rates-e.asp.

Government of Newfoundland and Labrador. (2006, June). *Reducing poverty: An action plan for Newfoundland and Labrador.* Retrieved February 23, 2009, from www.hrle.gov.nl.ca/hrle/poverty/poverty-reduction-strategy.pdf.

Government of Nova Scotia. (2006, May 11). *Nova Scotia's new Minister of Volunteerism.* Retrieved September 18, 2008, from http://gov.ns.ca/news/details.asp?id=20060511007.

Government of Ontario. (2008, February 19). *Accessibility for Ontarians with disabilities: Frequently asked questions.* Ministry of Community and Social Services. Retrieved February 23, 2009, from www.mcss.gov.on.ca/mcss/english/pillars/accessibilityOntario/questions/aodo/act2005.htm.

Gray, G. (1990). Social policy by stealth. *Policy Options*, March: 17–29.

Greenwood, J. (2005, January/February). Whither welfare? *Canadian Journal of Public Health* 96(1): 9–10. Retrieved August 26, 2008, from http://journal.cpha.ca/index.php/cjph/article/view/599/599.

Guest, D. (1980). *The emergence of social security in Canada*. Vancouver: University of British Columbia Press.

Guest, D. (1997). *The emergence of social security in Canada* (3rd ed.). Vancouver: University of British Columbia Press.

Guest, D. (2008a). Social security. In *The Canadian encyclopedia, Historica Foundation of Canada*. Retrieved August 26, 2008, from www.thecanadianencyclopedia.com/index.cfm?PgNm=TCE&Params=A1SEC828298#SEC828304.

Guest, D. (2008b). Family allowance. In *The Canadian encyclopedia, Historica Foundation of Canada*. Retrieved August 26, 2008, from www.thecanadianencyclopedia.com/index.cfm?PgNm=TCE&Params=A1ARTA0002718.

Gyarmati, D., Raaf, S.D., Palameta, B., Nicholson, C., & Hui, T.S. (2008, November). *Encouraging work and supporting communities: Final results of the Community Employment Innovation Project*. Retrieved February 3, 2009, from Social Research and Demonstration Corporation, www.srdc.org/uploads/CEIP_finalrpt_ES_ENG.pdf.

Hall, C. (2007). *Social work practice in community development*. Retrieved February 14, 2009, from Canadian Association of Social Workers, www.casw-acts.ca/public/community_e.pdf.

Hall, M., de Wit, M., Lasby, D., McIver, D., Evers, T., Johnston, C., et al. (2005, June). *Cornerstones of community: Highlights of the National Survey of Nonprofit and Voluntary Organizations*. 2003 revised. Statistics Canada, Small Business and Special Surveys Division Business and Trade Statistics Field. Retrieved August 31, 2008, from http://nonprofitscan.imaginecanada.ca/files/en/nsnvo/nsnvo_report_english.pdf.

Hall, M., Lasby, D., Gumulka, G., & Tryon, C. (2006, June). *Caring Canadians, involved Canadians: Highlights from the Canada survey of Giving, Volunteering and Participating*. Retrieved September 18, 2008, from Statistics Canada, www.statcan.ca/english/freepub/71-542-XIE/71-542-XIE2006001.pdf.

Hall, M., McKechnie, A.J., Davidman, K., & Leslie, F. (2001, June). *An environmental scan on volunteering and improving volunteering*. Canadian Centre for Philanthropy. Retrieved February 12, 2009, from http://nonprofitscan.imaginecanada.ca/files/en/misc/vol-scan.pdf.

Hall, M.H., Andrukow, A., Barr, C., Brock, K., deWit, M., Embuldeniya, D., Jolin, L., Lasby, D., Levesque, B., Malinsky, E., Stowe, S., & Vaillancourt, Y. (2003). *The capacity to serve: A qualitative study of the challenges facing Canada's nonprofit and voluntary organizations*. Canadian Centre for Philanthropy. Retrieved September 18, 2008, from http://nonprofitscan.imaginecanada.ca/files/en/nsnvo/capacity_to_serve_english.pdf.

Hall, M.H., Phillips, S.D., Meillat, C., & Pickering, D. (2003). *Assessing performance: Evaluation practices and perspectives in Canada's voluntary sector*. Canadian Centre for

Philanthropy/Centre for Voluntary Sector Research and Development. Retrieved September 16, 2008, from www.cvsrd.org/eng/docs/Policy%20and%20Practice/Assessing%20Performance.pdf.

Halseth, G., & Booth, A. (1998, November). *Paper #2: Community participation in the new forest economy: Discussion paper on concepts: Community development.* British Columbia Resource Communities Project: University of Northern British Columbia. Retrieved February 14, 2009, from www.for.gov.bc.ca/hfd/library/documents/bib95182.pdf.

Hamdad, M., & Joyal, S. (2007, December). *Satellite account of nonprofit institutions and volunteering, 1997 to 2004.* Catalogue No. 13-015-XIE, Statistics Canada. Retrieved August 31, 2008, from www.statcan.ca/english/freepub/13-015-XIE/13-015-XIE2007000.pdf.

Handel, G. (1982). *Social welfare in Western society.* New York: Random House.

Hanley, J. (2000). *Social work practice and government policy on cultural diversity: The case of Ontario and Quebec.* Paper presented at the International Federation of Social Workers and International Association of Schools of Social Work Joint Conference Proceedings, Montreal, July 29–August 2, 2000. Retrieved March 11, 2009, from www.mun.ca/cassw-ar/papers2/Hanley.pdf.

Hanvey, L. (2002, June). *Middle childhood: Building on the early years: A discussion paper.* Retrieved March 2, 2009, from National Children's Alliance, www.nationalchildren-salliance.com/nca/pubs/2002/hanvey.pdf.

Hareven, T.K. (1969, April). An ambiguous alliance: Some aspects of American influences on Canadian social welfare. *Social History: A Canadian Review* 3: 82–98.

Hay, D. (2008, October 8). *Investing in youth: Evidence from policy, practice and research.* Retrieved February 24, 2009, from Policy Research Initiative, www.policyresearch.gc.ca/page.asp?pagenm=rp_iy_bkg.

Hayden, J. (1997). *Neo-conservatism and child care services in Alberta: A case study: Five phases of policy directions: Overt policies.* Child Care Resource and Research Unit, Child Care Canada. Retrieved August 26, 2008, from www.childcarecanada.org/pubs/op9/op9.pdf.

Health Canada. (2002, September 2). *National plan of action for children: History.* Retrieved April 28, 2004, from www.hc-sc.gc.ca/dca-dea/npa-pan/main_e.html.

Health Canada. (2007a). *Canadian community health survey: Cycle 2.2, Nutrition (2004): Income-related household food security in Canada.* Retrieved February 3, 2009, from www.hc-sc.gc.ca/fn-an/alt_formats/hpfb-dgpsa/pdf/surveill/income_food_sec-sec_alim-eng.pdf.

Health Canada. (2007b). *First Nations, Inuit and Aboriginal Health: Brighter Futures and Building Healthy Communities.* Retrieved March 12, 2009, from www.hc-sc.gc.ca/fniah-spnia/promotion/mental/brighter_grandir-eng.php.

Health Systems Research Unit. (1997). *Review of best practices in mental health reform.* Federal/Provincial/Territorial Advisory Network on Mental Health. Clarke

Institute of Psychiatry. Ottawa: Health Canada. Retrieved February 15, 2009, from www.phac-aspc.gc.ca/mh-sm/pubs/bp_review/pdf/e_bp-rev.pdf.

HeartWood. (2009). *Programs and services.* Retrieved February 24, 2009, from www.heartwood.ns.ca/services.shtml.

Héber, B.P. & Luong, M. (2008, November). Bridge employment. *Perspectives on labour and income, 9*(11): 5-12. Statistics Canada. Retrieved February 28, 2009, from www.statcan.gc.ca/pub/75-001-x/75-001-x2008111-eng.pdf.

Heclo, H. (1981). Toward a new welfare state? In P. Flora & A.J. Heidenheimer (Eds.), *The development of welfare states in Europe and America* (pp. 383–406). New Brunswick & London: Transaction Books.

Herman, R.D. & Renz, D.O. (1998). What is not-for-profit organization effectiveness? *The not-for-profit CEO monthly letter 5*(6): 4–6. Retrieved September 16, 2008, from www.bloch.umkc.edu/mwcnl/research/whatis.pdf.

Henderson, W.B. (2009). Indian Act. In *The Canadian Encyclopedia.* Retrieved March 12, 2009, from Historica Foundation of Canada, www.thecanadianencyclopedia.com/index.cfm?PgNm=TCE&Params=A1ARTA0003975.

Henslin, J.M. (2003). *Social problems* (6th ed.). Upper Saddle River, NJ: Prentice Hall.

Herberg, C., & Herberg, E.N. (2001). Canada's ethno-racial diversity: Policies and programs in Canadian social welfare. In J.C. Turner & F.J. Turner (Eds.), *Canadian social welfare* (4th ed.), pp. 167–79. Toronto: Pearson Education.

Herd, D., Mitchell, A., & Lightman, E. (2005, February). Rituals of degradation: Administration as policy in the Ontario Works programme. *Social policy and administration 39*(1): 65-79. Retrieved September 16, 2008, from www.socialwork.utoronto.ca/fsw/fswsupport/sane/doc/RitualsOfDegradation.pdf.

Herman, R.D. & Renz, D.O. (1998). What is not-for-profit organization effectiveness? *The not-for-profit CEO monthly letter 5*(6): 4–6. Retrieved September 16, 2008, from HYPERLINK "http://www.bloch.umkc.edu/mwcnl/research/whatis.pdf" www.bloch.umkc.edu/mwcnl/research/whatis.pdf.

Heritage Community Foundation. (2005). *Understanding Canadian diversity in Alberta: Timeline of Canadian immigration policy.* Retrieved March 11, 2009, from www.edukits.ca/multiculturalism/student/timeline_e.html.

Hick, S. (1998). *Canada's unique social history: Canadian government policy goals.* Retrieved March 12, 2009, from www.socialpolicy.ca/cush/m8/m8-t6.stm.

Hick, S. (2004). *Social welfare in Canada: Understanding income security: An introduction.* Toronto: Thompson Educational Publishing. Retrieved February 28, 2009, from www.socialpolicy.ca/swc/book_g.htm.

Hirst, S. (2006, December 11). *Proceedings of the Special Senate Committee on Aging: Issue 2–Evidence.* Retrieved February 28, 2009, from www.parl.gc.ca/39/1/parlbus/commbus/senate/com-e/agei-e/02evb-e.htm?Language=E&Parl=39&Ses=1&comm_id=600.

Hiscott, R. (2002). *Trends: Longer hours, more stress*. A CBC News special feature: The way we work. Retrieved September 1, 2008, from CBC News Online, www.cbc.ca/news/work/nomore9to5/234.html.

Historical review. (1975). Supplement: Our way. *Saskatchewan Indian*, June 1975. Retrieved March 12, 2009, from www.sicc.sk.ca/saskindian/a75our06.htm.

History of the Indian Act. (1978). *Saskatchewan Indian* 1(3) (March 1978). Retrieved March 12, 2009, from www.sicc.sk.ca/saskindian/a78mar04.htm.

Hollander, M.J., Liu, G. & Chappell, N.L. (2009). Who cares and how much? The imputed economic contribution to the Canadian healthcare system of middle-aged and older unpaid caregivers providing care to the elderly. *Healthcare Quarterly* 12(2) (2009): 42–49. Retrieved May 27, 2009, from www.longwoods.com/product.php?productid=20660&cat=586&page=1.

Holmes, O.W. (1927). *Compania General de Tabacos de Filipinas v. Collector of Internal Revenue*, No. 42, 275 U.S. 87. Retrieved August 27, 2008, from FindLaw for Legal Professionals, http://caselaw.lp.findlaw.com/cgi-bin/getcase.pl?court=us&vol=275&invol=87.

Horn, M. (1984). *The great depression of the 1930s in Canada*. Historical booklet, No. 39. Ottawa: Canadian Historical Association.

Horner, J.S. (2002, January). Innovative projects aim to prevent family violence. *Let's Talk Families* 13(4): 7. Retrieved April 28, 2004, from Canadian Paediatric Society, www.familyservicecanada.org/_files/newsletters_families/parlons_famille_janv2002_e.pdf.

Howlett, D. (1992, May/June). The arithmetic, chemistry, and art of coalition projects. *Action Canada Dossier 37*: 7–9. Action Canada Network.

Hrab, R. (2004, January). *Private delivery of public services: Public private partnerships and contracting-out*. Research Paper #21. Retrieved August 28, 2008, from www.law-lib.utoronto.ca/investing/reports/rp21.pdf.

HR Council for the Voluntary and Non-profit Sector. (2008). Toward a labour force strategy for Canada's voluntary & non-profit sector. Retrieved February 6, 2008, from www.conseilrh.ca/about/HRC_Labour_Force_Study_R1.pdf.pdf.

HRDC (Human Resources Development Canada). (1994a, October). *Improving social security in Canada: A discussion paper*. Retrieved August 21, 2008, from www.canadiansocialresearch.net/ssrdiscussionpaper.htm#context.

HRDC (Human Resources Development Canada). (1994b). *Improving social security in Canada: Reforming the Canada Assistance Plan: A supplementary paper*. Hull-Ottawa: Minister of Supply and Services Canada.

HRDC (Human Resources Development Canada). (1998). *The Government of Canada's record on disability issues*. Retrieved June 28, 2000, from www.hrdc-drhc.gc.ca/common/news/9821b4.html.

HRDC (Human Resources Development Canada). (1999a). *Investing in children: Ideas for action.* Report from the National Research Conference held in Ottawa, October 27–29, 1998. Retrieved February 24, 2009, from www1.servicecanada.gc.ca/eng/cs/sp/sdc/pkrf/publications/nlscy/2002-000085/2002_000085_e.pdf.

HRDC (Human Resources Development Canada). (1999b, July). *Future directions: The challenges facing persons with disabilities.* Retrieved February 23, 2009, from www.hrsdc.gc.ca/eng/cs/sp/sdc/socpol/publications/reports/1999-000046/1999-000046.pdf.

HRDC (Human Resources Development Canada). (2000, March). *Reconnecting social assistance recipients to the labour market: Lessons learned: Final report.* Retrieved February 3, 2009, from www.hrsdc.gc.ca/eng/cs/sp/hrsdc/edd/reports/2000-000437/sarlm.pdf.

HRDC (Human Resources Development Canada). (2002, December). *Advancing the inclusion of persons with disabilities: A Government of Canada report.* Retrieved February 23, 2009, from http://gateway.cotr.bc.ca/Downloads/AdvnIncDisabil.pdf.

HRDC (Human Resources Development Canada). (2003). *Defining disability: A complex issue.* Office for Disability Issues. Retrieved February 23, 2009, from http://dsp-psd.communication.gc.ca/Collection/RH37-4-3-2003E.pdf.

HRSDC (Human Resources and Social Development Canada). (2005a). *Social economy: Questions and answers.* Retrieved January 11, 2009, from www.hrsdc.gc.ca/eng/cs/comm/sd/social_economy.shtml.

HRSDC (Human Resources and Skills Development Canada). (2005b, March 4). *The business case for work-life balance.* Retrieved September 1, 2008, from www.hrsdc.gc.ca/en/lp/spila/wlb/16benefits_costs_businesscase.shtml.

HRSDC (Human Resources and Social Development Canada). (2006a, June). *Low income in Canada: 2000–2002: Using the market basket measure—June 2006.* Retrieved August 23, 2008, from www.hrsdc.gc.ca/eng/cs/sp/sdc/pkrf/publications/research/2002-000662/SP-628-05-06e.pdf.

HRSDC (Human Resources and Social Development Canada). (2006b). *Advancing the inclusion of people with disabilities: People—Partnerships—Knowledge.* Retrieved February 23, 2009, from www.hrsdc.gc.ca/eng/disability_issues/reports/fdr/2006/advancinginclusion.pdf.

HRSDC (Human Resources and Social Development Canada). (2006c). *2006 Federal report: Advancing the inclusion of people with disabilities.* Retrieved February 23, 2009, from www.hrsdc.gc.ca/eng/disability_issues/reports/fdr/2006/brochure.pdf.

HRSDC (Human Resources and Social Development Canada). (2007). *2007–2008 Estimates: A report on plans and priorities.* Retrieved February 24, 2009, from www.tbs-sct.gc.ca/rpp/0708/hrsdc-rhdsc/hrsdc-rhdsc-eng.pdf.

HRSDC (Human Resources and Skills Development Canada). (2008a, October). *Low income in Canada, 2000–2006: Using the market basket measure: Final report.* Retrieved

March 1, 2009, from www.hrsdc.gc.ca/eng/publications_resources/research/cate-gories/inclusion/2008/sp–864–10–2008/sp_864_10_08e.pdf.

HRSDC (Human Resources and Skills Development Canada). (2008b, October 7). *Questions about New Horizons for Seniors.* Retrieved March 5, 2009, from www.hrsdc.gc.ca/eng/community_partnerships/seniors/nhsp/faq.shtml.

HRSDC (Human Resources and Skills Development Canada). (2009a). *First Nations and Inuit child care initiative.* Retrieved March 12, 2009, from www.hrsdc.gc.ca/eng/employment/aboriginal_employment/childcare/initiative.shtml.

HRSDC (Human Resources and Skills Development Canada). (2009b). *Indicators of well-being in Canada: Canadians in context—Households and families.* Retrieved February 24, 2009, from www4.hrsdc.gc.ca/indicator.jsp?lang=en&indicatorid=37#MOREON_2.

HRSDC (Human Resources and Skills Development Canada). (2009c). *Indicators of well-being in Canada: Work–employment rate.* Retrieved January 11, 2009, from www4.hrsdc.gc.ca/.3ndic.1t.4r@-eng.jsp?iid=13.

HRSDC (Human Resources and Skills Development Canada). (2009d). *EI Monitoring and assessment report 2008.* Retrieved May 24, 2009, from www.hrsdc.gc.ca/eng/employment/ei/reports/eimar_2008/index.shtml.

HRSDC (Human Resources and Skills Development Canada). (2009e). *Disability savings.* Retrieved February 23, 2009, from www.hrsdc.gc.ca/en/disability_issues/disability_savings/index.shtml.

Huebner, F. (1999). *A guide for the development of policies and procedures in Ontario's community literacy agencies.* Retrieved September 16, 2008, from Community Literacy of Ontario, www.nald.ca/litweb/province/on/CLO/policies/guide1/devpol-1.pdf.

Hughes, J., & Stone, W. (2004) Family and community life: Exploring the decline thesis. *Transition Magazine 34*(1) (Spring 2004): 7–12. Retrieved February 14, 2009, from www.vifamily.ca/library/transition/341/341.pdf.

Human Resources Council for the Voluntary & Non-Profit Sector. (2008). *Toward a labour force strategy for Canada's voluntary & non-profit sector.* Retrieved September 18, 2008, from www.conseilrh.ca/about/HRC_Labour_Force_Study_R1.pdf.pdf.

Hwang, S.W. (2001, January 23). Homelessness and health. *CMAJ (Canadian Medical Association Journal) 164*(2001)(2): 229–33. Retrieved February 3, 2009, from www.cmaj.ca/cgi/reprint/164/2/229.

Hylton, J.H. (2002). *Appendix C: Aboriginal health and healing: A review of best practices.* A background paper prepared for the Regina Qu'Appelle Health Region, Working Together Towards Excellence Project. Retrieved March 12, 2009, from www.rqhealth.ca/programs/aboriginal/pdf_files/appendix_c.pdf.

Ilcan, S., & Basok, T. (2004, June). Community government: Voluntary agencies, social justice, and the responsibilization of citizens. *Citizenship Studies 8*(2), 129–44. Retrieved August 25, 2008, from http://sjg.uwindsor.ca/ilcan/13355012.pdf.

INAC (Indian and Northern Affairs Canada). (1990). *The Canadian Indian*. Hull-Ottawa: Minister of Supply and Services Canada.

INAC (Indian and Northern Affairs Canada). (2008a). *Fact sheet: Aboriginal self-government*. Retrieved March 12, 2009, from www.ainc-inac.gc.ca/ai/mr/is/abgov-eng.asp.

INAC (Indian and Northern Affairs Canada). (2008b). *Statement of apology*. Retrieved March 12, 2009, from www.ainc-inac.gc.ca/ai/rqpi/apo/index-eng.asp.

INAC (Indian and Northern Affairs Canada). (2008c). *Backgrounder: Toward a new federal framework for Aboriginal economic development*. Retrieved March 12, 2009, from www.ainc-inac.gc.ca:80/ai/mr/nr/m-a2008/2-3077bk-eng.asp.

INAC (Indian and Northern Affairs Canada). (2008d). *Aboriginal Head Start in urban and northern communities*. Retrieved March 12, 2009, from www.ainc-inac.gc.ca/hb/sp/ecd/unc-eng.asp.

INAC (Indian and Northern Affairs Canada). (2008e). *Frequently asked questions: Measuring First Nations well-being*. Retrieved March 12, 2009, from www.ainc-inac.gc.ca:80/ai/rs/pubs/re/qna/qna-eng.asp.

INAC (Indian and Northern Affairs Canada). (2009a). *Urban Aboriginal strategy: Backgrounder*. Retrieved March 12, 2009, from www.ainc-inac.gc.ca/ai/ofi/uas/bkg-eng.asp.

INAC (Indian and Northern Affairs Canada). (2009b). *First Nations National Child Benefit Reinvestment (NCBR) Initiative: Proposal development & reporting guide*. Retrieved March 12, 2009, from www.ainc-inac.gc.ca/hb/sp/ncb/pubs/ri/ncbrg-eng.asp.

Indian residential schools. (2008). *CBC News*, October 20, 2008. Retrieved March 12, 2009, from www.cbc.ca/canada/story/2008/05/16/f-faqs-residential-schools.html.

Industry Canada. (2006a). *Corporate social responsibility: An implementation guide for Canadian business*. Retrieved August 28, 2008, from www.ic.gc.ca/epic/site/csr-rse.nsf/vwapj/CSR_mar2006.pdf/$FILE/CSR_mar2006.pdf.

Industry Canada. (2006b). *Service industries: Services sector overview—2006 October*. Retrieved January 11, 2009, from www.ic.gc.ca/eic/site/si–is.nsf/eng/ai02201.html.

Innovation Network Inc. (2005). *Logic model workbook*. Retrieved August 25, 2008, from www.innonet.org/client_docs/File/logic_model_workbook.pdf.

Institute on Governance. (2008a). *Governance basics: What is governance? Getting to a definition*. Retrieved September 16, 2008, from www.iog.ca/boardgovernance/html/gov_wha.html.

Institute on Governance. (2008b). *Governance basics: What is governance? Where governance fits*. Retrieved September 16, 2008, from www.iog.ca/boardgovernance/html/gov_whe.html.

International Federation of Social Workers. (2000 July). *Definition of social work*. Retrieved September 18, 2008, from www.ifsw.org/en/f38000138.html.

International Federation of Social Workers. (2005). *International policy statement on globalisation and the environment*. Retrieved January 11, 2009, from www.ifsw.org/en/p38000222.html.

Ismael, J.S. (Ed.). (1985). Introduction. In *Canadian social welfare policy: Federal and provincial dimensions* (pp. xi–xv). Kingston and Montreal: McGill-Queen's University Press.

Ismael, S. (2006). *Child poverty and the Canadian welfare state: From entitlement to charity*. Edmonton: University of Alberta Press.

Jaco, R.M. & Pierce, B.D. (2005). Social agencies and human service organizations. In J.C. Turner & F.J. Turner (Eds.), *Canadian social welfare* (5th ed., pp. 225–41). Toronto: Pearson Education Canada.

J.N. Mukongolo & Associates. (2007). *Child protection legislation in Ontario*. Retrieved February 24, 2009, from www.ontariodivorces.com/child-protection.html.

Jackson, A. (2003, February 24). *The U-turn budget?* Canadian Labour Congress. Retrieved February 4, 2004, from http://action.web.ca/home/clccomm/en_op-ed.shtml?sh_itm=495c1c61877f69c11dc45680d80c8728.

Jackson, A. (2004, March). *Asset-based social policies: A new idea whose time has come?* Retrieved March 1, 2009, from Caledon Institute of Social Policy, www.caledoninst.org/Publications/PDF/452ENG.pdf.

Jacobs, E., Storey, F., & Poirier, F. (1992, October 19). *Liberating our children, liberating our nations*. Report of the Aboriginal Committee Community Panel Child Protection Legislation Review in British Columbia. Retrieved May 13, 2004, from www.turtleisland.org/healing/liberate.doc.

Janzen, C., & Harris, O. (1997). *Family treatment in social work practice* (3rd ed.). Itasca: F.E. Peacock.

Jeffrey, K. (2008, February). *Youth policy: What works and what doesn't: A report of United Way Toronto*. Retrieved February 24, 2009, from www.perthcountyspc.ca/reports/UWT%20Youth%20Policy.pdf.

Jenson, J. (2003, November 21). *Social citizenship, governance and social policy*. Canada Research Chair in Citizenship and Governance. Retrieved February 3, 2009, from www.cccg.umontreal.ca/pdf/SocialCitizenshipGovernance.pdf.

Jenson, J. (2004a, September). *Canada's new social risks: Directions for a new social architecture*. CPRN Social Architecture Papers, Research Report F43, Family Network. Retrieved August 23, 2008, from Canadian Policy Research Networks, www.cprn.org/documents/31815_en.pdf.

Jenson, J. (2004b, January). *Catching up to reality: Building the case for a new social model*. CPRN Social Architecture Papers, Research Report F35, Family Network. Retrieved August 24, 2008, from Canadian Policy Research Networks Inc., www.cprn.org/documents/26067_en.pdf.

Jewell, L. (2005). Chapter 14: Mental health and community counselling, and private practice. In P. Hayduk, L. Jewell, & S. Konrad, *An introduction to counselling in*

Canada. Retrieved August 23, 2008, from Centre for Psychology, Athabasca University, http://psych.athabascau.ca/html/Resources/Psych388/CanadianSupplement/Chapter14/00_intro.shtml.

Jill Florence Lackey and Associates. (2004). *What is a needs assessment?* Retrieved February 26, 2004, from www.my.execpc.com/~lackassc/page3.html.

Jiwani, I. (2000). *Globalization at the level of the nation-state: The case of Canada's third sector.* Retrieved August 23, 2008, from www.ucalgary.ca/~innovate/issues/Inv2000-4.pdf.

Johnson, A.W. (1987). Social policy in Canada: The past as it conditions the present. In S.B. Seward (Ed.), *The future of social welfare systems in Canada and the United Kingdom: Proceedings of a Canada/UK colloquium, October 17–18, 1986, Ottawa/Meech Lake* (pp. 29–70). Halifax: Institute for Research on Public Policy.

Johnson, H. (2006). *Measuring violence against women: Statistical trends 2006.* Ottawa: Minister of Industry. Retrieved August 24, 2008, from Statistics Canada, 2006 Catalogue no. 85-570-XIE, www.statcan.ca/english/research/85-570-XIE/85-570-XIE2006001.pdf.

Johnson, L.C., McClelland, R.W., & Austin, C.D. (2000). *Social work practice: A generalist approach* (Cdn. ed.). Scarborough: Prentice-Hall Canada.

Johnston, P. (1983). *Native children and the child welfare system.* Toronto: Canadian Council on Social Development in association with James Lorimer and Company.

Jones, A. (2007). *The role of supportive housing for low-income seniors in Ontario.* Retrieved February 28, 2009, from www.cprn.org/documents/49552_EN.pdf.

Jones, C., Clark, L., Grusec, J., Hart, R., Plickert, G., & Tepperman, L. (2002, March). *Poverty, social capital, parenting and child outcomes in Canada: Final report.* Applied Research Branch, Strategic Policy, Human Resources Development Canada, Catalogue #SP-557-01-03E. Retrieved February 3, 2009, from www.dsp-psd.communication.gc.ca/Collection/RH63-1-557-01-03E.pdf.

Juby, H. (2003). Yours, mine, and ours: New boundaries for the modern stepfamily. *Transition Magazine 33*(4) (Winter 2003–2004). Retrieved February 24, 2009, from www.vifamily.ca/library/transition/334/334.html.

KAIROS. (2008, October 2). *KAIROS analysis of the 2008 federal budget.* Retrieved March 12, 2009, from www.kairoscanada.org/en/get-involved/urgent-actions/urgent-action/archive/2008/02/article/kairos-analysis-of-the-2008-federal-budget/?tx_ttnews%5BbackPid%5D=116&cHash=67d5578d14.

Kenny, J. (2008, November 13). *Jason Kenney, Minister of Citizenship, Immigration and Multiculturalism: Speaking notes for the Minister of Citizenship, Immigration and Multiculturalism at the Canadian Club.* Retrieved March 11, 2009, from www.cic.gc.ca/english/department/media/speeches/2008/2008-11-13.asp.

Kilbride, K.M., & Anisef, P. (2001). *To build on hope: Overcoming the challenges facing newcomer youth at risk in Ontario.* Retrieved March 11, 2009, from Ontario Council of Agencies Serving Immigrants, http://atwork.settlement.org/downloads/Build_On_Hope_Final_Report.pdf.

Kinsella, N.A. (2008). *Speaking notes: The Honourable Noël A. Kinsella, Speaker of the Senate of Canada, On the occasion of the formal opening of the International Conference on the United Nations Convention on the Rights of Persons with Disabilities, November 18, 2008*. Retrieved February 23, 2009, from http://sen.parl.gc.ca/nkinsella/PDF/Speeches/UN_Convention-e.pdf.

Kirmayer, G., Brass, M., & Tait, C.L. (2000, September). The mental health of Aboriginal peoples: Transformations of identity and community. *Canadian Journal of Psychiatry 45*(7): 607–16. Retrieved March 12, 2009, from https://ww1.cpa-apc.org/Publications/Archives/CJP/2000/Sep/InReview.asp.

Laird, G. (2007). *Shelter: Homelessness in a growth economy: Canada's 21st century paradox: A report for the Sheldon Chumir Foundation for Ethics in Leadership*. Retrieved February 3, 2009, from www.ccsd.ca/pubs/2007/upp/SHELTER.pdf.

LaRoque, E.D. (1994, March). Violence in Aboriginal communities. Reprinted from *The path to healing: Royal Commissions on Aboriginal Peoples*. Retrieved March 12, 2009, from http://dsp-psd.pwgsc.gc.ca/Collection/H72-21-100-1994E.pdf.

Latimer, J. (1998). *The consequences of child maltreatment: A reference guide for health practitioners*. Retrieved February 24, 2009, from Public Health Agency of Canada, www.phac-aspc.gc.ca/ncfv-cnivf/familyviolence/html/nfntsconsequencevio_e.html.

Lautenschlager, J. (1992). *Volunteering: A traditional Canadian value*. Voluntary Action Program, Canadian Heritage. Retrieved August 26, 2008, from www.nald.ca/fulltext/heritage/ComPartnE/Tradval1.htm.

Lazar, H. (2000, August). *The Social Union framework agreement: Lost opportunity or new beginning?* School of Policy Studies, Queens University, Working Paper 3. Retrieved August 24, 2008, from www.queensu.ca/sps/publications/working_papers/03.pdf.

LeBlanc, R. (1996). *Romeo LeBlanc, Speech: February 23, 1996: Presentation of the 1996 Native Role Models*. Retrieved May 13, 2004, from www.gg.ca/media/doc.asp?lang=e&DocID=140.

Lecomte, R. (2005). Distinguishing features of social work education in Canada. In J.C. Turner and F. J. Turner (Eds.), *Canadian social welfare* (5th ed., pp. 465–71). Toronto: Pearson Education Canada.

Leiby, J. (1977). Social welfare: History of basic ideas. In *Encyclopedia of social work* (17th ed., pp. 1512–29), vol. 2, Washington, DC: National Association of Social Workers.

Leitch, K. Kellie. (2007). *Reaching for the top: A report by the Advisor on Healthy Children and Youth*. Retrieved May 28, 2009, from www.cmha.ca/data/1/rec_docs/1737_advisor-conseillere_e.pdf.

LeRoy, S., & Clemens, J. (2003, September 25). *Ending welfare as we know it: Lessons from Canada*. National Center for Policy Analysis: Brief Analysis: No. 457. Retrieved August 26, 2008, from www.ncpa.org/pub/ba/ba457.

Liberal Party of Canada. (1997). *Securing our future together: Preparing Canada for the 21st century*. Ottawa: Author. Retrieved August 28, 2008, from http://libscam. godsandartists.com/sourcefiles/1997_redbook.pdf.

Liberal Party of Canada. (2004, June 1). *Seniors, the disabled, and family caregivers get a $2.5 billion boost*. Retrieved June 13, 2004, from www.liberal.ca/news_e.aspx? site=news&news=580.

Linda Graff and Associates Inc. (2006). *Excerpt from Canadian Government budget-cutting raises issues: A keyboard roundtable discussion in e-volunteerism*. Vol. VII, Issue 1, October–December, 2006. Retrieved September 18, 2008, from www.canadawho-cares.ca/pdfs/KRTon%20CVI%20Cut_LGexcerpt.pdf.

Lowe, E. (2007). Urban villages for urban settlers. *Transition Magazine 36*(4) (Winter 2006–2007). Retrieved May 13, 2004, from Vanier Institute of the Family, www.vifamily.ca/library/transition/364/364.html#3.

Luther, R. (2007). Access and equity in Ottawa: A snapshot of social service issues, institutional responses and remaining challenges regarding culture, race and language. *Our Diverse Cities*, Fall 2007, no. 4, pp. 39–43. Retrieved March 11, 2009, from Metropolis Canada, http://canada.metropolis.net/pdfs/ODC%20Ontario% 20Eng.pdf.

Lutherwood. (2009). *Residential treatment services*. Retrieved February 24, 2009, from www.lutherwood.ca/subsection2.aspx?id=12.

MacDonald, A., & Adachi, R. (2001, October). *Regulation of social work practice in Canada*. Paper prepared for the Social Work Summit—Montreal. Retrieved September 18, 2008, from CASW, www.caddssw-acddess.org/Regulation%20of% 20social%20work%20practice%20in%20Canada.rtf.

MacDonald, F. (2005). *Progress or regress: A critical examination of the Canadian government's shift to "autonomous" First Nations child welfare*. Retrieved March 12, 2009, from www.cst.ed.ac.uk/2005conference/papers/MacDonald_paper.pdf.

MacDonald, G. (2004, April). Book review: Child welfare: Connecting research, policy and practice. *Envision: The Manitoba Journal of Child Welfare 3*(1). Retrieved February 24, 2009, from www.envisionjournal.com/application/Articles/62.pdf.

MacKinnon, M.P. (2004, June). *Citizens' values and the Canadian social architecture: Evidence from the citizens' dialogue on Canada's future*. CPRN Social Architecture Papers, Research Report F42, Family Network. Retrieved August 25, 2008, from Canadian Policy Research Networks, http://cprn.org/documents/29860_en.pdf.

MacMurchy, H. (1932). *Sterilization? Birth control?* Toronto: Macmillan.

Mailloux, L., Horak, H., & Godin, C. (2002). *Motivation at the margins: Gender issues in the Canadian voluntary sector*. Retrieved September 18, 2008, from Voluntary Sector Initiative, www.vsi-isbc.org/eng/knowledge/motivation_margins/index.cfm.

Maioni, A. (2004, August). New century, new risks: The Marsh Report and the post-war welfare state in Canada. *Policy Options 25*(7): 20–23. Retrieved August 26, 2008, from Institute for Research on Public Policy, www.irpp.org/po/archive/aug04/maioni.pdf.

Makarenko, J. (2008, June 2). *The Indian Act: Historical overview.* Retrieved March 12, 2009, from Mapleleafweb, www.mapleleafweb.com/features/the-indian-act-historical-overview.

March of Dimes Canada. (2008). *Tracking the Canadians with Disabilities Act, AKA The National Disabilities Act.* Retrieved February 23, 2009, from www.marchofdimes.ca/dimes/national_programs/advocacy/current_issues/Tracking+the+Canadians+with+Disabilities+Act+AKA+The+National+Disabilities+Act.htm.

Marsh, L. (1950). *The welfare state: Is it a threat to Canada?* Proceedings on the Canadian Conference on Social Work, 1950. Ottawa: Canadian Conference on Social Work.

Marsh, L. (1975). *Report on social security for Canada.* Toronto & Buffalo: University of Toronto Press.

Martin, S.A. (1985). *An essential grace: Funding Canada's health care, education, welfare, religion and culture.* Toronto: McClelland and Stewart.

Mawhiney, A.M., & Hardy, S. (2005). Aboriginal peoples in Canada. In J.C. Turner and F. J. Turner (Eds.), *Canadian social welfare* (5th ed., pp. 118–33). Toronto: Pearson Education Canada.

McClintock, N. (2004). *Understanding Canadian volunteers.* Canadian Centre for Philanthropy. Retrieved May 20, 2009, from www.givingandvolunteering.ca/pdf/reports/Understanding_Volunteers.pdf.

McDonagh, A. (2002, October). *Globalization.* Retrieved January 11, 2009, from Workers' Educational Association of Canada, www.weacanada.ca/files/articles/25.pdf.

McDonald, G. (2005a). Evaluation in social welfare. In J.C. Turner and F.J. Turner (Eds.), *Canadian social welfare* (5th ed., pp. 307–15). Toronto: Pearson Education Canada.

McDonald, R.A. (2005b, October 21). *Comparative resource analysis of support services for First Nations people with disabilities.* Katenies Research and Management Services. Retrieved February 23, 2009, from www.afn.ca/cmslib/general/fndp.pdf.

McFadyen, S.D. (2006, April). *Women with disabilities in Nova Scotia: A statistical profile.* Nova Scotia Advisory Council on the Status of Women. Retrieved February 23, 2009, from http://women.gov.ns.ca/pubs2006_07/WomenDisabilities April06.pdf.

McFarlane, S., & Roach, R. (1999, September). *Strings attached: Non-profits & their funding relationships with government.* Canada West Foundation Research Bulletin No. 4. Retrieved August 31, 2008, from www.cwf.ca/V2/files/199914.pdf.

McGill University, School of Social Work, Greater Victoria Survey Committee. (1931). *Problems in family welfare: Relief and child development.* Montreal: Author.

McGilly, F. (1998). *An introduction to Canada's public social services: Understanding income and health programs* (2nd ed.). Don Mills: Oxford University Press.

McIntyre, L. (2003, March). Food security: More than a determinant of health. *Policy Options* 24(3): 46–51. Retrieved February 3, 2009, from www.irpp.org/po/archive/mar03/mcintyre.pdf.

McKenzie, B., & Morrissette, V. (2003, April). Social work practice with Canadians of Aboriginal background: Guidelines for respectful social work. *Envision: The Manitoba Journal of Child Welfare* 2(1).

McLachlin, B. (2008, June 16). *The law's response to an aging population.* Remarks of the Right Honourable Beverley McLachlin, P.C., Chief Justice of Canada: World Elder Abuse Awareness Day 2008. Retrieved February 28, 2009, from www.cnpea.ca/Ottawa%20Presentations%202008_files/Cheif%20Justice's%20speech%20final.pdf.

McMahon, M.O. (1994). *Advanced generalist practice with an international perspective.* Englewood Cliffs, NJ: Prentice Hall.

McQuaig, L. (1995). *Shooting the hippo: Death by deficit and other Canadian myths.* Toronto: Penguin.

Meinhard, A., & Foster, M. (2002). *Responses of Canada's voluntary organizations to shifts in social policy: A provincial perspective.* Centre for Voluntary Sector Studies. ISTR Conference Working Papers, Volume III, Cape Town Conference. Retrieved August 24, 2008, from www.ryerson.ca/cvss/WP19.pdf.

Meston, J. (1993). *Child abuse and neglect prevention programs.* Ottawa: Vanier Institute of the Family.

Michaud, S., Cotton, C., & Bishop, K. (2004, February). *Exploration of methodological issues in the development of the Market Basket Measure of low income for Human Resources Development Canada.* Statistics Canada. Retrieved February 3, 2009, from www.statcan.gc.ca/pub/75f0002m/75f0002m2004001-eng.pdf.

Mihorean, K. (2005). Trends in self-reported spousal violence. In K. AuCoin (Ed.), *Family violence in Canada: A statistical profile, 2005* (pp. 13–32). Catalogue No. 85-224-XPE. Ottawa: Statistics Canada. Retrieved February 24, 2009, from http://prod.library.utoronto.ca:8090/datalib/codebooks/cstdli/gss/gss18/85-224-xie2005000.pdf.

Milan, A. (2000). One hundred years of families. *Canadian Social Trends*, Spring: 2–12.

Milan, A., Vézina, M., & Wells, C. (2007). *Family portrait: Continuity and change in Canadian families and households in 2006.* Retrieved February 24, 2009, from Statistics Canada, www12.statcan.ca/english/census06/analysis/famhouse/pdf/97-553-XIE2006001.pdf.

Mishra, R. (1981). *Society and social policy: Theories and practice of welfare* (2nd ed.). London & Basingstoke: Macmillan Press.

Mitchell, B.A. (2005). *Canada's growing visible minority population: Generational challenges, opportunities and federal policy considerations.* Discussion paper commissioned by The Multicultural Program, Dept. of Canadian Heritage, Gatineau, Quebec, pp. 51–62. Retrieved March 13, 2009, from http://culturecanada.gc.ca/

keyrefsearch.cfm?query=veterans&pr=CHRWALK&prox=page&rorder=500&rprox=
500&rdfreq=500&rwfreq=500&rlead=500&sufs=0&order=r&mode=simple&cq=&
lang=eng&cmd=context&id=47ba83fb12d.

Montgomery, J.E. (1977). The housing patterns of older people. In R.A. Kalish (Ed.), *The later years,* pp. 253–61. Belmont: Wadsworth Publishing.

Morel, S. (2002, September). *The insertion model or the workfare model? The transformation of social assistance within Quebec and Canada.* Retrieved August 23, 2008, from Status of Women Canada, www.swc-cfc.gc.ca/pubs/pubspr/0662323467/ 200209_0662323467_e.pdf.

Moscovitch, A., & Drover, G. (1987). Social expenditures and the welfare state: The Canadian experience in historical perspective. In A. Moscovitch & J. Albert (Eds.), *The benevolent state: The growth of welfare in Canada* (pp. 13–43). Toronto: Garamond Press.

Muegge, J., & Ross, N. (1996, November). *Volunteers: The heart of community organizations.* Ministry of Agriculture and Food: Government of Ontario. Retrieved September 18, 2008, from www.omafra.gov.on.ca/english/rural/facts/ 96-017.htm.

Mullaly, R. (1997). *Structural social work.* Toronto: Oxford University Press.

Murray, S., & Mackenzie, H. (2007, March). *Summary: Bringing minimum wages above the poverty line: An economic security project report.* Retrieved February 3, 2009, from Canadian Centre for Policy Alternatives, www.growinggap.ca/files/Minimum%20 Wages%20SUMMARY.pdf.

Myers, G. (1914). *A history of Canadian wealth: Chapter 2: The ecclesiastical and feudal lords.* Chicago: CH Kerr & Co. Retrieved August 26, 2008, from http://yamaguchy. netfirms.com/7897401/myers/can_wealth/c_wealth_02.html.

National Advisory Council on Aging. (2005a). *Seniors on the margins: Aging in poverty in Canada.* Retrieved February 28, 2009, from dsp-psd.pwgsc.gc.ca/Collection/H88-5-3-2005E.pdf.

National Advisory Council on Aging. (2005b). The Changing Face of Long-Term Care. *Expression, 18*(4). Ottawa: NACA.

National Anti-Poverty Organization. (2003, October). *Brief to House of Commons Standing Committee on Finance.* Retrieved February 4, 2004, from www.napo-onap.ca/House%20of%20Commons.htm.

National Clearinghouse on Family Violence. (2002). *Family violence and people with intellectual disabilities.* Health Canada. Retrieved February 23, 2009, from www.phac-aspc.gc.ca/ncfv-cnivf/familyviolence/html/fvintellectu_e.html.

National Clearinghouse on Family Violence. (2006). *A one-stop source of information on family violence* (pamphlet). Retrieved February 24, 2009, from www.phac-aspc. gc.ca/ncfv-cnivf/familyviolence/pdfs/fv-2006-brochure_e.pdf.

National Clearinghouse on Family Violence. (2008). *Transition houses and shelters for abused women in Canada.* Retrieved February 24, 2009, from www.phac-aspc.gc.ca/ncfv-cnivf/familyviolence/pdfs/fem-2008Women_e.pdf.

National Food Security Assembly. (2005). *Affordable housing, income/wages and food security, sustainable livelihoods.* Retrieved February 3, 2009, from http://chd.region.waterloo.on.ca/web/health.nsf/DocID/50BD7DC4ED391B0E85256FDB006611F0/$file/Workshop_ThemeA.pdf?openelement.

National Seniors Council. (2007, November). *Report of the National Seniors Council on elder abuse.* Retrieved February 28, 2009, from www.seniorscouncil.gc.ca/en/research_publications/elder_abuse/2007/hs4_38/hs4_38.pdf.

National Youth in Care Network. (1998). *The real deal: Rights, resources and opportunities for youth in and from care in Ontario: Types of care and placements.* Retrieved April 29, 2004, from www.hri.ca/realdeal/care.htm.

National Youth in Care Network. (2007). *Youth in care.* Retrieved February 24, 2009, from www.youthincare.ca/people/youthincare.html.

NCW (National Council of Welfare). (1995). *The 1995 budget and block funding.* Ottawa: Author.

NCW (National Council of Welfare). (1999, Autumn). *Poverty Profile, 1997.* Ottawa: Author.

NCW (National Council of Welfare). (2003a, October 20). *Recommendations on the creation of the Canada social transfer: Presentation to the Liberal Caucus Social Policy Committee.* Retrieved August 27, 2008, from www.ncwcnbes.net/documents/publicstatements/Archives/2003_NCWPresentationtoSocialPolicyCommittee_cstENG.pdf.

NCW (National Council of Welfare). (2003b, Spring). *Welfare incomes 2002,* vol. 119. Ottawa: Author.

NCW (National Council of Welfare). (2006a, October). *Welfare incomes, 2005,* vol. 125, Minister of Public Works and Government Services Canada. Retrieved August 23, 2008, from www.ncwcnbes.net/documents/researchpublications/Research Projects/WelfareIncomes/2005Report_Summer2006/ReportENG.pdf.

NCW (National Council of Welfare). (2006b, Summer). *Poverty profile, 2002 and 2003.* Retrieved February 3, 2009, from www.ncwcnbes.net/documents/research-publications/ResearchProjects/PovertyProfile/2002-03Report_Summer2006/ReportENG.pdf.

NCW (National Council of Welfare). (2006c, August 24). *Staggering losses in welfare income.* Retrieved February 3, 2009, from www.ncwcnbes.net/documents/research-publications/ResearchProjects/WelfareIncomes/2005Report_Summer2006/PressReleaseENG.pdf.

NCW (National Council of Welfare). (2006d, August). *Number of people on welfare: Fact sheet #9.* Retrieved February 3, 2009, from www.ncwcnbes.net/documents/researchpublications/ResearchProjects/WelfareIncomes/2005Report_Summer2006/Factsheets/Factsheet09ENG.pdf.

NCW (National Council of Welfare). (2007a, March). *Poverty profile 2004: Poverty statistics, 2004: Depth of poverty: Average depth of poverty in dollars, by family type, 2004.* Retrieved February 3, 2009, from www.ncwcnbes.net/documents/researchpublications/ResearchProjects/PovertyProfile/2004/DepthPoverty-DollarsENG.pdf.

NCW (National Council of Welfare). (2007b, October). *Poverty profile 2004: Poverty statistics, 2004: Poverty and paid work: The working poor.* Retrieved February 3, 2009, from www.ncwcnbes.net/documents/researchpublications/ResearchProjects/PovertyProfile/2004/PaidWork-WorkingPoorENG.pdf.

NCW (National Council of Welfare). (2007c, September 18). *Bolder action needed to give Aboriginal children and youth a decent life.* Retrieved March 12, 2009, from www.ncwcnbes.net/documents/researchpublications/ResearchProjects/FirstNationsMetisInuitChildrenAndYouth/2007Report-TimeToAct/PressReleaseENG.pdf.

New Brunswick Association for Community Living. (1992). *A social policy framework for people with a mental handicap in New Brunswick.* Fredericton: Author.

Noel, A. (2006). The new global politics of poverty. *Global Social Policy 2006*(6): 304–33.

Novick, M. (2007, September). *Summoned to stewardship: Make poverty reduction a collective legacy.* Campaign 2000 Policy Perspectives. Retrieved August 27, 2008, from Campaign 2000, www.campaign2000.ca/res/dispapers/summoned_to_stewardship.pdf.

OCISO (Ottawa Community Immigrant Services Organization). (2007). *Welcome to OCISO.* Retrieved March 11, 2009, from www.ociso.org.

O'Connor, T. (2005). *Program evaluation and policy analysis.* Retrieved August 25, 2008, from Dr. Tom O'Connor, Program Manager of CJ and Homeland Security, Director, Institute for Global Security Studies, Austin Peay State University Ctr. at Ft. Campbell: Lecture Notes for PM 3760 Methods and Research for Administration, www.apsu.edu/oconnort/3760/3760lect08.htm.

OCSWSSW (Ontario College of Social Workers and Social Service Workers). (2003). *About OCSWSSW.* Retrieved September 18, 2008, from www.ocswssw.org/sections/about_ocsw/generalinfo.html.

Oderkirk, J. (1996). Government sponsored income security programs for seniors: Canada and Quebec pension plans. *Canadian Social Trends 40* (Spring): 8–15.

OECD (Organization for Economic Co-operation and Development). (1997). *Societal cohesion and the globalising economy: What does the future hold?* Retrieved August 27, 2008, from www.oecd.org/dataoecd/41/24/35391763.pdf.

Office of the Auditor General of Canada. (2006, November). *Report of the Auditor General of Canada to the House of Commons: An overview of the federal government's expenditure management system.* Minister of Public Works and Government Services Canada. Retrieved August 23, 2008, from www.oag-bvg.gc.ca/internet/docs/20061100ce.pdf.

Offord Centre for Child Studies. (2006). *What puts children at risk?* Retrieved February 24, 2009, from www.knowledge.offordcentre.com/need/child_need_07.html.

Offord Centre for Child Studies. (2008, July). *Home*. Retrieved February 24, 2009, from www.offordcentre.com.

Ogrodnik, L. (Ed.). (2008, October). *Family violence in Canada: A statistical profile, 2008*. Retrieved February 24, 2009, from www.statcan.ca/english/freepub/85-224-XIE/85-224-XIE2008000.pdf.

OHCC (Ontario Healthy Communities Coalition). (2004). *Inclusive community organizations: A tool kit: II An organizational change strategy*. Retrieved February 14, 2009, from www.ohcc-ccso.ca/en/webfm_send/181.

Olasky, M. (1992). *The tragedy of American compassion*. Washington: Regenery Publishing.

Omidvar, R., & Richmond, T. (2003, January). *Immigrant settlement and social inclusion in Canada*. Retrieved February 24, 2009, from Laidlaw Foundation, www.laidlawfdn.org/cms/file/children/richmond.pdf.

Ontario Council of Agencies Serving Immigrants (2007). *Settlement workers in schools (SWIS)—Background information: Settlement workers in schools*. Retrieved March 11, 2009, from http://atwork.settlement.org/sys/atwork_library_detail.asp?doc_id=1003365.

Ontario Human Rights Commission. (2007). *Human rights and rental housing in Ontario: Background paper*. Retrieved August 25, 2008, from www.ohrc.on.ca/en/resources/news/housingback/pdf.

Ontario Stepfamily Association. (2009). *Who are we?* Retrieved February 24, 2009, from www.angelfire.com/on3/onstep/whoarewe.htm.

Osberg, L. (2004). What is the real issue in the debt debate? In C. Ragan & W. Watson (Eds.), *Is the debt war over? Dispatches from Canada's fiscal frontline* (pp. 335–48). Montreal: Institute for Research on Public Policy.

Osberg, L. (2007, February 9). *The evolution of poverty measurement—with special reference to Canada*. Retrieved August 24, 2008, from http://myweb.dal.ca/osberg/classification/research/working%20papers/The%20Evolution%20of%20Poverty%20Measurement/PaperFebruary9The%20Evolution%20of%20Poverty.pdf.

Osborne, J.E. (1986). The evolution of the Canada Assistance Plan (CAP). In Task Force on Program Review, *Service to the public: Canada assistance plan*, June 10, 1985 (pp. 57–92). Ottawa: Minister of Supply & Services Canada. Retrieved September 6, 2008, from www.canadiansocialresearch.net/capjack.htm.

O'Sullivan, E. (2006, February). *The Community Well-Being (CWB) index: Well-being in First Nations communities, 1981–2001 and into the future*. Retrieved March 12, 2009, from Indian and Northern Affairs Canada, www.ainc-inac.gc.ca/ai/rs/pubs/re/wbc/wbc-eng.pdf.

Overton, J. (1991, Winter). Dissenting opinions. *Perception* 15(1): 17–21.

Pal, L.A. (Ed.). (1998). *How Ottawa spends, 1998–99—Balancing act: The post-deficit mandate* (pp. 1–30). Toronto: Oxford University Press.

Panel on the Role of Government. (2004). *Investing in people: Creating a human capital society for Ontario*. Retrieved August 31, 2008, from www.law-lib.utoronto.ca/investing/reports/rogenglish.pdf.

Panitch, M. (1998). Forty years on! Lessons from our history. *Entourage 11*(4): 9–16.

Pape, B. (1990, December). *Self-help/mutual aid.* Canadian Mental Health Association, Social Action Series. Retrieved June 8, 2004, from www.cmha.ca/english/sas/selfhelp.htm.

Paquet, G., & Shepherd, R. (1996). The program review process: A reconstruction. In G. Swimmer (Ed.), *How Ottawa spends, 1996–97: Life under the knife* (pp. 39–72). Ottawa: Carleton University Press.

Parliament of Canada. (2006, March). *Compendium of procedure: House of Commons legislative process: Types of bills.* Retrieved August 24, 2008, from www.parl.gc.ca/compendium/web-content/pdf-e/legislativeprocess-e/c_d_typesbills-e.pdf.

Partnerships British Columbia. (2003, June). *An introduction to public private partnerships.* Retrieved August 31, 2008, from www.partnershipsbc.ca/pdf/An%20 Introduction%20to%20P3%20-June03.pdf.

Patterson, L.L. (2006, May 4). *Aboriginal roundtable to Kelowna Accord: Aboriginal policy negotiations, 2004–2005.* Retrieved March 12, 2009, from www.parl.gc.ca/information/library/PRBpubs/prb0604-e.pdf.

Patterson, S.L., Memmott, J.L., Brennan, E.M., & Germain, C.B. (1992, September). Patterns of natural helping in rural areas: Implications for social work research. *Social Work Research and Abstracts 28*(3): 22–28.

Peterborough County, City Health Unit. (2008, January 31). *Child and family violence.* Retrieved February 24, 2009, from http://pcchu.peterborough.on.ca/IP/IP-child-family-violence.html.

Peters, Y. (2003, February). *Federally sentenced women with mental disabilities: A dark corner in Canadian human rights: Part 1–Overview of disability discrimination.* DisAbled Women's Action Network (DAWN) Canada. Retrieved February 23, 2009, from www.elizabethfry.ca/submissn/dawn/4.htm.

Philia [website]. (1997). *Enabling communities: Report to the J.W. McConnell Family Foundation.* Retrieved February 23, 2009, from www.philia.ca/cms_en/page1292.cfm.

Philipps, L.C. (1997). The rise of balanced budget laws in Canada: Legislating fiscal (ir)responsibility. *Osgoode Hall Law Journal 34*(4): 681–740. Retrieved August 23, 2008, from www.ohlj.ca/archive/articles/34_4_philipps.pdf.

Phillips, S.D. (2001, December). SUFA and citizen engagement: Fake or genuine masterpiece? *Policy Matters 2*(7) www.irpp.org/pm/archive/pmvol2no7.pdf.

PRI (Policy Research Initiative). (2004, August). *A life-course approach to social policy analysis.* A Proposed Framework, Discussion Paper. PRI Project, Population Aging and Life-Course Flexibility. Retrieved August 25, 2008, from http://policyresearch.gc.ca/doclib/PRI%20Lifecourse%20Final%20with%20cover%20 e.pdf.

Policy Research Initiative. (2003, December). *Backgrounder: Conference on asset-based approaches: Exploring the promise of asset-based social policies: Reviewing evidence from research and practice.* Retrieved February 3, 2009, from http://policyresearch.gc.ca/ doclib/AB_backgrounder_e.pdf.

PRI (Policy Research Initiative). (2004, August). *A life-course approach to social policy analysis.* A Proposed Framework, Discussion Paper. PRI Project, population Aging and Life-Course Flexibility. Retrieved August 25, 2008, from http://policyresearch.gc.ca/ doclib/PRI%20Lifecourse%20Final%20with%20cover%20e.pdf.

Policy Research Initiative. (2005, July). *What we need to know about the social economy: A guide for policy research.* PRI Project, New Approaches for Addressing Poverty and Exclusion. Retrieved January 11, 2009, from www.policyresearch.gc.ca/ doclib/Soc_Eco_Guide_E.pdf.

Policy Research Initiative. (2008, October 9). *Exclusion: The existing system works reasonably well.* Retrieved February 3, 2009, from www.policyresearch.gc.ca/ page.asp?pagenm=rp_ep_bkg.

Poverty and Human Rights Centre. (2007). *Human rights treaty implementation: The consensus on Canada.* Retrieved August 25, 2008, from www.povnet.org/ files/pov_hr_centre/PHR_june07_v3.pdf.

Preece, M. (2003). When lone parents marry: The challenge of stepfamily relationships. *Transition Magazine 33*(4) (Winter 2003–2004). Retrieved February 24, 2009, from www.vifamily.ca/library/transition/334/334.html.

Premiers' Council on Canadian Health Awareness. (2002, August). *Strengthening home and community care across Canada: A collaborative strategy: Report to the annual premiers' conference.* Retrieved February 28, 2009, from pubs.aina.ucalgary.ca/health/62478.pdf.

Priest, A., Cohen, M., Goldberg, M., Istvanffy, N., Stainton, T., Wasik, A., & Woods, K.M. (2008, February). *Removing barriers to work: Flexible employment options for people with disabilities in BC: Summary.* Retrieved February 23, 2009, from Canadian Centre for Policy Alternatives, www.policyalternatives.ca/documents/ BC_Office_Pubs/bc_2008/bc_removing_barriers_summary.pdf.

Privy Council Office. (1999, June 15). *The voluntary sector: Society's vital third pillar.* Retrieved February 17, 2004, from www.pco-bcp.gc.ca/volunteer/ backgrounder3_e.htm.

Proctor, E.K., & Davis, L.E. (1994, May). The challenge of racial difference: Skills for clinical practice. *Social Work 39*(3): 314–23.

Pross, P. (1986). *Group politics and public policy.* Toronto: Oxford University Press.

Pross, P. (1995). Pressure groups and lobbying. In M.S. Whittington & G. Williams (Eds.), *Canadian politics: Critical approaches* (2nd ed., pp. 425–53). Scarborough: Nelson Thomson Learning.

Public Health Agency of Canada. (2002, December 15). *Mental health promotion: Frequently asked questions.* Retrieved February 25, 2009, from www.phac-aspc. gc.ca/mh-sm/mhp-psm/faq-eng.php.

Public Health Agency of Canada. (2003). *Family and parenting: Nobody's perfect.* Retrieved August 23, 2008, from www.phac-aspc.gc.ca/dca-dea/family_famille/nobody_e.html.

Public Safety and Emergency Preparedness Canada. (2003, November). *Cost-benefit analysis of a community healing process.* Research Summary: Corrections Research and Development. Vol. 8, No. 6. Retrieved March 12, 2009, from www.publicsafety.gc.ca/res/cor/sum/_fl/cprs200311-eng.pdf.

Quarter, J. (1992). *Canada's social economy: Co-operatives, non-profits, and other community enterprises.* Toronto: James Lorimer.

Quebec. (2007). *Guide to government programs and services for families and children. Financial support for childcare.* Retrieved August 23, 2008, from www.mfa.gouv.qc.ca/services-en-ligne/guide-programmes-services/fiches/7.asp?lang=en&chapitre=7&fiche=0.

Quebec wants to coax people off welfare. (2008). *CBC News*, March 19, 2008. Retrieved February 3, 2009, from www.cbc.ca/canada/montreal/story/2008/03/19/qc-quebecwelfare0319.html.

Queen's International Institute on Social Policy. (2007). *The new poverty agenda: Reshaping policies in the 21st century: August 18–20, 2008: The theme.* Retrieved February 3, 2009, from www.queensu.ca/sps/conferences_events/qiisp/2008/index.php.

Quennell, F. (2007). *Frank Quennell's speech to announce the expansion of programs for children who witness domestic violence, May 22, 2007.* Retrieved February 24, 2009, from www.frankquennell.ca/speeches/Speech%20re%20expansion.docx.

Quesnel, J. (2008). Indigenous peoples from an international perspective: How is Canada faring? *Frontier Centre Policy Series, No. 41, April 2008.* Retrieved March 12, 2009, from www.fcpp.org/images/publications/41.%202008Apr%20Indigenous%20peoples%20in%20international%20perspective.pdf.

Rajan, D. (2004). *Violence against women with disabilities.* National Clearinghouse on Family Violence. The Roeher Institute for the Government of Canada. Retrieved February 23, 2009, from www.phac-aspc.gc.ca/ncfv-cnivf/familyviolence/pdfs/fv-2005femdisabl_e.pdf.

Raphael, D. (2006, July/August). Politics, political platforms and child poverty in Canada. *Policy Options*, July/August 2006, 99–103. Retrieved August 24, 2008, from www.irpp.org/po/archive/jul06/raphael.pdf.

RCAP (Royal Commission on Aboriginal Peoples). (1996a). *Highlights from the Report of the Royal Commission on Aboriginal Peoples: Looking forward, looking back.* Retrieved March 12, 2009, from www.ainc-inac.gc.ca/ap/pubs/rpt/rpt-eng.asp#toc.

RCAP (Royal Commission on Aboriginal Peoples). (1996b). Conclusions. In *Report of the Royal Commission on Aboriginal peoples: Looking forward, looking back.* Retrieved March 12, 2009, from www.ainc-inac.gc.ca/ap/pubs/sg/cg/cg13-eng.pdf.

Reed, P.B., & Howe, V. J. (2000). *Voluntary organizations in Ontario in the 1990s*. Statistics Canada and Carleton University. Retrieved February 14, 2009, from Statistics Canada, http://dsp-psd.pwgsc.gc.ca/Collection/Statcan/75F0048M/75F0048MIE2002002.pdf.

Reitz, J.G. (2003, May 30). *Social risks for newcomers to Canada: Issues respecting the role of government in Ontario*. Retrieved March 11, 2009, from www.law-lib.utoronto.ca/investing/reports/rp11.pdf.

Rektor, L. (2002, September). *Advocacy: The sound of citizens' voices: A position paper from the advocacy working group*. Voluntary Sector Initiative Report. Retrieved August 31, 2008, from www.vsi-isbc.org/eng/policy/pdf/position_paper.pdf.

Reyes, G.E. (2001, Summer). The policy making process and models for public policy analysis. University of Pittsburgh, Graduate School of Public and International Affairs. Retrieved December 27, 2008, from *Sincronia, A Journal for the Humanities and Social Sciences*, http://sincronia.cucsh.udg.mx/poan.htm.

Rice, B., & Snyder, A. (2008). Reconciliation in the context of a settler society: Healing the legacy of colonialism in Canada. In M.B. Castellano, L. Archibald, & M. DeGagné (Eds.), *From truth to reconciliation: Transforming the legacy of residential schools* (pp. 43–63). Retrieved March 12, 2009, from Aboriginal Healing Foundation, www.ahf.ca/pages/download/28_13322.

Rice, J. J., & Prince, M.J. (2000). *Changing politics of Canadian social policy*. Toronto: University of Toronto Press.

Richmond, T., & Shields, J. (2003, June). *NGO restructuring: Constraints and consequences*. Presentation to the 11th biennial social welfare policy conference, University of Ottawa, June 2003, Section "Evolution of social services delivery. Retrieved September 18, 2008, from Ontario Council of Agencies Serving Immigrants, www.ocasi.org/downloads/NGO_Restructuring.pdf.

Riessman, F. (1999). *Self help is more than support groups. An interview with Frank Riessman: Erik Banks*. National Self-Help Clearinghouse. Retrieved February 15, 2009, from www.bipolarworld.net/Treatments/Self%20Help/sh7.htm.

Robson, J. (2006). Assets, ownership and a new (and very Canadian) approach. In J. Robson & P. Nares (Eds.), *Wealth and well-being: Ownership and opportunity: New directions in social policy for Canada* (pp. 29–36). Social and Enterprise Development Innovations (SEDI). Retrieved March 1, 2009, from www.sedi.org/DataRegV2-unified/sedi-IDA/Assets%20Book%20English%20Version.pdf.

Roeher Institute. (1996). *Disability, community, and society: Exploring the links*. North York: Author.

Rogers, F. (2001). Mister Rogers takes off the cardigan. Robert Bianco, *USA Today*, August 27, 2001. Retrieved February 15, 2009, from www.usatoday.com/life/television/2001-08-22-rogers.htm.

Rogers, R.E., & Fong, J.Y. (2000). *Organizational assessment: Diagnosis and intervention*. Amherst, MA: Human Resource Development Press.

Rogow, S.M. (2002). *The disability rights movement: The Canadian experience.* International Conference on Autism, May 2002, Kamloops, B.C. International Special Education. Retrieved February 23, 2009, from www.internationalsped.com/magazines_articles/The%20Disability%20Rights%20Movement%20Ed.1.pdf.

Romanow, R.J. (2002, November). *Building on values: The future of health care in Canada: Final report.* Commission on the Future of Health Care in Canada. Retrieved August 26, 2008, from www.canadiandoctorsformedicare.ca/English/HCC_Final_Report.pdf.

Romanyshyn, J.M. (1971). *Social welfare: Charity to justice.* New York: Random House.

Romeder, J.M. (1990). *The self-help way: Mutual aid and health.* Ottawa: Canadian Council on Social Development.

Rondeau, G. (2001). *Challenges that confront social education in Canada: Canadian social work forum 2001.* Retrieved February 15, 2004, from CASW, www.casw-acts.ca/SW-Forum/CdnSWForum-Challenges.htm 7.

Ross, D.P. (1987). Income security. In S.A. Yelaja (Ed.), *Canadian social policy* (rev. ed., pp. 27–46). Waterloo: Wilfrid Laurier University Press.

Ross, D.P., Roberts, P.A., & Scott, K. (1998, October). *Variations in child development outcomes among children living in lone-parent families.* Retrieved February 24, 2009, from www.hrsdc.gc.ca/en/cs/sp/sdc/pkrf/publications/research/1998-001325/1998-001325.pdf.

Roy, C. (2001, August). *The services industries and trade in services.* Retrieved March 3, 2009, from Statistics Canada, www.statcan.gc.ca/pub/63f0002x/63f0002x2001036–eng.pdf.

Royal Commission on the Economic Union and Development Prospects for Canada. (1985). *Report* (Vols. 1, 2, and 3). Ottawa: Ministry of Supply and Services Canada.

Royal Commission on the Status of Women of Canada. (1977). *Report of the Royal Commission on the Status of Women of Canada (Chapter 6).* Retrieved February 3, 2009, from www.acswcccf.nb.ca/english/documents/Chapter%206%20Poverty.doc.

Russell, B. (1952, reprint 1985). *The impact of science on society.* London: George Allen and Unwin.

Saint-Martin, D. (2004, May). *Coordinating interdependence: Governance and social policy redesign in Britain, the European Union and Canada.* CPRN Social Architecture Papers, Research Report F41, Family Network. Retrieved August 24, 2008, from Canadian Policy Research Networks Inc., www.cprn.com/documents/29040_en.pdf.

Saskatoon Council on Aging. (2008). *Services.* Retrieved February 28, 2009, from www.scoa.ca/services/index.php?id=2.

Sauber, R. (1983). *The human services delivery system.* New York: Columbia University.

Saunders, R. (2004, January). *Passion and commitment under stress: Human resource issues in Canada's non-profit sector: A synthesis report.* CPRN Research Series on

Human Resources in the Non-Profit Sector No. 5. Retrieved September 18, 2008, from Canadian Policy Research Networks Inc., www.cprn.org/en/doc.cfm?doc=504#.

Saunders, R. (2005, June). *Lifting the boats: Policies to make work pay.* Retrieved March 1, 2009, from Canadian Policy Research Networks, www.cprn.com/documents/37297_en.pdf.

Schellenberg, G., & Maheux, H. (2007, April). Immigrants' perspectives on their first four years in Canada: Highlights from three waves of the Longitudinal Survey of Immigrants to Canada. *Canadian Social Trends*, Special Edition, 2007, pp. 2–34. Retrieved March 11, 2009, from Statistics Canada, www.statcan.ca/english/freepub/11-008-XIE/2007000/pdf/11-008-XIE20070009627.pdf.

Scott, B. (2004). *Establishing professional social work in Vancouver and at the University of British Columbia.* Retrieved February 14, 2009, from UBC Library, http://toby.library.ubc.ca/webpage/webpage.cfm?id=97.

Scott, D. (1914). Indian affairs, 1763–1841. In A. Shortt & A. Doughty (Eds.), *Canada and its provinces, Vol. IV* (pp. 695–725). Toronto, Glasgow: Brook and Company. Cited in Bélanger, C. (2005). *Quebec history: Marianopolis College: History of Canadian Indians, 1763–1840.* Retrieved March 12, 2009, from http://faculty.marianopolis.edu/c. belanger/QuebecHistory/encyclopedia/HistoryofCanadianIndians-1763-1840.htm.

Scott, K. (2003a). *Funding matters: The impact of Canada's new funding regime on nonprofit and voluntary organizations. Chapter 2: Financial capacity and sources of funding.* Retrieved February 14, 2009, from www.ccsd.ca/pubs/2003/fm/chapter2.pdf.

Scott, K. (2003b). *Funding matters: The impact of Canada's new funding regime on nonprofit and voluntary organizations: Chapter 5: How funding trends are affecting nonprofit and voluntary organizations.* Retrieved February 14, 2009, from www.ccsd.ca/pubs/2003/fm/chapter5.pdf.

Scott, K. (2005). *The world we have: Towards a new social architecture.* Retrieved August 21, 2008, from Canadian Council on Social Development, www.ccsd.ca/pubs/2005/world/world.pdf.

Scott, K. (2008). *The economic well-being of children in Canada, the United States, and Mexico.* Retrieved February 24, 2009, from Canadian Council on Social Development, www.ccsd.ca/pubs/2008/cina/TriEcono_English.pdf.

Seguin, G. (2009). *What are asset-based social policies?* Retrieved March 1, 2009, from Canadian Social Research, www.canadiansocialresearch.net/assets.htm.

Self-Help Connection. (2006). *Research on self-help: Self-help research opportunities.* Retrieved February 15, 2009, from www.selfhelpconnection.ca/research.htm.

Self-Help Resource Centre. (2008a). *Tips for the helping professional.* Retrieved February 15, 2009, from www.selfhelp.on.ca/resource/professional.pdf.

Self-Help Resource Centre. (2008b). *Self-help facts and definitions.* Retrieved February 15, 2009, from www.selfhelp.on.ca/resource/shfacts.pdf.

Seniors Canada. (2008, August). *The latest for seniors.* Retrieved February 28, 2009, from www.seniors.gc.ca/content.jsp?lang=eng&contentid=148.

Service Canada. (2007a, March 31). *Job futures: Social workers.* Retrieved September 18, 2008, from www.jobfutures.ca/noc/4152p3.shtml.

Service Canada. (2007b, March 31). *Job futures: Community and Social service workers.* Retrieved September 18, 2008, from www.jobfutures.ca/noc/4212p1.shtml.

Service Canada. (2008a). *Old Age Security (OAS) payment rates.* Retrieved August 23, 2008, from www1.servicecanada.gc.ca/en/isp/oas/oasrates.shtml#note.

Service Canada. (2008b, October 24). *Canada Pension Plan disability benefits.* Retrieved February 23, 2009, from www1.servicecanada.gc.ca/eng/isp/pub/cpp/disability/benefits/section1a.shtml.

Shapcott, M. (2008, September 21), *News flash: Feds extend housing/homeless investments but freeze dollars.* Retrieved February 3, 2009, from The Wellesley Institute, http://wellesleyinstitute.com/news-flash-feds-extend-housing-homeless-investments-freeze-dollars.

Shapiro, J. (2008, August 1). *Action planning toolkit: Developing a financial strategy.* Retrieved September 2, 2008, from CIVICUS, www.civicus.org/new/media/Developing%20a%20Financing%20Strategy.pdf.

Shields, J. (2003, January). *No safe haven: Markets, welfare, and migrants.* CERIS Working Paper No. 22. Retrieved August 28, 2008, from Joint Centre of Excellence for Research on Immigration and Settlement—Toronto, http://ceris.metropolis.net/Virtual%20Library/Demographics/wkpp22_shields.pdf.

Shillington, R. (2000, March 19). *Adding social condition to the Canadian Human Rights Act: Some issues.* Retrieved November 6, 2008, from Tristat Resources, www.shillington.ca/rights/chra-rp.pdf.

Shookner, M. (2002, June). *An inclusion lens: Workbook for looking at social and economic exclusion and inclusion.* Retrieved August 25, 2008, from Population and Public Health Branch, Atlantic Region, www.phac-aspc.gc.ca/canada/regions/atlantic/Publications/Inclusion_lens/inclusion_2002_e.pdf.

Singer, S.M. (2007, March 22). *Choices Mr. Flaherty, choices. ... Commentary on the Conservative government's budget.* Retrieved August 27, 2008, from Canadian Policy Research Networks, www.cprn.org/documents/47227_en.pdf.

Sladowski, P.S., & Hayes, E. (2007, March 14). *Mapping the communities agenda in Canada: An inventory of action, resources, programs and policies.* The Centre for Voluntary Sector Research and Development. Retrieved February 14, 2009, from http://cure-crfmu.org/docs/Communities_Agenda_Mapping_Inventory-revised.pdf.

Smith, E. (2004, March). *Nowhere to turn? Responding to partner violence against immigrant and visible minority women: Voices of frontline workers.* Retrieved March 11, 2009, from Canadian Council on Social Development, www.ccsd.ca/pubs/2004/nowhere/voices.pdf.

Smith, M. (2004). Interest groups and social movements. In M. Whittington & G. Williams (Eds.), *Canadian politics in the 21st century* (6th ed., pp. 213–30). Toronto: Nelson Thomson Canada.

Smith, R., & Torjman, S. (2004). *Policy development and implementation in complex files.* Retrieved February 14, 2009, from www.csps-efpc.gc.ca/Research/publications/pdfs/p125_e.pdf.

Social Planning Council of Metropolitan Toronto. (1997). *Policy statement on provincial devolution of responsibilities to municipalities and communities.* Retrieved March 16, 2004, from www.worldchat.com/public/tab/polstmnt.htm.

SPAN (Single Parent Association of Newfoundland). (2009). *Programs and services.* Retrieved February 24, 2009, from www.envision.ca/webs/span.

Special Senate Committee on Aging. (2007, March). *First interim report: Embracing the challenge of aging.* Retrieved February 28, 2009, from www.parl.gc.ca/39/1/parlbus/commbus/senate/com-e/agei-e/rep-e/repintfeb07-e.pdf.

Special Senate Committee on Aging. (2008, March). *Second interim report: Issues and options for an aging population.* Retrieved September 18, 2008, from www.parl.gc.ca/39/2/parlbus/commbus/senate/com-e/agei-e/rep-e/repfinmar08-e.pdf.

Special Senate Committee on Aging. (2009, April). *Final report on Canada's aging population: Seizing the opportunity.* Retrieved May 27, 2009, from www.parl.gc.ca/40/2/parlbus/commbus/senate/com-e/agei-e/rep-e/AgingFinalReport-e.pdf.

Special Senate Committee on Poverty. (1971). *Report of the Special Senate Committee on Poverty: Poverty in Canada.* Ottawa: Government of Canada.

Spencer, C. (2003). Grey power in Canada: Will baby boomers become a political force as they age? *GRC News* 22(2): 1-5. Retrieved February 28, 2009, from www.sfu.ca/grc/publications/grcnews/grcn_pdfs/vol22no2.pdf.

Sperling, J., & Lasby, D. (2007). *Giving and volunteering for education and research organizations in Alberta: Findings from the 2004 Canada Survey of Giving, Volunteering, and Participating.* Toronto: Imagine Canada. Retrieved September 18, 2008, from http://nonprofitscan.imaginecanada.ca/files/en/nsgvp/social_services_short_report_-_alberta.pdf.

Spicker, P. (2008). *An introduction to social policy: The politics of welfare.* Public Policy at the Robert Gordon University. Retrieved August 23, 2008, from www2.rgu.ac.uk/publicpolicy/introduction/contents.htm.

Splane, R. (1965). *Social welfare in Ontario, 1791–1893.* Toronto: University of Toronto Press.

SPRC (Social Planning and Research Council of Hamilton, Ontario). (2006, May). *Women and poverty in Hamilton.* Retrieved February 3, 2009, from www.sprc.hamilton.on.ca/Reports/pdf/SPRCWomen&PovertyReport.pdf.

SRDC (Social Research and Demonstration Corporation). (2005, Spring). *Whither welfare? Learning what works* 5(1): 6–9. Retrieved February 3, 2009, from www.srdc.org/uploads/volume_5_number_1-en.pdf.

Standing Senate Committee on Social Affairs, Science and Technology. (2006a, May). *Out of the shadows at last: Transforming mental health, mental illness and addiction services in Canada. Part 1.* Retrieved February 15, 2009, from www.parl.gc.ca/39/1/parlbus/commbus/senate/com-e/soci-e/rep-e/pdf/rep02may06part1-e.pdf.

Standing Senate Committee on Social Affairs, Science and Technology. (2006b, May). *Out of the shadows at last: Transforming mental health, mental illness and addiction services in Canada. Part V: Federal leadership.* Retrieved March 12, 2009, from www.parl.gc.ca/39/1/ParlBus/commbus/senate/com-e/SOCI-E/rep-e/pdf/rep02may06part2-e.pdf.

Standing Senate Committee on Social Affairs, Science and Technology. (2006c). *Community-based.* Retrieved September 2, 2008, from www.bcalliance.org/LinkClick.aspx?fileticket=SnPfyWjt7TA%3D&tabid=887&mid=1565.

Stanford, J. (2005). When taxes are good. *Perception* 27(3–4): 18–19. Retrieved January 3, 2009, from www.ccsd.ca/perception/2734/per2734.pdf.

Stapleton, J., & Tweddle, A. (2008, August). *Navigating the maze: Improving coordination and integration of disability income and employment policies and programs for people living with HIV/AIDS: A discussion paper.* Retrieved February 23, 2009, from www.hivandrehab.ca/EN/episodic_disabilities/documents/NavigatingtheMazeFinal.pdf.

Stasiulis, D., & Abu-Laban, Y. (2004). Unequal relations and the struggle for equality: Race and ethnicity in Canadian politics. In M. Whittington and G. Williams (Eds.), *Canadian politics in the 21st century* (6th ed.), pp. 371–97. Scarborough: Thomson Nelson.

Statistics Canada. (1997, Spring). Canadian children in the 1990s: Selected findings of the National Longitudinal Survey of Children and Youth. *Canadian Social Trends.* Catalogue No. 11-008-XPE. Retrieved February 24, 2009, from www.statcan.gc.ca/kits-trousses/pdf/social/edu04_0024a-eng.pdf.

Statistics Canada. (2002, November 6). *2001 Census: Families and households profile: Canada.* Retrieved February 28, 2009, from www12.statcan.ca/english/census01/products/analytic/companion/fam/canada.cfm.

Statistics Canada. (2003a, January). *2001 census: Analysis series: Canada's ethnocultural portrait: The changing mosaic.* Retrieved March 11, 2009, from www12.statcan.gc.ca/english/census01/products/analytic/companion/etoimm/pdf/96F0030XIE2001008.pdf.

Statistics Canada. (2003b). Census of population: Labour force activity, occupation, industry, class of worker, place of work, mode of transportation, language of work and unpaid work. *The Daily,* February 11, 2003. Retrieved March 11, 2009, from www.statcan.gc.ca/daily-quotidien/030211/dq030211a-eng.htm.

Statistics Canada. (2005). Study: Divorce and the mental health of children. *The Daily,* December 13, 2005. Retrieved February 24, 2009, from www.statcan.ca/Daily/English/051213/d051213c.htm.

Statistics Canada. (2006a, March). *Women in Canada: Fifth edition: A gender-based statistical report*. Retrieved March 12, 2009, from www.statcan.ca/english/freepub/89-503-XIE/0010589-503-XIE.pdf.

Statistics Canada. (2006b). *Measuring violence against women: Statistical trends, 2006*. Retrieved March 11, 2009, from www.statcan.gc.ca/pub/85-570-x/85-570-x2006001-eng.pdf.

Statistics Canada. (2006c, June 22). *2005 Canadian community health survey: Statistics Canada*. Cited in Public Health Agency of Canada, Aging and Seniors. Retrieved February 28, 2009, from www.phac-aspc.gc.ca/seniors-aines/archive/know2006_e.htm.

Statistics Canada. (2006d). Survey of financial security. *The Daily, December 7, 2006*. Retrieved February 28, 2009, from www.statcan.gc.ca/daily-quotidien/061207/dq061207b-eng.htm.

Statistics Canada. (2007a). General Social Survey: Navigating family transitions. *The Daily*, June 13, 2007. Retrieved February 24, 2009, from www.statcan.ca/Daily/English/070613/d070613b.htm.

Statistics Canada. (2007b, December). *Participation and Activity Limitation Survey 2006: Analytical report*. Retrieved February 23, 2009, from www.statcan.gc.ca/pub/89-628-x/89-628-x2007002-eng.pdf.

Statistics Canada. (2007c, May 3). *Income of Canadians*. Retrieved January 11, 2009, from www.statcan.gc.ca:80/daily–quotidien/070503/dq070503a–eng.htm.

Statistics Canada. (2007d). 2006 Census: Age and sex. *The Daily, Tuesday, July 17, 2007*. Retrieved February 28, 2009, from www.statcan.gc.ca/daily-quotidien/070717/dq070717a-eng.htm.

Statistics Canada. (2007e). Residential care facilities. *The Daily, Wednesday, May 30, 2007*. Retrieved February 28, 2009, from www.statcan.ca/Daily/English/070530/d070530d.htm.

Statistics Canada. (2008a, March). *Canada's changing labour force, 2006 Census*. Retrieved February 15, 2009, from www12.statcan.gc.ca/english/census06/analysis/labour/pdf/97-559-XIE2006001.pdf.

Statistics Canada. (2008b, January). *Aboriginal peoples in Canada in 2006: Inuit, Métis and First Nations, 2006 Census: Aboriginal peoples, 2006 Census: Census year 2006*. Retrieved March 12, 2009, from www12.statcan.ca/english/census06/analysis/aboriginal/pdf/97-558-XIE2006001.pdf.

Statistics Canada. (2008c). *Canadian demographics at a glance*. Retrieved March 11, 2009, from www.statcan.ca/english/freepub/91-003-XIE/91-003-XIE2007001.pdf.

Statistics Canada. (2008d, September). *Participation and Activity Limitation Survey 2006: Families of children with disabilities in Canada*. Retrieved February 23, 2009, from www.statcan.gc.ca/pub/89-628-x/89-628-x2008009-eng.pdf.

Statistics Canada. (2008e, July). *Participation and Activity Limitation Survey 2006: Labour force experience of people with disabilities in Canada*. Retrieved February 23, 2009, from www.mcss.gov.on.ca/NR/rdonlyres/92F72127-4EE4-46BE-A114-31ADD6415B33/3329/2006laborforce.pdf.

Statistics Canada. (2008f, September). *Residential care facilities 2006/2007*. Catalogue no. 83-237-X. Retrieved November 6, 2008, from dsp-psd.pwgsc.gc.ca/collection_2008/statcan/83-237-X/83-237-XIE2009001.pdf.

Statistics Canada. (2008g, November 25). *Suicides and suicide rate, by sex and by age group (Males)*. Retrieved February 28, 2009, from www40.statcan.gc.ca/l01/cst01/perhlth66b-eng.htm.

Statistics Canada. (2008h). Pension plans in Canada. *The Daily, Friday, July 4, 2008*. Retrieved February 28, 2009, from www.statcan.gc.ca/daily-quotidien/080704/dq080704a-eng.htm.

Statistics Canada. (2009a, January 9). Labour Force Survey, December 2008. *The Daily*, January 9, 2009, pp. 2–8. Retrieved February 3, 2009, from www.statcan.gc.ca/daily-quotidien/090109/dq090109-eng.pdf.

Statistics Canada. (2009b, May 8). Labour Force Survey, April 2009. *The Daily*, May 8, 2009. Retrieved May 27, 2009, from www.statcan.gc.ca/subjects-sujets/labour-travail/lfs-epa/lfs-epa-eng.pdf.

Status of Disabled Persons Secretariat. (1994). *Disability policy and programs in Canada: A brief overview*. Ottawa: Human Resources Development Canada.

Status of Women Canada. (1998). *Gender-based analysis: A guide for policy-making*. Retrieved August 25, 2008, from www.swc-cfc.gc.ca/pubs/gbaguide/gbaguide_e.pdf.

Stephenson, M., Rondeau, G., Michaud, J.C., & Fiddler, S. (2000). *In critical demand: Social work in Canada, Vol. 1, Final report*. Social Work Sector Steering Committee. Retrieved February 10, 2004, from www.socialworkincanada.org/pdf/vol1_en/toc_en.pdf.

Stevenson, K. (1999). Family characteristics of problem kids. *Canadian Social Trends*, Winter 1999: 2–6.

Stewart, J. (2002, September 10). *Speaking notes for The Honourable Jane Stewart, Minister of Human Resources Development Canada: To the International Social Security Association: Vancouver, B.C.* Retrieved December 27, 2008, from www.hrsdc.gc.ca/eng/cs/comm/speeches/hrdc/2002/020910_e.shtml.

St-Hilaire, F. (2002). *The debate on vertical fiscal imbalance and federal health care funding*. Paper presented at the 2002 Economic Outlook Forum, "What Is the Role of the Federal Government?," sponsored by the Canadian Association for Business Economics (CABE) and Moneco-Econtro, Kingston, August 29, 2002. Retrieved August 27, 2008, from Institute for Research on Public Policy, www.irpp.org/miscpubs/archive/021125e.pdf.

Stobert, S., & Cranswick, K. (2004). Looking after seniors: Who does what for whom? *Canadian Social Trends*, Autumn 2004 (74). Retrieved February 15, 2009, from http://dsp-psd.tpsgc.gc.ca/Collection-R/Statcan/11-008-XIE/0020411-008-XIE.pdf.

Strong-Boag, V. (1979 Spring). Wages for housework: Mothers' allowances and the beginnings of social security in Canada. *Journal of Canadian Studies* 14(1): 24–34.

Struthers, J. (1983). *No fault of their own: Unemployment and the Canadian welfare state, 1914–1941*. Toronto: University of Toronto Press.

Subcommittee on Population Health. (2008, April). *Population health policy: Issues and options: Fourth report of the Subcommittee on Population Health of the Standing Senate Committee on Social Affairs, Science and Technology*. Retrieved March 12, 2009, from www.parl.gc.ca/39/2/parlbus/commbus/senate/com-e/soci-e/rep-e/rep10apr08-e.htm#_Toc19360049.

Sudbury, F. & Rook, M. (2003, November 20). Needs-based access to residential care: Changing policy, practice and outcomes on southern Vancouver Island. *Stride Magazine*. Retrieved February 12, 2004, from www.stridemagazine.com/2003_11%20November/article_03.shtml.

Svenson, K.A., & Lafontaine, C. (1999, April 22). The search for wellness. In First Nations and Inuit Regional Health Survey National Steering Committee, *Results from the First Nations and Inuit regional health surveys* (pp. 181–216). Retrieved March 12, 2009, from http://uregina.ca/datalibrary/holdings/FN_regional_survey_ch6.pdf.

Sykes, S. (2008, May). *Life on the reef in the Canadian ocean: The "new" second generation in Canada: Discussion paper*. Retrieved March 11, 2009, from Policy Research Initiative, http://policyresearch.gc.ca/doclib/DP_div_Sykes02_200805_e.pdf.

Tamarack Institute for Community Engagement. (2006). *Serving the communities' agenda: Call #3—How can government advance the communities' agenda?* A conversation with Sherri Torjman, June 15, 2006. Retrieved February 14, 2009, from http://tamarackcommunity.ca/downloads/vc/GL_Notes_June15.pdf.

Tamarack Institute for Community Engagement. (2007). *About vibrant communities*. Retrieved February 3, 2009, from http://tamarackcommunity.ca/g2s1.html.

Tamarack Institute for Community Engagement. (2009). *Poverty reduction*. Retrieved February 3, 2009, from http://tamarackcommunity.ca/g3s3_3.html.

Taylor, G. (1969). *The problem of poverty, 1660–1834*. Seminar Studies in History, Kings College School. Wimbledon: Longmans, Green, & Company.

Taylor, J.L. (2009). Native people, government policy: European settlement and native status. In *The Canadian Encyclopedia*. Retrieved March 12, 2009, from Historica Foundation of Canada www.thecanadianencyclopedia.com/index.cfm?PgNm=TCE&Params=A1SEC824928.

Taylor-Butts, A. (2007). Canada's shelters for abused women, 2005/2006. *Juristat, Canadian Centre for Justice Statistics 27*(4), Catalogue No. 85-002-XIE. Retrieved February 24, 2009, from Statistics Canada, www.statcan.gc.ca/pub/85-002-x/85-002-x2007004-eng.pdf.

Teeple, G. (2000). *Globalization and the decline of social reform: Into the twenty-first century*. Aurora: Garamond Press.

THCU (The Health Communication Unit). (2001 April). *Introduction to health promotion program planning, Version 3.0*. Centre for Health Promotion, University of Toronto. Retrieved September 16, 2008, from www.thcu.ca/resource_db/pubs/ 930522026.pdf.

Thomas, A. & Skage, S. (1998). Overview of perspectives on family literacy: Research and practice. In A. Thomas (Ed.), *Family literacy in Canada: Profiles of effective practices* (pp. 5-24). Welland: Soleil Publishing. Retrieved February 5, 2009, from www.nald.ca/fulltext/family/LITENG.pdf.

Thompson, A.H., Howard, A.W., & Jin, Y. (2001). A social problem index for Canada. *Canadian Journal of Psychiatry 46*: 45–51. Retrieved August 24, 2008, from http://ww1.cpa-apc.org:8080/Publications/Archives/CJP/2001/Feb/Original.asp.

Thorburn, H.G. (2008). Pressure group. In *The Canadian encyclopedia, Historica Foundation of Canada*. Retrieved August 25, 2008, from www.thecanadianencyclopedia.com/index.cfm?PgNm=TCE&Params=A1ARTA0006467.

Thursz, D. (1977). Social Action. In J.B. Turner (Ed.), *Encyclopedia of Social Work* (17th ed., vol. 2, pp. 1274–80). Washington, D.C.: National Association of Social Workers.

Torjman, S. (1996, October). *The disability income system in Canada: Options for reform*. Ottawa: Caledon Institute of Social Policy. Retrieved February 23, 2009, from www.caledoninst.org/Publications/PDF/1-895796-72-5.pdf.

Torjman, S. (2005, September). *What is policy?* Ottawa: Caledon Institute of Social Policy. Retrieved August 24, 2008, from www.caledoninst.org/Publications/PDF/544ENG.pdf.

Torjman, S. (2007a, September 17). No small answers to big problems. *Toronto Star*. Retrieved January 11, 2009, from www.thestar.com/comment/article/256864.

Torjman, S. (2007b, May). *Organizing for neighbourhood revitalization*. Retrieved February 14, 2009, from www.caledoninst.org/Publications/PDF/633ENG.pdf.

Toronto Community and Neighbourhood Services. (2004). *Cracks in the foundation: Community agency survey 2003: A study of Toronto's community-based human service sector*. Retrieved September 18, 2008, from www.neighbourhoodcentres.ca/reportspub/Cracks-in-the-foundation-Feb-04.pdf.

Toronto Community and Neighbourhood Services. (2004, February). *Cracks in the foundation: Community agency survey 2003: A study of Toronto's community-based human service sector: Final report*. Retrieved February 5, 2009, from www.toronto.ca/divisions/pdf/cns_survey_report.pdf.

Townsend, P. (1993). *The international analysis of poverty*. Milton Keynes: Harvester Wheatsheaf.

Townsend, T., & Werwick, M. (2008). Hope or heartbreak: Aboriginal youth and Canada's future. *Horizons 10*(1) (March 2008): 4–6. Retrieved March 12, 2009, from Policy Research Initiative, www.policyresearch.gc.ca/doclib/HOR_v10n1_200803_e.pdf.

Townson, M., & Hayes, K. (2007, November). *Women and the employment insurance program*. Retrieved August 23, 2008, from Canadian Centre for Policy Alternatives, www.policyalternatives.ca/documents/National_Office_Pubs/2007/Women_and_the_EI_Program.pdf.

Treasury Board of Canada Secretariat. (2002, April 1). *Policy on alternative service delivery: 2.0 Preface*. Retrieved August 31, 2008, from www.tbs-sct.gc.ca/pubs_pol/opepubs/TB_B4/asd-dmps1_e.asp#_Toc853880.

Treasury Board of Canada Secretariat. (2008, April). *Guide on strategic planning: Tips and advice for IM or IT strategic plans.* Chief Information Officer Branch: Alignment and Interoperability Division, Final Draft – Version 1.0. Retrieved September 2, 2008, from www.tbs-sct.gc.ca/inf-inf/documents/strateg-plan/strateg-plan-eng.pdf

Treasury Board of Canada Secretariat. (2000, April 11). *SUFA template: Guide to federal government reporting.* Retrieved February 12, 2004, from www.tbs-sct.gc.ca/rma/account/sufa-ecus/temp-mod_e.asp.

Treasury Board of Canada Secretariat. (2006, September). *Backgrounder: Effective spending.* Retrieved September 18, 2008, from www.tbs-sct.gc.ca/media/nr-cp/2006/0925-eng.asp.

Treasury Board of Canada Secretariat. (2007, February 14). *Canada's new government acting to improve grant and contribution programs.* Retrieved January 11, 2009, from www.tbs-sct.gc.ca/media/nr-cp/2007/0214_e.asp.

Treasury Board of Canada Secretariat. (2008, April). *Guide on strategic planning: Tips and advice for IM or IT strategic plans.* Chief Information Officer Branch: Alignment and Interoperability Division, Final Draft – Version 1.0. Retrieved September 2, 2008, from HYPERLINK "http://www.tbs-sct.gc.ca/inf-inf/documents/strateg-plan/strateg-plan-eng.pdf" www.tbs-sct.gc.ca/inf-inf/documents/strateg-plan/strateg-plan-eng.pdf.

Trocmé, N., Fallon, B., MacLaurin, B., Daciuk, J., Felstiner, C., Black, T., et al. (2005). *Canadian incidence study of reported child abuse and neglect—2003: Major findings.* Retrieved February 24, 2009, from http://dsp-psd.pwgsc.gc.ca/Collection/HP5-1-2005E.pdf.

Turcotte, M. & Schellenberg, G. (2007). *A portrait of seniors in Canada.* Retrieved February 28, 2009, from Statistics Canada, www.statcan.ca/english/freepub/89-519-XIE/89-519-XIE2006001.pdf.

U of C Faculty of Social Work. (2007, July 20). *Children's mental health project: Introduction to children's mental health.* Retrieved February 24, 2009, from www.fsw.ucalgary.ca/cmhp/introduction.

Undoing the Kelowna agreement. (2006). *CBC News Online: Nov. 21, 2006: In depth: Aboriginal Canadians.* Retrieved March 12, 2009, from www.cbc.ca/news/background/aboriginals/undoing-kelowna.html.

UNICEF (United Nations Children's Fund). (2007). *Child poverty in perspective: An overview of child well-being in rich countries.* Innocenti Report Card 7, 2007 UNICEF Innocenti Research Centre, Florence. Retrieved February 24, 2009, from http://unicef-icdc.org/publications/pdf/rc7_eng.pdf.

United Nations. (1993). *Declaration on the elimination of violence against women.* General Assembly resolution 48/104 of December 20, 1993. Retrieved May 17, 2009, from www.unhchr.ch/huridocda/huridoca.nsf/(symbol)/a.res.48.104.en.

United Nations. (1995). *World summit for social development, Copenhagen 1995: Copenhagen Declaration on Social Development: Part A: Current social situation and reasons for convening the Summit.* Retrieved January 11, 2009, from www.un.org/esa/socdev/wssd/decl_parta.html.

United Nations. (1996). *Families: Victims of poverty and homelessness.* United Nations, International Day of Families, May 15, 1996. Retrieved February 24, 2009, from www.un.org/esa/socdev/family/idf/1996/Backg96.htm.

United Nations. (2002, May 12). *Indigenous people: Backgrounder: First meeting of permanent forum high point of UN decade.* Retrieved March 12, 2009, from www.un.org/rights/indigenous/backgrounder1.htm.

United Nations. (2006). *Background: International day of older persons: October 1, 2006.* Retrieved February 28, 2009, from www.un.org/events/olderpersons/2006/background.html.

United Way of Guelph. (2006). *Seniors and mental health and dementias: Research News, July 2006.* Retrieved February 28, 2009, from www.unitedwayguelph.com/newsletters/mental.html.

UNPAC (UN Platform for Action Committee Manitoba). (2006). *The economics of ability.* Retrieved February 23, 2009, from www.unpac.ca/economy/ability.html.

VIHA (Vancouver Island Health Authority). (2009). *Food security.* Retrieved February 3, 2009, from www.viha.ca/mho/food/Food+Security.htm.

Voluntary Sector Initiative. (2002, October). *A code of good practice on policy dialogue.* Building on an accord between the Government of Canada and the voluntary sector. Retrieved September 1, 2008, from www.vsi-isbc.org/eng/policy/doc/codes_policy.doc.

Voluntary Sector Initiative. (2004, April). *The voluntary sector initiative process evaluation, Final evaluation report.* Audit and Evaluation Directorate, Strategic Direction, Social Development Canada. Retrieved August 31, 2008, from www.vsi-isbc.org/eng/relationship/pdf/process_evaluation.pdf.

Voluntary Sector Steering Group. (2002, Autumn). *Building a stronger voluntary sector: How the VSI is making a difference.* Voluntary Sector Steering Group Report to the Voluntary Sector in Canada. Voluntary Sector Initiative. Retrieved August 28, 2008, from www.vsi-isbc.org/eng/about/pdf/building.pdf.

Volunteer Canada. (2001). *Rethinking volunteer engagement: International Year of Volunteers, 2001.* Retrieved September 18, 2008, from www.volunteer.ca/volunteer/pdf/RethinkingEng.pdf.

Volunteer Canada. (2004). *Trends in volunteerism.* Retrieved September 18, 2008, from www.volunteer.ca/en/volcan/other/x-trends.

Volunteer Canada. (2006). *The Canadian code for volunteer involvement.* Retrieved September 18, 2008, from http://volunteer.ca/volunteer/pdf/CodeEng.pdf.

Volunteer Canada. (2008). *Canadian Volunteerism Initiative (CVI): Overview.* Retrieved September 18, 2008, from http://volunteer.ca/en/about/programming/pastprojects/cvi.

VON Canada. (2004). *Caring for family caregivers: The unmet need for respite as a break, time out or relief from caregiving: VOICE demonstration project case study, August 2004.* Retrieved February 15, 2009, from www.projectvoice.ca/English/Documents/VON/von_e.html.

Voyer, J.P. (2005). A life-course approach to social policy. In *Exploring new approaches, PRI conference, synthesis report* (pp. 4–7). Retrieved August 24, 2008, from Policy Research Initiative, www.policyresearch.gc.ca/doclib/R6_Synthesis_report_e.pdf.

Wallace, B., & Richards, T. (2008, June). *The rise and fall of welfare time limits in British Columbia*. Retrieved August 26, 2008, from Vancouver Island Public Interest Research Group, www.vipirg.ca/welfare_time_limits_june_08.pdf.

Ward, L. (2002, June 14). *The First Nations Governance Act*. Retrieved May 13, 2004, from CBC News, www.cbc.ca/news/indepth/firstnations/indianact.html.

Watson-Wright, W. (2001, July). *The role of evidence in the development of national policies to enhance children's well-being: A Canadian case story (1990–2001)*. Retrieved January 26, 2009, from http://209.85.173.132/search?q=cache:aVLmENDVs4gJ:www.phac-aspc.gc.ca/ph-sp/implement/news_iuhpe-eng.ppt+%22policy+making+is+a%22&hl=en&ct=clnk&cd=10&gl=ca.

Webb, M. (2008). Federal equalization update for fiscal 2009–10: Ontario becomes a recipient. *Fiscal Pulse*, November 4, 2008. Retrieved January 26, 2009, from Scotia Capital, www.scotiacapital.com/English/bns_econ/fedequalupdate.pdf.

Weir, E. (2008, December 11). *Ontario's manufacturing crisis*. Retrieved January 11, 2009, from The Progressive Economics Forum, www.progressive-economics.ca/2008/12/11/ontario-manufacturing-crisis.

Weiss, L. (1998). *The myth of the powerless state*. Ithaca: Cornell University Press.

Westhues, A. (2002). Social policy practice. In F.J. Turner (Ed.), *Social work practice: A Canadian perspective* (2nd ed., pp. 315–29). Toronto: Prentice Hall.

Wharf, B. (2007) Introduction: People, politics, and child welfare. In L.T. Foster & B. Wharf, *People, politics, and child welfare in British Columbia* (pp. 1–9). Retrieved August 23, 2008, from www.ubcpress.ca/books/pdf/chapters/2007/PeoplePoliticsandChildWelfare.pdf.

White, D. (2003). *The rising profile of services and partnerships: What implications for analysing welfare state dynamics?* International Sociological Association Research Committee 19 on Poverty, Social Welfare and Social Policy. Retrieved August 25, 2008, from http://individual.utoronto.ca/RC19_2003/pdf/White_The_Rising_Profile_of_Services_and_Partnerships.pdf.

WHO (World Health Organization). (2002). *The Toronto declaration on the global prevention of elder abuse*. Retrieved February 28, 2009, from www.who.int/ageing/projects/elder_abuse/alc_toronto_declaration_en.pdf.

WHO (World Health Organization). (2009). *International classification of functioning, disability and health (ICF)*. Retrieved February 23, 2009, from www.who.int/classifications/icf/en.

WHO (World Health Organization). (2007). *Global age-friendly cities: A guide*. Retrieved February 28, 2009, from www.who.int/ageing/publications/Global_age_friendly_cities_Guide_English.pdf.

Wilensky, H., & Lebeaux, C. (1965). *Industrial society and social welfare*. New York: The Free Press.

Wilkerson, B., & Guscott, R. (2005, September). *Special report to the Premiers of Canada: Guidelines for working parents to promote and protect the mental health of their children*. Retrieved February 24, 2009, from www.parentsforchildrensmentalhealth.org/attachments/Premiers-Special-Report-Aug-2005.pdf.

Williams, C. (2005). *The sandwich generation*. Statistics Canada. Retrieved February 15, 2009, from www.statcan.gc.ca/pub/11-008-x/2005001/article/7033-eng.pdf.

Williams, C. (2006). Asset-building approaches and the search for a new social policy architecture in Canada. In J. Robson & P. Nares (Eds.), *Wealth and well-being: Ownership and opportunity: New directions in social policy for Canada* (pp. 53–67). Social and Enterprise Development Innovations. Retrieved March 1, 2009, from www.sedi.org/DataRegV2-unified/sedi-IDA/Assets%20Book%20English%20Version.pdf.

Willms, J.D. (2007). *Vulnerable children*. Retrieved March 7, 2009, from Investing in Children, www.investinginchildren.on.ca/Communications/articles/vulnerable%20children.htm.

Woodall, C. (2004). *Focal point: Silent voices in distress*. Retrieved May 27, 2004, from Diversity Now, www.diversitynow.ca/features/focalpoint/silentvoices.shtml.

Workers' Compensation Board of Saskatchewan. (2005, February 1). *Return-to-work program audit*. Retrieved February 23, 2009, from www.wcbsask.com/WCBPortal/ShowProperty/WCBRepository/pdfs/rtw_program_audit.pdf.

Yalnizyan, A. (1994). Securing society: Creating Canadian social policy. In A. Yalnizyan, T.R. Ide, & A.J. Cordell (Eds.), *Shifting time: Social policy and the future of work* (pp. 17–71). Toronto: Between the Lines.

Yalnizyan, A. (2005). *Divided and distracted: Regionalism as obstacle to reducing poverty and inequality*. Retrieved January 3, 2009, from Canadian Centre for Policy Alternatives, www.policyalternatives.ca/documents/National_Office_Pubs/ 2005/Social_Watch_2005.pdf.

Yalnizyan, A. (2008, May 1). *Why a growing income gap affects us all*. Retrieved January 11, 2009, from Canadian Centre for Policy Alternatives, www.policyalternatives.ca/documents/Manitoba_Pubs/2008/FastFacts_May1_08_GrowingGap.pdf.

You're not alone if you're online: Tips for healing on the Internet. (1997, June 16). *Healthy Way Magazine*. Retrieved February 15, 2004, from www.nb.sympatico.ca/Contents/Health/healthyway/archive/feature_sel1.html.

Zastrow, C. (2008). *Introduction to social work and social welfare: Empowering people* (9th ed.). Belmont, CA: Thomson/Brooks/Cole.

Zelenev, S. (2008). *Preventing abuse of older persons: Progress in implementing theMadrid International Plan of Action on Ageing*. Retrieved February 28, 2009, from www.cnpea.ca/frequently_asked_questions_files/Zelenev%20final%20v.%20full%20text.pdf.

INDEX